Free Trade versus Protectionism

To my beloved grandchildren Natacha and Nicholas

Free Trade versus Protectionism

A Source Book of Essays and Readings

By
Johannes Overbeek
Professor of Economics, University of the Virgin Islands

Edward Elgar
Cheltenham, UK • Northampton, MA, USA

Published by
Edward Elgar Publishing Limited
Glensanda House
Montpellier Parade
Cheltenham
Glos GL50 1UA
UK

Edward Elgar Publishing, Inc.
6 Market Street
Northampton
Massachusetts 01060
USA

A catalogue record for this book
is available from the British Library

Library of Congress Cataloguing in Publication Data
Free trade versus protectionism : a source book of essays and readings
/ compiled by Johannes Overbeek
    Includes index.
    1. Free trade—History.   2. Protectionism—History.
3. International economic relations—History.   I. Overbeek,
Johannes.
HF1711.F744   1999
382'.7'09—dc21   98–42879
                                                              CIP

ISBN 1 85898 971 X

Printed and bound in Great Britain by Bookcraft (Bath) Ltd.

Contents

v

Preface

The subject of free trade and protectionism is one of the oldest in economic science. This controversy has arisen out of various historical contexts. This book, which is mainly designed for courses in international economics, aims at examining this discussion over a long period of time. It starts with the mercantilists of the sixteenth and seventeenth century and it ends with contemporary authors living and publishing during the last decade of the twentieth century.

The task undertaken in this inquiry is to present a selection of readings with essays and annotations by the editor. Thus it brings before the public a source book which contains one of the great debates in economic theory from the days of mercantilism to present times. Hopefully it offers a tool which will be helpful in carefully scrutinizing the arguments advanced by both the advocates of free trade and those of protectionism. The presentation of the debate over a long period of time should also create historical perspective. As the German writer and scholar Goethe observed, a person with no knowledge of history must remain content to dwell in obscurity.

Needless to say that the two doctrines of free trade and protectionism are fundamentally opposed. The advocates of free trade usually contend that the best way to promote a nation's and the world's prosperity is by maintaining the utmost freedom for the exchange of all goods and services between a country's own people and residents of other nations. The proponents of free trade also often argue that an international division of labor generates mutual interdependence, obliges nations to work together thus promoting international peace. The advocates of protectionism on the other hand maintain that in order to promote domestic industry, agriculture, employment and income, the inflow of imports must be restricted. Some protectionists also state the view that greater self-sufficiency puts a nation in a better position to defend itself in case of war without unsuitable dependence on foreign sources of supply.

This book consists of seven parts starting with mercantilism and its critics. The two subsequent sections examine the free traders and protectionists of the nineteenth century. Two more portions are devoted to the evolution of the debate during the 1900–1940 period. The last two divisions review the discussion of the economics of free trade and protectionism during the second half of the twentieth century.

Each of the seven sections starts with a survey by the editor of the period under review in order to place the material before the reader in proper context. The selections themselves are preceded by the editor's introduction containing a short biography of the author and an explanation of the author's views. The individual writings speak for themselves. They consist mostly of compositions of men who have pondered long and hard over the issues that their essays address.

I feel indebted to many good friends for help, advice and secretarial assistance during the preparation of this book, in particular Dr Bernard A. Kemp, Mrs Margaret Hennessy and Ms Maaike Vergeer. I am especially thankful for the assistance and support of the Netherlands Institute for Advanced Study in the Humanities and Social Sciences (NIAS), its excellent staff and its former director Dr D.J. van de Kaa, which allowed me to work for five months without interruption at this manuscript. Needless to say that the steadfast support of the University of the Virgin Islands for my research endeavors has also been most welcome.

During the writing of this book I have greatly benefited from the assistance of the staffs of the Library of the University of the Virgin Islands, the Library of Congress, the Library of NIAS, and the Library of the Graduate Institute of International Studies in Geneva.

It remains for me to express my thanks to the authors and original publishers of the selections in this book for their kind permission to use their materials. As always, mistakes, misinterpretations and other errors are the editor's responsibility.

1. Mercantilism and its Critics

PREAMBLE

1

Mercantilism is the label commonly given today to the economic views and practices of European writers and statesmen between the end of the Middle Ages and the late eighteenth century. Like socialism, mercantilism was essentially a folk doctrine. As Jacob Viner states: 'it evolved in the light of the prevailing historical circumstances and values by simple inference from the apparent facts'.[1] Like some other historical realities, mercantilism drew greatly upon ideas and circumstances surviving from previous ages including feudalism. The three main phenomena which formed the basis of mercantilism were (1) the rise of strong national states such as Portugal, Spain, England and France, (2) the growth of the exchange and money economy and finally (3) the establishment of oceanic contacts with other continents.

The two major aims of mercantilist theory and policy were (1) the strengthening of the power of the state (political) and (2) the accumulation of wealth (economic). Those twin objectives were inseparably joined in the minds of the mercantilists. Political power could be used to conquer new markets, acquire colonies or monopolize trade routes which would bring in new wealth. Additional wealth could be used to equip armies and navies and thus defeat rivals. The accumulation of wealth made power possible and power led to more wealth. The most important and desirable form of wealth was treasure or precious metals. In other words, gold and silver, coined or uncoined were regarded as the only productive and tangible form of wealth. This preoccupation with gold and silver led to a particular kind of trade policy which is of interest to us. Countries which had no gold or silver mines and which were deprived of colonies where precious metals could be found had no option other

---

1 J. Viner, 'Mercantilist Thought', *International Encyclopedia of the Social Sciences* (D.L. Sills, ed.) vol. 4 (New York: Macmillan, 1968) p. 436.

than to acquire bullion by trade. A country therefore had to strive for a favorable or positive balance of trade. If exports exceeded imports an influx of precious metal was ensured. The proper motive for foreign trade was the procurement of precious metals. Usually the criterion was the total balance between all imports and exports not the bilateral balance with each trade partner. Because the centerpiece of mercantilist thinking consisted of an export surplus and the compensatory inflow of bullion, many of the policy proposals of mercantilist writers consisted of recommendations as to how to stimulate exports and hamper imports. From discouraging imports to protectionism is but one step, thus import prohibitions, quotas, tariffs and other protectionist measures became part of the stock and trade of mercantilist policy and recommendations.[2] Moreover, in order to have much to export, production had to be encouraged, mercantilism becoming a system of extensive state regulation of production and trade.

Impediments to trade were not new. During the Middle Ages petty rulers of towns and regions frequently harassed and hampered trade using tolls and other devices. Export restrictions based on the fear of depletion of commodities were also common. To some extent these exclusive town economies with their external barriers and internal trade measures set the pattern for the national economies which emerged subsequently.

What made mercantilism so different from the medieval order was that it was clearly dominated by a fear of goods. Production had to be encouraged but the resulting output had to be sent away and foreign commodities had to be blocked. This is of course typically a producer's point of view. Consumers love goods; the more the better. The producer however, wants to sell. Oversupply from domestic or foreign sources has to be avoided at all costs.

Mercantilism was also associated with the gospel of full employment. While production and exports created employment, a plentiful home supply and imports were a nuisance and a cause of unemployment. This ideology witnessed a splendid revival in the 1930s when the world was suffering from the Great Depression.

---

2   It may be observed here that the typical mercantilist author was not a dispassionate scholar analyzing the economy but a merchant or a professional writer deliberating on a specific topic of current interest.

2

Germany and Austria developed their own variety of mercantilism called Cameralism which lasted some 300 years. The word camera (Kammer in German) designated the place in which the royal treasure was located. Thus cameral affairs concerned the economy of the prince although in reality cameralism consisted as much of political science and law as of economics. However cameralism was not an inquiry into the abstract principles of prosperity in the Smithian sense. It was essentially an administrative technology, not a philosophy.

Cameralism arose in a semifeudal setting characterized by sharply divided political regions in Germany, economic backwardness and closed economies. According to the cameralistic conception, the state was a magnified family with a large farm as its property. The unity of this family with its holdings was symbolized by the prince.

Cameralism rested upon the fundamental assumption of total subordination of the individual to the state (the usual situation in small German principalities). As was to be expected, cameralism was less concerned with foreign relations and more interested in domestic affairs than was French or English mercantilism. In international relations the controlling principle of cameralism was to allow each country take care of its own national interest which meant *de facto* a policy of readiness for aggression and for resistance to aggression. At the same time, cameralism had even more faith in government regulation, a large population, protectionism and self-sufficiency than had its French and English counterparts. We also find certain cameralists such as Joseph von Sonnenfels (1733–1817) advocating such welfare measures as state care for the sick.

German cameralism continued well into the nineteenth century and influenced the romanticist movement and the members of the German Historical School (1843–1883) especially its 'younger' version. Many of these scholars who are also known as state or academic socialists managed to get a number of their proposals adopted by the German government once Germany was united after 1870.[3] Germany, by then the most powerful nation in continental Europe, became a model for

---

3 If socialism is defined as a belief in the state regulation of the entire economy in which the individual is seen as being subordinate to the state, mercantilism is in fact a doctrine of 'monarchal socialism'. See R. Gonard, *Histoire des Doctrines Economiques* (Paris: Librairie Valors, 1930) p. 49.

other countries to imitate. The Historical School like the Cameralists was strongly protectionist in outlook. The protectionist policies of Germany greatly contributed to the decline of the free trade philosophy which took place between 1880 and 1914 in Western Europe.

3

In countries such as England and France the retreat from mercantilism began in the late eighteenth century. The classical school including such forerunners as David Hume (1711–1776) rejected the mercantilist emphasis on the national supply of gold and silver and the balance of trade. Instead they claimed that trade conducted under individual initiative and free from government interference was inherently profitable to the individuals involved, their nations, as well as to the world community as a whole.

READING 1

Thomas Mun

Biography

Our first reading consists of a selection from *Discourse on England's Treasure by Forraign Trade* written by Thomas Mun (1571–1641) and published posthumously by his son John Mun in 1664. Thomas Mun was the third son of a London mercer during Queen Elizabeth's time.

Mun has been selected here because he develops the objectives and policies of a national mercantilist economy very systematically. This together with his persuasive powers made him 'The Prince of Mercantilism'. His book had great influence. Mun himself became a wealthy merchant and served as one of the directors of the East India Company from 1615 until his death.

Mun rose to prominence when in 1622 he was one of the merchants consulted by the English government to investigate and give advice on the economic depression of 1620 which had resulted in a loss of gold and silver and a drop in the exchange rate of the pound sterling.

Mun broke into print in 1621 with a small work entitled *A Discourse of Trade from England unto the East-Indies*. This tract of some fifty pages was designed to counteract the growing criticism of the East India Company which financed its spice trade largely by the export of gold and silver. Mun's argument was that the East India Trade was profitable because it brought into the country necessary and useful commodities which could only be bought elsewhere (mainly in Turkey) at three times the sterling cost. He also argued that a large proportion of these East Indian goods were re-exported at higher prices ensuring that England more than regained the bullion which had initially been sent to India.

Mun was a practicing professional merchant and his writings are handbooks for merchants and policy makers rather than essays on theoretical economics.

Mun was buried on July 21, 1641.

The Work

In *Discourse on England's Treasure by Forraign Trade* Mun broke indisputably with bullionists like Gerald de Malynes (1586–1641) who advocated such measures as the prohibition of the export of gold and silver, and tight exchange controls in order to increase the domestic stock of bullion. Mun on the other hand, sought to increase the national stock of precious metals solely through an excess of exports over imports. Mun argued that a private person can only enrich himself if he spends less than his income and, consequently, he drew the (wrong) conclusion that a nation can get rich only if it exports (earns) more than it imports (spends).

Therefore, in order to obtain a positive balance of trade Mun recommended that commercial policy should be fashioned in such a way as to ensure a chronic excess of exports over imports.[4] Mun himself had no less than twelve proposals to produce the desired inflow of precious metals.

The main measures Mun advocated were the cultivation of previously unutilized land, the domestic production of commodities hitherto imported (import substitution), the restriction of consumption of foreign luxury articles, the promotion of shipping and fisheries, the moderation of export duties, the lowering of import duties on foreign raw materials and articles designed for re-export and the imposing of heavy import duties (item 11) on imports destined for home

---

4   By balance of trade Mun meant both the visible items and the services in the current account of the total balance of payments.

consumption.[5]

Extract

The Means to Enrich this Kingdom and to Increase its Treasure

Although a Kingdom may be enriched by gifts received, or by purchase taken from some other Nations, yet these are things uncertain and of small consideration when they happen. The ordinary means therefore to encrease our wealth and treasure is by Forraign Trade, wherein we must ever observe this rule; to sell more to strangers yearly than we consume of theirs in value. For suppose that when this Kingdom is plentifully served with the Cloth, Lead, Tinn, Iron, Fish and other native commodities, we do yearly export the overplus to forraign Countries to the value of twenty two hundred thousand pounds; by which means we are enabled beyond the Seas to buy and bring in forraign wares for our use and Consumptions, to the value of twenty hundred thousand pounds; by this order duly kept in our trading, we may rest assured that the Kingdom shall be enriched yearly two hundred thousand pounds, which must be brought to us in so much Treasure; because that part of our stock which is not returned to us in wares must necessarily be brought home in treasure.

For in this case it cometh to pass in the stock of a Kingdom, as in the estate of a private man; who is supposed to have one thousand pounds yearly revenue and two thousand pounds of ready money in his Chest: If such a man through excess shall spend one thousand five hundred pounds per annum, all his ready money will be gone in four years; and in the like time his said money will be doubled if he take a Frugal course to spend but five hundred pounds per annum; which rule never faileth likewise in the Commonwealth, but in some cases (of no great moment) which I will hereafter declare, when I shall shew by whom and in what manner this balance of the Kingdoms account ought to be drawn up yearly, or so often as it shall please the State to discover how much we gain or lose by trade with forraign Nations. But first I will say something concerning those ways and means which will encrease our exportation which being done, I will then set down some other arguments both affirmative and negative to strengthen that

5   Source: T. Mun, *Discourse on England's Treasure by Forraign Trade* (London: Thomas Clark, 1664) (reprinted by A. Kelley in 1986) pp. 5–13.

which is here declared, and thereby to shew that all the other means which are commonly supposed to enrich the Kingdom with Treasure are altogether insufficient and mere fallacies.

The Particular Ways and Means to Encrease the Exportation of our Commodities, and to decrease our Consumption of Forraign Wares.

The revenue of stock of a Kingdom by which it is provided of forraign wares is either Natural or Artificial. The Natural wealth is so much only as can be spared from our own use and necessities to be exported unto strangers. The Artificial consists in our manufactures and industrious trading with forraign commodities, concerning which I will set down such particulars as may serve for the cause we have in hand.

1. First, although this Realm be already exceeding rich by nature, yet might it be much encreased by laying the waste grounds (which are infinite) into such employments as should no way hinder the present revenues of other manured lands, but hereby to supply ourselves and prevent the importations of Hemp, Flac, Cordage, Tobacco, and divers other things which now we fetch from strangers to our great impoverishing.

2. We may likewise diminish our importations, if we would soberly refrain from excessive consumption of forraign wares in our diet and rayment, with such often change of fashions as is used, so much the more to encrease the waste and charge; which vices at this present are more notorious amongst us than in former ages. Yet might they easily be amended by enforcing the observation of such good laws as are strictly practised in other Countries against the said excesses; where likewise by commanding their own manufactures to be used, they prevent the coming in of others, without prohibition, or offence to strangers in their mutual commerce.

3. In our exportations we must not only regard our own superfluities, but also we must consider our neighbours necessities, that so upon the wares which they cannot want, nor yet be furnished thereof elsewhere, we may (besides the vent of the Materials) gain so much of the manufacture as we can, and also endeavour to sell them dear, so far forth as the high price cause not a less vent in the quantity. But the superfluity of our commodities which strangers use, and may also

have the same from other Nations, or may abate their vent by the use of some such like wares from other places, and with little inconvenience; we must in this case strive to sell as cheap as possible we can, rather than to lose the utterance of such wares. For we have found of late years by good experience, that being able to sell our Cloth cheap in Turkey, we have greatly encreased the vent thereof, and the Venetians have lost as much in the utterance of theirs in those Countries, because it is dearer. And on the other side a few years past, when by the excessive price of Wools our Cloth was exceedingly dear, we lost at the least half our clothing for forraign parts, which since is no otherwise (well neer) recovered again than by the great fall of price for Wools and Cloth. We find that twenty five in the hundred less in the price of these and some other Wares, to the loss of private mens revenues, may raise above fifty upon the hundred in the quantity vented to the benefit of the publique. For when Cloth is dear, other Nations do presently practise clothing, and we know they want neither art nor materials to this performance. But when by cheapness we drive them from this employment, and so in time obtain our dear price again, then do they also use their former remedy. So that by these alterations we learn, that it is in vain to expect a greater revenue of our wares than their condition will afford, but rather it concerns us to apply our endeavours to the times with care and diligence to help ourselves the best we may, by making our cloth and other manufactures without deceit, which will encrease their estimation and use.

4. The value of our exportations likewise may be much advanced when we perform it ourselves in our own Ships, for then we get only not the price of our wares as they are worth here, but also the Merchants gains, the charges of ensurance, and fraight to carry them beyond the seas. As for example, if the Italian Merchants should come hither in their own shipping to fetch our Corn, our red Herrings or the like, in this case the Kingdom should have ordinarily but 25.S. for a quarter of Wheat, and 20.S. for a barrel of red hearings, whereas if we carry these wares ourselves into Italy upon the said rates, it is likely that we shall obtain fifty shillings for the first, and forty shillings for the last, which is a great difference in the utterance or vent of the Kingdoms stock. And although it is true that the commerce ought to be free to strangers to bring in and carry out at their pleasure, yet nevertheless in many places the exportation of victuals and munition are either prohibited, or at least limited to be done only

by the people and Shipping of those places where they abound.

5. The Frugal expending likewise of our own natural wealth might advance much yearly to be exported unto strangers; and if in our rayment we will be prodigal, yet let this be done with our own materials and manufactures, as Cloth, Lace, Imbroderies, Cutworks and the like, where the excess of the rich may be the employment of the poor, whose labours notwithstanding of this kind, would be more profitable for the Commonwealth, if they were done to the use of strangers.

6. The Fishing in his Majesties seas of England, Scotland and Ireland is our natural wealth, and would cost nothing but labour, which the Dutch bestow willingly, and thereby draw yearly a very great profit to themselves by serving many places of Christendom with our Fish, for which they return and supply their wants both of forraign Wares and Money, besides the multitude of Mariners and Shipping, which hereby are maintain'd, whereof a long discourse might be made to shew the particular manage of this important business. Our Fishing plantation likewise in New-England, Virginia, Greenland, the Summer Islands and the New-found-land, are of the like nature, affording much wealth and employments to maintain a great number of poor, and to encrease our decaying trade.

7. A Staple or Magazin for forraign Corn, Indigo, Spices, Raw-silks, Cotton wool or any other commodity whatsoever, to be imported will encrease Shipping, Trade, Treasure, and Kings customes, by exporting them again where need shall require, which course of Trading, hath been the chief means to raise Venice, Genoa, the low-Countreys, with some others; and for such a purpose England stands most commodiously, wanting nothing to this performance but our own diligence and endeavour.

8. Also we ought to esteem and cherish those trades which we have in remote or far Countreys, for besides the encrease of Shipping and Mariners thereby, the wares also sent thither and receiv'd from thence are far more profitable unto the kingdom than by our trades neer at hand. As for example; suppose Pepper to be worth here two Shillings the pound constantly, if then it be brought from the Dutch at Amsterdam, the Merchant may give there twenty pence the pound, and gain well by the bargain; but if he fetch this Pepper from the

East-Indies, he must not give above three pence the pound at the most, which is a mighty advantage, not only in that part which serveth for our own use, but also for that great quantity which (from hence) we transport yearly unto divers other Nations to be sold at a higher price: whereby it is plain, that we make a far greater stock by gain upon these Indian Commodities, than those Nations doe where they grow, and to whom they properly appertain, being the natural wealth of their Countries. But for the better understanding of this particular, we must ever distinguish between the gain of the Kingdom, and the profit of the Merchant; for although the Kingdom payeth no more for this Pepper than is before supposed, nor for any other commodity bought in forraign parts more than the stranger receiveth from us for the same, yet the Merchant payeth not only that price, but also the fraight, ensurance, customes and other charges which are exceeding great in these long voyages; but yet all these in the Kingdoms account are but commutations among our selves, and no Privation of the Kingdoms stock, which being duly considered, together with the support also of our other trades in our best Shipping to Italy, France, Turkey, the East Countreys and other places, by transporting and venting the wares which we bring yearly from the East Indies; It may well stir up our utmost endeavours to maintain and enlarge this great and noble business, so much importing the Publique wealth, Strength, and Happiness. Neither is there less honour and judgment by growing rich (in this manner) upon the stock of other Nations, than by an industrious encrease of our own means, especially when this later is advanced by the benefit of the former, as we have found in the East Indies by sale of much of our Tin, Cloth, Lead and other Commodities, the vent whereof doth daily encrease in those Countreys which formerly had no use of our wares.

9. It would be very beneficial to export money as well as wares, being done in trade only, it would encrease our Treasure; but of this I write more largely in the next Chapter to prove it plainly.

10. It were policie and profit for the State to suffer manufactures made of forraign Materials to be exported custome-free, as Velvets and all other wrought Silks, Fustian, thrown Silks and the like, it would employ very many poor people, and much encrease the value of our stock yearly issued into other Countreys, and it would (for this purpose) cause the more forraign Materials to be brought in, to the improvement of His Majesties Customes. I will here remember a

notable increase in our manufacture of winding and twisting only of forraign raw Silk, which within 35 years to my knowledge did not employ more than 300 people in the City and suburbs of London, where at this present time it doth set on a work above fourteen thousand souls, as upon diligent enquiry hath been credibly reported unto His Majesties Commissioners for Trade. And it is certain, that if the said forraign Commodities might be exported from hence, free of custome, this manufacture would yet encrease very much, and decrease as fast in Italy and in the Netherlands. But if any man allege the Dutch proverb, Live an let others live; I answer, that the Dutch-men notwithstanding their own Proverb, doe not onely in these Kingdoms, encroach upon our livings, but also in other forraign parts of our trade (where they have power) they do hinder and destroy us in our lawful course of living, hereby taking the bread out of our mouth, which we shall never prevent by plucking the pot from their nose, as of late years too many of us do practise to the great hurt and dishonour of this famous Nation; We ought rather to imitate former times in taking sober and worthy courses more pleasing to God and suitable to our ancient reputation.

11. It is needful also not to charge the native commodities with too great customes, lest by indearing them to the strangers use, it hinder their vent. And especially forraign wares brought in to be transported again should be favoured, for otherwise that manner of trading (so much importing the good of the Commonwealth) cannot prosper nor subsist. But the Consumption of such forraign wares in the Realm may be the more charged, which will turn to the profit of the kingdom in the Balance of the Trade, and thereby also enable the King to lay up the more Treasure out of his yearly incomes, as of this particular I intend to write more fully in his proper place, where I shall shew how much money a Prince may conveniently lay up without the hurt of his subjects.

12. Lastly, in all things we must endeavour to make the most we can of our own, whether it be Natural or Artificial; And forasmuch as the people which live by the Arts are far more in number than they who are masters of the fruits, we ought the more carefully to maintain those endeavours of the multitude, in whom doth consist the qreatest strength and riches both of King and Kingdom: for where the people are many, and the arts good, there the traffique must be great, and the Countrey rich. The Italians employ a greater number of people, and

get more money by their industry and manufactures of the raw Silks
of the Kingdom of Cicilia, than the King of Spain and his Subjects
have by the revenue of this rich commodity. But what need we fetch
the example so far, when we know that our own natural wares doe not
yield us so much profit as our industry? For Iron oar in the Mines is
of no great worth, when it is compared with the employment and
advantage it yields being digged, tried, transported, bought, sold, cast
into Ordnance, Muskets, and many other instruments of war for
offence and defence, wrought into anchors, bolts, spikes, nayles and
the like, for the use of Ships, Houses, Carts, Coaches, Ploughs, and
other instruments for Tillage. Compare our Fleece-wools with our
Cloth, which requires shearing, washing, carding, spinning, weaving,
fulling, dying, dressing and other trimmings, and we shall find these
Arts more profitable than the natural wealth, whereof I might instance
other examples, but I will not be more tedious, for if I would amplify
upon this and the other particulars before written, I might find matter
sufficient to make a large volume, but my desire in all is only to
prove what I propound with brevity and plainness.

READING 2

Philipp Wilhelm von Hornick

Biography

One of the leading Austrian cameralists Philipp Wilhelm von Hornick,
(1638–1712) studied and received his doctorate in law at the
University of Inglestadt in Austria. He then established himself in
Vienna to practice law, serving for a long time under the German
Emperor Leopold I who, mainly through heritage, helped to lay the
foundations of the Austrian–Hungarian Empire. His published work
attracted much attention and won him a post as privy councilor with
the Cardinal of Passau, who was at that time a German Prince. Passau
was a religious and commercial town in Bavaria near the Austrian
border.

The Work

In his political writings von Hornick claimed Charlemagne's ancient
empire for Austria. He actually advocated the use of force to wrestle
Alsace-Lorraine from France. More importantly, however, especially

for economists, is his *Oesterreich über Alles, wann Es Nur Will* ('Austria above all, if she only wants'). The book was published anonymously in 1684 and was reprinted twelve times. The book which is intensely mercantilist was intended to render Austria the most powerful state in Europe. The propositions made by von Hornick, deal with measures to secure self-sufficiency and economic growth but contain little analysis. In real mercantilist fashion von Hornick argued that:

(a) gold and silver should not leave the country,
(b) trade should be bilateral,
(c) only the most indispensable foreign goods such as raw materials should be brought in and exchanged for surplus domestic products,
(d) exports of manufactures and raw materials should be encouraged,
(e) wastelands and other resources should be actively exploited,
(f) the labor force should receive more training,
(g) population growth should be stimulated.

As a true mercantilist von Hornick always asserted the primacy of political objectives over economic ones. The balance of power surpassed the balance of trade in importance. His confidence in the paternal state and extensive regulation is naive but very typical for mercantilists (and neo-mercantilists). Von Hornick's book attracted much attention and it was of considerable influence in fashioning Austria's economic policy in the eighteenth century.[6]

Extract

Nine Principal Rules of National Economy

If the might and eminence of a country consist in its surplus of gold, silver and all other things necessary or convenient for its subsistence, derived so far as possible, from its own resources, without dependence upon other countries, and in the proper fostering, use, and application of these, then it follows that a general national economy

---

6   Source: Philipp Wilhelm von Hornick, 'Austria Over All if She Only Will', *Source Readings in Economic Thought* (P.C. Newman et al., eds) (New York: Norton, 1954) pp. 38–42.

(LandesOeconomie) should consider how such a surplus fostering, and enjoyment can be brought about without dependence upon others, or where this is not feasible in every respect, with as little dependence as possible upon foreign countries, and sparing use of the country's own cash. For this purpose the following nine rules are especially serviceable.

First to inspect the country's soil with the greatest care, and not to leave the agricultural possibilities or a single corner or clod of earth unconsidered. Every useful form of plant under the sun should be experimented with, to see whether it is adapted to the country, for the distance or nearness of the sun is not all that counts. Above all, neither trouble nor expense should be spared to discover gold and silver.

Second, all commodities found in a country, which cannot be used in their natural state should be developed within the country: since the payment for manufacturing generally exceeds the value of the raw material by two, three, ten, twenty, and even a hundred fold, and the neglect of this is an abomination to prudent managers.

Third, for carrying out the above two rules, there will be need of people, both for producing and cultivating the raw materials and for working them up. Therefore, attention should be given to the population, that it may be as large as the country can support, this being a well ordered state's most important concern, but, unfortunately, one that is often neglected. And the people should be turned by all possible means from idleness to remunerative professions; instructed and encouraged in all kinds of inventions, arts, and trades; and, if necessary, instructors should be brought in from foreign countries for this.

Fourth, gold and silver once in the country, whether from its own mines or obtained by industry from foreign countries, are under no circumstances to be taken out for any purpose, so far as possible, or allowed to be buried in chests or coffers but must always remain in circulation; nor should much be permitted in uses where they are at once destroyed and cannot be utilized again. For under these conditions, it will be impossible for a country that has once acquired a considerable supply of cash, especially once that possesses gold and silver mines, ever to sink into poverty: indeed it is impossible that it should not continually increase in wealth and property. Therefore,

Fifth, the inhabitants of the country should make every effort to get along with their domestic products, to confine their luxury to these alone, and to do without foreign products as far as possible (except where great need leaves no alternative, or if not need, wide-spread, unavoidable abuse, of which Indian spices are an example). And so on.

Sixth, in case the said purchases were indispensable because of necessity or irremediable abuse, they should be obtained from these foreigners at first hand, so far as possible and not for gold or silver, but in exchange for other domestic wares.

Seventh, such foreign commodities should in this case be imported in unfinished form, and worked up within the country, thus earning the wages of manufacture there.

Eighth, such opportunities should be sought night and day for selling the country's superfluous goods to these foreigners in manufactured form, so far as this is necessary, and for gold and silver; and to this end, consumption, so to speak, must be sought in the farthest ends of the earth, and developed in every possible way.

Ninth, except for important considerations, no importation should be allowed under any circumstances of commodities of which there is a sufficient supply of suitable quality at home; and in this matter neither sympathy nor compassion should be shown to foreigners, be they friends, kinsfolk, allies or enemies. For all friendship ceases, when it involves my own weakness and ruin. And this holds good, even if the domestic commodities are of poorer quality, or even higher priced. For it would be better to pay for an article two dollars which remain in the country than only one which goes out, however, strange this may seem to the ill-informed. There is no need of further elucidating these fundamental rules of a general national economy. Their reasonableness is obvious to every man of intelligence.

How to Institute Reforms in the National Economy Properly

I should like to begin with the above-mentioned fifth rule, and advise the Austrians to be content for a while with their own goods, with their own manufactures, however bad they may be at first, and to refrain from foreign ones, keeping their good gold and silver in their pockets. This would fit in with all the other rules, and everything else would follow from this alone. For the ninth rule is practically included in this fifth one; and if people would use nothing but domestic manufactures, the children and inhabitants of the country would be compelled (most of them gladly) to turn their hands to their own manufactures, and to work up the domestic raw materials. In this way the second rule would be greatly furthered. And since artisans go where they can get a living, and many foreigners would necessarily be out of work as a result of the prohibition of their products, and sometimes even lack our raw materials, they would be compelled to come to Austria, in order to seek work, necessary raw materials, and their living and to settle there ...

What is to be done about those merchants who are engaged solely in the importing business? They will be ruined – An advantage! For they are the very fellows who are impoverishing the country. It is therefore better that they should collapse than the commonwealth. They will be able to hold out, however until they obtain commissions from domestic wholesalers or financiers, or credit from them, or book-keeping with the manufacturers, or some other position or service (of which there will then be hundred times as many as there are ruined merchants), or invest any capital they may have in domestic manufactures. If they do not wish to be employed by the domestic factories, however, and they have no capital to invest, then such worthless rascals who, act only to the advantage of foreigners and to the harm of Austria, and who have not been able to do any more than earn their daily bread, are no more worthy of sympathy than downright fools.

Our Austrian manufactures will not be as good as the foreign ones. Such a claim is many cases a delusion of the Devil, who is hostile to the prosperity of Austria. Granted, however, that this would be an unavoidable evil, still it would not be unendurable. I will cite the prohibition of Hungarian wine in Austria, Styria and elsewhere. If you ask why wines are prohibited which are better than the domestic ones, and even cheaper, the answer will be: That the domestic gifts of providence may be utilized and prudently consumed, not despised, thrown away or ruined; that the highlands may be benefited and the limited cultivation of vineyards, an important source of regalian revenue, may not be abandoned; that thereby so much more money may stay in our pockets. It is the same with Hungarian salt, to which the Austrian is inferior. And yet the former is kept out and the latter retains control of the field. It is quite the proper thing, however, and can be applied ad literam to domestic manufactures. For if we have such principles in a few things, why do we not extend them to the great and many?

It is to be feared that we shall have to live at the mercy of domestic artisans and business-men, since they will raise their prices excessively when they are not restrained by foreigners. If the government supervises things as it should, and checks wantonness, this will not have to be feared. And if manufactures eventually become extensive, the people themselves will strive for money and bread, and make goods cheap through their plentifulness. Where foodstuffs, house-rent, and wages of servants, as well as raw materials or goods are inexpensive, as with us, and where wares are not brought from a distance and consequently are subject to no heavy charges from freight, tolls, or risks. it is hardly possible that they should be higher-priced than foreign ones (especially if the market is certain, and the goods do not have to lie long at interest). It might even be said that strangers do not make us gifts of these things, either; and it would be better, after all, if something must be sacrificed, to be a victim to one's own countryman rather than to a stranger, and to console one's self with the fact, already alluded to above, that it is better, although not every peasant can understand it, to pay two dollars for a domestic article, which remains in the country, than only one for a foreign one, which is exported. For what once goes out stays out. But what remains in domestic circulation involves no loss to the public, but is an advantage in several ways. The merchant himself, who invested it can profit by it again. The state is to be thought of a rich man, who has his money in many purses. If he takes something out of one and puts it into the other, he becomes no poorer thereby, For, although one purse becomes lighter. the other becomes that much heavier. He is master, however, of one as well as of the other. And this must be a leading principle of the national economy, or things will not go well.

But those nations whose manufactures we propose to prohibit will be angry and cut us off from such things as we may still need from them; our domestic goods hitherto taken by them will be left on our hands; our alliances and we ourselves will be deserted in time of need. Let them be angry who will. If they are enemies, we do not need to spare their feelings: if they are friends, they will excuse us if we, by eventually developing a good economy, get into a position not only to help ourselves, but also in case of need to be of more real service to them. We see how France is angry at the way England consigns to the flames all French wares that are discovered. And after all, let him who stands behind Job take a friendship which really aims only at plundering our purse. We have learned how much friends give us for nothing in an emergency.

READING 3

David Hume

Biography

We now turn our attention to David Hume (1711–1776) a Scottish philosopher, historian, man of letters and economist. He is known for his skepticism and empiricism, practicing the method of observation. He was raised in a cultural family, and was educated at home and at the University of Edinburgh which he left at the age of 15, as was then customary. For several years he read widely in the humanities. Following a brief period in a merchant's office in Bristol, he went to France in 1734 where he stayed for 3 years. His writing career had now begun.

In 1752 he became keeper of the Advocate's Library at Edinburgh, a position which allowed him to turn to historical writing. In 1763 he left England to become Secretary to the British Embassy in Paris. The society of Paris accepted him and was impressed by his learning, his acuteness of thought and his cheerfulness.

In 1766 he returned to London to become Undersecretary of State in 1767. Two years later he retired from public life and established his residence in Edinburgh where he remained for the rest of his life, enjoying the company of old and new friends including Adam Smith. He also continued to write new works and to revise earlier publications. Following a long illness he died in his Edinburgh house in 1776.

The Work

His major work lies in the fields of philosophy (*A Treatise of Human Nature*, 1739) and in history (*A History of England*, 1761). As an economist he favored economic individualism and (classical) liberalism. As a philosopher he was a Utilitarian, equating the useful with the good. His economic contributions were published in 1752 in a volume entitled *Political Discourses*. These essays have often been treated as self-contained. However, as far as Hume was concerned philosophy was at the center of all his writings and his treatment of economics reflect this. Even more than his friend Adam Smith (12 years his junior), Hume was a philosopher-economist. Hume has long been recognized as a major influence in the transition from mercantilism to classical economic thought. In the two essays published here he endeavors to bring down the curtain on mercantilist doctrine.

In his two essays, Hume makes five contributions to the theory of international trade and payments. First comes the price–specie flow mechanism. Hume presents this theory in the essay 'Of the Balance of Trade'. There he rejects the mercantilist preoccupation with a chronic surplus in the balance of trade. Making use of the (crude) quantity theory of money whereby the price level in a nation varies directly with the money supply, Hume showed that a policy aiming at a permanently favorable balance of trade was selfdefeating. If a country experiences an excess of exports over imports, specie will flow in. The country gaining gold and silver will experience a rise in its domestic price level while the opposite will happen in the country losing specie because of its import balance. Since quantities demanded by foreigners depend to some extent upon price, the exports of the country experiencing an inflow of bullion will fall. Its relatively high price level will also stimulate imports thus reversing the flow of specie. Simultaneously, the inverse process takes place in the foreign country suffering an outflow of gold and silver. Its price level will fall, its imports will be reduced and its exports will increase. Specie will start to flow in again. In conditions of free trade, says Hume, specie movements automatically correct trade imbalances. External trade and specie are akin to water in two connecting vessels constantly seeking a common level.

In his second essay 'Of the Jealousy of Trade', Hume demolishes the mercantilist view that a nation can only prosper at another's expense. Mercantilists always believed that one country's gain somehow led to an impoverishment of its neighbors. The idea of common economic growth was totally alien to them. Hume on the other hand argued that nations do benefit from the prosperity of other countries. In his second contribution to international economics, Hume explains that the economic development of countries other than England has benefited the British Isles. Through trade, England often acquired foreign commodities incorporating new technologies which were subsequently imitated and improved by domestic producers. Via this 'demonstration effect', the domestic advance of technology was enabled. Trade in other words fulfills an educational function.

In a third contribution Hume expresses the view that foreign competition has stimulating effects on the spirit of industry at home. Competitive pressures keep domestic producers on their toes so to speak.

Hume's analysis of the effects of one nation's prosperity upon its neighbors shows that he is a true believer in the natural harmony of interests. In a fourth contribution Hume clarifies that nations benefit from the prosperity of their neighbors. He argues that an expansion of industry and income abroad enhances foreign demand for 'our' products. A wealthy neighbor with high income will buy extensively from 'us'. This increased foreign demand will make 'us' prosper too and contribute to 'our' economic growth. Poor nations on the other hand, impoverish other countries as well, as they cannot take part in international exchange. Therefore Hume was inclined to pray even for the prosperity of France.

Finally, Hume realizes that the foreign demand for a specific domestic product may drop or disappear. Perhaps foreigners now produce the item themselves, perhaps they buy elsewhere. In modern language this would mean that a nation loses its comparative advantage position in the production of a particular commodity. Hume argues that nothing is to be feared from such events. An enterprising and civilized country can always divert some of its resources to the production of new items for which foreign markets can be found.[7]

Extracts

Of the Balance of Trade

It is very usual, in nations ignorant of the nature of commerce, to prohibit the exportation of commodities and to preserve among themselves whatever they think valuable and useful. They do not consider, that, in this prohibition, they act directly contrary to their intention; and that the more is exported of any commodity, the more will be raised at home, of which they themselves will always have the first offer.

It is well known to the learned, that the ancient laws of Athens rendered the exportation of figs criminal; that being supposed a species of fruit so excellent in Attica, that the Athenians deemed it too delicious for the palate of any foreigner. And in their ridiculous

7   Source: David Hume, 'Of the Jealousie of Trade'; 'Of the Balance of Trade' (E. Rotwein, ed.) *David Hume, Writings on Economics* (London: Nelson, 1955) pp. 60–66, 75, 77–82.

prohibition they were so much in earnest, the informers were thence called sycophants among them, from two Greek words, which signify figs and discoverer. There are proofs in many old acts of parliament of the same ignorance in the nature of commerce, particularly in the reign of Edward III. And to this day, in France, the exportation of corn is almost always prohibited; in order, as they say, to prevent famines; though it is evident, that nothing contributes more to the frequent famines, which so much distress that fertile country.

The same jealous fear, with regard to money, has also prevailed among several nations; and it required both reason and experience to convince any people, that these prohibitions serve to no other purpose than to raise the exchange against them, and produce a still greater exportation.

These errors, one may say, are gross and palpable: But there still prevails, even in nations well acquainted with commerce, a strong jealousy with regard to the balance of trade, and a fear, that all their gold and silver may be leaving them. This seems to me, almost in every case, a groundless apprehension; and I should as soon dread, that all our springs and rivers should be exhausted, as that money should abandon a kingdom where there are people and industry. Let us carefully preserve these latter advantages; and we need never be apprehensive of losing the former.

It is easy to observe, that all calculations concerning the balance of trade are founded on very uncertain facts and suppositions. The custom-house books are allowed to be an insufficient ground of reasoning; nor is the rate of exchange much better; unless we consider it with all nations, and know also the proportions of the several sums remitted; which one may safely pronounce impossible. Every man, who has ever reasoned on this subject, has always proved his theory, whatever it was, by facts and calculations, and by an enumeration of all the commodities sent to all foreign kingdoms.

The writings of Mr. Gee struck the nation with an universal panic, when they saw it plainly demonstrated, by a detail of particulars, that the balance was against them for so considerable a sum as must leave them without a single shilling in five or six years. But luckily, twenty years have since elapsed, with an expensive foreign war; yet is it commonly supposed, that money is still more plentiful among us than in any former period.

Nothing can be more entertaining on this head than Dr. Swift; an author so quick in discerning the mistakes and absurdities of others. He says, in his *short view of the state of Ireland*, that the whole cash of that kingdom formerly amounted but of 500,000$\mathcal{L}$.[8]; that out of this the Irish remitted every year a neat million to England, and had scarcely any other source from which they could compensate themselves, and little other foreign trade than the importation of French wines, for which they paid ready money. The consequence of this situation, which must be owned to be disadvantageous, was, that, in a course of three years, the current money of Ireland, from 500,000$\mathcal{L}$., was reduced to less than two. And at present, I suppose, in a course of 30 years it is absolutely nothing. Yet I know not how, that opinion of the advance of riches in Ireland, which indignation, seems still to continue, and gain ground with everybody.

In short, this apprehension of the wrong balance of trade, appears of such a nature, that it discovers itself, wherever one is out of humour with the ministry, or is in low spirits; and as it can never be refuted by a particular detail of all the exports, which counterbalance the imports, it may here be proper to form a general argument, that they may prove the impossibility of this event, as long as we preserve our people and our industry.

Suppose four-fifths of all the money in Great Britain to be annihilated in one night, and the nation reduced to the same condition, with regard to specie, as in the reigns of the Harrys and Edwards, what would be the consequence? Must not the price of all labour and commodities sink in proportion, and everything be sold as cheap as they were in those ages? What nation could then dispute with us in any foreign market, or pretend to navigate or to sell manufactures at the same price, which to us would afford sufficient profit? In how little time, therefore, must this bring back the money which we had lost, and raise us to the level of all the neighbouring nations? Where, after we have arrived, we immediately lose the advantage of the cheapness of labour and commodities; and the farther flowing in of money is stopped by our fullness and repletion.

Again, suppose, that all the money of Great Britain were multiplied fivefold in a night, must not the contrary effect follow? Must not all labour and commodities rise to such an exorbitant height, that no neighbouring nations could afford to buy from us; while their commodities, on the other hand, became comparatively so cheap, that, in spite of all the laws which could be formed, they would be run in upon us, and our money flow out; till we fall to a level with

---

8   The $\mathcal{L}$. stands for pound sterling, equivalent to 111 g of silver per pound (ed.).

foreigners, and lose that great superiority of riches, which had laid us under such disadvantages?

Now, it is evident, that the same causes which would correct these exorbitant inequalities, were they to happen miraculously, must prevent their happening in the common course of nature, and must for ever, in all neighbouring nations, preserve money nearly proportionable to the art and industry of each nation. All water, wherever it communicates, remains always at a level. Ask naturalists the reason; they tell you, that, were it to be raised in any one place, the superior gravity of that part not being balanced, must depress it, till it meet a counterpoise; and that the same cause, which redresses the inequality when it happens, must for ever prevent it, without some violent external operation.

Can one imagine, that it had ever been possible, by any laws, or even by any art or industry, to have kept all the money in Spain, which the galleons have brought from the Indies? Or that all commodities could be sold in France for a tenth of the price which they would yield on the other side of the Pyrenees, without finding their way thither, and draining from that immense treasure? What other reason, indeed, is there, why all nations, at present, gain in their trade with Spain and Portugal; but because it is impossible to heap up money, more than any fluid, beyond its proper level? The sovereigns of these countries have shown, that they wanted not inclination to keep their gold and silver to themselves, had it been in any degree practicable.

But as any body of water may be raised above the level of the surrounding element, if the former has no communication with the latter; so in money, if the communication be cut off, by any material or physical impediment (for all laws alone are ineffectual) there may, in such a case, be a very great inequality of money. Thus the immense distance of China, together with the monopolies of our India companies, obstructing the communication, preserve in Europe the gold and silver, especially the latter, in much greater plenty than they are found in that kingdom. But, notwithstanding this great obstruction, the force of the cause above mentioned is still evident. The skill and ingenuity of Europe in general surpasses perhaps that of China, with regard to manual arts and manufactures; yet are we never able to trade thither without great disadvantage. And were it not for the continual recruits, which we receive from America, money would soon sink in Europe, and rise in China, till it came nearly to a level in both places. Nor can any reasonable man doubt, but that industrious nation, were they as near us as Poland or Barbary, would drain us of the overplus of our specie, and draw to themselves a larger share of the West Indian treasures. We need not have recourse to a physical attraction, in order to explain the necessity of this operation. There is a moral attraction, arising from the interests and passions of men, which is full as potent and infallible.

How is the balance kept in the provinces of every kingdom among themselves, but by the force of this principle, which makes it impossible for money to lose its level, and either to rise or sink beyond the proportion of the labour and commodities which are in each province? Did not long experience make people easy on this head, what a fund of gloomy reflections might calculations afford to a melancholy Yorkshireman, while he computed and magnified the sums drawn to London by taxes, absentees, commodities, and found on comparison the opposite articles so much inferior? And no doubt, had the Heptarchy subsisted in England, the legislature of each state had been continually alarmed by the fear of a wrong balance; and as it is probable that the mutual hatred of these states would have been extremely violent on account of their close neigbourhood, they would have loaded and oppressed all commerce, by a jealous and superfluous caution. Since the union has removed the barriers between Scotland and England, which of these nations gains from the other by this free commerce? Or if the former kingdom has received any increase of riches, can it reasonably be accounted for by any thing but the increase of its art and industry? It was a common apprehension in England, before the union, as we learn from L'Abbé Du Bos, that Scotland would soon drain them of their treasure, were an open trade allowed; and on the other side the Tweed a contrary apprehension prevailed: with what justice in both, time has shown.

What happens in small portions of mankind, must take place in greater. The provinces of the Roman empire, no doubt, kept their balance with each other, and with Italy, independent of the legislature; as much as the several counties of Great Britain, or the several parishes of each county. And any man who travels over Europe at this day, may see, by the prices of commodities, that money, in spite of the absurd jealousy of princes and states, has brought itself nearly to a level; and that the difference between one kingdom and another is not greater in this respect, than it is often between different provinces of the same kingdom. Men naturally flock to capital cities, sea-ports, and navigable rivers. There we find more men, more industry, more commodities, and consequently more money; but still the later difference holds proportion with the former, and the level is preserved.

......

From these principles we may learn what judgment we ought to form of those numberless bars, obstructions, and imposts, which all nations of Europe, and none more than England, have put upon trade; from an exorbitant desire of amassing money, which never will heap up beyond its level, while it circulates; or from an ill-grounded apprehension of losing their specie, which never will sink below it. Could any thing scatter our riches, it would be such impolitic contrivances. But this general ill effect, however, results from them, that they deprive neighbouring nations of that free communication and exchange which the Author of the world has intended, by giving them soils, climates, and geniuses, so different from each other.

......

In short, a government has great reason to preserve with care its people and its manufactures. Its money, it may safely trust to the course of human affairs, without fear of jealousy. Or if it ever give attention to this latter circumstance, it ought only to be so far as it affects the former.

Of the Jealousy of Trade

Having endeavoured to remove one species of ill-founded jealousy, which is so prevalent among commercial nations, it may not be amiss to mention another, which seems equally groundless. Nothing is more usual, among states which have made some advances in commerce, than to look on the progress of their neighbours with a suspicious eye, to consider all trading states as their rivals, and to suppose that it is impossible for any of them to flourish, but at their expense. In opposition to this narrow and malignant opinion, I will venture to assert, that the encrease of riches and commerce in any one nation, instead of hurting, commonly promotes the riches and commerce of all its neighbours; and that a state can scarcely carry its trade and industry very far, where all the surrounding states are buried in ignorance, sloth, and barbarism.

It is obvious, that the domestic industry of a people cannot be hurt by the greatest prosperity of their neighbours; and as this branch of commerce is undoubtedly the most important in an extensive kingdom, we are so far removed from all reason of jealousy. But I go farther, and observe, that where an open communication is preserved among nations, it is impossible but the domestic industry of every one must receive an encrease from the improvements of the others. Compare the situation of Great Britain at present, with what it was two centuries ago. All the arts both of agriculture and manufactures were then extremely rude and imperfect. Every improvement, which we have since made, has arisen from our imitation, of foreigners; and we ought so far to esteem it happy, that they had previously made advances in art and ingenuity. But this intercourse is still upheld to our great advantage: Notwithstanding the advanced state of our manufactures, we daily adopt, in every art, the inventions and improvements of our neighbours. The commodity is first imported from abroad, to our great discontent, while we imagine that it drains us of our money: Afterwards, the art itself is gradually imported, to our visible advantage: Yet we continue still to repine, that our neighbours should possess any art industry, and invention; forgetting that, had they not first instructed us, we should have been at present barbarians; and did they not still continue their instruction, the arts must fall into a state of languor, and lose that emulation and novelty, which contribute so much to their advancement.

The encrease of domestic industry lays the foundation of foreign commerce. Where a great number of commodities are raised and perfected for the home-market, there will always be found some which can be exported with advantage. But if our neighbours have no art or cultivation, they cannot take them; because they will have nothing to give in exchange. In this respect, states are in the same condition as individuals; a single man can scarcely be industrious, where all his fellow-citizens are idle. The riches of the several members of a community contribute to encrease my riches, whatever profession I may follow. They consume the produce of my industry, and afford me the produce of theirs in return.

Nor needs any state entertain apprehensions, that their neighbours will improve to such a degree in every art and manufacture, as to have no demand from them. Nature, by giving a diversity of geniuses, climates, and soils, to different nations, has secured their mutual intercourse and commerce, as long as they all remain industrious and civilized. Nay, the more the arts increase in any state, the more will be its demands from its industrious neighbours. The inhabitants, having become opulent and skilful, desire to have every commodity in the utmost perfection; and as they have plenty of commodities to give in exchange, they make large importations from every foreign country. The industry of the nations, from whom they import, receives encouragement: Their own is also increased, by the sale of the commodities which they give in exchange.

But what if a nation has any staple commodity, such as the woollen manufacture is in England? Must not the interfering of our neighbours in that manufacture be a loss to us? I answer, that, when any commodity is denominated the staple of a kingdom, it is supposed that this kingdom has some peculiar and natural advantages for raising the commodity; and if, notwithstanding these advantages, they lose such a manufacture, they ought to blame their own idleness, or bad government, not the industry of their neighbours. It ought also to be considered, that, by the encrease of industry among the neighbouring nations, the consumption of every particular species of commodity is also encreased; and though foreign manufactures interfere with them in the market, the demand for their product may still continue, or even encrease. And should it diminish, ought the consequence to be esteemed so fatal? If the spirit of industry be preserved, it may easily be diverted from one branch to another; and the manufacturers of wool, for instance, be employed in linen, silk, iron, or any other commodities, for which there appears to be a demand. We need not apprehend, that all the objects of industry will be exhausted, or that our manufacturers, while they remain on an equal footing with those of our neighbours, will be in danger of wanting employment. The emulation among rival nations serves rather to keep industry alive in all of them: And any people is happier who possess a variety of manufactures, than if they enjoyed one single great manufacture, in which they will feel less sensibly those revolutions and uncertainties, to which every particular branch of commerce will always be exposed.

The only commercial state, that ought to dread the improvements and industry of their neighbours, is such a one as the Dutch, who enjoying no extent of land, nor possessing any number of native commodities, flourish only by their being the brokers, and factors, and carriers of others. Such a people may naturally apprehend, that, as soon as the neighbouring states come to know and pursue their interest, they will take into their own hands the management of their affairs, and deprive their brokers of that profit, which they formerly reaped from it. But though this consequence may naturally be dreaded, it is very long before it takes place; and by art and industry it may be warded off for many generations, if not wholly eluded. The advantage of superior stocks and correspondence is so great, that it is not easily overcome; and as all the transactions encrease by the encrease of industry in the neighbouring states even a people whose commerce stands on this precarious basis, may at first reap a considerable profit from the flourishing condition of their neighbours. The Dutch, having mortgaged all their revenues, make not such a figure in political transactions as formerly; but their commerce is surely equal to what it was in the middle of the last century, when they were reckoned among the great powers of Europe.

Were our narrow and malignant politics to meet with success, we should reduce all our neighbouring nations to the same state of sloth and ignorance that prevails in Morocco and the coast of Barbary. But what would be the consequence? They could send us no commodities: They could take none from us: Our domestic commerce itself would languish for want of emulation, example, and instruction: And we ourselves should soon fall into the same abject condition, to which we had reduced them. I shall therefore venture to acknowledge, that, not only as a man, but as a British subject, I pray for the flourishing commerce of Germany, Spain, Italy, and even France itself. I am at least certain, that Great Britain, and all those nations, would flourish more, did their sovereigns and ministers adopt such enlarged and benevolent sentiments towards each other.

2. Classical Liberalism and Free Trade in the Late Eighteenth and Nineteenth Century

PREAMBLE

1

Early liberalism consisted of a set of principles, a philosophy and a movement which was committed to freedom as a method and policy for government, as an organizing principle in society and as a way of life for the individual and the community. The term 'liberalism' is Spanish in origin and comes from the name of a Spanish political party, the 'Liberales' which early in the nineteenth century advocated constitutional government for Spain. Liberalism is the end product of centuries of development. In England the liberal spirit of the seventeenth and eighteenth century was nourished by a slow and persistent acquisition of liberties. In France it emerged during a period when the French royalty and nobility were parasitic and divorced from function. In the late eighteenth and early nineteenth century the two streams of thought merged into a coherent system of ideas and practical goals.

Early liberals sought to free individuals from the unjust hampering restraints imposed upon them by governments, institutions and traditions. Thus, classical liberalism stood for changes which diminished coercion or compulsory cooperation and which increased voluntary collaboration. The interference of the state had to be restricted and state policy had to be transformed into a vehicle for promoting the liberties of individuals and groups. To these ends, liberals stressed free contract and the rule of law in the political-juridical sphere and the importance of a free selfregulating market, unrestrained by monopoly or political intervention in the economic domain. Free international trade was seen as an essential complement to domestic economic freedom.

2

Economic liberalism or the theory and practice of economic liberty

29

held that economic and other freedoms are inseparable. Economic liberalism is merely part of a system of values centering on individual freedom. The government was not to interfere in economic life except as the custodian of the free market. Its function as guardian of the free market obliged it to enforce contracts, punish frauds, protect competition and maintain a stable currency. No law should confer special privileges on some and impose discrimination on others. Therefore, a law protecting certain industries and not others was antiliberal. Thus economic liberalism expressed itself as a demand for both the internal freedom of enterprise and the external freedom of exportation and importation.

Economic liberalism was formulated with precision by a group of French thinkers of the eighteenth century, called the 'Physiocrats', and the classical school of English economists. The Physiocrats believed in a beneficent, harmonious, selfoperating, physical order of nature which could be matched in the socio-economic sphere if the government limited itself to some basic functions and abstained from paternalistic interference in the economic process.[9] The famous expression 'laissez-faire' was coined by the Physiocrats signifying that governments were to refrain from intervening in the economic activities of individuals and enterprises allowing free scope to the working of the natural economic laws. Interference with the operation of the market must necessarily restrict output and make everybody poorer.

After the Physiocrats, Adam Smith's *Wealth of Nations* (1776) became the great source of ideas and policies distinctive to economic liberalism. In his system of laissez-faire economics the functions assigned to government were substantially similar to those of the Physiocrats. The state had to maintain inter-individual liberty, peace and justice, defense against foreign enemies and public works. Education and other tasks which the private sector would or could not undertake could also be assigned to governments. Wealth was created by production, and freedom in the market would enhance it. Producers, merchants and consumers being motivated by self-interest follow the dictates of their own interests and desires. But the 'invisible hand' guides producers to supply consumers' needs and households to

9   The notion of natural law comes from Sir Isaac Newton and his colleagues in
      the scientific revolution of the sixteenth and seventeenth century. They revealed
      that the operation of the universe could be explained rationally in terms of
      universal and immutable laws that operated smoothly and infallibly.

offer the resources necessary for enterprise. Thus the invisible hand directs each to serve the interest of the other in pursuing his own interest. This concept replaced the mercantilist idea whereby what one gains the other must lose. Competition would keep everybody in line. The government should follow a policy of laissez-faire leaving producers free to compete in the market. Households should also be free to sell their resources. In relation to other nations, free trade was the ideal formula. Peaceful, voluntary international economic exchange would allow for a better division of labor, greater productivity and a higher level of prosperity for all. Once again, the pursuit of individual advantage seemed admirably connected with the universal good of the whole. The other classical economists such as Ricardo, Malthus, Say and Bastiat produced somewhat different versions of classical economics. Yet the principle of economic freedom was maintained. When early liberalism appeared in a very nonliberal world, the liberal vision was comparatively radical. Later, towards the middle of the nineteenth century liberalism changed from a principle of social criticism to one of actual government practice. Freedom was the polestar of the public mind. When there was an evil to be dealt with, men looked almost instinctively for its cause in the manifestation of some arbitrary power which, needless to say, had to be removed. In countries such as England and the Netherlands where powerful Liberal Parties existed, the Liberals, whether in power or not, emphasized an economic program and policy which minimized state intervention and attempted to carry out the philosophy of economic freedom under the difficult conditions of progressive industrialization and urbanization. The triumph of free trade in England originated in 1846 when the Corn Laws were abolished.

In England a broad Liberal movement and a powerful Liberal Party existed. In the United States the Liberal Party was non-existent. In continental countries such as Germany and France a broad Liberal movement was also absent. In a number of European countries, therefore, classical liberalism did not fully develop. Liberal creeds did arise but they lacked a broad-based support group. As a result, liberalism failed often during the first half of the nineteenth century while in later decades it was unable to impose itself because of statism, socialism and nationalism which had already become the popular gospels. Yet from 1815 until 1914 liberalism spoke with great authority. Although it was never permitted to come to full fruition, this brief period of widespread influence sufficed to release man's productive powers as never before and to raise the standard of living in the western world to hitherto unknown levels. It transformed Great Britain into the workshop of the world and it created a world market for numerous goods and services.

3

In the second half of the nineteenth century, the principles of liberalism prevailed with varying degrees of effectiveness in practically all civilized countries. Yet, the actual practice of liberalism fell short of the theory and 'laissez-faire' was never fully applied. For one reason or another the state did sometimes intervene in economic and social affairs. Thus, between 1850 and 1900 a great deal of compulsory legislation dealing with sanitary, health and working conditions was passed.

The prosperity, security and tolerance which prevailed, favored dissent and produced a wide range of rival philosophic and political creeds. Central to that range stood classical liberalism. Increasingly, however, this outlook came under strong hostile attack. To the 'right' of liberalism stood the romantic, conservative, and authoritarian critics. To the left stood both the radical socialists and the more moderate socialist prophets. Despite a strong defense by such writers as Herbert Spencer in England and William G. Sumner in the United States, the liberal idea was now challenged at its very foundations. An important reason for this change in intellectual climate was, that by the end of the century universal suffrage was virtually established in most of the nations in Western Europe. Equality before the ballot box was now added to equality before the law. This marked the beginning of a change of permanent importance. The proletarian working class which emerged as the industrialization process proceeded, had no sympathy for the doctrine of liberalism. This emerging labor class and its leaders tended frequently to be socialist and radical in their political outlook. The urban workers wanted above all greater social and economic benefits through legislation. The concept of an impartial state gave way to the notion of a state which could be conquered and used for the attainment of class objectives. New political parties were committed to the use of the authority of the state in the interest of specific groups such as the dependent workers. The revolutionary socialists went further and argued that through revolutionary action the working class should transfer all political and economic power to itself.

With the growth of popular suffrage, political parties were

tempted, in order to capture the popular vote, to outbid each other in their promises of more social welfare legislation and more redistribution of income. The liberals of the late nineteenth century were no exception. They still talked the language of liberty but more and more their dominant drive was towards the redistribution of income, and wealth and the provision of social services. Increasingly, the original meaning of liberalism was drawn from that term, at least in England and the United States. In England the 'People's Budget' of Lloyd George in 1909 introduced large scale social legislation reflecting the changed outlook of the English liberal party.

The demand for the interventionist provider state was now rising and as the Liberals responded to it, it became more and more difficult to distinguish between the 'new' liberalism and the milder forms of socialism.

Thus around and after the turn of the century there was an increasing stress placed on such notions as social justice, social responsibility, social control, social rights and social welfare. What each of these concepts basically meant in concrete terms, was more taxes, more government interference and more coercive legislation. Officialdom, government interference and regulation tend to feed upon themselves. Every additional state encroachment strengthens the tacit assumption that it is the duty of the state to deal with all problems and to secure all benefits. Besides, each state interference tends to increase the need for additional administrative compulsions and restraints which result from the unforeseen evils and shortcomings of preceding interventions.

As public opinion in Europe and the United States moved away from classical liberalism towards more collectivist orientations, free trade was de-emphasized, self-sufficiency and protectionism were stressed and offensive activities for national preservation and aggrandizement became more common, culminating in World War I. This war further weakened whatever was left of genuine liberalism and its commitment to free trade. The same was true for the establishment of totalitarian socialist and fascist nations. External threats evoke response and response demands collective effort which is typically stimulated by nonliberal incentives and appeals. Thus the twentieth century has become the century of coercion and of state idolatry.

READING 4

Adam Smith

Biography

Adam Smith (1723–1790) who was to become the pioneer formulator of English classical economics was born in 1723 at Kirkcaldy (Scotland), a fisheries and mining town near Edinburgh. His father died three months before he was born and his mother, a talented woman, was left with the responsibility for his upbringing.

His early education was obtained in local schools. Thereafter he was educated at the Universities of Glasgow and Oxford. At Glasgow University he became a pupil of Francis Hutchinson from whom he learned the concept of a beneficent natural order. Later, Smith became a professor of logic, and then of moral philosophy at Glasgow University (1751). His first great work *The Theory of Moral Sentiments* materialized in 1759. Following 13 years at the University of Glasgow he accepted a position as tutor to the young Duke of Buccleuch from whom he received a pension which he held for the remaining years of his life. As a tutor he travelled, chiefly in France and Switzerland (1764–1766) where he met such leading thinkers as Turgot, Quesnay and Voltaire. By the time he began work on his *Inquiry into the Nature and Causes of the Wealth of Nations* (usually abbreviated to *The Wealth of Nations*) in 1764, he was already a man widely read in history and economics and versed in English and French philosophy. Smith also had a great insight into human nature and had learned much from the alert and successful people he had associated with. The *Wealth of Nations* was published in 1776. In 1778 he was appointed a commissioner of customs for Scotland, a post he held until his death in 1790. Like his friend David Hume, Adam Smith was a sober minded, composed and good natured individual.

The Work

Adam Smith lived in an age deeply impressed by a Newtonian order of nature which envisaged the universe as a vast machine whose parts were operated harmoniously according to a plan. This harmonious and beneficial functioning testified to the wisdom of its maker. Following the footsteps of Francis Hutchinson, Smith adopted the idea of a type of social Newtonianism in which the socioeconomic order is also modelled according to a beneficent pattern.

According to Smith the natural order is inherently simple, harmonious and beneficial.[10] The free play of self-interest, produces automatically a natural harmony of interests. The pursuit of private concerns by persons directed by liberty and justice would allow individuals not only to attain their own best advantage but would also promote the common good. Individuals are motivated by the desire to better their own condition. However, this obliges them to produce those goods and services required by other people. Therefore an 'invisible hand' leads self-seeking people to promote the public interest even though this was not their main intention. As far as Smith was concerned, the harmony of the interest principle operated both at the domestic and international level resulting in both the domestic and international economy being self-regulating. The idea of 'laissez-faire' was of course associated with the concept of minimum government intervention. Governments were often wasteful and corrupt, according to Smith, and the majority of legislation was either useless or damaging. It usually distorted the natural order preventing the invisible hand from harmonizing the private and the public benefit. Besides, governments which thwart the natural course of things are usually obliged to become oppressive and tyrannical in the process. Smith believed the mercantilist idea of wealth consisting of gold and silver to be a fallacy. He also questioned the usefulness of a positive balance of trade. He argued that real wealth consisted of consumable output produced by labor in conjunction with the other factors of production. Production could always be augmented by a better division of labor. Yet consumption remained the sole end of production. Trade, both domestic and international, was significant because it permitted a wider division of labor limited by the extent of the market. Larger markets increase productivity and more wealth (output) is generated. Money or treasure was vital as a means of payment, it facilitated the exchange of goods and services. However, by themselves, gold and silver coins were dead stock producing nothing. It was the production of goods and services that constituted

---

10   By the natural order Smith meant the operation of the unpremeditated propensities and impulses of individual men and women of which self-interest is the most important. Self-interest meant to Smith not only the desire for income but self-improvement in all its possible manifestations. See also: J. Viner, 'Adam Smith and Laissez-faire', *Essays in Economic Thought* (J.J. Spengler, W. R. Allen, eds) (Chicago: Rand, 1960).

a nation's prosperity not bullion.

As noted previously, Smith believed that foreign trade had an important function to fulfill. By enlarging the market and increasing the opportunities for a greater division of labor, foreign trade enhanced the creation of wealth.

Even although Smith considered domestic trade to be of more importance than international trade, he also discussed some of the advantages of foreign trade. Free international trade allows a nation to acquire goods not produced at home. A nation can benefit by the importing of items which can be made cheaper other than at home. This concept is now referred to as the principle of absolute advantage. Foreign trade also provides an outlet for the commodities produced in excess of domestic needs.[11] Individuals differ and this results in some having an advantage over others. This principle (of absolute advantage) also applies to countries because of climate, location, the availability of mineral deposits and the like; each nation has an advantage in the production of something. With territorial specialization, all nations will share in the gains from trade. Public policies involving artificial encouragement to exports or interference with imports will only distort international harmony and make everyone worse off. The promotion and preservation of free competition should therefore be the principal objective of economic policy.

In book IV of *The Wealth of Nations*, Smith vehemently attacks the mercantile system and its protectionist policies which benefits the narrow special interests of certain manufactures and merchants but overlooks the interests of the consumer. Restraints on imports create monopoly power and redirect capital away from more productive employment into the protected sectors. Bounties to promote exports, argues Smith, result in the payment to foreigners for the purchase of goods. Mercantilists still believe that these devices enrich the whole country. As Smith put it, bounties or export subsidies impose two different taxes upon people. First, money must be raised to pay the bounty. Second, as exports (for example cereals) are encouraged, the available domestic supplies drop. This imposes a second tax on the consumer in the form of higher prices which reduce people's real incomes. According to Smith, moderate duties could be justified under

---

11   This is a variety of the 'vent for surplus' theory which states that exports are an outlet for surplus commodities.

certain conditions. A particular industry, very important to the defense of a country, might require some protection. If a domestic tax is imposed upon the produce of a home industry it might be reasonable to impose an equal duty on the foreign equivalent to offset the domestic tax. Moreover, if foreign nations impose high duties upon a product of a given country, that nation might retaliate in order to bring the other country to terms. Finally, Smith believed that if protective taxes were lifted this should be done slowly and only after due warning.

In a more general sense Smith opposed protectionist state regulation and monopoly because they involved privilege. Much of this privilege if not it all, was due to government intervention. All too often (and here Smith anticipates public choice economics) the state was manipulated by special interest groups to create favored positions for themselves at the expense of others. In fact, much of Smith's criticism was in terms of the special immunities given and the vested interests of the merchants and manufacturers. Without government intervention to help them and given an active policy to promote competition, those in search of privilege were powerless. This led Smith to believe that state action is guilty until proven beneficent. Most of the problems the world was suffering from were simply the result of misguided past government regulation, inherited from centuries of interventionism with its militaristic and dynastic values. Sweep away all of these measures and the world would be a better place. International trade should create bonds of union and friendship among nations according to Smith. Mercantilism with its absurd policies has made it into a source of discord and animosity.[12]

Extracts

That wealth consists in money, or in gold and silver, is a popular notion which naturally arises from the double function of money, as the instrument of commerce, and as the measure of value. In consequence of its being the instrument of commerce, when we have money we can more readily obtain whatever else we have occasion for, than by means of any other commodity. The great affair, we always find, is to get money. When that is obtained there is no

---

12   Source: A. Smith, *Inquiry into the Nature and Causes of the Wealth of Nations*, Book IV (New York: Random House, 1937) pp. 398–439.

difficulty in making any subsequent purchase in consequence of it
being the measure of value, we estimate that of all other commodities
by the quantity of money which they will exchange for. We say of a
rich man that he is worth a great deal, and of a poor man that he is
worth very little money. A frugal man, or a man eager to be rich, is
said to love money; and a careless, a generous, or a profuse man, is
said to be indifferent about it. To grow rich is to get money; and
wealth and money, in short, are, in common language, considered as
in every respect synonymous.

A rich country, in the same manner as a rich man, is supposed
to be a country abounding in money; and to heap up gold and silver
in any country is supposed to be the readiest way to enrich it.

......

Others admit that if a nation could be separated from all the
world, it would be of no consequence how much, or how little money
circulated in it. The consumable goods which were circulated by
means of this money, would only be exchanged for a greater or a
smaller number of pieces; but the real wealth or poverty of the
country, they allow, would depend altogether upon the abundance or
scarcity of those consumable goods. But it is otherwise, they think,
with countries which have connections with foreign nations, and which
are obliged to carry on foreign wars, and to maintain fleets and armies
in distant countries. This, they say, cannot be done, but by sending
abroad money to pay them with; and a nation cannot send much
money abroad, unless it has a good deal at home. Every such nation,
therefore, must endeavour in time of peace to accumulate gold and
silver, that, when occasion requires, it may have wherewithal to carry
on foreign wars.

In consequence of these popular notions, all the different nations
of Europe have studied, though to little purpose, every possible means
of accumulating gold and silver in their respective countries.

......

'A country that has no mines of its own must undoubtedly draw
its gold and silver from foreign countries, in the same manner as one
that has no vineyards of its own must draw its wines. It does not seem
necessary, however, that the attention of government should be more
turned towards the one than towards the other object. A country that
has wherewithal to buy wine, will always get the wine which it has
occasion for; and a country that has wherewithal to buy gold and
silver, will never be in want of those metals. They are to be bought
for a certain price and as they are the price of all other commodities,

so all commodities are the price of those metals. We trust with perfect security that the freedom of trade, without any attention of government, will always supply us with the wine which we have occasion for: and we may trust with equal security that it will always supply us with all the gold and silver which we can afford to purchase or to employ, either in circulating our commodities, or in other uses.
......

If, notwithstanding all this, gold and silver should at any time fall short in a country which has wherewithal to purchase them, there are more expedients for supplying their place, than that of almost any other commodity. If the materials of manufacture are wanted, industry must stop. If provisions are wanted, the people must starve. But if money is wanted, barter will supply its place, though with a good deal of inconvenience. Buying and selling upon credit, and the different dealers compensating their credits with one another, once a month or once a year, will supply it with less inconvenience. A well regulated paper money will supply it, not only without any inconvenience, but, in some cases, with some advantages. Upon every account, therefore, the attention of government never was so unnecessarily employed, as when directed to watch over the preservation or increase of the quantity of money in any country.
......

It would be too ridiculous to go about seriously to prove, that wealth does not consist in money, or in gold and silver; but in what money purchases, and is valuable only for purchasing.
......

Consumable commodities, it is said, are soon destroyed; whereas gold and silver are of a more durable nature, and, were it not for this continual exportation, might be accumulated for ages together, to the incredible augmentation of the real wealth of the country. Nothing, therefore, it is pretended, can be more disadvantageous to any country, than the trade which consists in the exchange of such lasting for such perishable commodities. We do not, however, reckon that trade is disadvantageous which consists in the exchange of the hard-ware of England for the wines of France and yet hard-ware is a very durable commodity, and were it not for this continual exportation, might too be accumulated for ages together, to the incredible augmentation of the pots and pans of the country. But it readily occurs that the number of such utensils is in every country necessarily limited by the use which there is for them; that it would be absurd to have more pots and pans than were necessary for cooking the victuals usually consumed there; and that if the quantity of victuals were to increase, the number of pots and pans would readily increase along with it, a part of the increased quantity of victuals being employed in purchasing them, or in maintaining an additional number of workmen whose business it was to make them. It should as readily occur that the quantity of gold and silver is in every country limited by the use which there is for those metals; that their use consists in circulating commodities as coin, and in affording a species of household furniture as plate; that the quantity of coin in every country is regulated by the value of the commodities which are to be circulated by it: increase that value, and immediately a part of it will be sent abroad to purchase, wherever it is to be had, the additional quantity of coin requisite for circulating them: that the quantity of plate is regulated by the number and wealth of those private families who chose to indulge themselves in that sort of magnificence: increase the number and wealth of such families, and a part of this increased wealth will most probably be employed in purchasing, wherever it is to be found, an additional quantity of plate: that to attempt to increase the wealth of any country, either by introducing or by detaining in it an unnecessary quantity of gold and silver, is as absurd as it would be to attempt to increase the good cheer of private families, by obliging them to keep an unnecessary number of kitchen utensils. As the expense of purchasing those unnecessary utensils would diminish instead of increasing either the quantity or goodness of the family provisions; so the expense of purchasing an unnecessary quantity of gold and silver must, in every country, as necessarily diminish the wealth which feeds, clothes, and lodges, which maintains and employs the people. Gold and silver, whether in the shape of coin or plate, are utensils, it must be remembered, as much as the furniture of the kitchen. Increase the use for them, increase the consumable commodities which are to be circulated, managed, and prepared by means of them, and you will infallibly increase the quantity; but if you attempt, by extraordinary means, to increase the quantity too, which in those metals can never be greater than what the use requires. Were they ever to be accumulated beyond this quantity, their transportation is so easy, and the loss which attends their lying idle and unemployed so great, that no law could prevent their being immediately sent out of the country.

It is not always necessary to accumulate gold and silver, in order to enable a country to carry on foreign wars, and to maintain fleets and armies in distant countries. Fleets and armies are maintained, not with gold and silver, but with consumable goods. The nation which can maintain foreign wars there is the one which has the wherewithal. These resources are derived from the annual produce of its domestic industry, from the annual revenue arising out of its lands, labour, and consumable stock.

......

The importation of gold and silver is not the principal, much less the sole benefit which a nation derives from its foreign trade. Between whatever places foreign trade is carried on, they all of them derive two distinct benefits from it. It carries out that surplus part of the produce of their land and labour for which there is no demand among them, and brings back in return for it something else for which there is a demand. It gives a value to their superfluities, by exchanging them for something else, which may satisfy a part of their wants, and increase their enjoyments. By means of it, the narrowness of the home market does not hinder the division of labour in any particular branch of art or manufacture from being carried to the highest perfection. By opening a more extensive market for whatever part of the produce of the produce of their labour may exceed the home consumption, it encourages them to improve its productive powers, and to augment its annual produce to the utmost, and thereby to increase the real revenue and wealth of the society. These great and important services foreign trade is continually occupied in performing, to all the different countries between which it is carried on. They all derive great benefit from it, though that in which the merchant resides generally derives the greatest, as he is generally more employed in supplying the wants, and carrying out the superfluities of his own, than of any other particular country. To import the gold and silver which may be wanted, into the countries which have no mines, is no doubt, a part of the business of foreign commerce. It is, however, a most insignificant part of it. A country which carried on foreign trade merely upon this account, could scarce have occasion to freight a ship in a century.

It is not by the importation of gold and silver, that the discovery of America has enriched Europe. By opening a new inexhaustible market to all the commodities of Europe, it gave occasion to new divisions of labour and improvements, of art, which, in the narrow circle of the ancient commerce, could never have taken place for want of a market to take off the greater part of their produce. The productive powers of labour were improved, and its produce increased in all the different countries of Europe, and together with it the real revenue and wealth of the inhabitants. The commodities of Europe were almost all new to America, and many of those of America were new to Europe. A new set of exchanges therefore, began to take place which had never been thought of before, and which should naturally have proved as advantageous to the new, as it certainly did to the old continent.

I thought it necessary, though at the hazard of being tedious, to examine at full length this popular notion that wealth consists in money, or in gold and silver. Money in common language, as I have already observed, frequently signifies wealth; and this ambiguity of expression has rendered this popular notion so familiar to us, that even they, who are convinced of its absurdity, are very apt to forget their own principles, and in the course of their reasoning to take it for granted as a certain and undeniable truth. Some of the best English writers upon commerce set out with observing, that the wealth of a country consists, not in its gold and silver only, but in its lands, houses, and consumable goods of all different kinds. In the course of their reasoning, however, the lands, houses and consumable goods seem to slip out of their memory, and the strain of their argument frequently supposes that all wealth consists in gold and silver, and that to multiply those metals is the great object of national industry and commerce.

The two principles being established, however, that wealth consisted in gold and silver, and that those metals could be brought into a country which had no mines only by the balance of trade, or by exporting to a greater value than it imported; it necessarily became the great object of political economy to diminish as much as possible the importation of foreign goods for home consumption, and to increase as much as possible the exportation of the produce of domestic industry. Its two great engines for enriching the country, therefore, were restraints upon importation, and encouragements to exportation.

Of Restraints upon the Importation from Foreign Countries of such Goods as can be produced at Home

By restraining, either by high duties, or by absolute prohibitions, the importation of such goods from foreign countries as can be produced at home, the monopoly of the home market is more or less secured to the domestic industry employed in producing them.

That this monopoly of the home market frequently gives great encouragement to that particular species of industry which enjoys it, and frequently turns towards that employment a great share of both the labour and stock of the society than would otherwise have gone to it, cannot be doubted. But whether it tends either to increase the general industry of the society, or to give it the most advantageous direction, is not, perhaps, altogether so evident.

The general industry of the society never can exceed what the capital of the society can employ. As the number of workmen that can be kept in employment by any particular person must bear a certain proportion to his capital, so the number of those that can be continually employed by all the members of a great society, must bear a certain proportion to the whole capital of that society, and never can exceed that proportion. No regulation of commerce can increase the quantity of industry in any society beyond what its capital can maintain. It can only divert a part of it into a direction into which it might not otherwise have gone; and it is by no means certain that this artificial direction is likely to be more advantageous to the society than that into which it would have gone of its own accord.

Every individual is continually exerting himself to find out the most advantageous employment for whatever capital he can command. It is his own advantage, indeed, and not that of the society, which he has in view. But the study of his own advantage naturally, or rather necessarily leads him to prefer that employment which is most advantageous to the society.
......
Every individual who employs his capital in the support of domestic industry, necessarily endeavours so to direct that industry, that its produce may be of the greatest possible value.

The produce of industry is what it adds to the subject or materials upon which it is employed. In proportion as the value of this produce is great or small, so will like-wise be the profits of the employer. But it is only for the sake of profit that any man employs a capital in the support of industry; and he will always, therefore, endeavour to employ it in the support of that industry of which the produce is likely to be of the greatest value, or to exchange for the greatest quantity either of money or of other goods.

But the annual revenue of every society is always precisely equal to the exchangeable value of the whole annual produce of its industry, or rather is precisely the same thing with that exchangeable value. As every individual, therefore, endeavours as much as he can both to employ his capital in the support of domestic industry, and so to direct that industry that its produce may be of the greatest value; every individual necessarily labours to render the annual revenue of the society as great as he can. He generally, indeed, neither intends to promote the public interest, nor knows how much he is promoting it. By preferring the support of domestic to that of foreign industry, he intends only his own security; and by directing that industry in such a manner as its produce may be of the greatest value, he intends only his own gain, and he is in this, as in many other cases, led by an invisible hand to promote an end which was no part of his intention. Nor is it always the worse for the society that it was no part of it. By pursuing his own interest he frequently promotes that of the society more effectually than when he really intends to promote it. I have never known much good done by those who affected to trade for the public good. It is an affectation, indeed, not very common among merchants, and very few words need be employed in dissuading them from it.

What is the species of domestic industry which his capital can employ, and of which the produce is likely to be of the greatest value, every individual, it is evident, can, in his local situation, judge much better than any statesman or lawgiver can do for him. The statesman, who should attempt to direct private people in what manner they ought to employ their capitals, would not only load himself with a most unnecessary attention, but assume an authority which could safely be trusted, not only to no single person, but to no council or senate whatever, and which would nowhere be so dangerous as in the hands of a man who had folly and presumption enough to fancy himself to exercise it.

To give the monopoly of the home-market to the produce of domestic industry, in any particular art or manufacture, is in some measure to direct private people in what manner they ought to employ their capitals, and must, in almost all cases, be either a useless or hurtful regulation. If the produce of domestic can be brought there as cheap as that of foreign industry, the regulation is evidently useless. If it cannot, it must generally be hurtful. It is the maxim of every prudent master of a family, never to attempt to make at what it will cost him more to make than to buy. The tailor does not attempt to make his own shoes, but buys them of the shoemaker. The shoemaker does not attempt to make his own clothes, but employs a tailor. The farmer attempts to make neither the one nor the other, but employs those different artificers. All of them find it for their interest to employ their whole industry in a way in which they have some advantage over their neighbours and to purchase with a part of its produce, or what is the same thing, with the price or a part of it, whatever else they have occasion for

What is prudence in the conduct of every private family, can scarce be folly in that of a great kingdom. If a foreign country can supply us with a commodity cheaper than we ourselves can make it, better buy it of them with some part of the produce of our own industry, employed in a way in which we have some advantage. The general industry of the country, being always in proportion to the capital which employs it, will not thereby be diminished, no more than that of the abovementioned artificers; but only left to find out the way in which it can be employed with the greatest advantage. It is certainly not employed to the greatest advantage, when it is thus directed towards an object which it can buy cheaper than it can make. The value of its annual produce is certainly more or less diminished, when it is thus turned away from producing commodities evidently of more value than the commodity which it is directed to produce. According to the supposition, that commodity could be purchased from foreign countries cheaper than it can be made at home. It could, therefore, have been purchased with a part only of the commodities, or, what is the same thing, with a part only of the price of the commodities, which the industry employed by an equal capital would have produced at home, had it been left to follow its natural course. The industry of the country, therefore, is thus turned away from a more, to a less advantageous employment, and the exchangeable value of its annual produce, instead of being increased, according to the intention of the lawgiver, must necessarily be diminished by every such regulation.

By means of such regulations, indeed, a particular manufacture may sometimes be acquired sooner than it could have been otherwise, and after a certain time may be made at home as cheap or cheaper than in the foreign country. But though the industry of the society may be thus carried with advantage into a particular channel sooner than it could have been otherwise, it will by no means follow that the sum total, either of its industry, or of its revenue, can ever be augmented by any such regulation. The industry of the society can augment only in proportion as its capital augments, and its capital can augment only in proportion to what can be gradually saved out of its revenue. But the immediate effect of every such regulation is to diminish its revenue, and what diminishes its revenue is certainly not very likely to augment its capital faster than it would have augmented of its own accord, had both capital and industry been left to find out their natural employments.

Though for want of such regulations the society should never acquire the proposed manufacture, it would not, upon that account, necessarily be the poorer in any one period of its duration. In every period of its duration its whole capital and industry might still have been employed, though upon different objects, in the manner that was most advantageous at the time. In every period its revenue might have been the greatest which its capital could afford, and both capital and revenue might have been augmented with the greatest possible rapidity.

The natural advantages which one country has over another in producing particular commodities are sometimes so great, that it is acknowledged by all the world to be in vain to struggle with them. By means of glasses, hotbeds, and hotwalls, very good grapes can be raised in Scotland, and very good wine too can be made of them at about thirty times the expense for which at least equally good can be brought from foreign countries. Would it be a reasonable law to prohibit the importation of all foreign wines, merely to encourage the making of claret and burgundy in Scotland? But if there would be a manifest absurdity in turning towards any employment, thirty times more of the capital and industry of the country, than would be necessary to purchase from foreign countries an equal quantity of the commodities wanted, there must be an absurdity, though not altogether so glaring, yet exactly of the same kind, in turning towards any such employment a thirtieth, or even a three hundredth part more of either. Whether the advantages which one country has over another, be natural or acquired, is in this respect of no consequence. As long as the one country has those advantages, and the other wants them, it will always be more advantageous for the latter, rather to buy of the former than to make. It is an acquired advantage only, which one artificer has over his neighbour, who exercises another trade; and yet they both find it more advantageous to buy of one another, than to make what does not belong to their particular trades.

......

There seem, however, to be two cases in which it will generally be advantageous to lay some burden upon foreign, for the encouragement of domestic industry.

The first is, when some particular sort of industry is necessary for the defence of the country. The defence of the Great Britain, for example, depends very much upon the number of its sailors and shipping. The act of navigation, therefore, very properly endeavours

to give the sailors and shipping of Great Britain the monopoly of the trade of their own country, in some cases, by absolute prohibition, and in others by heavy burdens upon the shipping of foreign countries.
......

The act of navigation is not favourable to foreign commerce, or to the growth of that opulence which can arise from it. As defence, however, is of much more importance than opulence, the act of navigation is, perhaps the wisest of all the commercial regulations of England.

The second case, in which it will generally be advantageous to lay some burden upon foreign for the encouragement of domestic industry, is, when some tax is imposed at home upon the produce of the latter. In this case, it seems reasonable that an equal tax should be imposed upon the like produce of the former. This would not give the monopoly of the home market to domestic industry, nor turn towards a particular employment a greater share of the stock and labour of the country, than what would naturally go to it. It would only hinder any part of what would naturally go to it from being turned away by the tax, into a less natural direction, and would leave the competition between foreign and domestic industry, after the tax, as nearly as possible upon the same footing as before it.
......

As there are two cases in which it will generally be advantageous to lay some burden upon foreign for the encouragement of domestic industry; so there are two others in which it may sometimes be a matter of deliberation; in the one, how far it is proper to continue the free importation of certain foreign goods; and in the other, how far, or in what manner, it may be proper to restore that free importation after it has been for some time interrupted.

The case in which it may sometimes be a matter of deliberation how far it is proper to continue the free importation of certain foreign goods, is, when some foreign nation restrains by high duties or prohibitions the importation of some of our manufactures into their country. Revenge in this case naturally dictates retaliation, and that we should impose the like duties and prohibitions upon the importation of some or all of their manufactures into ours. Nations accordingly seldom fail to retaliate in this manner.

There may be good policy in retaliation of this kind, when there is a probability that they will procure the repeal of the high duties or prohibitions complained of. The recovery of a great foreign market will generally more than compensate the transitory inconvenience of paying dearer during a short time for some sorts of goods. To judge whether such retaliations are likely to produce such an effect, does not, perhaps, belong so much to the science of a legislator, whose deliberations ought to be governed by general principles which are always the same, as to the skill of that insidious and crafty animal, vulgarly called a statesman or politician, whose councils are directed by momentary fluctuations of affairs. When there is no probability that any such repeal can be procured, it seems a bad method of compensating the injury done to certain classes of our people, to do another injury ourselves, not only to those classes, but to almost all the other classes of them. When our neighbours prohibit some manufacture of ours, we generally prohibit, not only the same, for that alone would seldom affect them considerably, but some other manufacture of theirs. This may no doubt give encouragement to some particular class of workmen among ourselves, and by excluding some of their rivals, may enable them to raise their price in the home-market. Those workmen, however, who suffered by our neighbours' prohibition will not be benefited by ours. On the contrary, they and almost all the other classes of our citizens will thereby be obliged to pay dearer than before for certain goods. Every such law, therefore, imposes a real tax upon the whole country, not in favour of that particular class of workmen who were injured by neighbours' prohibition, but of some other class.

The case in which it may sometimes be a matter of deliberation, how far, or in what manner, it is proper to restore the free importation of foreign goods, after it has been for some time interrupted, is, when particular manufactures, by means of high duties or prohibitions upon all foreign goods which can come into competition with them, have been so far extended as to employ a great multitude of hands. Humanity may in this case require that the freedom of trade should be restored only by slow gradations, and with a good deal of reserve and circumspection. Were those high duties and prohibitions taken away all at once, cheaper foreign goods of the same kind might be poured so fast into the home market, as to deprive all at once many thousands of our people of their ordinary employment and means of subsistence. The disorder which this would occasion might no doubt be very considerable. It would in all probability, however, be much less than is commonly imagined, for the two following reasons:

First, all those manufactures, of which any part is commonly exported to other European countries without a bounty, could be very little affected by the freest importation of foreign goods. Such manufactures must be sold as cheap abroad as any other foreign goods of the same quality and kind, and consequently must be sold cheaper at home. They would still, therefore, keep possession of the home market.

Secondly, though a great number of people should, by thus restoring the freedom of trade, ordinary employment and common method of be thrown all at once out of their subsistence, it would by no means follow that they would thereby be deprived either of employment or subsistence. By the reduction of the army and navy at the end of the late war, more than a hundred thousand soldiers and seamen, a number equal to what is employed in the greatest manufactures, were all at once thrown out of their ordinary employment; but, though they no doubt suffered some inconvenience, they were not thereby deprived of all employment and subsistence. To the greater part of manufactures besides there are other collateral manufactures of so similar a nature, that a workman can easily transfer his industry from one of them to another. The greater part of such workmen too are occasionally employed in country labour. The stock which employed them in a particular manufacture before, will still remain in the country to employ an equal number of people in some other way. The capital of the country remaining the same, the demand for labour will likewise be the same, or very nearly the same, though it may be exerted in different places and for different occupations.

......

The undertaker of a great manufacture, who by the home markets being suddenly laid open to the competition of foreigners, should be obliged to abandon his trade, would no doubt suffer very considerably. That part of his capital which had usually been employed in purchasing materials and in paying his workmen, might, without much difficulty, perhaps, find another employment. But that part of it which was fixed in workhouses, and in the instruments of trade, could scarce be disposed of without considerable loss. The equitable regard, therefore, to his interest requires that changes of this kind should never be introduced suddenly, but slowly, gradually, and after a very long warning. The legislature, were it possible that its deliberations could be always directed, not by the clamorous importunity of partial interests, but by an extensive view of the general good, ought upon this very account, perhaps, to be particularly careful neither to establish any new monopolies of this kind, nor to extend further those which are already established. Every such regulation introduces some degree of real disorder into the constitution of the state, which it will be difficult afterwards to cure without occasioning another disorder.

READING 5

David Ricardo

Biography

David Ricardo (1772–1823) was born in London. He was the son of Anglo-Jewish parents who had emigrated from the Netherlands in 1760. His ancestors originally came from Portugal. Once in England his father became a prosperous member of the London Stock Exchange. David was the third of seventeen children. He received a conventional education in local schools and from private tutors. At the age of twelve he was sent to a special Jewish school in Amsterdam (Netherlands) where he stayed for two years. Upon his return to England he was employed by his father in the brokerage business. Soon after attaining majority he married a young Quakeress (Priscilla Anne Wilkinson) and embraced Christianity which resulted in a break with his father. At twenty-one he became a member of the Stock Exchange and went into business for himself where he displayed exceptional qualities. At the age of twenty-five he had already acquired a fortune as a dealer and broker in government securities. In 1814 he retired from the Stock Exchange, bought a country estate in Gloucestershire and settled down to the life of a country gentleman. In 1819 he entered the House of Commons as a member of an Irish pocket borough and became, within a short time, one of its most highly regarded members. As an independent and a classical Liberal he was usually found on the side of progress and reform. He favored parliamentary reform, greater freedom of the press and Catholic emancipation. He only spoke on a subject after long and careful consideration and he was a persuasive speaker. In his private relations he was kind and charitable and made generous use of his wealth supporting two schools and an almshouse from his own pocket. His untimely death in 1823, at the relatively young age of fifty-one, cut short his brilliant career.

The Work

Ricardo had become interested in economics after a perusal of Adam Smith's *Wealth of Nations*. On deciding to devote himself mainly to 'Political Economy' he began to write on the burning topics of the day. One of the most pertinent subjects of debate was the issue of the Corn Laws. In England corn includes any edible grain such as wheat, barley, rye and oats. For centuries the Corn Laws had consisted of duties placed on grain imports or of bounties placed on exports, all typically mercantilist devices. In the middle of the eighteenth century, England was still a food exporting country selling enough grain abroad to feed a million people per year. This situation changed dramatically during the second half of the eighteenth century. Population growth, urbanization and a series of bad harvests sharply reduced the food surplus. The Napoleonic wars and the interruption of trade with Europe further deteriorated the situation. Ten years following the French revolution of 1789, when its force was spent, Napoleon rose to power. For almost fifteen years he kept Europe in a state of almost continuous warfare.

As a result corn prices rose enormously, pasture land was converted into arable land and poorer soils were cultivated, while land already under cultivation was tilled more intensively. It was during this period that the problem of the Corn Laws began to reflect the class struggle. The rising corn prices benefited the landed gentry in the form of increased rents. The interests of the manufacturers and urban dwellers, however, diverged from those of the landowners. Higher corn and bread prices implied lower real living standards for the urban population and rising wage costs for the businessmen. The distribution of income was now sharply debated.

With the surrender of Napoleon in 1815 the Corn Law controversy was again revived. The landed proprietors feared that the cessation of hostilities on the continent would allow the domestic British market to be flooded with cheap foreign grains. Thus they proposed import duties on corn at nearly prohibitive levels which produced a storm of protest. It was during this climate of opinion that Ricardo thought and wrote.

Generally speaking Ricardo's main interest lay in the distribution of income. Ricardo wanted to determine the way in which the national income was divided into rents, profits and wages and which laws governed the proportion each claimant got. Ricardo focussed on the rental portion because he believed that this would determine the shares of the other factor payments.

Starting from a closed economy model in which agriculture was still the dominant industry, Ricardo hypothesized that the best quality land would be cultivated first. This was the land with the highest fertility and/or in the most advantageous location. While the quantity of high grade land available exceeded the amount demanded, there would be no rent. Everyone could avail of it just by taking possession. As the population continued to grow, food prices would increase resulting in inferior quality land, of the second class so to speak, being brought under cultivation. Those who owned land of the first class, by now would have a distinct advantage over the others, and competition between tenant farmers would increase for the permission to use it. The land of the second class would have to pay the same wages as the best land. However, while both categories of land received the higher market price for cereals, the first grade land would require fewer resources to produce it. As a result rent would emerge on the first grade land. This rent would be a surplus to be paid by the tenant farmer to the landowner and the amounts would depend upon the difference in quality of these two grades of land. With every step in the growth of population the country under consideration would be obliged to have recourse to still inferior farm land, because the law of diminishing returns would set clear limits on a more intense cultivation of the older lands. As soon as land of the third grade was being cultivated, rent would appear on the land of the second grade, and rents would rise on lands of the first quality. Obviously, the landlords would benefit from the process but eventually the profits on capital (it was assumed that in most cases the tenant farmer provided the necessary capital) would be squeezed. The farm workers were assumed to receive wages near the minimum required to keep body and soul together. If wages rose above that level (and here Ricardo followed Thomas R. Malthus) workers (1) would marry earlier and produce more children while (2) better and additional food would lower infant and child mortality rates increasing the working population and bringing down wages once again. If food prices continued to rise the tenant farmers would have to pay higher nominal wages while real wages remained unchanged. Yet the extra revenue which higher corn prices yielded would be exacted by the landlord in the form of a bonus called rent. As rents rose and real wages remained the same, profits would fall, thus destroying every incentive to accumulate capital. The conclusion was that at the end of the process a stationary society was bound to appear. This would involve a zero capital accumulation, a discontinuance of cultivation of new lands and an end to population growth. Another conclusion was that the interests of the landed proprietor were clearly opposed to those of the other classes of the community (quite a statement for somebody who had chosen to become a landowner himself). The policy proposals followed from the model. State intervention in the form of import duties on grain were disastrous. The lifting of those duties, partial or total, would lower corn prices. The need to resort to inferior land would vanish, rents would stabilize or drop and prosperity would reappear. Free trade and laissez-faire were the obvious policies to adopt. Ricardo argued this position in such pamphlets as 'The Influence of a Law Price of Corn on the Profits of Stock' (1815) and 'On Protection to Agriculture' (1822).

Ricardo's arguments impressed many people. The Corn Law controversy continued during the 1820–1840 period. In September 1838 the Anti-Corn Law Association was established in Manchester and a very effective campaign was undertaken to convert public opinion. It prepared the ground for the abolition of the Corn Laws in 1846 by the then Prime Minister Robert Peel. The immediate cause for the abolition was the failure of the potato harvest in Ireland and Scotland which caused widespread famine in those areas. However, without a change in public opinion abolition could not have been achieved.

Ricardo was an ardent free trader and strongly believed in competition. In his book *Principles of Political Economy and Taxation*, first published in 1817 he furnished the scientific basis for the practical rule of free trade (Chapter 7). Adam Smith's teachings had pointed out the advantages to a country specializing in the production of those goods it produced at lower costs than other nations. If other countries applied the same system to trade, everyone would be better off. Ricardo demonstrated that gain was also possible if one country is superior (in terms of low costs) to another country at every kind of production. If the 'superior' country concentrates on the production of those items where its advantage is at the greatest and the 'inferior' nation concentrates on those activities where its disadvantage is at the smallest, both will benefit if they trade. Ricardo illustrated this idea with a two country (Portugal and England) and two commodity (cloth and wine) model which was phrased in real terms, labor and units of commodities, rather than in terms of prices and costs.

In his example he conveys the fundamental point that beneficial international trade does not depend on the absolute levels of economic efficiency of the trade partners but merely on the differences in their relative costs of production (or differences in ratios of advantage) in the absence of trade. The analysis of the phenomena of rent and comparative advantage clearly show that Ricardo used the deductive abstract method rigorously. He builds up his system from a few premises. Then with relentless logic he manipulates a few variables and finally deduces some practical policy conclusion.

In the first reading which consists of two sections taken from 'On Protection to Agriculture' Ricardo explains that the recourse to lands of lesser fertility is not to the advantage of the English population. He also explains why a country should not worry about being dependent on corn imports.[13] In the second selection taken from his 'Principles' Ricardo explains the principle of comparative advantage.[14]

Extracts

It appears then that, in the progress of society, when no importation takes place, we are obliged constantly to have recourse to worse soils to feed an augmenting population, and with every step of our progress the price of corn must rise, and with such rise, the rent of the better land which had been previously cultivated, will necessarily be increased. A higher price becomes necessary to compensate for the smaller quantity which is obtained; but this higher price must never be considered as a good, it would not have existed if the same return had been obtained with less labour, it would not have existed if, by the application of labour to manufactures, we had indirectly obtained the corn by the exportation of those manufactures in exchange for corn. A higher price, if the effect of a high cost, is evil, and not a good; the price is high, because a great deal of labour is bestowed in obtaining the corn. If only a little labour was bestowed upon it, more of the labour of the country, which constitutes its only real source of wealth, would have been at its disposal to procure other enjoyments which are desirable.

......

Before I conclude, it will be proper to notice an objection which

13 Source: D. Ricardo, *On Protection to Agriculture* (London: John Mursey. 1822).
14 D. Ricardo, *Principles of Political Economy and Taxation* (London: Bell, 1891) Ch. 7.

is frequently made against freedom of trade in corn, viz., the dependence in which it would place us for an essential article of subsistence on foreign countries. This objection is founded on the supposition that we should be importers of considerable portion of quantity which we annually consume.

In the first place, I differ with those who think that the quantity which we should import would be immense; and, in the second, if it were as large as the objection requires, I can see no danger as likely to arise from it.

From all the evidence given to the Agricultural Committee, it appears that no very great quantity could be obtained from abroad, without causing a considerable increase in the remunerating price of corn in foreign countries. In proportion as the quantity required came from the interior of Poland and Germany, the cost would be greatly increased by the expenses of land carriage. To raise a larger supply, too, those countries would be obliged to have recourse to an inferior quality of land, and as it is the cost of raising corn on the worst soils in cultivation requiring the heaviest charges, which regulates the prices of all the corn of a country, there could not be a great additional quantity produced, without a rise in the price necessary to remunerate the foreign grower. In proportion as the price rose abroad, it would become advantageous to cultivate poorer lands at home; and, therefore, there is every probability that, under the freest state of demand, we should not be importers of any very large quantity.

But suppose the case to be otherwise, what danger should we incur from our dependence, as it is called, on foreign countries for a considerable portion of our food? If our demand was constant and uniform, which, under such a system, it would undoubtedly be, a considerable quantity of corn must be grown abroad expressly for our market. It would be more in the interest, if possible, of the countries so growing corn for our use, to oppose no obstacles to its reaching us, than it would be ours to receive it.

Let us look attentively at what is passing in this country before our eyes. Do we not see the effects of a small excess of quantity on the price of corn? What would be the glut, if England habitually raised a considerable additional quantity for foreign consumption? Should we be willing to expose our farmers and landlords to the ruin which would overwhelm them if we voluntarily deprived them of the foreign market, even in case of war? I am sure we should not. Whatever allowance we may make for the feelings of enmity, and for the desire which we might have to inflict suffering on our foe, by depriving him of part of his usual supply of food, I am sure that at such a price as it must be inflicted, in the case which I am supposing, we should forbear to exercise such a power. If such would be our policy, so would it also be that of other countries in the same circumstances; and I am fully persuaded that we should never suffer from being deprived of the quantity of food for which we uniformly depended on importation.

All our reasoning on this subject leads to the same conclusion, that we should, with as little delay as possible, consistently with a due regard to temporary interests, establish what may be called a substantially free trade in corn. The interests of the farmer, consumer, and capitalist, would all be promoted by such a measure; and as far as steady prices and the regular receipt of rents is more advantageous to the landlord than fluctuating prices and irregular receipt of rents, I am sure his interest well understood would lead to the same conclusion; although I am willing to admit, that the average money-rents, to which he would be entitled if his tenants could fulfil their contracts, would be higher under a system of restricted trade.
......

The same rule which regulates the relative value of commodities in one country does not regulate the relative value of the commodities exchanged between two or more countries.

Under a system of perfectly free commerce, each country naturally devotes its capital and labour to such employments as are most beneficial to each. This pursuit of individual advantage is admirably connected with the universal good of the whole. By stimulating industry, by rewarding ingenuity, and by using most efficaciously the peculiar powers bestowed by nature, it distributes labour most effectively and most economically: while, by increasing the general mass of productions, it diffuses general benefit, and binds together, by one common tie of interest and intercourse, the universal society of nations throughout the civilized world. It is this principle which determines that wine shall be made in France and Portugal, that corn shall be grown in America and Poland, and that hardware and other goods shall be manufactured in England.

In one and the same country, profits are, generally speaking, always on the same level; or differ only as the employment of capital may be more or less secure and agreeable. It is not so between different countries. If the profits of capital employed in Yorkshire should exceed those of capital employed in London, capital would speedily move from London to Yorkshire, and an equality of profits would be effected; but if in consequence of the diminished rate of production in the lands of England from the increase of capital and population wages should rise and profits fall, it would not follow that capital and population would necessarily move from England to Holland, or Spain, or Russia, where profits might be higher.

If Portugal had no commercial connection with other countries, instead of employing a great part of her capital and industry in the production of wines, with which she purchases for her own use the cloth and hardware of other countries, she would be obliged to devote a part of that capital to the manufacture of those commodities, which she would thus obtain probably inferior in quality as well as quantity.

The quantity of wine which she shall give in exchange for the cloth of England is not determined by the respective quantities of labour devoted to the production of each, as it would be if both commodities were manufactured in England, or both in Portugal.

England may be so circumstanced that to produce the cloth may require the labour of 100 men for one year; and if she attempted to make the wine, it might require the labour of 120 men for the same time. England would therefore find it her interest to import wine, and to purchase it by the exportation of cloth.

To produce the wine in Portugal might require only the labour of 80 men for one year, and to produce the cloth in the same country might require the labour of 90 men for the same time. It would therefore be advantageous for her to export wine in exchange for cloth. This exchange might even take place notwithstanding that the commodity imported by Portugal could be produced there with less labour than in England. Though she could make the cloth with the labour of 90 men, she would import it from a country where it required the labour of 100 men to produce it, because it would be advantageous to her rather to employ her capital in the production of wine, for which she would obtain more cloth from England, than she could produce by diverting a portion of her capital from the cultivation of vines to the manufacture of cloth.

Thus England would give the produce of the labour of 100 men for the produce of the labour of 80. Such an exchange could not take place between the individuals of the same country. The labour of 100 Englishmen cannot be given for that of 80 Englishmen, but the produce of the labour of 100 Englishmen may be given for the produce of the labour of 80 Portuguese, 60 Russians, or 120 East Indians. The difference in this respect, between a single country and many, is easily accounted for, by considering the difficulty with which capital moves from one country to another, to seek a more profitable employment, and the activity with which it invariably passes from one province to another in the same country.

It would undoubtedly be advantageous to the capitalists of England, and to the consumers in both countries, that under such circumstances the wine and the cloth should both be made in Portugal, and therefore that the capital and labour of England employed in making cloth should be removed to Portugal for that purpose. In that case, the relative value of these commodities would be regulated by the same principle as if one were the produce of Yorkshire and the other of London: and in every other case, if capital freely flowed towards those countries where it could be most profitably employed, there could be no difference in the rate of profit, and no other difference in the real or labour price of commodities than the additional quantity of labour required to convey them to the various markets where they were to be sold.

Experience, however, shows that the fancied or real insecurity of capital, when not under the immediate control of its owner, together with the natural disinclination which every man has to quit the country of his birth and connections, and intrust himself, with all his habits fixed, to a strange government and new laws, check the emigration of capital. These feelings, which I should be sorry to see weakened, induce most men of property to be satisfied with a low rate of profits in their own country, rather than seek a more advantageous employment for their wealth in foreign nations.

Gold and silver having been chosen for the general medium of circulation, they are, by the competition of commerce, distributed in such proportions amongst the different countries of the world as to accommodate themselves to the natural traffic which would take place if no such metals existed, and the trade between countries were purely a trade of barter.

Thus, cloth cannot be imported into Portugal unless it sells there for more gold than it cost in the country from which it was imported; and wine cannot be imported into England unless it will sell for more there than it cost in Portugal. If the trade were purely a trade of barter, it could only continue whilst England could make cloth so cheap as to obtain a greater quantity of wine with a given quantity of labour by manufacturing cloth than by growing vines; and also whilst the industry of Portugal were attended by the reverse effects. Now suppose England to discover a process for making wine, so that it should become her interest rather to grow it than import it; she would naturally divert a portion of her capital from the foreign trade to the home trade; she would cease to manufacture cloth for exportation, and would grow wine for herself. The money price of these commodities would be regulated accordingly; wine would fall here while cloth continued at its former price, and in Portugal no alteration would take place in the price of either commodity. Cloth would continue for some time to be exported from this country, because its price would continue to be higher in Portugal than here; but money instead of wine would be given in exchange for it, till the accumulation of money here, and its diminution abroad, should so operate on the relative value of cloth in the two countries that it would cease to be profitable to export it. If the improvement in making wine were of a very important description, it might become profitable for the two countries to exchange employments; for England to make all the wine, and Portugal all the cloth consumed by them; but this could be effected only by a new distribution of the precious metals, which should raise the price of cloth in England and lower it in Portugal. The relative price of wine would fall in England in consequence of the real advantage from the improvement of its manufacture; that is to say, its natural price would rise there from the accumulation of money.

READING 6

Jean Baptiste Say

Biography

While Ricardo defended free trade using the argument of comparative advantage, the French economist Jean Baptiste Say (1767–1832) began from a different perspective to arrive at basically the same conclusions.

Say was born in Lyons to a cultured Protestant merchant family. Following a good education he was sent to England at the age of 19 where he witnessed the early industrial revolution and was deeply impressed. Upon his return to Paris, two years later, he read Adam Smith's *Wealth of Nations* which he found to be a truly scientific study of economic problems. Smith's treatise seemed to provide an answer to the question as to why England, a country not particularly rich in terms of resources, was so far ahead of other nations. Economic liberalism, of which there was more in England than elsewhere, seemed to be the key to the question.

Bookish and inclined towards philosophy Say was closely associated with a group of intellectuals during the last years of the eighteenth century. Together they published a periodical called the *The Decade* (*La Décade*) which dealt with literary, philosophical and political issues.

In 1799 he became a member of the Committee of Finances of Napoleon Bonaparte. Say, however, made it known that he disagreed with some of the authoritarian measures taken by the Napoleonic government and this cost him his job.

In 1803 he published the first edition of his *Treatise on Political Economy* (*Traité d'Economie Politique*). Subsequent to his short career in politics he settled in a small town in Northern France and established a cotton spinning plant (1805) which prospered under his management. In 1813 he sold out his business and returned to Paris. The fall of Napoleon allowed him to resume his intellectual activity and a revised edition of his book appeared in 1814. The peace which followed the demise of Napoleon permitted Say to travel to England where he was received by Ricardo, Malthus and other scientists and academics. He even lectured at the University of Glasgow where Adam Smith had once taught.

New editions of his treatise appeared in 1817, 1819, and 1827. An English translation (from the fourth edition) was issued in 1821 and was widely used as a textbook in English and American universities. In 1817 the French government established a chair for him at the Conservatoire des Arts et Métiers. Finally in 1830 he became professor of political economy at the Collège de France, a position he held until his death in 1832. His other publications include *A Catechism of Political Economy* (*Cathéchisme d'Economie Politique*) (1817) and *A Complete Course in Political Economy* (*Cours d'Economie Politique*) published in six volumes (1828–1829).

The Work

Philosophically, Say was a classical liberal and an upholder of rationalism. As a scientist the search for truth and objectivity ranked for him above all other values.

Say admired the work of Adam Smith. He also accepted many, but by no means all of the ideas formulated by Malthus and Ricardo. Primarily his great achievement was the interpreting of the work of Adam Smith for the French people and the world. But he did not merely repeat the ideas of the famous Scottish writer. Say brought method, consistence, and order, into the statement of economic principles. He rearranged the ideas of Smith and his followers, filtered them, clarified them and in so doing produced a text which became widely used.

Apart from this meritorious work of popularization, Say produced a number of ideas of his own. In the second edition of his book Say explains the methods whereby wealth is produced, distributed and consumed. This pattern of production, distribution and consumption has remained for a long time the established standard in textbooks on economic principles. Economics itself was defined as the production, distribution and the consumption of wealth. Production was described as the creation of utility, meaning that there was no longer any difference between the making of goods or the provision of services.

As a man with an intimate knowledge of the business world, Say emphasized the role of the entrepreneur whose function differs from the capitalist investor. The English classicals had neglected this distinction. The entrepreneur plays a key role in the hiring of resources or resource services in order to produce those goods and services for which a market demand exists. In doing so he also assumes risks.

The theory for which Say is best known, however, is his 'Law of Markets'. Say himself had no doubt that this law would give meaning and substance to the tenets of classical liberalism including free trade. Say's Law came to light during the industrial revolution which had greatly increased output combined with some cyclical instability. It was feared that sufficient purchasing power would not be present to absorb the ever growing production of the industrial economy. Say responded to such concerns by pointing out that the production of goods and services tended of itself to generate purchasing power equal to the value of those goods and services. The very production of certain goods creates a demand for other goods, therefore supply is potential demand. Selling, in effect, constitutes buying and production creates a demand for other products. In terms of the circular flow model so popular in contemporary textbooks, production by virtue of the necessary cost payments by firms to the factors of production (or their owners) also creates the demand to purchase the goods. Say's Law or the Law of Markets, as it is also called, regards money as a veil. It is only used as a means of exchange. Money can be compared to a vehicle which merely transports products from one person to the next. It hides the fact that exchange is really barter, money is merely the medium through which we buy goods. In reality we buy with our previously supplied goods and services, therefore supply creates its own demand.[15] The somewhat more vulnerable argument of secondary importance added to Say's Law of Markets stated that a market glut or aggregate overproduction, even in the short run, was impossible. The overproduction of specific commodities is of course possible but if certain items are in surplus it is because of either misdirected production or a decline in the production of other commodities which create a market for commodities in surplus. Thus the appropriate cure for addressing an excess of certain items is not to reduce production but to increase and diversify it. Imbalances in output may also occur because governments erect artificial hindrances to their exchange. In such cases, economic crises are merely the reflection of political tactics. Efficient governments always stimulate production.

Say's considerations which stress the interdependence of aggregate demand and aggregate supply led him to draw several conclusions. First, the more numerous the producers, the better the markets, as it is with products that we buy. The success of one branch of industry promotes success in all the others. Second, economic freedom should be promoted and imposed restrictions on production by government or private monopoly are reprehensible. Unhampered domestic production creates prosperous markets for everyone's supply. Third, free trade is beneficial. Nations are interdependent. The purchase of goods from foreigners cannot take place without the availability of an export market for home product goods. A nation pays for imports with money but that money must first be earned with exports, i.e. the produce of its domestic industry. Therefore imports provide a nation with foreign markets. Tariffs and other obstacles to trade are harmful even to those who believe they benefit from them. The following reading also shows Say as an early precursor of modern Public Choice Economics.[16]

---

15   Say's Law is of course true in a barter economy. In a money economy, however, money is not only a means of exchange but also has the function of a store of value. This permits the owner of money not to spend it immediately after receipt but to hold on to it for a while for future use.

16   Source: J.B. Say, *Treatise on Political Economy or the Production, Distribution and Consumption of Wealth*, Vol. I (Boston: Wells and Lilly, 1821) Ch. 17. Footnotes are omitted.

Extract

By the absolute exclusion of specific manufactures of foreign fabric, a government establishes a monopoly in favour of the home producers of these articles, and in prejudice of the home consumers; that is to say, those classes of the nation which produce them, being entitled to their exclusive sale, can raise their prices above the natural rate; while the home consumers, being unable to purchase elsewhere are compelled to pay for them unnaturally dear. If the articles be not wholly prohibited, but merely saddled with an import duty, the home producer can then increase their price by the whole amount of the duty, and the consumer will have to pay the difference. For example, if an import duty of 1fr. per dozen be laid upon earthenware plates worth 3fr. per dozen, the importer, whatever country he may belong to, must charge the consumer 4fr.; and the home manufacturer of that commodity is enabled to ask 4fr. per dozen of this customers for plates of the same quality; which he would not do without the intervention of the duty; because the consumer could get the same article for 3fr.; thus, a premium to the whole extent of the duty is given to the home manufacturer out of the consumer pocket.

Should any one maintain, that the advantage of producing at home counterbalances the hardship of paying dearer for almost every article; that our own capital and labour are engaged in the production, and the profits pocketed by our own fellow citizens; my answer is, that the foreign commodities we might import are not to be gratis; that we must purchase them with values of home production, which would have given equal employment to our productive powers, not in those branches in which foreigners excel us, but in those, which we excel in ourselves; and with the product to purchase of others. The opposite course would be just as absurd, as if a man should wish to make his own coats and shoes. What would the world say, if, at the door of every house an import duty were laid upon coats and shoes, for the laudable purpose of compelling the inmates to make them for themselves? Would not people say with justice, let us follow each his own pursuit, and buy what we want with what we produce, or, which comes to the same thing, with what we get for our products. The system would be precisely the same, only carried to a ridiculous extreme.

Well may it be a matter of wonder, that every nation should manifest such anxiety to obtain prohibitory regulations, if it be true that it can profit nothing by them; and lead one to suppose the two cases not parallel, because we do not find individual householders solicitous to obtain the same privilege. But the sole difference is this, that individuals are independent and consistent beings, actuated by no contrariety of will, and more interested in their character of consumers of coats and shoes to buy them cheap, than as manufacturers to sell unnaturally dear.

What, then are the classes of the community so importunate for prohibitions of heavy import duties? The producers of the particular commodity, that applies for protection from competition, not the consumers of that commodity. The public interest is their plea; but self-interest is evidently their object. Well, but, say these gentry, are they not the same thing? Are not our gains national gains? By no means: whatever profit is acquired in this manner, is so much taken out of the pockets of a neighbour and fellow-citizen; and, if the excess of charge thrown upon consumers by the monopoly could be correctly computed, it would be found, that the loss of the consumer exceeds the gain of the monopolist. Here, then, individual and public interest are in direct opposition to each other; and, since public interest is understood by the enlightened few alone, is it at all surprising, that the prohibitive system should find so many partisans and so few opponents?

There is in general far too little attention paid to the serious mischief of raising prices upon the consumers. The evil is not apparent to cursory observation, because it operates piecemeal, and is felt in a very slight degree on every purchase or act of consumption: but it is really most serious, on account of its constant recurrence and universal pressure. The whole fortune of every consumer is affected by every fluctuation of price in the articles of his consumption; the cheaper they are, the richer he is, and vice versa. If a single article rises in price, he is much the poorer in respect of that article; if all rise together, he is poorer in respect to the whole. And, since the whole nation is comprehended in the class of consumers, the whole nation must in that case be the poorer. Besides which, it is crippled in the extension of the variety of its enjoyments, and prevented from obtaining products whereof it stands in need, in exchange for those wherewith it might procure them. It is of no use to assert, that, when prices are raised, what one gains another loses. For the position is not true, except in the case of monopolies; nor even to the full extent with regard to them; for the monopolist never profits to the full amount of the loss to the consumers. If the rise be occasioned by taxation or import-duty under any shape whatever, the producer gains nothing by the increase of price, but just the reverse, as we shall see by-and-by (Book III Chap. 7.): so that, in fact, he is no richer in his capacity of producer, though poorer in his quality of consumer. This is one of the most effective causes of national impoverishment, or at least one of the most powerful checks to the progress of national wealth.

For this reason, it may be perceived, that it is an absurd distinction to view with more jealousy the import of foreign objects of barren consumption, than that of raw materials for home manufacture. Whether the products consumed be of domestic or of foreign growth, a portion of wealth is destroyed in the act of consumption, and a proportionate inroad made into the wealth of the community. But that inroad is the result of the act of consumption, not of the act of dealing with the foreigner; and the resulting stimulus to national production, is the same in either case. For, wherewith was the purchase of the foreign product made? Either with a domestic product, or with money, which must itself have been procured with a domestic product. In buying from a foreigner, the nation really does no more than send abroad a domestic product in lieu of consuming it at home, and consume in its place the foreign product received in exchange. The individual consumer himself, probably, does not conduct this operation; commerce conducts it for him. None country can buy from another, except with its own domestic products.

In defence of import-duties it is often urged, 'that, when the interest of money is lower abroad than at home, the foreigner has an advantage over the home producer, which must be met by a countervailing duty.' The low rate of interest is, to the foreign producer, an advantage, analogous to that of the superior quality of his land. It tends to cheapen the products he raises; and it is reasonable enough that our domestic consumers should take the benefit of that cheapness. The same motive will operate here, that leads us rather to import sugar and indigo from tropical climates, than to raise them in our own.

'But capital is necessary in every branch of production: so that the foreigner, who can procure it at a lower rate of interest, has the same advantage in respect to every product; and, if the free importation be permitted, he will have an advantage over all classes of home-producers.' Tell me, then how his products are to be paid for. 'Why in specie, and there lies the mischief.' And how is the specie to be got to pay for them? 'All the nation has, will go in that way; and when it is exhausted, national misery will be complete.' So then, it is admitted, that, before arriving at this extremity, the constant efflux of specie will gradually render it more scarce at home, and more abundant abroad; wherefore, it will gradually rise 1,2,3, percent higher in value at home than abroad; which is fully sufficient to turn the tide, and make specie flow inwards faster than it flowed outwards. But it will not do so without some returns; and of what can the returns be made, but of products of the land, or the commerce of the nation? For there is no possible means of purchasing from foreign nations, otherwise than with the products of the national land and commerce; and it is better to buy of them what they can produce cheaper than ourselves, because we may rest assured, that they must take in payment what we can produce cheaper than they. This they must do, else there must be an end of all interchange.

Again, it is affirmed, and what absurd positions have not been advanced to involve these questions in obscurity? Since almost all the nations are at the same time consumers and producers, they gain by prohibition and monopoly as much in the one capacity as they lose in the other; that the producer, who gets a monopoly-profit upon the object of his own production, is, on the other hand, the sufferer by a similar profit upon the object of his consumption; and thus that the nation is made up of rogues and fools, who are a match for each other. It is worth remarking, that everybody thinks himself more rogue than fool; for, although all are consumers as well as producers, the enormous profits made upon a single article are much more striking than reiterated minute losses upon the numberless items of consumption. If an import duty be laid upon calicoes, the additional annual charge to each person of moderate fortune, may, perhaps, not exceed 12 or 15fr. at most; and probably he does not very well comprehend the nature of the loss, or feel it much, though repeated in some degree or other upon every thing he consumes; whereas, possibly, this consumer is himself a manufacturer, say a hat-maker; and, should a duty be laid upon the import of original hats, he will immediately see that it will raise the price of his own hats, and probably increase his annual profits by many thousand francs. It is the delusion, that makes private interest so warm an advocate for prohibitory measures, even where the whole community loses more by them as consumers, than it gains as producers.

But, even in this point of view, the exclusive system is pregnant with injustice. It is impossible that every class of production should profit by the exclusive system, supposing it to be universal, which, in point of fact, it never is in practice, though possibly it may be in law or intention. Some articles can never, from the nature of things, be derived from abroad; fresh fish, for instance, or horned cattle; as to them, therefore, import duties would be inoperative in raising the price. The same may be said of masons and carpenters' work, and of the numberless callings necessarily carried on within the community; as those of shopmen, clerks, carriers, retail dealers, and many others. The producers of immaterial products, public functionaries and fundholders, lie under the same disability. These classes can none of them be invested with a monopoly by means of import duties, though they are subject to the hardship of many monopolies granted in that way to other classes of producers.

Besides, the profits of monopoly are not equitably divided amongst the different classes even of those that concur in the production of the commodity, which is the subject of monopoly. If the master- adventurers whether in agriculture, manufacture, or commerce, have the consumers at their mercy, their labourers and subordinate productive agents are still more exposed to their extortion, for reasons that will be explained in Book II. So that these latter classes participate in the loss with consumers at large, but get no share of the unnatural gains of their superiors.

Prohibitory measures besides affecting the pockets of the consumers, often subject them to severe privations. I am ashamed to say, that, within these few years, we have had the hat-makers of Marseilles petitioning for the prohibition of the import of foreign straw or chip hats, on the plea that they injured the sale of their own felt hats; a measure that would have deprived the country people and labourers in husbandry, who are so much exposed to the sun, of a light, cool, and cheap covering, admirably adapted to their wants, the use of which it was highly desirable to extend and encourage.

In pursuit of what it mistakes for profound policy, or to gratify feelings it supposes to be laudable, a government will sometimes prohibit or divert the course of a particular trade, and thereby do irreparable mischief to the productive powers of the nation. When Philip II became master of Portugal, and forbade all intercourse between his new subjects and the Dutch, what was the consequence? The Dutch, who before resorted to Lisbon for the manufactures of India, of which they took off an immense quantity, finding this avenue closed against their industry, went straight to India for what they wanted, and, in the end, drove out the Portuguese from that quarter; and, what was meant as the deadly blow of inveterate hatred, turned out the main source of their aggrandizement. 'Commerce,' says Fenelon, 'is like the native springs of the rock, which often cease to flow altogether, if it be attempted to alter their course.'

Such are the principal evils of impediments thrown in the way of import, which are carried to the extreme point by absolute prohibition. There have, indeed, been instances of nations that have thriven under such a system; but then it was, because the causes of national prosperity were more powerful, than the causes of national impoverishment. Nations resemble the human frame, which contains a vital principle, that incessantly labours to repair the inroads of excess and dissipation upon its health and constitution. Nature is active in closing the wounds and healing the bruises inflicted by our own awkwardness and intemperance. In like manner, states maintain themselves, nay, often increase in prosperity, in spite of the infinite injuries of every description, which friends as well as enemies heap upon them. And it is worth remarking, that the most industrious nations are those, which are the most subjected to such outrage, because none others could survive them. The cry is then, 'our system must be the true one, for the national prosperity is advancing.' Whereas, were we to take an enlightened view of the circumstances, that, for the last three centuries, have combined to develop the power and faculties of man; to survey with the eye of intelligence the progress of navigation, of discovery, of invention in every branch of art and science; to take account of the variety of useful animals and vegetables that have been transplanted from one hemisphere to the other, and to give a due attention to the vast enlargement and increased solidity both of science and of its practical application, that we are daily witnesses of, we cannot resist the conviction, that our actual prosperity is nothing to what it might have been; that it is engaged in a perpetual struggle against the obstacles and impediments thrown into its way; and that, even in those parts of the world where mankind is deemed the most enlightened, a great part of their time and exertions is occupied in destroying instead of multiplying their resources, in despoiling instead of assisting each other; and all for want of correct knowledge and information respecting their real interests.

But, to return to the subject, we have just been examining the nature of the injury, that a community suffers by difficulties thrown in the way of the introduction of foreign commodities. The mischief occasioned to the country, that produces the prohibited article, is of the same kind and description: it is prevented from turning its capital and industry to the best account. But it is not to be supposed, that the foreign nation can by this means be utterly ruined and stripped of all resource as Napoleon seemed to imagine, when he excluded the products of Britain from the markets of the continent. To say nothing of the impossibility of effecting a complete and actual blockade of a whole country, opposed as it must be by the universal motive of self-interest, the utmost effect of it can only be to derive its production into a different channel. A nation is always competent to the purchase and consumption of the whole of its own produce, for products are always bought with other products. Do you think to prevent England from producing value to amount of a million, by preventing her export of woollen to that amount? You are much mistaken, if you do. England will employ the same capital and the same manual labour in the preparation of ardent spirits, by the distillation of grain or other domestic products, that were before occupied in the manufacture of woollen for the French market, and she will then no longer bring her woollen to be bartered for French brandies. A country, in one way or other, direct or indirect, always consumes the values it produces, and can consume nothing more. If it cannot exchange its products with its neighbours, it is compelled to produce values of such kinds only as it can consume at home. This is the utmost effect of prohibitions; both parties are worse provided, and neither is at all the richer.

Napoleon, doubtless, occasioned much injury, both to England and to the continent, by cramping their mutual relations of commerce as far as he possibly could. But, on the other hand, he did the continent of Europe the involuntary service of facilitating the communication between its different parts, by the universality of dominion, which his ambition had well nigh achieved. The frontier duties between Holland, Belgium, part of Germany, Italy, and France, were demolished; and those of the other powers, with the exception of England, were far from oppressive. We may form some estimate of the benefit thence resulting to commerce, from the discontent and stagnation that have ensued upon the establishment of the present system, of lining the frontier of each state with a triple guard of douaniers. All the continental states so guarded have, indeed, preserved their former means of production; but that production has been made less advantageous.

It cannot be denied, that France has gained prodigiously by the suppression of the provincial barriers and custom-houses, consequent upon her political revolution. Europe had, in like manner, gained by the partial removal of the international barriers between its different political states; and the world at large would derive similar benefit from the demolition of those, which insulate, as it were, the various communities, into which the human race is divided.

I have omitted to mention other very serious levels of the exclusive system; as, for instance, the creation of a new class of crime, that of smuggling; whereby an action, wholly innocent in itself, is made legally criminal: and persons, who are actually labouring for the general welfare, are subjected to punishment.

Smith admits of two circumstances, that, in his opinion, will justify a government in resorting to import-duties: 1. When a particular branch of industry is necessary to the public security, and the external supply cannot be safely reckoned upon. On this account, a government may very wisely prohibit the import of gunpowder, if such prohibition be necessary to set the powder-mills at home in activity; for it is better to pay somewhat dear for so essential an article, than to run the risk of being unprovided in the hour of need. 2. Where a similar commodity of home produce is already saddled with a duty. The foreign article, if wholly exempt from duty, would in this case have an actual privilege; so that a duty imposed has not the effect of destroying, but of restoring the natural equilibrium and relative position of the different branches of production.

Indeed, it is impossible to find any reasonable ground for exempting the production of values by the channel of external commerce from the same pressure of taxation, that weights upon the production effected in those of agriculture and manufacture. Taxation is, doubtless, an evil, and one which should be reduced to the lowest possible degree; but, when once a given amount of taxation is admitted to be necessary, it is but common justice to lay it equally on all three branches of industry. The error I wish to expose to reprobation is, the notion, that taxes of this kind are favourable to production. A tax can never be favourable to the public welfare, except by the good use that is made of its proceeds.

These points should never be lost sight of in the framing of commercial treaties, which are really good for nothing, but to protect industry and capital, diverted into improper channels by the blunders of legislation. These it would be far wiser to remedy than to perpetuate. The healthy state of industry and wealth is the state of absolute liberty, in which each interest is left to take care of itself. The only useful protection authority can afford them is, that against fraud or violence. Taxes and restrictive measures never can be a benefit; they are at the best a necessary evil; to suppose them useful to the subjects at large, is to mistake the foundation of national prosperity, and to set at naught the principles of political economy.

Import duties and prohibitions have often been resorted to as a means of retaliation: 'Your government throws impediments in the way of the introduction of our national products: are not we, then, justified in equally impeding the introduction of yours?' This is the favourite plea, and the basis of most commercial treaties; but people mistake their object: granting that nations have a right to do one another as much mischief as possible, which by the way I can hardly admit; I am not here disputing their rights, but discussing their interests.

Undoubtedly a nation, that excludes you from all commercial intercourse with her, does you an injury; robs you, as far as in her lies, of the benefits of external commerce; if, therefore, by the dread of retaliation, you can induce her to abandon her exclusive measures, there is no question about the expediency of such retaliation, as a matter of mere policy. But it must not be forgotten, that retaliation hurts yourself as well as your rival; that it operates, not defensively against her selfish measures, but offensively against yourself in the first instance for the purpose of indirectly attacking her. The only point in question is this, what degree of vengeance you are animated by, and how much you will consent to throw away upon its gratification. I will not undertake to enumerate all the evils arising from treaties of commerce, or to apply the principles enforced throughout this work to all the clauses and provisions usually contained in them. I will confine myself to the remark, that almost every modern treaty of commerce has had for its basis the imaginary advantage and possibility of the liquidation of a favourable balance of trade by an import of specie. If these turn out to be chimerical, whatever advantage may have resulted from such treaties must be wholly referred to the additional freedom and facility of international communication obtained by them, and not at all to their restrictive clauses or provisions, unless either of the contracting parties have availed itself of its superior power, to exact conditions savouring of a tributary character; as England has done in relation to Portugal. In such case, it is mere exaction and spoliation.

Again, I would observe, that the offer of peculiar advantages by one nation to another, in the way of a treaty of commerce, if not an act of hostility, is at least one of extreme odium in the eyes of other nations. For the concession to one can only be rendered effectual by refusal to others. Hence the germ of discord and of war with all it mischiefs. It is infinitely more simple, and I hope to have shown, more profitable also, to treat all nations as friends, and impose no higher duties on the introduction of their products, than what are necessary to place them on the same footing as those of domestic growth.

Yet, notwithstanding all the mischiefs resulting from the exclusion of foreign products, which I have been depicting, it would be an act of unquestionable rashness abruptly to abolish it. Disease is not to be eradicated in a moment; it requires nursing and management to dispense even national benefits. Monopolies are an abuse, but an abuse in which enormous capital is vested, and numberless industrious agents employed, which deserve to be treated with consideration; for this mass of capital and industry cannot all at once find a more advantageous channel of national production. Perhaps the cure of all the partial distresses, that must follow the downfall of that colossal monster in politics, the exclusive system, would be as much as the talent of any single statesman could accomplish; yet, when one considers calmly the wrongs it entails when it is established, and the distresses consequent upon its overthrow, we are insensibly led to the reflection, that, if it be so difficult to set shackled industry at liberty again, with what caution ought we not to receive any proposition for enslaving her?

But governments have not been content with checking the import of foreign products. In the firm conviction, that national prosperity consists in selling without buying, and blind to the utter impossibility gone beyond the mere imposition of the thing, they have of a tax or fine upon purchasing from foreigners, and have in many instances offered rewards in the shape of bounties for selling to them.

This expedient has been employed to an extraordinary degree by the British government, which has always evinced the greatest anxiety to enlarge the vents for British commercial and manufactured produce. It is obvious that a merchant, who receives a bounty upon export, can, without personal loss, afford to sell his goods in a foreign market at a lower rate than prime cost. In the pithy language of Smith, 'We cannot force foreigners to buy the goods of our own workmen, as we may our own countrymen; the next best expedient, it has been thought, therefore, is to pay them for buying.'

In fact, if a particular commodity, by the time it has reached the French market, cost the English exporter 100fr., his trouble, &c. included, and the same commodity could be bought in France at the same or a less rate, there is nothing to give him exclusive possession of the market. But, if the British government pays a bounty of 10fr. upon the export, and thereby enables him to lower his demand from

100 to 90fr. he may safely reckon upon a preference. Yet what is this but a free gift of 10fr. from the British government to the French consumer? It may be conceived, that the merchant has no objection to this mode of dealing; for his profits are the same, as if the French consumer paid the full value, or cost price, of the commodity. The British nation is the loser in this transaction, in the ratio of 10 percent upon the French consumption; and France remits in return a value of but 90fr. for what has cost 100.

When a bounty is paid, not at the moment of export, but at the commencement of productive creation, the home consumer participates with the foreigner in the advantage of the bounty; for, in that case, the article can be sold below cost price in the home, as well as in the foreign market. And if, as is sometimes the case, the producer pockets the bounty, and yet keeps up the price of the commodity, the bounty is then a present of the government to the producer, over and above the ordinary profits of his industry.

When, by the means of a bounty, a product is raised either for home or foreign consumption, which would not have been raised without one, the effect is, an injurious production, one that costs more than it is worth. Suppose an article, when completely finished off, to be saleable for 24fr. and no more, but its prime cost, including of course the profits of productive industry, to amount to 27fr., it is quite clear, that nobody will volunteer the production, for fear of a loss of 3fr.. But, if the government, with a view to encourage this branch of industry, be willing to defray this loss, in other words, if it offers a bounty of 3fr. to the producer, the production can then go on, and the public revenue, that is to say, the nation at large, will be a loser of 3fr. And this is precisely the kind of advantage, that a nation gains by encouraging a branch of production, which cannot support itself: it is in fact urging the prosecution of a losing concern, the produce of which is exchanged, not for other produce, but for the bounty given by the state.

Wherever there is anything to be made by a particular employment of industry, it wants no encouragement; where there is nothing to be made, it deserves none. There is no truth in the argument, that perhaps the state may gain, though individuals cannot; for how can the state gain, except through the medium of individuals? Perhaps it may be said, that the state receives more in duties than it pays in bounties; but suppose it does, it merely receives with one hand and pays with the other: let the duties be lowered to the whole amount of the bounty, and production will stand precisely where it did before, with this difference in its favour, viz. that the state will save the whole charge of management of the bounties, and part of that of the duties.

READING 7

Frédéric Bastiat

Biography

Frédéric Bastiat (1801–1850) French economist and publicist was born in Bayonne in the department of Landes, the son of a merchant. He became an orphan at the age of nine and was reared by an aunt and his grandfather. Bastiat went to school at Soreze where he received an encyclopedic education, studied English and won a prize in poetry. At age of 17 he began to work in an uncle's firm. He had little taste for commerce, his main interest being in economic treatises which led him to study Adam Smith and J.B. Say very carefully. In 1825 he inherited his grandfather's estate at Mugron. He left his uncle's firm to manage the property. However, he showed no more aptitude for agriculture than he had for commerce. Increasingly his life became a one of learning and with a friend he established a discussion group in his village (Mugron).

From an English newspaper (the *Globe and Traveller*) he learned of the free trade movement originated by Cobden in 1844. Encouraged by Cobden's example he set up an association for free trade (Association pour la Liberté des Echanges). This event occurred in 1846. Two years earlier, in 1844 he had a stirring article published in the *Journal of Economists* (*Journal des Economistes*, volume IX), dealing with the influence of protectionism on France and England. The article was published under the title 'On the Influence of French and English Tariffs on the Future of the Two Peoples' (De L'Influence des Tarifs Francais et Anglais sur l'Avenir des deux Peuples). The article created a sensation. The response encouraged Bastiat to publish his *Economic Sophisms* (*Sophismes Economiques*) in 1846 which on publication was rapidly sold out and was subsequently translated into English and Italian.

In 1846 Bastiat moved to Paris, became secretary of the Association for Free Trade, and increased his literary activity endangering his health in the process. He suffered from a lung and throat disease which eventually killed him. At the time of the 1848 revolution he was elected representative of the Landes province in the constituent assembly in Paris. He also gave lectures, made public addresses and wrote articles for a periodical entitled *Free Trade* (*Libre Echange*). Shortly before his death he began a systematic exposition of his economic ideas. Unfortunately, he only lived to finish the first volume, *Economic Harmonies* (*Les Harmonies Economiques*). The book is built around a central antithesis between coercive restraining institutions and those which arise spontaneously to adjust the reciprocal relations between individuals and the environment in which they live. Bastiat died in 1850 in Rome at the age of 49.[17]

The Work

Bastiat was not a profound thinker and made no major original contributions to economic theory. However, he was a clever and incisive writer endowed with a great gift enabling him to ridicule the ideas of his opponents. In Schumpeter's words he was the most brilliant economic journalist who ever lived. Bastiat will always be remembered for his wit and irony and his ability to drive home economic insights in the form of satire and parables.

According to Bastiat there are basically two schools of economics. The first school (and here he has the classical school in mind) studies, arranges and classifies facts and phenomena. It looks for cause and effect relationships and eventually draws conclusions on the laws whereby people prosper or perish. This school observes the natural order and favors freedom. The other school sees society as an object of experiment. A community is nothing but an inert mass on which the legislator can impose his own laws and rules. This school is interventionist by definition and advocates compulsion to achieve its aims.

As a member of the first school Bastiat believed that the institution of private property combined with economic freedom would spontaneously and progressively, create the prosperity to which we all aspire and to which dreamers and zealous reformers endeavored unsuccessfully to realize artificially and prematurely. Bastiat in other words had a strong conviction of non intervention by government

17   His major works are: (1) *Cobden and the League* (*Cobden et la Ligue*) 1845;
      (2) *Sophisms of Protection* (*Les Sophismes Economiques*), 1845, 1848; (3)
      Essays on Political Economy (*Les Petits Pamphlets*), 1850; (4) *Economic
      Harmonies* (*Les Harmonies Economiques*), 1850.

allowing a natural harmony of interests to be created by the spontaneous actions of individuals.

But interventionism or statism had another side. Interventionism in practice, always meant that the state interfered in the economy to satisfy the interests of specific groups at the expense of others while simultaneously pretending to serve the general interest. Thus Bastiat fought monopoly, protectionism and socialism. Monopolists and manufacturers as recipients of protection are allowed to make extra profit at other people's expense. Socialism advocates a redistribution of property and income to the advantage of certain groups at the expense of others. Thus monopoly, protectionism and socialism are exploitative devices whereby certain people make gains to the detriment of others. They represent an unnatural organization of society, i.e. spoliation, undermining its potential for a natural harmony of interests. With spoliation the concept of justice weakens, the political struggle intensifies, and hatred and disagreement are the final result.

Bastiat's opposition to protection as a form of government inventionism was also related to his particular views on utility and value. Free goods such as sunshine and rain have great utility but the idea of value is linked to that of service. In Bastiat's view, value is derived not from work or labor actually done, but from labor or effort saved. Thus value is measured in terms of the trouble or effort a buyer saves by making a purchase. If human effort is needed it is because of the existence of an obstacle between a human's need and satisfactions. In the real world services are rendered to those experiencing obstacles. The physician makes his living from people who are ill, the car driver's services are needed when there is a distance to overcome and the glazier's services are needed when a window is broken. Therefore the bigger the obstacle the higher the income. If an obstacle vanishes, and services are no longer required, the supplier in turn suffers. From a societal point of view, however, this does not apply. Society as a whole is better off with fewer diseases, shorter distances and fewer broken windows. The fewer obstacles present the more prosperous we are, as a community. If in the course of time, because of technological advances, goods and services can be obtained with less effort, humanity is better off. Both the decline in effort needed and the reduction of obstacles translate themselves into lower prices, putting more and cheaper goods at the disposal of all sections of a given population.

This theoretical framework underlies Bastiat's opposition to protectionism. Each time a government accedes to the demands of a specific group, profession or class protecting it from competition, by the use of, for example, tariffs or quotas, it raises the magnitude of an obstacle resulting in intensified demand for the protected group's goods or services. Therefore, with foreign goods harder to get and domestically produced goods more expensive some individuals are better off but society as a whole is worse off. This also explains why Bastiat always puts the interests of the consumer before those of the producer. In modern terms we could say that it is the state which misallocates resources, a phenomenon Bastiat clearly recognized and prompted him to write: 'The state is the great fiction by means of which everyone tries to live at the expense of everyone else.'

The following reading, the 'Petition of the Candlemakers', is one of the best examples of Bastiat's craft. In this petition the manufacturers of candles urge Parliament to pass a law requiring the closing of all windows, shutters, holes, chinks and other openings through which the intolerable competition of the sun is bringing light inside houses free of charge, thus threatening to destroy a native industry affording employment directly and indirectly to thousands of people. The petition clearly shows the conflict of interests between consumers and producers. The question is, should we prefer the benefits of free consumption of sunlight or should we have rather the so-called advantages of expensive production, i.e. the manufacturing of candles.[18]

Extract

To the Members of the Chamber of Deputies,

Gentlemen: You are on the right road. You reject abstract theories; abundance, cheapness, impress you but little. You concern yourself chiefly with the fate of the producer. You want to free him from foreign competition; in short, you want to reserve the national market to national labor.

We come to offer you an admirable opportunity to apply your – what shall we say? your theory? No, nothing is more deceptive than theory. Your doctrine? Your system? Your principle? But you do not like doctrines, you have a horror of systems, and, as for principles,

---

18   Source: F. Bastiat, 'Economic Sophisms', *Selected Readings in International Trade and Tariff Problems* (F.W. Taussig, ed.) (New York: Ginn, 1921).

you assert that there are no such things in a social economy; we will say, then, your practice, your practice without theory and without principle.

We are subjected to the intolerable competition of a foreign rival, enjoying, as it appears, conditions so far superior to ours, for the production of light, that he inundates our national market at fabulously reduced prices, for as soon as he shows himself our sales cease, all the consumers turn to him, and a branch of French industry whose ramifications are innumerable is all of a sudden smitten with utter stagnation. That rival, which is no other than the sun, wages a war with us so inexorable that we suspect he is stirred up by perfidious Albion (good diplomacy as times go!) since he treats that haughty island with a consideration dispensed with in our case.

We demand that you pass a law which shall ordain the closing of all windows, dormer-windows, reflectors, shutters, curtains, casements, bull's-eyes, shades, in short, of all openings, holes, slits, and fissures, through which the sun is accustomed to penetrate into houses, to the prejudice of the fine industries with which we flatter ourselves we have endowed the country, which could not without ingratitude abandon us to so unequal a conflict.

We beg you, gentlemen, not to look upon our request as a satire, and, at least, not to reject it without listening to the reasons that we advance in support of it.

And in the first place, if you close, as far as possible, all access to natural light, if you thus create a need of artificial light, what industry in France is there that would not in the end be encouraged?

If more tallow is consumed, more oxen and sheep will be needed, and we shall, in consequence, see an increase of artificial meadows, of meat, wool, leather, and, above all, of fertilizers, that basis of all agricultural wealth.

If more oil is consumed, we shall see the poppy, the olive tree, colza, more extensively cultivated. These rich and exhausting plants will opportunely benefit by the fertility that the breeding of cattle will have communicated to our soil. Our heaths will be covered with resinous trees. Numerous swarms of bees will gather on our mountains the perfumed treasures which to-day are uselessly dissipated like the flowers whence they originate. There is thus not a single branch of agriculture which would not be greatly developed.

The same is the case with navigation: thousands of vessels will be engaged in whale fishery, and before long we shall have a navy capable of maintaining the honor of France and of answering to the patriotic susceptibility of the undersigned petitioners, candle merchants, etc.

But what shall we say of the specialties of Paris? Imagine the gilding, the bronzes, the crystals in chandeliers, lamps, candlesticks, candelabra glittering in spacious warehouses by the side of which those of to-day are mere insignificant shops.

Down to the very resin-gatherer on his moorland heights, or to the sad miner in the depths of his dark gallery, there is no one who will not see his wages and his well-being augmented.

Reflect upon it, gentlemen, and you will become convinced that there is perhaps not a single Frenchman, from the wealthy shareholder to the humblest match-vendor, whose condition would not be ameliorated by the success of our request.

We foresee your objections, gentlemen; but you will not oppose us with a single one of them which you have not gathered in the antiquated books of the partisans of commercial freedom. We defy you to say one word against us which will not at once rebound against yourselves and against the principle which governs your entire policy.

Will you tell us that if we profit by this protection France will not profit, because the consumer will pay the cost of it?

We will answer you: You no longer have the right to invoke the interests of the consumer. When he was at odds with the producer, you sacrificed him on every occasion. You did it in order to encourage labor, to enlarge the field of labor. You ought to do it again for the same motive.

You yourselves have met the objection. When you were told that the consumer is interested in the free importation of iron, coal, sesame, wheat, textiles, you said Yes, but the producer is interested in their exclusion. Well, then! If the consumers are interested in the admission of natural light, the producers are interested in its interdiction.

But, you went on to say, the producer and the consumer are one and the same. If the manufacturer profits by protection, he will cause the farmer to profit. If agriculture prospers, it will open markets for the factories. Very well! If you grant us the monopoly of illumination during the day, we shall, in the first place, purchase quantities of tallow, coal, oil, resin, wax alcohol, silver, iron, bronze, crystals, to feed our industry, and, furthermore, we and our numerous supplies having grown rich, we shall consume much and spread comfort to all the branches of national industry.

Will you say that the sunlight is a free gift, and to reject free gifts would be to reject wealth itself under the pretext of encouraging the means of acquiring it?

Then observe that you are striking a mortal blow at the very heart of your policy; observe that hitherto you have always rejected the foreign product precisely because it approximates the character of a free gift, and all the more the more it approximates it. For compliance with the importunities of the other monopolists you had but a half-motive; for the granting of our demand you have a complete motive; and to reject our appeal on the ground that it is better grounded than those others would be to state the equation $+ \; x \; = \; + \; -$; in other words, it would be heaping absurdity upon absurdity.

Labor and nature combine in varied proportions, according to countries and climates, in the creation of a product. The part that nature contributes to it is always gratuitous; it is labor's part that gives it value and is remunerated.

If a Lisbon orange is sold at half the price of a Paris orange, it is because a natural, and consequently a gratuitous heat does for the one what the other owes to an artificial, and therefore a costly, heat.

Hence, when we get an orange from Portugal, it may be said that it is given us half gratuitously, half on account of the labor involved, or, in other words, at half price relatively to those of Paris.

Now it is precisely upon this half gratuity (pardon the word) that you base your argument for its exclusion. You say: How can home labor stand the competition of foreign labor, when the former has to do everything, and the latter has to do only half the work, the sun taking the rest upon itself? But if a half gratuity determines you to shut out competition, how is it that a complete gratuity would lead you to admit competition? You are either no logicians or, since you reject the half gratuity as injurious to our national labor, you must *a fortiori* and with twice the emphasis reject the complete gratuity.

Once more, if a product, coal, iron, wheat, or textiles, comes to us from outside, and we can obtain it with less labor than if we produced it ourselves, the difference is a gift which is granted us. That gift is more or less considerable, according as the difference is greater or less. It is a quarter, a half, three-quarters of the value of the product, if the foreigner asks only three-quarters, half, quarter payment. It is as complete as possible when the donor, as in the case of the sun for light, demands nothing. The point is, and we state it formally, to ascertain whether you desire for France the benefit of gratuitous consumption or the pretended advantages of onerous labor. Choose, but be logical; for inasmuch as you will shut out, as you do, coal, iron, wheat, foreign textiles, in proportion as their price approaches zero, how inconsistent it is to admit the light of the sun, whose price is actually zero throughout the entire day!

READING 8

John Stuart Mill

Biography

John Stuart Mill (1806–1873), British philosopher and economist, prominent as a publicist in the reforming age of the nineteenth century was born on May 20, 1806 in his father's house in London. The latter, James Mill, was a man of considerable eminence as a historian, philosopher, utilitarian and economist. He was also a friend of Jeremy Bentham and David Ricardo.

Tutored by his father, a strict disciplinarian, John began learning Greek and arithmetic at the age of three; Latin at the age of eight while the study of geometry, algebra, chemistry, physics and logic was undertaken somewhat later. At age thirteen he began the study of political economy. When he was fourteen he was sent to France to complete his education. There he stayed some time with the French economist Jean Baptiste Say. At the age of seventeen he began his career with the East India Company which lasted for thirty-five years. In 1856 he became chief of the examiner's office. On the dissolution of the company in 1858 he retired with an annual pension of 1,500 pounds, a considerable sum in those days.

During the 1830s Mill met Harriet Taylor, the wife of a London businessman. Mill cherished her friendship for twenty years. Two years after her husband's death, Mill married Harriet in 1851. Although she had little influence upon Mill's literary craft she did affect his thinking on such subjects as women's rights and social progress. Their marriage lasted seven years. Harriet Mill died in 1858. John Stuart Mill spent much of the rest of his life at a villa at St Veran, near Avignon (France).

The Work

Mill's career as a writer began in 1822 when he was only sixteen. He produced a number of articles and short essays and his great major work *A System of Logic* was published in 1841.

A year later his *Essays on Some Unsettled Questions of Political Economy* were published followed by his famous *Principles of Political Economy* (1848). As a result of these Mill's reputation as an outstanding thinker was firmly established. His *Principles* was used as a text until the end of the nineteenth century. In 1859, Mill issued his famous *On Liberty* which is still the classic plea for individual freedom.

In his *Principles* Mill restates classical economics, giving it new life at the same time. He rephrased many of the classical theories, clarifying them and adding many analytical discoveries of his own. However, Mill did not try to construct a new system. He only added improvements to the classical system trying at the same time to transform it into a more hopeful and progressive system of thought. In the process he achieved a degree of theoretical refinement and orderly presentation that is truly admirable.

Mill's ideas on protection appear in book 5 of his *Principles* where he deals with the special functions of government vis-à-vis the economy. Mill was well aware of the inclination of reformers to extend the province of government beyond due bounds. Although he found the arguments of the dogmatic liberals unsatisfactory, he still felt that the laissez-faire rule was a good general guide for action. Admitting some exceptions to the rule, Mill considered that the main occupation of central government should be to create a legal framework for freedom and equality and to provide services of the non-coercive type such as the giving of advice and information. The number of coercive interventions by the state should be limited to a minimum for the following reasons:

1. Personal freedom is a great good in itself and should not be infringed upon. In the commercial-business sphere restrictions are only justified when the advantages clearly outweigh the disadvantages. The burden of proof has be on the advocates of intervention.
2. A second reason consists of the danger excessive state activity entails for political freedom. As soon as the share of government activity as a proportion of the total grows beyond a certain point, political freedom would survive in name only. For example, there can be no freedom of the press when all publishing houses are branches of government.
3. State activity has a tendency to limit the spontaneous development of the individual which in Mill's view is an essential condition for

progress. Government omnipotence tends towards a passive population.

4. A final reason for opposing increased government intrusion was the trust that Mill placed on the spontaneous operation of the free market which contained the springs of self-interest. At the same time Mill saw the market as a superior collector of information.

Protection was seen by Mill as a form of negative government intrusion in economic affairs. Any departure from free trade needed extended justification. As far as Mill was concerned, the only conceivable excuse was provided by the infant industry argument. A limited amount of protection could be given for a specified period to young industries needing a chance to develop. However, in a letter written in 1868, Mill confessed that it might be preferable to subsidize these industries. The reason being that it would always be easier to get rid of a subsidy or bonus than to do away with tariffs which always tend to create special interests.

The first reading is taken from Mill's *Principles of Political Economy*. The second selection consists of two letters written by Mill rather late in his life. In the first of these letters he carefully qualifies his support for infant industries. The second letter is an admirable expression of Mill's final and considered views on the subject of protection with particular reference to the case of the United States.[19]

Extracts

From the necessary functions of government and the effects produced on the economical interests of society by their good or ill discharge, we proceed to the functions which belong to what I have termed the optional class; these which are sometimes assumed by governments and sometimes not, and which it is not unanimously admitted that they ought to exercise.

Before entering on the general principles of the questions, it will be advisable to clear from our path of these cases, in which government interference works ill, because founded on false views of

19 John Stuart Mill, *Principles of Political Economy*, Vol. II (London: Parker, 1848) Chapter 10.

John Stuart Mill, 'Letter to Archibald Michie of Victoria', 'Letter to the New York Liberal Club' *John Stuart Mill on the Protection of Infant Industries* (Cobden Club) (London: Cassell, 1911).

the subject interfered with. Such cases have no connection with any theory respecting the proper limits of interference. There are some things with which governments ought not to meddle, and other things with which they ought; but whether right or wrong in itself, the interference must work for ill, if government, not understanding the subject which it meddles with, meddles to bring about a result which would be mischievous. We will therefore begin by passing in review various false theories, which have from time to time formed the ground of acts of government more or less economically injurious.

Former writers on political economy have found it needful to devote much trouble and space to this department of their subject. It has now happily become possible, at least in our own country, greatly to abridge this purely negative part of our discussions. The false theories of political economy which have done so much mischief in times past, are entirely discredited among all who have not lagged behind of the general progress of opinion; and few of the enactments which were once grounded on those theories still help to deform the statute-book. As the principles, on which their condemnation rests, have been fully set forth in other parts of this treatise, we may here content ourselves with a few brief indications.

Of these false theories, the most notable is the doctrine of Protection to Native Industry; a phrase meaning the prohibition, or the discouragement by heavy duties, of such foreign commodities as are capable of being produced at home. If the theory involved in this system had been correct, the practical conclusions grounded on it would not have been unreasonable. The theory was, that to buy things produced at home was a national benefit, and the introduction of foreign commodities, generally a national loss. It being at the same time evident that the interest of the consumer is to buy foreign commodities in preference to domestic whenever they are either cheaper or better, the interest of the consumer appeared in this respect to be contrary to the public interest: he was certain, if left to his own inclinations, to do what according to the theory was injurious to the public.

It was shown, however, in our analysis of the effects of international trade, as it had often been shown by former writers, that the importation of foreign commodities, in the common course of traffic, never takes place, except when it is, economically speaking, a national good, by causing the same amount of commodities to be obtained at a smaller cost of labour and capital to the country. To prohibit, therefore, this importation, or impose duties which prevent it, is to render the labour and capital of the country less efficient in production than they would otherwise be; and compel a waste, of the difference between the labour and capital necessary for the home production of the commodity, and that which is required for producing the things with which it can be purchased from abroad. The amount of national loss thus occasioned is measured by the excess of the price at which the commodity is produced, over that at which it could be imported. In the case of the manufactured goods, the whole difference between the two prices is absorbed in indemnifying the producers for waste of labour, or of the capital which supports that labour. Those who are supposed to be benefited, namely the makers of the protected articles (unless they form an exclusive company, and have a monopoly against their own countrymen as well as against foreigners), do not obtain higher profits than other people. All is sheer loss, to the country as well as to the consumer. When the protected article is a product of agriculture – the wage of labour not being incurred on the whole produce, but only on what may be called the last instalment of it – the extra price is only in part an indemnity for waste, the remainder being a tax paid to the landlords.

The restrictive and prohibitory policy was originally grounded on what is called the Mercantile System, which representing the advantage of foreign trade to consist solely in bringing money into the country, gave artificial encouragement to exportation of goods, and discountenanced their importation. The only exceptions to the system were those required by the system itself. The materials and instruments of production were the subjects of a contrary policy, directed however to the same end; they were freely imported, and not permitted to be exported, in order that manufacturers, being more cheaply supplied with the requisites of manufacture, might be able to sell cheaper, and therefore to export more largely. For a similar reason, importation was permitted and even favoured, when confined to the productions of countries which were supposed to take from us still more than we took from them, thus enriching the country by a favourable balance of trade. As part of the same system, colonies were founded for the supposed advantage of compelling them to buy our commodities, or at all events not to buy those of any other country: in return for which restriction, we were generally willing to come under an equivalent obligation with respect to the staple production of the colonists. The consequences of the theory were pushed so far, that it was not unusual even to give bounties on exportation, and induce foreigners to buy from us rather than from other countries, by a cheapness which we artificially produced, by paying part of the price for them, out of our own taxes. This is beyond the point yet reached by any private tradesman in his competition for business. No shopkeeper, I should think ever made a practice of bribing customers by selling goods to them at a permanent loss, making it up to himself from other funds in his possession.

The principle of the Mercantile Theory is now given up even by writers and governments who still cling to the restrictive system. Whatever hold that system has over men's minds, independently of the private interests which would be exposed to real or apprehended loss by its abandonment, is derived from fallacies other than the old notion of the benefits of heaping up money in the country. The most effective of these is the specious plea, of employing our own countrymen and our national industry, instead of feeding and supporting the industry of foreigners. The answer to this, from the principles laid down in former chapters, is evident. Without reverting to the fundamental theorem discussed in an early part of the present treatise, respecting the nature and sources of employment for labour; it is sufficient to say, what has usually been said by the advocates of free trade, that the alternative is not between employing our own country-people and foreigners, but between employing one class and another of our own country-people. The imported commodity is always paid for, directly or indirectly, with the produce of our own industry: that industry being at the same time rendered more productive, since with the same labour and outlay we are enabled to possess ourselves of a greater quantity of the article. Those who have not well considered the subject, are apt to suppose that our exporting an equivalent in our own produce, for the foreign articles we consume, depends on contingencies: on the consent of foreign countries to make some corresponding relaxation of their own restrictions, or on the question whether those from whom we buy, are induced by that circumstance to buy more from us; and that if these things, or things equivalent to them, do not happen, the payments must be made in money. Now, in the first place, there is nothing more objectionable in a money payment than in payment by any other medium, if the state of the market makes it the most advantageous remittance: and the money itself was first acquired, and would again be replenished, by the export of an equivalent value of our own products. But in the next place, a very short interval of paying in money would so lower prices as either to stop a part of the importation, or raise up a foreign demand for our products, sufficient to pay for the imports. I grant that this disturbance of the equation of international demand would be in some degree to our disadvantage, in the purchase of other imported articles; and that a country which prohibits some foreign commodities, does, *ceteris paribus*, obtain these which does not prohibit, at a less price that it would otherwise have to pay. To express the same thing in other words; a country which destroys or prevents altogether certain branches of foreign trade, thereby annihilating a general gain to the world, which would be shared in some proportion between itself and other countries – does, in some circumstances, draw to itself, at the expenses of foreigners, a larger share than would else belong to it of the gain arising from that portion of its foreign trade which it suffers to subsist. But even this it can only be enabled to do, if foreigners do not maintain equivalent prohibitions or restrictions against its commodities. In any case, the justice or expediency of destroying one of two gains, in order to engross a rather larger share of the other, does not require much discussion: the gain, too, which is destroyed, being, in proportion to the magnitude of the transactions, the larger of the two, since it is the one which capital, left to itself, is supposed to seek by preference.

Defeated as a general theory, the Protectionist doctrine finds support in some particular cases, from considerations which, when really in point, involve greater interests than mere saving of labour; the interests of national subsistence and of national defence. The discussions on the Corn Laws have familiarized everybody with the plea, that we ought to be independent of foreigners for the food of the people; and the navigation laws are grounded, in theory and profession, on the necessity of keeping up a 'nursery of seamen' for the navy. On this last subject I at once admit, that the object is worth the sacrifice; and that a country exposed to invasion by sea, if it cannot otherwise have sufficient ships and sailors of its own to secure the means of manning on an emergency an adequate fleet, is quite right in obtaining those means, even at some economical sacrifice in point of cheapness of transport. When the English navigation laws were enacted, the Dutch, from their maritime skill and their low rate of profit at home, were able to carry for other nations, England included, at cheaper rates than those nations could carry for themselves: which placed all other countries at a great comparative disadvantage in obtaining experienced seamen for their ships of war. The Navigation Laws, by which this deficiency was remedied, and at the same time a blow struck against the maritime power of a nation with which England was then frequently engaged in hostilities, were probably, though economically disadvantageous, politically expedient. But English ships and sailors can now navigate as cheaply as those of any other country; maintaining at least an equal competition with the other maritime nations even in their own trade. The ends which may once have justified Navigation Laws, require them no longer, and there seems no reason for maintaining this invidious exception to the general rule of free trade.

With regard to subsistence, the plea of the Protectionists has been so often and so triumphantly met, that it requires little notice here. That country is the most steadily as well as the most abundantly supplied with food, which draws its supplies from the largest surface. It is ridiculous to found a general system of policy on so chimerical a danger as that of being at war with all the nations of the world at once; or to suppose that, even if inferior at sea, a whole country could be blockaded like a town, or that the growers of food in other countries would not be as anxious not to lose an advantageous market, as we should be not to be deprived of their corn. On the subject, however, of subsistence, there is one point which deserves more especial consideration. In cases of actual or apprehended scarcity, many countries of Europe are accustomed to stop the exportation of food. Is this, or not, sound policy? There can be no doubt that in the present state of international morality, a people cannot, any more than an individual, be blamed for not starving itself to feed others. But if the greatest amount of good to mankind on the whole, were the end aimed at in the maxims of international conduct, such collective churlishness would certainly be condemned by them. Suppose that in ordinary circumstances the trade in food were perfectly free, so that the price in one country could not habitually exceed that in any other by more than the cost of carriage, together with a moderate profit to the importer. A general scarcity ensues, affecting all countries, but in unequal degrees. If the price rose in one country more than in others, it would be a proof that in that country the scarcity was severest, and that by permitting food to go freely thither from any other country, it would be spared from a less urgent necessity to relieve a greater. When the interests, therefore, of all countries are considered, free exportation is desirable. To the exporting country considered separately, it may, at least on the particular occasion, be an inconvenience: but taking into account that the country which is now the giver, will in some future season be the receiver, and the one that is benefited by the freedom, I cannot but think that even to the apprehension of food-rioters it might be made apparent, that in such cases they should do to others what they would wish done to themselves.

In countries in which the system of Protection is declining, but not yet wholly given up, such as the United States, a doctrine has come into notice which is a sort of compromise between free trade and restriction, namely, that protection for protection's sake is improper, but that there is nothing objectionable in having as much protection as may incidentally result from a tariff framed solely for revenue. Even in England, regret is sometimes expressed that a 'moderate fixed duty' was not preserved on corn, on account of the revenue it would yield. Independently, however, of the general impolicy of taxes on the necessaries of life, this doctrine overlooks the fact, that revenue is received only on the quantity imported, but that the tax is paid on the entire quantity consumed. To make the public pay much that the treasury may receive a little, is no eligible mode of obtaining a revenue. In the case of manufactured articles the doctrine involves a palpable inconsistency. The object of the duty as a means of revenue, is inconsistent with its affording, even incidentally, any protection. It can only operate as protection in so far as it prevents importation; and to whatever degree it prevents importation, it affords no revenue.

The only case in which, on mere principle of political economy, protecting duties can be defensible, is when they are imposed temporarily (especially in a young and rising nation) in hopes of naturalizing a foreign industry, in itself perfectly suitable to the circumstances of the country. The superiority of one country over another in a branch of production, often arises only from having begun it sooner. There may be no inherent advantage on one part, or disadvantage on the other, but only a present superiority of acquired skill and experience. A country which has this skill and experience yet to acquire, may in other respects be better adapted to the production than those which were earlier in the field: and besides, it is a just remark, that nothing has a greater tendency to promote improvements in any branch of production, than its trial under a new set of conditions. But it cannot be expected that individuals should, at their own risk, or rather to their certain loss, introduce a new manufacture, and bear the burden of carrying it on, until the producers have been educated up to the level of those with whom the processes are traditional. A protecting duty, continued for a reasonable time, will sometimes be the least inconvenient mode in which the nation can tax itself for the support of such an experiment. But the protection should be confined to cases in which there is good ground of assurance that the industry which it fosters will after a time be able to dispense with it; nor should the domestic producers ever be allowed to expect that it will be continued to them, beyond the time strictly necessary for a fair trial of what they are capable of accomplishing.

There is only one part of the Protectionist scheme which requires any further notice: its policy towards colonies, and foreign dependencies; that of compelling them to trade exclusively with the dominant country. A country which thus secures to itself an extra foreign demand for its commodities, undoubtedly gives itself some advantage in the distribution of the general gains of the commercial world. Since, however, it causes the industry and capital of the colony to be diverted from channels, which are proved to be the most productive, inasmuch as they are those into which industry and capital spontaneously tend to flow; there is a loss, on the whole, to the productive powers of the world, and the mother country does not gain so much as she makes the colony lose. If, therefore, the mother country refuses to acknowledge any reciprocity of obligation, she imposes a tribute on the colony in an indirect mode, greatly more oppressive and injurious than the direct. But if, with a more equitable spirit, she submits herself to corresponding restrictions for the benefit of the colony, the result of the whole transaction is the ridiculous one, that each party loses much, in order that the other may gain a little.

......

TO ARCHIBALD MICHIE, of Victoria.

 '*Avignon*, December 7, 1868.

DEAR SIR, I am much honoured by your thinking it worth while to write so long and interesting a letter for the purpose of convincing me that the people of Victoria are not so far gone in Protectionism as they are thought to be. I have never laid stress on anything contained in the article in the *Westminster Review* which did not, to my judgment, look like a fair representation. I need not say how glad I should be to believe that the Victoria Protectionists are Protectionists only within the limits of my excepted case, i.e. that they only wish for temporary Protection to try the experiment of naturalizing foreign branches of industry. Unfortunately, the writings I have seen on their side of the question – I admit that they are not numerous – make no reservation of the kind, but advocate the general theory of Protection on the old ignorant grounds, and support it by the old stock fallacies, and refer to the stupidest authorities – British, American, and Continental – as a sanction for it. All this is very natural. The Protectionist theory appears plain common sense to persons thoroughly ignorant of the subject; and industries artificially fortified, even though it be professedly for a time only, raise up private interests which combine, as they have done in the United States, but too effectually to convert what was intended as a temporary expedient into a permanent institution (though the thick end of the wedge seldom follows the thin end at so short an interval as three years). These considerations have greatly shaken the opinion I expressed in my book; and though I still think that the introduction of a foreign industry is often worth a sacrifice, and that a temporary Protecting duty, if it was sure to remain temporary, would probably be the best shape in which that sacrifice can be made, I am inclined to believe that it is safer to make it by an annual grant from the public treasury, which is not nearly so likely to be continued indefinitely, to prop up an industry which has not so thriven as to be able to dispense with it.

I can readily believe that the Free Trade party in Victoria is swelled by the private self-interest of importing merchants; but a cause seldom triumphs unless somebody's personal interest is bound up with it. It would have been long before the Corn Laws would have been abolished in Great Britain if, besides the public interests concerned, those laws had not been contrary to the private interests of nearly the whole of the manufacturing and mercantile classes.

......

TO THE NEW YORK LIBERAL CLUB.

[On being elected a corresponding member of that body, Mill, in response to a hint from the Secretary, wrote the following letter on Protection].

January 20, 1871

DEAR SIR, ... You intimate that it might be acceptable if, in acknowledging your communication, I was to take the opportunity of expressing my opinion on the desirableness of a Free Trade policy for America. I cannot suppose that those who have thought me deserving of the distinguished honour conferred on me can have anything to learn respecting my opinion on a question of this nature. But I should not be doing justice to my sense of that honour, or to the interest I feel in the objects and in the prosperity of the Club, were I not to comply with the wish expressed by you in its behalf.

I hold every form of what is called Protection to be an employment of the powers of Government to tax the many with the intention of promoting the pecuniary gains of a few. I say the intention, because even that desired object is very often not attained, and never to the extent that is expected. But whatever gain there is

made by the few, and them alone; for the labouring people employed
in the Protected branches of industry are not benefited. Wages do not
range higher in the protected than in other employments; they depend
on the general rate of the remuneration of labour in the country, and
if the demand for particular kinds of labour is artificially increased,
the consequence is merely that labour is attracted from other
occupations, so that employment is given in the Protected trades to a
greater number, but not at higher remuneration. The gain by
Protection, when there is gain, is for the employers alone. Such
legislation was worthy of Great Britain under her unreformed
constitution, when the powers of legislation were in the hands of a
limited class of great landowners and wealthy manufacturers. But in
a democratic nation like the United States it is a signal instance of
dupery, and I have a highest opinion of the intelligence of the
American many than to believe that an handful of manufacturers will
be able to retain by fallacy and sophistry that power of levying a toll
on every other person's earnings which the powerful aristocracy of
England, with all their political ascendancy and social prestige, have
not been able to keep possession of.

The misapprehension and confusion of thought which exist on this
subject – misapprehension and confusion quite genuine, I allow, in the
Protectionist mind – arise from a very small number of oversights,
natural enough perhaps in those who have never thought on the
subject.

1. When people see manufactories built and hands set to work; to
produce at home what had previously been imported from abroad,
they imagine that all this is fresh industry and fresh employment over
and above that which existed before, and that whatever increased
production takes place in these particular trades is so much additional
wealth created in the country. The oversight is in not considering that
this additional labour and capital to which this production is due are
not created, but withdrawn from other employments in which they
would have added as much to the wealth of the country; and not only
as much, but more, since they would not have needed a subsidy out
of every consumer's pocket to make their employment remunerative.
That the apparent increase of employment produced by Protection is
a mere transfer from one business to another is true everywhere, but
is particularly obvious in America, since none will question that
labour and capital in the United States are in any danger of not finding
employment, or that the time is at hand when they will even be
obliged to submit to any diminution of wages or of profits.

2. There is a widely diffused notion that by means of Protecting duties on foreign commodities a nation taxes not itself but the foreign producers. Because foreign nations can really be made to suffer by being deprived of a beneficial trade, it is imagined that what the foreigners lose one's own country must gain. But this is a complete misunderstanding of the nature and operation of Protection. Duties on such foreign commodities as do not come into competition with home productions sometimes do fall partly on foreigners, unless the effect is frustrated by a similar policy in the foreign country. Such duties do not destroy any wealth, and may alter its distribution. But such is not the case with any duties so far as they have a protective operation. For their protective operation consists in causing something to be made in one place which in a state of freedom would be made in another, and whatever does this diminishes the total produce of the world's labour; for in a state of freedom everything naturally tends to be produced in the places and in the ways by which the cost incurred in labour and capital obtains the largest return. If this working of the ordinary motives to production is interfered with and producers are bribed at other people's expense to produce an article where they would not otherwise find it for their interest to do so, there is a loss to the world of a portion of its annual produce which would have been shared in some proportion or other between the importing and the exporting countries. America can in this way damage foreigners, but she cannot tax them, for she cannot avoid largely sharing their loss.

3. A notion very powerful in the minds of some Americans is that if they let in the competition of what they call the pauper labour of Europe they would reduce their own labourers to similar pauperism. Let me observe, by the way, that the labour which produces the exportable articles of Europe, and especially of England, is not pauper labour, but is generally the most highly paid manual labour of the country. But it is, of course, true that the general wages of labour in America are above the English level, and if these high wages were the effect of Protection, I for one should never wish to see Protection abolished. But it is not because of Protection that wages in America are high, it is because there is abundance of land for every labourer, and because every labourer is at liberty to acquire it. As long as this abundance of land relatively to population continues, wages will not decline. These high wages are not a special burden upon the New England cotton-spinner or the Pennsylvanian iron-master, but have equally to be paid in agriculture and in those numerous branches of manufacturing and other industries (the building trades, for example)

which every country necessarily carries on for itself. If those employ-ments which form the bulk of the industry of the country can pay the high American wages and yield besides the high American profits, and if there are other branches of manufacture which cannot do this unless the people of the United States consent to pay them a subsidy in the form of a large extra price, the former class of employments yield a greater return to the labour and capital of America than the latter, and it is for the interest of American production on the whole that the labour and capital of the country should be diverted from the employments which require to be subsidized to those which can maintain themselves without.

4. An argument in favour of Protection which carries weight with many Americans who are not deceived by the economic fallacies of Protectionism is that it is an evil to have the population of a country too exclusively agricultural, and that the interests of civilization require a considerable admixture of large towns. I acknowledge that there was no little force in this argument at a much earlier period of American development. But the time has surely gone by when the growth of the towns in the United States required any artificial encouragement. Even in those parts of the Union in which little or no protected industry is carried on towns spring into existence and into greatness with a rapidity more marvellous than even the extension of the cultivated area of your territory. The necessity of centres both for internal and foreign trade, the multitude of occupations which from the nature of things are not exposed to the competition of distant places, and the many kinds and qualities of manufactures which are kept at home by the natural protection of cost of carriage, ensure to the United States a town population amply sufficient for a country in which to be an agricultural labourer does not mean, as it has hitherto meant in England, to be an uneducated barbarian. I believe the most enlightened Americans are generally of opinion that at present it is the rural much more than the town population which is both the physical and the moral strength of the country.

To these various considerations I might add that the Protection lavished upon some favoured classes of producers is, even from the Protectionist point of view, a serious injury to other producers who depend on those for the materials of the instruments of their several businesses, and that the attempt to remedy this injustice by distributing Protection all round exhibits American producers in the ludicrous light of attempting to get rich by mutually taxing one another. But these points have already been placed in so strong a light that it is quite superfluous for me to insist on them. Rather would I endeavour to impress my conviction that the evils of Protection, though they may be aggravated by the details of its application, cannot be removed by any readjustment of those details; and that any Protection whatever, just in so far as it is Protection – just in so far as it fulfils its purpose – abstracts in a greater or a less degree from the aggregate wealth of mankind, and leaves a less amount of product to be shared among the nations of the earth, to the necessary loss of all nations whose industry is forced out of its spontaneous course by preventing them either from importing or from exporting any article which they would import or export in a state of freedom.

READING 9

Nicolaas Gerard Pierson

Biography

Nicolaas Gerard Pierson (1839–1909), the foremost Dutch economist of the nineteenth century was born on February 7, 1839 into a family of seven children one of whom died early. He grew up in a rather well-to-do environment. His father was a businessman, apparently a somewhat withdrawn person, but very reliable and solid. His mother was more assertive. She was also a pious woman, very good-natured and caring.

Nicolaas attended a French elementary school in Amsterdam and was further educated at an English high school in Brussels (Belgium). Pierson never attended a university but always showed a great capacity for self-study. Destined to enter the business world he went to Liverpool in 1858 to study the cotton trade, working for a brokerage firm which went by the name of Colin Campbell and Son. The same year he traveled to Louisiana (New Orleans) in the United States, again to gain a better understanding of the cotton business. Upon his return he published, at the age of 20, his first article 'Trade and Banking in the State of Louisiana' emphasizing the importance of a sound banking system, something Louisiana with a well-regulated banking system could be proud of. Pierson pointed out that defective legislation in many American states resulted in the establishment of numerous banks each issuing its own notes. This excessive credit creation resulted in inflation, rising imports and declining exports. As gold flowed out, credit had to be restricted and recession followed.

Louisiana with its model system did not suffer from these problems.

Although Pierson spent the next several years in the world of business and banking, his heart was with economics. In 1861 at the age of 22, Pierson gave a talk to a Dutch association of economists. On this occasion he discussed current methodology which was somewhat defective, he felt, because of the type of economics (heavily influenced by the French School) which then dominated Dutch thinking. In his talk Pierson emphasized the fact that the deductive method backed up by statistical and historical knowledge was the only feasible one. Throughout his entire career Pierson remained faithful to this approach. On later occasions Pierson often criticized the German Historical School for its careless work and its sloppy methodology.

In 1862 at the age of 23 Pierson married Catharina Rutgera Waller the daughter of a stock trader in Amsterdam with whom he remained for 47 years. Because of Catharina's health problems the couple remained childless.

In 1863 Pierson published 'The Future of the Dutch Central Bank' (De Toekomst der Nederlandse Bank). In his article he pleaded for the maintenance of the bank's monopoly as the creator of banknotes. Although he favored competition as a matter of principle, he opposed the creation of more than one bank of issue on the grounds that such a situation was likely to cause inflation. In this article as in later publications Pierson clearly defends a variety of monetarism as we know it today. In his writings on national and international economics he always emphasizes that increases in the money supply tend to cause inflation. Pierson stressed on various occasions that a nation's demand for cash balances (defined as coins and notes) is remarkably stable. For a country like the Netherlands around the 1880s it fluctuated around the figure of three hundred million guilders according to Pierson. Increments in the money supply are simple expelled. Liquid money does not yield a return. When the merchant experiences a strong increase in his cash balances he buys goods, securities or furnishes loans to others for their purchases. The extra purchases tend to result in higher prices. If foreign goods are bought the redundant money flows out.

Pierson's publication on central banking coupled with his other writings made a deep impression on Mr W.C. Mees, himself an economist and President of the Dutch Central Bank with whom Pierson was to meet for the first time in 1866. On the advice of Mr Mees, Pierson was appointed as one of the five managers of the Dutch

Central Bank in 1868.

Earlier that year Pierson had given six published lectures on the agricultural system in the Dutch Indies. Here Pearson argued that the existing Dutch policy of government-led cultivation and merchandising of tropical products had to be abandoned because it discouraged private enterprise, resulted in artificially low wages in the Dutch Indies and led to the demoralization of the local population. As individual ownership of the land was discouraged no incentive to produce existed. Thus stagnation of production and trade were the inevitable consequences. As an alternative, Pierson proposed a well-regulated system of private land ownership, freedom of enterprise and self-government in the villages. The lectures were expanded and became republished in 1877. Pierson's version of liberalism, rather typical for the middle of the nineteenth century, was always associated with some social change, more democracy, and increased public participation. Solutions to social problems had to be based on activities which involved individual initiative and self-help.

Pierson's work at the Central Bank involved him only a few hours per day which left him time for his private studies and research. In the early 1870s he published many articles with monetary problems and tax issues as his favorite subjects.

In the period 1875–1876 Pierson issued his first textbook in two volumes entitled *Elements of Economics (Grondbeginselen der Staathuishoudkunde)*. This book which was written for high school students turned out to be too difficult for them. In 1886 Pierson published a new simpler version of the book. The last edition, the fifth, appeared in 1905. In 1877 Pierson accepted a professorship of economics and statistics at the newly established Municipal University of Amsterdam. He kept this post until 1889 but refused payment as he felt that his other sources of income were sufficient. Earlier in 1875 when the University of Leiden celebrated its three hundredth anniversary he was awarded a honorary doctoral degree which made him a recognized member of the academic establishment. Between 1889 and 1890 Pierson published a two-volume treatise, *Principles of Economics (Leerboek der Staathuishoudkunde)* for use in universities and this was translated into English by A. A. Wotzel. The book assimilated marginalism, mainly in the Austrian tradition. In 1884 Mr Mees, President of the Central Bank, died and in fulfillment of his wishes Pierson became the new President of the Dutch Central Bank. He resigned from his teaching position and stayed in his new office until 1891 when he was invited to become the Minister of Finance in the newly formed liberal government. His philosophy of taxes comprised three basic principles: (a) the state needs revenues to fulfill its accepted functions, (b) taxes should not hamper production, (c) taxes should be based on the ability to pay. As a minister of finance Pierson abolished a number of the old indirect taxes and introduced some new ones such as a very moderate income tax.

The government of which Pierson was a part, lasted until 1894 after which he returned to his study, research and writing. In 1890 he had also become the chairman of the editorial staff of *The Economist* (*De Economist*) a Dutch publication which still survives.

In 1897 Pierson again entered the government this time serving as Prime Minister and Minister of Finance. This administration was marked by new social legislation. In response to strong popular demand, new laws regarding compulsory elementary education, health, housing and accident insurance were adopted. Here Pierson's philosophy was, that social legislation should serve to mitigate the excesses of laissez-faire. It should also respect the free enterprise system and promote its preservation. It was not supposed to be an overture to socialism. Socialistic legislation, on the contrary, attempts to replace the market economy by an entirely different order.

New elections in 1901 resulted in Pierson's resignation and he return once more to study and research. In 1904 the University of Cambridge (England) awarded him the degree of 'Doctor of Science'. In 1905 Pierson agreed with some reluctance to run for a seat in the lower house of parliament and was elected. After 1908 his health began to deteriorate which obliged him to resign from his duties.

Pierson died in 1909 at the age of 70. Throughout his life he had remained the same modest, mindful, tolerant and decent person. A devotion to scientific activity was always high among his priorities. As a realist he believed that facts were of paramount importance. He promoted the establishment of the Dutch 'Central Bureau of Statistics' in 1899, still the main fact-gathering agency in the country. Idealism in his view was also necessary. It gave man strength, optimism and confidence.

The Work

Pierson, whose reasoning was based on the concepts of the gold standard and international payments made mostly with bills of exchange, argued again and again that protectionism, while benefiting certain domestic industries, harmed others. He stressed on many occasions that imports and exports should balance in the long run. An artificial reduction in imports will therefore automatically reduce exports and thus damage the export industries. Pierson took as an example two countries A and B. If imports and exports balance, the demand (by B) for and supply of A's currency will also balance. In other words, the demand and supply of bills drawn on A and B will be in equilibrium. But if country A reduces its imports by such artificial measures as immoderate tariffs and still exports the same amount, the demand for its currency remains high while the supply drops. B's demand for drafts to make payments in A is now in excess of A's demand for bills drawn on B. The exchange rate will move against B so that the cost of buying A's currency in the foreign exchange market rises. It may go up to the point that it becomes cheaper for B to send gold to A to make payments. The import of gold in A increases the domestic supply of legal tender money, credit expands, the demand for commodities rises and prices go up. As A becomes relatively expensive, exports drop and a new balance but at a lower level of international trade is attained.

If a country such as England experiences a quasi permanent import surplus the situation is comparable no matter what protectionists may say. England is a typical case of a capital rich nation, says Pierson, exporting capital in the form of direct investment in colonial or foreign firms or through the purchase of foreign securities. England also 'exports' transportation services, insurance services and banking services. A capital export in the form of specie or coins would reduce the English money supply, resulting in lower prices and therefore more exports. Thus, initially the capital movement transforms itself into an outflow of goods. Yet there exist a flow in the opposite direction because foreign investments produce a flow of returns in the form of interest and profit payments and services also have to be paid for. With the large flow of transfers England is entitled to, one would assume that large amounts of specie would flow into this country. Perhaps this was true at an earlier stage where it expanded the English money supply, pushed up prices, increased imports and reduced exports. Yet in reality specie movements are now relatively small, says Pierson. Those foreigners owing money to both English investors and the suppliers of services require drafts drawn on English individuals, firms or banks. The demand is strong, the terms are favorable and thus the inducement to supply them by exporting to England is created.

Although English investors want their profit and interest payments in the form of monetary transfers, in reality there are products which enter the country. An artificial reduction of imports would again produce the known result: a lower level of mutual trade and investment.

A second obvious disadvantage of high tariffs is that the protected article becomes more expensive. The users of the item experience a decline in real income. If a worker gets ten guilders per week and goods rise in price by 25% his real income is reduced by the same amount. If widely used articles are taxed, a redistribution of the nation's income results at the expense of the lower income groups. Countries such as Germany and France, argues Pierson, by imposing considerable duties on wheat, have benefited the larger landowners but have made the majority of the population suffer.

Consider the problem when the protected article is used as an input by other industries. If country A puts a heavy duty on cotton yarn, this will stimulate the domestic spinning mills but the weaving mills will suffer. A tariff on foreign sugar may help the local sugar refiners but the jam producers incur losses. Higher duties on grain increase the costs of making gin and will probably reduce their exports. Again protection benefits some but harms others.

The third problem with protectionism is of a moral nature according to Pierson. The mere promise of protection by a government may generate greed among local producers who know they can readily increase their profits under the new tariffs. At the same time such promises sow discord among domestic suppliers because it is always impossible to satisfy all demands for protection. Protection also weakens people's character. It leads to a situation where individuals develop the art of turning government regulation to their own advantage so as to be eligible for some kind of state intervention and support. This is something very different from productive behavior.

Pierson is also notable for his criticism of some of the positions taken by the protectionists. Basically he distinguishes six of them.

(a) 'Protective duties create domestic employment'. This argument is meaningless, says Pierson, if one considers that exports and imports must balance in the long run. Protection merely displaces employment (and capital).

(b) 'Import duties need not increase the price of the protected items because domestic producers have an incentive to produce more thus increasing the supply'. This can be true, says Pierson, but protection may also encourage the formation of cartels or other combinations which typically reduce output to maintain an artificial agreed-upon high price. If producers collude successfully consumers are made to pay heavily for the protective measures.

(c) 'Import duties may make life more expensive for some and increase the incomes of others. As the latter spend more, prosperity spreads. Therefore, as consumers, some people may be losers but as producers they are winners'. According to Pierson this argument fails to prove that the gains exceed the losses. It is of course true, says Pierson, that if one group of people becomes more prosperous, others will benefit, but the condition is that the increased prosperity was obtained through greater effort and productivity and not at the expense of third parties. A shopkeeper will benefit if his clients earn larger incomes but not if the money was taken from him in the first place.

(d) 'The infant industry argument'. 'High import duties do have negative effects in the short run but in the longer run they may well awaken dormant productive forces in a country resulting in a more productive and versatile economy. Besides, protection will only be granted for a few years in order to give young industries a chance or to create favorable conditions for new activities'. Pierson observes at least three problems with this type of argument. First, he fears that protection does not awaken productive forces, it often stuns them. Experience shows that many protected industries are backward. The reason being that without the stimulating power of foreign competition, entrepreneurs tend not to keep up with the latest improvements in production. The power of routine is likely to prevail. In a large country like the United States, argues Pierson, domestic competition is very strong. Foreign competition is hardly needed as a spur. In a small country like the Netherlands high import duties would dampen innovative entrepreneurship. A second problem with temporary protection is that when tariffs are about to be lowered, the spokesmen of the protected industries will always argue that more time is needed to become truly competitive. Finally the infant industry argument assumes that lawmakers are very clear-sighted; that they know something entrepreneurs apparently do not know because otherwise the industries to be promoted would exist already. But what if the legislators got it wrong? Then the country will be settled with a high cost industry unable to function in a normal competitive environment.

(e) 'It is expedient for a country to have a rather high general tariff to be used as a bargaining weapon or enticement in trade negotiations. Even if it is admitted that lower tariffs may be desirable, a country which has already a low general tariff negotiates with no bargaining power. It has nothing to offer at the negotiating table when it comes to lowering duties reciprocally. It can only demand'. Pierson's reply to the 'empty hands argument' as he calls it, is to suggest that for a small country like the Netherlands the argument is irrelevant. In commercial treaties dealing with duties, the most favored nation clause, is usually one of the greatest importance. Under this arrangement the two negotiating countries grant to each other the advantages or favorable terms they have already conferred on others or which are likely to be extended to others in the future. For small countries like the Netherlands this has important implications. If it negotiates with a larger nation such as Germany, the latter will compare the benefit it may gain from the small country, i.e. lower tariffs and more exports to this nation, with the larger imports not merely from the small country with which it is negotiating, but also with the larger imports from all the other beneficiaries under the most favored nation clause. As a result small nations have little reason to be concerned with the 'empty hands' policy. The larger nations have little inclination to make concessions to the smaller ones no matter what policy they follow. Such concessions tend to change their entire tariff structure, yet the only gain is easier entry into a small market.

(f) Finally, there are those who argue that 'trade must be fair'. The Italian economist Pietro Verri was, according to Pierson, the first to advocate this view in his *Meditazioni Sull Economia Politica* (1771). 'Free trade may be fine', argues Verri 'but others have to practice it as well. If others protect their industry we'll do the same'. Pierson's reply is that there is no evidence that somehow country B has to protect merely because country A happens to do it too. Protection hampers indirect production and exchange. It forces a nation to produce at greater cost what it could buy more cheaply abroad. If country A raises its tariffs, an impediment to trade is brought into existence. If in response B does the same a second barrier is created. The first obstacle is certainly not reduced by the second. If foreigners raise their level of protection they reduce both their and our income, Pierson concludes. That should be reason enough for refraining from measures which produce the same result making matters worse.

Pierson also discusses the use of export premiums in some of his writings. Export premiums are in his view part of the protective system and should as such be rejected. Such premiums are merely gifts to foreigners. They lower the standard of living in the country which adopts them. If, for example, an industry in a given nation produces an item for one hundred cents per kilogram and sells it abroad for ninety five cents the entrepreneurs must deduct five cents per kilogram from their revenues. If it is the government who pays the premium, the loss is merely transferred to others. The nation which receives the subsidized merchandise should be thankful, says Pierson. Both its standard of living and its terms of trade improve. It is possible that in the short run certain industries are harmed but in the long run the importing country benefits. If country A subsidizes the export of refined sugar, the sugar refineries in country B may suffer. However, its population gets cheaper sugar and its jam industry, as was the case in England, may flourish as a result.

The reading that follows is taken from the English translation of Pierson's *Principles of Economics*. The remainder of his writings is not available in the English language.[20]

Extracts

The Revival of Protectionism

When, in the eighteenth century, economic thought had already progressed beyond the stage of merely touching the fringe of economic subjects, when it had begun to assume something of a scientific character, doubts very soon began to be entertained as to the advantage of high import duties and export bounties for the development of agriculture and manufactures. The Physiocrats, led by Quesnay, the founder of their school, were strongly opposed to protectionism; and although their arguments were not always sound,

20 N.G. Pierson, *Principles of Economics* (A.A. Wotzel, trans.), Vol. I, Ch. 8, Vol. II, Ch. 4 (London: Macmillan, 1912).

a man was soon to appear who selected what was good and rejected what was bad in their ideas, and who advocated free trade with a force and talent such as had never before been exhibited in defence of that principle. We know what influence Adam Smith has exercised, especially in the sphere of commercial politics. The principles which he advocated made their way by degrees into many countries, and, however strongly opposed, they gradually prevailed. Thirty or forty years ago there was every reason for believing that protectionism was in a hopeless decline, that it was, in fact, doomed. From this state of utter inanition, however, it has revived; on the continent of Europe, Holland is the only country that has not yet broken with free trade, and how many there are who urge her to do so!

Various causes have contributed to bring about the revival of protectionism; chief among these has certainly been the decline in the prices of many articles. The greater this decline, the louder has been the cry for protection. This is no mere coincidence. Never has protectionism been more flourishing than in the years which followed the Napoleonic wars, when there was also a great decline in prices, and now, as in the past, it is applied more especially to those industries of which the products have declined most in price. If prices could rise again, the chances of free trade would improve. The abolition of the English Corn Laws was brought about, not only by Cobden's Anti-Corn Law League, but also by the dearness of potatoes in 1846.

The connexion to which we are alluding can be easily proved. Decline in prices may result from increased productivity of labour and capital, from large imports, or from scarcity of currency. But whatever the cause of the decline, it is absolutely certain to produce depression in certain branches of agriculture or manufacture. If increased productivity of labour and capital be the cause, then – as has been shown in Chapter I. of this volume – the *entrepreneur* class as a whole will gain on the quantity what they lose on the price; but while some *entrepreneurs* will, in this way, gain more, others will gain less than would suffice to compensate them for the decline in price. If large imports be the cause, then those entrepreneurs will lose with whose products the imported articles enter into competition: capital and labour must desert their industries for others. Lastly, if the decline in prices be due to scarcity of currency, then wages do not always adjust themselves quickly to the change in the value of money; the margins from which *entrepreneurs* derive their profits become too small in places, so that depression ensues in certain branches of industry – a depression which will ultimately vanish, it is true, but which may last a considerable time if the workpeople are obstinate in their refusal to accept any reduction in their money wages. Thus there will be depression in every case; and although this depression is never so general as it is represented to be, although it is offset by prosperity in other branches of industry and by economy in expenditure on the part of consumers, still it produces anxiety in many quarters and causes people to look round for some means whereby the supposed evil may be remedied. One of these means is the system of high import duties, hence protectionism always flourishes in times of falling prices. And so soon as it has been decided by one or more States to increase their import duties, others are sure to follow; for there is a very general opinion that free trade, however excellent it might be if it were adopted by all nations, is altogether prejudicial to a country which, surrounded by States with high import tariffs, still persists in adhering to free trade.

Besides the decline in prices, however, something else has helped to bring about the revival of protectionism. There was a time when the principle of what is called *laissez-faire* was held in great reverence. In practice, this principle, which is opposed to State interference in economic matters, has never been entirely victorious, and even in science it has never received such homage as many (more especially German) writers would have us believe. It cannot be denied, however, that, under the influence of the French School, with its worship of the 'Natural Order' – a survival of the teaching of the Physiocrats – the principle of *laissez-faire* was for a time accorded a certain esteem, in excess of its merits. In this respect a change has come about in recent years; the feeling of esteem is now entertained by a few only; many people even regard the 'Natural Order' as a true model of disorder. People have come to take a more favourable view of State interference in economic matters in general, and in this way the kind of State interference known as protection has come to be seen in a more favourable light. Quite wrongly, in our opinion; for, just as it would be irrational to condemn protection solely because it hampered the operation of self-interest, so also would it be irrational to approve of it solely because it restricted freedom of trade. Our inquiry in the second chapter of this volume showed us that, in a great number of cases, self-interest certainly does impel people to perform actions which are prejudicial to the national welfare, but that in a far greater number of cases, it impels them to perform actions which promote the national welfare. It may therefore be considered that the onus of proof still rests with the advocates of those restrictive measures. But in these days there are many to whom this point of view does not appeal. Formerly, the salutary effects of *laissez-faire* were exaggerated; now they are not even admitted in cases where their existence is undeniable. Formerly, too much was expected from the free play of supply and demand; now too much is expected of State control.

There is yet a third cause underlying the revival of protectionism, namely, the growth of interest in the condition of the working-classes. On grounds, the justice of which we shall presently examine, many people are convinced that protection in agriculture, manufactures, and shipping is a means of providing employment, consequently of increasing earnings and preventing poverty. We should be grossly misjudging the motives of protectionists of the present day if we suspected them of designs to promote the interests of capital, the interests of *entrepreneurs*. The majority of them – to their credit be it said – have primarily the interests of the working-classes in view. They believe that the working classes, though deriving a certain measure of benefit from free trade in their capacity of consumers, suffer a more than corresponding loss from it in their capacity of producers; that protective duties, therefore, notwithstanding the increased prices to which they give rise, promote the welfare of the lower classes. This opinion, as may readily be understood, finds much support among the working-classes themselves; the extension of the franchise, therefore, was a gain to protectionism. It is no mere coincidence that the democratic countries – Germany, France, the United States of America – are protectionist countries. The adoption of universal suffrage in Holland would certainly not improve that country's chances of continuing to pursue a free trade policy.

The growing tendency to view the protectionist system with favour, to which these various causes have contributed, makes it necessary for us to devote a chapter to that system. At the end of our chapter on the course of foreign exchanges, we said a few words concerning one kind of protection; our main object then was to show the close connexion existing between the matter of which we are now about to treat and the theory of money. That connexion has, we hope, been remembered. It is quite useless to set about an inquiry into the manner in which protection affects production unless we already know the laws which govern the distribution of the precious metals, and have formed some notion of the causes in virtue of which the value of money is different in different countries. For those who satisfy these requirements the task is greatly simplified, as we shall endeavour to show. We will now recall the conclusions already arrived at, and we will use them as the basis of further arguments, designed partly with the view to meeting certain objections, and partly so as to enable the student to judge of those kinds of protection of which mention has not yet been made.

......

We wish to draw two conclusions from the foregoing.

The first is this. Given a country whose monetary circulation does not require a continuous increase, whose standard metal is not suffering constant depreciation in the world market, and whose ratio of exchange with foreign countries is not continually improving: the imports of that country will, as a rule, consist of goods and securities, even though it should have large sums annually owing to it by other countries. If occasionally it should import some gold or silver, it will part again with precisely as much of either metal as it has received, retaining, of course, what it requires for use in the industries.

There are countries to which far more, in fact, is owing than the amount of their own indebtedness, and of which this is true not merely in respect of a particular year, and in virtue of special causes, but regularly and in an increasing measure year by year. Say, for instance, that a country has large amounts of capital invested in foreign and colonial undertakings, and has therefore to draw the income yielded by that capital; suppose also that many of its people who have gone to distant lands to seek their fortune return every year bringing home their gains with them; that it has many ships employed in the carrying trade between foreign ports; that it earns interest and commission by granting credit to firms abroad; and lastly, suppose that it holds large amounts in foreign bonds, of which the coupons or dividend warrants become payable at regular interval. Under such circumstances a large balance would be due from abroad each year, and what we wish to prove now is that when a country is so situated it will receive the balance, not in the form of gold or silver, but in the form of goods or securities, always provided the conditions mentioned above be fulfilled.

For if the balance were to be paid in gold or silver, redundancy of money would quickly ensue. But redundancy of money leads to the raising of prices, and the raising of prices to increase of imports and decrease of exports. Thus the balance of payments would become unfavourable.

Great Britain furnishes a striking example of what has just been said. Her imports of merchandise are always greater than her exports, and the excess is rapidly increasing. In 1856–59, it amounted to £29,000,000 per annum only; but in 1865–69 it had reached £56,000,000; in 1875–79 £119,000,000; and in 1892–95, no less than £131,000,000 per annum. This made some people uneasy at first. They regarded it as proving that the country was consuming more than it produced, which shows that the teaching of the Mercantile school still retained some hold on people's minds. But it simply confirms the doctrine just propounded. Large sums become due to Great Britain every year with respect of interest, freight, commission, and profits, and in normal times, owing to the action of the banks, these sums will not be paid in gold; or in the event of part of them being so paid, the gold will be quickly exchanged for more useful things.

A condition the reverse of that of England may also exist. Take the case of a country that purchases foreign securities every year, or keeps constantly increasing the number and extent of its foreign undertakings. So long as the annual income derived from the securities and undertakings is less than the capital annually sent abroad, such a country will have to remit a balance abroad every year. But if the amount of money in circulation in the country is just sufficient; if, at the same time, the ratio of exchange with other countries does not alter, and the country's standard metal does not appreciate in the world market, the balance spoken of will be remitted in the shape of goods. Were it remitted in gold or silver, prices would drop, exports increase, imports diminish; and thus, by a change in the balance of payments, the exported bullion would be brought back into the country.

Our second conclusion has a practical bearing. What happens when a country restricts its imports by imposing high import duties? In that case the exports ultimately experience a similar reduction. Although the importance of this conclusion in forming an opinion of what is called the protective system must be evident to all, we will say a word or two to emphasize it.

Suppose that a country exports goods to the value of £50,000,000 per annum, for which it receives in payment –

£45,000,000 in goods and
£5,000,000 in securities.

Thus the account is settled in full. Presently, however, imports of foreign merchandise are so hampered by high import duties as to fall from £45,000,000 to £35,000,000. Thus the account no longer balances, and one of the following three things must happen.

The value of the annual imports of securities will have to increase by £10,000,000. But how is this to be brought about by increasing import duties? Such duties will not cause annual aggregate savings to increase; on the contrary, they will cause many articles to become dearer, so that there will be more likelihood of decreased than increased purchases of securities. The difficulty cannot therefore be solved in this way.

Or again, £10,000,000 worth of bullion will have to be imported. But is it likely that it will? In a period of increasing wealth Holland once increased her stock of bullion by some £7,000,000 to £8,000,000. This was between 1866 and 1876, and it took her 10 years to do it. At that time the Dutch currency needed replenishing; otherwise she would either not have acquired this additional £7,000,000 to £8,000,000, or else she would have got rid of them again after a short while. A country already possessing a sufficient, stock of money to meet the requirements of internal trade, cannot increase the stock without causing a rise in prices; and we know what happens then. The newly imported money can be held in reserve for a while, it is true; we should then observe a considerable increase taking place, either in the note circulation or in the deposits of the banks. But redundant money cannot remain idle for good, and as soon as it gets into circulation it begins to produce its usual effect.

The only remaining solution then would consist in a reduction of the exports of merchandise by £10,000,000, and that is, in fact, what would take place. In this way the account could be got to balance again. In some cases, it is quite clear what the articles are, of which less will be exported when the imports of certain other articles are obstructed. If Holland, with the view to fostering her cotton-spinning industry, were to prohibit the importation of yarns, many of her cotton-weaving businesses would be ruined, and her exports of woven goods would fall off considerably. Were she to close her ports to foreign wheat and rye, many grazing lands would be put under the plough once more, and there would practically be an end to Dutch exports of cattle, sheep, and dairy produce. Were she to place any check upon her imports of iron machinery, steam engines would become dearer in Holland, and this would have an adverse effect on Dutch exports of manufactured goods in general. Even the rise in freights, which would necessarily take place in consequence of rolling-stock and vessels having to reach Dutch ports in a partly empty condition, would have an injurious effect on Dutch exports, in consequence of imports being subjected to high duties. The social structure is not so simple, however, as to permit of our being always able to indicate exactly the articles, of which the exports will be impeded when high import duties are levied upon other articles. Still, there can be no reasonable doubt that any reduction of the total amount of yearly imports must sooner or later be followed by an equal reduction of the total amount of exports. A careful study of the causes which regulate the balance of payments will show this.

It would appear, therefore, that it is a mistake to suppose that 'native industry' is benefited when we apply the protective system; it is simply diverted into another channel. The increased import duties destroy just about as much native industry as they create. And we shall find in a later part of this work that in most cases such a change in a country's production as may be brought about in this way is not a change for the better.

Here, then, we have one of the most important conclusions to which we are led when we study the theory of foreign exchanges. By doing so we become acquainted with the relation between imports and exports; we are made to see that, regarded from the standpoint of society as a whole, the two acts of importation and exportation constitute but a single act, of which different people each perform the half, namely, the act of exchanging with foreign countries. There would be no need for proving this if every one were in the habit of paying goods and securities for such goods and securities as he himself had bought. But in most cases this does not take place, and hence we occasionally lose sight of the connection existing between what is done by the one and what is done by the other person. This connection is revealed by the theory of foreign exchanges. It is immaterial whether the people by whom goods are imported from abroad and those who pay the foreigner with other goods are identical; if they pay with gold or silver, and that gold or silver is indispensable for internal trade, prices then reach such a level as to bring about the return of the exported metal in exchange for various kinds of products, so that payment is made in products after all.

To sum up: so long as there do not exist any causes connected with the currency itself, and therefore productive of a constant afflux or influx of bullion, our current accounts with other nations must (taking one year with another and allowing for temporary disturbances) be settled on such terms as would be the case if every individual did pay his foreign debts in goods and securities, and did require the payment of any balances owed to him in the same manner.

......

We think it worthwhile to work out the following hypothesis.

Suppose that there arises in the world market a brisk demand for certain goods, which only one particular country produces; that country, however, has no need itself of foreign goods, and does not want to buy them at any price. Such a case, we admit, is inconceivable; but it is necessary to assume it if we wish properly to realize this truth, that, except for the purpose of effecting the transfer of capital, the payment of interest and other debts, or the purchase of gold and silver for conversion into currency, a country cannot export without importing to the same amount. At least it cannot in the long run.

Now, what will happen under the circumstances assumed? Gold and silver will be accepted in payment for the exported goods. At first this will produce no effect beyond depressing the rate of interest in the credit market; for this, as we know, is the usual effect of importing gold and silver. As the banks have less discounting and lending to do, their uncovered note circulation declines, and if nothing else were to happen the stock of money (of all kinds) would not increase. But the fall in the rate of interest will stimulate the demand for credit, so that new money will get into circulation. All goods will advance in price, therefore the labour price too will advance; nor will this movement be likely to end soon, for gold and silver will keep on flowing into the country.[21] But this cannot go on for ever, for the rise in export products must come to an end. There must come a moment when foreign demand for these products begins to decline, and the dearer they become, the greater this decline; at length there remains not a single foreign buyer in the market. It is not possible to determine in advance how far the price must rise before this state of things is reached, but there can be no doubt that it *must* ultimately be reached; for however much an article may be in demand, if it keeps constantly getting dearer, a time must come when there is no longer any sale for it. If a rise of 50 per cent does not suffice to stop the sale, then a rise of 100, or perhaps 1,000 per cent will take place. But ultimately a moment will come when all exports of the article shall cease.

It may, perhaps, be objected that we have overlooked an important point, namely, the trade in securities. Indeed, it is not inconceivable

---

21 Pierson defines the labor price as the sum-total of money derived from the application of a definite quantity of labor and capital under unprivileged conditions. In more modern terms the concept includes labor costs, a normal rate of return on capital invested in the firm, plus a regular compensation for the entrepreneur-owner. Economic profits are zero (ed.).

that in this particular case trade may develop great proportions. As a rule we may expect that when there is strong demand abroad for the products of a country, part of the profits, which accrue to, that country from its export trade, will be invested in securities. Suppose that this actually happens: that not only gold and silver, but also a large amount of securities come into the country in payment for the goods which it exports. We will go even further than this: we will suppose that at first only securities, and no bullion and specie whatever, are received for the exported goods; will this alter in any way the conclusion to which our argument leads? Only to the extent that under the new hypothesis a longer time might have to elapse before the exports ceased; but cease they ultimately would. For every foreign bond has its coupon sheet, and every coupon of such a bond, from the day on which its payment falls due, represents so much foreign indebtedness. The larger the imports of securities the greater does this yearly sum of foreign indebtedness grow. In fifteen or twenty years it amounts to a year's imports of securities; if it grows beyond that limit, it hastens the approach of the time just spoken of; for then gold will come into the country, not only in payment for the exported goods, but also to meet a constantly increasing portion of the maturing coupons. This shows that, as far as our argument is concerned, we may safely neglect the trade in securities. Whether the exports are paid for with gold, or with securities, they must ultimately cease, unless an import trade in goods to the same value be developed.

And there is reason to expect that this import trade will actually be forthcoming. The advance in the labour price will itself suffice to bring it about, since it will make it advantageous to import goods which have previously been supplied by home production. It is of particular importance that this point should be well understood. A change in the labour price, which results from increase or diminution of the amount of currency in a country, has an effect, not only on the exports and imports of that country, but also on its production. The production undergoes a change at many points, it assumes another form. When the labour price falls, the imports of certain articles cease to be profitable, because it then pays better to produce those articles at home; on the other hand, it becomes possible to export certain articles which foreign countries have hitherto been wont to obtain elsewhere, or to produce themselves. When the labour price goes up, the converse of all this takes place: imports are stimulated and exports checked. But in either case some industries will be benefited, others depressed. In many the number of enterprises will become inadequate, in others excessive. A certain shifting – a certain redistribution – of capital and labour will have become necessary. Perhaps agriculture will develop at the expense of cattle-rearing or vice versa, or both will decline in favour of manufactures, or else supersede the latter. That such changes entail suffering, nobody can deny: who has not heard of the loud complaints which arose in England at the beginning of the sixteenth century owing to the numerous conversions of arable into pasture land. We recalled in a previous chapter how, in alluding to that circumstance, the usually placid Latin of Sir Thomas More assumes a tone of unwonted warmth. For this reason all governmental action, which, without procuring any advantage such as would compensate for this evil, influences the course of international trade, is to be deprecated in the strongest terms. For such action influences the course of production at the same time. Some industries are promoted, but others are injured. Wealth is created, but also poverty. Here prosperity ensues, there depression. Fortunes are amassed, but fortunes are also lost. And how do the working-classes fare? New industries look out for young and able-bodied workpeople; the old industries that are ruined leave their aged workpeople unprovided for.

High Import Duties

Such, then, as a rule, is the effect of high import duties; wherever they decrease imports they also decrease exports, and whatever national industry they create, they destroy exactly the same amount. And frequently the process of destruction is much simpler than has here been assumed, for a protected article may be a raw material or an instrument of production, and then the injurious effects of protection on the unprotected industries become evident at once. Dear corn is bad for milling, yeast-making, and distilling; dear cattle fodder for butter and cheese-making; dear timber and cordage for the fishing and shipping trades; dear iron for steam navigation and a host of other industries; dear yarn is bad for weavers, dear cloth for printers. When prices of building materials rise, the building trades languish; a rise in the prices of implements and machinery means loss all round. To remedy these evils, recourse is made to the system of 'drawbacks': thus the miller, on exporting flour, is refunded a sum estimated to be the equivalent of the import duty comprised in the price of the corn, from which the exported flour has been made. But this system gives no help to the industries which produce little or nothing for export, and it can never be strictly applied, owing to the differences in the quantity of finished products which different manufacturers succeed in obtaining from the same quantity of raw material. The drawback is either too high or too low; generally too high, and then it operates as an export bounty.

There is yet another thing to be borne in mind. Since the same person cannot afford to pay the same sum of money twice over, therefore, whenever the prices of a large number of articles are increased, the demand for the other articles must of necessity decline. This is a conclusion from which it is impossible for protectionists to escape, however they may try to do so. But perhaps they will retort with the objection mentioned above as regards the labour price. Perhaps they will contend that under the system of protection, all money incomes will be increased, so that there will be no difficulty in paying the higher prices. This line of argument is, in fact, frequently adopted, but those who adopt it forget that in doing so they are conceding everything that can with reason be said against the system of protection by means of high import duties. It is quite true that if a large number of articles are protected, the labour price will go up considerably; but will it then be possible to maintain exports? Will not the foreign demand decline if for every article that used to cost x times 1s., the price now asked is x times 1s. 3d., or x times 1s. 6d.? The theory which we propounded at the end of the chapter on foreign exchanges, and which we are now putting forward again, is based upon this very increase of the labour price. If it be admitted that protection necessarily entails a rise in the labour price, then it is also admitted that high import duties act as a check on the production of articles of export; and that is precisely what we wished to show.

What are the arguments usually adduced against this? So far as we know there are only four which are deserving of serious consideration. It is contended:

1. That high import duties do not necessarily cause a reduction, they often merely cause a change, in the imports;
2. That even though they should entail a sacrifice on the nation, this sacrifice is compensated by an all-round expansion of the nation's industries;
3. That in countries where the wages of labour are high, high protective duties may prove to be a means of preventing the decline of those wages;
4. That such duties may be a means of averting temporary depression.

Let us examine these contentions.

I. The protectionists deny that high import duties must necessarily act as a check upon imports.

Yes, they say, the imports of the protected articles do and must diminish. It is the intention of the legislator that they should, but raw materials and instruments of production are imported instead. Less cloth will be imported, but more wool; less yarn, but more calico; less machinery, but more iron and coal. Nor does the imposition of protective duties necessarily disturb the balance of payments, because it distributes wealth, and increase of wealth induces imports of tropical and other produce, which cannot be raised at home.

Is this true? It is contended that the imports of raw materials and instruments of production will amount to as much as the previous imports of manufactured articles. In that case the demand for manufactured articles must have increased, and it must have increased in spite of the rise in prices of those articles caused by the import duties. Originally the import value of a manufactured article was made up of raw material worth a, fuel, repairs and renewals of machinery, etc., worth b, and wages of labour worth c, making a total of $a+b+c$. There are now obtained by importation: the raw material $= a$, and the fuel and requisites for renewal of machinery $= b$, that is to say, things to the value of $a+b$. Consequently there is a diminution of imports to the extent of c, unless the imports of raw material and instruments of production amount to more than has here been assumed, and this, as we have pointed out, can only be the case on the assumption that the demand for manufactured goods has increased. But no increase – on the contrary a decrease – of that demand is to be expected. The imports will amount, not to $a+b$, but say to $3/4a + 3/4b$, so that they will be less by $1/4a + 1/4b + c$.

We pass on, however. It may be that at first, while new factories have to be established and equipped, the decrease in imports of manufactured articles will be fully offset by increase in imports of other things. Possibly too, the demand for the dear articles will not be appreciably smaller than the former demand for the cheap articles. But, then, surely the consumers of the article that has been rendered dear will have to economize as regards other articles, and the question now arises. On what articles will they economize? On products of native industry? If so, we have another proof that protection destroys native industries. On products of foreign industry then? If so, imports will certainly decline and the balance of payments will no longer be maintained. No, says the protectionist, money wages and other money incomes derived from manufacture will rise, owing to the new industry which has been established; this will increase the demand both for articles manufactured at home and for articles manufactured abroad.

But will money wages and other money incomes derived from manufacture really rise, without one single ounce of gold having come into the country, since the balance of payments, as we are told, remains undisturbed? If so, the rise can only be a temporary one, and must be immediately followed by a decline. If money wages and other money incomes have risen, but not owing to increased fertility of the land, or to improved instruments of production, or better methods of applying those instruments, then, surely, the cost prices of articles of export must also have risen, and in addition foreign manufacturers will be in a better position to compete with home manufacturers in so far as the latter are not protected. All this must lead to an unfavourable balance of payments and to exports of bullion, and those exports must be continued until money wages, and other money incomes derived from manufacturing, have fallen back to their old level. One of two things: either we must assume that protective duties do diminish imports, and then we have every reason to believe that the labour price will rise; in that case, however, the usual argument falls to the ground. Or we must assume that protective duties do not diminish imports, but in that case no rise in the labour price can be expected. Should such a rise have been brought about, nevertheless, through accidental causes, it could not be maintained, for it would bring about a series of occurrences that would speedily put an end to it. And as soon as the labour price had fallen to its old level, those economies would have to begin, of which mention has been made, and we should again be confronted with the question as to the articles in respect of which the economies would have to be exercised. We know the two answers between which the protectionist has to choose, and both of them tell against his theory.

II. The first argument, therefore, is devoid of force. Let us examine the second, namely, that even though high import duties should entail a sacrifice on the nation, this sacrifice is compensated by an all-round expansion of the nation's industries. It is quite possible, say the protectionists, that many articles might be produced at home at prices lower than those at which they are imported from abroad, if the experiment were only made, but lack of knowledge, or of enterprise, prevents this experiment from being made. Now, if the State were to impose high import duties on such articles, the effect would be to stimulate enterprise; the nation discovers its powers and resources in a field in which these have not previously been applied, and in a short time new sources of livelihood are opened up to many. For a time the high import duties will have proved obstructive, they will even have diminished the national wealth. But that time will have been short, and the object gained will have been well worth the sacrifice.

It must be admitted that this argument is much better than the previous one. It is not based on a false conception of international trade; it does not deny that restriction of that trade is harmful, it makes no plea in favour of permanent, but only in favour of temporary protection. It will be the legislator's business to discover what goods are purchased abroad owing to lack of knowledge or initiative on the part of native entrepreneurs, and having obtained this information, he will be expected to tax such goods and not any others. On theoretical grounds there is nothing to be said against this argument, but on practical grounds the objections are all the greater. It assumes, on the part of the legislator, an amount of acuteness and industrial knowledge such as no legislator possesses. What if, inadvertently, he were to put a duty on goods which, after the removal of that duty, could never again be produced at a profit in the country? In that case his action would have the effect, not of awakening dormant energies, but of diverting a part of the national industry into a wrong channel, into a channel that led to the destruction of capital.

It is true that an industry has often been brought to prosperity by means of protection. In any twenty industries taxed by the legislator, there will perhaps be two or three which are capable of surviving. But it is never possible to know with certainty which those industries are; in order to obtain successful results with two or three, it is found necessary to levy duties on a long list of goods, so that the sacrifice is really much greater than it seems. And what is the legislator to do afterwards with the industries which, though protected, show themselves incapable of living? Is he to leave them to their fate? He can hardly bring himself to do that. Is he then to go on protecting them? If he does, the wealth of the nation suffers. The State which enters upon this path becomes involved in great difficulties, for the transition from protection to free trade is always accompanied by losses for some and by temporary lack of employment for a portion of the working-classes. These are objections which usually make the legislator hesitate. Many a country has suffered for years (and perhaps still suffers) under protection, because, in addition to the industries with a future, others had been brought into life whose existence depended upon the import duties, but which the legislature feared (and perhaps still fears) to abandon to destruction. Is it not better then to foster the development of industry by good technical education instead of having recourse to tariffs for that purpose? Protection is a costly remedy, and any mistakes made in applying it – mistakes which are unavoidable produce very harmful results.

There is another matter, too, which may as well be mentioned, although it does not come within the sphere of purely economic considerations. The protectionist would impose a sacrifice upon the whole nation with the object of fostering industry at certain points. But import duties of this kind do not impose a sacrifice on the whole nation; they do so only on the consumers of particular kinds of goods; it is they who have to bear the burden. Is this fair? Where it is a question of promoting the interests of the country as a whole, all its inhabitants should set aside a portion of their income, the one more, the other less. But whatever the standard for apportioning the burdens must be, it ought never to be the quantities of certain articles that people happen to consume. A Government, for example, thinks it possible, in a country where no clocks and watches are made, to establish the manufacture of those articles as a permanent industry, by imposing high import duties on clocks and watches. Before adopting such a course, it ought to consider whether it is fair to require a sacrifice, not of every one, in proportion to his or her ability to make the sacrifice, but only of those who buy watches and clocks, and in proportion to the amount of each such person's annual purchases of these articles. Why just these people and not the others should have to contribute towards the establishment of the clock and watch industry is not clear. It would be much better to have nothing to do with import duties, and to pay bounties for the manufacture of clocks and watches, or else to grant subsidies out of the Public Exchequer to the manufacturers of these articles. If recourse must be made to artificial means for establishing an industry, care ought to be taken not to employ means which violate the most rudimentary principles of the incidence of public taxation. It would be wrong to retort that this line of argument goes too far, inasmuch as it implies a condemnation of all import duties, even of those imposed for purely revenue purposes. In a properly regulated system of taxation, the various imposts are interrelated; one tax bears upon this, the other upon that section of the community. But protective duties stand by themselves; they impose burdens upon particular persons, not because it is deemed right that just those persons ought to bear them, but for entirely different reasons. In this there is a certain unfairness, of which, as a rule, people are not sufficiently mindful.

Lastly, it seems not unnecessary to call attention to the numbing, enervating influence usually exercised by the protective system. An industry that has been secured against foreign competition is seldom elastic, it is seldom abreast of the times.[22] In a very large country the evil consequences of this may not be very marked; native competition is so keen that the absence of foreign competition does comparatively little harm. In a small country the case is different: there the stimulus of foreign competition is indispensable, native competition being, of course, less keen in such a country. When people speak of the disadvantages of foreign competition, they would do well not to forget its advantages, not only for the consumer, but also for the producer. It is easy enough to surround a state with a high wall that keeps things out; it is by no means such an easy thing to reawaken the numbed faculties of an enervated body.[23] And the dangers which we are now describing are not imaginary, as experience has repeatedly shown. Even in France, industry was found to be lagging at many points when, in 1860, the protective duties were considerably reduced.

There may be some truth in the contention that protection awakens dormant energies; but it may with equal truth be asserted that protection often greatly retards progress. This, added to the other drawbacks, makes it inadvisable to promote industry by means of high import duties. It is most likely that the object in view will not be attained by these means. They may succeed in creating a few industries which had not previously existed, and we will assume this advantage to be lasting. Nevertheless, it will probably be outweighed by so many disadvantages, that the country which has had recourse to these means will regret it.

III. Again, it is contended that in countries where the wages of labour are high, protection is useful in preventing the decline of those wages.

High real wages may be the result of various causes – of high productivity of the instruments of production, of a small population,

---

22 The word 'elastic' is not the ideal translation of the word 'veerkrachtig' in the original text. 'Resilient' or 'responsive' is what is meant here (ed.).

23 The word 'debilitated' translates Pierson's thought better than the word 'enervated' (ed.).

and of a low rate of interest. We will suppose first that the high wages
are due to the great productivity of the instruments of production, and
we will ask ourselves whether, in such a case, protection may be
advantageous to the working-classes.

Those who contend that it may, forget that high real wages in this
case take the form of high money wages as compared with normal
prices. The state of things will be this. The workpeople will be
enjoying liberal wages in the shape of money; the employers will be
able to afford those liberal wages because the quantity of products
which each workman turns out will be greater than it is in other
places, where the instruments (or faculties) of production are less
productive. What goods will then be imported? Imports, as we know,
are only possible where there is difference of price. The question,
therefore, reduces itself to this: What goods will be offered at lower
prices outside rather than inside the high-wage country? It will
certainly not be those goods for the production of which the country
itself possesses special facilities; these, instead of costing less abroad,
will cost more; rather will it be those goods for the production of
which there are in the home country, fewer facilities, either
absolutely, or as compared with those which exist for the production
of other goods. And wherewithal are the imports to be paid for, if not
with the goods that are produced under more favourable conditions,
that is to say with the products of the particularly fertile soil, the very
rich mines, the specially trained operatives? In virtue of free trade, the
nation of which we are speaking will be able to benefit in a twofold
sense by its special facilities for production. It will benefit directly in
being able to procure for itself many things with less effort than is
required in order to procure the same things elsewhere; it will benefit
indirectly in being able, with the goods which it has special facilities
or faculties for producing, to purchase from abroad other goods for
the production of which it does not possess equal facilities or faculties.
High money wages in this case indicate a favourable ratio of
exchange; would there be any advantage in having a favourable ratio
of exchange and yet not exchanging? So far as the workpeople are
concerned, protection can here lead to no other result than the
reduction of their incomes as reckoned in goods. It leaves untouched
the direct advantages of the special facilities for production, but
nullifies the indirect advantages.

The high level of wages may also be due to the population being
small, that is to say, small in proportion to the amount of available
land. The labour price will then be high, agricultural rents, on the

contrary, very low. Both labourers and capitalists will share on favourable terms with the landowners, inasmuch as they will enjoy large money incomes – in this case high money wages will be consistent with a high rate of interest – while all kinds of agricultural produce will be cheap. Under free trade the exports will consist almost entirely of agricultural produce; the imports will consist mainly of manufactured articles. Will the exchange be disadvantageous? There can be no disadvantage in parting with the products of what is, for the greater part, virgin soil, and receiving by way of payment goods which have cost much labour.

But does not the foreign labourer, with his starvation wages, then enter into competition with the home labourer, who receives liberal wages? Certainly; but he asks for just as much goods as he offers, and how can that cause wages to decline ? It will, indeed, prevent wages in some trades from reaching as high a figure as they do in others. This, however, is no reason for levying high import duties, but a clear indication of the direction in which capital and labour could be employed with the best results.

There can be no doubt that in both of these cases protection does harm and nothing else. The third case – that of wages being relatively high owing to the rate of interest being low – is not quite so simple, and we must discuss it at somewhat greater length.

When speaking above of the labour price, we observed that all kinds of ratios may exist between the respective remunerations of labour and capital comprised in that price. A labour price of 2s. 6d., for instance, may represent wages of labour and of *entrepreneur* to the amount of 2s. per day, and interest at 7½ per cent. per annum on a capital of £100; but it may also represent 1s. 6d. in wages, and interest at 15 per cent. per annum on the same amount of capital. From this it follows that, in two countries, the labour price may be equally high, while there is a considerable difference between the two countries both as regards the rate of wages and the rate of interest, and if this be so a particular kind of exchange will be possible between the two countries. A given quantity of a certain commodity requires the labour of 10 men supported by a capital of £2,000 for one year. The cost price of that quantity of goods will now be:

In country A, where the rate of interest is 7½ per cent. and the wage is 2s. (reckoning the year as 300 working days) ....   £ 450

But in country B, where the rate of interest is 15 per cent.
and the wage is 1s.6d. per day 525

Thus in country B it will be greater by .... £ 75

A given quantity of another commodity requires the labour of 15
men supported by a capital of £500. The cost price of that quantity of
goods will be:

        In country A. . . . . £ 487 10 0
        In country B. 412 10 0

Thus in country B it will be less by £   75 10 0

We see now wherein the exchange between these two countries
may consist if the cost of transport be not too great. In the one
country it will be things requiring a relatively large employment of
capital, in the other it will be things costing a relatively large amount
of labour that will be cheap, and therefore likely to be exported. And
even though it should happen that the high-wage country wanted to
buy more goods from the high-interest country than the latter wanted
to buy of the former, this would not prevent the exchange taking
place. The equality between the 'labour prices' of the two countries
(in our example taken to be 2s. 6d. per day in each country) would
then be destroyed by the transfer of bullion, and this would become
a new cause of trade.

It need scarcely be said that such an exchange, should it be
possible, could not fail to influence the relation between wages and
interest in which it has its rise. It would tend to bring the rates of
wages and interest respectively nearer to the same level in the two
countries without doing away absolutely with the differences existing
between them. In the country where wages were low and interest was
high, the former would rise and the latter would decline to some
extent; in the country where wages were high and interest was low the
reverse would happen. It follows, therefore, that this trade is not
without certain adverse results for the workpeople in countries where
wages are high and interest is low. As consumers the workpeople
benefit by the fact that things which cost relatively much in labour
become cheaper, but it cannot be denied that as producers they suffer
to some extent. In this respect the workpeople in countries where
wages are low are more favourably situated; they gain not only as
consumers, but also as producers. They benefit as consumers owing

to the fall in the prices of things, in the production of which much capital has to be employed, and they benefit as producers owing to the increased demand for their labour.

This matter may be viewed from more than one standpoint. We may consider it from the point of view of the welfare of mankind in general, irrespective of nationality. In that case we might argue as follows. Where wages are very low, they are most in need of being raised; exchange between high-wage and low-wage nations, therefore, promotes the welfare of mankind in general. But we may also consider the matter from a purely national standpoint, and, starting from the assumption that high wages are beneficial, even where they exist in conjunction with a low rate of interest, we may question the merits of a trade which causes this state of things to change. We shall then be disposed to lend a ready ear to any proposals that are calculated to prevent such a change, and protective duties may be among the means proposed. Whenever, in a country such as we have been describing, heavy protective duties are imposed on goods which require for their production much labour and little capital, the effect will really be to benefit the working-classes of that country.

But with import duties of this kind, just as with those imposed for the purpose of fostering industries, the difficulty lies in the application. How is the Government to ascertain which imports have their origin exclusively in differences in the relation between wages and interest? In England, for example, wages are higher and interest is lower than in Holland, but of the goods traded in between the two countries, which are the ones that would not be traded in but for this cause? To answer this question would require a knowledge which nobody possesses. Between England and Holland there exist many disparities, some in favour of the one, and some in favour of the other country. The result of all these disparities is that England purchases certain articles from, and supplies certain other articles to, Holland. It would be impossible, however, to show in detail what part of this trade would disappear if the ratio between wages and interest were to become the same in both countries. A country which was desirous of checking, by means of import duties, such international trade as had its origin in unequal ratios between wages and interest, would have to adopt measures, the results of which would reach much further than was desired, and much further than was good for the working-classes, whose interests it was intended to promote.

It is very doubtful, too, whether this inequality of ratios, which we are now discussing, can ever be the sole cause of trade being carried on between two nations, whether it is ever anything more than a subsidiary cause. This question suggests itself if we consider that the difference in the rate of interest between two neighbouring countries is never very great, and is therefore very likely to be made good by freight and other expenses; it is only as between places which are far apart, and between which the freights are therefore never small, that the rates of interest differ materially. There can be no doubt that England owes a great part of her commerce to the abundance of capital which she possesses. Many countries would be unable to supply England with goods, if England were not in a position to pay ready cash for those goods, and to give long credit for her sales. But will it often happen that England imports goods solely because of her high wages, or exports goods solely because of her low rate of interest? In the abstract it may, but if it actually does, will it happen on such a scale as to exercise an appreciable influence on the level of wages?

Moreover, everything that tends to depress the rate of interest in a country where that rate is already low, promotes the transfer of capital from that country to other countries. Against such transfer legislation can do nothing. For instance, it cannot prevent imports of securities. Of what use, then, is protection here? Even though it were applied with the fullest knowledge of things, and with the utmost tact, it would prove unavailing, and in so far as it might prove the reverse, it would bring about the very thing which it was intended to prevent. If the English Government were to impose heavy duties on all articles, the importation of which into England is solely due to the ratio existing between wages and interest, and if, as a result, the rate of interest in England were to fall even lower than the low figure at which, as a rule, it already stands, British capital would seek permanent investment abroad to an extent even greater than it does already. What would have been gained as a result? Previously a cause of high wages was in operation; by means of high import duties a cause of low wages would have been set in operation as a counterpoise.

IV. And now a word concerning protection as a remedy against agricultural or industrial depression. Can protection ever prove a remedy for this evil? Wherever it causes exports to decline and limits home demand, it is the reverse of a remedy. In the interests of truth, however, it must be admitted that there is one special case in which we may look to protection as a remedy against depression. It is the case of which we spoke when we were endeavouring to explain the phenomenon of depression, namely, great development of agriculture in distant countries owing to increased transport facilities in those countries, and a consequent sudden fall in the prices of agricultural produce.

We cannot for one moment admit that such an occurrence would be a misfortune, although it is often spoken of as if it would. Rather would it be an inestimable boon, in so far as it would cheapen our daily bread. The reasons adduced by those who endeavour to prove the contrary are entirely devoid of weight. They commonly amount to this: prosperity for the farmers ensures prosperity for the whole community, because a rich farmer class either consumes much or saves much, and thus brings prosperity to the manufacturing industries in either case. The proposition is true only if the prosperity of the farmer has developed spontaneously, and has not been brought about by high import duties on corn. It would be as unreasonable to defend protection on the ground referred to, as it would be to argue thus: it is good for the shopkeeper to live in a wealthy neighbourhood; we will therefore take money from the shopkeepers and distribute it among the inhabitants of the neighbourhood; these people will then be able to spend largely.

We must remember, moreover, that high or low corn prices, so soon as the rents have adjusted themselves to the prices, are a matter of complete indifference to the tenant farmers. The real, and indeed the only person ultimately interested in high prices of agricultural produce – we cannot lay enough emphasis on the fact – is the landowner: a high import duty on corn is a tribute levied upon the whole community for his advantage; a means of altering the distribution of the social income in his favour, or of preventing the distribution of that income from being altered to his disadvantage. Such a tax is never productive of good results for the national welfare. If a country be flooded with foreign corn, so much the better for that country: still better would it be to be flooded with goods of every conceivable kind. For supply of foreign products and demand for native products are only different expressions for the same thing, and a plentiful supply at low prices in this case means that foreign countries are willing to exchange with us on terms which are greatly to our advantage.

But this, however incontrovertible it may be, detracts nothing from a truth already adverted to – as to the losses, which are invariably entailed by a sudden fall in corn prices. The results of such as all are not all losses: great advantages accrue at the same time; but the losses are suffered by some and the advantages are enjoyed by others. Wealth increases very much in some parts of the country and declines very much in others. Ultimately everything readjusts itself by means of migration of persons and capital – migration from one country to another, from one industry to another – but for a time the distress will be great in places. The evil lies in the suddenness, the unexpectedness of the occurrence; and the consequences are far-reaching: much capital invested in agriculture will be lost for good, owing to the rapid fall in prices. And this will affect the interests not only of the farmers but of the whole community. For, lack of capital in agriculture means inadequate cultivation of the soil, consequently inadequate production. A measure which aims at preventing the too rapid fall of corn prices tends to the advantage, not of the farmers and the rural tradespeople exclusively, but to the advantage of the whole population.

And such a measure might consist in the imposition of import duties for a short time import duties diminishing each year by 15 or 20 per cent. of their original amount, so that they would disappear altogether at the end of five or seven years. Suppose, for instance, that wheat suddenly falls in price from 50 shillings to 30 shillings per quarter. An import duty is then imposed, amounting to 20 shillings the first year, 17 shillings the second year, 14 shillings the third year, and so on. Every one now knows that before long the price must come down to 30 shillings – at least if supply and demand do not change. This fact can be allowed for by all who conclude agreements for the purchase or lease of land, while those who think that a price of 30 shillings per quarter of wheat would not cover their expenses, can either choose some other business, or else temporarily put their land to some other use. In this way the advantage of the permanent decline in price is not taken away, while the harmfulness of the sudden decline is obviated. At home the decline in price will now only come about by degrees.

What is there to be said against such a measure as this? The first objection to it is, that although it does help some, it does not help all. As a rule, a country imports certain kinds of agricultural and garden produce and exports others. The protective duty can never prove helpful to those who produce articles mainly belonging to the latter class. In Holland, for instance, such a duty would bring no advantage to producers of potatoes, flax, beetroot, barley, or greenstuffs. It has been computed that, of the 2,112,000 acres of arable land in Holland, only 1,235,000 acres are used for growing such produce as might be protected by means of import duties. And a large portion of this area is owned by persons who consume their own produce and are therefore not interested in high prices at all.

In the second place, we would observe – and this lends force to what we have just said – that a decline in corn prices is frequently accompanied by a decline in the prices of cattle and dairy produce. The loss to cattle breeders then meets with partial compensation in the cheapness of corn. To withhold this compensation would be unfair. A decline in corn prices is also accompanied by a decline in the prices of goods, in the manufacture of which corn is the raw material; a protective duty must therefore have adverse effects for the industries which produce those goods. It is true that in many cases these adverse effects might be obviated if temporary import duties were at the same time laid upon the produce of stock farms, and upon flour, starch, spirits and other things manufactured from corn; but if these things belonged to the category of export articles, import duties could do no good in this case, and the only possible remedy would be to grant export bounties. And so the one thing leads to the other. The sacrifices, which are temporarily required of the nation, are greater than they appear at first sight.

In the third place, the legislator must follow a fixed rule. If that which has here been assumed to have happened in agriculture should presently happen in some other branch of the national industry, he must again have recourse to the principles which he has once accepted. He will have to afford relief to every trade that is suffering from depression, and if import duties and export bounties should prove of no avail for the purpose, he must not shrink even from making grants of money to employers or workpeople. If he does this, he not only assumes a difficult task, but he also weakens in individual members of the community their sense of personal responsibility for action and for the choice of their own calling.

In the fourth place, to whom should the assistance be afforded? To all, or to a few only? When depression prevails in a trade, the one entrepreneur fails to secure even his wages, while the other has merely to forgo his surplus because he is working under favourable conditions. A general measure adopted by the State in the interests of a languishing industry will thus have for its result, that some, who are able without help to continue carrying on their business at a normal profit, are enriched at the cost of the Exchequer; for they are enabled to go on securing the special gains to which they have been accustomed. And this remark holds good not only as regards manufacturers, but also as regards farmers, where these are the owners of the land and have purchased it at low prices. For many farmers, the decline which has taken place in the prices of agricultural produce in our time simply means being no longer able to secure exceptionally large profits.

In the fifth place, when must assistance be afforded? Wheat declines from 50 shillings to 30 shillings per quarter: must we at once proceed to impose a temporary duty of 20 shillings per quarter? Certainly nobody could recommend such a step as this, as the decline might be quite temporary, in which case the duty would not only be unnecessary, but would do much harm, for it would enrich one section of the population at the expense of all the others. Rapid falls and rises are far from uncommon with such articles as corn, so that in this case hasty action must be carefully avoided. But in avoiding this mistake there is a great danger of not imposing the duty until after extensive harm has already been wrought by the depression. Thus the legislator must not act too soon, or too late, but just at the right moment. It is easier to preach this rule than to practise it, for who can tell which is the right moment? Who can even determine how high a duty will be necessary in order to procure for the farmers a temporary recompense for their loss? When, owing to increased production, the price of an article begins to decline, nobody can foretell when the point will be reached, at which equilibrium will be restored between supply and demand.

Taking into consideration all these difficulties, and remembering, moreover, that everywhere there exists a protectionist party, who would certainly not fail to oppose each successive reduction of the duty, we feel bound to maintain that there are grave objections against giving practical effect to such a policy as that just described. It is calculated to injure many trades; it leads the legislator into a field where he cannot act consistently; it affords assistance to many who need no assistance; moreover, as regards the duty itself, it is impossible to determine even approximately either for how long or at what rate it ought to be levied. We do not deny that the plan has its favourable aspects, but the unfavourable aspects predominate, and we do not therefore consider that this kind of protection is to be recommended.

There is little more to be said; nevertheless it may have occasioned surprise that we have left a very common argument unanswered. It is frequently contended that high import duties fall, not on the home consumer, but on the foreign producer, and that this being so, one of the chief objections usually raised against such duties falls to the ground. The duties, it is argued, do not make the goods any dearer, they are a means of shifting some of the burden of taxation on to the foreigner.

We have left this unanswered, because it can hardly be regarded as an argument in favour of protection. It might serve for the purpose of showing that high import duties do no harm in the country in which they are levied, that they make no change whatever in economic conditions in that country, and that they simply serve to fill the national treasury. Under no circumstances could the argument serve the purpose of presenting the protective system in a favourable light. If it be true that import duties are paid by the foreigner, in other words, that foreign prices decline to the full extent of the duties, then those duties afford no protection. The dutiable goods continue to be imported as before. A protectionist would then have to say that they had failed in their object. The object in view was to keep out foreign products; this was to be done by making those products dear, so that consumers might choose native goods. But if the foreign products do not become dear, if, in spite of the import duties, they are still to be had at the same prices as before, what has been gained? People will still continue to order them from abroad, and native industry will be in no way benefited.

The advocates of protection must therefore either incur the charge of merely advocating measures which do nothing whatever towards promoting the application of their system, or else they must drop the contention that the burden of the import duties is borne exclusively by the foreigner. That contention itself, moreover, cannot be persisted in. We certainly admit that import duties, if they are levied by a very large country and on an extensive scale, do depress foreign prices. If England were to put a very high duty on butter, butter prices outside England would decline. But this decline would not be equal to the duty; it would amount to less, because the English demand, however important it may be, is only a small part of the total demand for that article, and also because the decline in the price would lead to a decline in production, which, in its turn, would act as a check on the decline in the price. It is true that duties on imports are a means of replenishing the national Exchequer at the expense of the foreigner; but the sums which are made to flow into the national Exchequer at the foreigner's expense, never amount to the whole, they always amount to a part only of those duties; and where the duties are levied by a small country, that part is so small as to be scarcely worth considering.

This is the very reason why, in a small country, the effects of production are doubly injurious. In a large country the harm resulting from high import duties is, to a certain extent, mitigated by the effect of those duties on foreign prices, and in so far as the duties have an effect on foreign prices they are not protective. But in a small country this advantage is almost entirely lacking, because the demand of such a country is too small to exercise any appreciable influence on prices abroad.

And now one word more in answer to a question frequently raised. Are high import duties harmful even when similar duties are levied by foreign countries? Many people are doubtful about this. Free trade, we are sometimes told, would be a good thing if it were adopted universally, but if our export trade is being hampered by foreign countries, our national interests require us to levy high import duties. The system advocated by those who hold this view is called 'fair--trade,' by which is meant, to put it briefly, taxing the produce of those countries whose laws diverge from the principles of free trade.

The question must be stated clearly. It is not a question as to whether the policy of levying heavy import duties against states which hamper our export trade is to be recommended as a means of inducing those states to adopt a more liberal policy. That is a question of statesmanship on which the economist is not competent to express an opinion. All that it concerns us to inquire into is whether a policy of retaliation in matters of tariff legislation is or is not calculated to promote, or at any rate to prevent the decline of the national welfare. The foreigner taxes our goods; this does us a certain amount of harm. Will this harm be made any the less by our taxing the goods sent to us by the foreigner?

It requires an effort to follow the line of thought of those who could answer the above question in the affirmative. Whoever is of opinion that the injury resulting from restriction of exchange can be lessened by increasing that restriction, must entertain ideas regarding international trade quite different from those which one gradually acquires by close observation of that trade. The injury is not lessened, but remains as great as before, or it increases.

Foreign countries tax our goods. This taxation may be so heavy that all exports of such goods as we are able to produce become impossible. But then all imports will cease of themselves, except in the case of remittances of interest and the like, and it becomes quite unnecessary to revise our tariff. By doing so we should be making matters neither worse nor better, we should merely be fixing a bolt on a door which was already hermetically fastened.

This case is scarcely likely to arise, however. As a rule the foreign duty will not be so heavy as to make it altogether impossible to export, but will press on our goods only to such an extent that we shall be obliged to accept lower prices and unable to dispose of such large quantities of the goods. Our 'labour price' will therefore fall, and however deplorable this may be in itself, it will be the only means of enabling us to continue our export trade, even though it be on a more modest scale, and on less favourable terms than before. Now what will be the result, if we, in our turn, put a tax on imports? The labour price will rise again somewhat, and so a second, and perhaps a more deadly blow will fall on our export trade. The effect will be the same (not outwardly but essentially) as if the foreigner had still further raised the tariff on our goods. For let nobody imagine that we shall be gainers by the rise in the labour price. It would be easy to prove that the increase in money incomes will amount to less than the increase in the prices of the foreign products. Consequently there will be greater loss on all sides.

The advocates of retaliatory duties are not wrong in contending that the country which imposes such duties inflicts an injury on the foreigner, but they forget, as a rule, that in doing so it also inflicts an injury on itself. If it be desirable that we should suffer that injury for a time, if it should be considered, for instance, that by retaliation we shall bring the foreigner to reason, let it be adopted. We repeat that questions of statesmanship are outside the sphere to which we must confine ourselves here. But the country which resorts to retaliation should never forget that in doing so it makes a sacrifice, perhaps a very great sacrifice, and that it inflicts an injury not only on the foreigner, but on itself as well. That the foreigner should tax our products is one bad thing; but for us to retaliate by taxing his products is another bad thing, both for ourselves and for the countries with which we trade. The Government ought to know what steps to take in order to prevent the foreigner from adopting legislation hostile to our interests; that is the business of the Government. But it must not believe that it is mitigating an evil, when it is really aggravating it.

Export Bounties

The most usual form of protection having now been discussed in detail, it will be sufficient in dealing with its other forms to confine ourselves to essentials. Almost every kind of permanent protection suffers from the same defect – that of benefiting the few at the cost of the many; promoting particular branches of industry, but at the same time depressing others. Protection imparts no fresh vitality to production, but only promotes parasitic growths; it never adds to the wealth of the nation as a whole, rather does it diminish the national wealth to some extent, because it diverts a certain amount of production into paths in which it is less desired. International trade is the means which a country employs in order to save itself some of the effort of production; the principal part in a system which, as a whole, may be termed that of acquiring necessaries indirectly. Instead of producing x, the country produces y, and with that product it purchases from the foreigner 1 1/4; or 1 1/2 times x, perhaps even more. Hampering international trade by means of protective duties is like raising freights artificially, or blocking the entrances to our harbours. In outward appearance the effects are different, but in reality all impediments, no matter of what kind, placed in the way of international trade, have the same baneful results.

But, it may be asked, does this apply equally to export bounties? Can these be said to hinder international trade? Do they not, on the contrary, promote it? We may begin by observing that this is by no means a matter of certainty; it is quite possible for export bounties to make no difference whatever in the movement of trade. This will be the case where the new industries, which the bounties have called forth, draw labour and capital away from the industries which were already working for the export trade. Then one kind of export is simply substituted for another, and increased taxation is the sole outcome of the measure. It is the same as if the country had undertaken to pay a certain tribute annually to the foreigner.

It is conceivable, however, that exports will really increase. But if they do, then imports too must increase, otherwise the balance of payments will no longer be preserved. Of what will these increased imports consist? Of securities? There will be no reason to expect any increase in the imports of securities when taxation has been increased and savings have therefore been diminished; but even if the imports of securities should increase, they would have to do so by a proportionately larger amount each year, for the reason already stated, namely, that a country cannot become the owner of more foreign securities without becoming entitled to draw more in the shape of interest from foreign countries. And there would be another result: wages would decline; for a yearly increasing inflow of securities means a yearly increasing outflow of capital, and such a cause can only benefit interest at the expense of wages. But this last remark makes it additionally clear how untenable is the hypothesis that the increased imports will consist of securities, for a rise in the rate of interest checks imports of securities.

The question, as to what the additional imports will consist of, admits only one answer: they will consist of goods. Then what will the export bounties have achieved? They will have achieved what we have already stated to be the result of protection in any form; they will have destroyed just as much national industry as they have created, and there will be nothing to compensate for the sacrifices that have been made. The advocates of export bounties must admit that the total export figure either remains unchanged, or else increases as a result of the bounties. If that figure remains unchanged, then an injury is done to such industries working for the export trade as are unprotected; if it increases, then the import figure also increases, and it does so at the cost of the industries working for the home market. In either case taxation will have been increased by the amount of the bounties, while no increase will have taken place either in production itself, or in the gains derived from production.

The shortest, but also the most accurate, definition of export bounties is conveyed by saying that they are gifts to the foreigner. The cost price of an article is so much per pound. This signifies that if the article should fail to fetch that price, the capital and labour employed in its production would not secure the normal rate of recompense, that is to say, they would not earn as much as it is possible for them to earn under ordinary circumstances. But the foreigner is not prepared to purchase the article at that price; in other words, if we offer that particular article, he is not prepared to recompense the labour and capital, which we employ, at the rate which it would be possible for that labour and capital to secure if it were differently employed. The obvious inference to be drawn from this is, that we must not offer the article in question, and that we must employ our energies and instruments of production for other purposes. If the legislator now steps in and says that a part of the price – i.e. so much of it as the foreigner thinks excessive – shall be paid out of the public Exchequer, he acts in a mistaken way, for he encourages the very thing that should be avoided with the greatest care. The nation as a whole then suffers a reduction in its income; it accepts payment which is inadequate, that is to say, inadequate in relation to the normal gains procurable by the employment of capital and labour. Nobody but the foreigner benefits by this.

When we know the manner in which export bounties affect the country by which they are granted, then we also know the manner in which such bounties, when granted by foreign countries, affect the wealth of our own country. If France and Austria grant high bounties on exports of an article which Holland is in the habit of consuming, the result is a pure gain for Holland. It is a mistake to suppose that Dutch industries must decline or become less productive in consequence, for either the foreign bounties will cause Dutch imports to increase, in which case Dutch exports also will increase, or they will simply cause Dutch imports to *increase* so that for certain articles which Holland had previously been in the habit of importing, certain other articles will be substituted; but in that case, too, a number of industries which were not paying before in Holland, will be brought to a state of prosperity. What the foreign countries have lost through their bounties is so much gain for the countries to which they send their goods. Certain industries are injured, perhaps ruined; we do not wish to ignore this, nor may we do so. But that the income of the nation increases is incontestable.

READING 10

William Graham Sumner

Biography

William Graham Sumner 1840–1910, American economist, political scientist and sociologist was born in Paterson, New Jersey, October 30, 1840.

He was the son of Thomas Sumner, an English immigrant who came to America in 1836 and married there Sarah Graham also of English birth. Thomas Sumner was a machinist. He was a self-educated person of strict integrity, a total abstainer and a man of indefatigable industry. Although Sumner's parents were unable to endow him with the advantages of culture they gave him some sturdy qualities including industriousness, thrift, self-discipline and perseverance. When Sumner was eight, his mother died and his father married Eliza van Alstein a good but rather stern mother. When she died in 1859 Thomas married Catherine Mix of whom William grew very fond.

William obtained his early education in the public schools of Hartford, Connecticut and was fortunate enough to have some remarkable teachers. Sumner also studied independently. When he was only thirteen or fourteen he discovered Harriet Martineau's *Illustrations of Political Economy* – a book of stories and illustrations on classical economics – in the library of Hartford's Young Men's Institute. From 1852 to 1863 Sumner enjoyed the friendship and support of Reverend Dr E.R. Beadle who was also a scholar and continuously encouraged and stimulated Sumner.

In 1859 Sumner matriculated at Yale College. At that time Yale was traditional in its habits and rather old-fashioned in its education. But, even if formal education was a bit narrow, there was an intensive extra-curricular life which combined the social and the educational life of the college allowing Sumner to emerge as an accomplished debater.

Sumner's ambition was to obtain the best available ministerial training. On graduating from Yale College in 1863 he looked to Europe to achieve this ambition. With the help of his father and some benefactors such as William C. Whitney, Sumner traveled first to Geneva (Switzerland) and worked there as an English tutor. He concentrated on the private study of French and Hebrew and attended some lectures on religion at the University of Geneva. In 1869 he moved to the University of Göttingen for a two-year stay where he received formal instruction in Hebrew, German, theology and history. Sumner was fortunate enough to become versed in biblical science with the help of professors who taught him the rigorous and pitiless methods of investigation and deduction which were to characterize Sumner's later work. After a short stay at Oxford University in 1866, Sumner returned home.

In June 1866 Sumner was made a tutor in Yale College, a position involving some classroom teaching as well as tutoring. He kept this position for three years.

Having been ordained in 1869 an Episcopal Priest, he took up, in 1870, a post as an Episcopal Rector, in Morrison, New Jersey. The year 1870 was also the year when, at the age of thirty, he fell in love with Jeannie Elliot, a charming New York city merchant's daughter whom he was to marry in 1871. They had three sons.

Sumner recognized the fact that he was made for teaching and research and when Yale offered him the chair of Political and Social Science in 1872 he gladly accepted. He kept this position for 38 years and educated such famous people as economist Irving Fisher and President William Howard Taft. From 1872 to 1906 Sumner published a dozen books and about two hundred essays, letters and speeches. In the field of economics he produced some historical work on money and finance of which *History of American Currency* (1874) and *History of Banking in the United States* (1896) are examples. During the last twenty years of his career he turned increasingly to sociology. His major sociological study appeared in 1906 and was entitled *Folkways: A Study of the Sociological Importance of Usages, Manners, Customs, Mores and Morals*. This book is still regarded as a classic in its field.

At Yale Sumner emerged as an inspiring, effective and popular teacher. He did not merely instruct the minds of his students, but because of his moral qualities he also moved their souls. The secret of his greatness was in his natural qualities, his self-discipline, his industry and his high moral purpose. He was characterized by a fearless devotion to the truth. This trait was very close to that of his former teachers at Göttingen. Once his mind was satisfied as to what the truth was, he would boldly state it on every fitting occasion without regard for the consequences. As an exponent of laissez-faire liberalism and individualism he fought for sound money and free trade. He denounced protectionism, socialism, statism and the imperialist sentiment which developed late in the nineteenth century. His forthright expression of opinion caused him on occasion to be attacked by the press and he was also accused of coldness. True enough, sentimentalists and superficial reasoners found little favor with Sumner as it was his habit not to soften the facts in order to spare anybody's feelings. Sumner's ethical sense was very keen and perhaps because of his training for the ministry an element of the preacher was never entirely absent in his writings. This is especially true for his essays where he is at his best.[24] As a result he sometimes mixes positive and normative economics. He analyzes rigorously but also gives opinions on how things ought to be. In fact this adds spice to his essays which even up to the present day are still very good reading.

Sumner's most prolific period was from 1876 to 1897. Thereafter, his health deteriorated. It was after 1897 that Sumner radically shifted from economics and political science to sociological research. He had his first stroke in 1907 and he retired from Yale in 1909 having spent thirty-seven years there. During the same year he experienced another

---

24 In fact Sumner's writings can be divided into three categories, i.e. (a) histories of an economic nature, (b) biographies including the life of Alexander Hamilton and (c) essays on economic, political and social topics. His last work, *Folkways*, falls outside these categories.

stroke. Sumner died in 1910 and was buried in Gulford, Connecticut.

The Work

Not surprisingly, Sumner's views of free trade and protectionism were linked to his general world view. Sumner, who had been strongly influenced by the ideas of Herbert Spencer and Charles Darwin, believed that social scientists had to develop their disciplines in accordance with the theory of evolution. Self-realization was consistent with evolution. The only rational and true purpose of the individual was to strive for self-realization for as long as his or her powers endured. Thus Sumner favored societies which promoted and upheld such self-realization. This implied that the right kind of society followed a laissez-faire policy which supported freedom of contract and enterprise domestically and free trade and migration across boundaries internationally. Only such a policy would encourage peace, harmony and prosperity at home and throughout the world.

The doctrine of laissez-faire is a doctrine of freedom. As Sumner used the term, it implied the avoidance of all interference by the state except such as is necessary to protect and maintain the balance between the rights and duties of individuals which liberty and justice require. Social life in Sumner's view was governed by unchangeable laws. There is nothing (or very little) arbitrary or accidental in social phenomena which implies that there is little room for arbitrary intervention by man. Therefore, the field for legislation is narrow and the role of the state should be small. However, with the help of scientific and historical knowledge, reformers and statesmen could bring about changes in circumstances and facilitate adjustment to new conditions. Wise leaders make carefully studied corrections and prevent foolish interferences in personal and public affairs. Continuous state interference eventually prevents the state from fulfilling its proper function which is mainly to guarantee peace, order, property and liberty; right instead of might. Government should stand as an impartial arbiter above all individual, group and class interests. As soon as legislation is employed to regulate, according to the wishes of some at the expense of the desires of others, which is what interference usually implies, then the state is no longer the guardian of the interests of all, but the servant of the interests of those best able to control it.

The social doctor or tinker on the other hand believes that there are no laws of society and thus no limits to the possibilities of social manipulation by the state. Sumner was extremely critical of all the sentimentalists, unscientific reformers, and a priori philosophers who parade their fine sentiments when they propose their artificial schemes of social improvement or try to bring society into conformity with some preconceived plan. Such attempts were, according to Sumner, destructive to social welfare, and eventually to civilization itself. The secret of welfare lies in the leading of honest and industrious lives, in hard work, saving and capital accumulation. The social doctors and uplifters usually lead man astray by their assumptions and speculations. Their ideologies are often nothing but meaningless rhetoric which tyrannize men and undermine the possibilities of rational action. The greatest reforms which have been accomplished, consisted usually in the undoing of the harmful work of statesmen in the past. People do not usually appreciate the loss to society caused by the ignorance and folly of former statesmen and social philosophers. The worst ills from which civilized nations suffer, said Sumner, come from unwisely adopted laws. The best reforms consist of undoing them without injury to what is natural and sound.

Another important element of Sumner's world-view was related to the concept of 'antagonistic cooperation' by which Sumner meant that people usually cooperate when it is necessary but without abandoning their self-interest. Sumner's naturalistic studies had convinced him of the reality of man's struggle for existence and the competition for scarce resources. However, even primitive groups had painfully learned that individuals could best fulfill their long-term goals of self-preservation and self-improvement by replacing the law of the fist, with institutions which protected the individual and promoted peaceful cooperation. As the benefits of cooperation had become obvious to men, they had come together in the form of family, clan, tribe and nation. The modern market economy was a good if not the best example of such antagonistic cooperation. It had contributed widely to higher levels of productivity and material well-being. The system holds together all the parties involved by the use of impersonal forces. Although the participants have antagonistic as well as complementary interests, a high degree of social harmony is attained. In that sense Sumner updated Adam Smith's argument whereby the combined self-interest of individuals, led by an invisible hand, brought about social order and adjustment. Men still compete but their self-interest had become enlightened. As the process of antagonistic cooperation evolved, one could possibly envisage, a world community of peaceful nations trading freely with mutual benefit and harmony.

Sumner's recognition of the importance of extended antagonistic cooperation ensured his support for free trade. His fear of government interventions such as protective tariffs which appeared to him as disruptive and divisive, constituted evolutionary regression because they set one group up against another.

Yet in Sumner's writings one can find many more objections against protectionism. One important problem with a protective tariff is that it is a tax. All taxation beyond what is necessary for an efficient administration is crippling or wasteful argued Sumner. When the advocates of a protective tariff state that protectionism produces industries they are in effect saying that 'waste makes wealth.' However, it is not taxes but the use of brains and energy that create industries. Protectionism simply allows one industry to live as a parasite upon another. Labor and capital are driven into wasteful and disadvantageous employments.

Another source of distress with protectionism is that it is really, according to Sumner, a form of legalized robbery. It is another example of 'jobbery' of which history is replete. Sumner defined jobbery as any effort to gain additional income, not by honest and independent production, but by some sort of scheme to extort from somebody part of his product. The protective tariff was in Sumner's view the greatest job or swindle of all. You plunder your neighbor and then convince him that it is beneficial for him. Tariffs involve a redistribution of income from the hard working 'forgotten man or woman' to the jobbers and grabbers. The forgotten man is always the victim who pays the taxes. He is weak because he is unorganized and he is conveniently forgotten in all schemes which imply a transfer of income from his pocket into the purse of the plotters. But, says Sumner, the system of plundering produces nothing. On the contrary, in the end, it is self-destructive.

Third, protectionism demoralizes government. It is a system of graft and thereby encourages graft in general. It involves the business of lobbying and log-rolling. Protected interests gain power in Congress and determine the course of legislation. Congressmen learn to sacrifice the true public interest. The effect on business leaders is not any better. It teaches them to rely on lobbying and special legislation rather than on enterprise and effort, to hire lobbyists rather than laborers.

Finally, protectionism is a form of disguised socialism protecting the inefficient producer. Sumner defined socialism as any device or doctrine whose aim is to shield individuals from the difficulties or hardships of the struggle for existence and the competition of life by the intervention of the state. Such systems, said Sumner, ensure the survival not of the fittest but of the unfittest.[25]

Extract

It must be assumed, in any controversy about a matter of public interest and importance, that the parties to the controversy are candid and sincere in the desire to find out what is really true and wise, that is, what will be permanently beneficial to all. When the controversy is about some old abuse it cannot assume this shape purely and simply. Vested interests always grow up under an old social or political abuse, and no vested interest ever yet voluntarily sacrificed itself. On the contrary, interested parties always make vigorous defence of their privileges and their mischievous advantages. They have a stronger and more personal interest to organize, to spend money, and to work in defence of the wrong they enjoy, than others have to overthrow it. We see instances of this in the history of the struggle by which all abuses have been corrected. Privileged classes and orders of nobility have been dislodged from their privileges only after long struggles and bloody revolutions. Sinecures and pensions and rotten boroughs and the sale of commissions in the army, and established churches, have been overthrown, so far as they have been overthrown, only after vigorous conflicts. Our own history furnishes only one great instance, because we inherited only one great abuse. The overthrow of slavery, however, is a startling instance of what it costs to bring truth and right to pass, of how hard it is to vanquish prejudice and interest, and of the vigorous defence which vested interests make to every step of progress in truth and enlightenment.

The history of the conflict with these abuses brings out distinctly one or two other features of such struggles which we ought to notice.

I. In the first place *the mass of the people who suffer under the abuses are slow to perceive them*, and can only be stimulated to rise against them by great effort on the part of a few. The notion that

---

25 Sources: G. Sumner, *Protection and Revenue in 1877* (New York: G.P. Pulnam's Sons, 1881) pp. 1–5.
W.G. Sumner, 'What is Free Trade?', *The Forgotten Man and Other Essays* (A.G. Keller, ed.) (New Haven: Yale University Press, 1919), pp. 123–127.
W.G. Sumner, 'Protectionism, The Ism which Teaches that Waste Makes Wealth', *The Forgotten Man ...*, pp. 11–16.

every man can be left to see and reflect for himself and by some kind of spontaneous consent to meet others of similar intelligence in a common judgment and will, has no foundation in fact. The sphere in which a man is born and lives bounds his notions of what is proper and possible, and at most he judges from the examples he sees before him of success in life, what chances he has of bettering his condition, and what methods he should use to that end. He will not be actively discontented so long as his circumstances do not become worse, much less if they are really improving, and if the examples of great success which he sees and hears of are those of men who grow rich by stock-jobbing, 'financiering,' creating monopolies, lobbying for subsidies, or political scheming, he will not be likely by his own intellectual energy to perceive how many other roads to success, of a higher and more permanent order, might be open to him under another state of things. Such knowledge can only be won by study and travel, and the wide experience of life which enables men to see what might be as well as what is, and to escape from the limits of tradition and prejudice.

2. The second feature worth mentioning in the history of conflicts against great abuses is that *the defenders of abuses always conduct the defence by special pleas* of all, sorts and descriptions. The special plea for Robin Hood and Dick Turpin was that they gave liberally to the poor. The special plea for class privileges was that they sustained culture, refinement, and art. The special plea for monopolies was that energy and enterprise needed a stimulus and reward, and that monopolies produced arts which otherwise would not exist. The special plea for a state church is that it secures a corps of agents of civilization scattered into every hamlet. The special plea for rotten boroughs was that they enabled able statesmen to be kept in public life when they could not get elected by popular constituencies, at any rate without great expense. Many of these pleas are not without force, for few things are altogether evil, as few are altogether good. Special pleas on behalf of abuses have no coherence or consistency. They always eventually destroy each other, but when taken piece by piece they have no little popular effect. They do what the defenders of an existing abuse always want to do, they obscure and confuse the question. A glittering commonplace, or a burst of patriotic gush, or an appeal to some popular prejudice, will outweigh the closest and most irrefragable argument. Such means have sustained for generations institutions and abuses which every school-boy is now taught to despise.

Our free trade controversy presents anew all the same features of these old struggles against ingrained abuses. Public opinion can only be enlightened by great and prolonged effort to understand the mischief done by the protective system to wealth, and to all which depends upon wealth, viz., morals, education, culture, civilization, and national greatness. The opposition which we have to meet, also consists in the reiteration of platitudes, special pleas, misrepresentations of history, both here and abroad, inferences mixed up with facts, facts misapprehended, and vigorous denunciations of want of patriotism. We cannot join issue on any proposition or set of propositions on which a discussion can be carried on by established methods, to a clear result. Even those of our adversaries who claim to stand generally on the platform of right reason and common sense, and to be disinterested, are not ashamed to treat this question with ignorant and flippant neglect or contempt. Now when we consider that a very large body of persons, respectable in every point of view, claim that this question involves the most important consequences for the welfare of the whole people, it follows that those who treat it with neglect or contempt, simply bring in to question their own good sense or their own good faith.

It is important then to distinguish between the protectionists who think that free trade threatens their own vested interests, and those who believe that protection is a sound theory of national wealth. For the present I leave aside the former class. The pensioners and sinecurists declared that the greatness of England would depart whenever their incomes were cut off. Nothing could exceed their contempt for the meanness of a great nation which refused to tax the people a farthing a head to sustain a brilliant coterie of gentlemen and ladies as ornaments to the country. They declared that there were moral, social and political advantages of high importance which depended on keeping up the coterie in question. Our protectionists have made us familiar with the same old round of platitudes. A man who enjoys or thinks he enjoys advantages from an arrangement, will not easily be led to consent that this arrangement shall be abolished, because it is won at the cost of others.

What is Free Trade?

There never would have been any such thing to fight for as free speech, free press, free worship, or free soil, if nobody had ever put restraints on men in those matters. We never should have heard of free trade, if no restrictions had ever been put on trade. If there had been any restrictions on the intercourse between the states of this Union, we should have heard of ceaseless agitation to get those restrictions removed. Since there are no restrictions allowed under the Constitution, we do not realize the fact that we are enjoying the blessings of complete liberty, where, if wise counsels had not prevailed at a critical moment, we should now have had a great mass of traditional and deep-rooted interferences to encounter.

Our intercourse with foreign nations, however, has been interfered with, because it is a fact that, by such interference, some of us can win advantages over others. The power of Congress to levy taxes is employed to lay duties on imports, not in order to secure a revenue from imports, but to prevent imports – in which case, of course, no revenue will be obtained. The effect which is aimed at, and which is attained by this device, is that the American consumer, when he wants to satisfy his needs, has to go to an American producer of the thing he wants, and has to give to him a price for the product which is greater than that which some foreigner would have charged. The object of this device, as stated on the best protectionist authority, is: 'To effect the diversion of a part of the labor and capital of the people out of the channels in which it would run otherwise, into channels favored or created by law.' This description is strictly correct, and from it the reader will see that protection has nothing to do with any foreigner whatever. It is purely a question of domestic policy. It is only a question whether we shall, by taxing each other, drive the industry of this country into an arbitrary and artificial development or whether we shall allow one another to employ each his capital and labor in his own way. Note that there is for us all the same labor, capital, soil, national character, climate, etc., – that is, that all the conditions of production remain unaltered. The only change which is operated is a wrenching of labor and capital out of the lines on which they would act under the impulse of individual enterprise, energy, and interest, and their impulsion in another direction selected by the legislator. Plainly, all the import duty can do is to close the door, shutting the foreigner out and the Americans in. Then, when an American needs iron, coal, copper, woolens, cottons, or anything else in the shape of manufactured commodities, the operation begins. He has to buy in a market which is either wholly or partially monopolized. The whole object of shutting him in is to take advantage of this situation to make him give more of his products for a given amount of the protected articles, than he need have given for the same things in the world's market. Under this system a part of our product is diverted from the satisfaction of our needs, and is spent to hire some of our fellow-citizens to go out of an employment which would pay under the world's competition, into one which will not pay under the world's competition. We, therefore, do with less clothes, furniture, tools, crockery, glassware, bed and table linen, books, etc., and the satisfaction we have for this sacrifice is knowing that some of our neighbors are carrying on business which according to their statement does not pay, and that we are paying their losses and hiring them to keep on.

Free trade is a revolt against this device. It is not a revolt against import duties or indirect taxes as a means of raising revenue. It has nothing to say about that, one way or the other. It begins to protest and agitate just as soon as any tax begins to act protectively, and it denounces any tax which one citizen levies on another. The protectionists have a long string of notions and doctrines which they put forward to try to prove that their device is not a contrivance by which they can make their fellow-citizens contribute to their support, but is a device for increasing the national wealth and power. These allegations must be examined by economists, or other persons who are properly trained to test their correctness, in fact and logic. It is enough here to say, over a responsible signature, that no such allegation has ever been made which would bear examination. On the contrary, all such assertions have the character of apologies or special pleas to divert attention from the one plain fact that the advocates of a protective tariff have a direct pecuniary interest in it, and that they have secured it, and now maintain it, for that reason and no other. The rest is all afterthought and excuse. If any gain could possibly come to the country through the gains of the beneficiaries of the tariff, obviously the country must incur at least an equal loss through the losses of that part of the people who pay what the protected win. If a country could win anything that way, it would be like a man lifting himself by his boot straps.

The protectionists, in advocating their system, always spend a great deal of effort and eloquence on appeals to patriotism, and to international jealousies. These are all entirely aside from the point. The protective system is a domestic system, for domestic purposes, and it is sought by domestic means. The one who pays, and the one who gets, are both Americans. The victim and the beneficiary are amongst ourselves. It is just as unpatriotic to oppress one American as it is patriotic to favor another. If we make one American pay taxes to another American, it will neither vex nor please any foreign nation.

The protectionists speak of trade with the contempt of feudal nobles, but on examination it appears that they have something to sell, and that they mean to denounce trade with their rivals. They denounce cheapness, and it appears that they do so because they want to sell dear. When they buy, they buy as cheaply as they can. They say that they want to raise wages, but they never pay anything but the lowest market rate. They denounce selfishness, while pursuing a scheme for their own selfish aggrandizement, and they bewail the dominion of self-interest over men who want to enjoy their own earnings, and object to surrending the same to them. They attribute to government, or to 'the state,' the power and right to decide what industrial enterprises each of us shall subscribe to support.

Free trade means antagonism to this whole policy and theory at every point. The free trader regards it as all false, meretricious, and delusive. He considers it an invasion of private rights. In the best case, if all that the protectionist claims were true, he would be taking it upon himself to decide how his neighbor should spend his earnings, and – more than that – that his neighbor shall spend his earnings for the advantage of the men who make the decision. This is plainly immoral and corrupting; nothing could be more so. The free trader also denies that the government either can, or ought to regulate the way in which a man shall employ his earnings. He sees that the government is nothing but a clique of the parties in interest. It is a few men who have control of the civic organization. If they were called upon to regulate business, they would need a wisdom which they have not. They do not do this. They only turn the 'channels' to the advantage of themselves and their friends. This corrupts the institutions of government and continues under our system all the old abuses by which the men who could get control of the governmental machinery have used it to aggrandize themselves at the expense of others. The free trader holds that the people will employ their labor and capital to the best advantage when each man employs his own in his own way, according to the maxim that 'A fool is wiser in his own house than a sage in another man's house'; – how much more, then, shall he be wiser than a politician? And he holds, further, that by the nature of the case, if any governmental coercion is necessary to drive industry in a direction in which it would not otherwise go, such coercion must be mischievous.

The free trader further holds that protection is all a mistake and a delusion to those who think that they win by it, in that it lessens their self-reliance and energy and exposes their business to vicissitudes which, not being incident to a natural order of things, cannot be foreseen and guarded against by business skill; also that it throws the business into a condition in which it is exposed to a series of heats and chills, and finally, unless a new stimulus is applied, reduced to a state of dull decay. They therefore hold that even the protected would be far better off without it.

(A) The System of Which Protection is a Survival

1. The statesmen of the eighteenth century supposed that their business was the art of national prosperity. Their procedure was to form ideals of political greatness and civil prosperity on the one hand, and to evolve out of their own consciousness grand dogmas of human happiness social welfare on the other hand. Then they tried to devise specific means for connecting these two notions with each other. Their ideals of political greatness contained, as predominant elements, a brilliant court, a refined and elegant aristocracy, well-developed fine arts and *belles lettres*, a powerful army and navy, and a peaceful, obedient, and hard-working peasantry and artisan class to pay the taxes and support the other part of the political structure. In this ideal the lower ranks paid upward, and the upper ranks blessed downward, and all were happy together. The great political and social dogmas of the period were exotic and incongruous. They were borrowed or accepted from the classical authorities. Of course the dogmas were chiefly held and taught by the philosophers, but, as the century ran its course, they penetrated the statesman class. The statesman who had had no purpose save to serve the 'grandeur' of the king, or to perpetuate a dynasty, gave way to statesmen who had strong national feeling and national ideals, and who eagerly sought means to realize their ideals. Having as yet no definite notion, based on facts of observation and experience, of what a human society or a nation is, and no adequate knowledge of the nature and operation of social forces, they were driven to empirical processes which they could not test, or measure, or verify. They piled device upon device and failure upon failure. When one device failed of its intended purpose and produced an unforeseen evil, they invented a new device to prevent the new evil. The new device again failed to prevent, and became a cause of a new harm, and so on indefinitely.

2. Among their devices for industrial prosperity were (1) export taxes on raw materials, to make raw materials abundant and cheap at

home; (2) bounties on the export of finished products, to make the exports large; (3) taxes on imported commodities to make the imports small, and thus, with No. 2, to make the 'balance of trade' favorable, and to secure an importation of specie; (4) taxes or prohibition on the export of machinery, so as not to let foreigners have the advantage of domestic inventions; (5) prohibition on the emigration of skilled laborers, lest they should carry to foreign rivals knowledge of domestic arts; (6) monopolies to encourage enterprise; (7) navigation laws to foster ship-building or the carrying trade, and to provide sailors for the navy; (8) a colonial system to bring about by political force the very trade which the other devices had destroyed by economic interference; (9) laws for fixing wages and prices to repress the struggle of the non-capitalist class to save themselves in the social press; (10) poor-laws to lessen the struggle by another outlet; (11) extravagant criminal laws to try to suppress another development of this struggle by terror; and so on, and so on.

(B) Old and New Conceptions of the State

3. Here we have a complete illustration of one mode of looking at human society, or at a state. Such society is, on this view, an artificial or mechanical product. It is an object to be molded, made, produced by contrivance. Like every product which is brought out by working up to an ideal instead of working out from antecedent truth and fact, the product here is haphazard, grotesque, false. Like every other product which is brought out by working on lines fixed by *a priori* assumptions, it is a satire on human foresight and on what we call common sense. Such a state is like a house of cards, built up anxiously one upon another, ready to fall at a breath, to be credited at most with naïve hope and silly confidence; or, it is like the long and tedious contrivance of a mischievous schoolboy, for an end which has been entirely misappreciated and was thought desirable when it should have been thought a folly; or, it is like the museum of an alchemist, filled with specimens of his failures, monuments of mistaken industry and testimony of an erroneous method; or, it is like the clumsy product of an untrained inventor, who, instead of asking: 'what means have I, and to what will they serve?' asks: 'what do I wish that I could accomplish?' and seeks to win steps by putting in more levers and cogs, increasing friction and putting the solution ever farther off.

4. Of course such a notion of a state is at war with the conception

of a state as a seat of original forces which must be reckoned with all the time; as an organism whose life will go on anyhow, perverted, distorted, diseased, vitiated as it may be by obstructions or coercions; as a seat of life in which nothing is ever lost, but every antecedent combines with every other and has its share in the immediate resultant, and again in the next resultant, and so on indefinitely; as the domain of activities so great that they should appall any one who dares to interfere with them; of instincts so delicate and self-preservative that it should be only infinite delight to the wisest man to see them come into play, and his sufficient glory to give them a little intelligent assistance. If a state well performed its functions of providing peace, order, and security, as *conditions* under which the people could live and work, it would be the proudest proof of its triumphant success that it had nothing to do – that all went so smoothly that it had only to look on and was never called to interfere; just as it is the test of a good business man that his business runs on smoothly and prosperously while he is not harassed or hurried. The people who think that it is proof of enterprise to meddle and 'fuss' may believe that a good state will constantly interfere and regulate, and they may regard the other type of state as 'non-government.' The state can do a great deal more than to discharge police functions. If it will *follow* custom, and the growth of social structure to provide for new social needs, it can powerfully aid the production of structure by laying down lines of common action, where nothing is needed but *some* common action on conventional lines; or, it can systematize a number of arrangements which are not at their maximum utility for want of concord; or, it can give sanction to new rights which are constantly created by new relations under new social organizations, and so on.

5. The latter idea of the state has only begun to win way. All history and sociology bear witness to its comparative truth, at least when compared with the former. Under the new conception of the state, of course liberty means breaking off the fetters and trammels which the 'wisdom'of the past has forged, and *laissez-faire*, or 'let alone,' becomes a cardinal maxim of statesmanship, because it means: 'Cease the empirical process. Institute the scientific process. Let the state come back to normal health and activity, so that you can study it, learn something about it from an observation of its phenomena, and then regulate your action in regard to it by intelligent knowledge.' Statesmen suited to this latter type of state have not yet come forward in any great number. The new radical statesmen show no disposition to let their neighbors alone. They think that they have come into

power just because they know what their neighbors need to have done to them. Statesmen of the old type, who told people that they knew how to make everybody happy, and that they were going to do it, were always far better paid than any of the new type ever will be, and their failures never cost them public confidence either. We have got tired of kings, priests, nobles and soldiers, not because they failed to make us all happy, but because our *a priori* dogmas have changed fashion. We have put the administration of the state in the hands of lawyers, editors, litterateurs, and professional politicians, and they are by no means disposed to abdicate the functions of their predecessors, or to abandon the practice of the art of national prosperity. The chief difference is that, whereas the old statesmen used to temper the practice of their art with care for the interests of the kings and aristocracies which put them in power, the new statesmen feel bound to serve those sections of the population which have put them where they are.

6. Some of the old devices above enumerated (§2) are, however, out of date, or are becoming obsolete. Number 3, taxes on imports for other than fiscal purposes, is not among this number. Just now such taxes seem to be coming back into fashion, or to be enjoying a certain revival. It is a sign of the deficiency of our sociology as compared with our other sciences that such a phenomenon could be presented in the last quarter of the nineteenth century, as a certain revival of faith in the efficiency of taxes on imports as a device for producing national prosperity.

3. Protectionism in the Nineteenth Century

The nineteenth century was characterized by an increasing spread of nationalism. But as shall be seen, both its tone and content changed as the century progressed. The majority of the protectionists discussed in the following section had strong nationalist feelings. Protectionism and nationalism tend to go hand in hand as the writings of protectionist authors clearly show.

Nationalism could be defined as a state of mind whereby the individual feels that his or her supreme secular loyalty belongs to the nation state. As a doctrine, nationalism places the nation at the top of the scale of political values, that is, above the competing values of the individual, of regional entities, and of the international community. As noted before, nationalism and mercantilism were closely associated. However, during the nineteenth century new dimensions were added to nationalism. From about 1800 to 1848 nationalism became increasingly a movement of national emancipation and constitutional rights.

During the earlier part of the nineteenth century nationalists often sought as a goal, self-determination similar to that in existence in England and France. Political self-determination was the ultimate goal. This pre-1848 liberal nationalism was often quite mild and open. In countries such as the United States and Italy nationalism was basically a motivating force for national liberation and unification with liberty and peace as the product. It stressed individual liberty, especially in the case of the United States, and was thought to be compatible with a cosmopolitan outlook and foreign trade. In its early form, nationalism was frequently a middle class movement. As a principle of political self-determination, classical liberals such as John Stuart Mill viewed it favorably and frequently endorsed it, arguing that independent, liberal national states could prosper together.

But, the nineteenth (and the twentieth) century has shown that while nationalism might begin its career as a Sleeping Beauty it could end it as Frankenstein's monster. This was particularly true in the case of Germany, when it merged with elements of monarchism, socialism, racism and imperialism, where after 1848 the hostile, sinister and despotic characteristics of nationalism became more apparent. Nationalist writers compounded this with their increasing attacks on the rationalistic, individualistic, and cosmopolitan ideas of the Classicists. A short overview of the events that occurred in Germany aptly illustrates this evolution.

Before the seventeenth century the inhabitants of Europe gave their loyalties to their communities, feudal lords, princes, religious groups, or to other universal principles. In mercantilist times this situation changed with the emergence of the nation state. Germany in the late eighteenth century was still divided into a hotchpotch of princedoms, duchies, counties and free cities not infrequently ruled by capricious despots. There was little desire on the part of the inhabitants or their intellectual leaders to unify these areas into an integrated political entity. The French revolution changed this. The French revolutionaries were so convinced of the correctness of their ideas that they felt honor bound to spread them, if necessary by the sword. But what may seem beneficent and altruistic to the crusaders may often appear selfish if not satanic to the receivers. This was especially true for the Napoleonic invasions which took place after 1800. These wars seemed to be little else but instruments of a new military imperialism. French conquests generated a new kind of nationalism in the Germans, the Italians, the Spaniards and other European peoples. As far as the Germans were concerned the invasions by Napoleon brought home to them the advantages of belonging to a state large enough to defend itself effectively against foreign intrusion. A strong united Germany was good insurance against invasion. The German philosopher Johan Gottlieb Fichte (1762–1814) a forerunner to both nationalism and socialism, faced with the ideas which the French revolution presented to the German people, concluded that corruption and vice came from the outside. In his widely read 'Addresses to the German Nation' delivered in 1807–1808, the German nation is depicted as the victim of foreign (French) influences. He invited all German speaking people to rally around a German nation and subordinate their individual interests to the superior national objectives of the state.

In his book on economics, *The Closed Commercial State*, Fichte applied his nationalist ideas by outlining an austere utopian political community sealed off from foreigners. Here he endeavored to illustrate that true individual freedom could only be secured in a state which regulated the life of its citizens to the minutest detail. Free foreign trade was no longer permitted to private individuals and companies. Travel abroad was to be restricted to a few privileged scientists and artists. Domestically, Fichte advocated price and wage controls, a guaranteed right to work and the strict use of national paper money. Although Fichte's excursion into economics had little practical influence at the time, it was to have a marked effect on subsequent German economic, political and social thought.

2

As stated previously, defeat by Napoleon left a strong imprint on the Germans. Once Napoleon himself was eliminated, those German intellectuals who were nationalist in outlook began to reject all the principles upon which the French revolution had been based. These principles were viewed as oppressive foreign ideas which included rationality, liberalism, cosmopolitanism, humanitarianism, and individualism. German nationalist writers beginning with Johann Gottfried von Herder and Friedrich Gottlieb Klopstock condemned the ideas of the Enlightenment as being shallow. Increasingly they stressed instinct against reason, the power of historical tradition against rational attempts at progress, and the diversity of national character against universality. Increasingly they praised the virtues of their own nation while they vilified the character of others. As history has clearly shown this is a short road to hate and destruction. The open, cosmopolitan, liberal nationalism of the early nineteenth century was gradually replaced by a more narrow, closed and militant type of nationalism. This was also the case in other countries but overall, Germany stood out clearly as the leader.

From 1815 the French were great villains as far as the German nationalist writers were concerned. When England became the dominant country in the nineteenth century, in terms of wealth, power and achievements, German nationalist writers, engulfed by envy and resentment, turned against everything British including English political economy.

An enduring characteristic of German nationalist doctrine was its uncritical reverence for state power. The German people were well-prepared for this attitude. From before the term of the nineteenth century Germany was divided into small states usually governed in a despotic manner by princes, many of who were capricious, spendthrift, improvident and inefficient rulers. Young educated men suffocated in this narrow provincial environment which sometimes hindered normal development.

Many German nationalist writers and in particular the early ones, were part of a kind of romantic movement. They were repelled by the world in which they lived. The image of their ideal society was to be found in the premodern past. Thus they turned to the Middle Ages in which they found the wondrous fairyland lacking in the present. For them the state became an object of love and devotion because associated with it was the feudal patriarchal state of the past, a large family estate held together by bonds of love and mutual responsibility.

Finally, between 1815 and 1870, Germany was progressively unified but not by democratic methods. Consolidation of the states occurred under Prussian leadership using 'iron and fire'. Prussia was a strong monarchy and its traditions were based in those of war. Its state organization was military with its sovereign as the commander in chief. Germany was thus unified on a reactionary, state abiding and authoritarian basis. The Prussian Chancellor Otto von Bismarck being powerful showed a great ability in the smothering of whatever little liberalism was left in Germany. As a fervent nationalist, he hated the internationalist outlook of classical liberalism and managed to oppose it successfully.

The German middle classes who were often sympathetic to the ideas of liberalism were at a disadvantage because of their belated development. In England the liberal-minded middle classes, more numerous than in Germany, had been able to consolidate their influence on the political process before the emergence of the industrial/urban proletariat as a serious political force. In Germany these liberal-minded middle classes were overtaken by the first stirring of a socialist-proletarian revolution before they had a chance to assert themselves. When in 1848 a liberal type of revolution swept across Europe, small groups of desperate men surfaced in Germany, preaching revolutionary socialist doctrines. These revolutionaries alleged that the entrepreneurs and owners of productive resources were the real enemies of the people. Revolution, class war and expropriation were advocated as the appropriate policies. It was these events which seriously weakened the Liberal movement in Germany and drove the Liberal middle classes into the arms of the more tradition-minded Conservatives. In nineteenth century Europe, Liberals faced three powerful enemies. The old Conservative feudal order showed aversion to Liberals on account of their democratic convictions. The nationalists disliked liberalism because of its cosmopolitan flavor. The socialists opposed it because according to the teachings of economic liberalism, individuals should be rewarded according to their contribution to the national product which left the lowly skilled urban/industrial proletariat with meager incomes. In Germany romanticism also opposed liberalism. When later in the nineteenth century elements of all four doctrines combined into a new article of faith that was adopted by the post-1870 German government, German liberalism was definitely crushed.

Nationalism as it evolved in Germany, became associated with a variety of socialism known as State Socialism. Since 1848, German industry had progressed considerably and a new urban working class had come into being. Many of its members had become followers of Marxian revolutionary socialism. The Social Democratic Party established in 1869 was also founded on Marxian ideas. State Socialism was very much the work of university professors such as Gustav von Schmoller (1838–1917) who attempted to wean the working class from the revolutionary (international) Marxian versions of socialism by proposing such welfare state type measures as progressive income taxes and the redistribution of income. Such ideas fell on fertile ground with people like Bismarck who sought to consolidate and cement the national unity he had created. Laws dealing with sickness, accidents, invalidity, old age, duration of labor and the like were adopted under his reign.

In the course of the nineteenth century, German nationalism also mixed with racism, which in effect consisted mostly of anti-semitism. Jews were depicted as an international people without a fatherland. They were cosmopolitans who owed their emancipation to Enlightenment (foreign) doctrines. They were prominent in German economic life and their ideas were believed to be tainted by materialism and liberalism. As such, they were seen as the carriers of corruption and decay by the more militant nationalists.

It is an undeniable fact that the fervent nationalist is often also an 'antiman.' He is an antiforeigner and thus dislikes men of other nationalities. If Jews represent an international tradition, he will be anti-semitic. Numerous German nationalists in the nineteenth and the twentieth century viewed Jews as un-German and therefore disloyal by definition.

Finally, German nationalism (and in this it was not alone) merged with imperialism. As has been stated earlier, during the nineteenth century the character of nationalism changed. With the decline of mercantilist doctrines in the second half of the eighteenth century, the enthusiasm for acquiring colonies abated.

If free trade could allow all nations free access to each other's sources of raw materials and markets, why bother? After the loss of South America by Spain and Portugal in the early 1820s, few colonial empires remained. The British empire did remain but during the period 1815–1870 the British cared little for their empire. This meant, in effect, that there were no important colonial rivalries left in existence. When Germany became united and defeated France in 1870, it began to display a strong interest in colonial expansion. The French followed. The British then embraced once more the imperial outlook and even the United States felt pressured into expanding into the Pacific and the Caribbean. Thus, after 1870, a new era of nationalist imperialism and overseas expansion emerged. The imperialist nations engaged in a wild scramble for the remaining available territories in Africa and Asia. Nationalism had now become intolerant, expansionist and military. As the European nations tried to carve out colonial empires for themselves, mutual suspicion, hostility and armament increased, culminating in the Great War of 1914. Beyond doubt, World War I was predominantly a nationalist war.

The period of neo-colonialism or imperialism can be explained in terms of public choice economics. The rulers of the era, monarchs included, were similar to other people. They sought to maximize their benefit, utility or satisfaction and this satisfaction included both the enjoyment of material and psychic incomes. Psychic income had several components such as the expression of plain combativeness (the jingoes), respect, honor, prestige and above all power. Colonial undertakings usually involved a transfer, and/or increase of glory, prestige and power to the colonizing nation and thereby to its rulers. However, this pursuit of power had to be masked and made acceptable to the public.

Although the arguments of 'historical rights', 'civilizing mission', 'manifest destiny' and 'white man's burden' were widely used, much of the camouflaging and justification of imperial expansion was done by invoking 'realist' economic motives. When thinking is dominated by economic considerations as was frequently the case in western nations, rulers can increase their popularity by invoking such quasi economic arguments as 'we need new markets for our products'; 'we need space for our increasing population'; 'we need outlets for our capital'; and 'we need new reserves of raw materials'. These economic explanations and 'sanctifications' of neocolonialism were contradicted by the facts that the colonial trade was usually an insignificant part of all trade. Colonies did not constitute good markets because of the inhabitants' lack of purchasing power. Emigration from Europe was mainly to the United States, Canada and Australia, and only the very few went to live in the colonies permanently. Capital did flow from Europe (England, France, Germany, Belgium, Netherlands, Switzerland) but not to the colonies. It went mainly to the United States, Russia, Canada, Australia and New Zealand. Trade, people and money did not follow the flag. However, economic motives remained an essential part of the neocolonial nationalist propaganda because the real causes of imperialism were unsalable. The press (the yellow press in the United States) and the state schools turned out to be important auxiliaries for nationalist propaganda and manipulation. In particular in Germany and France, the schools were used to inculcate a strong sense of nationalism and a supreme devotion to the nation state.

While the industrial revolution advanced in such countries such as the United States, England, France and Germany, large scale rural–urban migration caused cities to expand and grow. With urbanization came the masses, the crowds and the easily led. It was precisely to this quasi-illiterate, credulous, weak-minded and property-less class that the new, cheap, popular press addressed itself. It was these new urban masses of the nineteenth century, who were the most amenable to the more belligerent versions of nationalism, racism and socialism. In the twentieth century, as is well known, these same crowds were easily impressed by the ideas of communism, fascism and redistributive socialism.

Political and economic nationalism go hand in hand. Economic nationalism is the policy of self-sufficiency. It is a body of economic theories and policies aimed at making the nation as independent of foreign economic influences as possible. It loosens the ties between the economic processes taking place within a nation and those occurring beyond that nation's boundaries. Mercantilism is a regime of economic nationalism. Both the old mercantilism of the pre-1750 period and the new mercantilism of the nineteenth century explained and justified the right of the state to control, regulate and restrict internal and international economic activity. This included protectionist measures such as tariffs, quotas and export subsidies. In the earlier part of the nineteenth century, mercantilism seemed to be a thing of the past, an historical curiosity, but with the return of political nationalism a number of mercantilist ideas and policies returned and were able to prolong themselves well into the twentieth century. History has shown that the free trade period of the nineteenth century was to last only a few decades. Free trade as a principle was unable to defend itself successfully against the onslaught of nationalist and statist ideas which once again aimed at the subordination of the individual to the state and government interference in economic life. The nationalist neomercantilism of the nineteenth century differed from the old mercantilism in its principal aim of generating an influx of precious metals. However, in many other ways the two mercantilisms resembled each other. Both postulated a conflict of national interests (and not a harmony of interests like the classical Liberals), both sought greater self-sufficiency, both tended towards protectionism and colonial expansion. Moreover the state had to be powerful in both the old and the new mercantilism.

It was the Germans who were best prepared to take the lead in the neomercantilist surge. As was explained before, cameralism dominated the economic thought of the German states and Austria for over three hundred years. Its confidence in government regulation, its emphasis on power and its striving for near-self-sufficiency, all became recognizable elements in the new mercantilism of the nineteenth century. German political and economic thinking and policy in the nineteenth (and the twentieth) century would have been different had it not been for the peculiar background of cameralism. When after 1870 a united Germany showed an interest in the building up of her own colonial empire, France, England, Italy, the United States and Russia joined in the scramble. As in the pre-1750 past, contest in peace time was once again waged with tariffs, preferential shipping privileges and colonial policy. World War I was the logical outcome of the post-1870 change in ideas and policies.

READING 11

Alexander Hamilton

Biography

Although mercantilism was harshly criticized by authors such as Hume and Smith, it was never eradicated. Badly wounded, it survived and revived, as the nineteenth century was to show. In Europe, the influence of Adam Smith was felt, and after 1815, tariffs were simplified or lowered and innumerable restrictions and interferences were modified or abolished. In the United States, however, Alexander Hamilton (1755–1804) and others were endeavoring to salvage from mercantilism the vital elements which they deemed essential to the building up of the young nation. Trade policy ranked high among their concerns. In a very real sense, the United States became the battleground for protectionism during the nineteenth century. Through Friedrich List (to be discussed later), the belief in protectionism was carried back to Europe where eventually it was to develop into a new variety of (neo)mercantilism.

Alexander Hamilton was born in Charlestown (1755) on the West Indian island of Nevis, which was then a British colony. He spent his youth mostly on the island of St Croix, now part of the US Virgin Islands, where he was apprenticed as a clerk. In 1772, at the age of 17 he went to New York and entered Kings College (now Columbia University). Having spent one year there, he joined the colonial side when the revolutionary war began. He distinguished himself in combat and ended up as George Washington's aide-de-camp and trusted advisor, with the rank of lieutenant colonel. Following the revolutionary war, Hamilton was drawn into politics. Hamilton's sense of authority and orderliness was outraged by the political disunion and weakness of the confederate government which led him to advocate an aristocratic, strongly centralized government. As a Secretary to the Treasury in Washington's cabinet from 1789 to 1795, he organized the financial system of the nation. He was also the President's chief advisor on domestic policy. Hamilton left the cabinet in 1795 but his influence as an unofficial advisor continued as strong as ever. George Washington and his cabinet consulted him on many matters of policy. When Washington retired in March 1797 and John Adams became the new President, Hamilton's influence in the government continued for some time, only ending when the two men began to quarrel. On July, 11, 1804 Hamilton and his long time political enemy Aaron Burr met for a duel in which Hamilton died. He left behind a wife and seven children who were heavily in debt. This debt was discharged with the help of friends.

The Work

Hamilton's mind was a disciplined instrument. He was realistic, efficient, intelligent and determined. At the same time, he was not an original thinker and he was not capable of philosophical depth or real psychological insight. His particular ability lay in the imaginative way he adapted existing ideas to the perceived needs of the young republic. Philosophically, he rejected both the laissez-faire economics of Adam Smith, and the ideas of Thomas Jefferson. The latter was eager to preserve the rural economy and favored a national government with very limited powers. Hamilton/thought more in terms of national honor, strength, security, authority, orderliness and prosperity. He favored a powerful central government/and vigorously stated the case for government intervention.

In his *First Report on the Public Credit* (1790), Hamilton recommended the laying of taxes and tariffs on luxuries such as whiskey, wines, tea and coffee. Such a policy he felt would reduce imports and promote a favorable balance of trade./

In his 'Report on Manufacturers' submitted to the House of Representatives in 1791, Hamilton does two things. First, he builds up the case for the establishment of manufactures in the United States. Second, he determines the means appropriate to this end. In the process, he considers the (mercantilism) policies which had been employed in other countries. In practice, this document has served to promote more extreme protectionist ideas and policies than Hamilton himself ever contemplated.

In an early passage of his 'Report', Hamilton argues that manufacturing involved seven benefits which included:

1. an increased division of labor;
2. an extension of the use of machinery;
3. additional employment to sections of the community ordinarily not suited for agricultural pursuits such as women and children (in this instance Hamilton had the English cotton mills in mind);
4. the promotion of immigration;
5. a widened scope for the diverse talents and abilities of people;
6. the furtherance of the 'spirit of enterprise';
7. the expansion of the home market for farm products (Hamilton felt that foreign markets were unreliable).

In a subsequent part, Hamilton discusses why the government should actively promote industry. Here he mentions such factors as people's reluctance to start new ventures. Moreover, a country like the United States (new and undeveloped), could not be expected to compete effectively in manufacturing and trade with western Europe. Here also we have his version of the 'infant industry' argument. In a final section of the 'Report', Hamilton outlines the policies which he believes to be appropriate for the encouragement of domestic industries. They included such regulations as (a) total prohibition of imports; (b) protective duties; and (c) bounties for innovative industrial (and agricultural) undertakings. Hamilton also believed that the benefits of free international trade were more imaginary than real. Foreign governments, he argued, did not hesitate to place obstacles in the way of US exports.[26] Therefore, the United States should not be afraid to adopt similar policies, including prohibitions, protective duties and subsides to encourage domestic industries.[27]

Extracts

It is now proper to proceed a step further, and to enumerate the principal circumstances from which it may be inferred that manufacturing establishments not only occasion a positive augmentation of the produce and revenue of the society, but that they contribute essentially to rendering them greater than they could possibly be without such establishments. These circumstances are:

1. The division of labor.
2. An extension of the use of machinery.
3. Additional employment to classes of the community not ordinarily engaged in the business.
4. The promoting of emigration from foreign countries.
5. The furnishing greater scope for the diversity of talents and dispositions which discriminate men from each other.
6. The affording a more ample and various field for enterprise.
7. The creating in some instances a new, and securing all a more certain and steady demand for the surplus produce of the soil.

Each of these circumstances has a considerable influence upon the total mass of industrious effort in a community; together they add to it a degree of energy and effect which are not easily conceived. Some comments upon each of them, in the order in which they have been stated, may serve to explain their importance.

---

26 It should be noted that until 1815 and even beyond that, foreign discriminatory legislation did impose injury upon American commerce.
27 A. Hamilton, 'Report on Manufactures' (1791), *State Papers and Speeches on the Tariff* (F.W. Taussig, ed.) (Cambridge: Harvard University Press, 1893), pp. 15–37, 62–68, 69–73.

As to the Division of Labor

It has justly been observed, that there is scarcely anything of greater moment in the economy of a nation than the proper division of labor. The separation of occupations causes each to be carried to a much greater perfection than it could possibly acquire if they were blended. This arises principally from three circumstances.

1st. The greater skill and dexterity naturally resulting from a constant and undivided application to a single object. It is evident that these properties must increase in proportion to the separation and simplification of objects, and the steadiness of the attention devoted to each, and must be less in proportion to the complication of objects and the number among which the attention is distracted.

2nd. The economy of time, by avoiding the loss of it, incident to frequent transition from one operation to another of a different nature. This depends on various circumstances, the transition itself, the orderly disposition of the implements, machines, and materials employed in the operation to be relinquished, the preparatory steps to the commencement of a new one, the interruption of the impulse which the mind of the workman acquires from being engaged in a particular operation, the distractions, hesitations, and reluctances which attend the passage from one kind of business to another.

3rd. An extension of the use of machinery. A man occupied on a single object will have it more in his power, and will be more naturally led to exert his imagination in devising methods to facilitate and abridge labor than if he were perplexed by a variety of independent and dissimilar operations. Besides this, the fabrication of machines in numerous instances becoming itself a distinct trade the artist who follows it has all the advantages which have been enumerated for improvement in his particular art, and, in both ways, the invention and application of machinery are extended.

And from these causes united, the mere separation of the occupation of the cultivator from that of the artificer has the effect of augmenting the productive powers of labor, and with them the total mass of the produce or revenue of a country. In this single view of the subject, therefore, the utility of artificers or manufacturers towards promoting an increase of productive industry is apparent.

2. As to an extension of the use of machinery, a point which, though partly anticipated, requires to be placed in one or two additional lights.

The employment of machinery forms an item of great importance in the general mass of national industry. It is an artificial force brought in aid of the natural force of man, and, to all the purposes of labor, is an increase of hands, an accession of strength, unincumbered, too, by the expense of maintaining the laborer. May it not, therefore, be fairly inferred that those occupations which give greatest scope to the use of this auxiliary contribute most to the general stock of industrious effort, and, in consequence, to the general product of industry?

It shall be taken for granted, and the truth of the position referred to observation, that manufacturing pursuits are susceptible in a greater degree of the application of machinery than those of agriculture. If so, all the difference is lost to a community, which, instead of manufacturing for itself, procures the fabrics requisite to its supply from other countries. The substitution of foreign for domestic manufactures is a transfer to foreign nations of the advantages accruing from the employment of machinery in the modes in which it is capable of being employed with most utility and to the greatest extent.

The cotton mill, invented in England within the last twenty years, is a signal illustration of the general proposition which has been just advanced. In consequence of it all the different processes for spinning cotton are performed by means of machines which are put in motion by water, and attended chiefly by women and children, and by a smaller number of persons, in the whole, than are requisite in the ordinary mode of spinning. And it is an advantage of great moment that the operations of this mill continue with convenience during the night as well as through the day. The prodigious effect of such a machine is easily conceived. To this invention is to be attributed essentially the immense progress which has been so suddenly made in Great Britain in the various fabrics of cotton.

3. As to the additional employment of classes of the community not originally engaged in the particular business.

This is not among the least valuable of the means by which manufacturing institutions contribute to augment the general stock of industry and production. In places where those institutions prevail, besides the persons regularly engaged in them, they afford occasional and extra employment to industrious individuals and families who are willing to devote the leisure resulting from the intermissions of their ordinary pursuits to collateral labors, as a resource for multiplying their acquisitions or their enjoyments. The husbandman himself experiences a new source of profit and support from the increased industry of his wife and daughter, invited and stimulated by the demands of the neighboring manufactories.

Besides this advantage of occasional employment to classes having different occupations, there is another of a nature allied to it, and of a similar tendency. This is the employment of persons who would otherwise be idle (and in many cases a burden on the community), either from the bias of temper, habit, infirmity of body, or some other cause, indisposing or disqualifying them for the toils of the country. It is worthy of particular remark that, in general, women and children are rendered more useful, and the latter more early useful, by manufacturing establishments than they would otherwise be. Of the number of persons employed in the cotton manufactories of Great Britain, it is computed that four sevenths nearly are women and children, of whom the greatest proportion are children, and many of them of a tender age.

And thus it appears to be one of the attributes of manufactures, and one of no small consequence, to give occasion to the exertion of a greater quantity of industry, even by the same number of persons, where they happen to prevail, than would exist if there were no such establishments.

4. As to the promoting of emigration from foreign countries. Men reluctantly quit one course of occupation and livelihood for another, unless invited to it by very apparent and proximate advantages. Many who would go from one country to another, if they had a prospect of continuing with more benefit the callings to which they have been educated, will often not be tempted to change their situation by the hope of doing better in some other way. Manufacturers who, listening to the powerful invitations of a better price for their fabrics or their labor; of greater cheapness of provisions and raw materials; of an exemption from the chief part of the taxes, burdens, and restraints which they endure in the Old World; of greater personal independence and consequence under the operation of a more equal government; and of what is far more precious than mere religious toleration, a perfect equality of religious privileges, would probably flock from Europe to the United States to pursue their own trades or professions, if they were once made sensible of the advantages they would enjoy, and were inspired with an assurance of encouragement and employment, will with difficulty be induced to transplant themselves with a view to becoming cultivators of land.

If it be true, then, that it is the interest of the United States to open every possible avenue to emigration from abroad, it affords a weighty argument for the encouragement of manufactures, which, for the reasons just assigned, will have the strongest tendency to multiply the inducement to it.

Here is perceived an important resource, not only for extending the population, and with it the useful and productive labor of the country, but likewise for the prosecution of manufactures without deducting from the number of hands which might otherwise be drawn to tillage, and even for the indemnification of agriculture for such as might happen to be diverted from it. Many, whom manufacturing views would induce to emigrate, would afterwards yield to the temptations which the particular situation of this country holds out to agricultural pursuits. And while agriculture would in other respects derive many signal and unmingled advantages from the growth of manufactures, it is a problem whether it would gain or lose as to the article of the number of persons employed in carrying it on.

5. As to the furnishing greater scope for the diversity of talents and dispositions which discriminate men from each other.

This is a much more powerful mean of augmenting the fund of national industry than may at first sight appear. It is a just observation that minds of the strongest and most active powers for their proper objects fall below mediocrity, and labor without effect is confined to uncongenial pursuits. And it is thence to be inferred that the results of human exertion may be immensely increased by diversifying its objects. When all the different kinds of industry obtain in a community, each individual can find his proper element, and can call into activity the whole vigor of his nature. And the community is benefited by the services of its respective members in the manner in which each can serve it with most effect.

If there be anything in a remark often to be met with, namely, that there is in the genius of the people of this country a peculiar aptitude for mechanic improvements, it would operate as a forcible reason for giving opportunities to the exercise of that species of talent by the propagation of manufactures.

6. As to the affording a more ample and various field for enterprise.

This also is of greater consequence in the general scale of national exertion than might perhaps, on a superficial view, be supposed, and has effects not altogether dissimilar from those of the circumstance least considerable of the expedients by which the wealth of a nation may be promoted. Even things in themselves not positively advantageous sometimes become so by their tendency to provoke exertion. Every new scene which is opened to the busy nature of man to rouse and exert itself is the addition of a new energy to the general stock of effort.

The spirit of enterprise, useful and prolific as it is, must necessarily be contracted or expanded in proportion to the simplicity or variety of the occupations and productions which are to be found in a society. It must be less in a nation of mere cultivators than in a nation of cultivators and merchants, less in a nation of cultivators and merchants than in a nation of cultivators, artificers, and merchants.

7. As to the creating, in some instances, a new, and securing in all a more certain and steady, demand for the surplus produce of the soil.

This is among the most important of the circumstances which have been indicated. It is a principal mean by which the establishment of manufactures contributes to an augmentation of the produce of revenue of a country, and has an immediate and direct relation to the prosperity of agriculture.

It is evident that the exertions of the husbandman will be steady or fluctuating, vigorous or feeble, in proportion to the steadiness or fluctuation, adequateness, of the markets on which he must depend for the vent of the surplus which may be produced by his labor; and that such surplus, in the ordinary course of things, will be greater or less in the same proportion.

For the purpose of this vent, a domestic market is greatly to be preferred to a foreign one, because it is, in the nature of things, far more to be relied upon.

It is a primary object of the policy of nations to be able to supply themselves with subsistence from their own soils; and manufacturing nations, as far as circumstances permit, endeavor to procure from the same source the raw materials necessary for their own fabrics. This disposition, urged by the spirit of monopoly, is sometimes even carried to an injudicious extreme. It seems not always to be recollected that nations who have neither mines nor manufactures can only obtain the manufactured articles of which they stand in need by an exchange of the products of their soils; and that if those who can best furnish them with such articles are unwilling to give a due course to this exchange, they must of necessity make every possible effort to manufacture for themselves; the effect of which is, that the manufacturing nations abridge the natural advantages of their situation through an unwillingness to permit the agricultural countries to enjoy the advantages of theirs, and sacrifice the interests of a mutually beneficial intercourse to the vain project of selling everything and buying nothing.

But it is also a consequence of the policy which has been noted, that the foreign demand of the products of agricultural countries is in a great degree rather casual and occasional than certain or constant. To what extent injurious interruptions of the demand for some of the staple commodities of the United States many have been experienced from that cause must be referred to the judgment of those who are engaged in carrying on the commerce of the country; but it may be safely affirmed that such interruptions are at times very inconveniently felt, and that cases not infrequently occur in which markets are so confined and restricted as to render the demand very unequal to the supply.

Independently, likewise, of the artificial impediments which are created by the policy in question, there are natural causes tending to render the external demand for the surplus of agricultural nations a precarious reliance. The differences of seasons in the countries which are the consumers make immense differences in the produce of their own soils in different years, and, consequently, in the degrees of their necessity for foreign supply. Plentiful harvests with them, especially if similar ones occur at the same time in the countries which are the furnishers, occasion of course a glut in the markets of the latter.

Considering how fast and how much the progress of new settlements in the United States must increase the surplus produce of the soil, and weighing seriously the tendency of the system which prevails among most of the commercial nations of Europe, whatever dependance may be placed on the force of natural circumstances to counteract the effects of an artificial policy, there appear strong reasons to regard the foreign demand for that surplus as too uncertain a reliance, and to desire a substitute for it in an extensive domestic market.

To secure such a market there is no other expedient than to promote manufacturing establishments. Manufacturers, who constitute the most numerous class after the cultivators of land, are for that reason the principal consumers of the surplus of their labor.

This idea of an extensive domestic market for the surplus produce of the soil is of the first consequence. It is, of all things, that which most effectually conduces to a flourishing state of agriculture. If the effect of manufactories should be to detach a portion of the hands, which would otherwise be engaged in tillage, it might possibly cause a smaller quantity of lands to be under cultivation; but by their tendency to procure a more certain demand for the surplus produce of the soil, they would at the same time cause the lands which were in cultivation to be better improved and more productive. And while, by their influence, the condition of each individual farmer would be ameliorated, the total mass of agricultural production would probably be increased. For this must evidently depend as much upon the degree of improvement, if not more, than upon the number of acres under culture.

It merits particular observation that the multiplication of manufactories not only furnishes a market for those articles which have been accustomed to be produced in abundance in a country, but it likewise creates a demand for such as were either unknown or produced in inconsiderable quantities. The bowels as well as the surface of the earth are ransacked for articles which were before neglected. Animals, plants, and minerals acquire an utility and value which were before unexplored.

The foregoing considerations seem sufficient to establish, as general propositions, that it is the interest of nations to diversify the industrious pursuits of the individuals who compose them; that the establishment of manufactures is calculated not only to increase the general stock of useful and productive labor, but even to improve the state of agriculture in particular; certainly to advance the interests of those who are engaged in it. There are other views that will be hereafter taken of the subject which, it is conceived, will serve to confirm these inferences.

Previously to a further discussion of the objections to the encouragement of manufactures, which have been stated, it will be of use to see what can be said in reference to the particular situation of the United States against the conclusions appearing to result from what has been already offered.

It may be observed, and the idea is of no inconsiderable weight, that however true it might be that a state which, possessing large tracts of vacant and fertile territory, was at the same time secluded from foreign commerce, would find its interest and the interest of agriculture in diverting a part of its population from tillage to manufactures; yet it will not follow that the same is true of a state which, having such vacant and fertile territory, has at the same time ample opportunity of procuring from abroad, on good terms all the fabrics of which it stands in need for the supply of its inhabitants. The power of doing this, at least, secures the great advantage of a division of labor, leaving the farmer free to pursue exclusively the culture of his land, and enabling him to procure with its products the manufactured supplies requisite either to his wants or to his enjoyments. And although it should be true that in settled countries the diversification of industry is conducive to an increase in the productive powers of labor, and to an augmentation of revenue and capital, yet it is scarcely conceivable that there can be anything of so solid and permanent advantage to an uncultivated and unpeopled country as to convert its wastes into cultivated and inhabited districts. If the revenue, in the mean time, should be less, the capital in the event must be greater.

To these observations the following appears to be a satisfactory answer:

1. If the system of perfect liberty to industry and commerce were the prevailing system of nations, the arguments which dissuade a country in the predicament of the United States from the zealous pursuit of manufactures would, doubtless, have great force. It will not be affirmed that they might not be permitted, with few exceptions, to serve as a rule of national conduct. In such a state of things each country would have the full benefit of its peculiar advantages to compensate for its deficiencies or disadvantages. If one nation were in a condition to supply manufactured articles on better terms than another, that other might find an abundant indemnification in a superior capacity to furnish the produce of the soil. And a free exchange, mutually beneficial, of the commodities which each was able to supply on the best terms might be carried on between them, supporting in full vigor the industry of each. And though the circumstances which have been mentioned, and others which will be unfolded hereafter, render it probable that nations merely agricultural would not enjoy the same degree of opulence, in proportion to their numbers, as those which united manufactures with agriculture; yet the progressive improvement of the lands of the former might, in the end, atone for an inferior degree of opulence in the meantime, and, in a case in which opposite considerations are pretty equally balanced, the option ought perhaps always to be in favor of leaving industry to its own direction.

But the system which has been mentioned is far from characterizing the general policy of nations. The prevalent one has been regulated by an opposite spirit. The consequence of it is that the United States are, to a certain extent, in the situation of a country precluded from foreign commerce. They can indeed, without difficulty, obtain from abroad the manufactured supplies of which they are in want, but they experience numerous and very injurious impediments to the emission and vent of their own commodities. Nor is this the case in reference to a single foreign nation only. The regulations of several countries, with which we have the most extensive intercourse, throw serious obstructions in the way of the principal staples of the United States.

In such a position of things the United States cannot exchange with Europe on equal terms, and the want of reciprocity would render them the victim of a system which should induce them to confine their views to agriculture, and refrain from manufactures. A constant and increasing necessity, on their part, for the commodities of Europe, and only a partial and occasional demand for their own in return, could not but expose them to a state of impoverishment compared with the opulence to which their political and natural advantages authorize them to aspire.

Remarks of this kind are not made in the spirit of complaint. It is for the nations, whose regulations are alluded to, to judge for themselves, whether, by aiming at too much, they do not lose more than they gain. It is for the United States to consider by what means they can render themselves least dependent on the combinations, right or wrong, of foreign policy.

It is no small consolation that already the measures which have embarrassed our trade have accelerated internal improvements, which upon the whole, have bettered our affairs. To diversify and extend these improvements is the surest and safest method of indemnifying ourselves for any inconveniences which those or similar measures have a tendency to beget. If Europe will not take from us the products of our soil upon terms consistent with our interest, the natural remedy is to contract, as fast as possible, our wants of hers.

2. The conversion of their waste into cultivated lands is certainly a point of great moment in the political calculations of the United States. But the degree in which this may possibly be retarded by the encouragement of manufactories does not appear to countervail the powerful inducements to affording that encouragement.

An observation made in another place is of a nature to have great influence upon this question. If it cannot be denied that the interests even of agriculture may be advanced more by having such of the lands of the State as are occupied under good cultivation than by having a greater quantity occupied under a much inferior cultivation, and if manufactories, for the reason assigned, must be admitted to have a tendency to promote a more steady and vigorous cultivation of the lands occupied than would happen without them, it will follow that they are capable of indemnifying a country for a diminution of the progress of new settlements, and many serve to increase both the capital value and the income of its lands, even though they should abridge the number of acres under tillage.

But it does by no means follow that the progress of new settlements would be retarded by the extension of manufactures. The desire of being an independent proprietor of land is founded on such strong principles in the human breast, that where the opportunity of becoming so is as great as it is in the United States, the proportion will be small of those whose situations would otherwise lead to it who would be diverted from it towards manufactures. And it is highly probable, as already intimated, that the accessions of foreigners who, originally drawn over by manufacturing views, would afterwards abandon them for agricultural, would be more than an equivalent for those of our own citizens who might happen to be detached from them.

The remaining objections to a particular encouragement of manufactures in the United States now require to be examined.

One of these turns on the proposition that industry, if left to itself, will naturally find its way to the most useful and profitable employment. Whence it is inferred that manufactures, without the aid of government, will grow up as soon and as fast as the natural state of things and the interest of the community may require.

Against the solidity of this hypothesis, in the full latitude of the terms, very cogent reasons may be offered. These have relation to the strong influence of habit, and the spirit of imitation, the fear of want of success in untried enterprises, the intrinsic difficulties incident to first essays towards a competition with those who have previously attained to perfection in the business to be attempted; the bounties, premiums, and other artificial encouragements with which foreign nations second the exertions of their own citizens in the branches in which they are to be rivaled.

Experience teaches that men are often so much governed by what they are accustomed to see and practice, that the simplest and most obvious improvements in the most ordinary occupations are adopted with hesitation, reluctance, and by slow gradation. The spontaneous transition to new pursuits in a community long habituated to different ones may be expected to be attended with proportionably greater difficulty. When former occupations cease to yield a profit adequate to the subsistence of their followers, or when there was an absolute deficiency of employment in them, owing to the superabundance of hands, changes would ensure; but these changes would be likely to be more tardy than might consist with the interest either of individuals or of the society. In many cases they would not happen, while a bare support could be insured by an adherence to ancient courses, though a resort to a more profitable employment might be practicable. To produce the desirable changes as early as may be expedient may, therefore, require the incitement and patronage of government.

The apprehension of failing in new attempts is, perhaps, a more serious impediment. There are dispositions apt to be attracted by the mere novelty of an undertaking, but these are not always those best calculated to give it success. To this it is of importance that the confidence of cautious, sagacious capitalists, both citizens and foreigners, should be excited. And to inspire this description of persons with confidence, it is essential that they should be made to see in any project which is new, and for that reason alone, if for no other, precarious, the prospect of such a degree of countenance and support from government as may be capable of overcoming the obstacles inseparable from first experiments.

The superiority antecedently enjoyed by nations who have preoccupied and perfected a branch of industry constitutes a more formidable obstacle than either of those which have been mentioned to the introduction of the same branch into a country in which it did not before exist. To maintain between the recent establishments of one country and the long matured establishments of another country a competition upon equal terms, both as to quality and price, is in most cases impracticable. The disparity in the one, or in the other, or in both, must necessarily be so considerable as to forbid a successful rivalship without the extraordinary aid and protection of government.

But the greatest obstacle of all to the successful prosecution of a new branch of industry, in a country in which it was before unknown, consists, as far as the instance apply, in the bounties, premiums, and other aids which are granted in a variety of cases by the nations in which the establishments to be imitated are previously introduced. It is well known – and particular examples in the course of this report will be cited – that certain nations grant bounties on the exportation of particular commodities to enable their own workmen to undersell and supplant all competitors in the countries to which those commodities are sent. Hence the undertakers of a new manufacture have to contend not only with the natural disadvantages of a new undertaking, but with the gratuities and remunerations which other governments bestow. To be enabled to contend with success, it is evident that the interference and aid of their own governments are indispensable.

Combinations by those engaged in a particular branch of business in one country to frustrate the first efforts to introduce it into another by temporary sacrifices, recompensed, perhaps, by extraordinary indemnifications of the government of such country, are believed to have existed, and are not to be regarded as destitute of probability. The existence or assurance of aid from the government of the country, in which the business is to be introduced, may be essential to fortify adventurers against the dread of such combinations, – to defeat their effects, if formed, and to prevent their being formed by demonstrating that they must, in the end, prove fruitless.

Whatever room there may be for an expectation that the industry of a people, under the direction of private interest, will upon equal terms find out the most beneficial employment for itself, there is none for a reliance that it will struggle against the force of unequal terms, or will of itself surmount all the adventitious barriers to a successful competition, which may have been erected either by the advantages naturally acquired by practice and previous possession of the ground, or by those which may have sprung from positive regulations and an artificial policy. This general reflection might alone suffice as an answer to the objection under examination, exclusively of the weighty considerations which have been particularly urged.

The objections to the pursuit of manufactures in the United States, which next present themselves to discussion, represent an impracticability of success arising from three causes: scarcity of hands, dearness of labor, want of capital.

The two first circumstances are to a certain extent real, and within due limits ought to be admitted as obstacles to the success of manufacturing enterprise in the United States. But there are various considerations which lessen their force, and tend to afford an assurance that they are not sufficient to prevent the advantageous prosecution of many very useful and extensive manufactories.

With regard to scarcity of hands, the fact itself must be applied with no small qualification to certain parts of the United States. There are large districts which may be considered as pretty fully peopled, and which, notwithstanding a continual drain for distant settlement, are thickly interspersed with flourishing and increasing towns. If these districts have not already reached the point at which the complaint of scarcity of hands ceases, they are not remote from it, and are approaching fast towards it. And having perhaps fewer attractions to agriculture than some other parts of the Union, they exhibit a proportionably stronger tendency towards other kinds of industry. In these districts may be discerned no inconsiderable maturity for manufacturing establishments.

But there are circumstances which have been already noticed with another view, that materially diminish everywhere the effect of a scarcity of hands. These circumstances are: the great use which can be made of women and children, on which point a very pregnant and instructive fact has been mentioned; the vast extension given by late improvements to the employment of machines, which, substituting the agency of fire and water, has prodigiously lessened the necessity for manual labor; the employment of persons ordinarily engaged in other occupations during the seasons or hours of leisure, which, besides giving occasion to the exertion of a greater quantity of labor by the same number of persons, and thereby increasing the general stock of labor, as has elsewhere been remarked, may also be taken into the calculation as a resource for obviating the scarcity of hands; lastly, the attraction of foreign emigrants. Whoever inspects with a careful eye the composition of our towns, will be made sensible to what an extent this resource may be relied upon. This exhibits a large proportion of ingenious and valuable workmen in different arts and trades, who, by expatriating from Europe, have improved their own condition and added to the industry and wealth of the United States. It is a natural inference from the experience we have already had, that as soon as the United States shall present the countenance of a serious prosecution of manufactures, as soon as foreign artists shall be made sensible that the state of things here affords a moral certainty of employment and encouragement, competent numbers of European workmen will transplant themselves effectually to insure the success of the design. How indeed can it otherwise happen, considering the various and powerful inducements which the situation of this country offers; addressing themselves to so many strong passions and feelings, to so many general and particular interests?

It may be affirmed, therefore, in respect to hands for carrying on manufactures, that we shall in a great measure trade upon a foreign stock, reserving our own for the cultivation of our lands and the manning of our ships, as far as character and circumstances shall incline. It is not unworthy of remark that the objection to the success of manufactures deduced from the scarcity of hands, is alike applicable to trade and navigation, and yet these are perceived to flourish, without any sensible impediment from that cause.

As to the dearness of labor (another of the obstacles alleged), this has relation principally to two circumstances: one, that which has been just discussed, or the scarcity of hands; the other, the greatness of profits. As far as it is a consequence of the scarcity of hands, it is mitigated by all the considerations which have been adduced as lessening that deficiency. It is certain, too, that the disparity in this respect between some of the most manufacturing parts of Europe and a large proportion of the United States is not nearly so great as is commonly imagined. It is also much less in regard to artificers and manufacturers than in regard to country laborers; and while a careful comparison shows that there is in this particular much exaggeration, it is also evident that the effect of the degree of disparity which does truly exist is diminished in proportion to the use which can be made of machinery.

To illustrate this last idea: let it be supposed that the difference of price in two countries of a given quantity of manual labor requisite to the fabrication of a given article is as ten, and that some mechanic power is introduced into both countries which, performing half the necessary labor, leaves only half to be done by hand, it is evident that the difference in the cost of the fabrication of the article in question in the two countries, as far as it is connected with the price of labor, will be reduced from ten to five in consequence of the introduction of that power.

This circumstance is worthy of the most particular attention. It diminishes immensely one of the objections most strenuously urged against the success of manufacturers in the United States.

To procure all such machines as are known in any part of Europe can only require a proper provision and due pains. The knowledge of several of the most important of them is already possessed. The preparation of them here is in most cases practicable on nearly equal terms. As far as they depend on water, some superiority of advantages may be claimed from the uncommon variety and greater cheapness of situations adapted to mill-seats with which different parts of the United States abound.

So far as the dearness of labor may be a consequence of the greatness of profits in any branch of business, it is no obstacle to its success. The undertaker can afford to pay the price.

There are grounds to conclude that undertakers of manufactures in this country can at this time afford to pay higher wages to the workmen they may employ than are paid to similar workmen in Europe. The prices of foreign fabrics in the markets of the United

States, which will for a long time regulate the prices of the domestic ones, may be considered as compounded of the following ingredients: The first cost of materials, including the taxes, if any, which are paid upon them where they are made, the expense of grounds, buildings, machinery and tools; the wages of the persons employed in the manufactory; the profits on the capital or stock employed; the commissions of agents to purchase them where they are made; the expense of transportation to the United States, including insurance and other incidental charges; the taxes or duties, if any, and fees of office which are paid on their importation.

As to the first of these items, the cost of materials, the advantage upon the whole is at present on the side of the United States; and the difference in their favor must increase in proportion as a certain and extensive domestic demand shall induce the proprietors of land to devote more of their attention to the production of those materials. It ought not to escape observation, in a comparison on this point, that some of the principal manufacturing countries of Europe are much more dependent on foreign supply for the materials of their manufactures than would be the United States, who are capable of supplying themselves with a greater abundance, as well as a greater variety, of the requisite materials.

As to the second item, the expense of grounds, buildings, machinery and tools, and equality at least may be assumed; since advantages in some particulars will counterbalance temporary disadvantages in others.

As to the third item, or the article of wages, the comparison certainly turns against the United States, though, as before observed, not in so great a degree as is commonly supposed.

The fourth item is alike applicable to the foreign and to the domestic manufacture. It is indeed more properly a result than a particular to be compared.

But with respect to all the remaining items, they are alone applicable to the foreign manufacture, and in the strictest sense extraordinary; constituting a sum of extra charge on the foreign fabric, which cannot be estimated at less than from fifteen to thirty per cent on the cost of it at the manufactory.

This sum of extra charge may confidently be regarded as more than a counterpoise for the real difference in the price of labor; and is a satisfactory proof that manufactures may prosper in defiance of it in the United States.

......

In order to a better judgment of the means proper to be resorted to by the United States, it will be of use to advert to those which have been employed with success in other countries. The principal of these are:

1. Protecting duties, or duties on those foreign articles which are the rivals of the domestic ones intended to be encouraged.

Duties of this nature evidently amount to a virtual bounty on the domestic fabrics, since by enhancing the charges on foreign articles they enable the national manufacturers to undersell all their foreign competitors. The propriety of this species of encouragement need not be dwelt upon, as it is not only a clear result from the numerous topics which have been suggested, but is sanctioned by the laws of the United States in a variety of instances; it has the additional recommendation of being a resource of revenue. Indeed, all the duties imposed on imported articles, though with an exclusive view to revenue, have the effect in contemplation; and, except where they fall on raw materials, wear a beneficent aspect towards the manufactures of the country.

2. Prohibitions of rival articles, or duties equivalent to prohibitions.

This is another and an efficacious mean of encouraging national manufactures; but in general it is only fit to be employed when a manufacture has made such a progress, and is in so many hands, as to insure a due competition and an adequate supply on reasonable terms. Of duties equivalent to prohibitions there are examples in the laws of the United States; and there are other cases to which the principle may be advantageously extended, but they are not numerous.

Considering a monopoly of the domestic market to its own manufacturers as the reigning policy of manufacturing nations, a similar policy on the part of the United States, in every proper instance, is dictated, it might almost be said, by the principles of distributive justice; certainly by the duty of endeavoring to secure to their own citizens a reciprocity of advantages.

3. Prohibitions of the exportation of materials of manufactures. The desire of securing a cheap and plentiful supply for the national workmen; and, where the article is either peculiar to the country, or of peculiar quality there, the jealousy of enabling foreign workmen to rival those of the nation with its own materials, are the leading motives to this species of regulation. It ought not to be affirmed that it is in no instance proper, but it is certainly one which ought to be adopted with great circumspection and only in very plain cases. It is

seen at once that its immediate operation is to abridge the demand and keep down the price of the produce of some other branch of industry, generally speaking of agriculture, to the prejudice of those who carry it on; and though if it be really essential to the prosperity of any very important national manufacture it may happen that those who are injured in the first instance may be eventually indemnified by the superior steadiness of an extensive domestic market depending on that prosperity, yet, in a matter in which there is so much room for nice and difficult combinations, in which such opposite considerations combat each other, prudence seems to dictate that the expedient in question ought to be indulged with a sparing hand.

4. Pecuniary bounties.

This has been found one of the most efficacious means of encouraging manufactures, and it is, in some views, the best, though it has not yet been practiced upon the government of the United States, unless the allowance on the exportation of dried and pickled fish and salted meat could be considered as a bounty, and though it is less favored by public opinion than some other modes, its advantages are these:

1. It is a species of encouragement more positive and direct than any other, and for that very reason has a more immediate tendency to stimulate and uphold new enterprises, increasing the chances of profit, and diminishing the risks of loss in the first attempts.

2. It avoids the inconvenience of a temporary augmentation of price, which is incident to some other modes, or it produces it to a less degree, either by making no addition to the charges on the rival foreign article, as in the case of protecting duties, or by making a smaller addition. The first happens when the fund for the bounty is derived from a different object (which may or may not increase the price of some other article according to the nature of that object); the second, when the fund is derived from the same or a similar object of foreign manufacture. One per cent duty on the foreign article, converted into a bounty on the domestic, will have an equal effect with a duty of 2% exclusive of such bounty; and the price of the foreign commodity is liable to be raised in the one case in the proportion of 1%, in the other in that of 2%. Indeed, the bounty, when drawn from another source, is calculated to promote a reduction of price, because, without laying any new charge on the foreign article, it serves to introduce a competition with it, and to increase the total quantity of the article in the market.

3. Bounties have not, like high protecting duties, a tendency to

produce scarcity. An increase of price is not always the immediate, though where the progress of a domestic manufacture does not counteract a rise, it is commonly the ultimate effect of an additional day. In the interval between the laying of the duty and a proportional increase of price, it may discourage importation by interfering with the profits to be expected from the sale of the article.

4. Bounties are sometimes not only the best, but the only proper expedient for uniting the encouragement of a new object of agriculture with that of a new object of manufacture. It is the interest of the farmer to have the production of the raw material promoted by counteracting the interference of the foreign material of the same kind. It is the interest of the manufacturer to have the material abundant and cheap. If, prior to the domestic production of the material in sufficient quantity to supply the manufacturer on good terms, a duty be laid upon the importation of it from abroad, with a view to promote the raising of it at home, the interest both of the farmer and manufacturer will be deserved. By either destroying the requisite supply, or raising the price of the article beyond what can be afforded to be given for it by the conductor of an infant manufacture, it is abandoned or fails; and there being no domestic manufactories to create a demand for the raw material which is raised by the farmer, it is in vain that the competition of the like foreign article may have been destroyed.

It cannot escape notice that a duty upon the importation of an article can no otherwise aid the domestic production of it than by giving the latter greater advantages in the home market. It can have no influence upon the advantageous sale of the article produced in foreign markets, no tendency, therefore, to promote its exportation.

The true way to conciliate these two interests is to lay a duty on foreign manufactures of the material, the growth of which is desired to be encouraged, and to apply the produce of the duty by way of bounty either upon the production of the material itself, or upon its manufacture at home, or upon both. In this disposition of the thing the manufacturer commences his enterprise under every advantage which is attainable as to quantity or price of the raw material. And the farmer, if the bounty be immediately to him, is enabled by it to enter into a successful competition with the foreign material. If the bounty be to the manufacturer on so much of the domestic material as he consumes, the operation is nearly the same; he has a motive of interest to prefer the domestic commodity, if of equal quality, even at a higher price than the foreign, so long as the difference of price is anything short of the bounty which is allowed upon the article.

Except the simple and ordinary kinds of household manufacture, or those for which there are very commanding local advantages, pecuniary bounties are in most cases indispensable to the introduction of a new branch. A stimulus and a support, not less powerful and direct, is, generally speaking, essential to the overcoming of the obstacles which arise from the competitions of superior skill and maturity elsewhere. Bounties are especially essential in regard to articles upon which those foreigners, who have been accustomed to supply a country, are in the practice of granting them.

The continuance of bounties on manufactures long established must almost always be of questionable policy, because a presumption would arise in every such case that there were natural and inherent impediments to success. But in new undertakings they are as justifiable as they are oftentimes necessary.

There is a degree of prejudice against bounties, from an appearance of giving away the public money without an immediate consideration, and from a supposition that they serve to enrich particular classes at the expense of the community.

But neither of these sources of dislike will bear a serious examination. There is no purpose to which public money can be more beneficially applied than to the acquisition of a new and useful branch of industry, no consideration more valuable than a permanent addition to the general stock of productive labor.

As to the second source of objection, it equally lies against other modes of encouragement, which are admitted to be eligible. As often as a duty upon a foreign article makes an addition to its price, it causes an extra expense to the community for the benefit of the domestic manufacturer. A bounty does no more. But it is the interest of the society in each case to submit to a temporary expense, which is more than compensated by an increase of industry and wealth, by an augmentation of resources and independence, and by the circumstance of eventual cheapness, which has been noticed in another place.

It would deserve attention, however, in the employment of this species of encouragement in the United States, as a reason for moderating the degree of it in the instances in which it might be deemed eligible, that the great distance of this country from Europe imposes very heavy charges on all the fabrics which are brought from thence, amounting from 15% to 30% on their value, according to their bulk.

......

5. Premiums.

These are of a nature allied to bounties, though distinguishable from them in some important features.

Bounties are applicable to the whole quantity of an article produced or manufactured or exported, and involve a correspondent expense. Premiums serve to reward some particular excellence or superiority, some extraordinary exertion or skill, and are dispensed only in a small number of cases. But their effect is to stimulate general effort; contrived so as to be both honorary and lucrative, they address themselves to different passions, touching the chords as well of emulation as of interest. They are, accordingly, a very economical mean of exciting the enterprise of a whole community.

There are various societies in different countries, whose object is the dispensation of premiums for the encouragement of agriculture, arts, manufactures and commerce, and though they are for the most part voluntary associations, with comparatively slender funds, their utility has been immense. Much has been done by this mean in Great Britain. Scotland in particular owes materially to it a prodigious melioration of condition. From a similar establishment in the United States, supplied and supported by the Government of the Union, vast benefits might reasonably be expected. Some further ideas on this head shall accordingly be submitted in the conclusion of this report.

6. The exemption of the materials of manufactures from duty.

The policy of that exemption, as a general rule, particularly in reference to new establishments, is obvious. It can hardly ever be advisable to add the obstructions of fiscal burdens to the difficulties which naturally embarrass a new manufacture; and where it is matured, and in condition to become an object of revenue, it is, generally speaking, better the fabric, than the material, should be the subject of taxation. Ideas of proportion between the quantum of the tax and the value of the article can be more easily adjusted in the former than in the latter case. An argument for exemptions of this kind in the United States is to be derived from the practice, as far as their necessities have permitted, of those nations whom we are to meet as competitors in our own and in foreign markets.

There are, however, exceptions to it, of which some examples will be given under the next head.

The laws of the Union afford instances of the observance of the policy here recommended, but it will probably be found advisable to extend it to some other cases. Of a nature bearing some affinity to that policy is the regulation which exempts from duty the tools and implements, as well as the books, clothes and household furniture, of foreign artists who come to reside in the United States; an advantage already secured to them by the laws of the Union, and which is in every view proper to continue.

7. Drawbacks of the duties which are imposed on the materials of manufactures.

It has already been observed as a general rule, that duties on those materials ought, with certain exceptions, to be forborne. Of these exceptions, three cases occur which may serve as examples. One, where the material is itself an object of general or extensive consumption, and a fit and productive source of revenue. Another, where a manufacture of a simpler kind, the competition of which with a like domestic article is desired to be restrained, partakes of the nature of a raw material from being capable by a further process to be converted into a manufacture of a different kind, the introduction or growth of which is desired to be encouraged. A third, where the material itself is the production of the country, and in sufficient abundance to furnish a cheap and plentiful supply to the national manufacturers.

Under the first description comes the article of molasses. It is not only a fair object of revenue, but being a sweet, it is just that the consumers of it should pay a duty as well as the consumers of sugar.

Cottons and linens in their white state fall under the second description. A duty upon such as are imported is proper to promote the domestic manufacture of similar articles in the same state; a drawback of that duty is proper to encourage the printing and staining at home of those which are brought from abroad. When the first of these manufactures has attained sufficient maturity in a country to furnish a full supply for the second, the utility of the drawback ceases.

The article of hemp either now does or may be expected soon to exemplify the third case in the United States.

Where duties on the materials of manufactures are not laid for the purpose of preventing a competition with some domestic production, the same reasons which recommend, as a general rule, the exemption of those materials from duties, would recommend, as a like general rule, the allowance of drawbacks in favor of the manufacturer. Accordingly, such drawbacks are familiar in countries which systematically pursue the business of manufactures, which furnishes an argument for the observance of a similar policy in the United States; and the idea has been adopted by the laws of the Union, in the instance of salt and molasses. It is believed that it will be found advantageous to extend it to some other articles.

8. The encouragement of new inventions and discoveries at home, and of the introduction into the United States of such as may have been made in other countries; particularly those which relate to machinery.

This is among the most useful and unexceptionable of the aids which can be given to manufacturers. The usual means of that encouragement are pecuniary rewards, and, for a time, exclusive privileges. The first must be employed according to the occasion and the utility of the invention or discovery. For the last, so far as respects 'authors and inventors,' provision has been made by law. But it is desirable, in regard to improvements and secrets of extraordinary value, to be able to extend the same benefit to introducers as well as authors and inventors; a policy which has been practiced with advantage in other countries. Here, however, as in some other cases, there is cause to regret that the competency of the authority of the national Government to the good which might be done, is not without a question. Many aids might be given to industry, many internal improvements of primary magnitude might be promoted, by an authority operating throughout the Union, which cannot be effected as well, if at all, by an authority confined within the limits of a single State.

But if the Legislature of the Union cannot do all the good that might be wished, it is at least desirable that all may be done which is practicable. Means for promoting the introduction of foreign improvements, though less efficaciously than might be accomplished with more adequate authority, will form a part of the plan intended to be submitted in the close of this report.

It is customary with manufacturing nations to prohibit, under severe penalties, the exportation of implements and machines which they have either invented or improved. There are already objects for a similar regulation in the United States, and others may be expected to occur from time to time. The adoption of it seems to be dictated by the principle of reciprocity. Greater liberality in such respects might better comport with the general spirit of the country; but a selfish and exclusive policy in other quarters will not always permit the free indulgence of a spirit which would place us upon an unequal footing. As far as prohibitions tend to prevent foreign competitors from driving the benefit of the improvements made at home, they tend to increase the advantage of those by whom they have been introduced, and operate as an encouragement to exertion.

READING 12

Daniel Raymond

Biography

Daniel Raymond (1786–1849) was the first American to publish a full length treatise on economic topics.[28] He was born in Connecticut and studied law in the school of Tapping Reeve at Litchfield. In 1814 he was admitted to the bar in Baltimore and became a lawyer. Raymond was the author of *Thoughts on Political Economy* (1820) which was for subsequent editions entitled *The Elements of Political Economy* (1823). Raymond became a political economist by chance. In his younger years his law practice did not occupy enough of his time and talents and so he turned to writing up his thoughts on political economy. Interestingly enough, full employment appears in his work as a major preoccupation if not an obsession and one wonders if this is somehow related to the idleness of Raymond's early years as a lawyer.

Matthew Carey, a convinced protectionist (see Reading 13), was greatly impressed by Raymond's work and offered $500 a year to the University of Maryland for the purpose of endowing a professorship of political economy, a position to be filled by Raymond. This offer however, came to nothing, and Raymond's work was never used as a textbook at American universities.

The Work

Raymond was one of the very first post-mercantilist nationalist writers. He was distinctively early American in that he wanted to break away from foreign systems of thought especially if they happened to originate in England.

Like so many nationalist writers following him Raymond in his writings:

---

28 For a summary and discussion of Raymond's theories see C.P. Neill, Daniel Raymond, *An Early Chapter in the History of Economic Theory in the United States* (Baltimore: Johns Hopkins Press, 1897), and E. Teilhac, *Pioneers of American Economic Thought in the Nineteenth Century* (New York: Macmillan, 1936).

(a) makes a strong distinction between the individual and the nation,[29]
(b) believes that political considerations must govern economic ones,
(c) places the nation rather than the individual at the centre of his analysis,
(d) makes the building of a strong state a very important priority,
(e) argues that where national and individual interests clash, the individual interests should be sacrificed,
(f) repudiates laissez-faire,
(g) rejects arguments for the international division of labor and free trade,
(h) states that colonies should be kept as long as the benefits exceed the costs, and
(i) advocates a balance between manufacturing and agriculture and looks with favor on self-sufficiency.

Raymond's work in particular is full of such statements as:

1. a nation is beyond the limits of time and space,
2. nations ought to consider only their own interest without any regard to that of other countries,
3. universal philanthropy is chimerical, and
4. governments are delegates of God-on-earth.

Raymond's argument contains in addition to nationalism elements of agrarianism (he is often quite close to the physiocrats) and socialism but his nationalism dominates the other two components. As an agriculturalist Raymond sometimes believes that land is the only source of wealth while agricultural labor is almost always the sole cause of wealth. As a socialist Raymond stresses that the 'artificial' rules of private property perpetuate economic inequality between the social classes which loosens national bonds. While God has the right to deprive man of his health and/or life, the government has the right to deprive him of his property. At a more general level, Raymond makes it clear that he regards the principles of private interest as narrow and contemptible and those of the public interest as noble.

---

29 Adam Smith and other classical economists believed that society is nothing more than the sum total of the individuals who compose it. The well-being and prosperity of the state was the aggregate of that of the individuals in the state. Therefore, national and individual interests were identical (ed.).

State action and interference are justified on those grounds. Raymond also emphasizes labor as being the only factor of production. He makes the (nebulous) distinction between on the one hand effective labor which creates the means of production i.e. national wealth and on the other hand productive labor which produces final consumer goods, i.e. private wealth.

It is difficult to extract a coherent logical picture from Raymond's work because his reasoning is often poorly disciplined and characterized by ill defined methods, a lack of cohesion, the use of problematic concepts and a frequent confusion of ideas.

What is one to think of an economist who argues that banks are institutions which enable money lenders to obtain usurious interest payments for their money? What can one say of an economist who does not believe in the usefulness of individual thrift and saving in order to allow for capital accumulation, and thus the increase of the nation's ability to produce 'national wealth'? In fact Raymond theorizes that national prosperity is maximized when the whole product of one year is consumed in the next. All surplus output should be burned or thrown in the ocean. Any excess of production above consumption, he argues, involves stagnation and distress.

Raymond's book is in many ways a reaction against the individualistic and cosmopolitic approach of the classical economists but his criticism of Smith is often narrow if not incorrect. Raymond rejects the idea that man tending to his own interest may well serve the general interest of mankind simultaneously. His reasoning is based on the hypothesis that a person following his self-interest may decide to engage in such activities as smuggling which can hardly be said to be an employment most useful to society. Raymond forgets however that Smith explicitly states that only the pursuit of private concerns *within the law* would produce social harmony. Smith makes it clear that self-interest which is ordinarily a virtue may degenerate into vice if not regulated by justice.

The definition of national wealth and of what it consists is of great importance to Raymond. He makes the distinction between individual and national wealth the basic principle upon which he constructs his system. Individual wealth consists of consumable commodities and other possessions of the individual. National wealth (a problematic concept to say the least) consists of a nation's capacity to produce goods – a stock of resources, physical as well as human. One reason[30] why the distinction between private and public wealth is so important to Raymond is that it establishes a role for government. It justifies government interference in the economy. National or social wealth he wrote, can best be promoted and nurtured by government action such as the protection of the domestic market.

The distinction between individual and national wealth had been made earlier by a Scottish writer, Lord Lauderdale (1759–1839) whom Raymond quotes approvingly. In his book *Inquiry into the Nature and Origin of Public Wealth* (1804) Lauderdale contrasts private and public wealth. Public wealth consisted mainly of items which possessed utility but which were not scarce, such as rivers and lakes in a sparsely populated country, while private riches consisted of everything which possessed utility while being scarce at the same time. Since value was derived from scarcity, private riches had value while public wealth was deprived of it. Raymond adopted the distinction put forward by Lord Lauderdale but gave a different interpretation to the two concepts.

Later we shall see how Friedrich List appropriated the notion of national wealth in order to make it the cornerstone of his protective argument.

One specific reason why Raymond favored the reduction of imports or protective tariffs was that such measures permitted full and constant employment of the labor force of a nation. Here we have the 'full employment' type of argument which has been used abundantly in the 1930s even by such economists as John Maynard Keynes. According to Raymond, protective tariffs not only provide full employment but also constant employment because domestic industry is shielded from the fluctuations of foreign demand. Obviously, Raymond strongly believes that the domestic market is always more stable than the foreign market. A second plea used by Raymond is now known as the 'infant industry' argument. The initial (average) cost of producing certain articles may be relatively high. Over time however, costs in a given industry (say textiles) may be lowered so that firms in that industry became more competitive. A third consideration is that protectionism increases the national wealth

---

30 If these resources are privately owned one may ask the question whether this is not individual wealth as well. If that is the case protectionism favoring the owners of the resources creates privilege just like Adam Smith said (ed.).

(physical and human capital). Because protection promotes industrialization it also fosters diligence, enterprise and expertise which are all included in Raymond's definition of national wealth. A fourth point which Raymond emphasizes is that in comparison with England, America in the early decades of the nineteenth century lagged behind in many ways. Because of early industrialization, the English worker was better equipped with skills and experience than his American counterpart, resulting in greater English competitiveness. In order to 'protect' American wages and to equalize the costs of production, Raymond recommends compensating tariffs. In this instance we are confronted with a mixture of two considerations, i.e. the pauper labor argument and the cost-equalization plea. Finally, Raymond deals with the issue of dumping. Tariffs are needed, he argues, in order to prevent British manufacturers from dumping their surplus products on the American market at 'demoralizing' prices, thus destroying domestic firms in the process.[31]

Raymond also points out how his new tariffs should be structured. As a rule they should not be reduced but raised frequently. Second, they should be lowest on those items which cannot be produced domestically and highest upon those goods produced by industries employing the greatest number of laborers. Raymond clearly shows here that he puts the maximization of employment above the optimal use of resources.

Although this is not the place to discuss Raymond's arguments in detail it may well be observed that following the Napoleonic Wars in Europe and the return of peace, the influx of British goods into the US expanded, causing some increases in American unemployment. Superficial observation prompted Raymond to argue that without protective tariffs and import prohibitions quasi-permanent unemployment was inevitable in the United States. However, Raymond should be accorded some credit for the bringing out of the fact that the classicals always assumed full employment to prevail, an assumption which might have been more clearly stated by them in order to avoid confusion. He also deserves some praise for his opposition to slavery.[32]

---

31 For a discussion of these arguments the reader is referred to textbooks on international economics which usually contain a chapter analyzing arguments for and against protection (ed.).

32 Source: D. Raymond, *The Elements of Political Economy*, Vol II, Chapter 9 (Baltimore: F. Lucas, 1823).

Extracts

In imposing duties on importations, governments have a twofold object. The one is to raise a revenue; the other, to secure to its own citizens some advantage or privilege, over the citizens of foreign governments, in the domestic trade and industry of the country. All writers on political economy admit the expediency of raising a revenue by imposts. The only questions that are ever made on this branch of the subject, respect the amount of the revenue that ought to be raised by imposts, and the mode of collecting it.

But the expediency of laying import duties, for the purpose of securing to citizens some advantage, or privilege, over foreigners, in the domestic trade and industry of the country, has been vehemently controverted by many of the most celebrated and popular writers on political economy, at the head of whom stands Adam Smith.

Imposts, bounties, drawbacks, and corn laws, are all branches of the same system. They are only different expedients for accomplishing the same object – the encouragement of the industry of the nation. Their object is to create an absolute or qualified monopoly, according as the duty amounts to an absolute or qualified exclusion of foreigners, from a participation in any particular branch of the trade or industry of the country. This system is opposed to that of free trade.

Although all nations have to a greater or less extent, adopted the monopoly system, with respect to their own domestic trade and industry, yet the policy of doing so, has been much questioned by a very numerous sect of politicians; and many, who admit the expediency of this policy, consider it wrong in itself, but rendered necessary, in order to counteract the restrictive measures of other nations.

Upon this question, the United States is at present divided into two parties; those who are in favour of, and those who are opposed to raising the tariff. One party contends, that the only object of imposts, should be the raising a revenue, the other, that this should be resorted to, for the purpose of creating a qualified monopoly of our own domestic trade, and for the purpose of encouraging manufactures. The former are the partisans of a free trade, the latter, of a restricted trade.

......

Upon all subjects relating to political economy, and especially upon the subject of protecting duties, it is ever to be remembered, that the public interests are paramount to individual interests – that a private mischief, or inconvenience, must be endured for the public good; and that when a political economist has shown that public and private interests are opposed, he has made out a case, in which the interposition of the government is necessary – he cannot be required to prove that private interests ought to give way – this is to be taken for granted.

In military tactics, it is a fundamental principle, that the army is ONE, and the general the head; no soldier is permitted to have a right, or an interest, opposed to the general good of the army. So, in political economy, it should be a fundamental principle, that the nation is ONE, and the legislature the head; no citizen should be permitted to have a right, or an interest, opposed to the general good of the nation. Until this comes to be admitted, and acted upon as a fundamental principle, political economy will remain in its present crude chaotic state, and cannot be subjected to the rules of science.
......

We often hear people talk about individual rights, in a strain that would lead one to suppose that national interests, and individual rights, were, in their opinion, often at variance. They seem to suppose, that the right of property is absolute in the individual, and that every one has a right to sell to whom he pleases, and to buy of whom he pleases; and that any interference by the government, in restraining the exercise of this right, is arbitrary and tyrannical. They will tell us, that government has no right to control them in the disposition of their property, merely with a view, that other citizens may derive a benefit from it.

This is a manifest error. Individual right to property is never absolute, but always relative and conditional. There is no such thing as perfect, absolute right, but in those things which are the gift of nature; such as life, liberty, strength, talents, personal beauty, etc. The right to property, is merely conventional or conditional, subject to such regulation as may be made respecting it, with a view to the general interest of the whole nation. No man has, or can have, a perfect exclusive right to property of any description. Every man in the community, has a qualified right to it, and under certain circumstances has a right to a living out of it. The public right to every piece of property in the nation, is superior to the private right of the individual owners. Hence, the right of the public to take any man's property from him, whenever it becomes necessary for the public good. If this were not so, the social compact would not be sustained; government could not be supported.

If individual right to property was absolute, government would have no right to take an individual's property from him, for any purpose whatever. The public has no right to deprive a man of his life, his liberty, his talents, his strength, his personal beauty, or of any other gift of nature, merely for the public good, and for the plainest reason in the world, because he does not derive any of these from the public – they are the gifts of his creator, and He alone has a right to deprive him of them. No man, or body of men, has a right to take them from him, unless they have been forfeited by some crime.

Upon the same principle that God has a right to deprive a man of health and life, government has a right to deprive him of his property. The former is the bounty of God, and held subject to his will. The latter is the bounty of the government, and held subject to its will. But for the social compact no man could have an exclusive right to any spot of this earth. The right of property is therefore a conventional right, and the public grants no title to property in derogation of the public weal. An individual may have a title to property, superior to the title of any other individual, or to any number of individuals, less than the whole, but it cannot be superior to the title of the whole, because the whole includes the title of the individual himself, as well as the title of every body else. Hence the right of the public to take a man's property for the purpose of making public roads, or erecting fortifications, or for any other purpose, which the public good may require. Hence the right of the government to levy and collect taxes in any manner the public interests may require. Hence the right to prohibit a man from selling his property to foreigners, or to buy from them those things he many want. The government has a clear and perfect right to make any regulations respecting property, or trade, which the public interests may require.

Every question, therefore, respecting a tariff, or protecting duties, must be a question of expediency, and not a question of right.
......

It may be admitted, that if individuals, or a nation, can buy an article cheaper than they can make it, they had better buy than to make, as a general rule; but to this general rule there are many exceptions, and these exceptions will embrace the policy of protecting duties to as great an extent, as has ever been contended for by the partisans of a restricted trade.

The doctrine, however, of buying, when we can buy cheaper than we can make, as illustrated, or rather as stated without illustration, by

Dr. Smith, is most erroneous and unsound, when applied to individuals. Had he explained what he means by 'buying cheaper than we can make,' the doctrine might, perhaps, have been admitted as correct. But, in the broad terms in which the doctrine is laid down, it is never adopted by prudent individuals and much less by nations. If an individual were to go upon the principle of buying, in the ordinary acceptation of the phrase, it would lead him to inevitable ruin. But every case of this kind, depends on its own circumstances.

It may, as an ordinary rule, be better for the tailor to buy his shoes from the shoemaker, than to make them himself, but it may be better to make them than to buy. If he has constant employment in his own trade, he had better buy his shoes than to make them. If he has not, it may be better to make than to buy them. If a tailor cannot sell his own work, he had better spend a week in making a pair of shoes, than to buy them with the price of an ordinary day's work. Whether it be better for a farmer to buy his own clothes, and shoes, than to make them, depends entirely on circumstances. Sometimes it is better to do the one, and sometimes the other. If he can buy them with some of the produce of his own industry, 'employed in a way which he has some advantage,' better to buy than to make them; if not, he had better make than buy them. A tailor, who can find employment in his trade only one half of his time, had better employ the other half in making shoes and raising corn, than to be idle that time, and buy his shoes and corn at any price, no matter how cheap. So, the farmer, who can only find a market for one half the product of his labour, will find it more for his interest to employ one half of his time in manufacturing various articles, than to buy those articles at any price whatever. If the tailor and shoemaker will take corn for their work, it will probably be better to buy than to make. This, however, will depend on the quantity they will give in exchange. This is a universal principle – a principle upon which all prudent men act. It applies to all classes of people, and to communities, as well as to individuals. This is the true meaning of the doctrine of buying, when you can buy cheaper than you can make. But, from the general unqualified manner, in which Dr. Smith lays down the doctrine, one would be led to suppose, that in his opinion at least, it would always be better for the tailor to buy his shoes and his corn, than to make the one, and raise the other, by his own labour; and that the farmer could never be profitably employed in making clothes and shoes.

This doctrine, when rightly explained, is as applicable to nations, as to individuals. The principles which are applicable to individuals, being often applicable to nations; but in order to apply then properly, we must consider nations as individuals, distinct in all their parts, and not as part individual only. The nation must be considered as one and indivisible. Let this be done, and we shall not be embarrassed with individual interests and rights, as contra–distinguished from national rights and interests. Individual interest is perpetually at variance with national interests. Hence the absurdity of supposing that, that which is beneficial to individuals, is also beneficial to the nation. An individual, or a class of the community, may be benefited by being permitted to import goods, free of duty, but it does not necessarily follow, that the nation would be benefited by it.

It may be beneficial to cotton and tobacco-planters, to be permitted to import cotton and woollen cloths for their own consumption, free of duty, from England, because in England they find a market for their produce. They can exchange 'some part of the produce of their own industry', employed in a way in which they 'have some advantage'. As regards the cotton and tobacco-planters, distinct from the nation, they are in the situation of the tailor and shoemaker, who have constant employment in their trades, when it is better for them to buy of each other, the respective products of their labour, than to make for themselves; but taking the whole United States together, as an individual, with a unity of rights and interests, and it may be better for it, to make its own cotton and woollen clothes, than to import them, even at any price; precisely for the same reason, that it is better for the tailor to make his own shoes, when he has nothing else to do, or to employ his unoccupied time in making shoes, than to remain idle, and buy them at any price.
......

The sophistry of Dr. Smith's reasoning consists in a great measure, in his not discriminating between national and individual interests. He considers the interests of some particular class of citizens, as identical with the interests of the nation, when in reality they are, perhaps, directly opposed. This is the only principle upon which it can be maintained, that, 'to give the monopoly of the home market to the product of domestic industry, in any particular art or manufacture must generally be hurtful'. A measure of government may interfere with the private interests of an individual, or a class of individuals; but if at the same time, it promotes in a greater degree, the interests of a larger class of individuals, it will be beneficial to the nation, and will promote national wealth.

But the question, whether the importation of manufactures should be prohibited, or the tariff raised, does not at all depend upon the fact, that they can be procured by the consumer cheaper in foreign countries, than in his own. Buying goods where they may be had cheapest, may be the best policy for some individuals, while buying them where they come dearest, may be the best policy of the nation. Mr. Smith's doctrine cannot be admitted, till he proves, that individual interests are never at variance with national interests.

......

To suppose, as many writers do, that monopoly of the home market, has a tendency to benefit the rich, instead of the poor, is most absurd. A monopoly of the home market for corn, may raise the price of corn to the consumer, it is true, but the effect is more than counterbalanced to the labourer, by the greater demand it creates for labour. Many writers have made the price of commodities, and the price of labour, matters of great importance in political economy; but their absolute, or rather nominal price, is of no importance whatever; – it is only their relative price that can affect the labourer. If a labourer is obliged to give five dollars a bushel for corn, and can, at the same time, get five dollars a day or his work, it is just as well for him, as though he could buy corn for fifty cents a bushel, provided he can, at the same time, get only fifty cents a day for labour. The money price of labour, is a matter of no consequence in any country, neither is the money price of the necessaries of life. The proportion which the price of labour bears to the price of the necessaries of life, is the only important thing, as it regards wages, and a monopoly of the home market, must invariably have a tendency to vary this proportion in favour of labour.

Another important advantage, arising from a monopoly of the home market, is the certainty and stability of the demand for the product of industry. All fluctuations in the demand for either the necessaries or comforts of life, produce want and distress among the labourers, who supply the demand. This nation is at present groaning under the distress, caused by a fluctuation in the demand for the product of labour. The national distress in England, arises from the same cause. The consumption does not equal the production, which, as has already been shown, necessarily produces distress. This is always liable to be the case, when the consumption depends on a foreign market. This market is liable to be interrupted by foreign nations. But this is not the case with a domestic market. In this, the demand is always steady, and usually increasing. It is not liable to be interrupted by foreign nations, so long as a nation maintains its independence.

If the whole product of English industry, was clean consumed annually by the English nation, there would be little or no distress – there would be no fluctuations in the demand for labour. The product of their industry is abundantly sufficient for the comfortable supply of all the people, and if it was all consumed in the country, there would necessarily, a much more equal division of this product take place. But as a part of the people depend on foreign nations, to consume the product of their labour, they are in a great measure, at the mercy of these nations. They may consume their produce, or not, as pleases them best. In proportion as foreign nations stop consuming British manufactures, in that proportion must British subjects be deprived of the means of procuring the necessaries of life.

These are not, however, the only advantages arising from a monopoly of the home market. As such a market tends to augment the quantity of national industry, and of course national wealth, it also tends to make the people more habitually industrious; and habits of industry constitute a portion of national wealth. A man, who is industrious from habit, has a greater capacity for acquiring the necessaries and comforts of life, than one in similar circumstances, with idle habits: so of a nation.

A monopoly of the home market, has the effect of increasing a nation's skill in the arts and sciences, because it affords a motive for improvement in them. Improvement in the arts and sciences, is as effectual a mode of increasing the capacity of a nation, for acquiring the necessaries and comforts of life, as improvement in the cultivation of its land. A skillful mechanic has a greater capacity for acquiring the necessaries and comforts of life, than a man of equal strength, without any mechanic art. A nation, thoroughly skilled in all the arts, possesses a more inexhaustible source of national wealth, than if it possessed mountains of gold; and it would be much better economy for a nation, to impose heavy taxes for the purpose of acquiring such a source of wealth, than for conquering provinces, containing mountains of gold.

The extensiveness of the manufacturing establishments in England, in consequence of which the manufacture is carried on with much more economy – the multitude of people they employ of every age and condition, at wages which barely supply them with the necessaries of life, and not even that, as the public maintains many of them some part of the year as paupers – the superior skill which these people have acquired in many branches of manufacture, render it utterly impossible for the people of this country to enter into competition with the English upon equal terms, and they never will be able to enter into such competition, until they are reduced to the necessity of working as hard and living as poor, as the English labourers, which it is to be hoped will never be their condition. A tariff, therefore, on British manufactures, adequate to counterbalance all these disadvantages, is necessary to enable our countrymen to engage successfully in the manufacture of a great variety of articles. But besides these, they must also be protected against the fluctuations in the market, caused by occasionally throwing into our market the surplus product of British manufacturer, and selling it, sometimes at half its original cost.

In a country where manufactories are so numerous and extensive as in England, there must necessarily be a surplus of production over the regular consumption, in many articles every year. It will be impossible to regulate the supply so exactly to the demand, as to prevent this; and where every branch of industry is pushed to the extreme, that it is in England, there is much more probability of a surplus than a deficiency in the supply. This surplus must be disposed of at some price, and if it only sells for half the original cost, it is better to sell it for that, than to keep it on hand in expectation of being able to throw it into the consumption of the following year at a saving price, and this the English manufacturers understand perfectly well. They, therefore, send this surplus, of which there must always be more or less of some particular articles in every manufactory, to the American market, and sell it at auction, often for one half the prime cost. This temporary supply causes a fluctuation in the American market, and reduces the price of the article below the cost of manufacturing it here, and breaks up our infant manufactories. After this is done, the English manufacturers can remunerate themselves by selling their goods in our market at a fair price, with but little competition from the American manufacturers.

If goods could be manufactured as cheap in this country as in England, a tariff would be necessary to protect the American manufacturer against the fluctuations caused by these irregular supplies.

There is no part of the statute book that requires such frequent revision, as the tariff law, although we sometimes hear it said, that a tariff should be permanent, and seldom, if ever changed; but this is a great error. A year does not pass in which the tariff upon some particular article may not be raised with advantage. The most general rule on this subject is, that a tariff ought not to be reduced, although it may frequently require to be raised. The next most general rule is, that a tariff should be lowest upon those articles which are not, or cannot be produced in the country, and highest upon those which employ the greatest number of people, or the greatest portion of the industry of the country. In pursuance of these two rules, the tariff should be frequently changed, and gradually raised upon different articles of domestic manufacture, as they spring up in the country.

If an existing tariff on a particular article is suddenly reduced, it will have the uniform effect of prostrating, and probably totally destroying that branch of manufacture. The reduction of a tariff is one of the harshest and most violent measures, that a government can possibly adopt. Suppose, the tariff to be reduced twenty per cent, upon some branch of manufacture, which occupied a numerous class of people. What will be the effect? These people probably did not make more than ten percent profit upon the whole amount of goods, they manufactured. This is a liberal allowance for profits on manufactures in any country. By reducing the tariff twenty per cent, the price of the goods would be reduced twenty percent, provided there should be a foreign supply, and of course, unless the American manufacturer used either more industry or more economy, which might not be in his power, he would lose ten per cent on all the goods, he manufactured. He would, therefore, be obliged to abandon his business, or be ruined.

A tariff should be laid with reference to the future beneficial effects it is to produce, rather than to its immediate effects. That is a miserable short-sighted policy, in private economy, and much more so in public, which looks only to the present, and disregards the future – it is killing the goose to get the golden egg. In private life, we look upon him as a wise man, who subjects himself to present privations and hardships, with a view to an ultimate benefit which shall overbalance the hardships. It is accounted wise, for a man, in his youth, to labour hard, and fare hard, that he may enjoy the good things of this life, more abundantly in old age. It is accounted wise for a man to go to great expense in clearing his lands, in building houses, mills, making roads and bridges, with a view to a future augmented product of the necessities and comforts of life. It is accounted wise for a man to spend many years as an apprentice, to learn a trade, which may be a source of wealth in after life. This he does, to increase his capacity for acquiring the necessaries and comforts of life. 'What is wise and prudent in the conduct of every private man, can scarce be folly in that of a great kingdom,' says Adam Smith.

It may be, and often is folly in a legislator, not to be longer-sighted in his schemes, than the wisest private individual. The schemes of the latter can only be adapted to the probable duration of this life, which can only be for a few years at most. The schemes of the former, may be adapted to the life of the nation, to which no limit can be priced. Upon the same principle then, that it is wise for an individual to make calculations, and adopt measures, which look ten or twenty years ahead, it may be wise for a legislator to adopt measures, which look centuries ahead. Although it may be more beneficial for the time being, for a nation to import, than to manufacture its own comforts of life, still that ought not to decide the question. The inquiry should be made, how will it be fifty years hence? Admitting, that for the first five years, domestic manufactures may come at double price, still if in ten, they will come at single price, and in twenty, at half price, we may be very sure that the present extra cost, is money well laid out for the nation, more especially, when it is considered that the annual product of labour cannot be accumulated, but must be annually consumed.

Although a high protecting duty may therefore prevent an individual from enjoying so great a portion of the comforts and luxuries of life, as he might otherwise do, or prevent him from accumulating so much private wealth, still national wealth is not thereby in the least degree diminished at any time.

From this it is not to be inferred that in all cases it would be advisable for government to secure to its own citizens the monopoly of the home trade, either by absolute prohibition of foreign importation, or by high protecting duties. All measures upon this subject should be regulated according to the existing circumstances of the nation; and the first thing to be ascertained is, whether the nation has full employment in its ordinary occupations, or whether the sum of national industry is likely to be augmented by such a measure. A great deal of mischief may be done by an imprudent restriction upon the freedom of trade – it may have the effect to diminish the consumption of the country, which will paralyze, instead of invigorating industry. But when the people of a nation have not fully employment, and a measure of this description will have the effect to give employment to a portion of them, it will promote the general prosperity of the country, and augment national wealth, although it may be adverse to the interests of some individuals.

READING 13

Henry Charles Carey

Biography

Henry Charles Carey (1793–1879), an American social scientist and publicist, was born in Philadelphia.[33] His father, Matthew Carey (1760–1839) had a pervasive influence on his life. The latter was an immigrant from Ireland who had made a name for himself as an unfriendly critic of British policies towards Ireland. In Philadelphia he set up a flourishing publishing firm. In 1819 Matthew organized the 'Philadelphic Society for the promotion of National Industry' which was an extreme pressure group advocating protectionism. George Friedrich List (to be discussed in a subsequent section) who was a founder member of the enormously influential German nationalist school of political economy, had been during his seven-year stay in Pennsylvania (1825–1832) in close personal contact with the Philadelphia group. In his writings Matthew always stressed the need for protective tariffs in order to encourage the American manufacturing industry and enlarge the domestic market for raw materials and for farm products. High tariffs had the additional advantage of injuring England, the country he hated above all.

Henry began his career at the age of eight in his father's firm and by the time he reached his early thirties he had become its head. He remained in that position for ten years. In 1835 he gave up active participation in the company and devoted himself to his other widespread business interests and to his career as a writer on economic matters. His output consists of some 13 volumes and thousands of pages of pamphlet and newspaper material which is a considerable amount for a self-taught writer who began writing rather late in his life. His most important books are:

An Essay on the Rate of Wages (1835)
Principles of Political Economy (1837–40) (3 vols)

---

33 Discussions of Carey's work can be found in: A.D.H. Kaplan, *Henry Charles Carey. A Study in American Economic Thought* (Baltimore: Johns Hopkins University Press, 1931) and E. Teilhac, *Pioneers of American Economic Thought in the Nineteenth Century* (New York: Macmillan, 1936).

The Past, the Present and the Future (1848)
The Harmony of Interests (1851)
The Principles of Social Science (1858–60) (3 vols)

John Stuart Mill commented on his *The Principles of Social Science* that it was the worst book he had ever toiled through. Joseph Schumpeter commented on his entire output that Carey subtracted rather than added to economic analysis. The reasons for these negative comments are not difficult to find. Like Raymond, Carey's work has practically no explanatory merit. His theorizing suffered from his lack of analytic powers, a misreading of American and European history and his strong ideological commitment to the concept of the ultimate harmony of interests. His writings are unsystematic, redundant, repetitious and long-winded.

Carey became well-known in the United States and his reputation as the prophet of protectionism increased during the period of high American tariffs which originated during the Civil War. Carey was also the first American economist to be translated into foreign languages and to acquire an international reputation. His renown was especially great in Germany where his nationalistic and protectionist views were in full harmony with German conditions and thought. It is interesting to observe that Carey had much in common with Thomas Mun (see Reading 1) who was also a wealthy businessman writing on economics. In substance Carey also had close ties with the mercantilists (see his thoughts on Colbert in the next reading) because of his emphasis on nationalism and protectionism.

The Work

Carey's work displays four important characteristics.

1. An optimistic belief in the essential harmony of interests.
2. A deep faith in the concept of association.
3. Opposition to the Ricardian theory of rent and the Malthusian theory of population.
4. Support for permanent protectionism.

Carey strongly rejected the more pessimistic elements in the classical school such as the idea of pressure of population on landed resources, being a cause of poverty and the concept of rising rents. Carey, who often mixes theology with economics feels that such ideas are an insult to the Creator who made a harmonious universe. In his opinion Malthus and Ricardo changed the Lord into a blunderer. In contrast to this Carey proclaimed the idea of 'harmony of interests of all classes of society', which he (and his followers) deemed to be the highest achievement of Carey's thought. Carey held that labor employed in association with capital would become more productive as society progressed and capital accumulated. Labor employing more capital would become increasingly better paid and would receive a constantly greater rate of return. Although the rate of return on capital itself would decline as it accumulated, the larger stock of capital would make the aggregate amount of profits greater thus establishing a harmonious relationship between capital and labor. Carey included cultivable land in capital because he regarded this land as the product of human endeavor. Thus land also became part of the harmonious order of events.

As stated previously, the power of association is very important in Carey's thought. Association is the ability of man to join together with his fellow-men. It is based on the division of labor and it develops the intelligence and individuality. Association is based on difference, it cannot take place to any great extent among people performing the same tasks. Free trade however, leads to specialization and association fails to occur. As a result, according to Carey, people become mindless and dull.

Population growth did not disturb Carey's belief in a harmonious order. Malthus had written that population, unchecked, has a constant tendency to draw level with and even to pass beyond the existing means of subsistence. This law of population was based upon the potential of populations to expand geometrically (or exponentially). Food however could not possibly increase by more than an arithmetic progression. This arithmetic increase was based upon the law of diminishing returns. According to Malthus a great deal of human poverty could thus be explained. Carey, however, considered such ideas to be an insult to the Creator. Carey attacked Malthus by arguing that man's food supplies are of animal and vegetable origin. These lower forms of life can also grow geometrically just like the human race. Carey does not take into account that although plants and animals can increase exponentially they need land to do so and Malthus's argument was based on the premise that land is fixed in supply and subject to diminishing returns. A further argument used by Carey (and here he relied on Herbert Spencer's 'Principles of Biology'), was that with the advance of civilization, man's intellectual and spiritual powers increase while his reproductive powers decline to the point where births and deaths just about balance. Needless to remark that there is no proof that man's reproductive capacity varies inversely with his development.

Carey also challenged Ricardo's theory of rent. Ricardo had argued that as the population grew and food prices rose, inferior grades of land (in terms of fruitfulness and/or location) are brought under cultivation. Since farmers outbid each other for the superior lands, the extra return per unit of labor and capital applied to these lands can be exacted by the landlord in the form of rent. Continued population expansion leads to the cultivation of even less productive areas resulting in the distribution of income becoming still more uneven with the landlord as the major benefiter. As far as Ricardo was concerned free trade in cereals (implying the abolition of the Corn Laws) would help to solve this problem as it tended to destroy the privileged monopoly position of the landed interests.

Carey, with some American examples in mind reversed the Ricardian sequence. Thus he argued that diminishing returns and rising rents are not a problem because in his view cultivation had commenced on the poorer soils. As population grew and society progressed, men acquired the ability to cultivate the richer but more resistant land. With better tools and more people, the better but less accessible land could then be farmed. Consequently, returns would increase and the share of output returned, as land rent would drop, which would take us right back to Carey's harmonious scheme of things. The fact remains, however, that Carey's thinking was deficient. What would happen when the more fertile lands were fully cultivated? With the population still increasing, lower quality lands would have to be used and/or more capital and labor would be applied to land already tilled, resulting in diminishing returns. Differential rent would reappear just as Ricardo predicted.

Carey also rejects free trade in favor of protectionism. Protection encourages domestic commerce and thus association, a phenomenon which ranks high on his list of priorities. Free trade, in his opinion, makes the distribution of income more uneven with merchant princes living in palaces surrounded by slums. In addition, free trade would cause soil exhaustion in countries such as America. Apparently forgetting that there are many ways to refresh the soil, Carey argues that the more agriculture borrows from the soil the more it can return to the land, provided the food producer is not too far removed from the consumer and his refuse. With international trade and agricultural exports, the link between producers and consumers is broken. When the soil becomes exhausted, the food producing country will end up exporting people as Ireland did. Foreign trade also is at the root of business fluctuations as it increases the distance between producers and consumers making the exchange of goods more irregular. Another problem with foreign commerce is that it increases enormously the 'wasteful transportation' of goods which Carey views as a tax to be paid by the exporter, so that in the case of the United States the costs of transportation to foreign countries absorbed the greater share of the farmer's profits.[34] Besides, transportation is morally undesirable. It removes the sailor and the wagon driver from their families while exposing them to the baneful influence of the grogshop and the brothel.

In conclusion Carey mainly favored protection as many others did before and after him because it acted as a shield, reducing dependence upon foreign nations and increasing 'balance' and self-sufficiency. It might be added here that Carey's harmony of interests was in reality a discordant, clashing harmony. If manufacturers were protected by a tariff everybody gained in the process. If other categories of people such as the consumers or users of imported inputs lost, nobody lost. Such was Carey's understanding of harmony. His interpretation of foreign trade was also essentially mercantilist. He saw it as a rather belligerent type of activity whereby one country forced its commodities upon others, not as an exchange in which all participants benefited.[35]

Extracts

From: The Second Letter in Reply to the London Times

In assuming, Mr. Editor, as you seem to do, that I regard protection as especially necessary for new countries, you are much in error. The societary laws are applicable to all countries alike, the great object to be accomplished being the promotion of that domestic commerce held

---

34 Carey actually states the curious (and erroneous) belief that the expenses of transportation increase geometrically as the distance from the market increases arithmetically.

35 The following excerpts are selected from: H.C. Carey, *Letters in Reply to the London Times* (Philadelphia: Collins, 1876), and H.C. Carey, *Letters to the President* (Philadelphia: Polock, 1858).

in so great regard by the illustrious founder of a real economic science.

France on the day of the assembling of the States General, in 1789, had made so little progress in the industrial arts that her markets were crowded with British wares; that her workshops were closed; that her workmen were perishing for want of food; and that the French school of art had almost entirely disappeared. The Few were magnificent – more so, perhaps than any other in Europe. The Many a large majority, were in a state closely akin to serfage, and ignorant almost beyond conception.

The Revolution, however, now coming, the people did for themselves what their masters had refused to do; re-establishing the system of Colbert, the greatest statesman the world has yet seen, and making protection the law of the land. Since then, counsels and kings, emperors and presidents, have flitted across the stage; constitutions almost by the dozen have been adopted; the country has been thrice occupied by foreign armies, and thrice has it been compelled to pay the cost of invasion and occupation; but throughout all these changes it has held to protection as the sheet-anchor of the ship of State. With what result? With that of placing France in the lead of the world in reference to all that is beautiful in industrial and pictorial art. With that of making her more independent, commercially, than any other country of the world. Why is this? For the reason that she enables her artisans to pass over the heads of other nations, scattering everywhere the seeds of that love of the beautiful in which consists a real civilization, and everywhere stimulating while defying competition; Britain, meanwhile, seeking everywhere to stifle competition by means of cheap labor, shoddy cloth, cinder iron, and cottons that, as recently certified to by British merchants in China, lose a third of their weight on their first immersion in the tub.

But a few months since Monsieur Michel Chevalier gave to his English friends an eulogium upon this shoddy system, saying, however, not a word as to the fact, that the tariff for which he claims the credit is the most intelligently, and the most effectively, protective of any in the world; not a word to show how perfectly it had been made to accord with the view presented in his then, as I think, latest work, and which read as follows:

'Every nation owes it to itself to seek the establishment of diversification in the pursuits of its people, as Germany and England have already done in regard to cottons and woollens, and as France herself has done in reference to so many and so widely different departments of industry, this being not an abuse of power on the part of the government. On the contrary, it is the accomplishment of a positive duty which requires it so to act at each epoch in the progress of a nation as to favor the taking possession of all the branches of industry whose acquisition is authorized by the nature of things.'

Prior to the date of the Cobden treaty, 1860, the regime of France, for almost seventy years, had been that of prohibition so nearly absolute as almost to preclude the importation of foreign manufactures of any description whatsoever. Prior to 1861, that of this country had for a like period of time, with two brief and brilliant exceptions, been that of revenue, and almost free-trade, tariffs dictated by subjects of the cotton king holding a full belief in the morality of human slavery, and in a sort of right divine to buy and sell their fellow-men. We have thus two contemporaneous systems differing from each other as light does from darkness, and may here with some advantage study their work as regards the great question now before us, that of civilization. The last four years prior to 1861 were in this country so much disturbed by reason of the great free-trade crisis of 1857 that, desiring to give every advantage to free-trade theorists, I prefer to throw them out, taking for comparison the year 1856, one in which the world at large was rejoicing in the receipt of hundreds of millions of gold from California and Australia; and when, if ever, our Southern States must have been growing rich and strong by means of the policy of which they so long had been the ardent advocates.

In that year the domestic exports of France amounted to $840,000,000, having far more than trebled in twenty-five years; doing this, too, under a system that, as we now are told, must have destroyed the power to maintain any foreign commerce whatsoever. Of those exports, $140,000,000 consisted of textile fabrics weighing 20,000 tons, the equivalent of 100,000 bales of cotton, and sufficient, perhaps, to load some five and twenty of the ships that, as I think, were then in use. The charge for freight was, as may readily be seen, quite insignificant, and for the reason that the chief articles of value were skill and taste, $100,000,000 of which would not balance a single cotton bale. Arrived out, the goods were all finished and ready for consumption; and, as a consequence of these great facts, there were no people retaining for themselves so large a proportion of the ultimate prices of their products as did those of France.

At that date two hundred and fifty years had elapsed since the first settlement of Virginia, and the whole country south of the Potomac, the Ohio, and the Missouri, had then been taken possession of by men of the English race the total population having grown to almost a dozen million. The territory so occupied contained, as I believe, more cultivable land, more coal, and more metallic ores, than the whole of Europe; and it abounded in rivers calculated for facilitating the passage of labor and its products from point to point. What now had become, in 1856, the contribution of this wonderful territory, embracing a full half of the Union, to the commerce of the world? Let us see! The cotton exported amounted to 3,000,000 bales. To this may now be added 100,000 hogsheads of tobacco, the total money value of the exports of this vast territory having been almost precisely $140,000,00 – barely sufficient to pay for the cargoes of five-and-twenty ships, of a joint burden of 20,000 tons, laden with the beautiful fabrics of France.

For the carriage to market of this cotton and tobacco how many ships were required? Thousands! How many seaman? Tens of thousands! Who paid them? The planters! Who paid the charges on the cotton until it reached its final consumer? The planter whose share of the two, three, or five dollars a pound paid for his cotton by his customers in Brazil, Australia, or California, amounted to but a single dime. It may, as I think, be safely asserted that of all people claiming to rank as civilized there have been none who have retained for themselves so small a portion of the ultimate prices of their products as have those who have been accustomed to supply raw cotton to Britain and to France

The first of all taxes is that of transportation, preceding as it does even the demands of government. Of this the Frenchman pays almost literally none, the commodities, taste and skill, which mainly he exports, being to be classed among the imponderables. The planter, on the contrary, gives nine-tenths of the ultimate prices of his products as his portion of the terrific tax, doing so for the reason that he is always exporting, in the forms of cotton and tobacco, the weighty food of mere brute labor, and the most valuable portions of the soil upon which that labor had been expended.

Throughout the world, as here among ourselves, the exporters of raw produce pay all the taxes incident to a separation of consumers from producers, the manufacturing nations profiting by their collection. Hence it is that while the former tend from year to year to become more dependent, the latter tend equally to become more independent, thus furnishing conclusive evidence of growing civilization.

The protected Frenchman, freed from the most oppressive of all taxes, grows in love of the beautiful, in love of freedom, in that love of his native land by which he is everywhere so much distinguished – each and every stage of progress marking growth of real civilization.

The unprotected men of the South, on the contrary, have been so heavily taxed on the road to their ultimate market as to have produced a constantly growing need for abandoning their exhausted lands, and a corresponding growth of belief in human slavery, which is but another word for barbarism.

Since the date above referred to, France and the South have passed through very destructive wars, but how widely different is their present condition; the one being more prosperous than ever before, the other remaining now so much impoverished as to excite the sympathy even of those who had most execrated the men and measures to which the rebellion had been due.

Such, Mr. Editor, have been the results of thorough protection on one side of the ocean and an absence of protection on the other. Choose between them!

From: *The Eleventh Letter to the President of the United States*

All men, Mr. President, desire to maintain commerce with each other – exchanging ideas and services, or commodities, in which those services are embodied. Some men desire to be employed in effecting exchanges for other men – standing between them, in the various capacities of sailor and wagoner, trader and transporter, all of whom are merely instruments to be used by commerce.[36]

The greater the diversity in the employments of society, the greater is the power to maintain commerce, and the less is the necessity for the use of the instruments above referred to – the greater is the tendency towards increase in the productiveness of the soil, the larger is the return to agricultural labor, the higher are the prices of the rude products of the land, the cheaper become those finished commodities required for the use of the farmer and the greater is the tendency towards that improvement of human condition, to which we are

---

36 For Carey commerce was an associative link between producer and consumer. The characteristic of commerce was stability, trade was its opposite. It required middlemen and was essentially spasmodic and thus perverted man and society (ed.).

accustomed to attach the idea of civilization.

The less, Mr. President, the diversity of employments, the greater is the necessity for the service of the ship and the wagon, the trader and transporter – the less is the commerce – the greater is the tendency towards exhaustion of the soil – the smaller is the return to agricultural labor – the lower are the prices of the rude products of the land – the dearer are clothing, knives, axes, and other finished products – and the greater is the tendency towards that deterioration of mans condition to which we are accustomed to attach the idea of barbarism.

......

At the return of peace in 1815, land was high in price – a market having been already made at home, for the most important of its products. Protection being discontinued, that market disappeared, and the result was seen, six years later, in the almost universal ruin of the farmers – judgments being everywhere entered up – mortgages being foreclosed – sheriffs' sales abounding to such an extent as, at length, to force the people of the agricultural states to the adoption of laws for staying the execution of the judgments of their courts-- and land falling to a fourth of the price at which it had sold, but seven years before. The sales of public land, and the revenue therefrom, had trebled in the period from 1814 to 1818–19 thus increasing the number of farmers, at the moment when the market for their products was gradually disappearing – and thus preparing the way for that decline in the price of the products of the farm, whose steady progress is exhibited in the figures already, Mr. President laid before you.[37]

The coal-miner, the smelter of ores, the cotton and woollen manufacturer, and all others engaged in the work of production are, Mr. President, like the farmer in the fact that they need stability and regularity – giving a steady circulation of labor and its products, and increasing their ability to add to the machinery required for their operations. That having been obtained, they are enabled, in each successive year, to profit by the experience of the past, and to give to the farmer a constantly increasing quantity of cloth, in exchange for

---

37 After the Napoleonic Wars imports were resumed, especially from England. In 1816 Congress passed the Tariff Act which was quite protectionist. The average rate of duty during the 5-year period 1816–1820 was about 25 per cent. In 1828 a new Tariff Act was passed greatly increasing the rates of duty. Strong opposition of the South resulted in the Compromise Tariff of 1833 which lowered rates again. Between that date and the early 1860s tariffs were relatively modest (ed.).

a constantly diminishing quantity of food and wool – the prices of the two tending steadily and regularly to approach each other. That stability, and that regularity of circulation, have, however, been to the people of the United States, things entirely unknown.

At times, as in the two periods ending in 1835 and 1847, it has been approached, but in every case, it has proved but a mere lure, for inducing men of skill and enterprise to waste their fortunes, and their time, in the effort to advance the interests of the community, with ruin to themselves.

From 1810 to 1815, mills and furnaces were built, but with the return of peace, their owners – embracing large and small capitalists, working – men and other, the most useful portions of the community were everywhere ruined, and the people who had been employed were turned adrift, to seek in the West the support they could no longer find at home. Land sales then, as we have seen, became large, and, next, the farmer suffered as the manufacturer had done before. From 1828 to 1834, such establishments were again erected, and the metallic treasures of the earth were being everywhere developed; but, as before, the protective system was again abandoned, with ruin to the manufacturer, accompanied by enormous sales of public land, and followed by ruin to the farmer. From 1842 to 1847, mills and furnaces were again constructed; and then, from 1848 to 1850, they were again closed; the effect being seen, in 1850–52, in the fall of flour to a price lower than had ever before been known. The perfect harmony of all true interests, and the absolute necessity for protection to the farmer, in his efforts to bring the artisan to his side and thus relieve himself from the heavy taxation to which he is now subjected, are here exhibited in the strongest light. No one, who studied the regular sequence of these facts, can hesitate as to full belief in that portion of the doctrine of The Wealth of Nations, which teaches, that the English system, based as it is upon the idea of cheapening all the raw materials of manufacture, 'is a manifest violation of the most sacred rights of mankind.'

In the last ten years, few mills or furnaces have been erected – the value of those in existence having been, in general, so far below the cost production, as to have afforded no reason for making any addition to their number.

The history of industry in no civilized country of the world presents such a scene of destruction as is found in the manufacturing, mining, and railroad operations of the Union. Of all the persons concerned in making those great improvements required for diminishing the distance between the consumer and the producer – for enabling the producers of wool, flax, and food readily to exchange for cloth and iron – and for reducing the prices of manufactured commodities, while raising those of the raw products of the earth a large majority have been ruined; and the result is seen in the facts, that the various metals are rising in price, as compared with flour and cotton that our farmers, as a rule, are poor – that, each successive year, the land is being more rapidly exhausted – and, that the country exhibits so many other evidences of declining civilization.

READING 14

Adam Heinrich Muller and Friedrich List

Before discussing Friedrich List a few words should be said about his friend Adam Heinrich Muller (1779–1826) who influenced him a great deal.

Muller was one of the founders and leading representatives of the so-called German Romantic School of Political Economy. The romantic movement began in the late eighteenth century and embraced art and literature as well as social thought. The movement was mainly confined to intellectuals, writers, artists and poets. In literature, romanticism reacted against rationalized convention and reason. In social thought romanticism opposed the ideals of the Renaissance and the Enlightenment, and rejected the concepts of natural law as well as those of liberalism, internationalism, rationalism, individualism and materialism. Romanticism must by definition repudiate rationalism and free scientific inquiry because rational analysis tends to destroy romantic illusions. It is no accident that the movement originated in Germany because the Napoleonic Wars had created great hardship in many German States. Romanticism and irrationalism always tend to receive a great stimulus from economic destitution and adversity as in times of great deprivation people tend to lose faith in the power of human reason. The fact that Germany was both politically and economically far behind countries such as France and England probably helps to account for the belated reappearance of philosophical battles which had already been decided on in other parts of Europe. Similar to socialism, which emerged later, romanticism was very much confined to intellectuals and can be thought of as an intellectual movement of anti-intellectualism.

Muller was born in Berlin, where he studied theology and

subsequently law and political science at the University of Göttingen. It was there he was taught to dislike rational thought. His best known book *The Elements of Politics* (*Die Elemente der Staatskunst*) appeared in 1809. In 1805 he was received into the Roman Catholic Church (a symbol of authority and tradition) and as Muller grew older his ideas became increasingly colored by Catholic thought. Through friends he became acquainted with the reactionary Austrian Minister of Foreign Affairs, Metternich. The latter appointed Muller to important positions within the Treasury and later as an observer at various international congresses. As an assistant and an advisor Muller helped Metternich in his work of oppression and intrigue.

In his writings Muller opposes the principles of liberalism and freedom with that of authority. Progress is contrasted with the value of tradition, while the idea of individual liberty is presented as hostile to the principle of binding ties to the state. Muller had a mystical view of the state. He also had a totalitarian outlook. The highest realization of community life, in his opinion, was the natural state. This state was to be regarded as an organism. The individuals living in a country were the cells of that organism and could not be thought of as living outside the totality of the state. The state stands between the past and the future. It allows a connection between past, contemporary and future generations thus binding society together through time. The state therefore is an end in itself and individuals should seek happiness in subordinating their interests to those of the state.[38] This conception of the state explains why Muller regarded the political and social organization of the Middle Ages as an ideal and why he suggested their restoration. In his opinion the Middle Ages offered an example of the ideal organic state with its authoritarian order of society and traditional hierarchy.

Muller's political and social views provided the foundations of his economic ideas in which the cameralist and nationalist elements are only too obvious. Muller rejected free enterprise and competition, because in his opinion they generated disorder and loosened traditional personal ties. Like Fichte he objected to free trade and preferred protection and economic self-sufficiency as a means of solidifying national unity. Free trade makes people citizens of the world and therefore weakens national cohesion, a perfect nightmare for an ardent

---

38 With such views it is not difficult to understand why the Nazis considered Muller as one of their ideological ancestors.

nationalist like Muller.

Muller's economic nationalism was reinforced by his monetary nationalism. His view of money is again mystical. He sees money only as being the economic form of union between men and state. He opposed both the use of gold and silver money and the adherence to some form of the silver or gold standard, on the grounds that bullion is cosmopolitan. It tends to destroy the link between man and his national state. Therefore Muller preached the virtues of inconvertible paper money because it was national. Paper money, a product of the issuing state, tied men closely to the state.

On the issue of international relations, Muller was even more outspoken than most mercantilists before him. The positive side of war, in his view, was that it created or reinforced national cohesion. Perpetual peace could not be an ideal in politics. Peace and war should supplement each other like rest and motion.

Though we may smile at the jungle of nebulous verbiage of Muller and his likes, in terms of influence Muller has been very important. This writer influenced Friedrich List as well as members of the historical school and the later so-called state socialists. The historical school and the state socialists in their turn have prompted through their writings and advice, a great deal of late nineteenth century legislation and political action in which Muller (and List) are clearly recognizable.

Friedrich List

Biography

Friedrich List 1789–1846 was born in the free town of Reutlingen in the state of Wurtemberg. His father was a prosperous tanner. List's early life was unremarkable. At an early age he was appointed to a clerkship in the city of Tubingen where he began to attend law lectures at the university. In 1814 he passed the actuaries examination and re-entered the administration as an accountant. By 1816 he had risen to the post of Ministerial Undersecretary. A year later he accepted a professorship in administration and politics at the University of Tubingen but his dissident political views caused his dismissal in 1819. In fact List used his professorship to attack the bureaucratic routine of the civil service in Wurtemberg. During the same period he had been involved in the publication of a reformist journal advocating change. Upon his dismissal from the university he became counsel to the 'German Commercial and Industrial Union' an association of manufacturers that he had helped to found. The association, which represented producers' interests (and not consumers' interests), wanted free trade for the whole of Germany and strong protection at the borders of the free trade area.

In 1820 he became a deputy of Reutlingen in the Parliament of Wurtemberg. There List took a Liberal line and advocated such reforms as the elimination of tolls on roads and feudal burdens resting on the land. He sought to introduce trial by jury and favored a reduction in the number of civil servants as well as the sale of some public domains. This brought him into conflict with the reactionary government. He was expelled from Parliament and sentenced to jail. Finally the Wurtemberg government agreed to allow him his liberty on condition that he left the country. List consented and eventually emigrated to the United States where he resided from 1825 to 1832. There he became involved with another manufacturers association – the 'Pennsylvania Society for the Promotion of Manufactures and the Mechanic Arts' – which was then the leading protectionist organization in the United States. List also acquainted himself with the ideas of Alexander Hamilton, the two Careys (father and son), and Raymond. At the request of the 'Pennsylvania Society' he wrote his first work 'Outlines of American Political Economy' (1827). He also became a coal mine and railways promoter.

List's period of residence in America deeply colored his economic views. He regarded the tariff controversy in the US as an excellent laboratory. It was during this period that the 'Tariff of Abominations' was passed by Congress (1828).

List took part in American political affairs and became the friend of Andrew Jackson. When the latter became President he named List as United States Consul in Leipzig. Upon his return to Germany he found that the tariff movement for which he had struggled earlier, had made rapid progress. In 1834 the economic union of Germany (Zollverein) was accomplished and a large domestic market had been created. However it was Prussia and not Austria (as List had hoped) which was to be the leader of the movement. As a result, the relatively low Prussian tariff of 10% was adopted as the common outside tariff. This was not to the taste of many manufacturers such as the iron-smelters and the flax spinners who wanted more protection. It was at this point that List became the theoretical spokesman of protection. Between 1837 and 1840 he stayed mostly in Paris reworking his theoretical system. Finally in 1841 he published his

National System of Political Economy. The book appeared at an opportune moment. In this work List expounded a theory of protection particularly suited to the demands of the youthful German industry. Following the publication of the book List settled permanently in Germany to continue his colorful career. In 1846 financial failures, ill-health and thwarted political ambitions led him to commit suicide at Kufstein in Tyrol where he had gone for a rest.

The Work

Like other writers, List was influenced by the environment in which he moved. Even in 1815 Germany was still a conglomeration of princedoms. Each individual state possessed a national currency and enforced obstructionist trade regulations towards other German states. To the outside world, however, the German states were not a closed unit – which resulted in heavy imports from England. It should also be remembered that List's book was written before 1844. The corn laws, the navigation laws and the generally protectionist tariff of Great Britain were still in existence.

List is difficult to summarize and sometimes hard to understand because there is always an admixture of a classical Liberal, a demagogue, a political reformer and a mercantilist in his make-up. This explains why his criticism of the economics of the classical group is often unmeasured. He criticized their teachings as the outcome of boundless cosmopolitanism, dead materialism and individualism as well as of false terminology. Classical writers, he argued, had failed to recognize the significance of the nation as the most important link between the individual and the human family. Economists such as Adam Smith looked at an imaginary world of peace and harmony whereas in reality, nations exist, going to war with each other and taking advantage of each other when they can. In such a world argues List, the principle of free trade cannot succeed. Actually it is far from clear whether List understood the teachings of the classicals. This applies especially to the comparative cost doctrine as stated by David Ricardo. Ricardo is only mentioned in relation to the theory of rent.

List also criticized the classical liberals for concentrating on the level of real income of individuals at the expense of the power to produce income. In fact List regarded the productive powers of a nation as being far more important than the level of income or output itself. This concept of productive powers, the core of List's argument, provided List with an effective instrument with which to defend the principle of protectionism.[39] For List, neither free trade nor protectionism was an end in itself but merely a means to achieve the greatest possible development of a nation's productive forces. In a sense one could argue that List set up a mercantilist framework in which the concept of productive powers (or industrial development) took the place of the older idea of a favorable balance of trade. These powers included not only manufactures and infrastructure but also human skills, intelligence, morality, thrift, suitable institutions and laws, arts and science, security for person and property, justice and even colonies (p.137). To develop these productive forces behind the shelter of protective duties was, according to List, the primary task of economic policy.

List also popularized the idea of stages in economic development which helped him to defend the 'need' for protection. Nations according to List may pass through the following five stages:

1. the hunting–fishing stage;
2. the pastoral stage;
3. the agricultural stage;
4. the agricultural and manufacturing stage;
5. the agricultural–manufacturing–commercial stage.[40]

The stages represent a continuous advancement in prosperity, power and civilization. National economic policies had to be designed to permit the nation state to move from a lower to higher phase of economic development. Up to stage three, free trade might be the appropriate policy. Free trade with more advanced nations would help the less developed countries to raise themselves from a state of 'barbarism' and make advances in agriculture. Once in phase three with some industry already emerging, nations should resort to a lengthy period of protectionism. England provided the best example of a country which had gone through the entire process and had

---

39 List borrowed the concept of productive powers from Daniel Raymond and also from a French writer by the name of Charles Dupin who defined productive forces as the combined forces of men, animals and nature applied to the work of agriculture, industry and commerce. The title of Dupin's book is *Situation Progressive des Forces de France* (1827) See: C. Gide, C. Rist, *A History of Economic Doctrines* (Boston: Heath, 1947), p. 286. List quotes Dupin approvingly (p. 375).

40 'Commercial' meant that the nation was actively involved in foreign trade.

reached the high point of economic development. Her manufactures were full-grown and she actively participated in world trade. Other countries such as America and Germany were in stage three or four and had the necessary materials and human resources to reach the highest stage. But in order to attain the ultimate phase of economic progress against competition from the more advanced countries (England), active government intervention in the form of appropriate protective policies was called for. Manufacturing industries do not arise spontaneously. Full-scale industrialization was to be achieved with the help of 'educational' tariffs protecting the 'infant' industries of the developing country.[41] Once the last phase is attained however and the country's productive forces have fully matured, the nation must gradually revert to free trade, said List. At this point free trade has to prevail to keep out indolence and to act as a spur to further progress.

List thought that the countries of the tropical zone did not have the gifts necessary to become manufacturing nations. In a tropical climate the appropriate intellectual and physical efforts cannot be made. Therefore these countries should remain on a free trade basis and exchange their tropical products for the manufactured goods produced by the countries in the temperate zone.

List also believed that disparity in stages of development often leads to inferiority and subjection (pp.127–131). Without industrial development, nations like Germany will be forever 'reduced' to supply mature nations such as England with farm products and raw materials.

The essence of the so-called infant industry argument is that young industries including navigation and fisheries often start with a cost disadvantage.[42] With protection this cost advantage may be overcome in the course of time.

---

41 List never mentions the term 'infant industries' (see next footnote) although in the literature the contention is often referred to as the 'infant industry argument'. The term 'infant manufacture' appears once in Hamilton's report. Raymond has used the term 'infant manufactories' at least once.

42 A French author by the name of J. A. Chaptal was probably one of the very first to use the term 'infant industries'. Thus he says in his *De L'Industrie Française* (1819) 'everywhere we feel that infant industries cannot struggle against older establishments cemented by time, supported by much capital, freed from worry and carried on by a number of trained, skilled workman, without having recourse to prohibition in order to overcome the competition of foreign industries'. It is certain that List was familiar with this author (see p. 375). Gide, Rist, *A History of … ,* p. 375.

When List states that once the last phase of economic evolution is attained a return to free trade is the best possible policy, he obviously talks like a classical liberal. However, his work is also filled with considerations which are totally mercantilistic in nature. List stresses repeatedly that the world of his days was not a peaceful world but a world of nation states with conflicting interests trying to wrest advantages from each other. Prosperity and power always go together according to List. Small countries like Holland or the Italian republics lacked a sufficient power base. As a result the bigger powers snatched away the commercial benefits they once enjoyed. Industrialization is often referred to as a necessary component of a true power base. Protective tactics are needed by nations such as Germany to build up their economies enabling them to defend their very existence. A country without an industrial apparatus always runs the risk of being reduced to an inferior status according to List (pp.130–131). England is often described as a country trying to keep the others down (p. 189). Policy makers in Britain designed the English navigation laws, the corn laws and the generally protective tariffs to prevent other nations from developing their productive powers, while English philosophers like Adam Smith lectured these same nations to adopt free trade so that England could continue to flood their markets with manufactured commodities. List apparently did not understand that writers such as Hume and Smith opposed most of the protective legislation still in existence in their country.

List is also a colonialist in the sense that he considers colonialism to be a normal phenomenon for a European nation approaching maturity (Ch. 15).

In addition List is to be suspected of imperialist inclinations when he argues that Germany in order to attain the last phase of full maturity needed an enlargement of territory (Ch. 15). Germany required 'natural' frontiers in the form of mountains, seas and rivers which made the incorporation of countries such as Belgium, Switzerland and the Netherlands into a German union desirable. List does not advocate military conquest but rather voluntary unification. The question remains what was supposed to happen when the countries mentioned wanted to remain independent? There is also a possibility that later on more belligerent minds have used his main idea to justify military expansion. In the twentieth century Germany did in fact occupy three out of the four nations mentioned.

Finally one finds in List's writings the beginning of the so-called 'white man's burden' type of argument (p. 419). Asia, List argues, is so worn and corrupted that regeneration can only come about by a transplantation of European institutions and morals supplemented by immigration from European nations. Thus, Europe is destined to take the whole of Asia under its guardianship and to diffuse its institutions, civilization and population over the entire region. This type of argument was further developed by the imperialist writers of the late nineteenth century.

In short List believed that countries which are young in terms of industrial and technical evolution cannot afford to follow free trade policies. Instead, they should adopt a protectionist course to stimulate national industrial growth. However List forgets that the different nations of the West were, in his days, the common heirs of a basic technology of industrial production, transportation and communication. This situation tended to synchronize their economic and industrial development much more than List supposed. Economic nationalism would only disrupt this correspondence.[43]

Extracts

Having attained to a certain grade of development by means of free trade, the great monarchies perceived that the highest degree of civilization, power, and wealth can only be attained by a combination of manufactures and commerce with agriculture. They perceived that their newly established native manufactures could never hope to succeed in free competition with the old and long established manufactures of foreigners; that their native fisheries and native mercantile marine, the foundations of their naval power, could never make successful progress without special privileges; and that the spirit of enterprise of their native merchants would always be kept down by the overwhelming reserves of capital, the greater experience and sagacity of the foreigners. Hence they sought, by a system of restrictions, privileges, and encouragements, to transplant on to their native soil the wealth, the talents, and the spirit of enterprise of the foreigners. This policy was pursued with greater or lesser, with speedier or more tardy success, just in proportion as the measures adopted were more or less judiciously adapted to the object in view, and applied and pursued with more or less energy and perseverance.

43 Source: F. List, *The National System of Political Economy* (New York: A. Kelley Publishers). Reprint of 1885 edition.

England, above all other nations, has adopted this policy.

......

The North American free states, who, more than any other nation before them, are in a position to benefit by freedom of trade, and influenced even from the very cradle of their independence by the doctrines of the cosmopolitan school, are striving more than any other nation to act on that principle. But owing to wars with Great Britain, we find this nation twice compelled to manufacture at home the goods which it previously purchased under free trade from other countries, and twice, after the conclusion of peace, brought to the brink of ruin by free competition with foreigners, and thereby admonished of the fact that under the present conditions of the world every great nation must seek the guarantees of its continued prosperity and independence, before all other things, in the independent and uniform development of its own powers and resources.

......

The popular school has assumed as being actually in existence a state of things which has yet to come into existence. It assumes the existence of a universal union and a state of perpetual peace, and deduces therefrom the great benefits of free trade. In this manner it confounds effects with causes. Among the provinces and states which are already politically united, there exists a state of perpetual peace thus maintained that the commercial union has become so beneficial to them. All examples which history can show are those in which the political union has led the way, and the commercial union has followed. Not a single instance can be adduced in which the latter has taken the lead, and the former has grown up from it. That, however, under the existing conditions of the world, the result of general free trade would not be a universal republic, but, on the contrary, a universal subjection of the less advanced nations to the supremacy of the predominant manufacturing, commercial, and naval power, is a conclusion for which the reasons are very strong and, according to our views, irrefutable.

......

The system of protection, inasmuch as it forms the only means of placing those nations which are far behind in civilization on equal terms with the one predominating nation (which, however, never received a perpetual right to a monopoly of manufacture at the hands of Nature, but which merely gained an advance over others in point of time), the system of protection regarded from this point of view appears to be the most efficient means of furthering the final union of nations, and hence also of promoting true freedom of trade. And national economy appears from this point of view to be that science which, correctly appreciating the existing interests and the individual circumstances of nations, teaches how every separate nation can be raised to that stage of industrial development in which union with other nations equally well developed, and consequently freedom of trade, can become possible and useful to it.

......

It would be most unjust, even on cosmopolitical grounds, now to resign to the English all the wealth and power of the earth, merely because by them the political system of commerce was first established and the cosmopolitical principle for the most part ignored. In order to allow freedom of trade to operate naturally, the less advanced nations must first be raised by artificial measures to that state of cultivation to which the English nation has been artificially elevated. In order that, through that cosmopolitical tendency of the powers of production to which we have alluded, the more distant parts of the world may not be benefited and enriched before the neighbouring European countries, those nations which feel themselves to be capable, owing to their moral, intellectual, social, and political circumstances, of developing a manufacturing power of their own must adopt the system of protection as the most effectual means for this purpose.

......

The nation derives its productive power from the mental and physical powers of the individuals; from their social, municipal, and political conditions and institutions; from the natural resources placed at its disposal, or from the instruments it possesses as the material products of former mental and bodily exertions (material, agricultural, manufacturing, and commercial capital.

......

The power of producing wealth is therefore infinitely more important than wealth itself; it insures not only the possession and the increase of what has been gained, but also the replacement of what has been lost. This is still more the case with entire nations (who cannot live out of mere rentals) than with private individuals. Germany has been devastated in every century by pestilence, by famine, or by civil or foreign wars; she has, nevertheless, always retained a great portion of her powers of production, and has thus quickly reattained some degree of prosperity; while rich and mighty but despot-and priest-ridden Spain, notwithstanding her comparative enjoyment of internal peace, has sunk deeper into poverty and misery.

......

The nation must sacrifice and give up a measure of material property in order to gain culture, skill, and powers of united production; it must sacrifice some present advantages in order to insure to itself future ones. If, therefore, a manufacturing power developed in all its branches forms a fundamental condition of all higher advances in civilization, material prosperity, and political power in every nation (a fact which, we think, we have proved from history); if it be true (as we believe we can prove) that in the present conditions of the world a new unprotected manufacturing power cannot possibly be raised under free competition with a power which has long since grown in strength and is protected on its own territory; how can anyone possibly undertake to prove by arguments only based on the mere theory of values, that a nation ought to buy its goods like individual merchants, at places where they are to be had the cheapest – that we act foolishly if we manufacture anything at all which can be got cheaper from abroad – that we ought to place the industry of the nation at the mercy of the self-interest of individuals – that protective duties constitute monopolies, which are granted to the individual home manufacturers at the expense of the nation? It is true that protective duties at first increase the price of manufactured goods; but it is just as true, and moreover acknowledged by the prevailing economical school, that in the course of time, by the nation being enabled to build up a completely developed manufacturing power of its own, those goods are produced more cheaply at home than the price at which they can be imported from foreign parts. If, therefore, a sacrifice of value is caused by protective duties, it is made good by the gain of a power of production, which not only secures to the nation an infinitely greater amount of material goods, but also industrial independence in case of war. Through industrial independence and the internal prosperity derived from it the nation obtains the means for successfully carrying on foreign trade and for extending its mercantile marine; it increases its civilization, perfects its institutions internally, and strengthens its external powers.

......

A nation which only carries on agriculture, is an individual who in his material production lacks one arm. Commerce is merely the medium of exchange between the agricultural and the manufacturing power, and between their separate branches. A nation which exchanges agricultural products for foreign manufactured goods is an individual with one arm, which is supported by a foreign arm. This support may be useful to it, but not so useful as if it possessed two arms itself, and this because its activity is dependent on the caprice of the foreigner. In possession of a manufacturing power of its own, it can produce as many provisions and raw materials as the home manufacturers can consume; but if dependent upon foreign manufacturers, it can merely produce as much surplus as foreign nations do not care to produce for themselves, and which they are obliged to buy from another country.

As between the different districts of one and the same country, so does the division of labour and the co-operation of the productive powers operate between the various nations of the earth. The former is conducted by internal or national, the latter by international commerce. The international co-operation of productive powers is, however, a very imperfect one, inasmuch as it may be frequently interrupted by wars, political regulations, commercial crises, etc. Although it is the most important in one sense, inasmuch as by it the various nations of the earth are connected with one another, it is nevertheless the least important with regard to the prosperity of any separate nation which is already far advanced in civilization. This is admitted by writers of the popular school, who declare that the home market of a nation is without comparison more important than its foreign market. It follows from this, that it is the interest of every great nation to make the national confederation of its productive powers the main object of its exertions, and to consider their international confederation as second in importance to it.

......

The popular school betrays an utter misconception of the nature of national economical conditions if it believes that such nations can promote and further their civilization, their prosperity, and especially their social progress, equally well by the exchange of agricultural products for manufactured goods, as by establishing a manufacturing power of their own. A mere agricultural nation can never develop to any considerable extent its home and foreign commerce, its inland means of transport, and its foreign navigation, increase its population in due proportion to their well-being, or make notable progress in its moral, intellectual, social, and political development: it will never acquire important political power, or be placed in a position to influence the cultivation and progress of less advanced nations and to form colonies of its own. A mere agricultural state is an infinitely less perfect institution than an agricultural–manufacturing state. The former is always more or less economically and politically dependent on those foreign nations which take from it agricultural products in exchange for manufactured goods. It cannot determine for itself how much it will produce; it must wait and see how much others will buy from it. These latter, on the contrary (the agricultural–manufacturing states), produce for themselves large quantities of raw materials and provisions, and supply merely the deficiency by importation from the purely agricultural nations. The purely agricultural nations are thus in the first place dependent for their power of effecting sales on the chances of a more or less plentiful harvest in the agricultural–manufacturing nations; in the next place they have to compete in these sales with other purely agricultural nations, whereby their power of sale, in itself very uncertain, thus becomes still more uncertain. Lastly, they are exposed to the danger of being totally ruined in their trading with foreign manufacturing nations, or new foreign manufacturing nations or new foreign tariff regulations whereby they suffer the double disadvantage of finding no buyers for their surplus agricultural products, and of failing to obtain supplies of the manufactured goods which they require. An agricultural nation is, as we have already stated, an individual with one arm, who makes use of a foreign arm, but who cannot make sure of the use of it in all cases; an agricultural–manufacturing nation is an individual who has two arms of his own always at his disposal.

. . . .

If the school maintains that protective duties secure to the home manufacturers a monopoly to the disadvantage of the home consumers, in so doing it makes use of a weak argument. For as every individual in the nation is free to share in the profits of the home market which is thus secured to native industry, this is in no respect a private monopoly, but a privilege, secured to all those who belong to our nation, as against those who nationally belong to foreign nations, and which is the more righteous and just inasmuch as those who nationally belong to foreign nations, possess themselves the very same monopoly, and those who belong to us are merely thereby put on the same footing with them. It is neither a privilege to the exclusive advantage of the producers, nor to the exclusive disadvantage of the consumers; for if the producers at first obtain higher prices, they run great risks, and have to contend against those considerable losses and sacrifices which are always connected with all beginnings in manufacturing industry. But the consumers have ample security that these extraordinary profits shall not reach unreasonable limits, or become perpetual, by means of the competition at home which follows later on, and which, as a rule, always lowers prices further than the level at which they had steadily ranged under the free competition of the foreigner. If the agriculturists, who are the most important consumers to the manufacturers, must also pay higher prices, this disadvantage will be amply repaid to them by increased demands for agricultural products, and by increased prices obtained for the latter.

......

Statistics and history, however, teach, on the contrary, that the necessity for the intervention of legislative power and administration is everywhere more apparent, the further the economy of the nation is developed. As individual liberty is in general a good thing so long only as it does not run counter to the interests of society, so is it reasonable to hold that private industry can only lay claim to unrestricted action so long as the latter consists with the well-being of the nation. But whenever the enterprise and activity of individuals does not suffice for this purpose, or in any case where these might become injurious to the nation, there does private industry rightly require support from the whole power of the nation, there ought it for the sake of its own interest to submit to legal restrictions.

......

The system of the school suffers, as we have already shown in the preceding chapters, for three main defects: firstly, from boundless cosmopolitanism, which neither recognizes the principle of nationality, nor takes into consideration the satisfaction of its interests; secondly, from a dead materialism, which everywhere regards chiefly the mere exchangeable value of things without taking into consideration the mental and political, the present and the future interests, and the productive powers of the nation; thirdly, from a disorganizing particularism and individualism, which, ignoring the nature and character of social labour and the operation of the union of powers in their higher consequences, considers private industry only as it would develop itself under a state of free interchange with society (i.e. with the whole human race) were that race not divided into separate national societies.

Between each individual and entire humanity, however, stands THE NATION, with its special language and literature, with its peculiar origin and history, with its special manners and customs, laws and institutions, with the claims of all these for existence, independence, perfection, and continuance for the future, and with its separate territory; a society which, united by a thousand ties of mind and of interests, combines itself into one independent whole, which recognizes the law of right for and within itself, and in its united character is still opposed to other societies of a similar kind in their national liberty, and consequently can only under the existing conditions of the world maintain self-existence and independence by its own power and resources. As the individual chiefly obtains by means of the nation and in the nation mental culture, power of production, security, and prosperity, so is the civilization of the human race only conceivable and possible by means of the civilization and development of the individual nations.

Meanwhile, however, an infinite difference exists in the condition and circumstances of the various nations: we observe among them giants and dwarfs, well-formed bodies and cripples, civilized, half-civilized, and barbarous nations; but in all of them, as in the individual human being, exists the impulse of selfpreservation, the striving for improvement which is implanted by nature. It is the task of politics to civilize the barbarous nationalities, to make the small and weak ones great and strong, but, above all, to secure to them existence and continuance. It is the task of national economy to accomplish the economical development of the nation, and to prepare it for admission into the universal society of the future.

A nation in its normal state possesses one common language and literature, a territory endowed with manifold natural resources, extensive, and with convenient frontiers and a numerous population. Agriculture, manufactures, commerce, and navigation must be all developed in it proportionately; arts and sciences, educational establishments, and universal cultivation must stand in it on an equal footing with material production. Its constitution, laws, and institutions must afford to those who belong to it a high degree of security and liberty, and must promote religion, morality, and prosperity; in a word, must have the well-being of its citizens as their object. It must possess sufficient power on land and at sea to defend its independence and to protect its foreign commerce. It will possess the power of beneficially affecting the civilization of less advanced nations, and by means of its own surplus population and of their mental and material capital to found colonies and beget new nations. By its Zollverein the German nation first obtained one of the most important attributes of its nationality. But this measure cannot be considered complete so long as it does not extend over the whole coast, from the mouth of the Rhine to the frontier of Poland, including Holland and Denmark. A natural consequence of this union must be the admission of both these countries into the German Bund, and consequently into the German nationality, whereby the latter will at once obtain what it is now in need of, namely, fisheries and naval power, maritime commerce and colonies. Besides, both these nations belong, as respects their descent and whole character, to the German nationality. The burden of debt with which they are oppressed is merely a consequence of their unnatural endeavours to maintain themselves as independent nationalities, and it is in the nature of things that this evil should rise to a point when it will become intolerable to those two nations themselves, and when incorporation with a larger nationality must seem desirable and necessary to them.

Belgium can only remedy by means of confederation with a neighbouring larger nation her needs which are inseparable from her restricted territory and population.

......

If, on the other hand, Germany could constitute itself with the maritime territories which appertain to it, with Holland, Belgium, and Switzerland, as a powerful commercial and political whole – if this mighty national body could fuse representative institutions with the existing monarchical, dynastic, and aristocratic interests, so far as these are compatible with one another – then Germany could secure peace to the continent of Europe for a long time, and at the same time constitute herself the central point of a durable Continental alliance.

......

As respects their economy, nations have to pass through the following states of development: original barbarism, pastoral condition, agricultural conditions, agricultural–manufacturing condition, and agricultural–manufacturing–commercial condition.

The industrial history of nations, and of none more clearly than that of England, proves that the transition from the savage state to the pastoral one, from the pastoral to the agricultural, and from agriculture to the first beginnings in manufacture and navigation, is effected most speedily and advantageously by means of free commerce with further advanced towns and countries, but that a perfectly developed manufacturing industry, an important mercantile marine, and foreign trade on a really large scale, can only be attained by means of the interposition of the power of the State.

The less any nation's agriculture has been perfected, and the more its foreign trade is in want of opportunities of exchanging the excess of native agricultural products and raw materials for foreign manufactured goods, the deeper that the nation is still sunk in barbarism and fitted only for an absolute monarchical form of government and legislation, the more will free trade (i.e. the exportation of agricultural products and the importation of manufactured goods) promote its prosperity and civilization.

On the other hand, the more that the agriculture of a nation, its industries, and its social, political, and municipal conditions, are thoroughly developed, the less advantage will it be able to derive from the improvement of its social conditions, from the exchange of native agricultural products and raw material for foreign manufactured goods, and the greater disadvantages will it experience from the successful competition of a foreign manufacturing power superior to its own.

Solely in nations of the latter kind, namely those which possess all the necessary mental and material conditions and means for establishing a manufacturing power of their own, and of thereby attaining the highest degree of civilization, and development of material prosperity and political power, but which are retarded in their progress by the competition of a foreign manufacturing power which is already farther advanced than their own – only in such nations are commercial restrictions justifiable for the purpose of establishing and protecting their own manufacturing power; and even in them it is justifiable only until that manufacturing power is strong enough no longer to have any reason to fear foreign competition, and thenceforth only so far as may be necessary for protecting the inland manufacturing power in its very roots.

......

In Adam Smith's time, a new maxim was for the first time added to those which we have above stated, namely, to conceal the true policy of England under the cosmopolitical expressions and arguments which Adam Smith had discovered, in order to induce foreign nations not to imitate that policy.

It is a very common clever device that when anyone has attained the summit of greatness, he kicks away the ladder by which he had climbed up, in order to deprive others of the means of climbing up after him. In this lies the secret of the cosmopolitical doctrine of Adam Smith, and of the cosmopolitical tendencies of his great contemporary William Pitt, and of all his successors in the British Government administrations.

Any nation which by means of protective duties and restrictions on navigation has raised her manufacturing power and her navigation to such a degree of development that no other nation can sustain free competition with her, can do nothing wiser than to throw away these ladders of her greatness, to preach to other nations the benefits of free trade, and to declare in penitent tones that she has hitherto wandered in the path of error, and has now for the first time succeeded in discovering the truth.

William Pitt was the first English statesman who clearly perceived in what way the cosmopolitical theory of Adam Smith could be properly made use of, and not in vain did he himself carry about a copy of the work on the Wealth of Nations.

......

It is a conclusion long arrived at by all thoughtful men, that a nation so thoroughly undermined in her religious, moral, social, and political foundations as Turkey is, is like a corpse, which may indeed be held up for a time by the support of the living, but must none the less pass into corruption. The case is quite the same with Persians as with the Turks, with the Chinese and Hindoos and all other Asiatic peoples. Wherever the smoldering civilization of Asia comes into contact with the fresh atmosphere of Europe, it falls to atoms; and Europe will sooner or later find herself under the necessity of taking the whole of Asia under her care and tutelage, as already India has been so taken in charge by England. In this utter chaos of countries and peoples there exists no single nationality which is either worthy or capable of maintenance and regeneration. Hence the entire dissolution of the Asiatic nationalities appears to be inevitable, and a regeneration of Asia only possible by means of an infusion of European vital power, by the general introduction of the Christian religion and of European moral laws and order, by European immigration, and the introduction of European systems of government.

READING 15

The German Historical School and Adolph Wagner

The Historical School

We noticed earlier that classical economics never really took root in nineteenth century Germany. One reason for this was, that it took for granted a degree of individual freedom and initiative which was lacking in Germany. In the German States and Princedoms there existed only a small segment of free enterprise while economic life was for the large part regulated by bureaucracies which usually applied cameralistic principles. Thus, the political, economic and intellectual climate of the first half of the nineteenth century definitely favored the creation of the so-called Historical School.

The German Historical School of Economics developed as a logical sequence to romantic thinking and in opposition to classical economics. Fichte, Muller and List are the precursors of this school. This heritage gave it its anti-individualistic tendency. It also lent the Historical School its anticosmopolitan, nationalist flavor. There existed however other intellectual influences which explain the contents of German historical economic scholarship. German scholars such as Friedrich Karl von Savigny (1779–1861), who taught jurisprudence at the University of Berlin, had already introduced the historical method in law. His purpose was to find a historical explanation and justification for the institutions and laws as they existed in Germany. Savigny wanted to prove the legitimacy of those laws and institutions despite the pretensions of rationalist reformers. Reformist codification in the light of rationalism and natural law had to be opposed. As a result of his successful efforts, the restraining influence of the natural law concept vanished almost completely from German jurisprudence.[44]

Another development outside economics was the overwhelming dominance of Hegelian philosophy among German universities. George Wilhelm Friedrich Hegel (1770–1831) also taught in Berlin, taking over the chair formerly held by Fichte. Society and culture were to be understood by the study of history in a philosophical fashion. History was seen as a kind of rational evolutionary process which unfolds inexorably and mechanically, revealing the intentions of the 'World Spirit', a kind of providential design. Thus, history unwinds according to a pattern. At the same time, the state was first and foremost in the scheme of things. According to Hegel the state preceded civil society and even the family. The Hegelian concept of the state thus provided a logical basis for absolutism under German monarchs and later for totalitarianism under the Nazis.[45] Liberty in Hegel's definition consisted of the conscious submission of the individual to the authority of the state which, needless to say, is not

---

44 Natural law consists of legal principles supposed to be discoverable by the light of nature or abstract reasoning, or to be taught by nature to all nations and men alike.

45 Karl Marx was a follower of Hegel. For Marx too, historical evolution was a basic concept.

the usual way more ordinary people view freedom. In spite of the fact (or perhaps because of it) of Hegel's work being full of mystical concepts, Hegel was successful.

The Historical School reacted against the English and French enlightenment and classical economics. The opposition to the classicals manifested itself (a) in the form of strong criticism and (b) in the seeking out of alternative objects of economic investigation.

(a)   The classical school's deductive method and its implications were rejected. Economic laws discovered through deduction, according to the members of the school, have no eternal and universal validity. If economic regularities can be found, they are essentially variable with time and place.[46] Each country's economic evolution was unique, therefore universal laws did not exist in economics.[47] A second charge leveled against the classicals was related to the alleged narrowness of their psychology. As the classicals saw it, man seemed to be solely moved by considerations of self-interest (which the historicists often confused with egoism thus distorting the views of the classical school). Instead, said the historicists, man's motives are more varied. He is also prompted by motives such as vanity, benevolence, love of power and the like. Although members of the classical school would probably not have disagreed with this, they would conceivably have answered that the premise of (enlightened) self-interest was the best available simplifying assumption used for analytical purpose.

Besides, it is no accident that this criticism came from German writers. The idea of an individual pursuing his private interest clashed with their more collectivist view of the nation as being more important than the individual.

(b)   On the positive side, the historicists devoted much time to detailed historical description of man's economic activity. His social environment and changes thereof received much attention and the elaboration of successive phases of economic development was a common feature in the writings of the

---

46 One problem with the Historical School was that its members sometimes tended to confuse the deductive method itself with the use made thereof.

47 One could argue that the members of the Historical School simply wanted to dismiss 'foreign' theories by saying 'such doctrines do not apply to us, we are in an entirely different situation'.

Historical School. Several members of the school wanted to build a new economic science based upon the careful examination of the successive stages of man's economic evolution. Yet the school did not really succeed in this effort.

The Historical School is usually divided into the older and the younger generation. Wilhelm Roscher (1817–1896), professor at the University of Göttingen and later of Leipzig, was the founder and leader of the older school. He was quite moderate and felt that history must be drawn upon to supplement theory. His major work was *Outline of Lectures on Political Economy according to the Historical Method* (1843). Other well-known members of the older school were Bruno Hildebrand (1812–1878) who wrote *Economics of the Present and the Future* (1848) and Karl Knies (1821–1898) author of *Political Economy from the Standpoint of the Historical Method* (1853).

Over the course of a few years another generation of historical economists appeared. They were determined to apply the historical method, as they conceived it, in a meticulous way to concrete studies. This new group was led by Gustav von Schmoller (1830–1917), a strong-minded man who ascended to an influential chair at the University of Berlin. His major work was entitled *Outline of General Economic History*, 2 vols, (1900–1904). Other notable economists of this group were Ludwig Joseph Brentano (1844–1931) who taught in Strasbourg, Vienna, Leipzig and Munich (he was more 'liberal' than the others) and Adolph Wagner (1835–1917) who will concern us later in more detail. Wagner taught for forty-seven years in Berlin.

The younger school was more hostile to economic theory than the older one. Economics in their hands, became increasingly identical to the study of economic history. Professors such as Schmoller and Wagner were also politically involved and their advice was often taken by Prussian political leaders such as Bismarck. By and large the members of the younger school stood for:

(a) A strong undemocratic militaristic German empire.
(b) German nationalism.
(c) Paternalistic attitudes and policies towards labor.
(d) Opposition to the Marxian type of socialism.
(e) Protectionism.

Since 1848 German industry had made great progress. A new urban working class had come into being and labor issues began to attract attention as they had done earlier in England and France. Also, the unity and strength of the emerging German nation were threatened by a labor movement which fanned the flames of class struggle and attempted to establish close ties with similar special interest groups in other countries. In 1872 the younger generation of the school came together in the town of Eisenbach and founded the 'Verein für Sozialpolitik' (Association for Social Policy) which declared war on economic liberalism and stood for participation in political activity and for social reform. A liberal journalist by the name of Heinrich Oppenheimer nicknamed this group of economists, social scientists and political analysts 'Katheder Sozialisten' (Socialists of the professorial chair) because so many of them were university teachers. Wagner and Schmoller participated. One of the fundamental aims of these 'parlor socialists' was to wean the factory workers from revolutionary international socialism and attach their loyalty to the Prusso-German monarchy. In this endeavor they made a number of the features of the socialist program their own, thus asking for the nationalization of certain industries such as the railways, and the introduction of various kinds of social laws such as insurance against illness, unemployment and old age. This new parlor socialism now incorporated some of the major ideas of Fichte, List, Rodbertus and Wagner. These requests were to be granted they argued, within the framework of the monarchial state. There can be little doubt that towards the close of the nineteenth century, socio-economic thought in Germany came to be dominated by the ideas of these socialists of the chair. Other European countries soon imitated this influential current of thought and action. In the United States a group of American scholars who had studied in Germany established the American Economic Association (1885) which at least in its very early phase was modeled after the 'Verein'. Among the practical results of the demands of the state socialists were the social laws and the higher tariffs enacted in Germany during the 1880s. These welfare state measures and trade restrictions were soon emulated throughout the world.

The dominance of the younger historical school in the academic world of Germany had many implications.[48] On the positive side one must admit that it might be a good idea to illustrate economic theory with historical examples. However it was not this very mild version of historicism which prevailed. The complete rejection of classical

---

48 The reign of the School lasted until the first decade of the twentieth century.

theory by the younger members of the school led to a paralysis of economic theorizing which ceased to be useful as a guide to action. It also barred German economists from participating in the refinements of economic theory which took place elsewhere. The example of the marginal revolution may be cited. Furthermore, the neglect of theoretical knowledge and the resulting lack of serious criticism of radical socialism helped the latter to take deep roots in Germany. As a result of the slighting of theory, few economists understood the concept of comparative advantage when in 1879 Bismarck shifted the policy of the German empire from free trade to protectionism. In a private conversation with the British historian William Ashley, Schmoller actually argued that tariffs could be looked on as international weapons which could be very useful if skillfully handled.[49] When after World War I Germany experienced its great inflation, its leading economists no longer remembered the quantity theory of money. Economic theory had ceased to be a guide of policy and when the great depression came, German economists had no effective advice to give.

Historical economics came to the United States as a number of young American economists such as Richard Ely attended German universities. Upon their return they implanted the approach of the historical school in the US. Economists such as John R. Commons (1862-1945) who taught at the University of Wisconsin called themselves institutionalists. They were critical of neoclassical economics. Commons even believed that government planning and control could be justified to ensure the socio-ethical ideal of welfare in the long run. Generally speaking, the institutionalists were inspired by the Historical School.

Adolph Wagner

Biography

Adolph Wagner (1835–1917) was born in Erlangen, the son of a professor of physiology. He grew up in Göttingen and studied jurisprudence and political economy in Heidelberg and Göttingen.

He taught at various universities before he was appointed to a chair of political economy at the University of Berlin which he held for 46

---

49 See W. Ashley, *The Tariff Problem* (3rd edn.) (London: King, 1911) pp. 30-31.

years. This period coincided almost exactly with the life-span of the new German Empire (1871–1918) of which he was an ardent supporter.

During the years 1882–1885 he served as a Conservative member in the lower house of the Prussian Diet. From 1910 onwards he was awarded life-time membership in the upper house.

Among his most important publications are *Foundations of Political Economy* (1876) and his *Science of Public Finance* (1872) consisting of four volumes.

The Work

Karl Rodbertus (1805–1875), an early exponent of socialist thought, was a major influence on Wagner's philosophy of 'social conservatism'.

Wagner's state socialism really begins with Rodbertus. This writer advocated the repudiation of laissez-faire, the nationalization of land and capital, the elimination of rent and profits as sources of revenue and a far-reaching redistribution of income. The institution of monarchy should however be preserved. Rodbertus's work also shows an extraordinary confidence in the power of the state as well as an utter indifference to individual freedom.

Wagner's state socialism was directed against international revolutionary socialism and aimed at the integration of the working classes into the German monarchic state. In spite of appeals to morality (he actually believed that economics should be part of an ethical science) his ideas were also designed to reinforce the power politics of the German governments.

In his various works on political economy and public finance Wagner favors amongst others the following proposals:[50]

(a) A more 'regulated' and 'ordered' system of production with higher wages, fewer hours of labor, assured employment, limits on employment of children and females, and insurance against sickness, incapacity and old age.
(b) Recognition of the principle of state assistance to advance the mass of the people morally, intellectually, physically,

50 See also W. H. Dawson, *Bismark and State Socialism* (London: Swann, 1890) pp. 156–158.

economically and socially.

(c) Nationalization of industries which showed a high degree of monopolization especially communication, transport, public utilities, insurance and banking.

(d) Regulation of postal and telegraph charges, railway tariffs, judicial charges, school fees and the like so that the lower income groups would pay less for these services than the more affluent households.

(e) Restructuring of financial arrangements in such a manner that a larger share of that portion which is currently distributed in the form of rent, interest and profit will be diverted into public channels.

(f) A more egalitarian distribution of income through the use of a progressive income tax, an inheritance tax, and luxury and capital gains taxes. Taxation should also be used to discourage certain types of consumption, such as the use of alcoholic drinks, and to the encouragement of healthier products.

(g) Corrective intervention in economic processes through such measures as protective tariffs.

Wagner also claimed to have discovered an empirical law of historical development. According to this law, state functions and public expenditures constantly expand with the progress of civilization. Wagner saw the state as an organ of moral solidarity and insisted upon the association of interests between individuals and classes of the same nation.[51] This attitude can be seen as a remnant of feudalism which considers men as being related to each other by ties of mutual obligation. In nineteenth century Germany, feudal institutions were disappearing but many of the feudal attributes still lingered on.

In conclusion, the state socialist often provided special interest groups, legislators and politicians with the arguments they needed to justify further intervention in economic processes. This included protectionism.

During World War I state intervention increased substantially in all participating countries because the state had to regulate production and consumption to make victory possible. Even in America, President

---

51 In part because of his nationalistic and anti-semitic arguments, the Nazis, once in power, celebrated Wagner as a precursor of national socialism. However, in spite of the totalitarian flavor of Wagner's proposals there remain very fundamental differences between Nazism and Wagner's state socialism.

Wilson mobilized the economy and an immense enlargement of federal bureaucracy was the result. When the war ended much of this bureaucratic machinery was dismantled but when Franklin D. Roosevelt, who had served in high office under Wilson, became President in 1933 many of the agencies, which under whatever name had existed during World War I, were revived. With the New Deal the largest bureaucracy in American history was created. In Europe, once the First World War was over, the bureaucrats who had acquired so much power were reluctant to give it up. Moreover, special interests had been created and liberty never returned to its prewar level. The Second World War bureaucratized the western world even more than the first and the second half of the twentieth century saw once again all-powerful governments regulating and controlling their economies.

In the following reading Wagner defends agricultural protectionism. It should be remembered that during the last decade of the nineteenth century the United States had begun to sell low-priced cereals abroad. Fast transport brought it cheaply to Europe and other importing nations. Inexpensive foodstuffs were good for the city dweller as they increased his real income. However, European farmers working on smaller plots found it often difficult to compete with American grains. At the same time the Prussian scholar probably also wanted to protect the interests of the large Prussian landowners.[52]

Extracts

The entire controversy, political and literary, concerning economic policy in relation to local and to foreign trade, centers essentially on the question which it has of late become customary to refer to as that of 'Agrarian State versus Manufacturing State', not a very happy terminology, since it is not definite and does not preclude misconceptions from the outset. In general it suggests, as we know, an economic development of the following character: A constantly increasing portion of the needs of a country for foodstuffs and raw materials is obtained more cheaply from abroad, partly from distant lands sparsely peopled and extensively cultivated; and this importation

---

52 Source: A. Wagner, 'Agrar-und Industriestaat' (1901), *Selected Readings in International Trade and Tariff Problems* (F.W. Taussig, ed.) (New York: Ginn, 1921) pp. 343–370.

is paid for by the export of domestic industrial products. This applies particularly to breadstuffs, and also to such raw and auxiliary materials for the different industries as can be, and in the past have been, produced at home in somewhat adequate quantity and quality, and at a not prohibitive cost, in accordance with climate, soil, and the historical development of agriculture and forestry.

......

In what follows we shall essentially deal only with the question of Agrarian versus Manufacturing State as presented by independent national and economic domains in their world-trade relations. But it will be well to bear in mind the foregoing considerations.

The effective factors in the entire historical movement, from the disruption of the old unity of natural home economics to the modern coordination of national economics with world economics and to the ever more enormous development of the latter, are chiefly two. But in this connection I do not deny the frequently important cooperation of other elements – notably that of legal systems, personal status (serfdom, freedom), private and public administrative law (relating to land, the trades, commerce); furthermore, that of manners morals, religion, indeed of *Kultur* as a whole. These matters, however, I shall not further enter into here. The two factors are: first, increasing population, as it is shown by birth-statistics; second, technological development – especially in the so-called industrial processes and in communication and transportation, but also in extractive industry, particularly agriculture.

In the 19th century, especially since the close of the great wars of the French Revolution, the factor of increasing population has unquestionably been of singular importance, greater, perhaps, than in any other period of history of like duration, that is, a period of from two to three generations. It was, of course, in its turn, strongly affected by the second factor, technological progress, based upon natural science, not only in manufactures but also in agriculture, in communication and transportation. The technology of steam is but one side, even though hitherto the most important one, of this progress. Without this new resource, which has increased the supply of food and other necessaries, a considerable portion of the people now living would never have come into existence. That is not too much to say. Within the boundaries of the present German Empire the population in 1816 was but 24,830,000; at the close of 1900, it was 56,360,000, in spite of a German emigration (chiefly overseas) estimated at more than six millions since 1820. Accordingly, the density of population in these 84 years has been more than doubled; it amounts now, 1900, to 104.2 per square kilometer, nearly comes up to that of Italy (113 in l901), it is almost four-fifths that of Great Britain and Ireland (132 in 1901; that of England and Wales alone is 215), and exceeds the almost stationary density of France (72 in 1901) by a half. The comparison of great domains like that of Germany with small ones of still greater density, like Belgium or Holland, is, it may be added, inadmissible for our problem. The latter domains, even though politically independent, are, nevertheless, in part only the highly developed industrial sections of the greater geographical commercial region of Northwestern Germany and Northeastern France.

In this great increase of native population, and the correlated marked development of our country from agrarian to manufacturing state, there is, to be sure, something great, significant, and gratifying.

But it has its dubious side as well. And this is either overlooked, or palliated or denied in toto, in the prevailing optimistic view of the glorifiers of that development, and in the view of those who advocate a general economic policy and an agrarian and commercial policy which would promote in ever increasing measure our evolution into a manufacturing state.

And here is where my standpoint, as well as that of others, deviates. We do not share that optimism. Not that we are 'Agrarians,' 'Reactionaries,' which we have so often been reproached, but because we believe that this evolution into a manufacturing state – not that it is altogether wrong – is in its newest phase too precipitately, too immoderately, carried out; that its reaction upon national life in general is in many ways dubious; that its solidity, its continuance, moreover its advance in the direction and with the rapidity that it has recently shown cannot be permanently assured. We do not deny, however, that economic developments such as those which have recently taken place in Germany are based upon profound, inherent causes; it may even be said that in a certain respect they bear the character of 'natural phenomena,' as it were. But, on the other hand, they are by no means as wholly removed from human will and the influence of purposeful human action, and in particular legislative and administrative measures, as a recent view – of which traces are to be found even in Brentano – assumes: a view which represents a reversion to the formerly prevailing conception of economics as a purely natural process.

Nor do we behold in the ever swifter increase of the native population; in the ever greater shifting of rural and urban populations, in a direction favorable to the latter; in the building up of more and more great cities, with larger and larger populations; in the crowding together of agglomerations of people in comparatively small industrial and mining regions; in the absolute stationeriness – at best – of agriculture, and its great relative decline; in the great increase, absolute and relative, of the population engaged in industrial, mining, and commercial pursuits: we do not, I say, behold in all this a phenomenon as wholly favorable as do our opponents. We ask ourselves, more cautious than they, whether this evolution answers the needs of the nation in general; whether it is a sound one, one that promises to endure, one whose permanence can be assured. Those are just the things we doubt.

And likewise we ·perceive in this development of prevailing conditions not a thing purely natural, removed as a matter of course from conscious human volition and guidance, but a thing towards which human will, as evidenced, among other things, in legislation and administration, can and should take a certain stand: with the aim and the prospect – a prospect not to be declined as impossible, and surely not as generally harmful – of intervening successfully in such development by moderate action. Not, by any means, directly, but indirectly by appropriate regulation of economic conditions, which in its turn will react effectually upon the shifting of population.

It is this conception of things and their interrelations which determines us to advocate an economic, agrarian, and foreign-trade policy which, though it does not render impossible such foreign trade as is indispensable, – the importation of foreign and exportation of domestic products, – seeks to put it upon its old and natural foundation: where those commodities which either cannot be produced at home at all or only in altogether insufficient quantity and inferior quality (things dependent upon more or less exclusively foreign conditions of soil and climate) are of course obtained from abroad and are paid for by the export of suitable domestic products – essentially, therefore, by the products of our industries and mines; where a great, increasing, and profitable international trade in partly and wholly manufactured articles and in raw materials of various sorts and qualities, in which each country has its own special superiority, is carried on to the advantage of all concerned, and is even encouraged; but where the products, particularly the ordinary agricultural ones, but also those of forest and mine, which, owing to conditions of climate and soil, we succeed in producing permanently or have naturalized by means of the recent developments of economic technology (beet sugar, tobacco) or can easily naturalize, and that at a reasonable cost, where, I say, these are increasingly developed at home to as high a degree as possible. And this we advocate for the justifiable and great object of making us more independent of the importation of such products from abroad, and of keeping our agriculture, which is the basis of economic activity, whether modern or ancient, on a good footing and making it capable of maintaining in profitable labor a larger number of people in the rural districts.

Moreover, we favor this particularly on account of the favorable effects upon the population in general of country life, away from the crowding of cities; the favorable effect of rural occupations as compared with the industrial, and almost all the other urban callings. And this, in its turn, reacts favorably upon the people as a whole, truly serves the interest of the nation; the health of the people, using that term in its broadest sense, is better conserved and increasingly fortified. The broad and thoroughly sound views of G. Hansen form the best basis for this conception of things and their relation.

This conception is, to be sure, opposed to that which still prevails in social economics and was formerly the only one represented according to which in these and similar questions the only problems concerned are those of economic values. These are indeed involved and require consideration. But they are not the only things concerned or to be considered. To attain the greatest economic success, the greatest measure of value, at the least possible cost, the smallest expenditure of labor, is the one great object aimed at in the familiar 'economic principle' or fundamental maxim of economics in national and international as well as in individual and private economy. But even in the case of the last, the pursuance of that principle is not the only right lodestar, particularly if thereby other important sides and especially the higher sides of the life of the individual are jeopardized, suffer, or are stunted. Even for the individual, therefore, it is dangerous, and as a general thing not right, to aim only at getting a maximum of economic reward, as expressed in economic values, for a minimum of personal labor, regard being had only to the quantity of exertion without any consideration of the nature of the work, of its reaction upon other sides of the life of the 'individual' concerned and upon the 'others,' his 'fellow-creatures,' his 'countrymen.' What throughout the ages has aroused, and still arouses, the opposition and antipathy of nations against the Jews dwelling in their midst and their predominantly one-sided mode of making a living, and likewise in the Orient excites the same sentiments against the Armenians, is precisely this ruthless pursuance of that 'economic principle' in individual economic life.

In public economy, however, every kind of labor and every achievement of labor, all division of labor, and every socioeconomic calling must be valued not according to its relation to the realization of that principle alone, not according to the measure in which it accomplishes that realization, but according to its general influence upon the national life as a whole. Here the pursuance of that principle cannot and must not be the only lodestar, because the economic interests which revolve about the element of economic value are not merely not the only ones, but are for the general life of the nation by far not the highest ones. The great question, 'What is a man profited, if he shall gain the whole world, and lose his own soul?' should be borne in mind in the discussion of these great economic issues. Only, in that connection, we must consider not alone the religious and ethical side but all sides of human life which are affected by the economic side. The question of the kind and quantity of labor does not resolve itself into the 'problem of value,' in consonance with that economic principle, but is related to the general problem of occupations, and that, again, includes the additional problem: what effect has the kind and quantity of work, the vocation, upon the other aspects of the life of the individual, and, in accordance with the prevalence of those kinds and quantities and vocations among the people, upon the national life in general? Questions such as these which economics, if it is really to become 'Social Economics,' and a historical and ethical science, cannot ignore. That was the error of the 'classical' political economy, and is still, in the main, even in Germany, the error of the modern and more highly developed science of economics. In the discussion of the 'practical problems' of commercial, agrarian, and manufacturing policy, and, in particular, of our problem of Agrarian versus Manufacturing State, in the manner of Dietzel, Brentano, and even Schaffle, this error is, in my judgment, striking.

It appears, among other things, in Brentano's reference to certain doctrines of Torrens and Ricardo regarding international trade. According to these, every country should aim to engage particularly in those branches of production in which its superiority, based upon natural conditions or upon historical development, is greatest. Inasmuch, then, as an international exchange of these products for other foreign ones in which though the first country is perhaps likewise superior, it is so in a less degree takes place, the result is an economic gain, a general benefit, for each of the countries concerned. At bottom this doctrine is, after all, only a dialectic subtlety. It contains, indeed, a grain of truth, but the quantitative element the question to what extent such as exchange will in the future be maintained in practice is, as is usual in that method, ignored. It is precisely here that the historical method in political economy has made good its challenge of the value of the mental gymnastics of the old school. I raised this objection as far back as my first edition. But now continuing the discussion, let me take up still another side of the question involved in that doctrine.

Assuming that a country is really permanently and decidedly superior to other countries in the production of certain, even important, articles superior to them in greater measure than in the case other commodities; assuming that it employs, accordingly, an ever greater part of its labor resources, its population, its capital, in the branches of production in which it particularly excels, for example in certain great branches of the textile and mining industries; that it supplies with the products indicated its home market and increasingly exclusive foreign markets; that, on the other hand, it allows its own production of other articles to decline more and more, and supplies its needs in those lines ever more exclusively from abroad. Then, to be sure, so long as production and trade maintain this character, it may be admitted that the countries concerned, and particularly the superior one, would reap an economic advantage, inasmuch as a greater quantity of commodities is obtained with a less expenditure of labor. If we were dealing exclusively with a problem of economic value, the result would be an unalloyed advantage. So far one may agree with Torrens, Ricardo, Dietzel, Brentano.

But is the question, as an economic one, to say nothing of its social and cultural aspect, settled thereby? By no manner of means! Leaving, again, the question of the assured permanence of that condition of production and trade entirely out of account, what would be the consequence of that condition during its continuance? Evidently that the nation with its great superiority in particular branches would restrict its national activity to those few. It would perhaps on that very account attain a special skill, but at the cost of a one-sided occupation of its population, the narrowing of their views, the most one-sided physical and mental development, the absence of all the advantages of the universality and variety of national production, and of the favorable reaction of this upon the national life in general. There would then perhaps be scarcely any agriculture, except a little to supply the local market with products difficult to transport from a distance; scarcely any industries except those in which the special superiority obtains, and those branches of production necessarily closely connected with them locally. The agricultural quota of the population would sink to a minimum, the manufacturing and mercantile would rise to a maximum; but here again the industries which are excelled in would constitute the greatest part. That things would hardly develop to quite such an extreme in reality must, indeed, be admitted. But if problems of economic value were really the only things to be considered, then such an extreme development would be the proper aim, to realize which as nearly as possible every effort should be made, every obstacle removed; and furthermore a development in the direction of this extreme would be the natural consequence of a regime of perfect freedom in trade and production. The 'country of superiority,' then, would have, for example, little outside of coal-mining and the metal and textile industries, and accordingly only miners, metal-workers, spinners, weavers, etc. among its laboring population. Can such a development – even though, from a 'purely economic' standpoint, that is, its relation to the solution of the problem of production, of value, it would be the most advantageous one – be really looked upon as conducive to the true, the abiding interest of the nation's economy, of its civilization, of the national life as a whole? To the question, put in this form, every man of sense will answer No. But it may, it must, be put in this form, because it is precisely in the hypothetical case of such an extreme condition of things as is always the case when one proceeds consistently that the untenable stands out most clearly. And though even England, even its chief manufacturing and mining centers, and our chief German manufacturing districts, those of Dusseldorf, Arnsberg, the Kingdom of Saxony, are as yet far removed from this hypothetically assumed extreme condition, yet they are approaching that development, and already exhibit some of its deplorable attendant phenomena, in the division of labor among their inhabitants, and in England in the decline of agriculture, and especially of the cultivation of grain. *Vestigia terrent.*

But the development of production and trade that we are considering would carry in its train still other effects an accompanying phenomena, an estimate of which is requisite in order to determine one's attitude towards the whole agrarian and manufacturing problem. The development that has in fact already taken place development for example in England, or in our manufacturing districts, which are essentially devoted to manufacturing for export exhibits the symptoms referred to in a degree quite sufficient to furnish food for thought. The necessary intermediary in these activities is trade, whose function must become all the more important, and its position consequently all the more controlling, the more complex the form assumed by export on its mercantile side, the more distant the territories it must seek, the more seriously it would be endangered by outside competition. The spirit of trade, or rather the trader spirit, must, therefore, become ever more specialized, one-sided, ruthless; must increasingly infect the entire national spirit, and assimilate it to itself. The more completely a country concentrated its efforts, in accordance with the above-mentioned doctrine, on some few industries in which it excels, the more would this spiritual, ethical, and even economic degeneration be bound to take place. To maintain at any cost the superiority in production, in sales; to employ every means for that object, every sort and form of competition; to open and reserve for itself every possible new market would be a necessity, a vital issue. The trader spirit, trader conceptions, trader interests, would dominate everything. What we see already in the extension of stock speculation to private circles, in real-estate speculation in our large cities and the incipient extension of it to places in the mountains and on the seashore prospectively rich in beautiful sites for foreign patronage or country outings, would penetrate more and more all the strata of society. What present-day England exhibits to us in sufficiently abhorrent form in her Boer War, its origin, its continuance, its object, the mode of warfare pursued are not these symptoms enough to bring out in sharp relief, as with a searchlight, the real nature of the trader spirit which takes possession of a whole people like the English, otherwise so worthy, when it has reached the stage of 'world-economic manufacturing and export State'? *Sapienti sat*, one would think! The picture, in good truth, is not an engaging one.

But these consequences are, to be sure, 'in accordance with nature,' even 'a natural necessity,' provided one has allowed the foundations of political economy to be shifted to this one-sided development. But whether this itself is a 'natural necessity' that is the question. Whoever – like the free traders, like Dietzel and Brentano as well – basing his view, it may be, upon the abovementioned doctrine of Torrens and Ricardo, simply answers in the affirmative, answers too easily. Whoever replies in the negative, or is doubtful about answering in the affirmative, at least takes the stand that a problem is in question here which cannot be solved offhand according to the cheap recipe of laissez faire: and this particularly because we are dealing, as is always the case in political economy, not only with 'natural tendencies of development,' but with things which are at all events also subject to human insight, will, and determination; and furthermore especially because the effects and attendant phenomena of the so-called natural economic development are of a character so grave that we cannot ignore the question whether in point of fact that development is inevitable.

We, myself and others, who in our view of the problem of Agrarian versus Manufacturing State differ with the free traders and the Socialists, do not believe so. We find, therefore, in a condition of things in which agriculture continues to flourish, and a greater number of people continue to be employed in rural labor even though this be brought about by an agricultural protective tariff, a blessing for the nation as a whole. And this even if, as a result, consumers should be obliged to pay somewhat higher prices, temporarily or even permanently, than those that would, for the time being, obtain under free trade. We hold that such a condition has a more assured continuity; that the progressive evolution of a more wholesome economic life would offer and secure to the nation as a whole a mode of life and a kind of prosperity better suited to the real economic, social, ethical, cultural, and political interests of the entire community than the feverish activity of the purely manufacturing state. Such a state draws an ever increasing part of its needs in foodstuffs and raw materials from abroad as long as it can, and they are not too dear and disposes of an ever increasing quantity of domestic manufactures abroad again as long as it can, and get a sufficient profit; not at prices, therefore, which would only allow the payment of starvation wages and cease to yield a satisfactory gain.

From this standpoint we favor 'agrarian' demands, not to serve 'bread-usury,' not even, primarily, for the sake of the landowners or farmers be they peasants of low, medium, or high degree, Junkers or lords of the manor but because we regard the maintenance of a part of the population, absolutely and relatively considerable, in landownership and farming, and the permanence of the economic efficiency of such inhabitants, as an essential requirement of the welfare and the enduring economic and social, as well as physical, ethical, cultural, and political soundness and security of the whole nation.

We do not conceal from ourselves or others the fact that, like all great things of which a nation stands in need: defensive strength, internal administration, justice, educational system, care of economic interests, etc. this 'maintenance of the permanent economic and human strength of the nation' by an adequate quota of vigorous rural inhabitants demands sacrifices. But we believe that here, as in the other cases mentioned, it is necessary to made these sacrifices for the sake of the higher object. Brentano, in his second series of articles, seeks to cast ridicule upon our theory by representing it as one that contemplates cultural 'supermen.' But raillery is out of place in a matter so serious. If an appropriate economic policy burdens the consumer, 'labor,' with a somewhat higher price of foodstuffs, even of bread whether and to what extent it does so is still an open question which is by no means determined by the usual 'statistical proofs' of the difference of cost between 'dutiable' and 'duty-free' grain this is a consequence, undesirable in one respect, but unavoidable. This should be counteracted by all possible means and certainly in part by express compensation, as we shall presently explain; but in so far as it cannot be prevented it should be accepted, and should be looked upon, and justified, as something that will help to guarantee to the nation as a whole a more tranquil, more assured general development, a thing that is certainly in the true interest of the working classes above all. In this circumstance, the nation, and not least the working classes, would receive, so to say, the 'equivalent' for any sacrifices it might have to make.

....

The assumptions of the rapid, and ever more rapid, development of the manufacturing state, whereby the economic center of gravity is shifted more and more to foreign trade, are, first and foremost, that foreign countries are willing and able to supply us with agricultural products in general, and in particular with such as we require, at reasonable rates; secondly, that the obtaining of such products, in great part overseas from the New World and other parts of the earth and from Eastern Europe, is sufficiently assured; thirdly, that our manufactures will find an adequately assured outlet – either in the countries furnishing the agricultural products or in others – at prices profitable to us, so that the expenses involved in home production (including an adequate return to enterprise and capital) are covered. Only in case, and in so far as all of these assumptions can be realized, is the system of the manufacturing state, described above, to be regarded as practicable and permanent. Otherwise, it threatens to give way and collapse – to say nothing of all its other objectionable aspects and consequences.

Let us examine these three assumptions. Of the first and second, a brief discussion will suffice for our purposes; in the case of the first some statistical data must be brought in, to show the extent of our dependence upon importations from abroad. The third assumption is the most important for our problem of the manufacturing state, and must consequently be examined more thoroughly. In the matter of agricultural imports, we are concerned first and foremost with breadstuffs, wheat and rye: next with other grains, including Indian corn: and finally with some kinds of meat and fats, and occasionally live-stock and eggs – altogether, in the main, human foodstuffs. To these we must add raw materials, such as material for spinning and weaving, skins, seeds, etc., and wood. A great part of these materials, especially those which we do not and cannot produce at home, are practically outside of the scope of our problem; for example, cotton, silk; these, like other 'colonial' goods, must be obtained from abroad. Wool, especially of the inferior grades, and skins, we shall also permanently have to obtain from foreign countries. Nor is it likely that there will be a dearth there of those articles – at least of cotton and perhaps silk, and of some kinds of wool – so long, at any rate, as the countries producing them do not themselves develop manufactures in these lines; a thing which, to be sure, is by no means improbable in the future. Thus it is with foodstuff, and among these with breadstuffs, that we are chiefly concerned.

......

We see from all these figures what immense values are involved, in the modern 'manufacturing states,' in the importation of foreign agricultural products, competing more or less with the domestic output. And yet the chief difficulty, as is admitted below, does not consist in obtaining these articles from abroad but, in finding foreign markets for the manufactures which (along with other credits – freight charges, interest on capital investments and on current debts, etc.) serve as part payment for the imports. (See below, section 3.)

In spite of the gigantic magnitude of these imports, there is no special cause for immediate concern as to whether, and under what conditions, we shall be able henceforth to satisfy our needs, at reasonable rates, in breadstuffs and in most of the other commodities which we and Great Britain draw from abroad. It may be readily admitted, too, that the importation of grain furnishes a desirable safeguard against our still considerably fluctuating harvests. With the present system of transportation, however, we should, as has been remarked above, by no means suffer any deprivation should we not draw regularly upon foreign grain in such large quantities. But on the other hand, we can by no means always be sure – and probably less so in the future than now – that foreign countries will not at times refuse us the importation of the foodstuffs and raw materials which we require, or make it difficult for us to obtain them, owing either to their own needs – caused, it may be, by bad home harvests – or to considerations pertaining to their economic and financial policy. I will call attention only to the Russian embargo on the exportation of rye at the time of the great failure of the crops in 1891–92; to the British plan, already in operation, of an export duty on coal; to the thought that has been entertained in cotton-growing countries – e.g., in the 60s, after the Civil War, in the United States – of putting export duties on cotton, and possibly on grain also, if it seems in any way practicable; for example, if the United States should be the only, or almost the only, country upon which Europe could draw for grain. After all duties on exports had been abolished, it was assumed that export duties, whether for financial or for protective purposes, had been 'definitely done away with' throughout the civilized world. England has taught us otherwise. She believes that the other countries cannot do without British coal, particularly coal of certain kinds, and will therefore bear the burden of the export duty on it. She suddenly goes to work in 1901, 'realistically' abandoning all 'principles' and adopts this means of imposing part of the cost of the Boer War upon foreign countries, – as an atonement for their siding with the cause of the Boers, the Britons might contemptuously add! Besides, purely political grounds of enmity, of unfriendliness, of intentional injury to the land and people which stand in need of foreign products, may lead to the prohibition of exports or to the imposition of a duty upon them, as a general measure or one directed against a particular country; for example, in war times under the pretext of a 'neutral' attitude this applying especially to grain.

But even if our importation of foreign commodities were not intentionally made difficult or prevented by such commercial, financial, or political policies, – the ability of foreign countries to supply our needs may be lessened, or cease altogether, temporarily or permanently. Temporarily, as has already been remarked, in the case of bad foreign harvests, as in the aforementioned case of Russian rye; as in the Civil War in the United States in the case of cotton, when its production ceased almost entirely, and its exports as good as entirely, during the course of the war. Permanently, if the native population in the exporting state greatly increases, if its needs for the products of the soil multiply, or its own industries develop to such an extent that it needs all or nearly all of its domestic raw materials itself. Particularly in the case of such important providers of our foodstuffs and agricultural raw materials as Russia and the United States must these contingencies be positively reckoned with in a not very distant future. In those countries too, then, agriculture must become more intensive, and the cost of production be increased in consequence. Under such circumstances, we shall, at best, obtain these continued supplies of grain etc. from those countries only at considerably higher prices, and therewith one much-stressed advantage of the manufacturing-state regime will disappear. These supplies may, moreover, to a great extent, become permanently impossible. The possibility, namely, of acquiring steadily increasing quantities of breadstuffs – wheat and rye – for a growing world-population, is, according to recent investigations, including inquiries into the natural climatic conditions requisite for grain culture, etc., much more limited than was formerly assumed by a widespread optimism, even though for the present there is little likelihood of a scarcity; in Argentina, for example, the area of cultivation could be greatly extended. When cultivation becomes more difficult and expensive, the 'problem of population' will loom up in the export countries also, and become more serious with us.

In export countries like Russia, moreover, the export of breadstuffs to foreign lands does not even now represent, or at all events does not always represent, a surplus beyond their own needs. It is at least in part derived from the reduction of home consumption, in certain districts (often under stress of taxes and debts), to a point where the pangs of hunger are barely allayed. Every improvement in living conditions – surely desirable from a humanitarian standpoint – of a not inconsiderable part of the Russian lower classes will diminish the amount of grain available for export. In short, every statesman, every political economist who thinks not only for the moment, and who has to do with economic policy, must even at the present time take into serious consideration the uncertainty of a permanently large, and not too expensive, importation of foodstuffs and of many raw materials, above all of breadstuff. This will necessarily lead him to adopt a cautious attitude on the 'problem of the manufacturing state.' The class-centered conception of mere commercialism, which thinks only of the immediate present and of its own advantage, cannot possibly be the guiding star of scientific thought or of rational, practical economics. Nor can the conception of our urban industrial workers, frequently equally short-sighted, and likewise stamped with class-selfishness, be the decisive factor. These people and those who lead and mislead them, – even assuming the good faith of the latter in such matters, – fix their attention only upon the momentary advantage of the lower price of grain, without concerning themselves about a lasting assurance of its continuance, or about the conditions involved. Even in the Social-Democratic camp, voices such as Schippel's or Calmer's, are like those of preachers crying in the wilderness and do not penetrate; nor, as we have seen, do they always dare to state plainly the necessary conclusions. But at least they do not belie the truth.

But even if the countries which export agricultural products were always willing and able to satisfy our necessary demands, we must take into account, besides, that in the case of a country occupying a geographical an political position such as does Germany, in time of war – a contingency which we, for well-known reasons, must reckon with more than most of the European states – imports can more readily be cut off. Great Britain, in particular, with its insular position and its supremacy at sea, assured at least for the time being, is more favorably situated than our fatherland, hemmed in as it is between Russia and the Slavic world on the one side, and France on the other. And yet even in England itself earnest voices have already been raised, pointing out the danger of being starved out; and in thoughtful mercantile circles, even within the grain trade itself, there has been serious discussion of the 'medieval idea – an idea which impresses bigoted free traders as downright insane – of maintaining great public storehouses of grain in England because the food supply of the country does not seem sufficiently assured through the processes of trade.

I do not wish to overrate the considerations thus brought forward; I admit even that the entire economic policy of a great state cannot be guided solely, or even primarily, by circumstances such as great political and military complications, which are, after all temporary and exceptional. They will, however, form an important subject of consideration for every thoughtful economist and statesman. Objections, and refutations, such have been attempted by H. Dietzel, Brentano, and others, have not convinced me, at least, of the opposite. In his second series of articles, Brentano again expresses nothing but scorn for these apprehensions, and calls them the weakest argument of his Agrarian opponents. That is a matter of opinion. I do not overrate it – a thing which Brentano does not mention – but I do not take it as lightly as he does, even though I may, in Brentano's opinion, be acting here again like 'clever Elsie' in the fairy tale.

More important, however, than all that has been set forth above – more important even than the uncertainty of a permanent profitable importation of agricultural products – is the question of the disposal of our own products, particularly of our manufactures, in foreign countries – in countries which export agricultural products, and in others. Here, too, the question arises: Will the countries always be willing, and able – and, for that matter, compelled – to absorb foreign products in general, and our manufactures in particular, and to pay adequately for them? Now we observe in those countries, again above all in the United States and Russia, – but in others also; Rumania and Argentina, for example, are making a beginning – strenuous efforts to render themselves more independent of the importation of foreign manufactures, to develop their own industries by means of high protective tariffs and other measures. And who can deny that these efforts have been crowned with great success, especially in the United States, but to some extent also in Russia and other agricultural countries, and that they are perfectly natural from the standpoint of the advocate of the manufacturing state? The difficulties involved in the disposal of the manufactures of the manufacturing states of Europe have, indeed, been steadily increasing. Above all in the foremost of these, England, they have in the last generation grown continuously greater; but even the Continental countries, Germany especially, are having the same experience. Before examining the case of England more closely, however, let us consider an objection which our opponents are fond of making.

This industrial development in countries which were formerly agricultural is, they say, only a consequence of the agrarian protective policy of our own and other grain-importing countries. If we obstruct the importation of agricultural products for those countries into our own they are compelled, or, at any rate, stimulated, to develop their own industries and to find in industrial protection compensation for our agricultural protection! It was only our agricultural protective policy that drove them into their more extreme manufacturing protective policy.

This assertion, however, presents the facts and the historical course of events in an altogether false light. The other countries proceeded with their commercial policy entirely independently of us. They did so, too, in spite of England's absolute free trade as regards agricultural products. The most important of them, especially the

United States and Russia, have long had, and still have, exorbitantly high tariff rates upon manufactures, and would have them even without our Continental agricultural imposts. They make, at best, some slight concessions in commercial agreements as, for example, in the Russo-German agreement. And certainly from the standpoint of the manufacturing state, according to which the chief economic advantage is to be found in manufacturing development, there is, as we have remarked, nothing to wonder at in this commercial policy of countries which were formerly agricultural. How these excessive imposts upon manufactures affect European, including German, exportation to those countries is well known (United States: McKinley Bill, Dingley Tariff, Russia, etc.!), not to mention the aggravation of the tariff by tricky devices, or the ad valorem duty system (United States). The possible profit upon exports of manufactures is thus substantially diminished for us, and consequently also the possible rate of wages (Saxon textiles, Berlin cloaks, etc., Viennese mother-of-pearl articles).

On no account, however, dare we Germans threaten countervailing measures and reprisals, lest the freetraders raise an outcry at once. Just remain 'nice and calm,' 'nice and quiet,' 'no grumbling,' by no means irritate the other party, the Yankee, the Russian, by raising our duties on agricultural products! What a pitiful exhibition was made in the winter of 1900–1901 by part of the freetrade press and by the mercantile interests! When those hectoring articles – of semi-official origin, it was said – appeared in the Russian press, in opposition to the contemplated raising of the German grain duties, our valiant merchants and their press promptly crouched under the lash, and soon themselves joined in blowing the foreign horn! We passed through a similar experience in the summer of 1901, at the time of the publication of the proposed German tariff. The 'freetraders' and their political partisans again solemnly pointed a warning finger to the 'bad impression abroad,' and explicitly raised that cry as confederates against such a tariff! So lacking were these gentry in pride and the spirit of independence – a symptom of the 'commercial spirit' of the manufacturing state. Very different certainly from that borne by the proud spirit of the Boers, that of the agricultural state.

To the emancipation from the necessity of importing West European manufactures – already begun, and in the case of the United States and Russia pretty well advanced – must be added a further circumstance. The other countries of Western and Central Europe – Britain above all – and in ever growing measure the United States also, compete sharply with us in the world market, in all the regions which offer a field for the disposal of our manufactures. Or, to put the matter with greater historical correctness, we Germans have been entering into ever more intense export competition with the other manufacturing countries, but the Americans are following us swiftly and have already in many directions overtaken us and the others, England included. Whence, otherwise, the well-known animosity of our British 'cousins' against us? It is easy enough to understand: we spoil their market, their prices, make their sales more difficult. Apart from a temporary favorable turn during the last few years, British exports have on the whole remained pretty stationary for decades, as will be set forth more fully below, and they have become less profitable. The whole system of the manufacturing state, however, is literally dependent on a continual increase of the export of manufactures and its maintenance with the highest possible profit, in order to provide for the growing need of agricultural products, no longer covered at home. The only prospect is that this condition of things will become increasingly acute. The recent commercial development of Great Britain is a striking proof of the probable future that awaits her – and all other countries with a one-sided development, wholly dependent upon the export of manufactures.

Commercial treaties with the countries which export agricultural products, and with others, may establish a modus vivendi, which, to be sure, is desirable. But they will not and cannot be of any effectual significance as regards the export of manufactures; and domestic agriculture will in the case of such treaties only too probably have to pay the score, as did ours in the Caprivi agreement. In specialties even the industrial countries, such as, for example, Germany, Great Britain, France, will always be able to complement each other more or less by reciprocal imports and exports. But whether they would do so permanently with much profit and with the requisite extension of trade, and in all the branches of such specialties, are open questions. And important as this may be, it scarcely suffices to procure for the one country the requisite great amount of same in the other country, and to insure its permanence. For each country strives, again, to equal the other country even in the specialties of that other, in order that it may be under less need of importing them.

A country which exports manufactures can, indeed, better its condition by technological progress, which may be stimulated by the existing sharp competition. And it is a gratifying fact that a part of the recent manufacturing advance in Germany, in the chemical, iron, electrical industries, etc., is to be traced to that cause. But we have neither a monopoly of those improvements, nor are the other Western and central European nations and the United States inferior to us in the capacity for technological progress. Whether Russia is so, or even the East-Asiatic countries, as is widely assumed, is still to be demonstrated. Here, again, I am not so optimistic as my opponents. Furthermore, the increase and improvement of manufactures, and the reduction of their cost, have their limits, even in the event of great technological progress. International competition, moreover, exerts a pressure upon prices and profits. Nor in its greed of gain does capital, 'without a country,' hesitate in the least to set up manufacturing plants abroad to compete with the home industries, whenever it pays to do so. This has long been done on a grand scale by British capital the world over. But it is done also by capital – Continental, French, Belgian, Swiss, and not least German – in Poland, Russia, Austria, America, etc., especially of late, by the transfer of manufacturing establishments and business concerns to foreign countries offering better prospects, isolating themselves by prospective tariffs, promising higher profits and lower wages for labor. This has been specially and justly stressed by Oldenberg. We shall very soon experience the same thing in China. Our position will thus be made still more unfavorable.

Accordingly, the universal cry is: new markets – in Asia, Africa, and wherever else something may still be expected. Assuredly, the proper result of the system. But it leads to a ruthless policy, to conflicts and combats, either with the government and people and manufacturing concerns of the regions themselves which it is desired to open up as new markets, or with the other competitors for the economic conquest of those regions. A ruthless 'Get out of the way, I want to take your place' is the outcome, – with all its grievous and mournful ethical, human, social consequences. The South African tragedy and the shocking method of warfare of the 'pious' Britons against the Boers, at which all Europe and America stand aghast, – where indeed is the ultimate cause for all this to be found but in that policy of expansion and robbery, aimed at the conquest of territory where some economic advantage may still be reaped? – though in this case there enters also the aura sacra fames, the desire for the possession of the Rand. But let there at least be no prating about 'Christianity.'

However, one might possibly disregard all that if this 'sales policy of the manufacturing state' yielded adequate and lasting results! After all that has been said, this still remains to be proved; and the recent developments of the trade of the most important manufacturing state, the British, has, as we shall see, demonstrated unmistakably that it is an illusion.

And when by the transfer of European and American industrial, commercial, and banking capital to countries which are the source of many agricultural products and which have hitherto furnished a market for our manufactures, competitive manufacturing establishments, with cheap labor, shall have been created; when the East Asiatics – Japanese, East Indians, Chinese – shall have been supplied with tools, machinery, technological experts, business managers, foremen; when they shall have been instructed in methods of production and provided with railroads etc. – what will the result be with those peoples? That they will have less need of our manufactures, will work up their raw materials at home, will compete with us in outside markets, nay, in our own domestic markets themselves – and all the more successful since they have at their disposal much cheaper labor. Many signs of such a state of affairs are already apparent, particularly in Japan and in India (cotton manufacture). Even if these civilized Asiatic nations are considerably inferior in intellectual originality and technological inventive ability to the European races, a thing perhaps too confidently taken for granted; even if their workmen, with poor pay, food, and mode of life, are less efficient than ours, and thus their low wages do not mean a correspondingly low cost of production; if, with the development above indicated, their scale of wages should soon be considerably raised – as is said to be the case already in Japan – and thus that disadvantage for us, as the competitors of those peoples, would be steadily diminished; those East Asiatics would nevertheless retain, at least for a considerable time, a decided advantage over us in cost of production. But that is the decisive factor! And in that factor lies the limit of our development of the manufacturing state: we should then have to sell at lower rates, that is, on the basis of lower wages and smaller profits, and could not even on such a basis do so with certainty of permanence.

READING 16

Paul Emile Cauwès and Felix Jules Méline

Biography

This last protectionist reading of the pre-1914 period deals with the

French return to high tariff walls. Between 1852 and 1870 France was governed by Charles-Louis Napoleon Bonaparte (Napoleon III) whose father was a younger brother of Napoleon I. During the latter period of his reign his economic advisor and friend Michel Chevalier had been able to convince him of the benefits of free trade. This led to such treaties as the Cobden–Chevalier Treaty of 1860 with England which included the suppression of export and import prohibitions, lower tariff schedules and the use of the most favored nation clause. The liberal measures of the Napoleon reign also comprised the abolition of navigation type of laws, (the monopoly of the carrying trade between the motherland and the colonies was given up, etc.) while tariffs in French colonies were cut to the bone.

In the mean time Germany wanted to eliminate France, to check her expansion, which eventually led to the war of 1870–1871 which was lost by France. Napoleon himself left for England and elections were held in France. A new provisional government with Adolphe Thiers at its head was formed. Thiers had been prominent in public affairs for decades. He was an opponent of Napoleon III and a staunch protectionist.[53] The liberal period was over.

The return to protectionism by the French can be traced to the intensification of nationalism which followed the defeat of 1870. This return was strongly influenced by two men, Paul Emile Cauwès the thinker, and Felix Jules Méline the doer.

During difficult periods in national life there will always be theorists who preach political and/or economic nationalism. This was the case with Cauwès after the defeat of 1870. Cauwès (1843–1917) studied law in Paris and received his PhD in 1865. He always had a strong preference for historical studies. First he taught law at the University of Nancy. In 1873 he was transferred to Paris to teach economics. From 1882 onwards he taught law again. In the 1870s, courses in economics were instituted in the faculties of law at various French universities. Very few of the classical liberals were appointed however. The new positions went mostly to individuals with training in law. Their legal background made them sympathetic to legislation and state interference in general. Often they knew little about the abstract theories of the French and English classical school.

Cauwès was familiar with the German and English languages and

---

53 See S.B. Clough, *France, A History of National Economics 1789–1939*, Chs VI, VII (New York: Charles Scribner's Sons, 1939).

was strongly influenced by Carey and List whom he quotes with approval.[54] The German Historical School was another obvious source of inspiration. He was deeply impressed by Germany's return to protection, which by 1879 became an established fact, and also the American tariffs. The Morill Tariff Act of 1861 was strongly protective. The Dingley Tariff of 1897 raised tariffs even more.

The Work

The main ideas of this leading academic exponent of the new economic nationalism were not very original. Their roots can be found in mercantilist writings and in the works of List, Carey and their precursors as well as in the writings of the German Historical School.[55]

For Cauwès economics was not really a science but rather the art of management of the nation state. This vision of economics is very close to the cameralistic viewpoint. The ultimate aim for Cauwès was to strengthen the nation state (especially his own) and economics had to provide the appropriate recipes. In terms of method he preferred the inductive method although the deductive method was not entirely neglected. Cauwès also reacted against political and economic internationalism. He believed that these forces had led to a weakening and neglect of the French military forces and therefore the defeat of 1870. Classical liberals had also depreciated the state. Cauwès saw the state as a moral being with the mission of developing the latent powers of the nation which in turn justified far-reaching state intervention.

The development of a nation's productive powers is the most important priority for a nation. Free trade is not as advantageous as it seems, argues Cauwès. Even if initially free trade brings in inexpensive goods which benefit the consumer, the development of the nation's industries under a protective umbrella will eventually enlarge the supply of relatively cheap commodities. Foreign industries under a free trade regime may conquer a domestic market such as the French

---

54 Cauwès published his 'lectures' in four volumes in 1893. See: P. Cauwès, *Cours d'Economie Politique* (Paris: Larose, Forcel, 1893). The first edition came out in 1879. A good summary of his thought can be found in the following doctoral thesis: R. Deplanta De Wildenberg, *Cauwès et L'Economie Nationale* (Dyon: Belvet, 1938).

55 The French translation of Carey's *Principles of Social Science* was published in 1861. List's book had been translated into French by 1851.

one. However once competition is eliminated monopoly prices will be imposed. Furthermore, consumers need not necessarily carry the whole burden of protection. If tariffs are raised, foreign firms may well lower their prices so as not to lose all their markets. Finally, free trade also means larger exports. The addition of foreign demand to domestic demand may well increase the prices domestic consumers pay for certain items.

According to Cauwès there are at least six situations in which economic protection is justified.

1. Industries which are related to national defense must be sheltered unconditionally in order to safeguard national independence.
2. Protection fosters harmony. Manufactures find a reliable domestic market in the countryside while farmers obtain stable markets in towns and cities.
3. If nations are at different stages of development the industries of the 'younger nations' will be wiped out by free trade which may result in a migration of people and financial capital. This justifies a regime of protection in nations which are 'late comers'.
4. Certain industries employ such a large volume of employees and capital that their demise would be a national disaster.
5. When relatively high domestic prices are the result of relatively high domestic taxes (gross receipts, taxes, excise taxes, business property taxes, etc.) which businesses have to add to their production costs, a compensatory duty equalizing relatively high domestic and relatively low foreign taxes is justified.[56]
6. Protection leads to diversification which engenders a more 'balanced' composition of the national product.

As far as the policies were concerned Cauwès recommended the usual battery of protective devices to stimulate domestic industry, e.g. tariffs, subsidies, cheap credit, premiums, and even honorary distinctions.

Cauwès also accepted List's picture of an ideal or normal nation with a larger territory, varied resources, a large population and access to the oceans. According to Cauwès, 'normal' nations establish colonies and thus give birth to new nations. Colonialism therefore was

---

56 It may be observed here that this proposal seeks to solve the problem of high taxation by yet another tax on the consumer (ed.).

part and parcel of Cauwès' economic nationalism. In his view, colonialism generated the following advantages.

(a) Colonization (by European powers) spreads civilization. Without it a large part of the world would remain 'barbarous' and uncultured.
(b) Colonies are a source of supply of specific raw materials and tropical foods.
(c) Colonies supply the motherland with outlets for her products and her financial capital.
(d) Colonies provide the colonizing country with assured openings for emigration.
(e) Colonial expansion generates a spirit of enterprise and initiative in the mother country.[57]
(f) Finally, colonies provide the colonizing nations with power and prestige.

Note that colonization is a logical extension of economic nationalism. The latter seeks greater self-sufficiency which automatically leads to the acquisition of colonies possessing whatever resources and outlets the mother country lacks.

Cauwès' observations did not fall upon deaf ears and after 1870 France joined the race for the acquisition of more colonies which eventually led increased confrontation with World War I as the ultimate outcome.[58]

In order to encourage the spread of his ideas Cauwès established the 'Association of National Political Economy' (1897) which comprised a number of politicians, academics and businessmen. This includes his friend Felix Méline who became the association's honorary president.

Cauwès did not go unchallenged. The representatives of the French classical school of economics whose influence was rapidly declining after 1870 argued that:

---

57 We are not told how (ed.).
58 In spite of the fact that the Third Republic engaged in one of the greatest colonial expansions in French history, there was little popular backing for it in the early 1870s. The trade with colonies was not very profitable, the French population grew slowly and did not need emigration outlets while the costs of colonization were always high to the average taxpayer (ed.).

(a) His 'Lectures' lacked good theory,
(b) His writings contained too many moral, legal, historical and political considerations which transformed his economics into some kind of normative chef's salad.
(c) With teachers like Cauwès, students at the French faculties of law increasingly received an economics education which was both anti-economic and anti-scientific.

While Cauwès was the thinker, his friend Méline (1838–1925) was the doer and thus became the leading political exponent of economic protectionism. A lawyer by training he was elected to the National Assembly in 1872. From 1883 to 1885 he served as Minister for Agriculture in the Cabinet of Jules Ferry. Between 1896 and 1898 he was both Prime Minister and Minister for Agriculture.

In 1905 Méline published a book entitled *Return to the Land* (*Retour à la Terre*) and from 1903 to 1925 he was a senator. Between 1915 and 1916 he was again Minister for Agriculture. However Méline's reputation is due mostly to the fact that he was the leader of the protectionist movement and the great defender of agriculture. As Secretary General of the tariff commission of the lower house (Chamber of Deputies) he was very effective in defending the protectionist conclusions of the final report. Thus the lower house adopted the majority of the main ideas of the report and this resulted in the 1892 protectionist legislation (often called the 'Méline Tariff') which broke definitively with the free trade system inaugurated in the 1860s.

In so far as the Méline Tariff contained a distinct principle, this was beyond doubt the idea of 'cost equalization'. This concept proposed that competition must occur on 'equal terms'. If the domestic producer has higher costs, tariffs should be tailored to equalize the domestic and foreign costs of production.

The problem with this argument is, that if taken seriously it would kill off most international trade at its inception. Another implication is that the idea intends to reward inefficiency. The less efficient the domestic producer, the higher his costs and thus the higher the amount of protection for which he qualifies. As the reading here below shows, the report also devotes much attention to agricultural protection. During the latter decades of the nineteenth century, European farmers experienced increasing difficulties in their attempts to compete with the relatively cheap American cereals and this further increased pressure for the protection of domestic farm products.

After the short war of 1870–1871 France had to pay an indemnity of five billion francs to Germany. This necessitated the pursuit of new sources of revenue (from tariffs etc.). Thus the new government was provided with an excuse to put an end to the liberal tariff system of the late empire. Early efforts in that direction had already been undertaken in the 1870s. However these attempts were not very successful mainly because of the failure of industrialists and agriculturalist to act together.

The first new tariff became law in 1881. It favored industry more than agriculture. The general increase in the tariff was about twenty-four per cent but this gain was watered down by existing trade treaties. In 1883 Meline became Minister for Agriculture. He used this position to push for more protection. In 1885 higher tariff rates were placed on foreign grains, livestock and alcoholic drinks. As in other countries during the same period, French policies moved in the direction of more protection. Nationalism and the strength of special interest groups forced commercial legislation in that direction. The new socialist parties (in France, Jean Jaurès was a popular socialist leader) often endorsed it too because they believed that protectionist legislation safeguarded jobs and wages.

In 1890 the French government submitted a new tariff bill to the Chamber of Deputies. Its object was (so stated the preamble), to guarantee French producers the ability to compete 'on equal terms' with foreigners. The bill was first presented to a tariff commission which consisted mainly of members of special interest groups who were all in favor of higher import barriers. Méline presided over the group as the secretary-general. The sponsors of the tariff revision argued that higher tariffs were needed (1) to stimulate industry and employment, (2) to maintain and raise wages, (3) to provide French industry with a secure home market and (4) to defend peasant proprietors. The success of the movement was facilitated by the fact that since 1890 the French government was dominated by a protectionist party, In addition the French economy experienced a recession, while other countries including Germany, Austria, Russia and the United States had given the example by adopting more protectionist policies. The report of the tariff commission (see reading) was presented and defended by Méline. The new tariff of 1892 actually became known as the Méline tariff. This new tariff provided for increases of approximately eighty per cent over the old rates. Manufactured products still enjoyed more protection than agricultural items but duties on food products were also raised. Most treaties concluded under Napoleon III had expired so France now enjoyed a great deal of independence in terms of commercial policy.

The new law also established the policy of tariff assimilation of the colonies. This meant free trade between the homeland and the colonies that had to adopt the French tariff. To the colonies this was an arrangement which turned out to be very disadvantageous. It also meant that the first steps towards a self-sufficient empire had been taken.

The new tariff (and this applies equally to the 1910 tariff) also implied the concept of 'combat tariff' or 'revenge tariff' in the sense that concrete powers were granted to the executive to erect special trade barriers including prohibitions on the products of countries which discriminated in any way against French exports.

The new tariff had several consequences. Like mercantilism, the new protectionism of the 1880s was justified in terms of national greatness and productive capacity. It was a theory of the state, rather than a theory of economics. It asserted what the state ought to be and ought to do. It also poisoned international relations (as did the old mercantilism) and the Méline tariff created conflicts with countries such as Italy, Switzerland, Spain and Portugal. While other countries joined in the protectionist race, free trade England became increasingly isolated. In 1902 Germany adopted a carefully crafted highly protectionist bill which inflamed the international atmosphere even further. There were also implications internally as a result of the Méline tariff.

As soon as an official protectionist policy had been adopted, pressure groups became better organized. They all raised their voice in pleas for more assistance. The tariff became the 'football of politics' and an instrument for the redistribution of income to the advantage of the more influential groups and classes. Many of the arguments used were rationalizations to conceal special privilege rather than genuine economic reasoning.

In France another tariff revision took place in 1910. New industries had arisen and they also wanted protection. Chemical and electric products were amongst these industries. The document actually resembled the German tariff schedule of 1902. The new bill raised duties on taxable goods by another 15–30 percent and the executive was given even more powers to retaliate with formalities, taxes, duties and the like if foreign powers attempted to impede the importation of French commodities. Needless to remark once again that the combination of protectionism and imperialism which nearly all nations practiced to some degree by 1900 contributed to the outbreak of hostilities in 1914.[59]

Extracts

It evolves upon me now to acquaint you with the principles which have guided your Commission, and the general reasons which justify its main contentions. As to the tariff details, the special reports will supply you with explanations of a kind to prove the correctness of the figures which we have adopted.

By a sort of tacit agreement, we excluded from the discussion, from the outset, all speculative controversies, all academic theories. We did not inaugurate our work by entering the lists in favor of free trade or of protection, as was done by previous tariff commissions. None of us maintained that France should be made to follow a policy of *laissez-faire et laissez-passer*, that she ought to resign herself to produce only what she could manufacture cheaper than others; finally, that the interest of the consumer transcended that of the producer and that everything should be sacrificed to him.

However, if theoretical questions did not form the subject of a regular debate, it is indubitable that they were found, with shades of distinction, at the basis of all the important resolutions. Tendencies towards free trade or protection collided with each other, as they always do, and it was evident from the first day that the Commission was divided into two distinct camps, entertaining different views and different aims.

The first, which formed a minority of the Commission, embraced the members whose economic ideal is manifestly the principle of commercial freedom; but the eminent and able men who compose it realize the actual situation too clearly to think for a moment of demanding an immediate application of their doctrine. They did not even urge that France should at present proceed a step further in that direction. They would be satisfied with the step taken in 1860, and it is towards this that they have steadily directed their economic policy. All their efforts have tended to maintain, in principle, the regime of the treaties of 1860, particularly the duties as a whole which were

---

59 Source: F. J. Meline, 'Report of the Tariff Commission', *Selected Readings in International Trade and Tariff Problems* (F.W. Taussig, ed.) (Boston: Ginn, 1921).

appended to them and which were but slightly modified in 1881.

The majority of your Commission brought another view to bear upon the actual situation of our country and upon the system best adapted to develop its riches and the well-being of its workers. It does not regard a protective tariff as an absolute principle, a sort of dogma, as has so long been done in the case of free trade; it sees in protection, as in free trade, only measures of international regulation of exchange good or bad according to time, place, the economic and financial condition of the different peoples. In its view, that is best for a nation which assures to it the greatest amount of work, since the greater the quantity of work, the greater is the amount of capital, and consequently of wages for the working masses.[60]

It is not astonishing that England has adopted free trade and urges all other nations to follow the same policy; her own interest indeed commands her to do so. When one enjoys, as she does, natural advantages which secure preeminence over most of the countries of the world, when one has an advance of over a century and superabundant production, it is easy to open the doors to all the world; for no one is feared at home, and other countries must at all costs be invaded. That is why Cobden was a true benefactor of his country in procuring for it in France, and, thanks to France, in all Europe, unexpected outlets.

Who would dare to maintain that the situation of France is in any respect whatever comparable to that of England? All the mighty agencies of production which nature has lavished upon England – iron, coal, etc.? An unequaled geographical position – have been parsimoniously granted to us, and we are but too often compelled to produce at a much higher cost than our rival. To these natural advantages must be added those which she derives from her formidable maritime power, the concentration of her industries, and the vast scale of her principal productions.

In treating with her we should never have lost sight of these causes of inferiority, insurmountable for us, and duties should have been imposed in accordance with them; we should, above all, never have forgotten that the domestic market of France is one of the finest and most envied in the world, that it represents an annual revenue of about 34 billion francs, and that it was folly to sacrifice a fortune so solidly acquired to the mere hope of increasing our exports. We know today

60 Statements like this clearly show a lack of basic economic knowledge (ed.).

how thoughtlessly, with what culpable generosity on our part, the
duties of 1860 were fixed; they were so much below the divergence
which differentiates production in the two countries, that a great
number of industries were endangered. Many would have been given
up but for the energy, the elasticity, of our industrial genius, the
ability of our workmen, and, above all, our admirable spirit of
economy which permits us to be satisfied with earnings often
ridiculously low; but they drag along painfully, unable to have full
play, and have for thirty years struggled, discouraged, with ever
increasing difficulties. The same error was committed when, after
negotiating with England, and impelled in the direction of imprudent
concessions, we negotiated with the other countries; and thus our
domestic market, of which we were the undisputed masters in 1860,
was delivered over to the progressive invasion of foreign products.

Treaties of 1860

Of course, we must not exaggerate anything, and we shall not go the
length of saying that the treaties of 1860 have ruined France. We will
even admit, if so desired, that for certain of our industries the existing
duties might have been lowered without detriment; but it should have
been done with discretion, defending French interests inch by inch,
instead of surrendering them, as was done, with closed eyes, in the
privacy of a cabinet of ministers.

If the treaties of 1860 did not produce all the untoward results that
might have been feared, it is because France at that time enjoyed a
comparative prosperity which it did not forfeit at once, and which, it
must be recognized, she owed in great part to the protective system
under which it was developed. And besides, she benefited, like the
rest of the world, by the great discoveries which at that period
transformed all the conditions of production. The powerful impulse
given to labor by the development of railway and of maritime
transportation, by the telegraph and the improvement of the postal
service, counterbalanced for a certain time the inadequacy of our
economic policy.

But what we are entitled to assert is that if the treaties of 1860 had
been better conceived in the interest of France and better drawn up,
if they had not by a deplorable condescension towards the foreigner
– the facts of which are known to us today – so gratuitously sacrificed
our agriculture and so many of our industries, France would not have
experienced the cruel trial which have been inflicted upon her. She

would be today, from an economic and financial point of view, in an infinitely better position; her industrial and her national capital would be greater.

Facts are at hand which fully demonstrate this contention; they prove that the upward movement of affairs in France in the ten years preceding the treaties of 1860 has, from that year on, shown retardation instead of acceleration.

......

The consequence is that France, which in 1859 was creditor of the foreigner to the amount 1,341,000,000 francs for the excess of exports over its imports of manufactured products, is now, 1888, only so to the sum of 1,098,000,000 francs. Even if we take the years 1889 and 1890, which our Exposition rendered so favorable to the export of our manufactured products, the excess of our exports is only, for 1889, 1,280,000,000; for 1890, 1,312,000,000 – that is to say, less than that of 1859.

We may judge from these few figures the benefit that France has derived from the treaties of 1860, of those treaties which were intended above all, in the conception of its author, to cause such a marvelous development of our export of manufactured products, and which have in reality only served to favor the invasion of our own market.

I know quite well that the objection is made that the general balance of trade is not to be found wholly in the tariff tables, that it is composed of many other factors, such as French investments abroad, the money spent by foreigners in France, the profit upon our exports, etc. We willingly admit all that, but it may well be conceded to us that the activities of international exchange such as is represented in the tariff tables, form, at all events, one of the very important factors of the general balance of trade, and we certainly have a right to note that the regime of 1860 does not seem to have improved that factor, but quite the contrary.

It is evident that we should be richer if our exports had been greater and our imports less; it is equally obvious that if the balance is considered from the point of view of the aggregate of French labor, it must be admitted that the balance yield to us by foreigners through the increase of their purchases has by no means compensated for that which they took from us by their sales.

Increase of Duties in Foreign Countries

If we look around us, on the other hand, we shall notice that the various countries of the world, with few exceptions, have pursued a policy distinctly different from ours. We shall remark, above all, that those that were subjected, like us, to the duties of 1860 and have altered them, have improved their economic situation, which presents a striking contrast to that of our country.

Let us not discuss America, which has developed so prodigiously under the shelter of the protective system that today she commits the error of exaggeration without any necessity. Let us not even talk of Russia which has likewise made such great progress for some years, because it would perhaps be retorted that it is an entirely new country which advances by a natural and irresistible impulse. But let us take Germany, let us take Austria-Hungary, which in the last decade have raised their duties in such considerable proportions, and let us see the results obtained. If we consider a period of ten years, from 1878 to 1888, we ascertain that in Germany exports did not cease to increase, while imports diminished in a significant measure. From the figure of 3,608,000,000 francs which exports had already attained in 1878, they rose in 1888 to 4,007,000,000. As to the imports, which attained in 1878 the sum of 4,892,000,000, they dropped in 1888 to 4,043,000,000. It follows that Germany, which in 1878 was a debtor, by reason of its excess of importations, to the extent of 1,284,000,000, was so only to the sum of 36,000,000 in 1888. If instead of going back ten years we should go back twenty years, the results would be still more striking. Doubtless this ascending movement could not continue indefinitely, and we freely admit that at present it seems to have come to a halt.

In Austria-Hungary the results have been less brilliant, but they are nevertheless very satisfactory. The exports, which in 1878 amounted to 1,363,000,000, rose to 1,581,000,000. As for the imports, they decreased from 1,150,000.000, the sum for 1878, to 1,110,000,000, the sum for 1888, to 407,000,000. It seems to us that a system which produces such results is not calculated to discourage those who may be tempted to imitate it.

These examples suffice to demonstrate, contrary to a thesis maintained for a long time and which still counts ardent followers, that a nation can defend its home market without for that reason sacrificing its exports. The United States had already clearly illustrated that truth, and the only resource left for challenging the authority of such an example was to represent it as an exceptional country which could not be compared with any other. But, surprisingly, the same phenomenon is produced in the very heart of Europe under conditions such as no longer permit the denial of its demonstrative force.

It is finally beginning to be understood that exports are primarily the consequence of prosperous production, in secure possession of the home market, impelled by its very successes to seek outlets abroad, capable, if need be, of sacrifices in order to procure them; that, on the contrary, a precarious production, one constantly threatened, unable to grow, and lacking capital, has a fatal tendency to retire within itself, and does not willingly risk going beyond the country's frontiers.

The results obtained in the various countries which for twenty years have made a point of defending their national production have indeed, been of a nature to strike French minds; they would suffice to explain the irresistible movement of treaties and the revision of our economic system in the direction of increasing the protection of the nation's labor.

That which has been done by other peoples compels us, indeed, to adopt measures at home, if we do not wish to be the only ones to suffer the consequences of their tariff policy. The inevitable result of the high duties behind which they entrench themselves is to throw back upon ourselves the entire surplus of production which seeks a market the world over and which formerly found assured outlets. If we look over the table of our importations of the last fifteen years we find them perceptibly increasing in proportion as the principal countries of Europe raise their tariff barriers. If we do not give heed to this, we shall end by becoming the drain of the whole of Europe. Is it right, is it wise, to persist in keeping our doors open when all others are proceeding to close theirs?

This reflux movement is encouraged and facilitated by some of our nearest competitors by the intentional lowering of the freight rates applied to the principal products directed towards our frontiers. In those countries the transportation industry is not regarded as an ordinary one, free, independent in its activities, with a right to seek its profits wherever it may find them. It is dependent upon production, and is considered primarily as an indirect means of lowering the general expenses of domestic labor and of offsetting the duties of the neighboring states. This constitutes a premium of singular efficacy upon exportation and we must in justice admit that certain of our competitors understand how to handle it with wonderful skill.

Upon all these points your Commission has been happy to find itself in agreement with the Government, which in its statement of the motives of the law submitted to us, has so conscientiously analyzed the economic evolution which is taking place everywhere today, and set forth so forcibly our need of adopting measures of preservation for the defense of our market.

Burdens which weigh upon French Production

To these general reasons drawn from the economic movements of the world, which would suffice to justify the revision of the duties of 1860, there must be added another which has arisen since that period, one peculiar to France, and upon which one cannot insist too strongly; for it is perhaps that which weighs most heavily upon our situation. We refer to the increase of financial burdens of every kind, which are a consequence of the fatal war of 1870. No other country is laboring under burdens so heavy, and it really requires the extraordinary powers of labor and of frugality of the French race to keep it from succumbing under such a load. If we only consider the per capita charge which interest on the public debt places on the inhabitants of the principal countries, we find that it is only 4 francs for the United States; for Germany 7.5 francs; for Russia 10 francs; for England 16.25 francs; while for France it is 33.75 francs.

The annual general burden is no less heavy; if we confine ourselves to the lowest figures, the least debatable ones, we still arrive at the conclusion that our budget of general expenses, which is three and a half billions, imposes upon every Frenchman a yearly burden of 92 francs (certainly more than 100 francs if one includes the local debts), while for Germany the burden is only 67 francs, for Italy 60 francs, for Austria 54 francs, for the United States 50 francs and for Belgium 41 francs.

The Hon. M. Pelletan, who has made such a conscientious and profound study of our financial situation, effects reductions in our budget which sensibly reduce its amount; but the divergence steadily remains about the same, to the detriment of France. According to him, the sum paid by a Frenchman in general taxes is only 66 francs yearly; but M. Pelletan calculates that that burden is 49.50 for the Englishman and that it varies for the other countries from 25 to 45 francs.

At all events, the expenditures for the war budget alone represent for the French an annual impost far greater than that of any other country. To the pecuniary tax it would be fair to add the burden, onerous in quite another way to French production, of obligatory universal military service. In the opinion of the manufacturers it is through that circumstance that we suffer the most in the state of armed peace which is crushing the principal nations of Europe. They are unanimous in declaring that military service, by taking our workmen in mid-career and at an age when their manual skill is most remunerative, inflicts an injury, often irreparable, upon their vocational instruction. It is thus that they account for the differences of accomplishment which our English or Belgian competitors attain in certain callings. Assuredly our workmen are inferior to none in intelligence and industry, and they should not be held responsible for the inevitable consequences occasioned by the compulsory interruption of their work. This is an additional reason for taking account of them in establishing our customs duties.

Wages

And now it is easy to calculate for every branch of production the increase of general expenses consequent upon our financial situation, and the special disadvantage which it inflicts upon our producers as compared to their foreign competitors. As was inevitable, it is principally in wages that it has made itself felt; nearly all had to be raised since 1860, the rise in certain industries mounting as high as 50 percent and even higher. And as a general thing it is wages that cause the principal divergence in the net cost of like French and foreign products. You will find this demonstrated on every page of the special reports relating to the different industries. This cause of inferiority weighs upon us all the more heavily since the products in which we excel are as a general thing those in which manual labor is a predominant factor.

What we have to defend in our customs duties, therefore, is manual labor, that is to say, the labor and the bread of our workmen. Upon the aggregate of general expenses our manufacturers have made the maximum possible reduction; there remains only manual labor to be squeezed, and unfortunately it is upon this that the inadequacy of our new economic regime would fall with fatal effect.

It cannot enter any one's mind to reduce the wages of our workmen, which, in certain branches of production, are manifestly insufficient. We ought, on the contrary, to strive with all our might to raise them, there is only one way to do it: to maintain the prices of our products at a sufficiently remunerative rate by preventing their excessive reduction through foreign competition. Thus the tariff question is connected with the social problem itself in its acutest form.

Let us take heed, moreover, that if we do not see our way to paying our workmen well, others will succeed in taking them from us, and they are doing so already. Everybody knows that it is by the employment of the best of our workmen and foremen that Russia, America, Germany, and China itself, manufacture today choice and tasteful articles of which we have hitherto had the monopoly. If this movement should become a little more general, we ask ourselves uneasily what may become before long of our artistic supremacy.

And finally, must we not take into account, if we wish to cover the question in all its aspects, the numerous laws submitted today to the consideration of the Parliament, having for their object the amelioration of the condition of our workmen; the law of responsibility for accidents, of pensions, and finally, so important, the one concerning the hours of labor, which in reducing the working day of women and children from twelve to ten hours inevitably leads to the same reduction for men? It is quite evident that all these laws if passed will constitute a heavy burden on production. Many manufacturers have stated to your Commission that for the majority of the industries a reduction of two hours of work, with wages unaltered, represented in net cost an increase of more than 20 percent, and they have requested that the tariff rates which we propose to you should be raised accordingly.[61]

It is evidently a necessity which will be forced upon us unless our foreign competitors should decide to follow our example and reduce their hours of labor to the same extent as ourselves. Barring that, the reduction of working hours would benefit only our rivals, to the great detriment of our workers.

We believe we have said enough to establish the imperative necessity of the revision of our customs duties by allowing a just compensation for French as compared with foreign production. We do not by any means propose for this purpose to return to the regime that preceded 1860, advantageous as it may have been to our country; times have advanced since then, the conditions of production have been transformed, many of our industries have taken a new direction, and to overthrow their processes from top to bottom would be fraught

---

61 This paragraph evidences the relationship between social legislation and protectionism (ed.).

with danger. Nobody, for that matter, either in agriculture or manufactures, demands such an extreme; there is no longer any question today of prohibition, or even of an immoderate protection. The French producer does not demand any privileges, he demands but one thing: justice.

He claims, as it is his right to do, that account should at last be taken of the excessive burdens which weigh upon his work, and of the causes of inferiority whose suppression does not depend upon him. In fixing the customs duties, he demands that the public authorities should estimate exactly the divergence which differentiates him from his foreign competitor, and that the figure set down in the tariff should represent that divergence.

Your Commission is of the opinion that such a claim is absolutely legitimate, and it is upon that basis that it has tried to found the very difficult work which you confided to it. It has sought for every branch of products, whether agricultural or manufacturing, the exact duty which seemed to it indispensable in order to insure their existence and free development. It, like the Government, considers that to invest our tariff rates with a real value, and to give French production courage and confidence, the first essential is to fix the minimum of the duty which will be assured to it, no matter what happens – below which it will not in future be permitted to sink. It is upon this fundamental principle that the economics of our tariff minimum rests – it is this which determines its peculiar character.

Upon this first point, we believe we have given our producers one of the greatest satisfactions, one of the most valuable guarantees, to which they could aspire.

There is another of no less importance, and which has since 1860 been the object of an incessant claim upon public attention.

Equality for Agriculture and Manufactures

At that period people were not intent upon apportioning in the tariff to each of our manufactures and to our agriculture the just share which was their due in the protection of the nation's labor. In order to favor the exporting manufactures other great and important manufactures were sacrificed which had a right to live and would certainly have developed if they had not been delivered over directly to a crushing competition. It is no mystery to any one today that the cotton, flax, and carded-wool manufactures, and many others too numerous to mention, have been a ransom for the others. It is in virtue of the same principle that agriculture was in like manner sacrificed to manufactures by putting its principal products on the absolutely free list.

It was our duty to repair these acts of gross injustice. Following a point of view different from that of the negotiators of 1860, we believed that we had no right to choose between the various branches of labor, to prefer one to another, but that we owed them all equality of treatment.

The preceding Chambers had already started on this road of reparation by abolishing for certain products the crying inequality of which agriculture had for so long a time been a victim. They ended by recognizing that all those products which are the fruit of labor have a right to equal protection, and that of all products it is those of the soil, if there should be a choice, which ought to be sacrificed the least, because they are at once the most necessary and yield the most to the country. For they borrow nothing from abroad and are pure gain for the public wealth.

We could not, therefore, hesitate to complete the work of the preceding legislatures by granting our agricultural production a thoroughgoing and scientific tariff. We were all the more obliged to do this since, besides the causes of inferiority which we have just analyzed, and which apply to agriculture as well as to manufactures, there are those which particularly affect our agriculture and which are daily growing more menacing to its future.

These causes, which have brought on the agricultural crisis which is not yet over, are well known today no one thinks any longer of denying them.

There is in the first place the considerable agricultural development of the nations of Central and Western Europe, such as Germany, Austria-Hungary, Russia, Rumania, whose agricultural products flow into our markets in ever increasing volume; not to speak of Italy and Spain, whose competition has become so formidable for our wines. But the chief of these causes is the entrance into line in the markets of Europe of young peoples favored by nature and by their financial situation with exceptional advantages: a virgin soil, costing next to nothing; for certain nations incredibly cheap labor; the absence of military imposts and the insignificance of the fiscal taxes. In 1860 those peoples were still dormant, and it is this circumstance that constitutes an excuse for the statesmen who disdained to take precautions to insure the future of our agricultural production. America was still so far off! As for India and Australia, who would have given them a moment's thought? One hardly thought even of Russia.

But lo and behold, all of a sudden the development of the means of transportation and communication, the rapid reduction of freight rates, brought those great markets in a few years to our doors, to such an extent that it was found that the grains of America and India, landed at Le Havre and Marseilles, could be had at lower rates than those from our chief centers of production. After grain, it is cattle, even cattle on the hoof, which, thanks to ingenious improvements in the construction of ships, tend to be substituted for French cattle; for meats, the facilities of importation are still greater.

The inevitable consequence of this movement has been to upset all the conditions of agricultural production. The Government recognizes this very fully when it declares in its statement of reasons 'that it tends more and more to make the world a single immense market in which all the parts are jointly responsible, and feel directly the repercussion of the agricultural and industrial crises which occur in any one of them.

......

Such, in their totality, are the general views which have actuated your Commission; its duty was, thus, clearly marked out: it was to recover in its entirety our agricultural production, and, doing what should have been done in 1860 and in 1881, to give it the same place in our customs duties that is given to the other branches of production.

But if it was easy to lay down the rule of equality and justice, it should be recognized that it was not so easy to apply it. Agriculture and manufactures are not separated by an impassable wall; there are points of contact between them where their interests seem to run into each other and yet cannot be blended and served at the same time. With the best will in the world it is impossible, on those special points, to give to them equal treatment: a choice must perforce be made and a preference given to the dominant interest.

It should in justice be recognized that your Commission has made the most serious and most sincere efforts with the object of conciliating them in the greatest possible degree. Its reporter, who has not always agreed with it, is obliged to declare that it has never lost sight of the rights of any of the great interests of the country and it has faithfully sought every means of giving them satisfaction.

How it was led to maintain the free entry of wool, of raw hides, of flax and silk, despite its desire to grant agriculture the same treatment as manufactures, is a thing which it is important to state very precisely. For, of all the questions which it has had to solve, this has certainly been the most delicate, the most difficult, the one which has agitated it the most and caused it the greatest distress.

Agricultural Duties

We have sought to present as accurately as possible the chief reasons which prompted the resolutions of your Commission upon one of the most difficult questions it had to solve in agricultural matters. That question settled, it easily agreed upon all the others, and it has allowed to our agricultural production as a whole the just protection to which it has been entitled for a long time, and which the treaties alone have prevented it during these last years from obtaining. Duties are raised on a great number of agricultural products, such as live-stock, and particularly meats, cheese, wines, beer, fish, oils, hops, etc., etc.

New duties are imposed on a great number of products which are allowed free admission by our conventional tariff regulations. Let us mention butter, oleomargarine, eggs, milk, poultry, lard, honey wax, fodder, fresh and dried vegetables, grapes and apples, hemp, oleaginous grains, brans, and, finally, wood, that product so important for our country and which is such a valuable source of income for the budget of the state.

If the Parliament ratifies these propositions, which we confidently hope, agricultural France will soon feel their beneficial effects; we shall soon see the revival and development of a great number of agricultural activities which have been discouraged by foreign competition and which ask only the possibility of living.

However, some of the agricultural societies do not feel satisfied, and urge that more could have been done; they complain, above all, that manufactured products have been granted an amount of protection greater than that accorded to those of agriculture. The agricultural protection, they say, averages only from 10 to 25 percent of the value of the articles, while the protection of manufactures ranges from 25 to 60 percent.

To these objections and criticisms we shall reply by pointing out, firstly, that if one wishes to judge of an undertaking so considerable as that of framing an agricultural tariff applicable to the whole of French agriculture it is not sufficient to single out some isolated points and complain of not having obtained everything.

It is necessary to consider what has been obtained, the whole scheme of the duties enacted, and compare them with the importance of the branches of labor which are to be protected; only thus can we understand their operation and estimate their beneficial effect upon the national production.

Now, if one takes the figures of the most exacting advocates of agriculture, who reckon the annual agricultural production at 25 billion francs, and analyzes these figures by applying to each article the duties voted by the Commission, one finds that more than 21 billions' worth of agricultural products are henceforth going to be protected. And, moreover, from the four billions remaining we should subtract nearly two billions' worth upon which agriculture does not demand any protection (straw, manure, tobacco, etc.).

Finally, it should be observed that if not all the agricultural products are protected – if some, to the regret of your Commission, had to be excepted – it is no less true that after the vote upon our tariffs there will not be a single agricultural industry in France that will not have a share of protection; for there is not a single one which, through the inevitable variety of its productions, will not be in line to profit by it.

As for the existing difference between the proportion of duties, according as they are applied to agriculture or to manufactures, this is an easy thing to explain and to justify. It is a consequence of the nature of things and does not impair the rights of anyone. If the taxes imposed upon agricultural products seem in general lower than those that protect certain manufactured ones, it is because they are levied upon a product that is simple and has not as yet undergone any transformation; thus it gets the entire benefit of the duty. The duties on wheat, corn, wood, hemp, oil, live-stock, oleaginous seeds, go entirely to agricultural production. But when these products are transformed by manufacture, it is absolutely necessary that the duty granted should be higher, lest it gets nothing; when wood is transformed into furniture, oleaginous seeds into oil, he begins by paying, on the wheat, the corn, the oleaginous seeds that he buys, the duties granted to agriculture, and it is the part of justice that should be taken into account. The duty that protects him represents only the difference which constitutes his special protection.

As to the total duty, great as it may be, it protects agriculture as much as manufactures, since, if manufacturing industry were crushed by foreign competition, it would be unable to buy French agricultural products. When the starch and farina industries prove unsuccessful, it is wheat and potatoes that suffer; when foreign sugar invaded our market, the culture of the beet languished.

What we say about agriculture in its relation to manufactures is equally applicable to the various manufacturing industries when compared with each other. That which is concerned with the earliest stage of production is as a general thing very moderately protected; those which come last in the series of transformations seem, on the contrary, to enjoy exorbitant duties; but that is only apparently true.

In the textile industries, for example, spinning gets an average protection of only 12 percent for the numbers most used; but when we pass from the thread to the unbleached cloth, from the unbleached to the dyed or printed cloth, from the dyed or printed cloth to the finished garment, when each one of these processes of manufactures has been allowed its due share, it is obvious that the last duty, which embraces all the others, is necessarily very high; but it will be seen by what we have just said that it would be a serious error to believe that it benefits the industry concerned exclusively.

Observation is of prime importance in the matter of the tariff; it replies in advance to the objection so often repeated, and so inaccurate, that the duties voted by your Commission are exorbitant and prohibitive.

Your Commission may, therefore, justly claim that in its fixing of the duties it applied the same principles to agriculture as to manufactures, and that it held the balance even between all French workers. Upon that point there never has been a shadow of difference among its members; they were so thoroughly convinced of the intimate solidarity which unites the two great branches of our national production that it never for a single moment entered their minds to establish a difference, or even a shade of difference, between the one and the other.

Duties on Manufactures

After the agricultural tariff it remains to examine the lines of our tariff on manufactures and to acquaint you with the general ideas which led to their revision. In the case of agriculture, it was the first time that its situation was examined throughout from the point of view of customs protection, and your Commission had, in a way, everything to do. As regards manufactures, the situation was very different; since 1860 the duties which govern them have been the subject of ceaseless discussion, and the truth has come out on every hand. It is recognized now that the fundamental evil of the treaties of 1860 was the unequal treatment of the different industries; certain ones have been adequately protected, some even liberally so; others have been wholly sacrificed. In the first rank of the latter we must place the cotton industry, the linen industry, that of carded wool.

It was the chief care of your Commission to give these great industries their due. It is upon them that the duties have been increased the most; but it is evident that these increases are justified.

Some of these increases are merely a correction of purely material errors in the assessment and calculation of the duties. Thus the tariff on embroideries was fixed in such a way that the duty on embroidered cloth was in many cases lower than that on the plain cloth upon which the embroidery was applied, so that the importer needed only to dab a bit of embroidery on the plain cloth in order to escape the payment of duty on the embroidery and a part of the duty on the cloth. In the case of oilcloths and rubber goods we have discovered like anomalies.

But there is another point in our work of revision to which it is important to call attention, because it is perhaps the one which has exacted the most considerable labor on the part of your Commission. Since 1860, and particularly since 1881, a great transformation, and one which is accentuated every day, has taken place in the course and development of the various industries. The advances of science are constantly modifying the processes of manufacture, substituting one product for another and creating new industries of whose existence there was no indication a few years ago. It is to this new state of things that it was requisite to adapt our new tariff; hence the necessity of new duties, the alteration of old ones, and, above all, a complete change of classification.

As a consequence our tariff will necessarily appear more complicated than the old one; but it was an inevitable complication. You will recognize in it a proof of the conscientious care which your Commission has brought to bear upon its work.

The change of classifications has in many instances resulted in raising certain duties; but it should in justice be pointed out that others have been lowered, and it is the total amount, the average of the duties, that we must take into consideration, if we wish to obtain an exact estimate of the actual result of our new tariffs.

You know now in what spirit and by what processes your Commission decided to settle upon the minimum tariff requisite for the protection of our agriculture and our manufactures. We have thus affirmed the intimate solidarity of all the branches of our national production, and we hope that the Chamber will be as deeply impressed with it as ourselves; the success of the work which we are undertaking depends upon it. The feeling of that solidarity is very vivid today in the working masses. Their sound sense and their spirit of justice are repelled by inconsistencies and selfish calculations. They do not admit that one should be protectionist for one's self and free trader for others, and fail entirely to understand the language of the representatives of certain Chambers of Commerce who demand high duties for certain industries, and yet constantly insist that the economic policy of France is being turned into a deplorable course. If one wishes to assume such an arrogant attitude one should at least be logical and carry out one's theory to its full extent.

Application of the Double Tariff

There remains still for us to explain to you the resolutions of your Commission regarding the application of our minimum tariffs to foreign countries; we come thus to the very important question of the actual working of our new economic system.

The Government proposed to us that we attack the problem by the adoption of a double tariff; a minimum tariff and a higher general tariff which would be based upon a variable augmentation of the figures of the minimum tariff. The general tariff would be our common tariff, applicable in principle to everybody. As for the minimum tariff, it would constitute a tariff of favor which would be conceded to the nations which would accord to us corresponding advantages, and particularly to those which would allow us to get the benefit in their markets of the same advantages as our foreign competitors – that is to say, those that would treat us on the level of the most favored nation.

A question of great importance was that of determining in what shape, for what length of time, and subject to what conditions the minimum tariff could be granted to any country. Was it to be by means of a genuine treaty; that is, by reciprocal agreements binding the two parties and establishing in an irrevocable manner, pending their duration, the rates of the tariff? Should it not, on the contrary, be granted as a simple reduction of the general tariff, but a reduction which we should be empowered to modify at will, if the necessity for such action were demonstrated to us?

Upon this capital point the Government expressed the desire to reserve to itself its liberty of action and decision. It declared to us that in its opinion the time had not yet come to say that it absolutely renounced the principle of the treaties. It expressed itself formally only upon one point; and that is that if treaties were ever entered into, the concessions made to foreigners should never fall below the figures of the minimum tariff. It admitted, for the rest, that it would be expedient to except from those treaties the duty on cereals and on live-stock.

It is the whole body of these declarations that we are going to pass in review, acquainting you in the case of each with the opinion of your Commission.

Single Tariff

And, in the first place, it adopted without hesitation the principle of the double tariff, which seemed to it particularly adapted to those who are opposed to treaties. No one, it should be mentioned, suggested a single tariff applicable to the world at large without distinction. That absolute system presents, in fact, obvious disadvantages and dangers. The first of these disadvantages would be the forcing of the protective idea beyond measure, as all the nations that have adopted that system have done. When the same tariff is applied to all, that is, even to the countries which have a really prohibitive system, the natural result is a great increase of tariff rates. That is a road upon which we do not wish France to enter.

But the single tariff would have a defect far more serious, that of compromising the interests of our export trade, which we propose to protect by every means in our power. The single tariff would cause us to lose the benefit of the concessions which we can expect in offering our minimum tariff, and especially the advantages which our competitors might gain in foreign markets – that is, the treatment of the most favored nation. If we exclude ourselves from the possibility of granting favors to others, what right have we to demand any from them?

It is true that the reply is made that the single tariff would not exclude measures of reprisal against nations which would be tempted to inflict a rigorous treatment upon our products, and that the menace of such reprisals sufficed to secure to certain nations which have the single tariff the tariff of the most favored nation. But is not this, by the admission of the advocates of the single tariff themselves, a condemnation of that very system?

The policy of reprisals is the most dangerous of all: it should not be resorted to except in case of the utmost extremity; one never knows where it may lead or what it may cost, and it may well be conceded to us that the method that can without reprisals accomplish the desired aim and protect our export trade is incontestably superior to all others.

So our Commission espoused without hesitation the principle of the double tariff. It agrees with the Government in holding that the general tariff should constitute the common duty applicable to all, and that the minimum tariff should not be conceded to the foreigner except under certain forms and conditions.

As for the form, there are only two means of making the concession: either a law which binds only ourselves or an agreement which binds equally those with whom it is entered into. We have already practiced both systems; it is only by a law that we conceded to England, and quite recently to Greece, the benefit of our contractual tariffs. It is by special conventions that we have accorded the most favored nation treatment to other countries, such as Austria, Hungary, Turkey, Mexico.

But besides these conventions, which embrace only a pledge of principle and of relative favor, the consequences of which may be varied by the contracting parties, there are those whose aim it is to bind in close union the nations that sign them, by fixing for their entire duration, in an immutable fashion, the customs system of the contracting countries. These conventions are termed treaties. The distinctive character of the treaties consists in the embodiment in their text of the sum total of the tariffs concerning the entire production of the contracting nations, and in the pledge of leaving them untouched pending their entire duration.

There are, then, two possible ways of granting the minimum tariff in the form of a convention. It may be conceded as a simple treatment of favor under the general tariff, but without taking any pledge to maintain its figures indefinitely. In that case the result of the convention does not sensibly differ from that of the law. To concede our minimum tariff by a convention of that kind is only to promise to the nation to which we grant the concession our lowest tariff rate; but we owe it nothing more and we retain the power to alter and raise the actual figures of that tariff should the necessity for such action be demonstrated to us. In short, we promise only one thing; that is, never to apply our general tariff pending the duration of the convention to the nation with which we have made that agreement.

There is a second way of according our minimum tariff, and that is by incorporating it in a genuine treaty and thus fixing the figures for the entire duration of the treaty. In this system, the minimum tariff would take the place of our actual contractual tariffs, with the sole difference that it would be applied in bloc while our contractual tariffs have been formed by sections and by successive layers.

System of Treaties

Confronted with these two systems, your Commission decided, by a very large majority, that if the first was considered acceptable, the second should henceforth be abandoned. It was of the opinion that the interest of our country commanded it not to enter into any more treaties and to remain master of its tariff. It seemed to it that the economic situation of the world imposed that measure of prudence upon us more than upon others. We have for ten years been witnessing a revolution in the condition of production, and the respective situation of the various nations is constantly being modified with a dizzying rapidity. One that amounted to nothing yesterday is all of a sudden revealed as a formidable agricultural or industrial rival; a few years may enable it to crush all its competitors. There was a time when distance, the difficulty of communication, and the high rates of transportation were, for the majority of nations, particularly those of Europe, a bulwark more efficacious than customs duties. Today that advantage is denied them and everything is against them. Who would dare to assert that matters will stop here and that the future holds no new surprises for us?

One must bow to the force of circumstances and recognize that today all the markets tend more and more to draw near to each other, and that the distance which separates them will steadily keep on diminishing.

It is, therefore, the struggle of the strongest against the weakest that is beginning, and we must prepare to sustain it without discouragement but likewise without illusion. We must be ready for everything, ready, consequently, to recast our economic system should new dangers, impossible to foresee today, menace our national production. We may hope that such a necessity will not make itself felt for a long time to come, but it would be most presumptuous not to take it into account.

Even should the precaution be needless, it would, in any case, have the advantage of reassuring our producers, of giving them a feeling of security for the morrow and confidence in the future. Before our producers themselves we must place our workingmen, who are the first victims of these displacements of production. If we wish to wrest them from the temptation to emigrate to the fortunate lands which are preparing to supplant us, we must protect and defend their labor. In order to do that we must attend to the means of securing those objects.

4. The Decline of Economic Liberalism and the Idea of Free Trade during the 1900–1940 Period

PREAMBLE

1

The leading exponents of nineteenth century political and economic liberalism believed that their doctrines were in harmony with the spirit of the new industrial age. It has been noted, however, that the nineteenth century also produced another race of thinkers emphasizing conflict and contradiction. Many of these publicists: nationalists, conservatives, socialists, radicals and totalitarians to mention but a few, had little in common except for their hostility to liberalism. Common wisdom has it that impartiality, detachment and critical thinking are the major defining characteristics of intellectuals. Yet the nineteenth and twentieth centuries have shown that intellectuals can allow themselves to be carried away by political passion and commitment and can become adept at suspending their critical faculties. Instead of restraining the passions of the laymen, intellectuals have often inflamed them. Intellectuals often wield power through the spoken and written word. Experience suggests that when intellectuals have been converted to a set of beliefs, it is often merely a question of time for their views to become the driving force of politics. Many of these literates directed their criticism at the harmonized version of society and intellectual order from which liberalism began and preached state interference and national self-assertion instead. It was noticed earlier that the Historical School in Germany opposed liberalism and supported a program of social legislation and protectionism. This school became extraordinarily influential in Germany and abroad.

In the 1880s interventionist ideas began to influence the political decision making process once again. After Germany's victory over France in 1870, a marked change took place in the international atmosphere. In 1878, Bismarck, the German Chancellor, avowed his faith in tariff protection as a German national policy. In the 1880s

283

Germany increased its tariffs, adopted a whole new system of factory legislation and social insurance and nationalized the railways as well as the telegraph and telephone systems.

Feelings of damaged national prestige in France pushed the Third Republic in the same direction. Other countries such as Austria, Italy and Russia which had young industries also raised their tariffs. This movement of declining economic liberalism continued until 1914. Pro-labor legislation can also be an inducement to the raising of tariffs as it increases the costs of production and weakens the competitive power of domestic industry. This was certainly an important factor in the numerous tariff reforms that took place after 1880 in Germany and elsewhere.

One problem with interventionism is that each time the nation state extends its activities, it encourages dependence. The state becomes increasingly the institution through which all is to be accomplished. Therefore the extension of state activities encourages the emergence of special interest groups. Thus after 1880 special interest groups serving manufacturers, labor and farmers emerged or became stronger. Manufacturers and farmers wanted to retain national markets for themselves and thus they asked for protection. Labor groups, in order to insure wages and employment, naturally wanted protection against the products of 'cheap' foreign labor. In a period of rising national sentiment, special interest groups will often align themselves to the national interest in order to achieve their objectives. They realize quickly that by using nationalistic arguments, their proposals have a better chance of being readily accepted by both policy makers and the public.

In summary, between 1875 and 1914, substantial changes involving government with economic life occurred. The increasing interference of the state with exchange relations gave a new impetus to imperialism producing economic friction and political entanglement which finally led to World War I.

Perhaps the greatest error of the old liberals of the nineteenth and even the early twentieth century, was their assumption that what appeared rational and reasonable to them would be accepted by the majority of the people. Obviously, the liberal vision with its emphasis on liberty, the market economy and free international trade had brought with it freedom, prosperity and peace. When late in the nineteenth and early in the twentieth century the majorities in many countries preferred the doctrines of nationalism, interventionism and collectivism, many of the old liberals felt helpless as these doctrines seemed to fly in the face of their most deeply held beliefs about human nature.

2

World War I destroyed the old order and it could be said that the twentieth century was born in 1918. The hundred years between 1815 and 1914 witnessed the creation of a world economy with most of its members integrated through a well-developed network of trade and finance. London was at its center. The convulsions of the war burst the cake of custom and put an end to the world economic order and the climate of opinion which had, to varying degrees, dominated the 1815–1914 period. By 1918 the world had changed irreversibly.

The First World War necessitated for the first time the thorough mobilization of the productive resources of all the major belligerent states so that almost every aspect of economic life became the ultimate concern of government. The disrupting of the peacetime channels of trade also put tremendous pressure upon the warring nations. The result was far-reaching government intervention in the national economies and an almost complete control of foreign trade and financial transactions. After the war many of the wartime controls were abandoned. Yet, a great deal of technical knowledge with regard to managing an economy had been acquired. Thus, the war had permitted (however clumsily) the establishment of the precedent of a planned economy. The readiness to intervene became much greater. During and after the period of war, practically all the European nations and the United States showed an eagerness to assign more power to their governments and to expand the sphere of government. After the war the values of the liberal world seemed to have become unreal and all the old guideposts and landmarks somehow seemed irrelevant.

3

The tariff history of the interwar period shows how far countries were able to move from economic liberalism. The peace treaty of Versailles broke up the Austro-Hungarian and Ottoman empires. New political units were established, all desirous of erecting their own autonomous tariff systems. Each of the new units tried to develop a rounded economy by the granting of protection to its weaker industries. In countries such as Canada and Australia notable advances in the direction of industrialization had been made during the war. But some of these 'war babies' needed protection in order to survive in the more competitive post-war environment, and protection they got. In countries such as France and Germany, agricultural protection was sometimes defended on two grounds. First, the Great War had demonstrated the importance of easy access to domestic food supplies. Second, some policy makers felt that the peasantry was a stable and desirable element in the population. With the growth in strength of radical parties, the peasantry had to be preserved and protected, particularly after 1925 when international competition in food products sharpened.

Once the war was over the United States had become a creditor country. Creditor countries have to keep their tariffs low so as to allow other countries to import and earn the money to make interest payments and eventually repay their debts. Yet in 1922 the US congress approved the Fordney–McCumber Act which established the highest tariff up to that time.

In England the commitment to free trade was weakened by the fact that her efforts to reestablish her former position as a major exporter were not very successful. Besides, especially after 1925, the British pound was overvalued which made English products expensive generating economic stagnation during the second half of the 1920s.

4

During the 1920s the international economy was disrupted by the linked problems of German reparations and inter-allied war debts. Germany had to pay the costs of the war which were set at $33 billion over a period of thirty years. However, this was estimated to be about four times the amount she was able to pay. There was also the problem of inter-allied war debts. The US had lent about $10 billion, Britain $8.7 billion and France $2 billion. But England and France had been borrowing as well, especially from the US. During the 1920s a rather unhealthy chain of capital movements evolved. Interest rates were comparatively high in Germany. As a result American private investors poured loans into Germany. Some of these funds were used to make reparation payments to England, France, Belgium and Italy. The recipients in turn used the money to discharge their debts to countries such as the United States. When in the late 1920s American interest rates rose and the flow of loans from the US to Germany dried up, the whole system broke down.

After World War I, monetary policies became increasingly divorced from international considerations. To varying degrees a period of monetary nationalism had begun. The pressures of the war had caused most of the belligerent states and many of the neutral nations to abandon the gold standard although the sharpness and extent of the break varied from country to country. As a result the link between national price systems was broken and prices in different countries were free to move independently. Inflation went to various lengths and in Germany and Austria the currencies became virtually worthless. However, between 1922 and 1925, at least in Europe, inflation was stopped by a series of successful stabilization efforts. The piece of machinery which replaced the gold standard was named the gold exchange standard. The US dollar and the British pound would remain convertible into gold at a fixed price. This made the US and England into the core countries. The non-center countries that is countries not themselves on the gold standard, would align their currencies to the pound or the US dollar. Monetary reserves were kept in dollars and pounds which connected them indirectly to gold. The snag in the system was that gold reserves in the core countries had to be large as claims on sterling and dollars accumulated. Britain with its low gold reserves was the weak link within the system. A sudden request, perhaps due to a crisis of confidence, for conversion of dollars or pounds into gold could make the system crash. This is what happened to England in 1931. Once England abandoned the system there no longer existed a coherent international monetary arrangement.

5

During the second half of the 1920s the world was back on what looked like a normal course. In spite of some unfavorable developments such as higher tariffs, world trade expanded. The Great Depression of 1929–1933 changed the picture completely and must be considered as another watershed comparable to World War I. The US depression was almost entirely domestic in origin. The US entered a recession in the summer of 1929, several months before the stock exchange crash in October. When banks began to fail the money supply shrank. The banking system in the US was archaic and the monetary policies of the Federal Reserve were incredibly poor. During the depression of August 1929–March 1933 money GNP in the US declined by 50%. Real GNP fell by 33% whereas industrial production dropped by 53%. Unemployment rose to 25% of the labor force. Given the dominant position of the US economy and of the dollar in the world economy and the fact that exchange rates were fixed, the American depression spread rapidly to the rest of the world. In 1930 the US struck a heavy blow to the world economy by imposing unprecedented duties on imports. The so-called Smoot–Hawley Tariff Act of 1930 created much resentment abroad. Protectionist forces in Congress paid little attention to the argument that a great creditor nation must be willing to accept imports if it expects to receive payment on its loans. The combined circumstances made world trade shrink to about half its predepression level.

The Great Depression was a great divide. In the US it undermined faith in the free market philosophy and gave rise to the welfare state which began with the first term of President Franklin D. Roosevelt in 1933. In Germany the depression helped Adolph Hitler's rise to power, and it played into the hands of such totalitarian countries as Italy and Japan. In the democratic European nations it made the Soviet system appear respectable, undermined whatever faith in economic liberalism was left and gave rise to the Keynesian revolution in economic ideas. It also led to far reaching government interventions similar to those that had prevailed during World War I. The international economic order collapsed and the world witnessed an international crisis of enormous proportions. The result was that every nation looked out for itself which meant tariff wars, quotas, competitive currency depreciations and exchange controls. In the end this created more problems than it solved.

The interwar period has demonstrated that the international division of labor and the economic interdependence of nations are not only sources of prosperity but also factors greatly contributing to world peace. When the liberal world economic order and its institutions were abandoned, nations became far more belligerent. Yet in spite of this the liberal free trade tradition remained strong among many professional economists even if their appeals did not always reach the policy makers of the period. The following readings demonstrate this attachment.

READING 17

Frank William Taussig

Biography

Frank William Taussig (1859–1940), a foremost economist of his age was born in St. Louis, Missouri. He was regarded as America's greatest teacher of economics during the first three decades of the twentieth century. His father had emigrated from Prague to the United States in 1846 and was quite successful in business. His mother was the daughter of a Protestant teacher who emigrated to America in 1848 from a village in the Rhineland (Germany).

Taussig was educated at a public school whereafter he attended a college named Smith Academy. From there, he went to Washington University and in 1876, he transferred to Harvard University. At Harvard, he took economics and history. After his graduation in 1879, came the European tour which allowed him to spend the winter of that year at the University of Berlin studying Roman Law and Political Economy. Returning to Harvard in September 1880, he accepted a position as Secretary to President Eliot of Harvard. This was not a full-time job and he had enough time to complete his PhD in 1883. The topic of his dissertation dealt with the history of tariff legislation in the United States.

In 1885, he became an instructor at Harvard and he advanced quickly to the rank of full Professor of Economics in 1892, a position which he held until his retirement in 1935. In 1888, he published his classic work *The Tariff History of the United States* which established his reputation. In the same year, he married Edith Thomas Guild of Boston. Taussig became the father of one son and three daughters. In 1896, he was appointed to the editorial chair of the *Quarterly Journal of Economics*, a position he kept for 40 years. As an editor, he was tolerant but firm.

From 1905 to 1911, the bulk of his energies went into the composition of his *Principles of Economics* (1911) which appeared in two volumes. It quickly became one of the most widely used textbooks. The section on international trade is outstanding as one would expect. Taussig who had great admiration for Ricardo and Böhm–Bawerk was at his best in the field of applied economic theory. His work was also remarkable for its historical perspective.

In 1910, his first wife died and eight years later he married Laure

Fisher. In 1917, at the request of President Wilson, Taussig accepted the chairmanship of the newly created US Tariff Commission which was to study the then existing tariff structure and make recommendations for its revision. As the leading US authority on international trade, he was an obvious choice.

In 1919, when the war was over, he joined the 'Advisory Committee on Peace' as Economic Advisor to President Wilson. In this function, he spent several months in Paris at the Versailles peace conference. He notes in Chapter 36 of his 'Principles dealing with international trade, that the politicians, legislators and other public men present at this conference were unable to discuss the subject of international trade and protectionism in terms other than mercantilistic ones.

In 1920, Taussig returned to Harvard as a teacher, researcher and chairman of its economics department. A book of collected essays *Free Trade, the Tariff and Reciprocity* appeared in 1920 and his last major piece of work in the field of international commerce was *International Trade* (1927).

Taussig resigned his chair at Harvard in 1935 and began a revision of his *Principles of Economics*. The fourth and last edition appeared in 1939. Taussig died on November 11, 1940 in Cambridge, Massachusetts.

The Work

In the sphere of international economics, his major concerns were with the elaboration of a unified general theory of international trade, the analysis of the international trade mechanism under nonspecie monetary systems and the analysis and history of protectionism.

In the reading which follows, Taussig recognizes that the real implications of international trade are often misunderstood as people tend to see the first and most obvious effects of a given policy while neglecting to inquire into the long-term effects of the same policy. Besides, most people's ideas do not get beyond the stage of sales and of money dealings to begin with. The final remarks on the problems related to the influence of special interest groups are also worthy of notice.[62]

---

62 F.W. Taussig, *Principles of Economics* (4th edition), Vol. 1, Chapters 36, 37 (New York: The Macmillan Company, 1939).

Extracts

Protection and Free Trade. The Case for Free Trade

1. The main argument in favor of free trade between nations has been already indicated. It is a simple corollary from the principles of the division of labor. Exchange between individuals brings the same kind of gain whether they live in the same village or in widely separated districts; things are obtained more easily and abundantly than by each person's producing for himself. The reasoning which shows that it is advantageous for the farmer to exchange with the village blacksmith, Maine with Florida, New England with the Mississippi Valley, California with the rest of the Union, makes out a strong *prima facie* case in favor of free exchange between the United States and England, between France and Germany. The burden of proof may be fairly said to rest on those who assert there is gain from the contrary policy.

Most of the common arguments in favor of restrictions upon trade, by protective duties or otherwise, are fallacious. Many are crudely Mercantilistic, resting on an assumption that imports are bad and exports good. The so-called unfavorable balance of trade is made much of; what is expended on imports is deemed so much wasted or lost. It is supposed that a decline in imports or an increase of exports necessarily brings money into the country; and the notion persists that herein there is a gain – one which results directly from a balance of money secured, not thru those recondited effects on money incomes and foreign prices which were analyzed in the preceding chapter. Few among those who speak of a gain in exports as profitable ever heard of the last-named process or are able, unprepared, to understand it. They think of exports as bringing in money, and imports as taking money out, and money is the be-all and end-all of their economic thinking. Even if it is pointed out that a continuing excess of exports is due to other than merchandise transactions and does not bring in specie, the notion still persists that exports somehow mean gain and imports loss. The elementary truth that exports are but a means of procuring the imports on easier terms than the same goods could be got by making them at home – this is rarely grasped, or, if once grasped, is soon let slip.[63]

Mercantilist notions, universally discarded tho they are by the well informed, affects the policy of nations not only by strengthening the movement toward protection, but in other ways also. The public railways of most countries make special rates for exported goods, on the theory that this sort of movement deserves especially to be fostered. In the United States, the rate regulating authority – the Interstate Commerce Commission – sanctioned the same principle. Shipping subsidies are granted by many countries, and colonies acquired and maintained at great expense, with the same object in view. The United States government spends large sums in gathering information about opportunities for export and in promoting otherwise the export market; while various semi-public agencies and museums cooperate for this supposedly praiseworthy object. Underlying almost all activity of this sort is the persistent belief that there is something peculiarly profitable in international trade, and that the profit appears in the sale of the exports – a belief which exaggerates the importance of the trade and misconceives the nature of the real gain from it.

Perhaps the ancient association of foreigner with enemy still lingers. People do not worry when New England buys coal from Pennsylvania; but when coal is bought from Nova Scotia, dire consequences are supposed to ensue. Half a century ago (more or less) the region which is now British Columbia was claimed by the United States to be part of its territory. Had the Oregon question been settled at that time in accord with the American claims, no one would have questioned that the resources of British Columbia in lumber, coal, and fisheries were of advantage to Americans. But once a border line is drawn, the situation is supposed to change; and that which would have brought us gain in the way of more abundant and cheaper supplies is fraught with peril precisely because these supplies came from a foreigner.

2. Some of the popular arguments in favor of protection call for

---

63 What is true in this regard of the common talk of businessmen and newspaper writers is hardly less true of legislators and other public men. While I was in Paris in 1919, deputed to serve in the re-ordering of trade relations after the war, I found it quite hopeless to attempt to carry on discussion in other than the bald mercantilistic terms. All the representatives of the various allied countries presented their wishes and claims once for all on the basis that any measure promoting the exports of a country was *ipso facto* beneficial and any permitting larger imports *ipso facto* harmful.

brief consideration: that it creates a home market; that it makes employment; and that it raises wages or keeps them high.

When imports are checked, and the things previously imported are made at home, a home market is supposed to be created. It is created; but is not, as protectionists commonly state or imply, an additional market. Another and different market is substituted. Here again most people's ideas do not get beyond the range of sales and of money dealings. When the linen manufacture (say) is established, those engaged in it buy food and other supplies and here, it is supposed, is an additional market for food. The real 'market' – that is, the real exchange – is of food for linens. That same market existed when linens were imported and food or other things were exported in payment. To cut off imports is to cut off exports also; it means simply the substitution of exchange within the country for exchange between countries. The essential question is whether for a given quantity of food (i.e. of labor exerted in producing that quantity) more linen is got in one way than in the other. The very fact that linen can be got cheaper by importation indicates that the foreign market is better than the domestic. The home market argument is most frequently used in the United States with reference to the farmers, who are supposed to get benefit from a greater demand for their products because of the establishment of manufactures. The presumption is, however, that they do not gain but lose; the 'market' which is created offers less in exchange for their products than does the foreign market.

A special form of the home market argument, also much used in the United States, is suggested by the truck farm. Suppose a manufacturing town is established in consequence of protection: the near-by farmers profit by the sale of milk, vegetables, and the like. There farmers do in fact profit; but simply because, while they sell all their produce in the town, they purchase from that town a very small share, if any, of the particular things there made. If they had previously exported all their vegetables and dairy products, and if the manufacturing town, after the duty, supplied precisely the goods which they had previously procured by importation, they would lose, not gain. The truck farmers, in truth, are ordinarily within the limited circle of real beneficiaries from protection. They gain, however, not as farmers, but as landowners. They are like the lucky holder of sites in or near to a newly established town. The great mass of farmers do not gain, but lose – those who supply most of the needs of the manufacturing population and who buy most of its products. The non-landholding people of the manufacturing town also fail to gain. As will appear more fully in the sequel, neither employers nor workmen are permanently better off. Only those gain in the end whose sites, whether agricultural or urban, happen to be more advantageously situated under the new distribution of the population.

Closely connected with the home market argument is that about employment. That protective duties add to the demand for labor seems patent to the everyday man and especially to the workingman. When imports are kept out, is it not clear that more employment exists for the workmen who make at home the things formerly imported? Here again people see only the first and most obvious results, and do not stop to think what other results must follow. If there are less imports, there will be less exports; and labor, if employed more in the new way, is employed less in the old. One of the most persistent of economic errors is the notion that employment is an end, not a means; and one of the hardest things to fasten in the average person's thinking is that the end to which employment should be directed is the increase of the national income – the total flow of consumable goods and of services which constitutes the real revenue of the community. Most working-men oppose labor-saving appliances and welcome arrangements which seem to increase the demand for labor. And most of them are instinctively protectionists, since the same fallacies are current in arguments for protection as in arguments for increasing the employment of labor. The workmen of any one group or set are concerned solely with their own share of the national income. Anything which adds, or seems to add, to the demand for their particular kind of labor is of course welcomed; and then, by an easy transition from the particular to the general, it is inferred, that all labor is more in demand because of the circumstances which increase the demand in this particular direction.

One form of this argument – that employment is created – alleges that there is always unemployed labor and always unemployed capital. Put on a duty, bring this labor and capital together for making an article previously imported – and is there not a gain? The answer is that this problem is far removed from the protective controversy. Unemployed labor is a grave social evil; unemployed capital is a real waste. Some proportion of unemployment, no doubt, is inevitable both for labor and for capital; it results from shifts between occupations, from the processes of change and transition from progress in industry. To minimize it, is among the most important of public tasks; it is also among the most difficult. But there is no ground for supposing that a system of protection would permanently affect it one way or the other.

If a new industry is stimulated in a country by a protective duty, it by no means follows that the labor which is unemployed is adapted to that particular industry or is in a place where it can take advantage of the new opportunities. Those who are out of a job cannot drop at once into the new places provided. Transfer and adaptation require time. And even supposing the improbable outcome that the unemployed labor and capital were really brought together in an industry created by protection – the solution of the problem would be but temporary. Inventions and improvements, redistribution of industries and of population, crises with all their dislocating effects, would ere long cause the problem to present itself again. A country quite without international trade, shut within its own borders, would still be confronted with unemployment, as with other evils, so long as its industry rested on private property, complex division of labor, free movement of labor and capital; so long as there were hopes and fears, successes and failures, in the business world.

3. The great depression of the third decade of this century led to a new turn in the use of the make-employment argument for the support of protective duties. The appalling numbers of the unemployed spurred endeavors to find work for them not only in the fields traditionally thought proper for public expenditure – roads, bridges, buildings for the civil service, men-of-war – but also in operations of the 'private' kind such as workman's dwellings. In these operations the prime object was to create employment. While the resulting product was to be as abundant or useful as possible, the accruing utility was a secondary matter; the main thing was to provide work. Surely it was better, both for the unemployed and the rest of the community, that they should do something than that they should be supported in idleness. Did it not follow that one effective way was to impose duties on imports which would cause things to be made within the country rather than brought in from abroad? True, it might not be easy – as has just been indicated – to fit the unemployed labor into the new industries. Perhaps also, even after the labor had been placed and trained, the product might not be turned out as cheaply as it could be procured by importation. Still, was it not better to employ the labor in this way than to let it stand idle? and did not some net addition to the community's real income thereby accrue? The answer would seem to be quite the same for protective duties as for any of the other works promoted by public funds.

And yet the answer is not quite the same; there is a ground for distinction. The construction of roads, bridges, public buildings, even workmen's dwellings is not likely to continue indefinitely on a suddenly enlarged scale. Sooner or later people will see that this cannot go on without end, – that after all it is but a stop-gap. One may feel some assurance that it will be followed by a period of quiescence; after a while operations of the kind, as they are resumed, will proceed on the scale adapted to current needs. It becomes plain that the sudden huge expenditure is 'wasteful', that is, entails a comparatively disadvantageous application of the community's resources.

The measures are seen to be temporary. But when it comes to protective duties this insight is slow to come, may never come. The vested interests stubbornly oppose any return to the previous and more advantageous channels of industry. All the fallacies and catch words are brought into play: domestic labor against foreign labor, foreign invasions of our markets, the money lost in payment for imports, and so on. Sometimes it happens that by a lucky stroke an industry is called into being which proves able to hold its own even without the prop of a duty – the case of protection to young industries, of which more is said in the next chapter – and then this exceptional outcome is declared to be the common one. All experience proves that when protective duties are once imposed it is extremely difficult to get rid of them, even tho they were originally advocated as mere emergency measures. At the start, they may be more 'wasteful' than other ways of making employment or less so; but either way they are more likely to be retained indefinitely.

4. In the United States by far the most common and most effective argument in favor of protection is that it makes wages high or enables wages to be high. With many persons it is an accepted article of faith that American wages can be kept high, and the American standard of living can be maintained, only if there is protection against the goods made by the cheaper labor of other countries.

With this belief goes another closely similar: that free trade may be advantageous between regions which have the same general range of wages – the same 'standard of living' – but is harmful to a country of high wages when carrying on trade with one of low wages. Between different parts of the United States, or between the United States and Canada, or between Great Britain and Germany unfettered exchange, it is said, may be permissible. But not so when the United States and Germany confront each other in the exchange – least of all, if a country like Japan or China stands on the other side! This fear of universal levelling rests on ignorance or misunderstanding of the causes that lead to the differences between countries in money wages, in prices, in general prosperity. There is here the same ignorance and misunderstanding as in the argument from pauper-labor competition. None put forward in favor of protection are more specious and widely held, none are more fallacious.

Evidently the argument is not of universal application. How could there be any exports at all, if lower wages always gave the foreigner an advantage? As much is exported (virtually as much) as is imported. The exported goods are made by laborers who get high wages in the United States; yet these goods, so far from being undersold in foreign countries, are themselves underselling those of the foreigners. The explanation is simple: the effectiveness of labor in the exporting industries is great, and therefore high wages and low prices coexist. And that effectiveness is the *cause of* the high money wages; and these wages, again, may or may not be accompanied by high prices of the domestic commodities which are outside the realm of international trade. This whole subject cannot be understood except in connection with the principle of comparative advantage. In those industries in which the United States has a comparative advantage in effectiveness, high wages can be paid, and yet low prices accepted, with profit to the employing capitalists. In those in which there is no such advantage, the current high wages cannot be afforded. In this latter class, tho labor be as effective as in competing foreign countries and tho the industries in that sense are well adapted to the country, they encounter the difficulty that other industries are still better adapted, yield still larger returns, and set up a prevalent high rate of wages which these less advantageous industries cannot sustain.

Of course it is true that, when once industries which possess no sufficient advantage have been established under the shelter of protective duties, high wages can be maintained *in those industries* only by the continuance of the duties. This sort of situation – the existence of industries dependent on duties – was historically the occasion of the protectionist argument about wages. Wages have always been higher in the United States, than in other countries. Before a protective system was adopted, it would have been absurd to say that they were due to any such system. When new industries are called into existence by protection, they must, of course, in order to secure their workmen, pay the same wages as are generally prevalent; and once they are established, it can be maintained with reason that high wages to their workmen are dependent on protection. As long as the workmen remain in those industries, the high wages they receive are so dependent.

The free trader argues that if the duties were given up and the protected industries pushed out of the field by foreign competitors, the workmen engaged in them would find no less well-paid employment elsewhere. Presumably they would betake themselves to the exporting industries, in which labor is advantageously applied. The protectionist answers that there would then be 'overproduction' in those industries – that more goods would be produced, prices would be lower, and then wages lower. No, replies the free trader – there would be more goods, but not lower prices or lower wages. For there is a new demand for these exportable goods. The new exports must be paid for by imports; there is a new foreign 'market', replacing the lost domestic 'market'. Goods are imported which were formerly made by protected industries. The eventual result, says the free trader, is that more workmen will be turned to the advantageous industries, and more goods will be exported in exchange for more imports; there will be higher wages (in terms of commodities) all around within the country, resulting from the more productive direction of its labor.

In all this reasoning, the free trader is right. There are some further questions concerning the effect of the supposed change on money wages, which will be presently considered; but these do not affect the essentials of the argument. Of course the reasoning applies only to the long-run course of events. It assumes that labor (and capital, too) will shift from a less profitable to a more profitable industry; that when a protected industry is deprived of support, and those engaged in it are confronted with the alternative of either accepting lower wages or quitting, they will quit and go to better-paid occupations. Any such process of transition is difficult and trying. When carried out on a very large scale – say by the sudden abandonment of a protective system under whose shelter many industries have grown up – it may cause for the time something like disaster. The extent to which existing industries are in fact dependent on protection is commonly exaggerated by both its advocates and its opponents, but none the less the question of vested interests is a very troublesome one. It may be deemed better, on the whole, to let things stand, or change them very slowly and cautiously, rather than incur the disturbance and damage of a radical change. But all this does not affect the question of principle, which is not squarely presented unless we ask what would have been the best policy from the outset.

The question of wages – to anticipate for a moment – is at bottom one of productivity. The greater the productivity of industry at large, the higher will be the general level of wages. There are very intricate problems as to the precise nature of this connection, and as to the shares of the total which go respectively to wages, interest, business profits, and rent. Under certain contingencies, it is conceivable that protective duties will affect the process of sharing, and so will influence wages otherwise than thru their effect on the total product. But these are rare contingencies and are negligible for the discussion of the main problem. Whatever lessens a country's general productivity tends to lower wages. Protection aims to restrict the geographical division of labor; in doing so, it ordinarily turns industry into less advantageous channels (possible exceptions will be considered in the next chapter). Ordinarily it lowers general productivity, general prosperity, general wages.

5. One phase of the wages argument appears in the proposition, much heard in the United States of late years, that duties should be so adjusted as to 'equalize cost of production' between this country and foreign countries. This has been propounded as a 'scientific' solution of the tariff problem. When the labor cost of a commodity, it is said, is higher in the United States, let a duty be imposed sufficient to enable the domestic producer to meet his foreign competitor on terms of equality – and then let them fight it out.

It needs little reflection to show that such a policy, consistently followed, means the complete wiping out of all the advantages from international trade, nay, the wiping out of international trade altogether. The greater the disadvantage of a country in producing a given commodity, the more labor must be given to producing it, and the higher will be the expenses of the employers. In proportion as the efficiency or productivity of labor is less, more must be paid out in wages to secure the greater amount of labor required per unit of output; then 'labor cost' is so much higher; and duties must be made correspondingly high if the labor cost is to be equalized. Any commodity, however unsuited to the industrial possibilities of a country, can be produced in it if only its price is made high enough; and by keeping out foreign competitors, there is no limit (short of the possible extinction of demand) to the rise in price. If the principle of equalizing cost were consistently carried out, we should exert ourselves most strenuously to promote by high duties the domestic production of an article according as we gain most from its importation and lose most by its domestic production. No doubt, the persons who propose the principle would probably refrain from pushing it to its logical conclusion. They would shrink from clapping on duties high enough to cause lemons to be grown in Maine, or (to use Adam Smith's familiar illustration) grapes in Scotland; tho all this could be done if labor costs were unflinchingly equalized. They think only of the commodities for which the domestic disadvantages are not glaring. But the difference is only one of degree. There is no rational reason for saying that a disadvantage in labor cost – that is, a disadvantage in industrial effectiveness – of twenty per cent should be offset by a protective duty, but that one of fifty, one hundred, two hundred per cent should not be so offset.

One thing is to be said in favor of the notion: duties should certainly not *exceed* the rates necessary to 'equalize labor cost'. If they so exceed, there is the possibility that a domestic monopoly may levy additional burdens on the consumers. This possibility arises if competition among the domestic producers is not free. As will presently appear, no special benefits to the protected producers accrue, and no monopoly profits are derived, if domestic competition keeps prices down to the level of expenses of production. Where there is a possibility of monopoly and of abnormal profit to the protected capitalists, it is not unreasonable to say that, if they must have protective duties, these should not be greater than suffice to enable the industry to be carried on. But it is absurd to urge that the proposal, even in this form, is a 'scientific' solution of the protective question. It simply amounts to saying that protection should not be carried to the point where it may foster monopoly.

6. The strength of the general presumption against protection will be made clearer by a consideration of the working of protective duties in greater detail.

When a duty is imposed on a commodity, its price usually rises by the amount of the duty. It does so usually, but not necessarily; and even in those cases where this normal result is to be looked for it does not always come at once, but often only in the end. Strictly, the result is to be expected only if the commodity is produced under free competition and under the conditions of constant return. Ordinarily a duty, like any tax on a commodity, increases by so much the expense of getting the article to market. The amount of the tax or duty must be added to the price charged to the consumer if the producer is to get his usual return. But a rise in price has its effect on demand. Very likely the same quantity cannot be sold at the higher price. The producer, none the less, may not be able to lessen the supply with any promptness; he may have a large plant committed to making the particular thing. For a while, therefore, price may be raised by less than the amount of the tax; conceivably it may not be raised at all. Only as supply is slowly adjusted to the new situation will normal conditions be regained and the price raised so as to recoup the producers and dealers for their increased expenses of production. Hence it is true that a duty on imports, and indeed any tax on a commodity, may fall for a while on the producer, foreign or domestic; while yet in the end it falls with its full weight on the consumer.

So long as the commodity continues to be imported, this rise in price brings a tax, but no national loss. It is true that the consumers are in effect deprived of so much of their incomes; but what they lose, the public treasury gains. Taxes are presumably levied for useful public purposes; they do not stand for waste. If the needed revenue had not been got by customs duties, it would have been got in some other way, and the same amount of tax would have been levied on the public.

Suppose, however, that after the duty has been imposed, domestic producers supplant the foreigners. They charge higher prices than the foreigners did; they *must* charge higher prices, in order to get a profit. If they could bring the commodity to market at the same price as the foreigner, there never would have been any importation. The fact that the domestic producers did not enter the field before the duty was imposed, shows that they are under a disadvantage. When they are stimulated by the duty to enter the field and sell their article at a higher price than the imported one had previously cost, the consumer pays the tax in precisely the same way as if the article continued to be imported – that is, in the shape of higher prices. Only, there is in this case no revenue to the public treasury. The extra price stands for so much bonus to the domestic producers, to enable them to maintain themselves in a disadvantageous industry. And it represents so much national loss. In most discussion of protective duties, at least in the United States, the common assumption is that the creation of a domestic industry, supplying a commodity which was previously imported, represents so much gain. Strictly, the reverse is the case. The payment of duties on continued imports brings no loss; the loss arises when the domestic supply supplants the imports, and duties are no longer paid.

Hence where the principle of free trade is consistently followed, a customs duty on an article is accompanied by an internal tax of the same amount on the domestic product. Then the combined taxes operate solely to bring in revenue, and have no effect on the direction of industry within the country. Such was the system which Great

Britain long followed with complete consistency. Her customs duties were limited to a few articles of general consumption, such as tea, coffee, cocoa, sugar, beer, spirits, tobacco. On beer and spirits, an internal tax was imposed at the same rate as the customs duty. The other articles were such as would not be produced within the country; the duties on them were of a purely revenue kind. Sometimes, in popular discussion, it is said that the imposition of any duties whatever is inconsistent with the principle of free trade. Obviously, this is a mistake; it is only the imposition of duties that cause a substitution of domestic products for imported that conflicts with the principle.

When a customs duty operates to bring into existence a domestic industry, the domestic producers do not make unusual gains; that is, they do not if the commodity is brought to market under competitive conditions. Very likely those who take the initiative in producing the article make unusual profits on the first imposition of a duty. In time, however, profits will fall to the normal level, and at that normal level prices will be higher than foreign prices only if a real disadvantage handicaps the domestic producers. In other words, nobody gains, and the community loses – the loss consisting in its paying more for the protected article than it would have had to pay without the protection.

Where there are not competitive conditions, – where there is a monopoly, complete or partial, permanent or temporary – the domestic producers may make unusual gains. To the extent that they do so, another item enters into the account. There may not only be some national loss, but in addition a shift of income from one set of persons to another set. The commodity may be produced at higher expense within the country, and may have to sell on that account for a higher price than if imported. It may sell for a price still higher, because the domestic producers are in a position to keep out competition and make unusual gains. It may even happen that the imposition of a duty enables domestic producers who are under no disadvantage at all, and who could bring the article to market as cheaply as the foreigners, to form a combination and exact a price higher than the competitive one. In such a case there is no national loss at all. What the consumers lose the monopolists gain.

Naturally enough, this last-mentioned case is precisely that in which protection is least popular, tho in a sense least harmful. Where the protected producers make no unusual gains, the system is supposed to work not unfairly. But the direct robbing of Peter to pay Paul, which seems to appear in case of monopoly, strikes the popular imagination at once and leads to indignation; even tho, on critical consideration, it appears that Paul gains merely what Peter loses and that the community as a whole is no worse off. The more distant consequences on general industrial effectiveness which strict economic analysis brings out are within the ken of comparatively few persons.

The ease with which popular feeling can be roused against a monopoly has led to the frequent allegations by opponents of protection that it breeds monopoly. It was once remarked to a congressional committee of investigation that 'the tariff is the mother of all trusts', and the aphorism became the text of many free trade sermons. Its truth is limited. The causes of combination are deeply rooted in the industries of modern times. They are found mainly in the development of production on a great scale; a tendency so far-reaching cannot be ascribed to a single external cause.

It is true, however, that protective duties have sometimes brought combination more easily and at an earlier date, and sometimes have increased the gains from it. This is likely to be the case where the situation is ripe for consolidation within the country, but not ripe for international consolidation – a stage of development not uncommon, especially in the United States during recent years. The tendency to combination, strong and far-reaching tho it is, does not work out its results automatically, irrespective of favoring causes or legislative influences, or international complications. Protective duties in the United States have been at times during the last generation a favoring cause. Tho the trust problem is in is essence very different from that of protection – a graver problem and of far larger social consequence – the two may interlace.

Just as protective duties may bring unusual gains to some capitalists, if these can keep out competitors, so they may bring exceptionally high wages to some workmen, on the same condition of keeping out competition. This is commonly less easy for the workmen; but it is not impossible, at least for considerable stretches of time. It is feasible most of all in occupations of the handicraft sort, calling for special acquired skill and not subjected to the machine processes. Such was until recent times glass blowing. Certain kinds of glass, especially window glass, called for the services of the blowers, whose trade was not easily learned. They had a tight union, restricted entrance to the trade, and maintained exceptionally high wages. The employers in this industry also combined; so that there was a double monopoly of capitalists and workmen, promoted by very high import duties. The two favored sets alternately quarreled and joined forces, with the advantage in the end, as usual in such cases, to the employers. Here, as elsewhere, new inventions came in, and the application of machinery tended to deprive the handicraft workmen of their special advantage. But so long as the old conditions remained the tariff system may be said really to have kept up wages – not wages of workmen in general, but those of a limited group. And in such cases, as in that of government industries, workmen in general are likely to regard this advantage to a small group with approval, even tho it may mean higher charges to consumers and to the great body of the workmen as consumers. Anything that means high wages to any set of manual laborers finds favor with the labor leaders and doubtless with the dumb rank and file also; partly from mere clannish sympathy, but mainly from inability to distinguish between the causes that bring advantage to all and those that bring advantage to a favored few only.

Protection and Free Trade. Some Arguments for Protection

1. The simpler aspects of the protective controversy have been considered in the preceding chapter – those which bring out most strongly the case for free trade. They tend to show that the increase in price due to a protective duty represents a net loss. But there are ways in which the loss may be offset. The consideration of the various possible modes of offset brings out those arguments for protection which have some validity.

First there is a possible influence on the terms of international exchange. The first effect of a duty is almost always to lessen imports. Even if it be a purely revenue duty, it will lessen them; the rise in price will cause a decline in consumption, unless demand happens to be quite inelastic. If the duty is protective and operates to stimulate domestic production, the decline in imports will be more certain and greater. Hence the movement of specie will be into the country. Then will ensue the train of consequences (always supposing the flow of specie to be considerable and continued) already familiar to the reader. Prices and incomes rise within the country, and fall in foreign countries. Exports in time begin to be checked, as the prices of exported articles rise, imports are stimulated, as the prices of imported articles fall. The length of this period of transition, and the extent of the change before it comes to an end, depend on the play of reciprocal demand. If the commodities exported from a country are of a sort insistently demanded in foreign countries; and if, on the other hand, the commodities which it imports are not such as to be consumed more largely as their prices fall – then the change may be considerable. Eventually equilibrium is reestablished; exports diminish and imports increase until payments again balance. When this stage is finally reached, the country that imposed the duty will have higher money incomes and higher prices. The higher incomes will be of no benefit so far as domestic purchases go, since within the country prices have risen in the same proportion. But they will be of advantage in the purchase of things imported.

In such a case, there is a balance of loss against gain. The consumers lose as purchasers of the protected articles, that is, of those made at home under the influence of the duties; but they gain as purchasers of things that continue to be imported. Even if the particular articles subjected to the duties are completely shut out, there will remain imports of other articles. Thus in the United States protective duties have served to prohibit completely the importation of many manufactures; but tea, coffee, sugar, tropical articles of all sorts, sundry raw materials, some finer manufactures, have continued to come in. All these, if the reasoning of the preceding paragraph holds good, are got in reality more cheaply because of the duties. It is true that some of the things imported, being still subject to duty, are absolutely raised in price; but for this advance there is a full recompense in the revenue received by the public treasury and in the relief (presumably) from other taxes. But even these imports are not raised in price by the full amount of the duties – there is some offset because foreign prices in general have fallen, and domestic money incomes have risen.

How far is reasoning of this sort applicable to the concrete facts? Precisely to the same extent as the general reasoning on the distribution of the gains from international trade. How difficult it is to verify this in detail has already been shown. Take the case of the United States during the half-century following the Civil War, when a system of high protective duties was steadily maintained. Throughout the period a whole series of other factors influenced international trade, some in one direction some in the other. The protective system, in so far as it restricted imports, made for gain in terms of exchange, the high tariff contributing something toward a higher range of money incomes. How far the gain from this source served to offset the loss from the fact that the domestic commodities were produced at higher cost and sold at higher prices is impossible of calculation. In any event no such possibility is reckoned with at all in the popular controversy. Most people who try to persuade the public on one or another side of the tariff question reason only about what is 'good for business,' about employing labor, higher prices to consumers, extortionate monopolies. Even the simpler questions really involved, as to the general effects of the geographical division of labor, they perceive but vaguely; the more intricate ones here considered are quite beyond the understanding not only of the average man but of the average writer on protection.

It is obvious that all countries could not play this game. No one of them has a monopoly of imposing import duties. A condition of mutual grasping and recrimination may be imagined, in which each country tries to get from the other all it can, with the eventual result that, while some advantage accrues to one among them in the form of high money incomes, considerable loss to that country and to the rest is entailed from the curtailment of the advantageous division of labor. Commercial strife has come perilously near this state in modern times; but the immediate object held in view by the combatants has never been that of getting some of the imports cheaper.[64] The motives and objects have invariably been of a semi-mercantilist sort: to check imports and yet to market more and more exports. Reciprocity movements are a compromise resulting from this familiar sort of contest.

2. The argument for protection to young industries points to another way in which the main argument in favor of free trade can be fairly met and the initial loss from protection offset. The gist of it is that an industry really advantageous for a country may be prevented from arising because of ignorance, lack of experience, all the obstacles that impede success in unfamiliar undertakings. Stated in another way, the argument is that while the price of the protected article is temporarily raised by the duty, eventually it is lowered. Competition sets in, it is said, and brings a lower price in the end. The free trader asks, why any need of a duty if the domestic producer is really able to sell at a lower price than the foreigner? The protectionist answer is that the reduction in domestic price comes only with the lapse of time. At the outset the domestic producer has difficulties and cannot meet foreign competition. In the end he learns how to produce to best advantage, and then can bring the article to market as cheaply as the foreigner, even more cheaply. Most persons who use this second form of the argument (alleging the eventual reduction of domestic prices)

64 Remember that these lines were written in the late 1930s (ed.).

are but dimly aware of its identity with that for protection to young industries. But the two arguments are one and the same, resting on the premises of temporary obstacles and eventual success.

The theoretical validity of this argument has been admitted by almost all economists. The question is how far and under what circumstances there is ground for applying protection with prospect of this good result. The argument was first used (in such a way as really to make an impression) in the United States during the earlier part of the nineteenth century, when this country was in the transition from dominantly agricultural and commercial conditions to the stage of modern manufacturing. It was carried from the United States to Germany by its best-known advocate, Friedrich List, who applied it to Germany in her transition during the middle of that century from semi-medieval to modern conditions. The United States was then a 'young' country, and Germany, though an old country, had manufacturing industries that were young so far as modern ways were concerned. In both countries there was force in the contention that manufactures with machinery, power, large-scale operation, were certain to arise in any case, or at least had an advantageous opportunity; and that the process of transition and growth could be made easier, and a beneficial result could be reached at an earlier date, by a temporary handicap on the developed competitors of older countries. England of course was the country then in the van, against which such shelter was sought.

List and the other more moderate advocates of nurturing protection said that duties for this purpose should be moderate and should be temporary. They should be moderate – not to exceed say 25 per cent – because, if the domestic industry was at a great disadvantage in the beginning, there was little prospect that it would ever reach independence. They should be temporary – not to endure more than twenty or thirty years – because in the end, by supposition, the domestic industry would not need them, and ought to be able and willing to face foreign competition. It was further added that agricultural commodities and raw materials give no field for this sort of protection. Their geographical distribution is determined chiefly by unalterable physical conditions. Only in manufacturing industries can the legislator have a prospect of encouraging young industries with good results.

These limitations on the argument are reasonable; more particularly the exclusion of agricultural articles. The government can do much to promote efficiency in agriculture; but chiefly by diffusing education improving the conditions of tenure, promoting science. There are respectable arguments, as will presently appear, for duties on such articles; but they are of a very different kind from this one, which looks to promoting eventual cheapness. The United States long levied protective duties on wool, but never with any prospect of getting wool cheaper thereby. Germany and France levied duties on grain, as England did until 1846 and after 1931; but in none of these cases was there any prospect of thereby securing domestic supplies more cheaply.

The other limitations seem also reasonable; but in actual experience it is not so clear that they must be observed in order to secure the desired result. Not only moderate duties, but very heavy ones, may set things going, and eventually lead to an independent domestic industry. Of this possibility the recent history of the silk manufacture in the United States supplies an illustration. A duty of 60 per cent on silks was imposed during the Civil War (1864). The object at first was revenue. Then a domestic industry grew up; and the duty was maintained, even increased (especially in 1897). Competition became active, and great improvements were introduced. The silk manufacture has indeed been the last of the textile industries to be adjusted to the machine processes; but this development seems to have been promoted in the United States by the establishment of the industry under the shelter of protection. It is certain that advances in manufacturing methods have taken place; it is probable that some branches of the industry, tho not all, have reached the stage where the fabrics can be put on the market as cheaply as they can be imported. Nor is it inconsistent with this outcome that the domestic producers still clamor for protection. They are simply in the habit of doing so. Most business men know very little outside the immediate range of their business. If foreign competition has been long shut off by a high duty, they are ignorant of its possible effects; and if there is a proposal to permit it again, they object on general principles even tho they are quite able to hold their own. The protective system, especially when exaggerated stress is laid on it thru party politics, begets an abject fear of all foreign competition. Notwithstanding this common attitude of the domestic producers, it is quite possible that the object of protection to young industries was in fact attained; tho the only certain way to ascertain this would be to remove the duties and let the domestic producers meet the foreigners on even terms.

While it is possible that protection to young industries may be successfully applied where advantages in production rest not on natural grounds but on acquired skill, it is extremely difficult to say how far there is a probability of such success. The question is part of one much wider – the general causes of the advance of the arts. Economic history shows that the spread of the various trades and manufactures in different countries has taken place by no 'natural' process, and that 'artificial' factors, such as governmental encouragement, the emigration of skilled artisans, the social and political organization of a country have been of large, often dominant, effect. It would be absurd to apply to the conditions of medieval and early modern times a theory of natural advantages and of settled differences in comparative advantages. On the other hand, the lesson of history seems to be that other modes of encouragement have been more effective than protective duties; such as rational education, free industry, abatement of social barriers, promotion of invention by patents and trade-marks. In very modern times – with the wide diffusion of industrial education, the ease of communication, the technical press, the eager search for all ways of investing capital at a profit – the argument for protection to young industries would seem to have lost much of its force. None the less, possibilities still exist, as in the case of the silk manufacture just cited. Unfortunately the decisive test – eventual removal of duties – is one which domestic producers are likely always to oppose; and so long as their opposition is successful it will be difficult to ascertain in any particular case whether the community ultimately gets a real gain sufficient to offset the initial loss.

......

4. While subsidies – direct payments to domestic producers – are the one form of protection available to the shipping trade, in other industries there is a choice between subsidies and import duties. During the seventeenth and eighteenth centuries, the period of unblushing mercantilism, subsidies were freely applied over a wide range. In the course of the nineteenth century, they were gradually dropped, few remaining at its close. Their disappearance was the result in part of the administrative difficulties inevitable in guarding them from abuse, even more of the general features of the great changes in all these matters during the post-war period of the twentieth century that direct subsidies or bounties again came to be paid on a large scale in the most varied parts of the world, – not only on the Continent and in Great Britain, but in countries as different as Australia and British India. In Great Britain, once the tenacious upholder of free trade principles, bounties were given on articles of

the kind for which the free trade reasoning had been supposed to have the greatest validity, such as agricultural products (wheat and sugar beet). This change, like so many others among the unexpected disruptions brought on by the war of 1914–18, rested on interests, prejudices, trains of reasoning in which the economic aspects were either glossed over or deliberately set aside; an aspect of the situation of which more will be said presently.

Bounties or subsidies are a less popular and hence a more vulnerable method of protection than import duties. Import duties, while in essentials they come to much the same thing as bounties, can be defended by a host of persuasive tho fallacious arguments. The direct payment of money to a favored industry presents in unmistakable form the question whether it is really worth-while thus to tax the community. From the free traders' point of view, this very simplicity is an argument in favor of using in all cases bounties and subsidies rather than import duties. The general recognition of the need of taking account of the repugnance to bounties is shown by the fact that they are not often granted without limit of time; they are usually for a stated period only, after which they cease either at one stroke or by gradual steps. It is rare that any provision for automatic cessation or reduction is made when protective duties are imposed.

It is this difference between subsidies and protective duties – as to probability of permanence – which signifies most. As regards lasting effects, the economic difference is in the ways in which the lessening of the national dividend is worked out. The real enduring consequences are the same. In the case of duties, the ultimate outcome is that the prices of the taxed articles are higher than they would otherwise be; while yet the government gains no revenue. Bounties, on the other hand, cause no rise in prices of the subsidized articles, even tho the industries are such as could not be carried on without them. The bounties are a drain on the public revenue and merely serve to offset the inability of the assisted industries to produce the articles as cheaply as they could be had thru importation. This is the gist of the free-trade reasoning – the economic reasoning. In the end, no individuals gain, but the community loses. All else is but qualification and explanation.

The first effect in both cases, however, is that somebody gets gains at the expense of somebody else; and in both it is the stage of initial gains which is most conspicuous and bulks largest in popular discussion. In both cases, again, the stage of high gains may last for a considerable period. The more imperfect competition is, the longer will the gains last; if there is a well-entrenched monopoly, indefinitely long. Whatever the conditions – pure competition, imperfect competition, monopoly – what we hear loudest from the free traders is talk about ill-gotten gains, plundering one set of people at the expense of another, robber barons; while the protectionists avow that they are increasing the demand for labor, helping the workingman, fostering domestic industries, keeping the money in the country. In all of which there is – as regards the short-period consequences – a modicum of truth on both sides, yet little understanding of the heart of the question: whether government by either sort of legislation can succeed in directing industry into more productive channels and so in raising the total national income of goods and services.

5. Considerations as to general social soundness are supposed by some to strengthen the case for free trade, by others that for protection. But it is doubtful whether a strong case can be made out on such grounds either way. It is said by the protectionists that diversified industry brings social and educational advantages and that a community whose occupations have a very narrow range will be deficient in intelligence and adaptability. In view of the degree of industrial diversity which is certain to appear under any circumstances in a modern country of advanced civilization, this sort of vague allegation has no probative force. Free traders have argued on the other hand that a diversity of industries secured by the promotion of manufactures at the expense of agriculture is more likely to bring bad social and political consequences rather than good ones. Manufactures mean large-scale production, concentration in comparatively few hands of management and of ownership, dependence of workmen on wages by hire, increasing inequality. They mean, too, crowding in cities, and the temptation to exploit women and children. In the earlier part of the nineteenth century arguments of this sort were much used in the United States against protection. They were not without weight; they may not have quite lost their weight. The soundest parts of our American nation are in those regions of the North where agriculture is still the dominant industry. But after all the mode in which an industry is conducted and the character of the people engaged in it are more important than the nature of the industry itself. The workingmen of the English manufacturing districts in Lancashire, Yorkshire, and Scotland are better social stuff than the agricultural laborers of eastern Germany and probably even than most of the peasant proprietors of France. Protection and free trade are minor factors as compared with the diffusion of education, the general range of intelligence, the

distribution of wealth and income, the demarcations of social classes, political and industrial freedom.

A special application of social and political arguments was made in Germany in the opening years of the twentieth century, combined with reasoning of a strictly economic sort. There the controversy was between the advocates of the *Agrarstaat* and of the *Industriestaat*, the former being in favor of duties on grain and other agricultural products, the latter opposed to them. To the former – the protectionists – dependence on foreign countries for indispensable foodstuffs always seems to entail evils and dangers. An agricultural population, or at least a population with a due proportion settled on the land, is thought to be better social material than one mainly engaged in manufactures. A great development of manufactures, moreover, and a dependence on foreign markets for disposing of the products, bring uncertainty. Hostile tariffs, or the loss of the advantage in production on which the exportation rests, may put an end to the trade and endanger the established industries. Finally – and here the crux of the arguments was reached – the relations between the European manufacturing countries and the overseas countries which developed during the last quarter of the nineteenth century were regarded as essentially temporary – temporary, that is, compared with a nation's life history. The supply of food, and especially of wheat, from the United States, Argentina, Canada, rest on methods of cultivation which could not be permanently maintained. The continuous use of the soil for the same crops can be kept up only so long as new land remains available. Sooner or later – and it will be soon, say these protectionists – the virgin lands will all be occupied; and then a conserving cultivation, with varied crops, must come. Meanwhile, population in the new countries increases rapidly, their own consumption of foodstuffs becomes greater, their economic situation becomes steadily less favorable to the exportation of grain and the like.

Hence – so the argument ran – those old countries in which great manufactures develop, based on an exchange of the manufactured products with imported food, must face the possibility, nay the probability, of an eventual revulsion. Food will no longer be obtainable by importation. The manufacturing population must then go back, in part at least, to the land. But this population, under the stimulus of plentiful employment and cheap food, will have become large, and an endeavor to support it at home will meet all the obstacles of diminishing returns from land. The example of England is held up as a warning. Her great population, which the country's own resources cannot possibly supply with food and materials, is necessarily dependent on foreign trade, and must be constantly uneasy lest trade with other countries may fail.

There is much validity in this train of reasoning. As put forth by careful thinkers, it admits the *prima facie* loss from protection. In the present generation food is indeed got cheaper by foreign trade, and the exchange of manufactures for food is for the time being advantageous. Some of the ardent protectionists hesitate in this sort of admission, as people commonly hesitate and minimize in such concessions to their opponents; but the admission must be made. It must be admitted also that the process of checking the growth of manufactures by making foodstuffs dear is a trying one. It is a sacrifice to the future which in the present generation may be unpopular. But where the sentiment of nationality is strong and the welfare of coming generations is prized, such sacrifice may be willingly made.

To go into all the details of the controversy on *Agrarstaat* and *Industriestaat* would pass the limits of this book. The free traders aver that in a country of great extent and diversified climate like Germany, no such extreme development of manufactures as in England is to be looked for; that the probability of failure of supplies from food-exporting countries is exaggerated; that if there comes eventually a check to the exchange of manufactures for food, it will be by no sudden disastrous halt, but by a gradual process to which industry and population can adjust themselves; and finally that, for the present generation, the burden of import duties is heavy and that the chief beneficiaries are a small knot of large landed proprietors. The main economic argument of the protectionists, as to the future failure of food supplies, raises a question difficult in many directions – namely, how far it is wise to go in the restriction of immediate satisfactions for the sake of a distant and more or less uncertain future. Shall we now for example husband our coal supplies, which we know to be limited? Or shall we use them freely according to present needs, partly indifferent to the distant future, partly trusting to possible discoveries and improvements for other sources of heat and power? Shall the Germans (and the English, too) maintain a policy of free trade and of dependence on distant countries for food and materials needed now, without speculating too anxiously upon the continuance of these supplies in the uncertain future? It is easy to err in endeavoring to provide too solicitously for coming generations. Such are some of the large problems which the protective controversy presents in a country like Germany – problems which give fair ground for differences of opinion, and involve considerations much weightier than those usually put forward by protectionists in the United States.

6. A similar phase of the tariff controversy developed in England. True, the steps towards a manufacturing nation (*Industriestaat*) had been irrevocably taken, and the question was as to the best means of remaining with safety and prosperity in this far-developed stage. It would seem at first sight that here a policy of free trade alone is tenable. Yet the reaction against it appeared in England also, and was not without the support of effective arguments. These arguments, so far as they are of weight, turn mainly on the expediency of reciprocity arrangements.

In the preceding pages it has been said more than once that exaggerated importance is commonly attached to a country's exports. For a country in England's situation, however, there is substantial ground for watching the exports with special care and perhaps with some anxiety. They are the means for obtaining indispensable imports. The alternative of producing the imports at home – of turning the labor and capital from making the things exported to making those now imported – hardly exists. England must import; and in order to import, she must export. Hence everything which lessens the market for exports must cause concern. Among the ominous possibilities is the imposition of protective duties elsewhere. It is a matter of large consequence for England to maintain in other countries an open market for herself. Hence the advocacy of imperial federation or imperial preference duties as a means of inducing the colonies to relax, if not to give up, their duties on English goods; and hence the advocacy of duties on foreign goods in England, as a means of chaffering with other countries in negotiations for the reciprocal reduction of tariff barriers. In England, as in all countries, the vulgar fallacious arguments in favor of protection play a large part in the popular controversy: such as increased employment for home labor, support of domestic industry, tribute to foreigners in payments for imports, and so on. But these arguments are more insidiously dangerous in England than anywhere else. That country depends for its very existence on manufacturing industries which are able to face the competition of the world. If once these industries, one and all, cannot face foreign competition – if they really must lean on protection against foreigners – her future is dark. The only solid ground for advocating duties on all the manufactured products is that some industries are still in the van and that an all-inclusive system would enable the diplomats to haggle more effectively for the admission of their products into other countries. And the only ground for preferential arrangements with the colonies is to induce them to admit English goods with no duties or with duties lower than those imposed on non-British goods.

In general, a retaliatory policy, that is, the levy of duties on imports in retaliation for duties elsewhere on a country's exports, makes the economic situation not better, but worse. If Germany levies duties on English goods, the advantages from the division of labor between the two countries are lessened by so much. If England then levies duties on German goods, those advantages are lessened by so much more. If, indeed, one takes the Mercantilist view of foreign trade and assumes that its chief object is to procure a market for the exports, then retaliation and reciprocity assume a different aspect. Then a country becomes always intent on increasing its exports and always uneasy at increasing its imports; and then it will perhaps consent to admit some imports more freely only if tempted by a bait of selling some exports more freely. So long as this state of mind exists, there is at least a possibility of securing an eventual relaxation of restrictions by first imposing restrictions.

What may be the substantial grounds for expecting a real extension of international trade through reciprocity treaties, it is difficult to say. Adam Smith remarked that this matter was not for the economist but for 'that crafty and insidious animal called the statesman or politician.' The staunch free traders aver that other countries will go their way undisturbed by retaliatory duties or preferential offers, or will make concessions that are only nominal; and that the initiating country herself will suffer at once from her own restrictions, and in no way gain in the end. On the other hand, it must be admitted that the Mercantilist notions persist with extraordinary tenacity. The immense majority of persons think of a reduction of duties not as a gain to their own country but as a favor shown to the foreigner; and conversely they think of tariff reductions by foreigners as the opportunity to sell more goods abroad and profit thereby.

7. The growth of protection during the closing years of the nineteenth century and the opening years of the twentieth was a remarkable phenomenon, in view of the weight of rational opinion against most of the arguments commonly advanced for it. During the generation following the repeal of the English corn laws in 1846, the indications seemed to be that free trade, or at least a great relaxation of customs barriers, would extend over the civilized world. But in the

decade 1870–80 the current began to turn the other way. Country after country moved toward protection, and even in England, the home of free trade, signs of reaction appeared. The protectionist movement is explicable on various grounds. The growth of nationalist feeling was one important cause. Protection seems, to most people, a 'national' policy, and in fact is so, in the sense of causing exchanges to be made within a country rather than between countries. The principle of free trade has a certain cosmopolitan flavor, and assumes as well as promotes a spirit of peace and good will among the nations. Another cause was the admitted need of a thorough reconstruction of economic theory. This promoted skepticism as to free trade, which was one of the cardinal doctrines of the older school; although no part of the system of the older economists has stood the test of time and criticism better than their reasoning about international trade. Still another cause was the competition of overseas countries with the agricultural producers of the Continent. The landed interest there, formerly indifferent or hostile to duties, joined in the demand for protection against underselling foreigners. At all events, during the generation preceding the war of 1914–18 a wave of protection succeeded the previous one of free trade.

After the war of 1914–18, the wave of protection mounted higher and higher, and free trade was quite swept away. In part this arose from the same causes as those of the pre-war period. Economic theory gave more and more attention to imperfect competition, and to the play of demand rather than to any steadying influence of supply. It cannot be said that the essential conclusions concerning international trade, as stated in the preceding pages, were seriously impugned; but their exposition could not be so confident and dogmatic. As regards the whole wide range of state action for directing the channels of industry, a less confident tone about international trade was the result of the growing belief that there must be more of conscious and deliberate control of economic activity; more planning all around, not merely in the international distribution and diversification of industry but also in monetary systems, the ordering and steadying of domestic industry. Much of this was brought about by the extraordinarily severe depression which set in after 1929, the distracting confusion of the industrial and monetary situation, the resort to any and every means which might somehow promise to promote stability. In the field of international trade the most important element was the intensification of nationalist feeling. That led to an even more stringent protectionist policy than before the war in the United States and in continental countries, and to the definitive adoption by Great Britain of a bargaining and 'quid pro quo' policy. The extreme form of protectionism appeared in Germany; the advocacy of autarchy (*Autarkie*), which came from people of the most various sorts, – mystics, idealists, fanatics, political and economic leaders. It called for isolation in every country and complete economic independence, above all for Germany. Such a consummation obviously was not feasible unless a country had a large and diversified area. The proclaimed ideal was both effect and cause of the demand for political changes. Its realization might be deemed not impossible for the United States, or for a newly created state or confederation in the middle of Europe. The British Commonwealth might conform to it after a fashion. Even though it could not give promise either of complete free trade within the range of that huge and unwieldy Commonwealth, or of complete isolation from non-members, it might bring about such moderation of protection in the several constituents of the Commonwealth as would maintain a great part of the advantages from free trade while still placating the demand for friendly trading with your countrymen and aloofness from others.

In all this there was more froth and foam than in the pre-war period, more loose talk and superficial thinking; and also more attention, even though not of a wiser sort, to other than economic considerations. So far as the economic aspects go, there was little to say beyond what had been threshed out again and again. It was a time when aspects other than economic were forced on men's minds more and more; both the relations of social classes to each other and those of nations and peoples. These matters of political, social and ethical philosophy are in part quite within the range of economics, but in good part go beyond it. So far as international trade is concerned, the reasonings and conclusions of our science are based on the assumption of continued peaceful dealings. Their trend is against war, against the blocking and disruption of trade. It is toward amity, good will, cooperation in all the dealings of men with each other.

8. In the United States a severely protective tariff was maintained for half a century after the Civil War. The financial exigencies of the war caused high duties to be levied, and in subsequent years these were retained. A rigid and all-inclusive system of protection grew up, and persisted without serious modification (barring a brief reaction in 1894–97) during the post-war period, – indeed with a marked accentuation in 1922 and in 1930.

The economic effects of this system it is impossible to follow empirically. We have seen that its effects on the terms of international exchange are so interwoven with those of other factors that no unraveling is possible. Even more baffling is the task of following or measuring its effects on general prosperity. The protectionists, on this subject as on the rate of wages, have preached and protested that all good things come from their tariff. Such talk results naturally from the exigencies of partisan conflict and the need of simple arguments for the mass of voters. So loud and persistent has been the talk that for many persons, even for many who are not unintelligent or uneducated, it has become an article of faith that the prosperity of this country rests on the protective tariff. Yet there is no greater delusion. A multitude of factors explain our general welfare – vast resources, a far-spread division of labor within the country, a free, active, and intelligent population. Has not this North American region been for several centuries, under all sorts of economic and political conditions, the envy of the world? But to trace in detail the part played by any one factor in promoting or retarding the enviable outcome is well-nigh impossible. Certain it is that, so far as the tariff is concerned, we must rely chiefly on general reasoning. The first and obvious effect of protection is to turn industry into less advantageous channels; and there is, in my judgement, no good case to rebut this general conclusion and to establish a balance of gain from such a tariff system as the United States has had since the Civil War.

Yet it should be said that on many articles the duties were but nominal. These are the articles which were made as cheaply within the country, and (competition being active) were sold as cheaply. The mere imposition of a duty does not raise prices. It does so only if a foreign supply is cut off and a more expensive domestic supply is thereby induced, or a domestic monopoly fostered. The extent to which manufacturing industry in the United States is dependent on the tariff system is vastly exaggerated by the protectionists. One would suppose, from their doleful predictions, that not a chimney would smoke but for the tariff. In fact, the United States is certain to be a great manufacturing country under any conditions. So much is assured by its resources of coal and minerals and by the ingenuity and enterprise of its people. Its comparative advantage is by no means confined to agriculture. But this same consideration indicates that the free traders went too far in ascribing ill effects to all the parts of the protective system. It did not change the course of industry so greatly as their charges implied. The country would be as prosperous, would have industries as diversified, without a high tariff as with it. The quantitative effect of a protective tariff is commonly exaggerated in all countries, not in the United States only.

9. The conditions on which depends the maintenance of manufactures in a country like the United States deserve a moment's consideration. The usual cause of advantage in manufactures is better machinery and methods. Take the case of the shoe manufacture, which has been cited as one of our efficient and independent industries. Shoes are not imported; they are beginning to be exported in considerable quantities. The Americans have taken the lead in the invention and perfection of machinery for making them. But machinery can be bought or copied. The Germans, perhaps, can copy it, and then, working it with cheaper labor, can undersell the Americans. This is often true of the Germans, or at least was so; they have been good imitators, though slow originators. It is said that American steel skates, devised and perfected in the United States, were copied to the smallest detail in Germany, and then, being made there with cheaper labor, were imported into this country. This sort of imitation is not usually possible; since for the operation of machinery a force of intelligent and skillful mechanics is often as necessary as the machinery itself, and is much more difficult to secure. But the thing is possible, if not always at least in many cases; and the more so if machinery becomes automatic. The salvation of the industry then is, in a country like the United States, incessantly to improve machinery. Constant progress is the condition of maintaining the comparative advantage. Once the same methods – that is, the same effectiveness of labor – prevail the world over, than the country where wages are lower can sell cheaper.

It is commonly said that the United States is likely to have an advantage in those manufactures where machinery is much used. This is true; but the real explanation is not often given. The mere use of labor-saving machinery does not give an advantage. Machinery represents only one way of applying labor. It is the use of labor-saving machinery to a greater degree or in a more ingenious way that enables the output to be comparatively cheap even though the wages of laborers are high. In those industries which are adapted to the machine processes, American labor is *likely* to be more efficient. Which those industries are, cannot be settled by any rule. The march of invention is irregular. Sometimes Americans take the lead, sometimes Englishmen, sometimes Germans or Frenchmen. It is proverbial that Americans have a more than creditable record in this sort of competition; and the economic corollary is that they do well to confine their manufacturing activity to those industries in which they seem able to keep in the van.

In some cases in the recent history of manufacturing industry in the United States, it is to be admitted that this process of getting the lead seems to have been promoted by protection. That is, protection to young industries has been successfully applied. The object has been attained by a rude, blundering, expensive method; but we must grant that attained it has sometimes been. The silk manufacture has already been cited as an example. Possibly the iron and steel manufacture presents another. But this latter case is more doubtful, because the question always arises whether such an industry, already established on a moderate scale in the country, would not probably have grown to independence under any circumstances. The steady increase and thickening of population and the growing scarcity of free land tended in any event to bring about the development of other than agricultural industry. The great streams of immigration and the altered conditions of labor supply thereby brought about strengthened still more this tendency. The tariff system, even where it may seem to have acted in the way of protection to young industries, often merely quickened development which would have come soon enough without it.

In this review of the tariff problem nothing has been said of some of its more obvious bad aspects – the pressure of interested producers to obtain measures favorable to themselves, the contributions of a semi-corrupt character to party chests, the log rolling by which each legislator strives in the general scramble to secure duties that will be of benefit, or at least will be thought of benefit, to his own constituents. The tendency in popular government for each representative to press the real or supposed interests of his special constituents is the greatest evil of democracy. It has been experienced to the full in tariff legislation. But it appears in many directions, in things good as well as in things doubtful – in education, harbor improvements, the postal service, public control of railways and other industries. Something of the sort must be faced whenever the State undertakes to direct and regulate matters of immediate economic consequence. We should give attention chiefly to the general outcome, under such working conditions as the existing state of political machinery makes possible; and from this point of view the question of protection also must be judged.

READING 18

Arthur Cecil Pigou

Biography

Arthur Cecil Pigou (1877–1959), Professor of Political Economy at Cambridge University from 1908 to 1943, was born at Ryde, on the Isle of Wight on November 1877. Of Huguenot descent and the son of a retired army officer, Pigou won an entrance scholarship to Harrow, a famous private boarding school. In 1897, he went up to King's College, Cambridge as a history scholar. During his third year, he embarked upon the study of economics. He began to lecture on economics in 1901 and in 1908 he succeeded Alfred Marshall as Professor of Political Economy. He held the chair for 35 years. It was primarily through Pigou that the Marshallian tradition was handed down and became the focus of the Cambridge School of Economics. Pigou was still very active when Keynes published his *General Theory*. In spite of health problems which developed after 1927, he outlived Keynes by thirteen years.

The Work

His principal contribution was to the field of welfare economics, a subject he helped to create. In 1912, he published *Wealth and Welfare* later transformed into *The Economics of Welfare* (1920). In this work, Pigou saw the possibility of a divergence between what he called the marginal private product and the marginal social product of an investment. The private production of a commodity can have negative, disturbing or other costly effects on third parties. A factory which pollutes the air does not carry all the costs of production. In today's terminology, an externality is imposed upon outsiders. Alternatively, there may also be situations in which a private enterprise fails to be the recipient of all the benefits of its operations. A firm planting trees may remain uncompensated for the climatic benefits it occasions. Thus, from society's viewpoint, sometimes too many of some goods are produced and sometimes too few and that is because (in contemporary terms) social costs diverge from private costs. According to Pigou, social welfare is maximized when the marginal social and private products are equal. Pigou recommended the imposition of taxes or fines on activities which created losses in welfare and subsidies on activities which created gains.

An implication of this type of analysis is that there are cases where the pursuit of private actions does not harmonize with the public interest. Therefore, this kind of argument could involve a weakening of the traditional liberal position, and give ammunition to advocates of government intervention. In 1912, Pigou himself was still very much a classical liberal and was thinking in terms of small changes within the framework of a free enterprise society.

During the last years of the nineteenth and the early years of the twentieth century, tariff reform was a subject of acute political controversy in England. As a publicist and a speaker, Pigou threw himself in the public debate arguing the case of free trade. In 1903, he published *The Riddle of the Tariff* and in 1906 *Protective and Preferential Import Duties*. During these years, Pigou was a cheerful, social person and a popular speaker, very different from the rather eccentric recluse he became in later years.

In the two publications mentioned above, Pigou also opposed the ideas of Joseph Chamberlain (1836–1914): British statesman, famous as a champion of social reform, imperial expansion and consolidation and tariff reform. Chamberlain wanted higher tariffs to supply the revenue necessary for the social reforms he advocated. He was also worried by the effects of increasing German and American competition and the protective tariffs which Germany and the United States had adopted. Chamberlain was convinced that new economic bonds rather than free trade were necessary to preserve and enhance the cohesion of the British Empire. His solution was the abandonment of free trade and the adoption of reciprocal preferential arrangements among the various parts of the Empire. Chamberlain withdrew from politics in 1906 for health reasons and died in 1914. Although he failed to convince his country at that particular time, he was a forerunner and inspirer of the themes (social reform, abandonment of laissez-faire, adoption of protectionism) that were to increasingly dominate British politics in the interwar period.

The first reading taken from *The Riddle of the Tariff* discusses free trade and protectionism in more general terms. At the time of writing, England was still on the gold standard. The second reading taken from the same work discusses the preferential arrangements advocated by

Mr. Joseph Chamberlain.[65]

The Riddle of the Tariff

We may now pass from current cries to current problems. The first of these – one, be it observed, which has been brought into prominence, not by the recognized leaders of any political party, but by a number of more or less irresponsible journalists and pamphleteers – is whether it would not be well for a considerable portion of the national revenue to be raised from Customs duties upon imports which compete with the products of home industries. I put the question in this form because I am anxious to be as fair as possible to those who are dissatisfied with our existing Free Trade policy. It must be confessed that partially protective taxes have not been credited by certain 'Cobdenite' writers with the contribution which they yield to the national exchequer, and it is plainly erroneous, when discussing their general merits and demerits, to ignore this aspect of the matter.

Nevertheless, I am bound to add, in passing, that, if the usual method of describing the subject of controversy is unduly favorable to Free Traders, the one which is here adopted is hardly less so to their opponents. For, though, in theory, it is quite easy to imagine a fiscal system consisting of partially protective taxes, whose amount is strictly limited by the money requirements of the State, in practice such a conception is very unlikely to be realized. Many of the import duties of the United States were originally levied, during the war period, for purely revenue purposes.[66] They were coupled with corresponding excise duties, and were adjusted to the necessities of national expenditure. When peace was restored, however, the excise was abolished, and the revenue motive for the tariff was very shortly crushed by the protective motive. The right position of affairs was reversed, national expenditure came to be adjusted to the yield of the protective duties, and various extravagant expedients had to be devised for disposing of an entirely unnecessary surplus. Does not the suggestion that old-age pensions could be more readily instituted, if Mr. Chamberlain's tariff proposals were carried through, indicate – apart altogether from the merits of that particular social policy – that

---

65 A.C. Pigou, *The Riddle of the Tariff*, Chapters 2 and 5 (London: R. Brimley Johnson, 1904).
66 Pigou has the civil war in mind here (ed.).

dangers of this class cannot safely be ignored even in our own country?

That point, however, need not be further pressed. I pass to compare the merits of two tariff systems, yielding the same revenue, but differing from each other in that one does, and the other does not, incidentally protect native producers. At the outset it must be observed that the popular distinction between protective and non-protective taxes is one of degree and not of kind. To some extent every import duty 'protects' – that is to say, shelters from foreign competition – one or more home industries. For competition is not solely between goods of the same class and the same name. Tea, for instance, competes in the market with other beverages, and the tea-duty undoubtedly affords a slight degree of 'protection' to the brewing interest. The real question, therefore, is not between Free Trade and Protection, but between a less and a greater amount of the latter. I make this observation because certain writers seem to imagine that when they have pointed out an inaccuracy in the use of the *phrase* Free Trade, they have demonstrated an absurdity in the *policy*. Consequently, it is as well to state quite definitely that by Free Trade I mean a system in which the protective element is slight and accidental, and, by Protection, one in which it is considerable and avowed.

A question typical of those involved in any comparison between the two systems is whether it would be for the good of the country as a whole that the £5,000,000 now collected upon imported tea should be assessed, instead, upon imported iron and cotton goods. Of course, considerations based upon the pathological effects of tea-drinking must be ruled out of the discussion. That commodity is taken simply as a convenient instance of one which is imported, but is not produced at home. In order to understand the Protectionist argument, let us put ourselves at the point of view of a group of English manufacturers in some industry that is face to face with severe foreign competition. They see, perhaps, that not only their foreign, but their home markets also, are being gradually taken away from them; that continental manufacturers, working under less stringent factory laws, and employing workmen who are contented with a lower rate of wages, are able to offer their commodities for sale at prices with which they themselves are unable to compete. They see their profits dwindling, and the expansion of their industry checked. Many of their number are driven to contract their sales, and some of them either to abandon their business altogether or to transfer it to another place. Meanwhile, many of the workmen engaged in the industry are thrown out of work, while the wages of those still employed have to be reduced. Whole families are brought down to a state of poverty, and the distress to which they are subjected very likely reacts permanently upon the physical, mental, and moral efficiency of their children. The evil is obvious to everybody, and nothing could be more natural than the view that the importation of cheap foreign goods, out of which it directly arises, should be checked by means of a moderate import duty.

Now, if we were entitled to confine our attention to the immediate and direct effect which this remedy would have upon the particular trade in question, the foregoing argument would be a perfectly valid one. But in economics, as in most other sciences, the 'things which are seen' by the superficial observer are often of much less importance than 'the things which are not seen.' The statesman must look beyond the immediate to the ultimate results of the measures that he proposes, and he must take account of their influence not only upon the industry which they are primarily designed to benefit, but also upon the other constituent parts of the community. When this is done in the present instance, the situation quickly assumes an altered aspect. For what precisely is the malady with which we are confronted? Primarily it is a case of dislocation of industry. The symptoms which have been catalogued above are by no means confined to businesses in which foreign competition plays an important part. On the contrary, they appear in an aggravated form whenever the push and energy of growing firms begin successfully to attack the market of old-established rivals. When new machinery and new processes are invented, their presence is still more marked. Plant representing large capital outlay is rendered worthless, and there is much temporary unemployment. These symptoms are the inevitable concomitant of movement, and movement is the very essence of modern life. It is not because of Free Trade, but because the industrial army is continually advancing, that the road is strewn with abandoned baggage and lagging men. Dislocation through foreign competition is only a single species of a far larger genus. People who are prepared to welcome mechanical inventions for the sake of their ultimate contribution to national wealth, and in spite of the temporary disturbances which they almost always create, cannot logically object when the same result, accompanied by the same disadvantages, is introduced by foreign competition.

The real problem for us to consider, therefore, is not the temporary incidents of the process of adjustment between the trade of different nations, but the ultimate effects of Free Trade and Protection respectively upon the real income of the United Kingdom. Let us return, then to the tea duty. The detriment inflicted upon the people of the country by that impost is measured by the amount of the duty actually paid, together with an additional loss of satisfaction arising from the fact that, in consequence of the enhanced price, a reduced quantity of tea is consumed. If the same amount of revenue were collected from imported manufactures, both these elements of sacrifice would, other things equal, remain the same. In addition to them, however, there would be a further loss arising from the fact that industry would be diverted from its natural course. Owing to the enhanced price of the protected articles, British labor and capital would be attracted to the business of producing them instead of to some other business in which it would otherwise have been employed. Capital and labor may, however, be presumed, in a country where enterprise is free, to gravitate towards different occupations in such relative quantities as to yield, directly and indirectly, a greater amount of desired commodities than could be produced under any other arrangement. The productive powers of the nation, in seeking the most profitable employment, are drawn by that very fact to those in which they are most efficient. When, therefore, a given quantity of capital and labor is artificially restrained in an occupation, from which it is being impelled away by the broad economic forces of the time, there must, in general, be a loss of total efficiency. If, in the normal course, it would have been devoted to the manufacture of bicycles to be sent abroad in exchange for bonnets, it will yield, when held down, through the operation of a protective tariff, to the direct production of bonnets, a smaller quantity of these than it could have obtained by the indirect method of exchange. Thus, protective taxes, so far as they really do protect any native industry, inflict upon the country imposing them the evil of a less efficient employment of its resources, in addition to the other sacrifices which all Customs duties necessarily involve. They may confer a benefit upon a particular group of producers, but only at the cost of a more than equivalent loss to the rest of the community. For this reason they are economically inferior to a Customs tariff of the kind now established in England.

But it may be answered: 'This reasoning would be all very well if our Free Trade system involved foreign competition merely with one or two of our minor products. As a matter of fact, however, it causes us to be threatened on every hand, and, so far from rendering the employment of our resources more efficient, makes it very doubtful if we shall long have an opportunity of employing them at all. It may, perhaps, be true that it causes goods to be cheaper; but what is the use of this if, through the destruction of our industries, we find ourselves without the money wherewith to buy them?'

In order to answer this very plausible objection, it is necessary to look a little more closely at the nature of international trade. Foreigners sell goods in England with a view, as a rule, to carrying away the proceeds to their own country. That payment must be made somehow is obvious. The critical question for us concerns the way in which this has to be done. The three generally recognized methods are: first, the remittance of bills of exchange drawn upon the foreign purchasers of English goods and services; secondly, the direct shipment of gold; and, thirdly, the export of securities. So far as the first of these methods is adopted, there is no great difficulty in seeing that the importation of foreign goods cannot possibly injure our industries as a whole. For, *ex hypothesi*, it is by the augmentation in the exported products of certain of them that payment for the extra imports is made. What the development of foreign trade does in this case is exactly typified by our bicycle and bonnet illustration. It enables capital and labor to be transferred from producing a particular class of goods for home consumption to producing other goods, which can be sent abroad in exchange for them, and which will purchase a greater quantity of them than we could, by the same effort, have produced directly for ourselves.

The second possible method of payment is by direct shipment of gold. It is fairly clear that, for a non-mining country like England, this cannot possible be more than a temporary expedient. The case is, however, instructive, because of the light it throws upon a common difficulty. To many people it seems obvious that, if another country, through greater natural resources, cheaper labor or less stringent factory laws, has an advantage over us in every direction, it must necessarily be able to offer every exportable commodity in our markets at a lower price than our own producers can afford to take. As a matter of fact, however, so far from such a result being necessary, an elementary acquaintance with monetary theory at once shows that it is absolutely impossible. For, if it be not so, let us assume that such a state of affairs exists. What is the immediate result? Plainly, that all our purchases are made abroad, and that no foreigner purchases anything from us. Consequently, there is an instantaneous and enormous flow of bullion away from this country to equate the balance. Consequently, prices at once move downwards in

England and upwards abroad, and the movement of bullion does not stop until they have so adjusted themselves that it has become profitable for foreigners to purchase in England goods equivalent in value to those which we purchase from them. We are then exporting those commodities for the production of which we are at a less comparative disadvantage, and importing those for which our disadvantage is greater, just as, in Socratic phrase, a bad cook may exchange his services with someone who, while superior to him in the culinary art, is still more superior in that of literature or shoemaking. The ultimate effect of trade in this, as in the former case, is merely to divert our capital and labor from a less to a more advantageous occupation. Shipments of gold serve to bring price-levels into conformity with this fundamental circumstance of international exchange, and the fear that foreigners may offer us everything at a lower figure than our own compatriots could accept arises from ignorance of a simple theorem, upon which all economists are agreed.

The third and last way in which imports may be paid for is by the export of securities. When this method is adopted, there is, it may be said, no reason why foreign trade should not destroy one group of our industries without giving any corresponding stimulus to another. To this suggestion I reply, first, that, as a matter of fact, all the available evidence goes to show that England is not at present paying for any considerable part of her imports in this way. The statement that 'the sum of our investments abroad is diminishing is not, as yet,' – in the words of Mr. A.L. Bowley – 'supported by statistics that will stand critical examination.' Even, however, if the fact were otherwise, it does not follow that any permanent reduction of employment would be involved. The capital withdrawn from investment abroad would almost certainly be reinvested in England; for, after all, the people, who sell securities, are individuals, and there is no reason to suppose that they will take to treating capital as income merely because it is repaid to them by foreigners. The supply of capital in England would, therefore, be increased, the rate of interest would fall, and industrial enterprise would be stimulated. Foreign 'underselling' would not prevent this result, because prices here would be reduced through the change in discount rates and the inflow of commodities from abroad, while they would be raised in foreign countries through the corresponding outflow of commodities. International price-levels would thus be adjusted to the conditions of exchange as effectively as in the preceding case, though by a slightly different method.

The argument in favor of Free Trade is not, therefore, in any degree weakened by the suggestion of general underselling. On the contrary, the fear that such a result may come about is seen to rest upon inadequate economic analysis. It remains true, therefore, that taxes of a protective character are more injurious than other taxes to the material wealth of the country, and that the amount of the injury varies directly with the amount of the Protection. It is possible, of course, that the actual material loss may be, in part, counterbalanced by the application, through longer hours of labor and so forth, of greater efforts to production, but the only difference thus made is that leisure is sacrificed instead of goods.

These are merely the material disadvantages of Protection. Unfortunately, however, they do not stand alone. Over and above the economic danger, we have to reckon with the political one. 'Le protectionisme,' says M. Yves Guyot in a notable phrase, 'remplace la concurrence économique par la concurrence politique.'[67] Under it there is – to put it at the lowest – a not inconsiderable chance that manufacturers, confronted with competition, will expend energies, which might best be devoted to discovering more economical methods of work, in the sordid trade of 'persuading' and 'influencing' legislators. From this it is not impossible that 'log-rolling' may develop, different industries making treaties of mutual support in the scramble for tariff doles. This is hardly a prospect to be anticipated with enthusiasm; for one of the things of which Englishmen are proudest is the comparative purity of their political institutions. It is *possible*, of course, that these might withstand the blast of corrupt solicitation, to which the adoption of any form of protective policy would inevitably expose them; but he would be a bold man who, with history before him, would venture to predict that it is *likely*. Indeed, there can be little doubt that the fourteen academic economists, who recently discussed this matter in the *Times*, were voicing the conclusions of the great body of educated opinion, when they wrote: 'There are also to be apprehended those evils other than material which Protection brings in its train – the loss of purity in politics, the unfair advantage given to those who wield the powers of jobbery and corruption, unjust distribution of wealth, and the growth of 'sinister interests.'

......

The argument of the last chapter was a general one, and needs to

---

67 Protectionism replaces economic competition by political competition (ed.).

be supplemented by the consideration of exceptional cases. One of these is supposed by many popular writers to arise when Free Trade on the part on one country is met by Protection on the part of others. The theoretical basis for Cobden's policy is imagined to consist in his mistaken prophecy that foreign nations would follow in the tariff footsteps of England. We are triumphantly informed that this has not been the case, that our fiscal system is not Free Trade at all, but merely Free Imports, and that the latter is a lame and halting makeshift to which the ordinary arguments of economic text-books are inapplicable. This opinion is not only erroneous, but is evidence of incomplete acquaintance with English tariff history. The advantage which a policy of Freedom possesses over one of Protection does not, and has never been believed to, depend upon its being reciprocated. The high Customs duties of foreign countries do, indeed, inflict an injury upon us. They have this result, however, simply because they put a check upon exchange. They impose a burden upon the outward branch of our foreign trade, which, of course, diminishes both our exports and our imports. If this country were to add a further burden upon the inward branch of it, she would diminish them both still further. The mere fact that impediments exist can give no ground for modifying the reasoned opinion that impediments are bad, and ought, whenever possible, to be removed. It is, therefore, altogether misleading to set up a kind of antithesis between Free Imports and Free Trade. The former policy is a part of the latter, and the only part which we, as a nation, have complete power to realize.

In the second place, it is sometimes argued that the 'orthodox' arguments against Protection are inapplicable to the problems of to-day, because they do not take sufficient account of the increasing mobility of capital. A tariff, it is suggested, may serve to check the emigration or stimulate the immigration of this important 'factor of production,' and may thus indirectly result in a benefit to the protecting nation as a whole. This argument has been countenanced by Mr. Balfour in his pamphlet (p. 16), and by Professor Ashley in his recent book on the Tariff Problem. The latter writer gives a list of a number of English firms which have, since the heightening of the tariff walls of other countries, set up factories within the protected area, and he comments in these terms: 'Adam Smith argued that Protection could only divert capital from one industry to another ; the Protectionists can reply that in many instances it has attracted fresh capital into the country' (p. 79). This argument appears to me thoroughly unsound. In so far as Protection is economically injurious

to a country, it diminishes the profit which capital can expect to reap there, and hence the inducement which is held out to it to come or to remain in that part of the world. Analysis, in short, suggests that a policy of Protection would, in this matter, have an effect precisely the opposite of that which Professor Ashley attributes to it. It is impossible to confute this general reasoning by adducing instances of individual migration. The worthlessness of these, and the weakness of Professor Ashley's position, is clearly brought out in the following extract from Professor Marshall's Presidential Address to Section F of the British Association in 1889. Speaking in reference to the discussions excited by the McKinley Bill, he said: 'An old fallacy has reappeared in a new form in an argument, which has attracted much attention both here and in America, that the Act must have benefited America, because it has led to the investment of a few hundred thousand pounds of English capital in starting tin-plate and lace works, etc., in America. Protection always puts capital into some industries: that movement is 'seen'; but before we can regard it as a net gain we must make sure that there is not an equal or greater, though 'unseen', leaking of capital out of other industries which the new tariff indirectly injures; and for every £100,000 that the Protection policy causes to be sent from England to be invested in American factories, it probably keeps away at least £1,000,000 that would otherwise have been sent there to be invested in railways and agriculture.'
......

In the three groups of problems to which this discussion has hitherto been confined, the center of interest has been the United Kingdom. The question has been whether or not any scheme of tariff manipulation would be likely to confer a direct or indirect benefit upon the inhabitants of these islands, and the conclusion reached has been a negative one. Now, however, the scene must be shifted. In passing to the proposals with which Mr. Chamberlain's name is more intimately associated, we rise from the level of national to that of Imperial policy. The problem, therefore, becomes more complex, the elements involved more numerous, and the relations between them more subtle. The simplest division of the subject is threefold. First, there is the strictly business question as regards the United Kingdom, whether, namely, a system of Imperial preference would mean an economic gain to the people of these islands. Secondly, there is the same business question concerning the people of the mother-country, her colonies and dependencies taken together. Lastly, there is the political question, whether Mr. Chamberlain's plan would help forward the consolidation of the Empire by promoting unity of spirit and aim among its different parts.

These three questions are perfectly distinct. The considerations upon which an answer to the first two should be founded are predominantly economic, while those which lie behind the last are chiefly general and historical. A satisfactory decision as to whether Mr. Chamberlain's policy ought to be supported or opposed can only be reached after a careful examination of them all. It cannot be condemned offhand upon the ground that it would be economically disadvantageous to the United Kingdom, or even upon the further ground that it would involve a material loss to the empire as a whole. For in matters of statecraft, sentiment may often be more important than shillings, and the most profitable course of action need not necessarily be the best. In this chapter, therefore, each of these three questions will be considered in turn, the business problem from the mother-country's point of view being taken first.

Now in this there is involved a somewhat difficult comparison. For a balance has to be struck between a debit and a credit account, neither of which it is possible to summarize with any degree of accuracy. We have no precise information as to the amount, either of the duties which Great Britain will be asked to impose upon foreign imports, or of the special advantages which the colonies are willing to grant to her in return. Nor is this the worst. For, even if some entirely definite scheme were before the country, we could never be certain that the limits of our sacrifices were really expressed therein. For, when once a policy of this kind has been started, it is apt to develop within itself an expansive power, which can neither be calculated before-hand nor resisted when it appears. In order to secure equivalence between the advantages accorded to our different colonies and dependencies, it might, ere long, become imperative that imports, which nobody at present has the least intention of taxing, should be brought within the purview of our Customs tariff. A beginning might be made with duties upon wheat and mutton only, but there can be no guarantee that these would not be driven to take unto themselves further duties upon fish, butter, cheese, vegetables, and eggs; perhaps even, to quote Sir Michael Hicks-Beach, upon 'the tea, the cocoa, the rice, the fruit that comes to us from India and the Crown Colonies.' Certainly, as Lord Ripon pointed out in the House of Lords, 'we could not give a preference to the self-governing colonies without considering the extent of the claims which India might have to preference upon her side.' We are told, again, 'that the new policy could not extend to taxes on raw materials, and no one imagines that such taxes would be proposed in the first instance. But they have already been suggested by those interested in Canadian timber and in the wool and skins sent us by Australia; and how long could South Africa, which sends us hardly any food, and large quantities of raw materials, be satisfied without them?'

Nor is the danger confined to the probable expansion of the *number* of imports subjected to taxation. There is also a considerable chance that the *amount* of individual duties would have to be raised above what was originally proposed. It is almost certain that the colonists would form an exaggerated estimate of the advantages which the new policy would confer upon them. Professor Davidson has told us that its inauguration would inevitably be followed by a tremendous boom in Manitoba and the Canadian North-West. 'Settlers would pour in; thousands of acres would be broken; the land companies would flourish, and advertise, and flourish more; railways would be projected, perhaps begun; new town sites would be laid out, existing hamlets would mortgage their future, and all would go merry as a marriage-bell.' But '*the preferential wheat boom will burst like other booms*. Then will come Canada's second thought about the preference, and that will be accompanied by gritting of the teeth'. When that time arrives, is there not bound to arise a loud and urgent demand for an increase in the rate of our preferential duty? Great Britain, it will be said, has, by her policy, tempted the Canadian farmer to move westward; she has directly caused, and is, therefore, in honor bound to cure, the evils of the boom. It will not be easy for a Government, anxious to promote good feeling within the Empire, to resist appeals of this kind. There is grave reason to fear that they may be unpleasantly numerous, and that the amount of our duties may, in response, be steadily increased.

Let us assume, however, for the sake of argument, that these dangers are imaginary, and that the debit side of the preferential account may fairly be calculated upon the basis of the duties imposed in the first instance. These, everybody is agreed, must fall upon articles of food, most probably upon grain and meat. That being the case, it will be observed that they are necessarily of a protective character. Every one of the chief colonial food products – and the same thing is true of Australian wool – is produced in large quantities at home. Nobody has suggested that it would be practicable to impose a corresponding excise upon the staples of British farming. Consequently, there is no escape from the conclusion that those interested in English, Scotch, and Irish agriculture will be sheltered from a certain amount of foreign competition to which they would otherwise be exposed. An incidental result of preference is partial agricultural protection.

Now, in the second chapter it was pointed out that Protection in general involves a sacrifice through the diversion of labor and capital from occupations in which they have greater, to others in which they have less, relative advantage. Protection of agriculture in an old country is, beyond all dispute, responsible for this class of sacrifice. In addition, however, it possesses two further highly objectionable features. In the first place, an increase in the crop yield can, *ceteris paribus*, only be brought about at continually increasing cost. If tariff arrangements compel a gradual movement of workmen into the textile industries, it does not necessarily follow that the average output per man is less after the change than before. In agriculture, however, in accordance with the physical law, to which economists give the name of *diminishing returns*, this result does follow. Agriculture is, therefore, one of those industries which, from an economic point of view, it is especially undesirable to protect. Partly involved with this consideration, there is a second point which will be more readily appreciated by the general reader. Protection to manufactures involves a detriment to the nation's annual income of real wealth. Protection to agriculture involves, over and above this, a further detriment to the manner in which that income is distributed among the different sections of the community. For, under it, rents inevitably tend to rise, and the circumstances of the land-owning class are improved. But there can be no doubt whatever that landlords are, on the average, already much better off than the artisan and laboring population. Consequently, agricultural protection leads to a larger proportion of the diminished total of the country's wealth falling to the relatively rich, and a smaller proportion to the relatively poor.

......

From these expressions of opinion two inferences of importance may be drawn as to the nature of the advantages which the mother-country is likely to receive. In the first place, the amount of any possible preference is limited by the revenue requirements of the colonies. It is a practical necessity for most of them to raise the great body of their revenue by indirect taxation. In the case of Canada, though the Dominion is constitutionally entitled to have recourse to direct taxes, it is in fact debarred from doing so lest its demands should clash with those of the separate provinces, to the governments of which this source of revenue is the only one open. With the other self-governing colonies the case is, for various reasons, similar. Upon such a matter Lord Brassey should be an authority of weight, and in June last he is reported to have declared 'that he knew positively that it was practically impossible for the self-governing colonies to make any material reduction in the duties now levied on British manufactures. The income obtained from their Customs was essential to enable them to carry on their governments, and there was no available means of obtaining that income from other sources.' This necessity of collecting a given revenue from import taxes is not, indeed, fatal to a reduction in the duties upon British imports, so long as other imports, to which part of the burden can be shifted, exist in sufficient quantities. Unless, however, these other imports are of a different kind from those sent by the United Kingdom, it would have to be considered how far the highly-taxed foreign articles would be ousted from the colonial market by their favored British rivals. In so far as this result occurred, the loss of revenue in one direction would not really be compensated by a corresponding increase in another, and though, no doubt, the fall in the rate of duty would be accompanied by a growth in the total quantity of the imports upon which it was levied, it is very doubtful whether the Customs receipts would be restored by this means to their old amount. The exigencies of the colonial revenue systems are thus seen to present a serious obstacle to a reduction of the duties upon imports from the mother-country.

In the second place, a further difficulty arises from the keen desire of the colonists to foster their own manufacturing industries. Mr. Fielding, in introducing his last Budget in the Canadian House of Representatives, described the attitude of the Dominion's delegates at the Colonial Conference in this way: 'We told them (Mr. Chamberlain and Mr. Gerald Balfour) that, if the imperial Government was prepared to adopt the preferential policy and give our products exemption from the duties now imposed, or hereafter to be imposed, on foreign goods, we would be prepared to grant some further preference, subject to certain conditions which we clearly laid down. *We frankly stated that we could not undertake to give that further preference in a manner which would operate to the disadvantage of our own industries. As between the British manufacturer and the Canadian manufacturer we thought we had gone as far in the way of reduction of duties as we could.'* There is reason to suppose that in this matter the Canadian attitude is typical of that of the self-governing colonies as a whole. It is in accord with a resolution recently passed by the council of the Protectionist Association of Victoria, which the *Times* correspondent declares 'fairly to represent the attitude of the Protectionists and the Protectionist press in Australia,' and also with the form of preferential concession, which Mr. Seddon is reported to favor in New Zealand.

These two sets of considerations taken together give ground for the general conclusion that the preferences granted to Great Britain in return for her concessions would take the form, almost exclusively, not of a reduction in the duties upon British imports, but of a substantial addition to those already imposed upon the competing imports of foreign countries. The representatives of the Cape and Natal at the Colonial Conference confined themselves to this single proposal, offering a 25 per cent, or equivalent all-round increase on foreign imports, and similar offers constituted an important factor in the suggestions made on behalf of the other colonies. The preference we may look for, in short, is one, not over the colonial, but over the foreign manufacturer, and by way, not of diminution in the duties against us, but of increase in those against our rivals.[68]

This point is important for more reasons than one. In the first place, since our new Imperial policy is to involve the imposition of a positive and obvious detriment to foreign traders both in this country and in the colonies, the chance that it may provoke 'reprisals' is increased. It is not a question of whether or not Germany and other countries would be morally justified in resorting to measures of that kind, but whether, as a matter of fact, they would be likely to do so. Now, as recently as April last, Baron von Richthofen hinted to the British ambassador that, if 'large portions of the British Expire were to give preferential treatment to Great Britain, it would be very difficult to obtain the consent of the Reichstag to the prolongation of most-favored nation treatment to Great Britain herself.' This suggestion may have been, and, indeed, at the time when it was made, probably was, little more than a piece of diplomatic bluff. But it is idle to deny that it points to a danger which is real, and which would probably become very serious if the colonial preferences were to take the form which has been anticipated, and if the mother-country were to reciprocate the policy of her daughter States. There is a very great

68 This is in fact what happened at the Ottawa agreement of 1932. Under these arrangements tariffs within the Empire were not lowered but they were raised to those countries outside it. This preferential system within the British Commonwealth was the most important (ed.).

probability that we should become involved in continued tariff discussions, occasional tariff wars, and, in view of the present temper of the nation, in the permanent upkeep of a clumsy and expensive 'big revolver'. Such advantage as we received in colonial markets would be accompanied both by a considerable loss of advantage in the foreign markets, and by the erection at our own ports of a bargaining tariff economically less advantageous than the present one. When it is remembered that British exports to foreign countries are about three times as great as those to the self-governing colonies, it appears only too likely that the advantages conferred upon us in return for our preferential duties would, when taken in conjunction with their indirect results, not merely fail to balance, but actually increase the amount of our sacrifice.

For the sake of argument, however, that point also may be waived, and it may be assumed that England's relations with foreign countries would remain unimpaired. It is, then, only necessary to consider the direct effect of colonial preference upon British well-being. To begin with, it is obvious that an advantage conferred upon us by increased taxation of our rivals will be less than one involving decreased taxation of ourselves. For, whereas, in the latter case we should be placed in a more favorable position relatively both to foreign and to colonial competitors, in the former it is only our relation to the foreigner that is affected. Whereas diminished duties might lead, not only to an increase in our share of colonial trade, but also to an increase in the total in which we shared, the kind of preference, which the mother-country is likely, as a matter of fact, to receive, cannot possibly bring about the second of these results. It may oust our rivals from existing, but can never create new trade.

It is necessary, however, in this connection, to note Sir Robert Giffen's opinion that 'almost all the high duties, of which our manufacturers complain, give no protection to colonial manufactures, because the particular manufactures which would compete do not, in fact, exist in the colonies'. If this view be correct, there is clearly less difference, from our point of view, between a preference given through increased duties on foreign imports and one given through diminished duties on those of British origin than at first sight appears. It must, however, be observed that other high authorities do not accept Sir Robert's view of the situation, and that textiles, which 'form more than half of the Canadian imports from Great Britain' are considered by Professor Davidson to compete directly with the native colonial manufactures. But I need not insist upon this point, because, in the light of a further fact, also noted by Sir Robert Giffen, the whole matter assumes a secondary importance. This fact is that a large part of the foreign imports of some of our colonies consists of classes of goods, such as foodstuffs and raw materials, which it is quite impossible that the United Kingdom would in any case supply. In view of this, Sir Robert's conclusion is that the *maximum* of trade which, under present conditions, could possibly be transferred from foreign to British hands 'is thus reducible to a very small sum when we take account only of those imports where foreign countries are our competitors.'

It may be rejoined that, as the colonies develop, their capacity for purchasing goods from abroad will increase, while preference granted to them by the mother-country would itself help forward their development. This statement is no doubt true, but it is open to the following replies: first, the development of the colonies is certain to involve a great expansion of their native manufacturing industries, and, in view of the similarity between their 'natural advantages' and our own, the goods in which they are likely soonest to become self-sufficing are just those which we are best able to export; secondly, even upon the extreme supposition that the preference granted to their agriculture would indirectly lead to a doubling of their capacity to purchase manufactures from abroad, the result would still be insignificant. Even 'Tariff Reformer' in the *Times* has not ventured to suggest that British exports to the colonies could be increased by more than £10,000,000 a year.

Let us take this generous estimate and see what it amounts to. Its author naïvely implies that this £10,000,000 would measure the increase of our exports, not merely to the colonies, but to the world at large. This is, of course, ridiculously superficial. The analysis of the case, to which economists in general would subscribe, is in this wise. The new fiscal arrangements of the colonies would lead to certain foreign exporters being supplanted in their markets by English rivals. Consequently, the foreign productive force which would otherwise have been devoted to the manufacture of these exports would have to seek new employment. A large part of it would probably find this in some branch either of foreign or of home trade. It would thus come, directly or indirectly, into competition with other groups of British exports, and would injuriously affect the market for them. Ultimately, therefore, our increased exports to the colonies would, in large measure, represent, not an addition to, but merely a diversion of, our total export trade. Further, even the increase of total exports would afford an entirely misleading and exaggerated measure of our national *advantage*. This would, in reality, consist only of the difference between the real cost of making these exports and that of making for ourselves the goods obtained from abroad in exchange for them. It would be represented, in commercial phrase, by the addition made, not to our turnover, but to our profits, and could not possibly be other than very small indeed.

When we come, therefore, to strike the balance between the debit and the credit side of the Preferential account, we find that, whereas the former is serious and substantial, the latter is bound, even under the most favorable circumstances, to be small. When we recall, further, the danger of reprisals on the part of foreign countries, the probability that our duties would expand both in number and amount, and the stimulus they would afford to the advocates of general protection, there can be little doubt that, as a matter of plain business, the policy of Imperial Preference would be an unprofitable one to the people of these islands. To mitigate the justice of this plea, two further considerations, on the borderland between the financial and the military, are sometimes advanced. In the first place, it is said that England ought to submit to whatever sacrifice Mr. Chamberlain's policy may involve, in order, by developing the agricultural resources of the colonies, to insure for herself an adequate food-supply in time of war. In view of the development of the Canadian wheat-fields, which is certain to come about in any case, this argument appears to me unnecessary. In view of what is known of the relations between nations, it strikes me as perverse. For is it not obvious that continental nations, at war with us, would be far more likely to seize wheat in transit to our shores from outlying portions of our own Empire, than if it came, as now, from the United States of America? In the latter case, as Sir George Trevelyan said at Birmingham a little while ago, 'America would place herself at the head of the neutral countries of the world, and would insist that wheat should go to British ports under neutral flags as freely as in times of peace; and, if America took that attitude, no European Government, however hostile to us, would venture to say her nay.' It is true that, if the United States herself were our opponent, the stress of the argument would be in the opposite direction, but it is surely better to insure against the more, than against the less, probable contingency, and nobody will deny that America is, of all the great Powers, the one with which we are least likely to become embroiled.

Finally, Mr. Chamberlain's supporters retreat from the naval to the military argument, and counsel us, cost what it may, artificially to develop the population of the colonies in order to increase our fighting force. I cannot here discuss the broad problems which this suggestion raises, but will merely observe in reply that, if this be our aim, preferential tariffs upon food are by no means the best way to promote it. Apart from the question of how far they would increase, and how far merely divert, population from one industry to another, it is easy to see that more direct methods, such as subsidies out of the Imperial Treasury for the construction of colonial railways, would be a far cheaper way of attaining the same end. Nothing could be effected by 'Preference,' which a straightforward policy of 'Bounties' would not effect much better.

So far of the business problem in its most inclusive sense, from the standpoint of the United Kingdom. To some minds, the conclusion to which we have been led would be decisive upon the whole issue. Professor Davidson, for example, has declared: 'We may lay it down as a cardinal rule of colonial policy, that no portion of the Empire should be expected to sacrifice what it conceives to be its economic interests to promote the good of the rest.' There may be others, however, who would reject this view as insular and selfish, and would proclaim themselves ready to see England lose, if by so doing she could promote a greater or an equal gain to the remainder of the King's dominions. To such persons the important point is the effect of Imperial Preference upon the economic interests of the Empire as a whole. Granted that the mother-country loses, will her loss be balanced by the colonies' gain? Now, if the arguments, which have already been employed in this chapter, are sound, the only possible answer to this question is a decisive and clear-cut negative. Had it been proposed that the setting up of new taxes in England should be matched on the side of the colonies by a reduction in their duties upon English imports, the total effect of the change might conceivably have been to make trade somewhat freer than before, and thus to facilitate the more advantageous employment of Imperial resources. Even in this case, in view of the enormous excess of British trade that would be adversely, over colonial trade that would be favorably, affected, no such result could come about unless the additions to English duties were at a rate quite insignificant compared with the remission granted in the colonies. Such an arrangement is, of course, exceedingly improbable, and would not, in any event, come within the range of practical politics. In the present instance, moreover, it has been shown that, so far from the colonists' *quid pro quo* taking the form of reduced duties, it will have precisely the opposite character. They, as well as we, are to raise their tariff against foreign imports. We are to pay more than is necessary for our food in order to buy it in the colonies, and they are to adopt a parallel policy with regard to manufactured goods. Each party to the bargain is to inflict a considerable injury upon himself, in order to confer a small benefit upon the other. Both parties taken together are deliberately to cut themselves off from some of the advantages on international trade, and the imperial unit is to become more protective against the rest of the world, without the compensating advantage, obtained in a true Zollverein, of becoming more free-trading within its own borders.

Mr. Chamberlain's proposals are, therefore, to be condemned from the imperial, as well as from the national, business standpoint. There remains, however, the political aspect of the problem. It is asserted that the adoption of the new policy would promote imperial solidarity and a spirit of unity and goodwill between the mother-country and the colonies. Upon this matter there is no denying that Mr. Chamberlain speaks as an expert. His opinion is, however, in conflict both with the views of ex-colonial governors, like Lord Brassey and Lord Jersey, and with the evidence which history supplies. He may appeal, of course, to the analogy of the German Zollverein, and point to its beneficent work in preparing the way for that completed union which Bismarck consummated. But, as has been pointed out again and again, a Customs union among adjacent States, by which tariff barriers are broken down and intercommunication freed, is not really parallel to a system of preferential tariffs among fiscal entities separated from one another by thousands of miles of ocean, and differing enormously in their economic circumstances. Nor is it as though this latter system were something entirely new and untried. In the first half of the nineteenth century, colonial preference was an established policy. The conditions of the time were, of course, different from those existing to-day, but they were more akin to them than the circumstances of pre-Bismarckian Germany. And how did the policy work? So far from cementing the Empire together 'the colonial preferences did a great deal to create in England a dislike for the colonies; ... there arose a powerful party demanding the abolition of these preferences and prone, in the heat of argument, to denounce a connection which made such sacrifices necessary.' When an experiment has already been tried and has conspicuously failed, strong arguments are needed to induce us to renew it. In this case, however, the arguments are all upon the other side. Nobody can deny that the difficulties to be overcome in adjusting matters equally among our different colonies and dependencies would be enormous, and that many opportunities for irritation and friction, both among them and between each of them and the mother-country, would inevitably arise. Is it not a fact that the gossamer thread of disinterested affection often binds more closely than any 'cash nexus,' and is there not a real danger that, by appealing to the lower motives of our colonists, we might seriously impair the uniting force of those that are higher? Furthermore, it is necessary to remember that if this great Imperial policy were to fail, it would not be easy to abandon it. The old preferences of sixty years ago were not done away without rousing very bitter feelings among the colonists. To grant them a second time and again to withdraw them would be scarcely possible without the risk of grave disaster. There is at present no evidence of a tendency on the part of the Empire to 'fall to pieces and separate atoms'; but it is doubtful if the same could be said, should it ever come to be subjected to so severe a strain as this. The economic argument against Mr. Chamberlain's policy is a strong one. To many, however, the political argument seems, in the side-light thrown upon it by history, to be still stronger, and, by itself, to make imperative the rejection of the ex-Colonial Secretary's scheme.

READING 19

Ludwig Elder von Mises

Biography

Ludwig von Mises, economist and social philosopher, was born on September 29, 1881 in the city of Lemberg in the Austrian-Hungarian Empire. His father, Arthur Elder von Mises, was a construction engineer employed by the Austrian railroads. After attending a gymnasium (a secondary school that prepares students for universities) he entered the University of Vienna. There he studied economics with teachers like Friedrich von Wieser and Eugen von Böhm-Bawerk, the followers of Carl Menger who was the founder of the Austrian school of economics. In 1906, the university conferred upon him the degree of Doctor of Law and Social Sciences.

After a short while, he accepted the post of Economic Advisor to the Austrian Chamber of Commerce, a position he held until 1934. In 1914, he was called to active duty in the Austro-Hungarian army, where he served as a captain of the artillery in the Russian Ukraine. In 1913, he had been admitted to the Faculty of Law at the University of Vienna as an unsalaried lecturer. In 1918, he received the title of Associate Professor but remained unsalaried. From 1920 onwards, von Mises held non-accredited private seminars which took place in his office in the Chamber of Commerce. Here eager young intellectuals gathered around him to debate economic and philosophical issues. From this circle emerged such scholars as Friedrich von Hayek and Gottfried Haberler.

When the political situation in Austria became increasingly turbulent, von Mises left his country. At the invitation of its director, William Rappard, he taught at the Graduate Institute of International Studies in Geneva, Switzerland, between 1934 and 1940. In 1938, at the age of 57, he married Marget Sereny-Herzfeld whom he had known for a long time.

During his stay in Geneva, von Mises anxiously observed the advance of Nazism in Germany and Austria and in 1940, shortly after World War II broke out, he emigrated to the United States. From 1940 to 1944, he was a guest of the National Bureau of Economic Research in New York which combined with other research grants enabled him to finance his writings.

After World War II, he was appointed visiting professor of the Graduate School of Business Administration at New York University. Von Mises retired in 1969. During that year, he was also named 'Distinguished Fellow' of the American Economic Association. He died on October 1973 at the age of 92 and was survived by his wife, Marget and his two stepchildren.

The Work

Until about the 1970s, the influence of von Mises's writings was very limited because his ideas and proposals were simply buried under the avalanche of enthusiasm which was present for Keynesian economics. Especially during the 1945–1970 period, the influence of Keynes on technical economic doctrine and practical economic policy was overwhelming.

Any individual who challenged the theoretical edifice and/or the policy proposals of the Keynesian system experienced an almost certain intellectual death. Yet this is precisely what Ludwig von Mises did. His rejection of the then 'New Economics', his criticism of totalitarian and democratic socialism, his opposition to interventionism and his disapproval of the welfare state made him unpopular with many.[69] Only after 1970, when Keynes's theories were losing their influence and doubts began to emerge about the fundamentals of the Keynesian system and interventionism, did von Mises's work begin to receive more widespread attention.

Von Mises's opposition to tariffs and other forms of economic nationalism are part of his rejection of all social doctrines which imply that there exists irreconcilable conflict between group interests. The groups consist mostly of nations, linguistic communities, classes and races. Mercantilists believed that the interests of nations were incompatible. Logically they deduced that war was an inherent and eternal pattern of international relations. With the achievements of the liberal philosophers and the classical economists of the eighteenth and early nineteenth century, there emerged for the first time in human history a social philosophy demonstrating the long run harmonious coexistence of different groups and people.

The unhampered market economy occupied a central position in this doctrine. In a free enterprise system, people can only improve their own position by serving others better and more efficiently. As the division of labor becomes more complex, social cohesiveness is brought about by mutual interdependence generated by the market economy. Thus the classical economists wanted to liberate economic transactions from the interventions and regulations imposed upon them by the mercantilists. Limited government became the explicit political goal of the classical liberals.

Until about the middle of the nineteenth century, Western man was moving towards the establishment of democracy and the evolution of the market economy. International cooperation was becoming peaceful and with it came an unprecedented rise in the standard of living, followed by a period of great artistic and literary achievement. However, after 1860, doctrines emphasizing conflict between nations, classes and races once again became increasingly popular. With the increasing popularity of these 'destructionist' doctrines, as von Mises called them, genuine liberalism and individualism gave way to nationalism, socialism, racism, and statism in general.[70] The ordeal of civil wars, two world wars, revolutions, enslavement, and

---

69 The best summary of von Mises's ideas can be found in his main work *Human Action, A Treatise on Economics* (1949).

70 Statism can be defined as the concentration of economic controls and planning in the hands of a highly centralized government (ed.).

totalitarianism were the inevitable result of the philosophies of irreconcilable conflict and dissociation which became popular after 1860. As soon as people begin to believe that their own group cannot thrive except at the expense of other communities, any peaceful arrangement between groups is out of the question. According to von Mises, the destructionist ideas, although they emerged as the urban masses grew in importance, were not advanced by those multitudes. The masses are dull, mentally inert and always seek shortcuts for thought. They have never created new ideologies. The doctrines of nationalism, racism, socialism and interventionism which have proved so detrimental to social cooperation and almost destroyed Western civilization, were produced by intellectuals who often came from the 'higher' classes. These intellectuals mostly consisted of teachers, professors, government employees, labor union leaders, preachers, political party officials, editors and leisured ambitious men and women anxious to gain the headlines by the expression of radical views. The statist and interventionist ideas were propagated from the chairs of universities and from the pulpit. They were disseminated by the press, by novels and plays, by the radio and the movies. It was the intellectuals who, in Western nations, converted the masses to political and economic nationalism, socialism, racism and interventionism.

A further reason why von Mises opposed protectionism is that tariffs, quotas and other instruments of economic nationalism created privileged castes. Caste membership as it existed in certain countries assigned to each individual certain privileges and/or certain disqualifications. In a truly free-market society castes do not exist because privileges are not granted. Social harmony is thus promoted. Tariffs and other interventionist measures always favor one group over the remainder of the population. If a country puts a quota, a tariff on foreign sugar it changes its own sugar producers into a privileged caste. An antagonism between the interests of the domestic sugar producers and the rest of society is created. Social harmony is impaired. Therefore, interventionism creates a new caste system and the caste conflicts that go with it. The following reading dated May 5, 1943, was unpublished until it appeared in *Money, Method and the Market Process* in 1990.[71]

---

71 *Money, Method and the Market Process* (R.M. Ebeling, ed.) (Norwell: Kluwer Academic Publishers, 1990) pp. 137–154.

Extracts

1

Autarky and its Consequences

Terminological Remarks

There is considerable ambiguity concerning the terminology to be used in dealing with the problems of international economic relations. It seems therefore expedient to start with a clear definition of some terms.

Chauvinism is the overvaluation of one's own nation's achievements and qualities and the disparagement of the other nations. As such it does not result in any political action.

Patriotism is the zeal for one's own nation's welfare, flowering, and freedom. But the patriots disagree with regard to the means to be applied for the attainment of this end.

The *free traders* (liberals in the old sense attached to the term liberalism, today mostly disparaged by the self-styled 'progressives' as orthodox, reactionaries or economic royalists, as Manchestermen, or as supporters of laissez faire) want to make their own nation prosperous by free trade and by its peaceful incorporation into the world-embracing commonwealth of the international division of labor. They recommend free trade not for the sake of other nations, but from the viewpoint of the rightly understood or long-term interests of their own nation. They are convinced that even if all other nations cling to protection, a nation best serves its own welfare by free trade.

The *nationalists*, on the contrary, believe that a nation cannot further its own well-being but by inflicting harm upon other nations. *Aggressive* or *militaristic nationalism* aims at conquest and at the subjugation of other nations by arms. *Economic nationalism* aims at furthering the well-being of one's own nation or of some of its groups through inflicting harm upon foreigners by economic measures, for instance: trade and migration barriers, expropriation of foreign investments, repudiation of foreign debts, currency devaluation, and foreign exchange control.

Economic nationalism results in war if some nations believe that they are powerful enough to brush away, by military action, the measures of foreign countries which they consider as detrimental to their own interests.

The free traders want to make peace durable by the elimination of the root causes of conflict. If everybody is free to live and to work where he wants; if there are no barriers for the mobility of labor, capital, and commodities; and if the administration, the laws, and the courts do not discriminate between citizens and foreigners, the individual citizens are not interested in the question where the political frontiers are drawn and whether their own country is bigger or smaller. They cannot derive any profit from the conquest of a province. In such an ideal – Jeffersonian – world of democracy and free trade war does not pay.

The nationalists, on the contrary, assert that peace itself is an evil and that war is, as the English writer John Ruskin said, 'the foundation of the arts and of all the high virtues and faculties of man.' Consequently the Nazis considered it as the most desirable state for a nation 'to be always at war,' and Mussolini exalted 'the dangerous life.' The Japanese clung to the same tenets.

Pacifism is the belief that all that is required for the abolition of war is the building up of an international organization and the establishment of an international world court whose rulings should be enforced by a world police force.

The noble-minded founders of the League of Nations were guided by this type of pacifism. They were right in their idea that autocratic governments are warlike, while democratic nations cannot derive any profit from conquest and therefore cling to peace. But what President Wilson and his collaborators did not see was that this is valid only within a system of private ownership of the means of production, free enterprise, and unhampered market economy. Where there is no economic freedom things are entirely different. In our age of statism and socialism, in which every nation is eager to insulate itself and to strive toward autarky it is quite wrong to assert that no man can derive any gain from conquest. Every citizen has a material interest in the nullification of measures by which foreign governments injure his economic interests.

Autarky or *economic self-sufficiency* is a state of affairs where there is no foreign trade at all; every nation consumes only goods produced within its own borders. No contemporary nation is ready to admit openly that it strives toward autarky. But as every nation is anxious to restrict imports and as exports must fall concomitantly, we can characterize the economic policies of the last decade preceding the present war as autarkic.

2

The Rise of Modern Protectionism

In the 'sixties of the nineteenth century, public opinion was almost unanimous in the assumption that the world was on the eve of an age of everlasting free trade and peace. True, there was only one big nation which had unconditionally espoused the principle of free trade: Great Britain. But there seemed to prevail a general tendency all over Europe toward a step-by-step abolition of trade barriers. Every new commercial treaty between civilized and politically advanced nations brought a reduction in tariffs and included the most favored nation clause. The teachings of Ricardo and John Stuart Mill, of Cobden and Bastiat, met with general approval. People were optimistic enough to expect that trade barriers and war were doomed to disappear with other remnants of the dark ages like despotism, intolerance, slavery and serfdom, superstition, and torture.

However, the greater part of the world still had tariffs. There were two groups of protectionist countries.

There were, on the one hand, the countries of the European continent which had long since embarked upon a Mercantilist policy of protection. People were convinced that these nations would soon learn that protectionism does not further but seriously checks their own material well-being and would turn to free trade.

There were, on the other hand, the former colonies, the countries peopled by the descendants of European settlers. These countries had in earlier days considered import duties as the most expedient means for taxing their citizens. Their tariffs had originally only fiscal purposes. With the progressive evolution of economic civilization and the increase of population figures these tariffs changed their character and provided ample protection to the growing domestic industries. In the middle of the nineteenth century they were, especially in the United States, already more effective in this regard than those of the then most protectionist European powers, Austria and Russia. However, the optimists hoped that at least the United States would outgrow what they qualified as the remnants of its colonial past.

The optimists were entirely wrong. The protectionist nations did not abandon protection, but raised their tariffs; furthermore, the free trade countries themselves turned toward protection. Great Britain and Switzerland, once the champions of free trade, are today fanatically devoted to the most radical methods of economic nationalism.

3

Remarks on the Theory of Foreign Trade

The return to protectionism, the progressive aggravation of trade restrictions through the multiplication of import duties and through the application of new methods for prevention of imports, and the evolution of the tariff system into a system under which all kinds of commercial transactions with foreigners (even tourism, the consultation of foreign doctors and education at foreign schools) require a special license on the part of the authorities – all these are not the outcome of a change in the theory of foreign trade. The desperate attempts of the advocates of protection to refute the statements of the classical economists concerning the consequences of free trade and protection failed lamentably. All they could demonstrate was that under special conditions the interests of some groups of the population can derive temporary benefits from protection. But the economists have never denied this. What they asserted was:

1. If protection is granted to one branch of production or to a few branches only, those privileged are benefited at the expense of the rest of the nation.

2. If protection is granted to the same extent to all branches of domestic production nobody can possibly derive any net profit. What a man profits on the one hand qua producer, he loses on the other hand qua consumer. Moreover, everybody is hurt by the fact that production is diverted from those lines in which its physical productivity is highest; all nations and every individual are injured by the fact that less favorable conditions of production are exploited, while some more favorable remain unused.

3. It is vain to try to 'improve' the balance of trade by import restrictions. But for capital transactions (foreign investments and foreign loans and the payments resulting therefrom), gifts and tributes, the total value of the commodities sold and the services rendered to foreigners exactly equals the value of the goods and services received.

4. The advantage derived from foreign trade lies entirely in importing. The exports are only the payment for the imports. If it were possible to import without exporting at all, the importing country

would not suffer, but enjoy prosperity.

It has been asserted again and again that conditions have changed since the days of Ricardo and that his conclusions are no longer valid under present conditions. This, however, is a fallacy too.

Ricardo assumes that there is no mobility of capital and labor, but that on the other hand there is some mobility for commodities. (If there is no mobility at all for commodities either, then every nation lives in perfect autarky and there is no question of any foreign trade.) The conditions assumed by Ricardo changed in the course of the nineteenth century. Millions of workers emigrated from the comparatively overpopulated countries and immigrated into the comparatively underpopulated countries offering more favorable conditions for labor and consequently higher wage rates. Today things have changed and the state of affairs is by and large the same as in the time of Ricardo. Migration is almost impossible. The international capital market is disintegrated. The capitalists shun foreign investments because discriminatory taxation, expropriation and confiscation, foreign exchange control and repudiation of debts make them too risky. The governments of those counties whose capitalists could consider foreign investment are ready to put an embargo upon capital export because they view it as contrary to the interests of the most influential domestic pressure groups, labor, and farming.

In a world of perfect mobility of capital, labor, and products there prevails a tendency toward an equalization of the material conditions of all countries. Those parts of the earth's surface which offer more favorable natural conditions of production attract more capital and men than those offering less propitious ones. There are areas more densely populated and areas less densely populated. Freedom of migration and capital transfer tend to make the difference of comparative overpopulation and comparative underpopulation disappear. They tend toward an equalization of wage rates and rates of interest and concomitantly of standards of living.

In a world of immobility of men some countries are comparatively overpopulated, others comparatively underpopulated. There are conspicuous differences in wage rates and in standards of living. The restrictions imposed upon the mobility of capital intensify this outcome.

Ricardo has demonstrated what the consequences of free trade in such a world are. His law of comparative cost has never been disproved. Even if all other countries cling to protection, every nation best serves its own interests by free trade.

4

Big Business and Protection

For the self-styled 'progressives' big business is the scape-goat for all evils. The selfish class interests of the capitalists and entrepreneurs, they say, have pushed the nations toward hyper-protectionism. Modern nationalism is but the ideological disguise of the class interests of the exploiters.

However, big business is not afraid of foreign competition. The American motor car producers and the German electric companies do not fear that any foreign competitor could supersede them on their domestic market. Neither do they ask for protective duties in those foreign countries into which they want to export, indeed their interests are considerably hurt by the import duties of these countries. If they are not ready to lose these markets, they are forced to build subsidiary plants in protected countries and to produce at a higher cost. Instead of supplying the consumers with merchandise manufactured in big scale plants located at the sites offering the most advantageous opportunities, they are compelled to produce a good deal of their output in smaller plants located in less appropriate places. But for protectionism it would never have occurred to Mr. Ford to fabricate cars in Canada, in France, in Germany, and in some other countries. The characteristic feature of present-day big business is that the enterprises own subsidiaries in many countries. They are not interested in the continuation of production of the subsidiaries.[72] They would, in the absence of protection, concentrate their whole production in those plants in which costs are lowest.

If it were true that big business is favored by protection, there would be no protection in this age of violent anti-capitalism. It can hardly be denied that the general trend of the economic policies of all countries in the last decades was to inflict as much harm as possible on big business.

The present structure of business and the location and the size of the single plants are adjusted to the conditions brought about by protectionism. A transition to free trade would cause a general

---

72 The reader should keep in mind that these passages were written in 1943 (ed.)

reshuffling, as many plants are now located in places where production costs are so high that they cannot, when unprotected, compete with industries operating in places offering more propitious opportunities. The vested interests of many enterprises are therefore opposed to free trade. But this is not the cause of protection, it is rather its outcome. If there had not been any protection at all, the capitalists would not have invested their funds in places in which profit can only be expected under protection.

While some enterprises are menaced by free trade, the interests of the bulk of industry and of the whole nation are not. On the contrary! Everybody would be benefited, if production were discontinued where the physical input needed for the attainment of one unit of output is higher, and were to expand where the input required is lower.

Under free trade for products and capital and under immigration barriers for labor, there would prevail in America a tendency to prefer those branches of manufacturing in which wages form a smaller part of the total costs of production. The country would favor more the expansion of the heavy industries and less those branches which require comparatively more labor. The resulting imports would bring about neither bad business nor unemployment. They would be compensated by an increase in the export of goods which can be produced to the highest advantage in this country. They would raise the standard of living both in America and abroad.

American processing industries do not need any protection. They are, but for some special branches, like Paris dressmaking and English cloth, paramount in the world. Natural conditions of production are extremely favorable in this country, the supply of capital is more abundant than anywhere else, the ingenuity of the entrepreneurs, the efficiency of the inventors and the designers, and the skill of the workers are unsurpassed. The technical equipment of the plants and the methods of business management are unparalleled.

The main argument advanced in favor of American protectionism is the wage rate argument. The American standard of living, people say, has to be protected against the 'dumping' of industries producing at lower labor costs.

Real wages are higher in this country than in almost all other countries because America is comparatively underpopulated, while most of the other countries are comparatively overpopulated. As immigration is restricted, there does not prevail a tendency toward an equalization of wage rates. In those countries in which physical conditions of production are less favorable than in America, wage rates must be lower. There would be but one means to raise the extremely low standard of living in China: to let the Chinese freely emigrate to countries in which natural conditions of production are more favorable, capital is more abundant, and population is comparatively less dense.

The comparatively high state of market real wage rates, i.e., wage rates as they would be in the absence of any trade union pressure and compulsion, in this country is not an outcome of protectionism and does not need to be safeguarded by tariffs. The abolition of protection would not lower the American standard of living, but raise it. American processing industries would concentrate their efforts upon those branches in which their superiority is highest. Their products would buy on the world market a greater amount of those products whose production would be discontinued in this country because American superiority is lower in those fields. The total amount of American consumption would increase, not decrease.

Money wage rates may drop. But they would drop less than the prices of consumers' goods, now artificially raised by protection.

5

Protection and Defense

It has been asserted that the nations strive after autarky because they are warlike and want to be independent of foreign supply.

The truth is that Germany strove after autarky and therefore wanted to conquer more *Lebensraum*, i.e., a territory so large and so rich in natural resources that the Germans would live in economic self-sufficiency at a standard not lower than that of any other nation.

Moreover, economic nationalism is not a phenomenon peculiar to aggressive nations. Peace-loving nations are no less imbued by the spirit of economic nationalism than militaristic peoples.

It may be reasonable to explain the protection (operated by a government wheat monopoly) which Switzerland grants to its domestic wheat production as a defense measure. But it is impossible to apply the same explanation to the Swiss import restrictions upon china, glassware, and silver plates. The country applies the quota system to passenger cars although there is no domestic production and no hope that such a production could be bolstered up!

6

Protection and Government Control of Business

A nation's policy forms an integral whole. Foreign policy and domestic policy are closely linked together, they are both a system. Economic nationalism is the corollary of the present-day domestic policies of government interference with business and of national planning as free trade was the complement of domestic economic freedom. There can be protectionism in a country with domestic economic freedom. There can be protectionism in a country with domestic free trade, but where there is no domestic free trade, protectionism is indispensable. A national government's might is limited to the territory subject to its sovereignty. It does not have the power to interfere directly with conditions abroad. Where there is free trade, foreign competition would in the short run already frustrate the aims sought by the various measures of government intervention with domestic business. When the domestic market is not to some extent insulated from the foreign markets, there can be no question of government control. The farther a nation goes on the way toward public regulation and regimentation, the more it is pushed toward economic isolation.

We do not have to deal with the problem whether economic interventionism, i.e., government interference with business, can attain the ends aimed at by the government and by the 'progressives' who endorse this system. Its champions – the German 'Sozialpolitiker,' the right wing of the British Fabians, the American Institutionalists, the moderates among the New Dealers and many other groups – have contended that interventionism is feasible and workable as a permanent form of social economic organization. They have claimed that it is as far from socialism as it is from capitalism, that it stands as a third solution of the problem of society's economic organization midway between communism and laissez faire, and that while retaining the advantages of both it avoids the disadvantages inherent in both of them. However, modern economic theory has demonstrated in an irrefutable way that this alleged third method is contrary to purpose, and that the various measures of government interference with business not only do not attain the ends sought but, on the contrary, must result in a state of affairs which – from the viewpoint of the government and the supporters of its policy – is even much more unsatisfactory than the conditions which they wanted to alter.

Neither do we have to deal with the lessons to be learned from historical experience. For more than sixty years all governments of civilized nations have experimented with various modes of economic interventionism. The outcome was always the same: manifest failure. The *Sozialpolitik* of the German Reich, inaugurated at the end of the 'seventies of the nineteenth century and solemnly publicized by the old Kaiser's imperial message of November 17, 1881, and the American New Deal are the outstanding examples.

From the viewpoint of the subject with which this paper deals we have to stress another point. Every act of government interference with business raises the domestic costs of production and thus disarranges the conditions for competition. Under free trade it would immediately result in a drop of sales on the part of domestic producers, in restriction of output and in discharging of workers. People would quickly realize that the system of interventionism does not work and that it causes unemployment and bad business. They would ask for a return to the conditions prevailing before the government interfered, i.e., for repeal of the detrimental measure.

But things are different if there is protection preventing foreign business from competing on the domestic market or at least rendering such competition more expensive. Then the domestic entrepreneur can react to the increase of costs through raising prices. The government and the supporters of its policy triumph; they are convinced that their methods of improving the material well-being of the workers have succeeded. What they do not see is that the public has to pay the bill and that the workers are burdened with higher prices. The same is valid with regard to wage raises brought about by the trade union compulsion and pressure. Wage rates on the unhampered labor market are higher in the United States than – with the exception of New Zealand – in any other country. Natural conditions of labor are more favorable, and capital is more abundant in this country; on the other hand immigration is restricted. If the American trade unions try to raise wage rates above this market level – a high level indeed, when compared with that of the rest of the world – the same problems present themselves. The immediate manifest failure of the trade union methods can only be avoided by a rise of prices which requires protection.

If there were free trade in United States, prices – due allowance being made for transportation costs – could not rise above world market levels. An employer whom the unions have forced to pay wages higher than his business can afford would have to restrict output and to discharge workers.

If the industry concerned exports a part of its products, it is in a special position. It is not free to raise the prices of the exported commodities. But protectionism provides another way out. The domestic producers form a cartel, charge monopoly prices on the domestic market and compensate for the losses incurred in selling abroad at low prices by a part of the monopoly profit. This was especially the case with Germany. Germany, which is forced to export a great part of its manufactures, was, from the end of the seventies of the nineteenth century to the outbreak of the First World War, far ahead of all other nations in matters of *Sozialpolitik* and trade unionism. Its much admired and glorified system of *Arbeiterschutz*, social insurance and collective bargaining, could work only because German industries, sheltered by all-round protection, built up cartels and sold on the world market much more cheaply than at home. The alleged success of the 'soziales Königtum der Hohenzollern' and of the German Social Democrat party was apparent. In their capacity as consumers, the workers themselves had to bear the burden. Cartel and monopoly were necessary complements of German interventionism.

Popular legends have misrepresented the fact. They teach that the trend toward monopoly is inherent in capitalism. The German champions of government control of business have repeated again and again that private enterprise, if left free and not restrained by government control, must result in monopolization and that this inextricable tendency makes nationalization of business necessary. They passed over in silence the fact that cartelization was only possible because government and parliament had decreed import duties; that the law itself ordered the entrepreneurs to form a cartel if they refused to so do of their own accord, as was, for instance, the case with potash; that the Prussian government itself in its capacity as owner and operator of coal mines joined the coal cartel.

It is a characteristic feature of present-day governments and political parties that they promise in the same breath low prices to the consumers and high prices to the producers. But as it is beyond the power of any government to make prices lower than they would be on the competitive market unhampered by government interference, what results is always only a policy of raising prices. The governments pretend to fight monopoly, but they never take recourse to the measure which would render vain in most of the branches of industry all attempts to bolster up a monopoly, namely the abolition of import duties.

That the governments and the parliaments favor monopoly prices is clearly evidenced by their actions with regard to international monopolistic schemes. If the protective tariffs result in the formation of national cartels in various countries, international cartelization can in many cases be attained by mutual agreements between the national cartels. Such agreements are often very well served by another pro-monopoly activity of governments, the patents and other privileges granted to new inventions. However, where technical obstacles prevent the construction of a national cartel – as is almost always the case with agricultural production – no such international agreements can be built up. Then the governments interfere again. The history between the two world wars is an open record of state intervention to foster restriction and monopoly by international conventions. There were schemes for wheat pools, rubber, tin and sugar restrictions and so on. Of course most of them collapsed soon. But this failure was rather an outcome of government inefficiency than of government preference for competitive business.

We have to realize that even protectionism cannot make government interference with business work and achieve the ends sought. All that it can bring about is to delay for a shorter or longer time the appearance of the undesired consequences of interventionism. Its failure must finally become manifest. The schemes to raise by decree or by trade union pressure the income of the wage earners above the height fixed by the unhampered market must necessarily sooner or later result in mass unemployment prolonged year after year; protection can only temporarily postpone this effect, but does not brush it away. But it is exactly this temporary adjournment which the supporters of interventionism aim at. It disguises the futility and ineptitude of their cherished policies. If the detrimental effects of their measures were to appear immediately, the public would more quickly understand their vanity. But as they are delayed, the champions of government control and trade unionism have in the meantime the opportunity to boast that the employers were wrong in predicting that the artificially raised wage rates and the burdens imposed upon business by discriminatory taxation and by labor legislation would make their plants unprofitable and hamper production.

Economic nationalism is the necessary complement of the endeavors to interfere with domestic business conditions.

7

Protectionism on the Part of Creditor Nations

The tariff barriers against imports are especially nonsensical when erected by creditor nations. If the debtor nations in accordance with the terms stipulated pay interest and repay the principal of the debts and if they do not hinder the foreign investors taking out the business profits earned, their balance of trade must show an excess over imports, i.e., become favorable. Concomitantly the balance of trade of the creditor nations becomes unfavorable. The terms 'favorable' and 'unfavorable' are, of course, misleading. It is not unfavorable to be a rich nation and to receive large payments of interest, dividends, and profits from abroad. Great Britain was in the past century the world's richest nation, not although, but because it had a very 'unfavorable' balance of trade.

The United States, in the years of its glorious geographic and economic expansion, had offered very propitious investment opportunities for foreign capital. The capitalists of Western Europe provided a part of the capital needed for the construction of American railroads and for the building up of American mining and American processing industries. Then later the Americans began to repatriate the stocks and bonds owned by foreigners; these operations made the nation's balance of trade active. With the First World War things changed. America became a creditor nation, the greatest capital exporting nation. Its favorable balance of trade – in the years 1916 to 1940 the excess of exports over imports was about 30 billion dollars – had now another significance; it was the outcome of the loans granted abroad and of investments in foreign countries.

But at the same time American tariff policy made the payment of interest and the transfer of dividends more burdensome to the debtor nations. The same policy was applied by the other creditor nations, for instance Great Britain, France, the Netherlands, Belgium, and Switzerland. The debtor nations were, it is true, not very enthusiastic about the payments they had to make; debtors mostly are not very anxious to keep to the terms of the contract. But the conduct of the creditor nations, which sensibly prejudiced their interests, provided them with an opportune pretext for refusal to pay. They took recourse to currency devaluation, foreign exchange control, moratoriums and some of them even to open repudiation and bankruptcy.

The policy of the creditor nations was especially paradoxical in the case of the German reparations and the inter-allied debts. If Germany had really paid reparations out of her own funds – and not out of foreign, mostly American credits granted to her – these payments would have rendered necessarily the receiving countries' balance of trade 'unfavorable'; their imports would have exceeded their exports *because* they collected reparations. But this effect appeared, from the viewpoint of mercantilist fallacies, as a tremendous mischief. The Allies were at the same time anxious to make Germany pay and not to get the payments. They simply did not know what they wanted. But the Germans knew very well what they themselves aimed at. They did not wish to pay. They succeeded.

The same holds true with regard to the inter-Allied debts.

8

Totalitarianism and Autarky

Ferdinand Lassalle, the founder of the German Social Democrat Party and the eloquent champion of government control of business, is credited with the dictum: 'The State is God.' Eminent scholars, for instance Ambassador Carlton Hayes, call nationalism a new religion, the creed of our day.

People distinguish between the parties of the Left and the parties of the Right. The former, they say, are the 'progressives,' the supporters of government control of business, the socialists and the communists; the latter the 'reactionaires,' the nationalists. This classification is spurious. The socio-economic tenets of both groups differ only in minor points. They both aim at full government control of business. It is difficult to decide to which of these two totalitarian groups the most eminent intellectual harbingers of present-day 'unorthodoxy' are to be assigned. There is no doubt that Lassalle was also the forerunner of German National Socialism and the first German who aimed at the *Führer* position. The Frenchman Georges Sorel, the advocate of the 'action directe,' i.e., violent trade union activities and general strike, was the preceptor both of Lenin and Mussolini. The socio-economic program of Italian Fascism, the *stato corporativo*, is an exact replica of the schemes of British Guild Socialism; its most lucid exposition is the book of the English Fabians and enthusiastic pro-Soviet writers, Sidney and Beatrice Webb: *A constitution for a Socialist Commonwealth of Great Britain* (1920). Not only Mussolini, but many outstanding French collaborationists and

German Nazis (for instance, Werner Sombart) were Marxian readers before they turned to the 'Right.'

The truth is that modern nationalism is a corollary of the domestic policy of government control of business. It has been demonstrated that government control of business would manifestly fail already in the short run if the country is not isolated from the rest of the world. A government aiming at full regimentation of business must aim at autarky too. Every kind of international economic relations impairs its power to interfere with domestic business and limits the exercise of its sovereignty. The state cannot pretend to be an omnipotent god if it has to bother about its citizens' ability to compete with foreign business. The outcome of government interference with business is totalitarianism, and totalitarianism requires economic self-sufficiency.

The same is valid with regard to self—proclaimed socialist states, that is states which have openly nationalized all economic enterprises and boast of this achievement. Socialism, when not operated on a world scale, is imperfect, if the socialist country depends on imports from abroad and therefore still has to produce commodities for sale on a market. It does not matter whether these foreign countries to which it has to sell and from which it has to buy are socialist or not. Socialism must always aim at autarky.

Protectionism and autarky mean discrimination against foreign labor and capital. They not only lower the productivity of human effort and thereby the standard of living for all nations; they create moreover international conflict.

There are nations which for lack of adequate resources cannot feed and clothe their population out of domestic resources. These nations cannot aim at autarky, but by embarking upon a policy of conquest. With them bellicosity and lust of aggression are the outcome of their adherence to the principles of government control of business. This was the case with Germany, Italy, and Japan. They said that they wanted to get a fair share of the earth's resources, thus they aimed at a new distribution of the areas producing raw materials. But these other countries were not empty; their inhabitants were not prepared to consider themselves as an appurtenance of their mines and plantations. They did not long for German or Italian rule. Thus there originated conflicts.

9

Sovereignty in the Present World

The principle of national sovereignty does not stand in the way of international division of labor and of peaceful collaboration of all nations within the framework of the world-embracing Great Society, provided that every nation unswervingly clings to the policies of democracy and capitalism. In the socio-economic setting of market society (laissez faire, laissez passer) the state is not an omnipotent God, but – as Lassalle used to say disparagingly – just a 'night-watchman.' The state is not an end, much less the only and supreme end, but simply a means for the promotion of the citizens' welfare. The acknowledgment of the indispensableness of private ownership of the means of production and of unhampered market exchange restricts the exercise of sovereignty. Although formally free in the exercise of their powers, the individual governments are subject to the supremacy of a principle which prevents the rise of international conflicts.

If the state administered in accordance with the ideas of economic interventionism, statism, and socialism, sovereignty becomes unlimited and absolute. The totalitarian state pretends to be omnipotent, supreme and above any principle, law, rule or consideration for anybody and for anything. Nothing counts but its 'sacred egoism.' Right is what the state declares to be such.

This excessive notion of national sovereignty is incompatible with the present state of economic evolution. It cannot coexist with international division of labor. It wrongs all other nations and must result in strife.

Mankind is not free to return from a higher state of division of labor to a lower state. Autarky of every nation would impair very sensibly the standard of living of all peoples. There are today no such things as domestic affairs of an individual nation which do not affect the well-being of the rest of the world. Every nation has a material interest in the other nations' economic well-being because maladministration of one country hurts all other nations too.

If a national government hinders the most productive use of its country's resources, it hurts the interests of all other nations. Economic backwardness of a country with rich natural resources challenges all those whose conditions could be improved by a more efficient exploitation of this natural wealth.

Protectionism and autarky result in a state of affairs in which a country's resources are not used to the extent that they would be under free trade. For instance, the fact that the tariffs of those nations whose soil offers the most favorable physical opportunities for the production of wheat – the United States, Canada, and Argentina – hinder the import of manufactures would, even in the absence of European tariffs on wheat, compel Europeans to grow wheat on a soil which is less fertile than millions of acres of untilled soil in those countries better endowed by nature.

A country's economic insulation impairs not only the material well-being of its own citizens. It is no less detrimental to the economic interests of foreigners. This is why, in the middle of the past century, Great Britain and France induced China to open its harbors and why the United States applied a similar policy with regard to Japan.

10

The United States and World Affairs

Not only economic isolation, political isolation too is unfeasible in the present world.

The Western Hemisphere was once safe against aggression. Thousands of miles of ocean separated it from possible invaders. The airplane has radically changed this state of things. The American isolationists have not yet realized this fact.

They argue this way: 'It is a very deplorable fact that the peoples of Europe are fighting one another, that they have wrecked their glorious civilization and that they are consequently doomed to starvation and misery. It is no less deplorable that similar things happen in Asia. Unfortunately we cannot save them from disaster. They themselves have to learn that peaceful cooperation would be more beneficial to them than war and mutual extermination. We cannot police the whole world. All we can do is to look out for ourselves and to preserve the Western Hemisphere's independence. We will keep neutral, will not interfere with other continents' affairs and thus preserve our American way of life.'

But it is not without concern for America what happens in the rest of the world. The establishment of two big totalitarian empires, one on the other side of the Atlantic, one on the other side of the Pacific, would have been a tremendous menace to America's political independence. The German nationalists had always emphasized that the last goal of their ambitions was the conquest of a large colonial domain on the American continent. The present writer is not familiar with the Japanese language and does not know whether Japanese economists and publicists were equally frank in their printed utterances. But he knows from conversations with many Japanese professors and students that they considered the Americans and not the Chinese, their main enemies.

For the sake of its own vital interests America cannot remain neutral in world affairs and cannot live in political isolation. It has to realize that every international conflict will sooner or later involve America too and that it must be its main concern to establish a post-war order which will make the peace last.

There have been suggested various plans for such a scheme for a durable peace. Nobody can foretell today which of them will be put into execution.[73] However, all these proposals must imply a close and permanent cooperation either among all nations or at least among one group of nations, those united today in the war. If conflicts are not eliminated, there can be no question of a durable political alliance. But protectionism and still more autarky provoke conflicts.

The Second World War was not caused by Nazism alone. The failure of all other nations to erect in time a barrier against a possible aggression was no less instrumental in bringing about the disaster than the plans of the Nazis and the other Axis powers. If the Nazis had expected to encounter on the first day of hostilities a united and adequately armed front of all those nations which later came united in fighting them, they would never have ventured an assault. But collective security is unrealizable among nations bitterly fighting one another in the economic sphere. Economic nationalism has divided the peace-loving nations. If the United Nations do not succeed in brushing away economic nationalism, postwar conditions will not differ from those prevailing in the years between the two World Wars. Then a third and much more dreadful war is unavoidable.

Every nation has to choose. The United States too. The alternative is; unity among the peace-loving nations or return to the chaos out of which new conflict will originate. But unity is incompatible with protection. Every day experiences anew that the good neighbor policy among the American republics comes into collision with economic nationalism. How should Latin America and the European

---

73 This was written before the United Nations Charter was drafted on January 1, 1942 (ed.).

democracies enter into a close political collaboration with the United States if their citizens suffer from American foreign trade policies?

If economic nationalism is not abandoned the most radical disarmament will not prevent the defeated aggressors from entering anew the scene of diplomatic intrigues, from building up new blocks and spheres of interest, from playing off one nation against the others, from rearming and finally from plotting new attacks. Economic nationalism is the main obstacle to lasting peace.

READING 20

Lionel Robbins

Biography

Lionel Robbins (1898–1984) was born on November 28, 1898, in Middlesex, England, the son of Rowland Richard Robbins and Rosa Marion Robbins. Upon completion of his secondary education he entered University College, London and then volunteered for war service. He saw active duty on the Western Front and returned to his home country in 1918 seriously wounded.

In 1920, he entered the London School of Economics (LSE) as an undergraduate and was taught by such people as economist Edwin Cannan and left-wing political scientist Harold Laski. Cannan represented a healthy common sense approach to economics deepened by a critical scholarly study of the history of economic ideas. Robbins graduated in 1923 and subsequently worked for a year as a research assistant to William Beveridge. In 1924 he married Iris Elizabeth with whom he had one son and one daughter.

From 1924 to 1925 Robbins was a tutor in economics at New College Oxford. In 1925 he was offered a lectureship at LSE. There he remained, apart from a second short spell at New College, Oxford (1928–29). In 1929, at the age of 31 he was appointed Professor of Economics at LSE, a position he held until 1961.

In the England of the 1920s, economics was still dominated by the somewhat tired orthodoxy of the Cambridge school of Alfred Marshall. Robbins escaped these narrow intellectual horizons successfully and found much inspiration in the works of Knut Wicksell, Philip Wicksteed and Ludwig von Mises. He was also influenced by Friedrich von Hayek whom he brought to LSE from Vienna (1928).

In 1932 Robbins wrote his first major work entitled *An Essay on the Nature and Significance of Economic Science* which eventually became a methodological classic. The book consisted of a reasoned statement of the methodology and philosophy of economics and was written in lucid and elegant prose. Robbins was actually the first economist to use the idea of scarcity as the central organizing concept of economic theory. He defined economic science as the systematic study of the relationship between ends and scarce means which have alternative uses.

In 1934 Robbins published a book entitled *The Great Depression*. This work was obviously influenced by the Austrian theory of the trade cycle which attributed the depression of the 1930s primarily to under-saving. This led to a major disagreement between Robbins and Keynes who saw things differently and who advocated expansionist policies combined with some sort of protectionism to counter recessionary circumstances. Later in his career however, Robbins accepted the idea of some form of macro-economic stimulation to remedy widespread unemployment. During World War II Robbins and Keynes worked well together as government advisors and they were both members of the British team negotiating the Bretton Woods Agreements.

Many of Robbins' later writings were devoted to the history of economic thought. His best-known book in this field was *Robert Torrens and the Evolution of Classical Economics* (1958). Via his discussion of Torrens, who had contributed to many of the economic controversies of the first half of the nineteenth century, Robbins was able to comment indirectly on those controversies. Robbins was also a dedicated and appreciated teacher and his lectures and seminars profoundly affected many young economists of the period.

Like Keynes, Robbins' interests were broad: he served as a trustee of the National and Tate Galleries, and in 1961, he accepted the chairmanship of the Financial Times, a position he held until 1970. In recognition for his distinct services Robbins was made a Life Peer in 1959 taking the title of Baron Robbins of Clare Market. Robbins died in 1984 at the age of 86.

The Work

In the first reading taken from *The Economic Basis of Class Conflict*, Robbins critically examines why in the interwar period (1920–40) nations elevated ever greater obstacles against international trade with the apparent aim to obtain long term gains.[74] First, there is the ideal of self-sufficiency. Second there is the argument that certain industries should enjoy protection because they are critical to national security. Third, there are those who believe that protectionism can improve a nation's terms of trade. Duties on foreign goods have also been advocated as a kind of bargaining chip to negotiate with other countries for the reciprocal reduction of their trade barriers.

Finally, there is always the well-known infant industry argument. Then there are the short-run contentions. Notorious is the argument that keeping out imports encourages domestic employment. This plea always has a special appeal during recessions and depressions. Moreover, there is the suggestion that trade restrictions must necessarily accompany the kind of national planning fashionable in the 1930s. As the argument says, national planning in combination with free trade leads to chaos. Robbins also explains that protectionism has been promoted by the fact that under the free trade conditions a nation can only hope to keep those industries which enjoy the greatest comparative advantage. Certain inefficient lines of industry will have to go which of course creates depressive circumstances in the areas where these industries are located. Thus, certain policies, beneficial as they may be in the long run hurt certain groups in the short run.

The general public, however, is often more impressed by the visible short-run effects of a given policy than by the less visible beneficial long-term implications. Therefore, says Robbins, a powerful intellectual tradition of adherence to the free enterprise system and free trade is most important to counteract the shortsightedness of the public. Yet, as Robbins notes, the intellectual resistance against government interference and statism in general had weakened in the 1930s even among professional economists.

Besides, the policies of interventionism typical for the post World War I period had made the movement of resources from one industry to another, much more difficult which increased the pain of adjustment when an industry declined.

Robbins also discusses how the reversal of the free trade policies started in the 1870s when a united Germany moved towards protectionism. At the same time the rapidly expanding sales of cheap American wheat also propelled some European nations into taking

---

74 L. Robbins, *The Economic Basis of Class Conflict and Other Essays in Political Economy* (London: Macmillan, 1939) pp. 107–134.

protectionism measures. The First World War precipitated the decline of the spirit of classical liberalism and then, the Great Depression with its large scale unemployment often drove governments into taking desperate measures.

The second set of readings are taken from Robbins' book *Economic Planning and International Order*.[75] They describe the *international* significance of obstacles to free trade. Protectionism destroys the international division of labor and the elevation of tariffs in one nation can plunge other countries into depression. Robbins also briefly reviews Keynes's position on protectionism in the early 1930s. Finally, the readings include a few remarks by Robbins on the issue of statism versus classical liberalism.

Extracts

The Cause of Increased Protectionism

Introduction
The object of this memorandum is to examine the fundamental reasons for the great increase of protectionism which has been characteristic of the commercial policies of the last half-century.

We can all agree that this increase is something which needs to be explained. The last half-century has been a period of rapid increase of all means of communication. The railway systems of the world have been extended and consolidated. Shipping services have been increased and made more reliable. Today the aeroplane is making distance still more negligible. Yet, in spite of all this, we find that the nations of the world are busily engaged in erecting ever greater and greater obstacles to the increased volume of trade which these developments make possible. An inhabitant of another planet, informed of the scientific progress of the last hundred years, might expect to discover a world organized to take advantage of the increased division of labor which these increased facilities for communication permit. If he actually paid a visit of inspection he would find the queer animals which inhabit this earth devoting much of their energy to what must appear to be a sort of self-frustration, destroying with one hand the riches which the other has created.

75 L. Robbins, *Economic Planning and International Order* (London: Macmillan, 1937), pp. 41–55, 319–323, 325–326.

Why has this come about?

National Interest and Protectionism

If the different parts of the world were organized into one state, there is no reason to suppose that the existence of inter-local obstacles to trade would be regarded as desirable. It has been characteristic of the development of modern states that, within their boundaries, the obstacles to trade have been removed. The formation of the German Empire, the reforms of the French Revolution, are conspicuous examples of a process which, when there has existed a sufficiently powerful state machine, has everywhere been thought to be desirable. If by the accident of history the Roman Empire had persisted and its dominions had been continuously coterminous with the borders of the known world, it is hard to believe that the persistence of local barriers to free exchange would have been thought to be consistent with the greatest benefit of the majority of its inhabitants. Whether a world state was organized on individualist or on socialist lines, a division of labor not limited by artificial territorial divisions would clearly be in the interests of the majority of its citizens.

But the world is not organized on these lines. It is organized into a number of territorial groups, constituted very largely as a result of historical accident. The controllers of these states do not profess to legislate for the benefit of the world as a whole. They claim only to legislate for the benefit of their own members; and though from time to time they may pay lip-service to international solidarity – this is much less obligatory now than it used to be – there can be no doubt that if there were a conflict between the interests of the world as a whole and those of their own group they would unhesitatingly choose the latter.

It follows therefore, if we are to examine the evolution of policy, that we must take as our starting point the interests, real or imaginary, of the national state. We need not enquire why the economic activities of the world as a whole are not deliberately organized with a view to the benefit of the majority of its inhabitants; given the absence of an international authority, there is no problem there. We must ask rather why it is that the policies of the different national states are such as to create international disharmony.

Now, it is conceivable that there may be a real clash between the interests of the world as a whole as regards trade and the interests of particular national groups. As we shall see later on, it is doubtful whether real clashes of this sort have played a very large part in bringing about the present international chaos. But it is obviously possible that such clashes may exist; and in a vague way, many people believe that they do exist. It will be convenient therefore to commence our investigation by enquiring in what way they may arise.

To do this, two issues must be very clearly separated. We must separate the question of what people want, of how they conceive their interests, from the question of how best they actually may secure what they want. It is obvious that disharmonies may arise, either as a result of differences in opinion as to the best way in which ultimate aims may be realized. It is conceivable that the different nations of the earth may entertain fundamentally different conceptions regarding the ultimate aims of national policy and that disharmony may arise in this way. Or it is conceivable that they may each be striving after the same thing and yet, by reason of differences of opinion regarding the best way to get it, their policies may create disharmony.

Let us commence with disharmonies originating in the ultimate aims of policy. If the government of a particular area regards it as an end in itself that the organization of production should be self-sufficient, it is obvious that its trade policy will be inimical to international division of labor. From time to time such ideals of self-sufficiency have indeed exercised some influence on political thought. It was held by Plato and other Greek philosophers that foreign trade was in itself to be regarded inimical to the atmosphere of the ideal state. The austerity of the alleged self-sufficiency of Sparta was contrasted favorably with the cosmopolitan atmosphere of Athens, whose prosperity depended on foreign trade. In recent times similar views have been held by less worthy and less interesting writers: Fichte, Adam Müller and the so-called Romantic school of German economists, whose writings have unquestionably influenced the thought of the leaders of present-day Germany, exalted the idea of the *Geschlossene Handelsstaat*. To eat home-grown rhubarb has been held to be more virtuous than the consumption of the foreign lemon. But it is doubtful how far ideas of this sort have been responsible for the development of policy. From time to time they may have been used to defend measures introduced for other reasons. But although at the present time they are undoubtedly rapidly attaining great ascendancy in those parts of the world now given over to barbarism, their influence on policy elsewhere has probably not been very great.

But although it is possible to exaggerate the influence of the idea of self-sufficiency as a means of preserving the characteristic *ethos* of the national state, it is important not to under-estimate the influence of the ideal of economic self-sufficiency, regarded, not as an end in itself, but as a means of military defence. It has always been conceded by free traders that, if the location of any particular form of production within the borders of the national state was regarded as essential to security against outside attacks, then measures designed to foster this industry could not be regarded as contrary to national policy. Even before the Great War considerations of this sort played some part in the determination of policy. The German agrarian policy was defended on military grounds. Since the war, experience of the difficulties which may arise in case of blockade or widespread interruption of international commerce has led to a vast extension of such measures. The extensive protection of industries capable of being used for munition-making has also been defended on this ground.

The cost of such measures is obvious. The factors of production which are used for producing expensive supplies at home might have been used to obtain them less expensively from abroad by exchanging goods for whose production local conditions are better fitted. It is arguable moreover that, even granting the necessity for regarding the danger of war as a permanent factor in international relations, much protection is ill-conceived. The experience of the last war, while it undoubtedly shows the value of security from blockade, has shown also the advantages of the riches which come from international commerce. It is not possible to have both of these, and it is not certain that in the majority of cases the latter is of less importance. But in recent years such considerations have tended to lose influence. As the danger of widespread international conflict becomes more acute, the area of military protectionism increases.

It is possible, however, to regard policies based on circumstances of this kind as being essentially abnormal. It is still arguable that the average citizen, even the citizen of the lands of hatred and mass murder, regards war as an evil which ought eventually to be eliminated, and conceives the main object of policy to be the inception of conditions in which the non-military requirements of the race are satisfied as far as the niggardly provisions of nature make possible. It is arguable, that is to say, that the main aims of national policy may still be conceived as being the maximization of the ingredients of real incomes other than security and military power. We may proceed therefore to enquire whether, in the realization of such aims, the interest of one national group may conflict with the interests of others, that is to say, whether one country can gain by a policy of trade restriction.

Now, it is certainly possible to conceive of cases in which, by erecting obstacles to trade, one national group may gain at the expense of others. Theoretical economics demonstrates clearly that, in certain circumstances, it is possible that a tariff may have the effect of turning the 'terms of trade' in favor of the inhabitants of the country imposing the tariff – that is to say, of bringing it about that they get more imports for a given quantity of exports. This, after all, is only what we should expect from the most general propositions of the theory of exchange. We know that if particular groups of producers happen to occupy a position of strategic advantage in the market, then by suitable restrictions they can secure monopolistic gains. Obviously this must apply not only to industrial groups but to geographical groups also.

In fact, however, it is possible greatly to over-estimate the applicability of this argument. The circumstances in which an unequivocal gain of this sort is realizable do not often occur in practice. The geographical group which attempts to turn the terms of trade in its favor will find, as likely as not, that it is merely inviting new competition in other quarters. Moreover, the whole argument depends upon the assumption that conditions in the outside world remain unchanged, that other nations pursue a passive policy in the face of isolated protection. In practice these conditions are not likely to be realized. The erection of a protective tariff by the members of one national group is likely to be countered by the erection of protective tariffs elsewhere: and though it is not *certain* that all the possible gains will be canceled out, the probabilities are overwhelmingly in favor, not merely of cancellation, but also of net impoverishment all round.

Exactly the same considerations apply to the other arguments by which it is attempted to establish the possibility of a permanent gain from the erection of protective tariffs. Other things being equal, for instance, it is possible that the erection of a bargaining tariff may result in a lowering of tariffs, in which case these tactical manoeuvres will have been productive of lasting benefit. But experience suggests that in practice other things are not equal. It is probable that the erection of a bargaining tariff will bring about a situation in which that tariff becomes permanent – to say nothing of the increases elsewhere which its erection may have occasioned. Similarly, it has always been conceded that cases are conceivable where protection to infant industries may result in national benefit. But again experience shows that such a form of assistance is almost always abused. The industry is called into being and the tariff is not removed. If there be a case for the fostering of infant industries by national states, a subsidy rather than a tariff seems to be the appropriate instrument: it is much less likely to be prolonged once the occasion for its use has disappeared.

The foregoing arguments apply to the possible long-run gains from protection. It appears that the prospects of such gains are very slender. If we restrict our view to the immediate effects, however, there are other cases where some benefit may be conceived. If a tariff is imposed at a time when trade is bad and a considerable margin of the factors of production are unemployed, it is possible that the result may be a net gain of production; though it is almost certain that the gain involved will not be as great as that which might have been achieved if the unemployed factors of production had been re-employed by recovery under free trade conditions. It is possible, too, that if a general tariff is imposed at a time when the central bank of the country, imposing the tariff, is losing gold, some credit contraction may be made unnecessary, though the tariff itself will be productive of some permanent maldistribution of resources and its existence will be no safeguard whatever against a similar drain of gold in the future.

It is notorious that arguments of this sort have played a considerable part in determining the policies which have been actually adopted during the recent depression. But the result of such policies indicates the consideration which has obviously been overlooked. If, in an otherwise stable world, a single nation has recourse to such policies, it may conceivably snatch for itself some gain – or, perhaps better said, some avoidance of loss. But if such policies are applied simultaneously by a number of nations, their effects, so far from being productive of gain all round, have in fact cumulative results of a negative order. If all countries impose emergency tariffs at a time of crisis, the effect is likely to be deflationary. More unemployment is produced than would have occurred in the absence of such policies. It is probably true that much of the increase in the height of international obstacles to trade has taken place in this way. But it is difficult to argue that the world is richer than it would have been if no such increase had taken place.

In recent years the case for trade restriction has sometimes been argued from a different point of view. It has been defended as a policy of national planning. To protect planned industry at home it is necessary, it is said, to restrict foreign imports. The tariff is essentially to be regarded as an instrument of the 'scientific' control of economic activity, which is to replace the individualistic 'chaos' of the free market and private enterprise.

Such a view, however, betrays a most paradoxical conception of the aims of national planning. If national planning is intended to bring 'economic' advantage – if, that is to say, it is desired for the sake of 'wealth' rather than military power, aesthetically pleasing layout of the countryside, etc. – it must surely be designed to use the national resources in the most productive manner. Now, resources will not be used in the most productive manner if they are used to produce at home what could be obtained more cheaply from abroad. It is the essence of the case for free exchange that it permits local resources to be specialized to produce the things which they are best fitted to produce and thus to procure, by way of exchange from abroad, *more* of the things which they cannot produce so efficiently at home. A national plan which does not proceed on the same principle is not a national plan but a national muddle.

Against all this, however, and against the case for free trade in general, it is sometimes argued that the advantages of international division of labor are really very small. The technique of modern machine production, it is said, renders the location of industry a matter of comparative unimportance. There may be some sacrifice in greater self-sufficiency; but it is more than compensated by the greater stability of a more autonomous system. Such arguments find support, not only among those who attach importance to the abracadabra of planning, but also among those monetary reformers who hold that their attempts to secure the advantages of a constant domestic price level would be considerably eased by the diminution of the dependence of particular industries on events in other parts of the world.

All this is surely very much in the air. The sacrifices involved by a policy of self-sufficiency must depend essentially upon the size and natural equipment of the particular national area in question. They would be one thing for an area such as Belgium or Holland. It is perhaps arguable that, *if* the benefits to be secured by a policy of national planning undisturbed by outside forces were very great, an area such as the United States might make such an experiment without catastrophic impoverishment. But for smaller areas, more dependent upon international trade, such a policy would inevitably be catastrophic. Vague talk about national planning which takes no account of the differences in the international situation of different national areas is not merely useless, it is positively misleading.

Further enquiry only tends to strengthen this conclusion. If modern machine technique is to be maintained (and it is the existence of modern machine technique which is usually the pretext for this type of argument), it is clearly impossible that the different national areas should become entirely self-sufficient. The necessity for obtaining raw-material supplies makes that out of the question for almost every national area in the world. Yet, if trade in raw materials is to continue, there must be also some trade in finished products. The distribution of natural resources between the different national areas is not such as to permit trade to be carried on only by the exchange of one kind of raw material for others. If the exporters of raw materials refuse to import manufactured articles, then the would-be importers of raw materials will be unable to secure the means of paying for them. The dislocation which would thus be occasioned in a world which hitherto had been organized for fairly extensive international trade for all must more than counterbalance the extremely doubtful benefits of increased national planning. The distribution of men and natural resources in different parts of the world is not such as to permit the existing national areas to plan far towards self-sufficiency without danger of grave loss. Here as elsewhere the belief that it can be otherwise rests on the naive assumption that, while one nation plans to produce everything save raw materials at home, others will pursue a more or less free trade policy.

But even if this were not so, it would still be untrue to argue that the existence of modern technique renders the international division of labor any less advantageous. The case for international division of labor rests on differences of costs. So long as the costs of production of different commodities are different in different areas, so long will it be advantageous for each area to specialize on producing those things in which its costs of production are least and to procure the rest by way of exchange from elsewhere. And these cost differences depend in the last resort on the different relative scarcities in the different parts of the world of the different factors of production – depend, that is to say, on the existence of differences of efficiency wages, differences of rents, differences of raw-material costs, differences of transport charges, etc. And there is really no presumption that modern technique renders any less essential nice attention to these particulars. Rather the contrary indeed. Moreover, in so far as the achievement of the economies of large-scale production depends upon large markets, the general case against trade restriction is all the greater. There may be some national areas, such as the United States of America, offering so wide a market that the maximum economies of mass production can be secured at home. But in the majority of cases it is safe to say that limitations on trade are a definite hindrance to the achievement of these economies. The world would be much richer today if markets were more extensive.

The Causes of Increased Protectionism

If all this is true it follows that, save as a means of securing military security – and a rather dubious means at that - policies of protection are not likely to secure to the inhabitants of different nations any of the aims which most of them would acknowledge if they were seriously to reflect on these matters. The problem we are trying to solve, the problem, namely, of the causes of the increased protectionism characteristic of the last fifty years of world history, finds no solution in consideration of the actual benefits to be secured by policies of restrictionism. The phenomenon of increased protectionism is essentially a manifestation of irrationality.

What, then, are the roots of this irrationality, and why is it more prevalent at the present day than in earlier times? To see this it is necessary to look a little more closely at the influences shaping policy and the general conditions under which these influences are exerted.

It is a fundamental argument for free trade that the market tends to bring about that specialization of the use of national resources which is conductive to the greatest national income measured in price terms. But this argument, while it promises advantage for the majority of the inhabitants of the national area, does not promise advantage for lines of industry in which the comparative advantage of the area in question is less. The process whereby, under free trade, international division of labor is brought about, has thus a double aspect. It brings prosperity and expansion to those industries in which the advantages of local specialization are greatest, but it brings loss and depression to those industries whose products it is more expedient to obtain by way of exchange from elsewhere. The argument of those free traders who sometimes suggest that the disappearance of any industry as a result of foreign competition is the result of gross inefficiency on the part of the management of that industry is false. Under free trade conditions an area cannot keep within its borders branches of *all* types of industry; it will keep only those branches in which it has the greatest comparative advantage, the rest will tend to disappear. It is childish to suppose that we can have at once the benefits of territorial division of labor and the range of industries characteristic of national isolation.

Now, in conditions of equilibrium such a state of affairs would be advantageous for everyone. But equilibrium seldom exists. The general conditions of supply and demand are continually changing, and with them must change the conditions of most advantageous specialization. In such circumstances some groups suffer disadvantage. Unless the members of these groups are willing to transfer their services to other lines of production they may suffer some impoverishment. Such cases of hardship attract attention. The general public, which, as Bastiat explained, is always more impressed by what is seen than by what is not seen, perceives the losses of the groups which are being squeezed and tends to ignore the general gains which are made elsewhere. Unless there exists a body of vigilant and informed opinion continuously active to resist the appeals of special interests for protective measures, the tendency to impose such measures is very strong. The group is always active to defend its own interest. The society of consumers is unfortunately often passive and unorganized.

But it is not only under such conditions that the tendency to protection is active. It sometimes happens that changes in general trade conditions bring it about that, in order to maintain international equilibrium, some credit contraction is necessary within a national area. In such circumstances the disadvantages of such contraction are not limited to special groups. The effects of the contraction are widespread. Although general considerations of long-period advantage are all against resort to protection, considerations of short-term alleviation seem all in its favor. Again, if there is not a powerful intellectual tradition of adherence to free trade principles, the arguments for imposing restrictions may appear almost overwhelming.

Now in the modern world resistance of this sort has been conspicuously lacking. It is probably true to say that the majority of competent economists are still convinced believers in the advantages of free exchange. But their numbers are few: and in recent years the weight of their advice has been greatly weakened by dissensions upon special issues. It is probable that the majority of the English economists, for instance, who for special reasons of monetary policy were willing to countenance a departure from free trade in England in 1931, would have still acknowledged the validity of the general arguments for free trade. But the confusion caused in the minds of the general public by their attitude was great, and the abandonment of the policy of free trade by Great Britain substantially weakened the resistance to free trade all over the world.

Moreover, it must not be forgotten that the political resistance to protectionism which used to be maintained by the parties of the Left, so long as these parties were inspired by the nineteenth-century liberal tradition, has in recent years greatly weakened, if it has not ceased altogether. The modern socialist, fascinated by the prospect of political power and the possibility of a little planning in his own national area, is apt to regard arguments relating to the advantages of international division of labor and exchange as having only academic importance. And if, as is very likely, he is supported financially by groups of workers whose employment may be endangered by the incidence of foreign competition, he may be as willing as the politician of the Right to support a protectionist policy. Modern socialists, though they may still render lip-service to the ideals of international economic co-operation, in fact, for the most part, support policies which lead in exactly the opposite direction.

This weakening of the intellectual resistance to the persistent tendency of lay opinion to acquiesce in measures of protection is paralleled by important changes in economic organization which make the apparent ravages of foreign competition more conspicuous and damaging. In a system in which movement of resources from one branch of industry to another is easy, the damage caused even to particular groups by foreign competition is likely to be very small: capital and labor can be rapidly transferred to other lines of occupation and the benefits of increased cheapness are shared by all but the owners of fixed resources specialized to one line of production. But if mobility is hindered by the existence of monopolistic obstacles of one kind or another, then the damage to the groups affected is likely to be of much longer duration. If rigidity of wages impedes the absorption of displaced labor into other industries, if restrictions on investment and artificially sustained monopoly impede free enterprise, then the difficulties of the transition are likely to be considerably enhanced. It is well known that obstacles of this sort, themselves the product of the decline of economic liberalism, are characteristic of the economic organization of most countries in the post-war period; and it should be noted that their effect tends to be cumulative. The existence of protective tariffs gives rise to monopolistic obstacles. The existence of monopolistic obstacles gives rise to resistance to free exchange. Resistance to free exchange increases the difficulty of new adaptation. New protection is therefore granted; and the accumulation of obstacles to international trade makes the incidence of change in the remaining parts of the system which are free much more oppressive and productive of sharp disequilibrium. In the panic atmosphere of general depression measures which would have been resisted in times of good trade are willingly agreed to. There are few politicians nowadays who can refrain from measures which promise hope of any alleviation of unemployment, however ultimately damaging such measures may promise to be: and even the number of economists who are willing to suffer unpopularity by drawing attention to long-period considerations is diminishing. Understanding of the 'exceptional' difficulties of any particular political or industrial situation is an easy way to a reputation for great sagacity. There are snug jobs for safe men in the quasi-corporative state.

The Growth of Protectionism

The growth of protectionism in Europe during the last sixty years affords ample vindication of this diagnosis.

The turning point in the tariff history of the last century was Bismarck's re-imposition of the iron and steel duties at the end of the 'seventies. Up to that time the tendency had been in the opposite direction. The free trade movement had moved from victory to victory, and it did not seem absurd to suppose that within a short period comparatively free exchange would become general. The fall of Delbrück and the creation of the new German tariff changed all that. Henceforward protectionism was to grow.

This reaction was the result of a conjunction of influences. On the one hand the growth of an anti-liberal social philosophy in the German universities had provided intellectual weapons for the representatives of special interests. The Historical School, which was then dominant, was imperialist, anti-utilitarian and anti-intellectualist in outlook. It was led by men who had never really understood the classical arguments for freedom of trade, and whose idea of the good society was typified by army barracks and the Prussian landed estate. This created an intellectual atmosphere favorable to the growth of protectionist ideas among the masses. The prolonged crisis which followed the collapse of 1873 provided the economic atmosphere in which the intellectual reaction could be politically effective.

In the same way, the growth of agrarian protectionism later on was the product of a conjunction of painful economic change and confused thinking. Throughout the 'seventies and the 'eighties the competition of the agricultural products of the new world caused difficulties to the agricultural interests of Europe. Again German economists provided the appropriate apologia for policy. The ideal of a 'just balance' between agriculture and industry, which from the 'economic' point of view is completely devoid of meaning, was exalted by such men as Wagner and Oldenberg. The agricultural interests were not slow to make political terms with the representatives of industry. Henceforward agrarian protectionism and industrial protectionism advanced hand in hand.

But the reversal of free trade policy which had been achieved up to the outbreak of the Great War was slight compared with what has happened since. The war itself produced a great extension of the branches of industry devoted to the manufacture of war materials. When the war was over, it was desired as far as possible to safeguard these industries against the consequences of a falling-off of demand for their products and the increased competition from similar industries abroad. The creation of new states and the fear of new wars afforded a pretext for high protection for manufacturing industries in areas which, from a purely economic point of view, would have been well advised to concentrate on other developments. Resistance to the changes brought about by the catastrophe of the war is a conspicuous feature of the policy of the post-war period; and protectionism is one of the manifestations of this tendency.

By the middle of the 'twenties of this century another influence was making itself felt. The great increase of agricultural production which had come about during the war years and in the period succeeding the war, produced a depression among agricultural producers. The absence of opportunities for migration deprived the agricultural populations of the most obvious relief from their distresses. Fear of war on the one hand, and fear of the socialism of the urban populations on the other, led the politicians of the day to grant to the agrarian interest ever-increasing measures of protection.

The effects of all this were cumulative. The products of the new world, deprived of easy access to the markets of the old, showed a greater tendency to fall in value. The capacity of the inhabitants of these areas to import manufactures was diminished. In a desperate attempt to maintain international equilibrium they themselves imposed tariffs on industrial products, thus increasing the difficulties of the manufacturing countries and rendering the market for their own products less stable. For a time the incidence of these measures was warded off by the inflationary expansion of the pre-1929 period. But when the boom broke, their effects were manifest and the speed of restrictionism redoubled.

In the Great Depression all these tendencies were multiplied.

Widespread unemployment, the contraction of markets, the political uncertainty and unrest which has accompanied it, drove one government after another into policies which, in happier times, better judgment would have restrained. Since the autumn of 1931 and the abandonment of the gold standard by Great Britain, to the other causes making for restrictions there has been added instability of exchange rates. The depreciation of the pound sterling and the currencies which followed the pound sterling, meant increased financial difficulty to those countries which remained on gold. To meet these difficulties resort has been had, not merely to high protection, but even to more rigorous forms of restrictionism. In many important commodities trade is limited within narrowly imposed quantitative margins. It is a conspicuous feature of the history of the last few years that in Europe at least the recovery has been predominantly a recovery of trade within the different national areas. In 1937 world industrial output was over 20 per cent above the 1929 level: the volume of world trade had not reached the 1929 level.

Strategic Considerations

If the foregoing analysis is correct, two conclusions seem to follow.

In the first place, since the growth of protectionism is essentially a manifestation of the progressive development of wrong ideas regarding its effects, it follows that only by the progressive education of public opinion to more correct ideas can the process be reversed. From time to time something may be achieved by tactics. Distressed governments may be manoeuvred into a position in which, without settled views as to policy, they adopt measures conducive to greater freedom of trade. But in the long run the chronic disposition to succumb to the temptation of the seen, rather than the calculated, effects of policy, can only be resisted by an educated public opinion. Without a spiritual revival which shall recover something of the sturdy independence of the men who, without hope in their time, laid the foundations of the liberties of Europe, the prospects of such resistance are small.

In the second place, since the intensification of protectionism is to be ascribed to the cumulative effects of all kinds of restrictive policies, of which protectionism is only one, it follows that this process of education is likely to be much more effective, if it is part of a frontal attack on measures conducive to restrictionism and instability in general, than if it is limited only to an attack on limitations on international trade. There is much more hope of inducing the public to tolerate the absence of protection to special interests if the incidence of change on these special interests is minimized by an absence of hindrances to transfer to other lines of enterprise. The public is much more likely to tolerate the disturbances incidental to tariff reduction, if at the same time it has not to contemplate the disturbances incidental to monetary instability. Only by a general rehabilitation of the principles of sound policy can the present vicious circle be broken.

......

Let us turn first to the planning of trade; and let us first examine the international significance of tariffs. We can then pass by an easy transition to more rigorous forms of planning.

If we review things in the large, it should be fairly clear that the effect of national protection is a diminution of international trade. We may admit the possibility that, owing to the imposition of tariffs on one class of commodity, markets elsewhere for other commodities may become so congested that new international outlets are sought. We may admit, too, that it is conceivable that the threat of the imposition of tariffs by one nation may lead to the lowering of tariffs by others – although, at this time of day, the suggestion that this sort of thing usually happens is not really very plausible. But speaking broadly there can be no doubt that tariffs, like obstacles to navigation, tend to diminish trade.

Now it is just as well that we should have clear ideas of the concrete significance for the world of today of a substantial diminution of international commerce. It means the decline of shipping. When Mr. Keynes, the other day, urged that 'goods should be homespun wherever it is reasonably and conveniently possible', he was urging that the ports of the world should be allowed to decay and that ships and international railways should be devoted chiefly to carrying passengers. It means, therefore, the decline as centers of international trade of such cities as London, Liverpool, Amsterdam, Hamburg, Shanghai, Alexandria. The lively bustle of the great *entrepôts* must cease 'wherever it is reasonably or conveniently possible'. It means, too, the decline of all those industries which have specialized in producing for export, the agriculture of the New World, the manufactures of the Old. The Lancashire cotton industry must henceforward look chiefly to home markets. British engineering must no longer seek a market in foreign parts. For a very long time to come, national planning in this sense means, not merely the protection of home industry, it must also mean the creation of depressed areas. The limitation of imports necessarily means the limitation of exports.

It may not always be true, as the popular free-trade argument has sometimes suggested, that the limitation of imports into a particular area necessarily means an exactly commensurate limitation of exports from that area. But it certainly does mean a commensurate limitation of exports from *other* areas. For the imports of one area are the exports of other areas and if all areas limit imports, they limit exports also. The 'depressed areas' are largely a by-product of economic nationalism.

But this consideration is not decisive unless international trade is to be regarded as an end in itself. And clearly it is not this: it is merely a means to an end, the satisfaction of demand. The function of international trade is not to maintain the export trades regardless of the demand for their products: it is to satisfy demand more adequately. If it could be shown that the contraction of international trade was conducive to more effective satisfaction of demand, more effective use of the productive resources of mankind, then, despite the agonies of the transition, it might be regarded as a change to be welcomed.

But this is not so. A contraction of international trade which is due, not to spontaneous changes in the direction of demand, but to the imposition of obstacles, must mean that the factors of production are used less efficiently, that demand in general is satisfied less adequately, than otherwise would be the case. For the restriction of trade means the restriction of the international division of labor. And the restriction of the international division of labor means that the cost of production is greater, the variety of products is less, than circumstances other than the obstacles necessitate. It means that the wrong goods are produced in the wrong places and that demand which could have been met goes unsatisfied. There may be those who gain from such a restriction as there are those who gain from earthquakes and shipwrecks. But their gain is an increased share of a volume of production which is less than might otherwise have been the case. And if earthquakes and shipwrecks become general, the probability of eventual individual gain becomes small. Who can seriously believe that the world at large is richer as a result of the various national restrictions which have led to the present contraction of international trade?

It is important to be clear on this point. It is sometimes thought that the advantages of international trade and the division of labor which it makes possible are confined to the exchange of those products which are impossible to produce at home. The different nations should produce all that they can within their own borders, it is said. But beyond that, there is an advantage in procuring by way of exchange, commodities which, for geological or climatic reasons, it is *impossible* to produce at home. It is thought to be highly enlightened to urge the national authorities that protection can go 'too far'. The import of pepper is advantageous; only the import of pigs is a mistake.

But this is a misapprehension. The advantages of division of labor do not consist merely in permitting us to obtain by way of exchange *only* those things which we cannot produce for ourselves. They consist rather in permitting us to obtain by way of exchange *everything* save those commodities which we are best at producing. The advantages of international division of labor are essentially that it permits the inhabitants of each area to concentrate the application of their resources on those lines of production in which they are most efficient, getting what else they want for their own consumption by way of exchange with abroad. If each produces what he can best contribute to the common pool, the common pool is at maximum relative to the opportunities available. Costs are lower, prices are less, than otherwise would be the case.

This rule is completely general. It applies quite clearly to the case where the inhabitants of different areas have differences of absolute efficiency at different kinds of production. It is obviously sensible for the inhabitants of Sheffield to concentrate on the production of high-grade steel and to abstain from attempting to force bananas in glass-houses, and for the inhabitants of tropical areas to concentrate on the production of bananas and to leave high-grade steel products to centers more favorably situated. But our rule applies no less to the case where the advantages of absolute efficiency are all on one side. It might well be the case that the fertility of certain sites in the City of London was greater than the fertility of lands in East Anglia. But nevertheless it would not be sensible to use them for growing wheat. It is better that they should be used for the purposes for which their efficiency is greatest, leaving the wheat to be grown elsewhere. To employ resources in any but their most valuable use involves waste; that is to say, it involves satisfying less demand in price terms than would otherwise be possible.

Now it is just this diversion of resources from their most productive uses which is the effect of protective tariffs. If, under competitive conditions and reasonably full employment, the cost of producing an article in a certain area is greater than the price it fetches in the world market, it follows that there are other lines of production in that area which offer more valuable results. The fact that costs are above prices means that the prices of other products which can be produced in that area permit a higher remuneration of the factors of production than the prices of this product would warrant. If the price of wheat is such as to make growing wheat on urban sites an unremunerative enterprise, that is because the other uses to which the site can be put command a higher value in the market. If wages are too high for certain lines of domestic agriculture to be profitable, that means, under competitive conditions, that the labor in question can produce a higher value elsewhere. If a protective duty is imposed which so raises the prices of imports competing with a certain line of business that business in that line becomes profitable, it follows that the factors of production there are devoted to producing something which, in the absence of the duty, would be less valuable, in preference to something which would be more valuable. It is this which is meant when it is said that protection involves discrimination against export. It brings it about that relatively more resources are employed producing directly for home consumption, relatively less producing for home consumption *indirectly*, by producing for export things to exchange for commodities produced abroad. It is thus that the international division of labor is diminished.

We can see this very vividly if we consider the results of the agrarian policy of Europe. As we have seen already, in recent years, the governments of Europe have erected higher and higher obstacles to the importation of agricultural products. Since the middle of the twenties, tariffs on agricultural imports have in some cases increased by several hundreds per cent. In Germany and Italy in particular, the duties have not only been such as to preserve from competition existing supplies, they have even called into being an additional volume of production.

The effect of all this on the immediate prosperity of the world has been disastrous. The areas which have specialized on supplying these excluded products have been plunged into depression. Faced with severe exchange difficulties, they themselves have resorted to tariffs. The manufacturers of Europe have suffered accordingly. Even the payment of interest on debt in some cases has been suspended. The movement of new capital has diminished almost to zero. No one who has perused the relentless analysis by which Sir Frederick Leith Ross has established these facts can doubt the harmfulness of the impact effects of recent agrarian protectionism.

But putting all this on one side as appertaining to the difficulties of the 'Transition', it must surely be obvious that the long-run effect must be to produce consequences which, from the international point of view, cannot be regarded as other than irrational. Even if the tremendous changes involved in reversing the trend of half a century could be carried through overnight, and the mobile resources of the world redistributed without friction in the lines of production appropriate to the new obstacles, it would surely be a mistake to do so. From the international point of view, there can be no justification for the production at high costs in Europe of agricultural products which could be produced at low costs in Australia and the Argentine, nor for the production in Australia and the Argentine at high cost of manufactures which could be produced at low costs in Europe. The thing is ridiculous. If it were not for the division of the surface of the earth into separate national areas it would not be thought of. Even in the most favorable conditions, the only possible gainers would be the owners of land and fixed resources in the protected industries. And if, as an indirect effect of these measures, protectionism abroad is increased, it is doubtful whether even these will benefit.

All this would probably be admitted by a majority of informed opinion nowadays. The evils of agrarian protectionism have become so conspicuous that their existence is not open to serious question. Today the intelligent apologists of such measures do so on avowedly political grounds, the desirability of safeguarding food supplies in time of war, the undesirability of falling foul of the rural electorate, the difficulty of breaking down the monopolistic obstacles which the rural laborer displaced by foreign competition might encounter in his search for employment. And so on. Mr. Walter Elliot and the landlords of East Prussia may continue to declaim the rustic argument that anything which puts money into the pockets of agriculturists is good for the world as a whole. But intellectually their position becomes less and less defensible.

But while the results of agricultural protection would be fairly generally judged to be bad, there is much more division of opinion about the protection of manufactures. It is often urged that the technique of manufacturing industry at the present day renders international division of labor much less advantageous than in the past. You can make almost anything anywhere nowadays, it is said. It does not much matter where your plant is located.

This sounds impressive. But it is really rather shallow. It may be true that it is physically possible to produce almost anything anywhere. But it does not follow at all that it is economical to do so. It is all a matter of costs. As we have seen, the advantage of international division of labor is *not* that it permits you to get from elsewhere only those products which you cannot produce at home, but rather that it permits you to get from elsewhere all products in whose manufacture your costs of production are not lower than anywhere else. So long as the costs of production are different for different commodities in different areas, so long will it be advantageous for the inhabitants of each area to specialize in producing the things in which their costs of production are least and to procure the rest from elsewhere. Now these cost differences depend in the last resort on differences of the relative scarcities in different parts of the world of the different factors of production – depend, that is to say, on the existence of differences of efficiency wages, differences of rents, differences of raw material costs, transport charges and the like. There is really no presumption that such differences have ceased to exist with the coming of modern technical methods. Nor is there any presumption that the use of such methods renders any less essential nice attention to such matters. On the contrary, indeed, it is the first essential of the successful conduct of any kind of productive enterprise. Thread is produced on spindles ('manufacture') and butter is produced in churns ('agriculture'). But there is not one shade of difference between the two types of production as regards the relevance of costs and prices as indices of their most efficient location.

We can see this even more clearly if, for a moment, we assume the contrary. If it really be true, as is asserted by the apologists for industrial protection, that the technique of modern manufacture makes the location of particular industries a matter of economic indifference, then it would follow immediately that there should be no real difficulty in establishing a manufacturing industry anywhere without the aid of a tariff. If it is really true that you can produce anything anywhere as economically as anywhere else, then it may well be asked why all this bother about protection? If the cost of production in any one part of the world is just as low as anywhere else, there should be no need of protective duties to make possible the existence of any type of industry deemed desirable.

But of course it is not so. In the absence of tariffs, the distribution of manufacturing industry between different areas would be very radically different. This is not a matter of conjecture. It is a proposition to which the most elementary facts of modern industry bear witness. How many of the branch factories which have been set up in different areas by the great international patent-holding companies to escape local tariffs would have come into being at all in the absence of such obstacles? Clearly very few. It needs a high tariff to bring them at all. And it needs a high tariff, too, to keep them prosperous once they have been established.

Confronted with facts of this sort, the advocate of industrial protection usually retreats upon the argument for large markets. Unless the market is secured by tariffs, it is said, the benefits of large-scale production can never fully be realized. The tariff eliminates the insecurity which is inimical to the development of large business. It is, as it were, the instrument of rationalization.

This is really the weakest position of all. To say at the present day that the multiplication of tariffs is conducive to the existence of wide and secure markets is so absurd a misreading of the facts that it scarcely seems necessary to spend time refuting it. It is of course conceivable that particular manufacturing units might run at less cost if a market were assured to them by a tariff, though we usually hear more of such arguments before the tariff is granted than when it has come into operation. But to concentrate upon this possibility to the neglect of the virtual certainties of a situation where there exist tariff-making powers on the part of a multiplicity of governments is surely to lose all perspective. For every case where the existence of tariffs has permitted such economies, there could be established many more where it prevents them coming into existence. Can it really be supposed that the economies of American mass production would be anything like so great if each of the forty-eight states of the Union were surrounded by a tariff? Is it very sensible even to argue that these economies would be lost if the federal tariff itself were to be lowered?

The fact is that, from the international point of view, planning by tariffs must necessarily be unsatisfactory, if only by reason of the complete unsuitability of the different areas of administration. It does not need much reflection to perceive that the nature of the existing tariff systems of the world is entirely contingent upon the accidental arrangement of the divisions over which the various sovereign states have authority. If the German Empire had not happened to include large manufacturing districts whose inhabitants could be made to pay the high prices necessary for the maintenance of the incomes of East Prussian landowners, there would have been no purpose in the erection of barriers to agricultural imports in that area – just as there would be very little purpose in the erection of barriers to the importation of coal into Great Britain. Some of the areas are large, such as Soviet Russia and the United States. Some are small, such as

Belgium, New Zealand and the republics of Central America. But one and all have this common characteristic, that as units for the organization of production they have no relation to anything which is relevant to this purpose. They have been determined by wars, royal marriages, accidental geographical discovery and the haggling of politicians at conference tables – by almost anything, in short, but consideration of their suitability for the administration of economic resources. Whatever may be the validity of the arguments by which the desirability for this or that nation of fostering this or that industry may be established – and, as the classical free-trade argument has shown, most of these arguments are pretty fragile – from the international point of view the whole thing is absurd. It is conceivable that a world authority with perfect knowledge might in certain cases have occasion to interfere with the free working of private enterprise. But whether this is so or not, it is certain that the lines on which it would intervene would differ completely from the lines on which tariffs are planned by national governments. Rational world planning would attempt to extend the international division of labor. National planning by tariffs has the effect of restricting it.

......

But let us cast our net a little wider. If war is not to be regarded as an ultimate good in itself, the avoidance of war is obviously a national interest. War destroys wealth. It destroys happiness. It destroys the subtle checks and controls which make civilized society possible. Under modern conditions even the cost of preparing for war bids fair to constitute a burden which will more than absorb all the fruits of technical progress.

It has sometimes been thought that this danger may be mitigated by a sacrifice of material well-being. If the various national states would organize their affairs on a basis of economic self-sufficiency, it is said, the dangers of war due to economic causes would be minimized. The inhabitants of each nation would be free to develop their own lives in their own way without the friction which comes from 'economic entanglement' among nations. This was the view of the philosopher, Johann Gottlieb Fichte. It is the official apologia for the policy of contemporary Germany; and, in our own less pretentious atmosphere, it has received the support of no less an authority than Mr. John Maynard Keynes.

'I sympathize', says Mr. Keynes, 'with those who would minimize, rather than maximize economic entanglement among nations. Ideas, knowledge, science, hospitality, travel - these are the things which should of their nature be international. But let goods be homespun wherever it is reasonably and conveniently possible ... a greater measure of national self-sufficiency and economic isolation among countries than existed in 1914 may tend to serve the cause of peace rather than otherwise.'

The idea is plain. To secure peace, some sacrifice – Mr. Keynes thinks it need not be great – of the wealth which comes from international division of labor is desirable.

But unfortunately it seems to rest upon delusion. We will not pause to enquire how long 'ideas, knowledge, science, hospitality, travel' are likely to remain free when goods are 'as far as is reasonably and conveniently possible' homespun – though developments in those parts where such policies are now being applied scarcely seem to warrant much optimism here. But we must recognize that this policy is incapable of being generalized. Mr. Keynes, whose outlook in recent years sometimes appears disconcertingly insular, may be right in supposing that, within the Empire, it would be possible at some sacrifice to reach greater self-sufficiency than in the past, though there is reason to suppose that he greatly underestimates the sacrifice. There are certain other national groups in a similar position. But it is really ridiculous to suppose that such a policy is possible for the majority, given their present national boundaries. Given the present political divisions of the world, to recommend autarky as a general policy is to recommend war as an instrument for making autarky possible.

No doubt Mr. Keynes would repudiate this. For, despite all the damage he has done to liberal policies in recent years, he is still the man who wrote the *Economic Consequences of the Peace*, one of the most magnificent gestures in defence of the great principles of peace and international justice of this or any other age. It would be absurd to depict Mr. Keynes in any way as a war-monger. But, if the analysis of these pages is correct, it is not absurd at all to depict war-mongering as the eventual consequence of the policies which, in a fit of premature discouragement at the absence of quick success of his earlier internationalism, he has been led, half desperately, half frivolously, to adopt. In all this he has been less logical than his predecessors. The philosopher Fichte, who recommended similar policies, saw more clearly on these matters.

'It has always been the privilege of philosophers to sigh over wars', wrote this rather prematurely *echt* Nordic type. 'The present author does not love them more than anyone else. But he believes in their inevitability in the present circumstances and deems it uncalled for to complain of the inevitable. In order to abolish war, it is necessary to abolish its cause. Every state must receive what it intends to obtain by war and what *it alone* can reasonably determine, that is its natural frontiers. When that is accomplished it will have no further claims on any other state since it will possess what it had sought'.

In fact the danger is even greater than this. For even if it were physically possible for the different national states to attain self-sufficiency at *some* level of real income, it is quite out of the question that they should attain it at the *same* level. So long as the inhabitants of the different states were prevented from bettering their position by exchange or by migration, some self-sufficient states would be richer than others. It would always be possible to hope that things would be improved by a forcible enlargement of frontiers. The populations of the East will be increasing long after the population of the West has become stationary or declining. If they are forcibly prevented from foreign trade, they are not likely to forget that, at no very distant date in the past, it was deemed justifiable to break down similar prohibitions on their part with cannons and bayonets. Who can believe that it is possible, year in year out, for the inhabitants of the richer countries of the world to withdraw into economic self-sufficiency without raising up against themselves combinations of the poorer Powers which are truly fearful to contemplate?

......

In the days of the decay of the great historical religions, men have deified the idea of the nation. They have made devotion to particular political machines a fanatical idolatry. They have erected a mythology of the state, or the race, more ridiculous, more inconsistent, more cruel than the superstitions of ancient barbarism. And because there is more than one state, there is conflict among the idols. Nothing can be more certain than that if we can find no ideals more compelling than this, much of what is best in human achievement hitherto must perish.

But is this really so difficult? Dostoievsky once said that if we try to love all humanity we shall only end by hating all humanity. No doubt this is profoundly true. But international liberalism does not bid us love humanity. It seeks only to persuade us that co-operation between the different members of humanity is advantageous for the furtherance of individual ends. In this respect; it is true, it is merely the plan of a mechanism more efficient than the world of independent nations. Yet nevertheless the idea of the way of living with which it is associated is something more than that. A society which preserves spontaneity and freedom, with its manifold play of mind on mind and its world-wide heritage of art and learning – this surely is a conception as congenial to the aspirations of men who are not spiritually sick as any nationalism which turns inwards.

Nationalism is something which must be surpassed. There was probably never a moment in the history of the world when such a task seemed so difficult to accomplish. But it can be accomplished if our hearts and minds tell us that it is necessary; and it must be accomplished if all that we regard as most valuable is not to perish in the wreck of our common civilization.

5. Protectionist Arguments during the 1900–1940 Period

PREAMBLE

In the interwar period, ideas of hegemony, domination, nationalism, collectivism, and oppression began to prevail in extreme form, in the Soviet Union, Italy, and Germany. In other countries these ideas existed in less drastic varieties. Some degree of economic autarky was always part of these conceptions.

Communism was the first major twentieth century totalitarian revolt against the Western liberal way of life. After the seizure of power in 1917, the communist regime in the Soviet Union nationalized the means of production in a wholesale way and the public ownership was extended even further in later years. The economy became a planned economy which meant basically that a planning commission and not the market made production decisions. All state enterprises were told by the planning commission what to produce and how much. They were also informed about the prices they were to establish and to whom to deliver. A five year plan was the base plan so to speak, while details were set by one year plans. Actually, there was little background for the concept of a planned economy in Marxist or pre-revolutionary thought. However, the idea was greatly encouraged by Lenin's admiration for the 'war socialism' of the German war economy with all its controls during World War I.

After the revolution in Russia, foreign trade became a state monopoly which lasted until 1988. In 1920, a people's commissariat for foreign trade was formed and special trading departments were created under it. Each department specialized in imports or exports (or both) of specific commodities. Trade was organized on a bilateral basis with the idea that the imports and exports from and to a trade partner should balance approximately. In effect, Soviet trade policy appears to have aimed at virtual self-sufficiency in as many fields as possible and to use foreign trade only as a device to make compensation for gaps that could not be filled by domestic producers. Self-sufficiency was also encouraged by military security considerations, by the risk that a Western country might interrupt trade with the Soviet Union (by imposing an embargo etc.), and the chronic shortage of foreign exchange. Thus, Soviet foreign trade has remained small as compared to its GNP. Yet imports had their importance as a source of essential materials, machinery, and know-how. This pattern of foreign trade characterized by extreme economic nationalism became rather typical for all totalitarian countries. It is also reminiscent of the trade planning in democratic and/or 'capitalist' countries in wartime.

2

All forms of totalitarianism rose from a system ruined by stasis, social exhaustion, a fatigued economy, a shattered class structure and an unhinged political apparatus. Italy was no exception. Immediately after World War I, the economic conditions were chaotic. Unemployment and inflation were rising and in the general election of 1919; the socialist party won 2 million out of a total of 5.5 million votes. The leadership of that party had passed into the hands of the radical left which openly advocated the establishment of a proletarian dictatorship. The Italian middle class became convinced that a revolution was pending and that the liberal democratic state was unable to stave off the danger. Fascists used the opportunity to present themselves as the uncompromising enemies of Italian socialism. Thus in 1922, at the invitation of the king and with the support of the army, the bureaucracy and big business, Benito Mussolini, the leader of the Italian Fascist party, was invited to become premier. The elections in 1924, though undoubtedly fraudulent, gave the Fascists their desired majority and secured Mussolini's power.

Not surprisingly Fascism regarded itself as a rejection, a complete and uncompromising denial of the principles of individualism, liberalism, internationalism, and democracy. The liberal ideas of individual freedom, free enterprise, and enlightened self-regard were seen as concepts that were disintegrating and divisive. Marxism with its ideas of class war was also regarded as a system breaking up the nation.

Following Hegel, Fascism repudiated the idea of peace and international harmony. It implied a return to an authoritarian order based upon the supremacy of the state and the subordination of the individual. The leaders were not to be elected and were not to be held responsible to the people. On the contrary, the people were to be responsible to the leaders.

Fascism is antipacifist and in the end nearly all fascist activity is devoted to the preparation for what it regards as the inevitable and beneficial struggles which form the life of nations. In the case of Italy, Germany and Japan totalitarianism eventually widened itself into world imperialism.

In the economic field, Fascism rejected the concept of a free market economy. The idea was that the classical liberal economic model was outmoded and that it was the duty of the state to impose 'economic order' on the nation. Thus the liberal state was to be replaced by the corporate state.

In Italy, the corporate idea began as an answer to occasional concrete problems arising out of unrest in industry. In the 1930s the system had been put forward as a reasoned system to answer the general indictment of capitalist production. The corporate law on the constitution and function of corporations, was not passed until February 1934. On November 1934, 22 corporations were inaugurated. They were supervised by the Ministry of Corporations. Workers, businessmen, artisans and industrialists were all organized in those 22 divisions in accordance with the economic function performed by their particular trade or industry. The main idea of the corporation was that the conflicting interests of owners, workers, technicians, and the state were to be brought together in a single unit operation under public control. The corporations were given the powers to fix wages, to regulate entry into industry, to control production, to settle disputes and to draft collective labor contracts. In fact, the corporations conformed to the nationalist idea of a highly organized, highly centralized state.

As time went by, the Fascist state imposed controls, including price and wage controls, over all forms of economic activity, including foreign trade. Tariffs on industrial products were constantly increased as were subsidies, thus making the home market quite safe for the domestic industrialists. Overvaluation of the Italian lira badly affected Italian exports and thereby employment. This situation combined with capital flights during the 1930s forced the government to cut down imports more with such devices as import prohibitions, quotas and exchange controls.

After the Ethiopian war (1935–36), the Fascist dictatorship embarked on a full-scale war economy when the decision was made to pursue a policy of economic autarky. For example, in an effort to make Italy self-sufficient in wheat, heavy duties were imposed, which had the effect of making the Italian wheat price three to four times that of the world price. In the end Mussolini's foreign policy and actions with its emphasis on military strength necessarily pressed the

Fascist government into fierce economic nationalism.

World War II, which was started by the major Fascist powers, ended in complete defeat for them. Had those powers won the war, it is possible that very few resources would have remained private. Italian Fascism might ultimately have culminated in some form of dictatorial socialism. Just like its counterparts in other places, the Italian brand of Fascism hardly made any contributions to economic thought. The Italian Fascists thought that it did not pay to have a clear theoretical framework and a precise program. They rather counted on their mystique, their enthusiastic will, and their direct action.

3

As was the case with Italy the Nationalist-Socialist movement in Germany grew out of the bitter aftermath of World War I. The German Empire collapsed in 1918. The great inflation of the early 1920s destroyed all savings and turned the impoverished German middle class into economically and socially displaced persons. The Great Depression hit Germany very severely and resulted in 6 million unemployed out of a population of 65 million.

Adolf Hitler, the leader of the National Socialists, who had never been a man of the left, found an even better soil in the anti-democratic traditions of the German Empire than Mussolini. The Nazi ideology could conquer Germany because it did not encounter enough determined intellectual resistance. The fundamental tenets of the Nazi ideology such as interventionism, authoritarianism and racism did not differ substantially from the earlier political, social and economic ideologies generally accepted in Germany. In the 1920s Hitler, who was a very smart vote-getter, presented himself as an insignificant man in the face of world-wide conspiracies. Here was an 'honest' German surrounded by Jews, traitors in government, radical socialists, Bolsheviks, Western imperialist nations, wealthy industrialists and department store owners all intent on robbing the ordinary German. While radical socialists preached civil war and revolution, Hitler and his Nazi followers advocated a doctrine based on such ideas as the purity of the German race, a corporate order, and the leadership principle. The leader would be the great unifying factor, and submission to the state embodied by its leader was essential. The state itself was to be totalitarian in the sense that it had to intervene in every aspect of public and private life. Although Hitler's program differed from that of Mussolini, they both were fundamentally similar expressions of the collectivist outlook, the type of society in which the individual is seen as being subordinate to a social collectivity such as the state.

In 1933, Germany joined the ranks of the Fascist powers and as stated earlier, the German form of Fascism was known as National Socialism or Nazism. In the economic field, Nazism was characterized by a thoroughgoing interventionism.

The development of economic controls, like most other aspects of Nazi economic policy, did not conform to a preconceived plan. Regulations were issued and measures were taken as they became necessary. State control of the economic system was steadily extended. Although private property and enterprise were not directly threatened, their independence was gradually restricted and their status was altered.

Domestic and foreign economic policy were characterized by the following features:

(a) Consumption was checked through high levels of taxation and wage controls which stabilized wages at depression levels.
(b) Inflation was kept down by price controls.
(c) Investment was redirected by prohibiting the flotation of private capital and by issuing large numbers of government bonds. The government also borrowed heavily from private banks.
(d) German agriculture became heavily protected by import quotas and tariffs. As Nazi Germany prepared itself for war, its leaders strove towards autarky, and agricultural self-sufficiency was a high priority.
(e) Capital exports were kept down in order to keep capital in the country and to avoid depletion of foreign exchange reserves.
(f) Foreign exchange was rationed by a system which required that importers first had to acquire a foreign exchange certificate for each individual transaction. Only upon presentation of the certificate could foreign exchange be obtained.
(g) Finally a system of bilateral clearing agreements with trade partners was established involving settlement of reciprocal claims and debts. For example, the German government would conclude an agreement with another country, say Bulgaria, setting up an account in both countries. Importers and others who had to make payments would pay in their own money in their national account the sums owed to foreign creditors. Exporters and others entitled to payments from the other country would be compensated in

their own currency from this account. The system obviously worked best when bilateral debts and claims balanced. This balance almost never happened in the case of Germany and its trade partners.

The combination of exchange controls and bilateral clearing made state control of foreign trade complete, which allowed the German authorities to pursue their drive for military power and economic self-sufficiency. De facto Germany moved continuously in the direction of Fichte's *Closed Commercial State*.

As time went by, state direction and regulation of Germany's economic life became ever more intrusive and ended up by becoming a form of state capitalism. By 1943, the vestiges of the private enterprise economy had been mostly replaced by a planned economy which fitted rather well with National Socialist conceptions. There can be little doubt that had Nazism prevailed, private interests would have been further collectivized.

4

The story of Great Britain during the 1930s is the record of a country drifting away from the concepts of the free play of market forces and multilateralism towards increased state intervention and bilateralism. In this, Britain resembled other democratic countries during the same period.

Before World War I, Britain had provided economic leadership. London was the financial capital of the world and the Bank of England came close to functioning as the world's central bank. After the war, Britain no longer supplied stewardship. World leadership was offered to the United States, now the richest and most powerful industrial nation in the world, and was declined.

Once the war was over, Britain's efforts to reestablish her former position as a trader were not very successful. Between 1925 and 1930, when many countries enjoyed a reasonable degree of prosperity, the British economy remained depressed. One reason was that in 1925 the pound sterling had been linked to gold again but at pre-war parity. This amounted to an overvaluation of the pound by 10 per cent, making British goods expensive on world markets. The high American tariffs were also detrimental to British exports.

The Great Depression, which started in 1929 in the US caused a contraction of world income and demand. Between 1929 and 1931, the value of British merchandise exports declined by nearly 50 per cent and the value of invisible exports fell by about 40 per cent. When after 1927 foreign banks began to convert some of their claims against London into gold, the pressure on the gold linked pound became unbearable, and in September 1931, Britain abandoned the gold standard and let the pound float. Within days the pound lost 25 per cent of its value. This was the signal for the Bank of England to adopt a policy of cheap (or cheaper) money in 1932. Between February and June, the Bank of England reduced the discount rate from 6 per cent to 2 per cent.

Both the Great Depression and the loss of British export markets increased unemployment and strengthened the protectionist case. Until 1930, Britain had mainly been a free trader. However, in February 1932, the British government adopted the 'Import Duties Act' which imposed a general duty of 10 per cent *ad valorem* on all imports into the United Kingdom. Empire goods were excepted as well as items named on a free list containing most raw materials and foodstuffs. The Act also set up an 'Import Duties Advisory Committee' to recommend additional duties. Within a few years most manufactures were subjected to 20 per cent duties. Another measure of state control of foreign trade came six months later with the adoption of the 'Imperial Duties Act'. At that time agreements were concluded in Ottawa between the United Kingdom and the British Commonwealth under which all participants agreed to extend to each other increased import preference.[76]

What was achieved was rather in the form of increases in Dominion tariffs on foreign goods than a reduction of tariffs within the Commonwealth. In 1933, the system of Imperial preference was extended to the Crown Colonies.

Agricultural protection followed industrial protection. The 'Agricultural Marketing Act' of 1933 provided for agricultural protection and internal assistance. This policy measure included quotas, direct and indirect subsidies, and such steps as the creation of marketing schemes.

After 1932, the British government also concluded a series of bilateral trade agreements with foreign countries. Such arrangements

76   The British Commonwealth can be defined as a free association of autonomous entities which had been former dependencies of Britain and who recognize the British monarch as the symbolic head of their association. They also have chosen to maintain ties of friendship and practical cooperation with England.

included one-sided promises by Britain's trade partners not to increase tariffs or quotas and various modifications of trade barriers.

The above mentioned measures of trade nationalism were accompanied by acts of monetary nationalism. Before World War I, and even in the 1920s, Britain had been a major lender of funds. In 1931 however, the British government imposed a complete though unofficial embargo on foreign new issues of bonds in Britain. Under the new rules, foreign borrowers needed Treasury permission to borrow in London, for which permission was hardly ever granted. In 1933, this embargo was relaxed in favor of the British Empire nations. The immediate purpose to the embargo on foreign investments was to facilitate the domestic cheap money policy.

The drift away from the international liberal system implied in the British policies of the 1930s was in line with Keynes's ideas on international trade during the period. As Reading 22 shows, Keynes believed that international trade had lost part of its beneficence and advocated a policy of tariff protection and even increased self-sufficiency.

5

Whereas countries such as the Soviet Union, Italy and Germany experienced authoritarian collectivism, the remaining democracies of the 1920s and 1930s, including Britain and the United States, were all characterized by the steady advance of the milder varieties of gradual collectivism. The practice of gradual collectivism was not always the result of a specific collectivist design. It rather came from efforts to deal with specific grievances and to provide particular benefits. Highly organized, strategically placed special interest groups were nearly always behind such endeavors. The legislative measures resulting from the actions of such organized interests profoundly affected the social order in the democratic countries by shifting important socio-economic benefits from one group to another, from one occupation to another, or from one region to another. Labor policies, subsidies, and protective tariffs were in this category. In a democratic society, the granting of some privileges will nearly always be followed by the granting of more privileges. Once the state abandons the principle of special privileges to none, it becomes almost automatically committed to the principle of special privileges to all. A tariff for one industry will make irresistible the demand of other industries for equal protection. In a system of gradual democratic collectivism in which the state distributes privileges, the beneficiaries usually receive more income for less effort. Special favors are not received by working harder but by working less. Thus the grand total effect of the system is to diminish the production of wealth.

In addition, the very concentration on income transfers diverts attention from the springs of economic prosperity and may have the effect of increasing the ignorance about its sources. The American Smoot–Hawley Tariff of 1930, which raised the average tariff from an average of 38 per cent to an average of 53 per cent, was an example of a state sponsored distribution of privileges. Public choice theory helps to understand the role of interest groups and their connection to creeping collectivism.

Public choice theory is a discipline that applies economic analysis to decision making in the public sector. The point of departure is the self-interest postulate. Economists have used this postulate to explain how markets work. Public choice analysis extends this assumption to politics. Individuals are assumed to choose from available alternatives those that further their own interests and to make those choices in a rational manner. If the pursuit of such rewards as personal income and power motivates individuals in the private sector, there is every reason to believe that the same factors motivate them in the political sector. However, the structure of incentives and constraints on behavior differ sharply under the two institutional orderings.

When it comes to voting, any given individual will compare the expected benefits of voting for a candidate with the costs. Voters will tend to support those political candidates whom they believe will supply them with the most net benefits. The costs of informed voting can be substantial as they include the time spent acquiring information about political issues and the candidates. A consumer who buys in the market place has every reason to be well-informed because it yields a high rate of return. This is not the case when it comes to voting at the ballot box. In the political arena, information has a low rate of return because one vote will not be decisive in the ultimate outcome of an election. Because of high costs and negligible benefits, most people will therefore decide not to incur the costs of being well-informed. As a result, political indifference and ignorance tend to prevail in democracies. This is called the 'rational ignorance effect'. Consequently, few voters are able to understand the implications of such issues as tariff legislation or export subsidies.

Politicians and legislators are also assumed to act in their own interest. This inclination will translate itself into the desire to get elected or reelected.

The rational ignorance effect creates a vacuum in the political process which tends to be filled by special interest groups which are in the business of obtaining advantages for the members of the organized group at the expense of the less organized. It is obvious that special interest groups have an overriding interest to get politicians on their side and will therefore often help them finance their election campaigns, expecting favorable legislation in return once the elections are over. The vote-seeking politician on the other hand has little incentive to support the interests of the largely uniformed and disinterested majority if only because that majority may not even know what its interests are. Of course, while the election campaigns are on, politicians may well make humanitarian and patriotic statements giving the impression that they stand for the general good. Once in office, however, they have every inducement to support special interest legislation because it pays them to do so. In order to make it difficult for even alert voters to recognize the costs imposed upon them, politicians and legislators will have the inducement to make special interest issues complex. Also, when special interest proposals can be made to look ethical or patriotic, they have a greater chance of being translated into concrete policy proposals. Thus, economic groups have a tendency to appropriate as their own, the whole amalgam of emotional attitudes associated with patriotism and nationalism. The idea is to make special private interests seem public. Every special interest group can and often will harp on national solidarity as a justification for demanding a degree of protection. Tariffs, for instance, have been presented as a patriotic obligation to agriculture or industry. In addition, the interest in international cooperation is not special to any particular group but is general and widely dispersed. Thus this interest does not give birth to effective organizations pressing and bargaining for their concerns to be considered. This again is a form of bias in organizational structure which tends to weaken international solidarity. These considerations were abundantly clear during the years when the American Smoot–Hawley Act of 1930 was being proposed.

Also, the American form of government facilitates the expression of special interests that could not gain such easy recognition under different systems. For instance, with the established practice of public hearings by the standing committees of Congress, the interest groups won for themselves an institutional connection with the government which seems almost as assured as the position of the political parties.

'Rent-seeking', defined as actions taken by individuals and groups to change public policy in order to gain personal advantage at the expense of others has gained prominence in the twentieth century. With the continuous advance of democratic gradual collectivism which involves heavy income transfers from one group to the next, the pay-off to rent-seeking increases. The steady increase of the number of special interest groups has been the predictable result. In other words, if government spending becomes an important source of income for all kinds of groups and people, including factory workers, farmers, welfare recipients and others, the inducement is created for these people to become even better organized. This situation will allow them to put additional pressure upon the government. A vicious circle is thus created.

Throughout the 1920s, agriculture remained depressed in the United States. In 1922, the Fordney–McCumber Act increased all tariff rates. The Act originated in a feared deluge of cheap European commodities, a desire to protect new war industries, and an anxiety to pacify the farmers who were well-represented in the US Senate. The Act sought to withdraw the nation from the economic world just like other moves attempted to isolate it from the political world. The new tariff rates (about 38 per cent on average) did not help the farmers very much. By making it difficult for America's trade partners to sell industrial goods in the US, these countries could not earn the dollars needed to buy American farm products. Thus the farmers often could not keep and extend their foreign markets.

As is wellknown, towards the late 1920s, Congress attended to the serious business of raising tariffs again. In his presidential campaign in the year 1928, Herbert Hoover had promised to raise American tariffs to help farmers who still experienced difficulties as a group. During the preparatory phase which began in the special session of Congress called in June 1929, a veritable orgy of log-rolling took place. To obtain the assistance of urban legislators, congressional members favoring higher duties on farm products had to agree to support an increase in tariffs on manufactured items as well. The Chairman of the Senate Finance Committee, Reed Smoot, happened to be a reckless protectionist who insisted on increasing the tariff rate on Cuban sugar for the advantage of western beet interests. He was, like many other promoters of the agricultural interest, quite willing to grant corresponding favors to manufactured goods. Therefore, what started as a limited piece of legislation became, because of the concessions to different private interest groups and regional interests, an all compassing Act with 890 of the 1,125 changes being increases. The passage of the Smoot–Hawley Act with the highest tariff level in the United States history (the average ad valorem duty rate became 53.2 per cent), caused a wave of foreign protests with many tariff reprisals, quotas, and other trade barriers as a result. The timing of the Act was unfortunate as it coincided with the Great Depression. It also signalled that the United States did not have the slightest intention of playing the economic and political role that her economic importance required.

After World War I, the United States had become the world's greatest creditor nation. The world owed the US large sums in war debts and private debts. At the same time, throughout the 1920s, American exports exceeded imports, while American banks poured loans into European countries. Thus these nations were piling up debts beyond their strength. In fact, the US should have been prepared to facilitate the importation of European commodities. In reality she did the very opposite.

The Smoot–Hawley tariff ignored foreign interests. At the same time it paid no attention to the vital interests of a substantial percentage of the American population, i.e. the American importing interests, the American exporting interests, and the American consumers. The reason was that all these three bodies were largely unorganized and incapable of making their voices heard above the clamor of the well-organized, powerful special interest groups in agriculture and industry. It is true that after the elections of 1932 with President Roosevelt in the White House, there was a mild change of heart. In 1934, the Reciprocal Trade Agreement Act was passed which represented an effort to obtain foreign tariff reductions in exchange for domestic concessions. One important feature of the new law was that it gave the President of the United States the power to negotiate trade agreements with other countries without approval by Congress. Such agreements usually consisted of bilateral tariff concessions with other countries. The law also stipulated that the most-favored nation clause could still be applied, but it related only to non-agricultural products. In fact, the bilateral trade agreements did not cut very deeply into the American tariff. In the world as a whole, protectionism continued to hold the upper hand until World War II. The total level of international trade shrank dramatically between 1930 and 1939.

READING 21

Benito Mussolini

Biography

Benito Mussolini (1883–1945) was born in a tiny Italian village named Predaggio near Forli in the Romagna region. His mother was an elementary school teacher and his father a local blacksmith. The smithy was the club for his father's political cronies, mainly consisting of anarchists and radical socialists. The Mussolinis lived in rather poor conditions partly because his father spent so much time discussing politics in taverns and most of his money on his mistress.

Benito was a restless child. In school he was disobedient, unruly and aggressive. On several occasions he attacked a fellow pupil with a pen-knife and was expelled from school. But, he was also quick and clever. From high school he proceeded to a teachers training college and for a short while he became an elementary school teacher. Then he also began a process of self-tuition, reading Hegel, Sorel, Nietzche and others. In the process Mussolini acquired all the strengths and weaknesses of the autodidact. In order to avoid military service he went to Switzerland at age 19 where he stayed from 1902 to 1904. There he moved from job to job often earning his living as a bricklayer or mason. Most of his time was spent in Lausanne, Zurich and Geneva. He apparently attended some lectures by Vilfredo Pareto at the University of Lausanne and was nearly always involved with anarchist and socialist groups. In 1904 the Swiss authorities expelled him for falsifying his passport.

In 1912 Mussolini became the editor of the official socialist newspaper *Avanti*. Until 1914 Benito was basically a revolutionary Marxist filled with strong hostile feelings towards the state. As he saw it, general elections and democracy were simply a form of bourgeois craft and deceit. As an anti-militarist, anti-nationalist and anti-imperialist journalist, Mussolini opposed Italy's entry into World War I. Yet soon afterwards he turned around and became strongly in favor of war participation. As a result he was made to resign from *Avanti* and was expelled from the socialist party. He entered the army, was wounded and returned home as a convinced anti-socialist. In 1916 Mussolini married Rachele Guidi, a daughter of his father's widowed mistress, with whom he had five children. In 1917 the former combatant founded the first Fascist organization mainly consisting of dissatisfied ex-soldiers. In 1921 the National Fascist Party officially came into existence. As was explained earlier, in 1922 Mussolini was charged with forming a new government in Italy. Over time he established an authoritarian state conserving the monarchy. In the early years of his government, the Italian dictator restored order and stabilized the economy which earned him praise from many European and American politicians.

In the 1930s, Mussolini started his imperial adventures and established friendly relations with the German dictator Adolph Hitler. As Germany's ally, Italy became involved in World War II. From the beginning, the war went badly for Italy and Italian military ventures in such areas as Greece and North Africa ended in failure. In 1943 Fascists and non-Fascists managed to dismiss Mussolini from office. With the German assistance a new Fascist (puppet) government was formed in which the Italian dictator had only a minor say. The Second World War ended in defeat and in 1945 Mussolini and his mistress were killed by communist guerilla fighters.

The Work

As a young man Mussolini had read writers such as Hegel, Sorel, Nietzsche and Machiavelli. Of course he did not read all the works of these people, only portions. From Hegel he had learned that the state was a 'Divine Idea' as it existed on earth. From Sorel he had become acquainted with the concept of violent action. Nietzsche was also one of those writers who doubted the classical liberal vision of society as a set of rational and responsible individuals. The German author despised democracy and lauded the superman. As is wellknown, Machiavelli in his book *The Prince* drew up a program to guide a strong ruler in how to seize and preserve political power.

Mussolini did not elaborate a comprehensive theory of society. He tried to combine revolutionary radicalism with conservative nationalism and not surprisingly his ideas are full of contradictions. In his speeches, which were most effective, he even did not always get the figures right. At the same time, he was always willing to admit that his brand of Fascism rejected theory in favor of action, while he also knew that to be vague can be the shortest route to power. A meaningless noise is that which divides the least.

One does not find any specific statements by Mussolini on free trade or protectionism. But his economic nationalism was the necessary counterpart of his political nationalism, his corporatism and his desire to create an Italian Empire. In the following readings dating from the 1930s, the Italian dictator clearly states his views on these issues.[77]

Extracts

The Concept of Fascism

The Corporation is established to develop wealth, political power and welfare of the Italian people. These three elements are conditioned by one another. Political strength creates wealth, while wealth, in its turn, invigorates political action. I wish to call your attention to what I mentioned as our scope, namely the welfare of the people. It is necessary that at a certain moment these institutions which we have created shall be felt and noticed directly by the masses as instruments through which they improve their standard of life .... The laborer, the peasant, should be able at a certain moment to tell himself and his dear ones: 'If I am to-day effectively better off, I owe it to the institutions which the Fascist Revolution has created' ... To-day we are burying economic liberalism, the Corporation plays that part in the economic field, which the Grand Council and the Militia do in the political. Corporativism means a disciplined, and therefore a controlled economy, since there can be no discipline which is not controlled. Corporativism overcomes Socialism as well as it does Liberalism: it creates a new synthesis.

......

Above all, Fascism, the more it considers and observes the future and the development of humanity quite apart from political considerations of the moment, believes neither in the possibility nor the unity of perpetual peace. It thus repudiates the doctrine of Pacifism – born of a renunciation of the struggle and an act of cowardice in the face of sacrifice. War alone brings up to its highest tension all human energy and puts the stamp of nobility upon the peoples who have the courage to meet it. All other trials are substitutes, which never really put men into the position where they have to make the great decision – the alternative of life or death. Thus a doctrine which is founded

---

77   Sources: H. Finer, *Mussolini's Italy* (London: Victor Gollancz Ltd, 1935) p. 502.
     E. Weber, *Varieties of Fascism* (Princeton: D. Van Nostrand, 1964) pp. 149–152.

upon this harmful postulate of peace is hostile to Fascism. And thus hostile to the spirit of Fascism ... are all the international leagues and societies which, as history will show, can be scattered to the winds when once strong national feeling is aroused by any motive – sentimental, ideal, or practical. This anti-pacifist spirit is carried by Fascism even into the life of the individual; the proud motto of the Squadrista, 'Me ne frego' (I do not fear), written on the bandage of the wound, is an act of philosophy not only stoic, the summary of a doctrine not only political – it is the education to combat, the acceptance of the risks which combat implies, and a new way of life for Italy. Thus the Fascist accepts life and loves it, knowing nothing of and despising suicide; he rather conceives of life as duty and struggle and conquest, life which should be high and full, lived for oneself, but above all for others – those who are at hand and those who are far distant, contemporaries, and those who will come after ...

Such a conception of life makes Fascism the complete opposite of that doctrine, the base of the so-called scientific and Marxian Socialism, the materialist conception of history; according to which the history of human civilization can be explained simply through the conflict of interests among the various social groups and by the change and development in the means and instruments of production. That the changes in the economic field ... have their importance no one can deny; but that these factors are sufficient to explain the history of humanity excluding all others is an absurd delusion. Fascism, now and always, believes in holiness and in heroism; that is to say, in actions influenced by no economic motive, direct or indirect. And if the economic conception of history be denied ... it follows that the existence of an unchangeable and unchanging class war is also denied. And above all Fascism denies that class war can be the preponderant force in the transformation of the world. These two fundamental concepts of Socialism being thus refuted, nothing is left of it but the sentimental aspiration – as old as humanity itself – towards a social convention in which the sorrows and the sufferings of the humblest shall be alleviated. But here again Fascism repudiates the conception of 'economic' happiness ... Fascism denies the materialist conception of happiness as a possibility, and abandons it to its inventors, the economists of the first half of the nineteenth century: that is to say, Fascism denies the validity of the equation, wellbeing = happiness, which would reduce men to the level of animals, caring for one thing only – to be fat and well-fed – and would thus degrade humanity to a purely physical existence.

After Socialism, Fascism combats the whole complex system of democratic ideology; and repudiates it, whether in its theoretical premises or in its practical application. Fascism denies that the majority, by the simple fact that it is a majority, can direct human society; it denies that numbers alone can govern by means of a periodical consultation, and it affirms the immutable, beneficial, and fruitful inequality of mankind, which can never be permanently leveled through the mere operation of a mechanical process such as universal suffrage. The democratic regime may be defined as from time to time giving the people the illusion of sovereignty, while the real effective sovereignty lies in the hands of other concealed and irresponsible forces. Democracy is a regime nominally without a king, but it is ruled by many kings – more absolute, tyrannical, and ruinous than one sole king, even though a tyrant. This explains why Fascism, having first in 1922 (for reasons of expediency) assumed an attitude tending towards republicanism, renounced this point of view before the March to Rome; being convinced that the question of political form is not today of prime importance.

A party which entirely governs a nation is a fact entirely new to history, there are no possible references or parallels. Fascism uses in its construction whatever elements in the Liberal, Social, or Democratic doctrines still have a living value; it maintains what may be called the certainties which we owe to history, but it rejects all the rest – that is to say, the conception that there can be any doctrine of unquestionable efficacy for all times and all peoples. Political doctrines pass, but humanity remains; and it may rather be expected that this will be a century of Fascism. For if the nineteenth century was the century of Individualism (Liberalism always signifying individualism) it may be expected that this will be the century of collectivism, and hence the century of the State.

Every doctrine tends to direct human activity towards a determined objective; but the action of man also reacts upon the doctrine, transforms it, adapts it to new needs, or supersedes it with something else. A doctrine then must be no mere exercise in words, but a living act; and thus the value of Fascism lies in the fact that it is veined with pragmatism, but at the same time has a will to exist and a will to power, a firm front in the face of the reality of 'violence'.

The foundation of Fascism is the conception of the State. Fascism conceives of the State as an absolute, in comparison with which all individuals or groups are relative, only to be conceived of in their relation to the State.

The Fascist State has drawn into itself even the economic activities of the nation, and through the corporative social and educational institutions created by it, its influence reaches every aspect of the national life and includes, framed in their respective organizations, all the political, economic and spiritual forces of the nation.

The Fascist State is an embodied will to power and government; the Roman tradition is here an ideal force of action. According to Fascism, government is not so much a thing to be expressed in territorial or military terms as in terms of morality and the spirit. It must be thought of as an empire – that is to say, a nation which directly or indirectly rules other nations, without the need for conquering a single square yard of territory. For Fascism, the growth of empire, that is to say the expansion of the nation, is an essential manifestation of vitality, and its opposite a sign of decadence. People which are rising, or rising again after a period of decadence, are always imperialist; any renunciation is a sign of decay and of death.

Fascism is the doctrine best adapted to represent the tendencies and the aspirations of a people, like the people of Italy, who are rising again after many centuries of abasement and foreign servitude. But empire demands discipline, the co-ordination of all forces and a deeply felt sense of duty and sacrifice; this fact explains many aspects of the practical working of the regime, the character of many forces in the State, and the necessarily severe measures which must be taken against those who would oppose this spontaneous and inevitable movement of Italy in the twentieth century, and would oppose it by recalling the outworn ideology of the nineteenth century ... for never before has the nation stood more in need of authority, of direction, and of order. If every age has its own characteristic doctrine, there are a thousand signs which point to Fascism as the characteristic doctrine of our time. For if a doctrine must be a living thing, that is proved by the fact that Fascism has created a living faith; and that this faith is very powerful in the minds of men, is demonstrated by those who have suffered and died for it.

READING 22

John Maynard Keynes

Biography

John Maynard Keynes (1883–1946) whose life coincided with two world wars, the fall of old empires, the decline of England, the emergence of new despotisms and the Great Depression was born on the June 5, 1883. By coincidence he came into the world in the very same year that Karl Marx passed away. Keynes was born in Cambridge, England, in a family of three children. John Neville Keynes, his father, first taught philosophy and economics at Cambridge and then became a university administrator. He was also the author of a little book *Scope and Method of Political Economy*, (1890) which became a standard work on the methodology of economics. His college educated mother, Florence Ada Keynes, was once a mayor of Cambridge.

Keynes received his elementary education at St Faith's preparatory school in Cambridge and then entered Eton (1897), a famous private secondary school. At Eton, with its variety and lack of regimentation, he was in an environment where his manifold interests could mature. He also developed good debating skills. From Eton he went to Cambridge University (King's College) where he continued to study the classics, history, mathematics and, towards the end of his training, economics. He attended Marshall's lectures and further improved his ability as a forceful and persuasive speaker. Nonconformism became one of his fundamental characteristics.

When Keynes had to decide what to do next after his graduation, he concluded that he had to take the Civil Service exam. He passed second with his worst mark in economics. This meant that he missed the Treasury and was appointed to the India Office in 1907. Here he had ample time to work on his fellowship dissertation which dealt with probability. During his two years at the India Office he also collected materials for a book published in 1913 entitled *Indian Currency and Finance*. It contained an analysis of the gold exchange standard under which a country pegs its currency to that of a gold standard country.

In 1909 Keynes accepted a fellowship at King's College where he lectured on a regular basis until 1915. He now had a secure academic base. In 1909, he became editor of the *Economic Journal*, a strategic position he kept until just before his death.

Keynes entered the Treasury in 1915 after the war had already broken out. In 1919, the Treasury found it appropriate to nominate him as its principal financial representative at the Paris Peace Conference. In this advisory capacity he was present at the peace talks. Soon Keynes arrived at the conclusion that the peace treaty was going to be vindictive, unjust, and unworkable, so he resigned in September 1919. Thereupon he wrote his *Economic Consequences of the Peace* in which he argued that:

(a) the key institutions of pre-war Europe had been fragile to begin with,
(b) the war had shaken them profoundly,
(c) the victors had left unresolved the economic problems of post-war Europe,
(d) the imposition of large reparations on a weakened Germany were impossible to fulfill.

The book also contained highly uncomplimentary portrayals of the 'Great Four' who represented the Allies at the peace negotiations. This was especially true for President Woodrow Wilson. The publication was a success and now Keynes started a life of controversy which was terminated only by his death.

Upon his return to King's College, he continued to work on post-war related problems. In 1922, he published *A Revision of the Treaty*, in which he updated the material presented in the *Economic Consequences of the Peace*. In 1923, he came out with a new work entitled *Tract on Monetary Reform* which was written against the background of weakened England and the monetary disorders that World War I had left in its wake. In this pamphlet Keynes broke with the desirability of the gold standard which in his view jeopardized a country's freedom to pursue an independent economic policy. Thus he favored a managed currency with exchange rates being allowed to fluctuate more freely than under the gold standard. From this publication onwards one finds in Keynes's publications always a plea for the management and/or control of something, be it money, interest rates, exchange rates, international trade, or aggregate demand.

In 1925, the pattern of European reconstruction came near completion, and it was after that date that Keynes began to concentrate on the problems of employment and unemployment. England suffered more from unemployment than other nations because she emerged from the war impoverished and her overseas markets had been lost.

Besides, much of its industrial equipment was outdated while the pound sterling was overvalued which hurt England's exports. During the same year Keynes married ballerina Lydia Lopokova, a great dancer and apparently a great personality.

During the late 1920s Keynes worked on what became *A Treatise on Money* (1930). He was also an active member of the English Liberal party which he tried to steer away from 'laissez-faire' and into the direction of interventionism. In his earlier days, Keynes was primarily an applied economist and a persuader. With the *Treatise* he became a tool-maker. This two-volume work contained his views on monetary theory and policy. In this text he remained faithful to a vision he had already expressed on earlier occasions. In his view, investment opportunities were diminishing while saving habits persisted. When the savings are not absorbed by investment the circular flow is interrupted and the economy becomes depressed. He thus demonstrated the 'need' for a managed economy.

In 1936, Keynes published *The General Theory of Employment Interest and Money*. The work was very successful, in part because the world was still suffering from mass unemployment and the new work seemed to point towards a solution. The central message was that economic stagnation was mainly due to a lack of aggregate demand and that fiscal policy could cure depression and unemployment. Thus Keynes once more made the case for government activism and interference. The views on free trade and protectionism expressed in the *General Theory* were not very different from those set down in his article 'National Self-Sufficiency'. Interestingly enough he also devoted 17 pages to leading mercantilist writers whose doctrines he cited with approval.

In 1937 Keynes suffered his first heart attack and was forced into a slower pace of life. With the war coming, and although he was not in good health, he prepared a little book entitled *How to Pay for the War* (1940). Here he presented a plan in which a portion of all wage earners' pay would be automatically invested in government bonds which would not be available for redemption until the war was over.

In 1940, the Chancellor of the Exchequer (the English equivalent of the American Secretary of the Treasury) appointed Keynes as one of his advisors and assigned him to work on the problems of war financing. When in 1942 these issues seemed to be under control, Keynes became concerned with plans for a post-war reconstruction. He was now an inside advisor and maker of policy. In 1943, Keynes published a scheme for an international cooperative body designed to deal with post-war monetary problems. The plan included a proposal for the establishment of a supranational monetary authority. Thus Keynes expanded the role of management and control to the international field. The American plan, known as the White Plan, was published almost simultaneously. Finally, a compromise scheme in which some elements of the Keynes Plan survived came about and eventually became the Bretton Woods System with the International Monetary Fund as its main institution. As an advisor to the British government, Keynes also became involved in direct negotiations with the US. All the missions, journeys and negotiations exhausted him almost to collapse and on April 21, Easter Day, he died from a sharp heart attack at age sixty-two.

It has often been said that Keynes has been inconsistent and that he changed his mind too easily. Some of that may be true. Yet, although he fathered many different proposals and plans, his main objective was always the full employment of resources. He tended to distrust the operation of automatic adjustment mechanisms and put his faith in economic management and control by policy makers and government officials. Besides, in practically all his writings he opposes some accepted mode of thought while his tendency to break with tradition is clear enough.

The Work

In an article written in March 1931 entitled 'Proposals for a Revenue Tariff', Keynes showed his apprehension about the effects of free trade on a country such as Britain. Opposing a policy of deflation and wage cutting Keynes espoused the adoption of tariffs. Later, this piece and other writings were published in a collection entitled *Essays in Persuasion*. Part of this writing is reproduced below.

Keynes returned to this issue in a notorious article entitled 'National Self-Sufficiency' published in 1933 in *The New Statesman and Nation* in England and *The Yale Review* in the United States. In this article, Keynes publicly deserted the free trade doctrine. The main theme of this piece was that greater self-sufficiency and economic isolation were desirable for his own country. The fewer economic entanglements the better. International trade and capital movements, in so far as they were inevitable, had to be monitored. He also criticized what he called 'individualistic and decadent capitalism'.[78]

Extract

Proposals for a Revenue Tariff

Do you think it is a paradox that we continue to increase our capital wealth by adding both to our foreign investments and to our equipment at home, that we can continue to live (most of us) much as usual or better, and support at the same time a vast body of persons in idleness with a dole greater than the income of a man in full employment in most parts of the world – and yet do all this with one quarter of our industrial plant closed down and one quarter of our industrial workers unemployed? It would be not merely a paradox, but an impossibility, if our potential capacity for the creation of wealth were not much greater than it used to be. But this greater capacity does exist. It is attributed mainly to three factors – the ever-increasing technical efficiency of our industries (I believe that output per head is 10 per cent greater than it was even so recently as 1924), the greater economic output of women, and the larger proportion of the population which is at the working period of life. The fall in the price of our imports compared with that of our exports also helps. The result is that with three-fourths of our industrial capacity we can now produce as much wealth as we could produce with the whole of it a few years ago. But how rich we could be if only we could find some way of employing *four*-fourths of our capacity to-day!

Our trouble is, then, not that we lack the physical means to support a high standard of life, but that we are suffering a breakdown in organization and in the machinery by which we buy and sell to one another.

There are two reactions to this breakdown. We experience the one or the other according to our temperaments. The one is inspired by a determination to maintain our standards of life by bringing into use our wasted capacity – that is to say, to expand, casting fear and even prudence away. The other, the instinct to contract, is based on the

---

78   Sources: J.M. Keynes, 'Proposals for a Revenue Tariff', *Essays in Persuasion* (New York: Norton, 1963) pp. 272–280.
J. M. Keynes, 'National Self-Sufficiency', *The Collective Works of John Maynard Keynes* (D. Moggridge, ed.) Vol. XXI (London: Macmillan Press, 1982) pp. 235–243.

psychology of fear. How reasonable is it to be afraid?

We live in a society organized in such a way that the activity of production depends on the individual businessman hoping for a reasonable profit, or at least, to avoid an actual loss. The margin which he requires as his necessary incentive to produce may be a very small proportion of the total value of the product. But take this away from him and the whole process stops. This, unluckily, is just what has happened. The fall of prices relatively to costs, together with the psychological effect of high taxation, has destroyed the necessary incentive to production. This is at the root of our disorganization. It may be unwise, therefore, to frighten the businessman or torment him further. A forward policy is liable to do this. For reasoning by a false analogy from what is prudent for an individual who finds himself in danger of living beyond his means, he is usually, when his nerves are frayed, a supporter, though to his own ultimate disadvantage, of national contraction.

And there is a further reason for nervousness. We are suffering from *international* instability. Notoriously the competitive power of our export trades is diminished by our high standard of life. At the same time the lack of profits in home business inclines the investor to place his money abroad, whilst high taxation exercises a sinister influence in the same direction. Above all, the reluctance of other creditor countries to lend (which is the root-cause of this slump) places too heavy a financial burden on London. These, again, are apparent arguments against a forward policy; for greater activity at home due to increased employment will increase our excess of imports, and Government borrowing may (in their present mood) frighten investors.

Thus the *direct* effect of an expansionist, policy must be to cause Government borrowing, to throw some burden on the Budget, and to increase our excess of imports. In every way, therefore – the opponents of such a policy point out – it will aggravate the want of confidence, the burden of taxation, and the international instability which, they believe, are at the bottom of our present troubles.

At this point the opponents of expansion divide into two groups – those who think that we must not only postpone all ideas of expansion, but must positively contract, by which they mean reduce wages and make large economies in the existing expenditure of the Budget, and those who are entirely negative and, like Mr. Snowden, dislike the idea of contraction (interpreted in the above sense) almost as much as they dislike the idea of expansion.

The policy of negation, however, is really the most dangerous of all. For, as time goes by, it becomes increasingly doubtful whether we *can* support our standard of life. With 1,000,000 unemployed we certainly can; with 2,000,000 unemployed we probably can; with 3,000,000 unemployed we probably cannot. Thus the negative policy, by allowing unemployment steadily to increase, must lead in the end to an unanswerable demand for a reduction in our standard of life. If we do nothing long enough, there will in the end be nothing else that we can do.

Unemployment, I must repeat, exists because employers have been deprived of profit. The loss of profit may be due to all sorts of causes. But, short of going over to Communism, there is no possible means of curing unemployment except by restoring to employers a proper margin of profit. There are two ways of doing this – by increasing the *demand* for output, which is the expansionist cure, or by decreasing the *cost* of output, which is the contractionist cure. Both of these try to touch the spot. Which of them is preferred?

To decrease the cost of output by reducing wages and curtailing Budget services may indeed increase foreign demand for our goods (unless, which is quite likely, it encourages a similar policy of contraction abroad), but it will probably diminish the domestic demand. The advantages to employers of a *general* reduction of wages are, therefore, not so great as they look. Each employer sees the advantage to himself of a reduction of the wages, which he himself pays and overlooks both the reduction of the incomes of his customers and the reduction of wages which his competitors will enjoy. Anyway, it would certainly lead to social injustice and violent resistance, since it would greatly benefit some classes of income at the expense of others. For these reasons a policy of contraction sufficiently drastic to do any real good may be quite impracticable.

Yet the objections to the expansionist remedy – the instability of our international position, the state of the Budget, and the want of confidence – cannot be disposed of. Two years ago there was no need to be frightened. To-day it is a different matter. It would not be wise to frighten the penguins and arouse these frigid creatures to flap away from our shores with their golden eggs inside them. A policy of expansion sufficiently drastic to be useful might drive us off the gold standard. Moreover, two years ago the problem was mainly a British problem; to-day it is mainly international. No domestic cure to-day can be adequate by itself. An international cure is essential; and I see the best hope of remedying the international slump in the leadership of Great Britain. But if Great Britain is to resume leadership, she must be strong and believed to be strong. It is of paramount importance, therefore, to restore full confidence in London. I do not believe that this is difficult; for the real strength of London is being under-estimated to-day by foreign opinion, and the position is ripe for a sudden reversal of sentiment. For these reasons I, who opposed our return to the gold standard and can claim, unfortunately, that my Cassandra utterances have been partly fulfilled, believe that our exchange position should be relentlessly defended to-day, in order, above all, that we may resume the vacant financial leadership of the world, which no one else has the experience or the public spirit to occupy, speaking out of acknowledged strength and not out of weakness.

An advocate of expansion in the interests of domestic employment has cause, therefore, to think twice. I have thought twice, and the following are my conclusions.

I am of the opinion that a policy of expansion, though desirable, is not safe or practicable to-day, unless it is accompanied by other measures which would neutralize its dangers. Let me remind the reader what these dangers are. There is the burden on the trade balance, the burden on the Budget, and the effect on confidence. If the policy of expansion were to justify itself eventually by increasing materially the level of profits and the volume of employment, the net effect on the Budget and on confidence would in the end be favorable and perhaps very favorable. But this might not be the initial effect.

What measures are available to neutralize these dangers? A decision to reform the grave abuses of the dole, and a decision to postpone for the present all new charges on the Budget for social services in order to conserve its resources to meet schemes for the expansion of employment, are advisable and should be taken. But the main decision which seems to me to-day to be absolutely forced on any wise Chancellor of the Exchequer, whatever his beliefs about Protection, is the introduction of a substantial revenue tariff. It is certain that there is no other measure all the immediate consequences of which will be favorable and appropriate. The tariff which I have in mind would include no discriminating protective taxes, but would cover as wide a field as possible at a flat rate or perhaps two flat rates, each applicable to wide categories of goods. Rebates would be allowed in respect of imported material entering into exports, but raw materials, which make up an important proportion of the value of exports, such as wool and cotton, would be exempt. The amount of revenue to be aimed at should be substantial, not less than 50,000,000 pounds and if possible, 75,000,000 pounds. Thus, for example, there might be import duties of 15 percent on all manufactured and semi-manufactured goods without exception, and of 5 percent on all food stuffs and certain raw materials, whilst other raw materials would be exempt. I am prepared to maintain that the effect of such duties on the cost of living would be insignificant – no greater than the existing fluctuation between one month and another. Moreover, any conceivable remedy for unemployment will have the effect, and, indeed, will be intended, to raise prices. Equally, the effect on the cost of our exports, after allowing for the rebates which should be calculated on broad and simple lines, would be very small. It should be the declared intention of the Free Trade parties acquiescing in this decision to remove the duties in the event of world prices recovering to the level of 1929.

Compared with any alternative which is open to us, this measure is unique in that it would at the same time relieve the pressing problems of the Budget and restore business confidence. I do not believe that a wise and prudent Budget can be framed to-day without recourse to a revenue tariff. But this is not its only advantage. In so far as it leads to the substitution of home produced goods for goods previously imported, it will increase employment in this country. At the same time, by relieving the pressure on the balance of trade it will provide a much-needed margin to pay for the additional imports which a policy of expansion will require and to finance loans by London to necessitous debtor countries. In these ways, the buying power which we take away from the rest of the world by restricting certain imports we shall restore to it with the other hand. Some fanatical Free Traders might allege that the adverse effect of import duties on our exports would neutralize all this; but it would not be true.

Free Traders may, consistently with their faith, regard a revenue tariff as our iron ration, which can be used once only in emergency. The emergency has arrived. Under cover of the breathing space and the margin of financial strength thus afforded us, we could frame a policy and a plan, both domestic and international, for marching to the assault against the spirit of contractionism and fear.

If, on the other hand, Free Traders reject these councils of expediency, the certain result will be to break the present Government and to substitute for it, in the confusion of a Crisis of Confidence, a Cabinet pledged to a full protectionist programme.

National Self-Sufficiency

What fault have we to find with this?[79] Taking it at its surface value – none. Yet we are not, many of us, content with it as a working political theory. What is wrong?

To begin with the question of peace. We are pacifist today with so much strength of conviction that, if the economic internationalist could win this point, he would soon recapture our support. But it does not now seem obvious that a great concentration of national effort on the capture of foreign trade, that the penetration of a country's economic structure by the resources and the influence of foreign capitalists, that a close dependence of our own economic life on the fluctuating economic policies of foreign countries, are safeguards and assurances of international peace. It is easier, in the light of experience and foresight, to argue quite the contrary. The protection of a country's existing foreign interests, the capture of new markets, the progress of economic imperialism – these are a scarcely avoidable part of a scheme of things which aims at the maximum of international specialization and at the maximum geographical diffusion of capital wherever its seat is ownership. Advisable domestic policies might often be easier to compass, if, for example, the phenomenon known as 'the flight of capital' could be ruled out. The divorce between ownership and the real responsibility of management is serious within a country when, as a result of joint-stock enterprise, ownership is broken up between innumerable individuals who buy their interest today and sell it tomorrow and lack altogether both knowledge and responsibility towards what they momentarily own. But when the same principle is applied internationally, it is, in times of stress, intolerable – I am irresponsible towards what I own and those who operate what I own are irresponsible towards me. There may be some financial calculation which shows it to be advantageous that my savings should be invested in whatever quarter of the habitable globe shows the greatest marginal efficiency of capital or the highest rate of interest. But experience is accumulating that remoteness between ownership and operation is an evil in the relations between men, likely or certain in the long run to set up strains and enmities which will bring to nought the financial calculation.

---

79   In the preceding section of this article, Keynes briefly discussed the free trade doctrine (ed.).

I sympathize, therefore, with those who would minimize, rather than with those who would maximize, economic entanglement between nations. Ideas, knowledge, art, hospitality, travel – these are the things which should of their nature be international. But let goods be homespun whenever it is reasonably and conveniently possible; and, above all, let finance be primarily national. Yet, at the same time, those who seek to disembarrass a country of its entanglements should be very slow and wary. It should not be a matter of tearing up roots but of slowly training a plant to grow in a different direction.

For these strong reasons, therefore, I am inclined to the belief that, after the transition is accomplished, a greater measure of national self-sufficiency and economic isolation between countries than existed in 1914 may tend to serve the cause of peace, rather than otherwise. At any rate the age of economic internationalism was not particularly successful in avoiding war; and if its friends retort that the imperfection of its success never gave it a fair chance, it is reasonable to point out that a greater success is scarcely probable in the coming years.

Let us turn from these questions of doubtful judgement, where each of us will remain entitled to his own opinion, to a matter more purely economic. In the nineteenth century the economic internationalist could probably claim with justice that his policy was tending to the world's greatest enrichment, that it was promoting economic progress, and its reversal would have seriously impoverished both ourselves and our neighbors. This raises a question of balance between economic and non-economic advantage of a kind which is not easily decided. Poverty is a great evil; and economic advantage is a real good, not to be sacrificed to alternative real goods, unless it is clearly of an inferior weight. I am ready to believe that in the nineteenth century two sets of conditions existed which caused the advantages of economic internationalism to outweigh disadvantages of a different kind. At a time when wholesale migrations were populating new continents, it was natural that the man should carry with them into the New Worlds the material fruits of the technique of the Old, embodying the savings of those who were sending them. The investment of British savings in rails and rolling stock to be installed by British engineers to carry British emigrants to new fields and pastures, the fruits of which they would return in due proportion to those whose frugality had made these things possible, was not economic internationalism remotely resembling in its essence the part ownership of the A.E.G. of Germany by a speculator in Chicago, or of the municipal improvements of Rio de Janeiro by an English spinster. Yet it was the type of organization necessary to facilitate the former which has eventually ended up in the latter. In the second place, at a time when there were enormous differences in degree in the industrialization and opportunities for technical training in different countries, the advantages of a high degree of national specialization were very considerable.

But I am not persuaded that the economic advantages of the international division of labor today are at all comparable with what they were. I must not be understood to carry my argument beyond a certain point. A considerable degree of international specialization is necessary in a rational world in all cases where it is dictated by wide differences of climate, natural resources, native aptitudes, level of culture and density of population. But over an increasingly wide range of industrial products, and perhaps of agricultural products also, I became doubtful whether the economic cost of national self-sufficiency is great enough to outweigh the other advantages of gradually bringing the producer and the consumer within the ambit of the same national, economic and financial organization. Experience accumulates to prove that most modern mass-production processes can be performed in most countries and climates with almost equal efficiency. Moreover, as wealth increases, both primary and manufactured products play a smaller relative part in the national economy compared with houses, personal services and local amenities which are not the subject of international exchange; with the result that a moderate increase in the real cost of the former consequent on greater national self-sufficiency may cease to be of serious consequence when weighed in the balance against advantages of a different kind. National self-sufficiency, in short, though it costs something, may be becoming a luxury which we can afford if we happen to want it. Are there sufficient good reasons why we may happen to want it?

The decadent international but individualistic capitalism, in the hands of which we found ourselves after the War, is not a success. It is not intelligent, it is not beautiful, it is not just, it is not virtuous – and it doesn't deliver the goods. In short, we dislike it and we are beginning to despise it. But when we wonder what to put in its place, we are extremely perplexed.

Each year it becomes more obvious that the world is embarking on a variety of politico-economic experiments, and that different types of experiment appeal to different national temperaments and historical environments. The nineteenth century free trader's economic internationalism assumed that the world was, or would be, organized on a basis of private competitive capitalism and of the freedom of private contract inviolably protected by the sanctions of law – in various phases, of course, of complexity and development, but conforming to a uniform type which it would be the general object to perfect and certainly not to destroy. Nineteenth-century protectionism was a blot upon the efficiency and good sense of this scheme of things, but it did not modify the general presumption as to the fundamental characteristics of economic society.

But today one country after another abandons these presumptions. Russia is still alone in her particular experiment, but no longer alone in her abandonment of the old presumptions. Italy, Ireland, Germany have cast their eyes, or are casting them, towards new modes of political economy. Many more countries after them will soon be seeking, one by one, after new economic gods. Even countries such as Great Britain and the United States, though conforming in the main to the old model, are striving, under the surface, after a new economic plan. We do not know what will be the outcome. We are – all of us, I expect – about to make many mistakes. No one can tell which of the new systems will prove itself best.

But the point for my present discussion is this. We each have our own fancy. Not believing that we are saved already, we each would like to have a try at working out our own salvation. We do not wish, therefore, to be at the mercy of world forces working out, or trying to work out, some uniform equilibrium according to the ideal principles, if they can be called such, of *laissez-faire* capitalism. There are still those who cling to the old ideas, but in no country of the world today can they be reckoned as a serious force. We wish – for the time at least and so long as the present transitional, experimental phase endures – to be our own masters, and to be as free as we can make ourselves from the interferences of the outside world.

Thus, regarded from this point of view, the policy of an increased national self-sufficiency is to be considered not as an ideal in itself but as directed to the creation of an environment in which other ideals can be safely and conveniently pursued.

Let me give as dry an illustration of this as I can devise, chosen because it is connected with ideas with which recently my own mind has been largely preoccupied. In matters of economic detail, as distinct from the central controls, I am in favor of retaining as much private judgement and initiative and enterprise as possible. But I have become convinced that the retention of the structure of private enterprise is incompatible with that degree of material well-being to which our technical advancement entitles us, unless the rate of interest falls to a much lower figure than is likely to come about by natural forces operating on the old lines. Indeed the transformation of society, which I preferably envisage, may require a reduction in the rate of interest towards vanishing point within the next thirty years. But under a system by which the rate of interest finds, under the operation of normal financial forces, a uniform level throughout the world, after allowing for risk and the like, this is most unlikely to occur. Thus for a complexity of reasons, which I cannot elaborate in this place, economic internationalism embracing the free movement of capital and of loanable funds as well as of traded goods may condemn this country for a generation to come to a much lower degree of material prosperity than could be attained under a different system.

But this is merely an illustration. The point is that there is no prospect for the next generation of a uniformity of economic systems throughout the world, such as existed, broadly speaking, during the nineteenth century; that we all need to be as free as possible of interference from economic changes elsewhere, in order to make our own favorite experiments towards the ideal social republic of the future; and that a deliberate movement towards greater national self-sufficiency and economic isolation will make our task easier, in so far as it can be accomplished without excessive economic cost.

There is one more explanation, I think, of the reorientation of our minds. The nineteenth century carried to extravagant lengths the criterion of what one can call for short the financial results, as a test of the advisability of any course of action sponsored by private or by collective action. The whole conduct of life was made into a sort of parody of an accountant's nightmare. Instead of using their vastly increased material and technical resources to build a wonder-city, they built slums; and they thought it right and advisable to build slums because slums, on the test of private enterprise, 'paid', whereas the wonder-city would, they thought, have been an act of foolish extravagance, which would, in the imbecile idiom of the financial fashion, have 'mortgaged the future'; though how the construction today of great and glorious works can impoverish the future no man can see until his mind is beset by false analogies from an irrelevant accountancy. Even today we spend our time – half vainly, but also, I must admit, half successfully – in trying to persuade our countrymen that the nation as a whole will assuredly be richer if unemployed men and machines are used to build much needed houses than if they are supported in idleness. For the minds of this generation are still so beclouded by bogus calculations that they distrust conclusions which should be obvious, out of a reliance on a system of financial accounting which casts doubt on whether such an operation will 'pay'. We have to remain poor because it does not 'pay' to be rich. We have to live in hovels, not because we cannot build palaces, but because we cannot 'afford' them.

The same rule of self-destructive financial calculation governs every walk of life. We destroy the beauty of the countryside because the unappropriated splendors of nature have no economic value. We are capable of shutting off the sun and the stars because they do not pay a dividend. London is one of the richest cities in the history of civilization, but it cannot 'afford' the highest standards of achievement of which its own living citizens are capable, because they do not 'pay'.

If I had the power today I should surely set out to endow our capital cities with all the appurtenances of art and civilization on the highest standards of which the citizens of each were individually capable, convinced that what I could create, I could afford – and believing that money thus spent would not only be better than any dole, but would make unnecessary any dole. For with what we have spent on the dole in England since the War we could have made our cities the greatest works of man in the world.

Or again, we have until recently conceived it a moral duty to ruin the tillers of the soil and destroy the age-long human traditions attendant on husbandry if we could get a loaf of bread thereby a tenth of a penny cheaper. There is nothing which it was not our duty to sacrifice to this Moloch and Mammon in one; for we faithfully believed that the worship of these monsters would overcome the evil of poverty and lead the next generation safely and comfortably, on the back of compound interest, into economic peace.

Today we suffer disillusion, not because we are poorer than we were – on the contrary even today we enjoy, in Great Britain at least, a higher standard of life than at any previous period – but because other values seem to have been sacrificed and because, moreover, they seem to have been sacrificed unnecessarily. For our economic system is not, in fact, enabling us to exploit to the utmost the possibilities for economic wealth afforded by the progress of our technique, but falls far short of this, leading us to feel that we might as well have used up the margin in more satisfying ways.

But once we allow ourselves to be disobedient to the test of an accountant's profit, we have begun to change our civilization. And we need to do so very warily, cautiously and self-consciously. For there is a wide field of human activity where we shall be wise to retain the usual pecuniary tests. It is the state, rather than the individual, which needs to change its criterion. It is the conception of the Chancellor of the Exchequer as the chairman of a sort of joint-stock company which has to be discarded. Now if the functions and purposes of the state are to be thus enlarged, the decision as to what, broadly speaking, shall be produced within the nation and what shall be exchanged with abroad, must stand high amongst the objects of policy.

READING 23

Reed Smoot and Willis C. Hawley

Biography of Reed Smoot

American legislator and Mormon leader, Reed Smoot (1862–1941) was born in Salt Lake City, Utah, on January 10, 1862, as the son of a textile producer. In 1874, he moved with his parents to Provo, Utah County, Utah, where he attended Mormon Church schools and academies. In 1879, he graduated from the Brigham Young Academy (now Brigham Young University) at Provo and became prominent in various industrial enterprises (banking, mining, livestock raising, and manufacture of woolen goods) in Salt Lake City and Provo. In 1879, he married Alpha Eldredge with whom he had three sons and three daughters. In 1895, he was named President of the Utah Stake of the Church of Jesus Christ of Latter–day Saints (the Mormon Church) and he became an apostle of that Church in 1900.

Smoot was elected to the US Senate in 1903 at age 41 and served as a Republican in the Senate until 1933 when he was defeated in the Roosevelt landslide of 1932. He is best known as the co-author of the Smoot–Hawley Tariff Act of 1930. After his defeat, Smoot retired to Salt Lake City. He died in St Petersburg, Florida, on February 9, 1941, and was buried in Provo, Utah.

The Work of Reed Smoot

Reed Smoot did not have any original ideas or arguments to offer on the topics of protectionism or free trade. His (mercantilist) understanding of international economics was that of an average

American businessman of the early part of the twentieth century with no international experience. Four important elements of Smoot's protectionist philosophy were the following:[80]

1. Smoot was especially eager to protect Utah's interests and in particular the infant sugar and woolen industries of that state in which he had a personal financial stake.
2. Smoot had always been heavily involved in the affairs of the Mormon Church. The tithes of the Church had mainly been invested in Utah's sugar factories.
3. The 'apostle of protectionism', as he was sometimes called, was firmly convinced that somehow self-sufficiency, prosperity and protectionism were intimately connected. In that sense he was, like Hawley, an economic nationalist. Without tariff protection, he thought, the American living standard would slide back. Many firms would not be able to make it, and farmers and wage earners would be paid the kind of pittance they received in Asian, Latin American, and Caribbean countries such as Cuba.
4. The American Senator thought that American farmers needed a strong domestic urban market for their products and that without protection, industrial/urban jobs would vanish and so would the home market for farm products.

In 1918, a Republican Congress was elected, and in 1920, the Republican Senator Warren G. Harding became President of the United States. Not surprisingly, Smoot took the isolationist position and opposed US membership of the League of Nations. As a confidant of the new President and a senior member of the Senate Finance Committee, Reed Smoot was ready to work on a new protectionist bill which came in the form of the so-called Fordney–McCumber tariff bill in 1922. The bill contained many provisions of special interest groups which Smoot fully supported. Farm products especially became heavily protected.

In 1923, Reed Smoot became chairman of the influential Senate Finance Committee. As such, he had more control over tariff legislation than ever before. At the same time, during the 1920s, he met Presidents Harding, Coolidge, and Hoover on many occasions.

---

80   J. B. Allen, 'The Great Protectionist, Senator Reed Smoot of Utah', *Utah Historical Quarterly*, Vol. 45, Number 4 (Winter 1977).

When it came to tariff matters, he seemed to have their confidence. Thus, his senatorial career culminated in the preparation of a tariff act that bore his name and which approximated his ideal more closely than any other. The Smoot–Hawley Act passed the Senate and the House in 1930 and President Hoover signed it.

Biography of Willis C. Hawley

Willis C. Hawley (1864–1941) was born on a farm near Monroe, Benton County, Oregon on May 5, 1864. He attended rural district schools and after high school he moved to Willamette University at Salem, Oregon. He graduated in 1884 with a BS degree. Hawley then became an educator at various institutions. For sixteen years he taught history and economics. Between 1893 and 1902, he was President of Willamette University.

In 1885, he married Anna Geisendorfer with whom he had three children. Between 1906 and 1932, he represented the First Oregon Congressional District in the House of Representatives as a Republican. When the Smoot–Hawley Bill was introduced in the House, he was the chairman of the powerful House Ways and Means Committee which allowed the co-sponsor of the Act to facilitate its adoption. When he lost in the 1932 election, he returned to Salem and resumed the practice of law. He died in Salem on July 24, 1941.

The Work of Willis Hawley

As the article published in the *New York Times* on June 1, 1930, (reproduced below) shows, Hawley's defence of the Tariff Law was hardly more sophisticated than the arguments brought forward by Senator Smoot.[81] Hawley basically claims that American industry and labor must be protected against 'unfair' competition, 'improper' trade practices, and exclusion from advantageous participation in American markets which Americans have created and maintained.

Hawley's arguments did not go unchallenged in the House. John N. Garner, for instance, minority leader in the House and ranking Democratic member of the Ways and Means Committee, saw things differently. He claimed that 'no greater fraud was ever perpetrated upon the American people than the claim of proponents of the

---

81   *New York Times*, Section 3, pages E1 and E11 (June 1, 1930).

Smoot–Hawley Act that it is designed to protect American labor. Its real purpose is to exploit, not to protect the millions of American working men as well as the farmers and the businessmen.'[82] He added that the formulation of this bill had developed into a wild scramble on the part of selfish interest groups to secure the assent of Congress.

Once the Smoot–Hawley Act was signed by the President, other nations retaliated. Economic nationalism followed the signing of the bill, and before 1931 was over, some 25 countries had made extensive tariff revisions upward or were planning to do so citing the United States commercial policy as justification. In retrospect, the Smoot–Hawley tariff, which raised the average ad valorem rate for dutiable articles to 53.2 per cent, was a blunder, national and international, in producing an economically compartmentalized world. Because of the Great Depression (1929–1933), which caused a world-wide decline in purchasing power, a relatively high exchange rate of the dollar and the Smoot–Hawley tariff, exports in current dollar value fell from $5,241 million in 1929 to $1,611 million in 1932. Imports declined from $4,399 million to $1,323 million.[83]

The Smoot–Hawley Tariff Act of 1930 Itself

As the reading taken from the Tariff Act of 1930 shows, the main principle upon which the Act was constructed was that the tariff rate upon a given article or product should equalize the difference in the costs of production of that article or product in the United States and the principal country abroad. In other words, the tariff should make uniform the difference between the domestic and foreign costs of production.

There are of course two problems with this idea. First, it is difficult if not impossible to know which costs are to be equalized. Not all producers in the importing countries have the same costs. The same applies to producers in the exporting nations. Second, if taken seriously, the cost equalization argument means that domestic trade barriers have to be sufficiently high to place the least efficient domestic producers on equal footing with the most efficient foreign

---

82   *Ibid.*, page E1.
83   H.N. Scherber et al., *American Economic History* (New York: Harper and Row, 1976) p. 358.

manufacturers. This would of course be sufficient to bring practically all foreign trade to a halt.

The 1930 Tariff Act also pays attention to 'unfair trade practices'. Such methods of competition could even lead to total exclusion from entry of the relevant products. As is evidenced in the reading, the definition of what constitutes an 'unfair practice' is vague enough to make it an ideal tool for special interests who want to wall-off world trade.

Finally the Smoot–Hawley Act has a provision related to the idea of discrimination against American commerce. The first problem here is that often enough discrimination is difficult to trace and prove. A second problem is that such discrimination may be a retaliatory move by an American trade partner against such laws as the Smoot–Hawley Act itself. Punitive reactions on the part of the United States may then trigger a real tariff war.[84]

Extracts

For the Tariff
By Willis C. Hawley

The present tariff law became effective on Sept. 22, 1922. When it was passed, the world had not returned to normal conditions in production and industry, in trade and commerce. During the past eight years important new developments in manufacture and production have occurred, new competitors have entered the field, new price levels have been established and intensive drives have been made by old and new competitors upon our agricultural and industrial activities. A protective tariff is intended as an alert guard protecting our industries and labor against unfair competition, improper trade practices and exclusion from an advantageous participation in our markets, which markets our people have created and maintain.

Aims to Aid Labor

It is the purpose of our protective tariff policy to make our country

---

84   *New York Times*, Section 3, pages E1 and E11 (June 1, 1930).
     'Smoot–Hawley Tariff Act', *U.S. Statutes at Large*, Vol. 46, Pt. 1 (April 1929–March 1931) June 1930 (Washington: US Government Printing Office, 1931).

self-sufficient and self-sustaining; to afford our agriculture, industry and labor a proper opportunity in the American market. Under this system we have multiplied our national wealth, developed our resources, maintained a high standard of living and afforded our wage earners an unprecedented remuneration for their toil. It has made this a land of opportunity for brains, industry and ability of every kind. Our population is rapidly increasing. It is necessary to develop commensurately to meet our growing needs. Every branch of human activity is called upon to expand to provide for our people.

A nation that has the opportunities we have that does not provide conditions, so far as law can do so, for the employment of its people, fails greatly in its duty toward them.

The pending bill gives due consideration to the nations wage earners. Twenty-seven million of our people earn their daily living by being on some payroll who with their families comprise more than half our population. To the extent of their use, foreign made articles which supplant in our markets articles that can properly be made here deprive our own workers of labor and wages consequent thereto.

The pending bill is a readjustment of existing rates; it chiefly relates to agriculture and to industries for which the present law does not adequately provide. It is frankly a protective tariff bill framed to meet the legitimate needs of our day. It is intended to be a structure under whose protection all America will prosper.

Whenever a Republican tariff has replaced a Democratic tariff our imports have increased. The annual average imports under the Wilson act were $760,000,000, but were increased to $998,000,000 under the Dingley act. Under the Underwood act the annual average was $2,871,000,000, but under the Fordney act it has been $4,052,000,000.

That is, better protection to American products and labor has largely increased the prosperity and well-being of our people and at the same time materially increased the foreign trade. There is every reason to believe that history is ready to repeat itself and that the pending bill, when enacted into law, will not only benefit our own people but enlarge our foreign trade.

Will the readjustments in the pending bill benefit or burden the consumer? There is no exclusively consumer class in this country except those who render no service or produce no products. All others are both producers and consumers. The prime necessity for any producer, if he is to continue, is a profitable market sufficient to absorb the output. The wage earners, of all kinds, are our largest consumers by number, but they are producers as well. If conditions arise in which their services are no longer required or the employment is discontinued, they are the first to be affected. What they want is a job. Unemployment for a very short time will many times offset any increase that may occur when the pending bill becomes a law. Nor is there any occupation to which this will not apply.

Duty and Price

In my opinion, based upon the past history of protective tariffs, prices will vary with supply and demand, under our competitive system, and the condition of the markets will be a primary factor in determining rise or decline in prices. A tariff duty is only one factor in determining the price at which an article will sell. There is no historical or economic basis for the wild statements that the duties proposed will cost the purchasers great sums. These are issued by those desiring to prejudice the bill in the public mind, having no regard for economic facts.

The proper test is made by offsetting any additional cost against benefits derived. Such a test taken over a period of time will show advantage on the side of benefits. If space afforded, it would be easy to multiply examples to show the accuracy of this observation.

A duty is not necessarily added to the price. Protection is intended to establish and maintain industries in this country, induce mass production and afford them a market. Profits usually accrue not from limited but from mass production. Tin plate and aluminum wares are good illustrations. When duties were imposed upon these articles it was argued by our opponents that prices would be greatly increased. The fact is that you can now buy American tin and aluminum wares of better quality and heavier weight cheaper here than anywhere else.

A price may be increased to the full amount of the duty or to a part of it or it may not increase at all. Prices may even decline; this is a common experience, especially under mass production. Which of these alternatives will apply depends on the markets and other economic factors, whose future operations can only be estimated on the basis of past experience.

This outcry that costs to American consumers will be increased at all times by the full amount of the duties, and probably much further increased by what is vaguely called 'pyramiding', has always been raised, but this has not been our experience, for if this were true each protective tariff act would not have multiplied production, increased employment, consumed enormous quantities of raw materials, fostered trade and commerce at home and abroad, sustained extensive and costly systems of public and private improvements and, in a word, prompted and maintained the general prosperity.

It has been asserted that the pending bill proposes the highest rates of duty in our history. 'Let facts be submitted to a candid world'. Since 1890 six tariff acts have been put on the statute books, four by the Republicans and two by the Democrats; the figures I now give relate to dutiable imports only.

Under the Republican protective tariffs, the weighted average ad valorem on dutiable imports are as follows, for the whole period each was in force:

			Per Cent
McKinley act	....	1890–1894	48.39
Dingley act	....	1897–1909	46.49
Payne act	....	1909–1913	40.73
Fordney act	....	1922–1930	38.22
Pending bill	....	1930	41.22

That is, the ad valorem under the pending bill, based upon 1928 dutiable imports is 7.17 per cent below the McKinley act, 5.27 per cent below the Dingley act, 0.49 per cent above the Payne act, and 2.47 per cent above the ad valorem of the Fordney act, for the year 1928, which is the year on which the computations are based for the pending bill. Under each of the above acts the country enjoyed an increasing and continued prosperity. Whether the rates were higher or lower than those proposed, each served its purpose well. It is in the memory of all that the Underwood free trade act resulted in national distress.

Our foreign trade includes both imports and exports, and the average ad valorem on all imports, both free and dutiable, under protective tariffs are as follows:

	Per Cent
McKinley act	23.01
Dingley act	25.47
Payne act	19.32
Fordney act	13.83
Pending bill	15.97

The pending bill is therefore lower than all others on all imports combined, excepting on the Fordney act. The two items to which the increase in the pending bill are specially due are the greatly increased rates on agricultural products and transfers from the free list. For the relief of agriculture in addition to an increase in rates, the bill proposes to stimulate and make profitable the growth of products not now grown in quantities sufficient for our requirements, and so reduce the amount of crops now grown in excess of such requirements.

The average ad valorem for dutiable imports entered in 1928, if computed on the rates in the pending bill, is 41.22 per cent or an increase of 2.47 per cent over the average ad valorem for the year 1928, under the present law. Distributing this increase between imports due to agriculture and all other imports, and taking into consideration that the increase in ad valorem on agricultural items is three times that on all other imports not related to agriculture, and also taking into consideration the amounts of dutiable imports under each it is apparent that of this increase of 2.49 per cent, 1.54 per cent is for agriculture and 0.95 per cent for all other industries. This is further borne out by the statement of the Tariff Commission that 68 per cent of the increases are related to agriculture and 32 per cent to all other industries.

There has been a tendency during the consideration of the bill for some producers to contend for satisfactory readjustments in rates affecting them and to oppose similar consideration for other producers. It has, however, been the policy of those in charge of the legislation to accord equal consideration to all, believing this to be a just national policy, and that a partial prosperity cannot be maintained.

After long and detailed consideration, I am led to the conclusion that the changes made in the rates of duties are justified and in the public interest.

The Smoot–Hawley Act

SEC. 336. Equalization of Costs of Production.

(a) Change of Classification or Duties. – In order to put into force and effect the policy of Congress by this Act intended, the commission (1) upon the request of the President, or (2) upon resolution of either or both Houses of Congress, or (3) upon its own motion, or (4) when in judgement of the commission there is good and sufficient reason therefor, upon application of any interested party, shall investigate the differences in the costs of production of any domestic article and of any like or similar foreign article.[85] In the course of the investigation the commission shall hold hearings and give reasonable public notice therefor, and shall afford reasonable opportunity for parties interested to be present, to produce evidence, and to be heard at such hearings. The commission is authorized to adopt such reasonable procedure and rules and regulations as it deems necessary to execute its functions under this section. The commission shall report to the President the results of the investigation and its findings with respect to such differences in costs of production. If the commission finds it shown by the investigation that the duties expressly fixed by statute do not equalize the differences in the costs of production of the domestic article and the like or similar foreign article when produced in the principal competing country, the commission shall specify in its report such increases or decreases in rates of duty expressly fixed by statute (including any necessary change in classification) as it finds shown by the investigation to be necessary to equalize such differences. In no case shall the total increase or decrease of such rates of duty exceed 50 per centum of the rates expressly fixed by statute.

(b) Change to American Selling Price. – If the commission finds upon any such investigation that such differences can not be equalized by proceeding as hereinbefore provided, it shall so state in its report to the President and shall specify therein such ad valorem rates of duty based upon the American selling price (as defined in section 402 (g)) of the domestic article, as it finds shown by the investigation to be necessary to equalize such differences. In no case shall the total decrease of such rates of duty exceed 50 per centum of the rates expressly fixed by statute, and no such rate shall be increased.

(c) Proclamation by the President. – The President shall by proclamation approve the rates of duty and changes in classification and in basis of value specified in any report of the commission under this section, if in his judgement such rates of duty and changes are shown by such investigation of the commission to be necessary to equalize such differences in costs of production.

---

85   The word 'commission' refers to the United States Tariff Commission which
      was composed of six members. Those six individuals were appointed by the
      President with the advice and consent of the Senate (ed.).

SEC. 337. Unfair Practices in Import Trade.

(a) Unfair Methods of Competition Declared Unlawful. – Unfair methods of competition and unfair acts in the importation of articles into the United States, or in their sale by the owner, importer, consignee, or agent of either, the effect or tendency of which is to destroy or substantially injure an industry, efficiently and economically operated, in the United States, or to prevent the establishment of such an industry, or to restrain or monopolize trade and commerce in the United States, are hereby declared unlawful, and when found by the President to exist shall be dealt with, in addition to any other provisions of law, as hereinafter provided.
(b) Investigation of Violations by Commission. – To assist the President in making any decisions under this section the commission is hereby authorized to investigate any alleged violation hereof on complaint under oath or upon its initiative.
......
(d) Transmission of Findings to President. – The final findings of the commission shall be transmitted with the record to the president.
(e) Exclusion of Articles from Entry. – Whenever the existence of any such unfair method or act shall be established to the satisfaction of the President he shall direct that the articles concerned in such unfair methods or acts, imported by any person violating the provisions of this Act, shall be excluded from entry into the United States, and upon information of such action by the President, the Secretary of the Treasury shall, through the proper officers, refuse such entry. The decision of the President shall be conclusive.

SEC. 338. Discrimination by Foreign Countries.

(a) Additional Duties. – The President when he finds that the public interest will be served thereby shall by proclamation specify and declare new or additional duties as hereinafter provided upon articles wholly or in part the growth or product of, or imported in a vessel of, any foreign country whenever he shall find as a fact that such country:

(1)   Imposes, directly or indirectly, upon the disposition in or transportation in transit through or reexportation from such country of any article wholly or in part the growth or product of the United States any unreasonable charge, exaction, regulation, or limitation which is not equally enforced upon the like articles of every foreign country; or

(2)　　　　　Discrimination in fact against the commerce of the United States, directly or indirectly, by law or administrative regulation or practice, by or in respect to any customs, tonnage, or port duty, fee, charge, exaction, classification, regulation, condition, restriction, or prohibition, in such a manner as to place the commerce of the United States at a disadvantage compared with the commerce of any foreign country.

(b) Exclusion from Importation. – If at any time the President shall find it to be a fact that any foreign country has not only discriminated against the commerce of the United States, as aforesaid, but has, after the issuance of a proclamation as authorized in subdivision (a) of this section, maintained or increased its said discriminations against the commerce of the United States, the President is hereby authorized, if he deems it consistent with the interests of the United States, to issue a further proclamation directing that such products of said country or such articles imported in its vessels as he shall deem consistent with the public interests shall be excluded from importation into the United States.

(c) Application of Proclamation. – Any proclamation issued by the President under the authority of this section shall, if he deems it consistent with the interests of the United States, extend to the whole of any foreign country or may be confined to any subdivision or subdivisions thereof; and the President shall, whenever he deems the public interests require, suspend, revoke, supplement, or amend any such proclamation.

(d) Duties to Offset Commercial Disadvantages. – Whenever the President shall find as a fact that any foreign country places any burden or disadvantage upon the commerce of the United States by any of the unequal impositions or discriminations aforesaid, he shall, when he finds that the public interest will be served thereby, by proclamation specify and declare such new or additional rate or rates of duty as he shall determine will offset such burden or disadvantage, not to exceed 50 per centum ad valorem or its equivalent, on any products of, or on articles imported in a vessel of, such foreign country; and thirty days after the date of such proclamation there shall be levied, collected, and paid upon the articles enumerated in such a proclamation when imported into the United States from such foreign country such new or additional rate or rates of duty; or, in the case of articles declared subject to exclusion from importation into the United States under the provisions of (b) of this section, such articles shall be excluded from importation.

6. The Economics of Free Trade during the Second Half of the Twentieth Century

PREAMBLE

1

Physical destruction was one of the most obvious consequences of World War II. In Europe, undermaintenance of plant and uneven economic investment added to this region's difficulties. Agricultural land had often been overcropped or neglected while the cattle stock had become exhausted. Europe's economic condition had been made worse by heavy public debts, inflation, and a complete breakdown of the system of multilateral trade and payments. Moreover, countries like England had accumulated new debts abroad. The situation in Japan resembled that of Europe. As a result economic and social disorganization, turmoil and agitation often prevailed.

The United States and Canada, on the other hand, witnessed the expansion of their basic industries, including agriculture. Their industries had not suffered and had benefited from the war-related demand which facilitated full employment, technological modernization, and expansion. Thus at the end of the war the United States (and to a lesser extent Canada) had the productive capacity to supply the items which the world was demanding.

As the United States emerged from the war as the strongest and economically the most important nation, it also had overwhelming bargaining power.

The interwar period had witnessed the collapse of the international payments and trade system which was not altogether unrelated to America's refusal to play its proper role in international relations. During and after the Second World War however, the United States government was determined not to withdraw into isolation but instead to take the lead in establishing a liberal, multilateral, non-discriminatory trading system. International cooperation was to be the keystone of the new order.

Global conflict inspired the Allies (principally the United States and Britain), to design the post-war international economic order from scratch. The architects of the new system believed that they had learned the lessons of the interwar period. Reconstruction and integration were now paramount. In 1944, the representatives of the Allies met at Bretton Woods, New Hampshire, to create the post-war monetary system based upon the plans of Harry Dexter White (US) and John Maynard Keynes (UK). The overwhelming bargaining power of the United States ensured that the new institution resembled the American plan rather than the British. Two basic new institutions emerged as a result of the Bretton Woods conference. The first agency, the International Monetary Fund (IMF) came to life in 1947 with a capital of \$8.8 billion.[86] It was basically an international currency pool from which members might be allowed to borrow in order to correct temporary deficiencies in their balance of payments. The fund also had to supervise the existing system of fixed exchange rates. The IMF system involved an exchange rate regime that pegged national currencies to gold or to the dollar (which was itself pegged to gold). Adjustments in exchange rates were allowed, but if inevitable, they had to be orderly and public spirited. While the Fund was to assist countries with short-term problems, the second basic institution, the International Bank of Reconstruction and Development, was to supply long-term credit for reconstruction and development purposes. Thus, the World Bank, as the institution was often called, was mainly concerned with long-term investment for productive purposes.

The participants at the Bretton Woods conference were also interested in the creation of an International Trade Organization (ITO) which should establish and supervise the rules for a relatively free international trade system. In line with this thinking, several states proposed an ITO, but the organization never materialized. However, in 1947 twenty-three nations met in Geneva and signed an agreement (1948) in which governments pledged to work for the elimination of discriminatory practices and the reduction of tariffs and other trade barriers. This General Agreement on Tariffs and Trade (GATT) was quickly converted into an organization with an office in Geneva where regular meetings of the dignitaries were planned. In the 1947 agreement the participants decided:

---

86 For more details see: R. Solomon, *The International Monetary System 1945–1981* (New York: Harper & Row, 1982).

1. To do away with discriminatory practices and to apply the most favored nations clause to all member states.
2. To abolish quantitative restrictions and not to adopt new ones.
3. To attempt to reduce tariffs.
4. To consult other members of the agreement before making some drastic policy change.

So far (1998), eight rounds of multilateral trade negotiations under GATT, have taken place.

The new international organizations especially the IMF, the GATT, and the World Bank had their inevitable shortcomings, and without strong American support they might not have survived. Fortunately, in 1945, and after, Uncle Sam no longer behaved like Uncle Shylock as had been the case after 1918. Instead, during and after World War II, the United States provided generous help which culminated in the Marshall Plan of 1948, named after the American Secretary of State, George Marshall, who proposed it in 1947.

From the American point of view, the plan would promote free multilateral trade because it would pour scarce dollars into the trade system. The plan would also speed up recovery and reduce the pull of the Soviet Union and its imperialist policies. Between 1948 and 1952, some $13 billion was made available to European nations. Central and Eastern European nations did not participate. They were governed by puppet communist governments and were increasingly dragged into the orbit of the Soviet Union. There is no doubt that the Marshall Plan was an act of great generosity and extraordinary vision.[87] The Plan also provided for the creation of an Organization of European Economic Cooperation (OEEC) with headquarters in Paris. It served as a clearing house for the Marshall Aid. At the same time the members of the organization were supposed to gradually eliminate trade quotas, and the institution also was assumed to promote economic consultation and collaboration. Originally membership consisted of the 16 European recipients of Marshall Aid. West Germany and Spain joined later. In 1960, The United States, Canada, and Japan took up membership and the name of the organization was changed to Organization for Economic Cooperation and Development (OECD). Originally, the new organization was supposed to liberalize

---

87   Japan's equivalent of the Marshall Plan was called the Dodge Plan (1949) which worked in a similar way.

the international mobility of the production factors; labor, entrepreneurship, and capital. In the end, it became more of a consultative body and a useful medium for the discussion and coordination of matters of common concern in economic and social policy.

In 1950, a new intra-European institution consisting of the OEEC countries was established with an American contribution of $500 million. The organization helped to promote free multilateral trade within the OEEC. The so-called European Payments Union (EPU) provided member nations with a clearing house for settling mutual financial claims resulting from current trade. Up to the limit of a quota a debit nation could pay its debts to the EPU in its own money. Beyond that quota, it had to pay in gold or dollars. Credit countries got a credit from the Union and received the rest in gold or dollars. The EPU was a success. In eight years the Union settled about $46 billion of transactions with a working capital of only $350 million.

Via the Marshall Plan, the OEEC, and the EPU, the United States had (indirectly) encouraged regional European integration. Economic integration consists of uniting two or more separate economies into one economic unit. In 1946, Belgium, the Netherlands and Luxemburg had already formed a customs union which ultimately involved free trade amongst themselves with a common tariff schedule for outsiders. The union received the name of Benelux. In 1951 the European Coal and Steel Community was established. The idea was to produce a gradual removal of duties on coal and steel. Subsidies, restrictions and discriminatory devices also had to be eliminated under the guidance of a supranational authority. The Benelux countries, France, West Germany and Italy, participated.

Progressively there developed a movement towards European economic integration. One reason behind this was the realization of the catastrophic implications of large scale wars and the importance of preventing another conflict. If Europe were to operate as an economic unit, political rivalries and tensions would be sharply reduced or even eliminated. Thus in 1957, six countries – France, West Germany, Italy, Belgium, the Netherlands and Luxembourg – signed the Treaty of Rome establishing the European Economic Community (EEC or EC) which provided for the gradual abolition of trade barriers, the free movement of labor, services and capital and the harmonization of economic policies. This first phase was supposed to be followed by full economic association and eventually political integration. Other countries joined the club, and in 1992, the Treaty on European Union

(Treaty of Maastricht) was signed providing for a very high degree of political, economic and social integration.

All the American-led initiatives towards a liberal organization of world trade and regional organization turned out to have very positive results. At the same time a fundamental conflict between interventionist domestic policies and a free trade international order remained.

2

Once the European recovery was well in progress, the world began to witness about two decades (1950—1970) of unusually rapid economic growth. Between the late 1940s and the early 1970s, Western Europe, the United States and Japan saw their economies expand at high rates within the framework provided by the new trade order. National incomes rose fast while international economic contacts expanded even faster. The GATT rounds of multilateral trade negotiations encouraged substantial cuts in tariffs and other barriers to trade although agricultural products did not share in this successful liberation of commerce.

Judged by the increase in trade and incomes, the new open-minded trade order was an enormous success. Besides freer trade and the new spirit of international cooperation, many other factors contributed to the increase in prosperity such as:

1. The catching up factor. The stagnation resulting from the Great Depression and the World War had created extra opportunities for growth. On the demand side, many wants had remained unsatisfied, creating a belated urge to acquire commodities. On the supply side, there was much potential for making up lost ground in the area of technology. After the war Western Europe and Japan were technologically backward compared with the United States, creating many opportunities for profitable investment.
2. The education factor. Education and training systems were often reorganized and upgraded with the aim to improve the quality of the labor force and to offer more equal chances to all. Productivity improved as a result.
3. The labor factor. Western Europe especially, benefited from large supplies of labor which ensured that wages lagged behind prices. This allowed the member nations to remain competitive

in the world market. The supply of labor force mainly came from workers moving out of agriculture, refugees from Central and Eastern Europe, immigrants from the poorer areas of Southern Europe, and from the increasing participation of women in the labor force.

Although the industrial countries showed great strength, many primary product producing countries also enjoyed considerable expansion. Even the countries of the Soviet bloc experienced good growth at times. Within the Eastern bloc, intra-bloc trade developed rapidly and came to dominate the trade of its members.

3

Even if the 1950–1970 period was a period of increasing prosperity, it was also one of rising inflation. Most Western governments were committed to full employment or near full employment which in a conventional Keynesian approach had to be achieved through expanding aggregate demand. When in 1961 John F. Kennedy became President of the United States, he became quickly committed to a policy of fiscal expansionism. Even if the Bretton Woods arrangement worked rather satisfactorily in the 1950s and 1960s, the system had a serious flaw. Under the arrangement, national currencies were tied to the dollar while the dollar itself was convertible to gold at $35 an ounce. Non-American governments or their central banks had the obligation to maintain the exchange rate between their currency and the dollar by buying and selling operations. One problem with the Bretton Woods arrangement was that the system did not impose any kind of fiscal and monetary discipline on the United States and its center currency, the dollar. The rising tide of American inflation slowly but surely lifted the system's anchor off the bottom. The $35 an ounce price of gold became increasingly unrealistic. Between 1957 and 1971, US liquid liabilities to foreigners rose from $13.6 billion to $62.2 billion while the American gold stock fell from $22.9 billion to $10.2 billion. Thus, central bankers lost confidence in the ability of the United States to convert dollars into gold at $35 an ounce. When under President L.B. Johnson the United States tried to combine the financing of a war in Vietnam with greatly increased social expenditures, speculation on the overvalued dollar became such that in 1971 his successor, President Nixon, announced measures which in fact suspended the convertibility of the dollar at $35 an ounce.

After 3 years of hesitation, the main trade partners of the US announced that they would no longer peg their currencies. The Bretton Woods system had collapsed and the era of floating exchange rates had begun. Fixed exchange rates, relatively free trade and expansionary welfare state types of fiscal and monetary policies contradicted each other. Domestic economic nationalism cannot easily be combined with free trade internationalism.

The inflations of the 1970s led, in many countries, to relatively tight monetary policies designed to squeeze inflation out of the system. These policies combined with higher oil prices, higher taxes, and the inevitable negative incentives with regard to work, saving and investment implicit in the welfare state, resulted in a deceleration of growth rates and recession. The post-war boom was definitely over, and as always, when an economy experiences a period of quasi-stagnation, protectionism raises its head. The revival of protectionism, now characterized by the use of non-tariff trade barriers, started around 1974. Relatively freer trade survived nevertheless, one reason being that the GATT sponsored Tokyo Round of multilateral trade negotiations (1973-79) initiated by President Richard Nixon resulted in a tariff cut of 33 per cent, spread over a period of eight years.

4

Between 1973 and 1980 the US economy, still the world's most powerful economy, experienced stagflation, a term which refers to the simultaneous occurrence of economic stagnation and relatively rapid inflation. When president Ronald Reagan came into office in 1981, he proposed a package of policies called 'supply side economics.' The plan was based on personal income tax reductions, diminutions in business taxes, curtailments in nondefense government spending and reductions in government regulation.

The Federal Reserve, in the mean time, applied strict monetary policies to combat an inflation rate of about 10 per cent. While inflation fell to about 4 per cent in 1982, the economy experienced a sharp recession in 1981-82. Yet, a long recovery started in the winter of 1982-83 which lasted until 1989 and which also benefited other countries. However, the long expansion of the economy was accompanied by serious strains such as frictions in world trade, large budget deficits in the US (and other countries) and a build-up of American household and corporate debt. In the 1990-91 period, under the Bush administration, the US economy began to sputter because in

1990 another recession had started. Although this reversal of economic activity was a rather mild one it lingered on which helped Bill Clinton to defeat George Bush and become President of the United States. The recovery in the US started late in 1991 but it was too weak to be widely noticed. Only in 1993 did the improvement solidify. For the US, the years 1994 and 1995 were years of sustained expansion.

Other industrial countries did not fare very well in the period 1991–93 and operated below their capacities. This situation affected US exports negatively. However, in 1994, things began to turn around and in 1995 the international outlook seemed brighter than it had for years. It may be said to be surprising that in spite of the international recession of the early 1990s the North American Free Trade Agreement and the Uruguay Round negotiations fared so well. Often enough, global recessions with increased unemployment, undermine confidence in free trade ideas and measures.

In July 1994 both the International Monetary Fund and the World Bank celebrated their half-century birthday. Clearly some of the tasks they were originally set up to perform were no longer needed in 1994. As we saw earlier, the architects of the Bretton Woods system aimed at post World War II economic reconstruction and integration and wanted to foster, through international trade, the kind of international symmetrization which existed during the 1860–1914 period. The cornerstone was a system of fixed exchange rates which the IMF had to supervise. At the same time this institution had to supply short-term credit to countries with balance of payments problems. The World Bank was to promote economic reconstruction and development with the help of long-term credit. The disappearance in 1971 of the fixed-exchange rate system deprived the IMF of an important role. Also the growth of private capital markets had reduced countries' dependence on the funds of both the IMF and the World Bank.

However, at present the Fund still has a responsibility to see that the economic policies of its members take into account their international effects. Nations should still collaborate and promote relatively stable exchange rates and orderly exchange arrangements. The Fund also found a new role in helping the countries of Central and Eastern Europe including Russia. It is only proper that the IMF should now (1996) assist the weak governments of those countries with advice and loans combined with insistence on appropriate economic reforms.

The World Bank should perhaps concentrate more on the very

poorest nations such as those located on the African continent. The not so poor countries can rely on the world capital markets which now function in an orderly manner. Next to long-term loans for development purposes the World Bank could provide the borrowers with the kind of analysis and judgement which commercial banks cannot give. The Bank may even consider furnishing more training facilities for government officials and other key employees in order to improve economic management at the micro and macro levels. With its rich operational experience and knowledge and its high-grade research facilities the bank has much to offer in this area.

Economic integration is the process of uniting two or more separate economies into a closer economic union that each has with the rest of the world. The European Community (EC) which started its career in 1957–58 is the most famous example of a common market and is now moving towards economic union which is the highest degree of economic integration. In the so-called Maastricht Treaty of 1991 the members of the European Community agreed to envisage a common currency and a European Central Bank overseeing a single monetary policy. Progress toward this economic and monetary union would take place in stages.

During the late 1980s and the early 1990s the growth of regionalism in Western Europe made some American policy makers fear that barriers against US exports could be erected. Some form of economic integration was also perceived as contributing to political and economic stability and democracy in neighboring countries. As far as a number of American legislators and publicists were concerned, this applied especially to Mexico. Also, if this country could become more prosperous, mature and stable, immigration into the US would slow down. All such thoughts led to the idea of creating a North American Free Trade Agreement (NAFTA) which would include the United States, Canada and Mexico. Thus after a period of negotiations, the NAFTA came into existence and was ratified by Congress in November 1993. The arrangement went into effect on January 1, 1994. Over a period of fifteen years a large free trade zone would be created containing some 360 million consumers. In free trade areas member countries remove trade barriers among themselves but continue to levy their own tariffs for non-member countries. Free traders generally favored the NAFTA. The anti-NAFTA coalition in the United States consisted mainly of organized labor, populists, protectionists, environmentalist and consumer groups. If NAFTA had been defeated in the US the anti-NAFTA coalition would almost certainly not have stopped there. They might have tried to torpedo the then ongoing GATT negotiations (Uruguay Round) followed by the building of a protectionist wall around the United States. As was to be expected, a year after the NAFTA endorsement by Congress, new jobs had already been created in both the US and Mexico while American investment in Mexico remained approximately at levels experienced in earlier years. In December 1994, American, Canadian and Mexican leaders announced their intention to welcome Chile as the next member of NAFTA. In so far as economic integration eliminates trade barriers and liberates commerce, the endorsement of NAFTA must be considered a victory for those who believe in free trade and harmony.

In December 1993, the eighth round of GATT negotiations was completed after seven years of bargaining. The negotiators of 117 nations were successful in bringing about a broad-ranging multilateral trade liberalization. At the same time a new organization, the World Trade Organization (WTO), was created to administer the latest as well as earlier agreements. The official signing of the pact took place on April 15, 1994 in Marakesh, Morocco. The conclusion of the Uruguay Round should be seen as a victory for free traders even if the pact is not perfect from the free trade viewpoint. Failure to complete the Round successfully would have undermined business confidence in the world and might have provoked the erosion of the open trading system. Key provisions of the new trade agreement include the following:

(a) Remaining manufacturing tariffs are cut by another 30 per cent.
(b) Quantitative limits on manufactured imports, including textiles and apparel, are prohibited. The same applies to voluntary import restraints.
(c) The Multi-Fiber Arrangement will disappear within a period of ten years.
(d) Farm subsidies in industrialized countries will be trimmed and agricultural import quotas will be converted to tariffs which themselves will be reduced over time.
(e) New global rules are established for services which include banking, insurance, high-tech consulting etc.
(f) Intellectual property rights such as patents, copyrights, trade marks and trade secrets are now governed by a new international code and are better protected.
(g) The new arrangement will standardize the methodology different

countries use to conduct investigation of dumping.

(h)   There will be tighter rules on the settlement of disputes.

The early architects of the post-war trade order had designed a comprehensive international organization: the International Trade Organization (ITO). This organization involved a set of rules of conduct with regard to international trade as well as an organization to interpret and enforce those rules. However this organization failed to come into existence as we saw earlier.

The Uruguay Round also created a new organization called the World Trade Organization (WTO), to replace the 46-year-old GATT. Policy makers had recognized that GATT needed a stronger institutional standing so the creation of a new association became an important objective of the Uruguay Round. The WTO charter provides legal authority for a Director General, a secretariat and a staff. The highest body is a Ministerial Conference to be held every other year. The WTO charter also includes a strengthened and unified dispute settlement mechanism which will be more automatic. Although the WTO will not be a United Nations organization, it is expected to be an institution of stature equal to the IMF and the World Bank.

The new pact is really an agreement for the twenty-first century in which trade barriers will be low and in which transportation and communication will be cheap. The exports of emerging economies will rise and protectionists in the older industrialized countries will again be alarmed. They will conveniently forget that increased exports give developing countries more money to spend on imports from the relatively rich countries. When trading partners become wealthier, high benefits are possible as long as economic linkages are not disrupted. The relatively rich countries, moreover, tend to import cheap labor intensive products, which raises real incomes in those countries. Besides, the fast growing emerging economies will offer savers in the older industrialized nations relatively high returns on their overseas investments.

The overall effect of the growth of third world economies as well as those of Central and Eastern Europe is likely to be beneficial. Wages in the rich world are not necessarily threatened by cheap third world labor. As always high wages are justified by high productivity. As long as the older mature economies can maintain high standards of education, good management and superior infrastructure they will be able to maintain and improve their living standards and enjoy the benefits of free trade at the same time.

READING 24

Henry Hazlitt

Biography

Henry Hazlitt (1894–1993) was born in Philadelphia in 1894. His father died soon after his birth and there was not much money in the family. After attending high school he went to City College in New York which he could not afford to finish. He started his career in 1913 as a reporter for the *Wall Street Journal*. During World War I he served in the Army Air Service.

After the war he worked for a number of newspapers including the *New York Evening Post* and the *New York Sun*. He developed a great capacity to study on his own and between 1930 and 1933 he became the literary editor of *The Nation* in which he criticized Roosevelt's New Deal. In 1934 he joined the *New York Times* where he wrote most of the economic and financial editorials. Hazlitt met Ludwig von Mises when he came to the United States and the two quickly became friends. Together they defended the gold standard as a viable policy. From 1946 to 1966 he was in charge of the 'Business Tides' column for *Newsweek*. Thereafter he became syndicated columnist for the *Los Angeles Times* syndicate. Both Grove City College in Pennsylvania and Bethany College in West Virginia awarded him an honorary Doctoral degree. During his later years he was also a Distinguished Advisor to the Ludwig von Mises Institute. At the age of 98 his pen fell silent.

The Work

Hazlitt wrote 18 books but he achieved lasting fame with his *Economics in One Lesson* first published in 1946. The book deals mainly with the economic fallacies which have become so current since 1945. The book was revised twice, in 1962 and 1978. It has sold over a million copies but as Hazlitt himself states in a postscript: 'politicians did not learn much from it.' International trade issues are discussed in Chapters XI and XII.

In an article written in 1969 for the *National Review* (May 20), Hazlitt examines some aspects of the new protectionism of the late 1960s. There the author also touches upon a theme later developed by Melvin Krauss in his book *The New Protectionism, The Welfare State and International Trade.* Krauss develops the point that the welfare state by weakening the economy may lead to protectionism.[88]

Hazlitt explains that many nations are affected by a pathological dread of imports combined with an unhealthy yearning for exports. People who can be reasonable and sensible when it comes to domestic trade can be incredibly muddleheaded when foreign trade is the issue, says Hazlitt. Imports and exports evolve together and more of the one leads to more of the other. If an American exporter sells goods (or services) to a British firm and is paid in British pounds he may use those pounds to buy British commodities. If he sells the pounds (through his bank or a dealer) to an American importer who wants to use them to buy British items the result is the same: exports are paid for by imports and vice versa. If the transaction had been conducted in terms of American dollars the outcome would not have been different. The British importer would not have been able to conclude the deal unless some earlier British exporter had built up a credit in dollars as a result of a previous export to the US.

As an example of confused thinking Hazlitt cites the example of making loans to the countries to stimulate exports regardless of whether these loans are repaid or not. However, if loans enabling foreigners to buy from a given country are not or partially repaid then the lending nation is giving goods away. A nation cannot get richer by parting with goods without compensation. It merely impoverishes itself.

Export subsidies are in the same category of false stimulations to export trade. What export subsidies really mean is that goods are sold by the exporter for less than what it costs to produce them. The taxpayer pays the difference.

Still others favor foreign aid as a means to promote exports, employment and incomes. Individual exporters may gain by such policies but the nation and its taxpayers must lose.

In the *National Review* article of 1969 Hazlitt examines some aspects of the new protectionism of the late 1960s. Although during such GATT rounds as the Kennedy Round tariffs were cut, nearly all countries looked for loopholes. And thus the non-tariff barriers emerged stronger than ever. What lies behind this new protectionism? According to Hazlitt the answer is that welfare-state policies lead to

---

88   H. Hazlitt, *Economics in One Lesson* (New York: Crown Publishers, 1979).
      H. Hazlitt, 'The New Protectionism', *National Review* (May 20, 1969).

high levels of government spending, budget deficits and the issuance of more paper money. The inflationary expansion of the money supply combined with fixed exchange rates (the article was written in 1969) leads necessarily to balance-of-payments deficits especially when countries are inflating at different rates. The next stage is that countries will try to eliminate their balance-of-payments deficits by protectionist measures and direct controls over selected items such as investing abroad or travel. The real remedy says Hazlitt lies in the abandoning of the welfare state and the inflationary policies that led to the new protectionism.

READING 25

Gottfried Haberler

Biography

Gottfried Haberler (1900–1995) was born on July 20, 1900 in Purkersdorf near Vienna, Austria. He studied economics at the University of Vienna under Friedrich von Wieser and Ludwig von Mises. Haberler received his doctorate in law in 1923 and in economics in 1925. A two year stay (1927–1929) in England and the United States as a Fellow of the Rockefeller Foundation permitted him to study at the University of London and Harvard University. Upon his return to Austria he became lecturer and later Professor of Economics and Statistics at the University of Vienna (1928–1936, with interruptions).

In 1931 he married Friederike Kaan. Between 1934 and 1936 he was employed as an economic expert at the financial section of the League of Nations, Geneva, Switzerland. He was appointed Professor of Economics (1936) and later Galen L. Stone Professor of International Trade at Harvard University where he remained until his retirement in 1971. After that he was for many years a resident scholar at the American Enterprise Institute for Public Policy Research, a well-known think-tank in Washington, DC. In 1963 he was President of the American Economic Association.

Haberler was one of the great figures of international economics in the twentieth century. In a paper published in 1930 ('The Theory of Comparative Costs and its Use in the Defense of Free Trade') Haberler played a crucial role in the construction of the modern theory of international trade. He reformulated the Ricardian laws of comparative advantage on the basis of opportunity costs rather than labor value. The problems he discussed in this paper were further developed in his book *The Theory of International Trade* which first appeared in German in 1933. Haberler made his international reputation with his volume *Prosperity and Depression* first published in 1937. The fourth and last revision appeared in 1964. The book, which has become a classic, critically analyzed and synthesized numerous trade cycle theories.

In the 1960s Haberler became convinced that the Bretton Woods system of fixed exchange rates should be replaced by a system of freely fluctuating exchange rates. Other economists such as Milton Friedman and Fritz Machlup agreed. In fact, in the 1970s the world did abandon the Bretton Woods system as it was conceived in 1944. Throughout his career Gottfried Haberler has maintained his faith in the superiority of classical liberal economic policies. He has always believed in competitive markets, private enterprise, free trade and minimal government interference in the economy. Clearly, these views have not always been in fashion especially in the 1930s and the post-World War II period.

The Work

In the first reading taken from the Cairo lectures delivered in Egypt (1959), Haberler discusses the contributions which international trade can make to the economic development of low-income countries. The second short piece is taken from an introduction by Haberler to a 1988 reprint of the Cairo lectures and the Pioneers lecture (1987). It briefly discusses the so-called 'Prebisch belief' in the secular tendency of the terms of trade to deteriorate for the food and raw materials producing less developed countries (see also section on twentieth century protectionist writers in this book). The last reading has been borrowed from a paper entitled 'Liberal and Illiberal Trade Policy: The Messy World of the Second Best' (1988). It discusses the extent to which world trade is again subject to quantitative restrictions.[89]

---

89   G. Haberler, *International Trade and Economic Development* (San Francisco: International Center for Economic Growth, 1988) pp. 7-8, 21-31.
G. Haberler, 'Liberal and Illiberal Trade Policy: The Messy World of the Second Best', *The Quest for National and Global Economic Stability* (W. Eizenga et al, eds) (Dordrecht: Kluwer Academic Publishers, 1988) pp. 56-58.

Extracts

Trade and Development

I shall now positively and systematically state what I think the contribution of international trade to economic development was in the past and what it can be in the future. My overall conclusion is that international trade has made a tremendous contribution to the development of less developed countries in the 19th and 20th centuries and can be expected to make an equally big contribution in the future, if it is allowed to proceed freely. It does not necessarily follow that a 100 per cent free trade policy is always most conducive to most rapid development. Marginal interferences with the free flow of trade, if properly selected, may speed up development. But I do not want to leave any doubt that my conclusion is that substantially free trade with marginal, insubstantial corrections and deviations, is the best policy from the point of view of economic development. Drastic deviations from free trade can be justified, on development grounds – and this is very nearly the same thing as to say on economic grounds – only if and when they are needed to compensate for the adverse influence of other policies inimical to economic development, for example, the consequences of persistent inflation or of certain tax and domestic price support policies. Let me guard against a possible misunderstanding. If I say that drastic interferences with the market mechanism are not needed for rapid development, I refer to trade policy and I do not deny that drastic measures in other areas, let me say, land reform, education, forced investment (if the projects are well chosen), etc. may not speed up growth. But I shall in these lectures not further elaborate on those matters.

I shall make use of the so-called classical theory of international trade in its neoclassical form associated with the names of Jacob Viner, James Meade, and Bertil Ohlin, to mention only a few. I shall not try to modernize the theory more than, say, Ohlin and Meade have done, although I shall make an attempt to spell out in some detail the implications of classical trade theory for economic development, an aspect which has perhaps been somewhat neglected. On the other hand, I shall, of course, avoid using the caricature of the theory which is often presented as a portrait by its critics.

Later I shall then take up in detail objections to the orthodox conclusions and shall consider alternative or rival theories put forward by the critics of the orthodox theory.

Let us then start with first things first. International division of labor and international trade, which enable every country to specialize and to export those things that it can produce cheaper in exchange for what others can provide at a lower cost, have been and still are one of the basic factors promoting economic well-being and increasing national income of every participating country. Moreover, what is good for the national income and the standard of living is, at least potentially, also good for economic development; for the greater the volume of output the greater can be the rate of growth – provided the people individually or collectively have the urge to save and to invest and economically to develop. The higher the level of output, the easier it is to escape the 'vicious circle of poverty' and to 'take off into self-sustained growth' to use the jargon of modern development theory. Hence, if trade raises the level of income, it also promotes economic development.

All this holds for highly developed countries as well as for less developed ones. Let us not forget that countries in the former category, too, develop and grow, some of them – not all – even faster than some – not all – in the second category.

In most underdeveloped countries international trade plays quantitatively an especially important role – that is, a larger percentage of their income is spent on imports, and a larger percentage of their output is being exported, than in the case of developed countries of comparable economic size. (Other things being equal, it is natural that the 'larger', economically speaking, a country, the smaller its trade percentages.) Many underdeveloped countries are highly specialized also in the sense that a very large percentage of their exports consists of one or two staple commodities. I am sure that here in Egypt, which depends on cotton for more than 60 percent of its exports, I need not cite further examples for that.

This high concentration of exports is not without danger. One would normally not want to put so many of one's eggs into one basket. But the price of diversification is in most cases extremely high. I shall touch on that topic once more. At this point, let me simply say that a high level of concentrated trade will, in most cases, be much better than a low level of diversified trade. How much poorer would Brazil be without coffee, Venezuela, Iran and Iraq without oil, Bolivia without tin, Malaya without rubber and tin, Ghana without cocoa, and I dare say, Egypt without cotton. The really great danger of concentration arises in the case of deep and protracted slumps in the industrial countries – slumps of the order of magnitude of the Great Depression in the 1930s. In my opinion, and here I am sure the overwhelming majority of economists in the Western World agrees, the chance that this will happen again is practically nil.

The tremendous importance of trade for the underdeveloped countries (as well as for most developed ones, with the exception of the U.S. and the U.S.S.R., which could, if need be, give it up without suffering a catastrophic reduction in their living standard) follows from the classical theory of comparative cost in conjunction with the fact that the comparative differences in cost of production of industrial products and food and raw materials between developed countries and underdeveloped countries are obviously very great, in many cases, in fact, infinite in the sense that countries of either group just could not produce what they buy from the other.

The classical theory has been often criticized on the ground that it is static, that it presents only a timeless 'cross-section' view of comparative costs and fails to take into account dynamic elements that is, the facts of organic growth and development. Of modern writers, it was especially Professor J.H. Williams of Harvard and recently Gunnar Myrdal who have voiced this criticism of the classical doctrine and have demanded its replacement by a dynamic theory. This type of criticisms is, in fact, about as old as the classical theory itself. Williams mentions many earlier critics and especially the German writer Frederich List who more than anyone else in the 19th century has attacked the classical theory on exactly the same grounds, that is, for being 'unhistorically static', with the same vehemence and the same strange tone of bitterness and irritation as the modern writers.

Now it is true that the theory of comparative cost is static; it is also true that the economies of most countries are changing and developing and that the theory should take account of that fact. But it is not true that a static theory, because it is static, is debarred from saying anything useful about a changing and developing economic world. There is such a thing as 'comparative statics', that is, a method for dealing with a changing situation by means of a static theory. How much can be done by means of comparative statics (as distinguished from a truly dynamic theory) depends on the type of problem at hand. I contend that the problems of international division of labor and long-run development are such that the method of comparative statics can go a long way towards a satisfactory solution. That does not mean, however, that a dynamic theory would not be very useful. Unfortunately, not much of a truly dynamic theory is available at present. What the critics of the static nature of traditional theory have given us over and above their criticism and methodological pronouncements is very little indeed and thoroughly unsatisfactory. But a well known Burmese economist, H. Myint, has recently reminded us that the classical economists, especially Adam Smith and J.S. Mill, were by no means oblivious to the indirect, dynamic benefits which less developed countries in particular can derive from international trade. Going beyond the purely static theory of comparative cost, they have analyzed the 'indirect effects' of trade (as J.S. Mill calls them) and thereby presented us with at least the rudiments of a dynamic theory, which Myint aptly calls the 'productivity' theory of international trade. Let us then inquire how we can deal, by means of the theoretical tools on hand, with the problems of change and development. The tools on hand are the static theory of comparative cost and the semi-dynamic 'productivity' theory.

For our purposes I will distinguish two types of changes which constitute economic development – those that take place independently of international trade, and those that are induced by trade or trade policy.

As far as the first group – let me call them autonomous changes – is concerned, I can see no difficulty resulting from them for the applicability of the classical theory of comparative cost. Such changes are the gradual improvement in skill, education and training of workers, farmers, engineers, entrepreneurs; improvements resulting from inventions and discoveries and from the accumulation of capital – changes which in the Western World stem for the most part from the initiative of individuals and private associations, but possibly also from conscious Government policies.

These changes come gradually or in waves and result in gradually increasing output of commodities that have been produced before or in the setting up of production of goods that had not been produced earlier. Analytically, such development has to be pictured as an outward movement of the production possibility curve (often called substitution or transformation curve). Depending on the concrete turn that autonomous development (including improvements in transportation technology) takes, the comparative cost situation and hence volume and composition of trade will be more or less profoundly affected. But since these changes only come slowly and gradually and usually cannot be foreseen (either by private business or Government planners) in sufficient detail to make anticipatory action possible, there is no presumption that the allocative mechanism as described in the theory of comparative cost will not automatically and efficiently bring about the changes and adjustment in the volume and structure of trade called for by autonomous development.

I turn now to the second type of changes in the productive capabilities of a country which are more important for the purposes of my lectures, namely those induced by trade and changes in trade including changes in trade brought about by trade policy. Favorable as well as unfavorable trade-induced changes are possible and have to be considered. Alleged unfavorable trade-induced changes have received so much attention from protectionist writers from List to Myrdal (which has induced free trade economists, too, to discuss them at great length), that there is danger that the tremendously important favorable influences be unduly neglected. Let me, therefore, discuss the latter first.

If we were to estimate the contribution of international trade to economic development, especially of the underdeveloped countries, solely by the static gains from trade in any given year on the usual assumption of given production capabilities (analytically under the assumption of given production functions or given or autonomously shifting production possibility curves) we could indeed grossly understate the importance of trade. For over and above the direct static gains dwelt upon by the traditional theory of comparative cost, trade bestows very important indirect benefits, which also can be described as dynamic benefits, upon the participating countries. Let me emphasize once more that the older classical writers did stress these 'indirect benefits' (Mill's own words). Analytically we have to describe these 'indirect', 'dynamic' benefits from trade as an outward shift (in the northeast direction) of the production possibility curve brought about by a trade-induced movement along the curve.

First, trade provides material means (capital goods, machinery and raw and semifinished materials) indispensable for economic development. Secondly, even more important, trade is the means and vehicle for the dissemination of technological knowledge, the transmission of ideas, for the importation of know-how, skills, managerial talents and entrepreneurship. Thirdly, trade is also the vehicle for the international movement of capital especially from the developed to the underdeveloped countries. Fourthly, free international trade is the best anti-monopoly policy and the best guarantee for the maintenance of a healthy degree of free competition.

Let me now make a few explanatory remarks on each of these four points before I try to show how they fit into, and complement, the static theory of comparative advantage.

The first point is so obvious that it does not require much elaboration. Let us recall and remember, however, the tremendous benefits which the underdeveloped countries draw from technological progress in the developed countries through the importation of machinery, transport equipment, vehicles, power generation equipment, road building machinery, medicines, chemicals, and so on. The advantage is, of course, not all on one side. I stress the advantage derived by underdeveloped countries (rather than the equally important benefits for the developed countries) because I am concerned in these lectures primarily with the development of the less developed countries.

The composition of the export trade of the developed industrial countries has been changing, as we all know, in the direction of the types of capital goods which I have mentioned away from textiles and other light consumer goods. This shift has been going on for a long time; it is not a recent phenomenon. But it has proceeded rapidly in recent years, and there is no reason to doubt that it will continue.

Secondly, probably even more important than the importation of material goods is the importation of technical know-how, skills, managerial talents, entrepreneurship. This is, of course, especially important for the underdeveloped countries. But the developed countries too benefit greatly from cross-fertilization aided by trade among themselves and the less advanced industrial countries can profit from the superior technical and managerial know-how, etc., of the more advanced ones.

The latecomers and successors in the process of development and industrialization have always had the great advantage that they could learn from the experiences, from the successes as well as from the failures and mistakes of the pioneers and forerunners. In the late nineteenth century the continental European countries and the U.S. profited greatly from the technological innovation and achievements of the industrial revolution in Great Britain. Later the Japanese proved to be very adept learners and Soviet Russia has shown herself capable of speeding up her own development by 'borrowing' (interest free) immense amounts of technological know-how from the West, developing it further and adopting it for her own purposes. This 'trade' has been entirely one-sided. I know of not a single industrial idea or invention which the West has obtained from the East. Today the underdeveloped countries have a tremendous, constantly growing, store of technological know-how to draw from. True, simple adoption of methods developed for the conditions of the developed countries is often not possible. But adaptation is surely much easier than first creation.

Trade is the most important vehicle for the transmission of technological know-how. True, it is not the only one. In fact this function of trade is probably somewhat less important now than it was a hundred years ago,because ideas, skills, know-how, travel are easier and quicker and cheaper today than in the nineteenth century. The market where engineering and management experts can be hired is much better organized than formerly. There is much more competition in this field as well as in the area of material capital equipment. In the early nineteenth century Great Britain was the only center from which industrial equipment and know-how could be obtained, and there were all sorts of restrictions on the exportation of both. Today there are a dozen industrial centers in Europe, the US, Canada, and Japan, and even Russia and Czechoslovakia, all ready to sell machinery as well as engineering advice and know-how.

However, trade is still the most important transmission belt. What J.S. Mill said 100 years ago is still substantially true: 'It is hardly possible to overrate the value in the present low state of human improvement, of placing human beings in contact with persons dissimilar to themselves, and with modes of thought and action unlike those with which they are familiar ... Such communication has always been, peculiarly in the present age one of the primary sources of progress.'

The third indirect benefit of trade which I mentioned was that it also serves as a transmission belt for capital. It is true that the amount of capital that an underdeveloped country can obtain from abroad depends in the first place on the ability and the willingness of developed countries to lend, which is of course decisively influenced by the internal policies in the borrowing countries. But it stands to reason – and this is the only point I wanted to make at this juncture – that, other things being equal, the larger the volume of trade, the greater will be the volume of foreign capital that can be expected to become available under realistic assumptions. The reason is that with a large volume of trade the transfer of interest and repayments on principle is more easily effected than with a small volume of trade; and it would be clearly unrealistic to expect large capital movements if the chance for transfer of interests and repayments is not good. There is, furthermore, the related fact that it is much easier to get foreign capital for export industries with their built-in solution of the retransfer problem than for other types of investments which do not directly and automatically improve the balance of payments. This preference of foreign capital for export industries is regrettable because other types of investment (such as investment in public utilities, railroads, manufacturing industries) may often (not always) be more productive and may make a greater indirect contribution, dollar per dollar, to economic development by providing training to native personnel and in various other ways than export industries which sometimes (by no means always) constitute foreign enclaves in native soil. If the direct and indirect contribution of non-export industries to national income and economic development are in fact greater than those of the export industry, they should be preferred, because their indirect contribution to the balance of payments position will then also be such as to guarantee the possibility of smooth retransfer of principle and interest – *provided* inflationary monetary policies do not upset equilibrium entailing exchange control that then gets in the way of the transfer. But with inflationary monetary policies and exchange control practices as they are in most underdeveloped countries, the preference of foreign capital for export industries is readily understandable and must be reckoned with and foreign capital in export is better than no foreign capital at all.

The fourth way in which trade benefits a country indirectly is by fostering healthy competition and keeping in check inefficient monopolies. The reason why the American economy is more competitive – and often more efficient – than most others is probably to be sought more in the great internal free trade area which the U.S. enjoys rather than in the anti-monopoly policy which was always much more popular in the US than in Europe or anywhere else. The importance of this factor is confirmed by the fact that many experts believe that the main economic advantages of the European Common Market, towards the realization of which the first steps have just been taken, will flow from freer competition rather than merely from the larger size and larger scale production which it entails.

Increased competition is important also for underdeveloped countries, especially inasmuch as the size of their market is usually small (even if the geographic area is large). A reservation has nevertheless to be made. The first introduction of new industries on infant industry grounds may justify the creation of monopolistic positions, depending on the size of the country and the type of industry. But the problem will always remain how to prevent the permanent establishment of inefficient exploitative monopolies even after an industry has taken root and has become able to hold its ground without the crutches of import restrictions.

The general conclusion, then, is that international trade, in addition to the static gains resulting from the division of labor with given (or autonomously changing) production functions, powerfully contributes, in the four ways indicated, to the development of the productive capabilities of the less developed countries. Analytically, we have to express that, in the framework of modern trade theory, by saying that trade gradually transforms existing production functions; in other words, that a movement along the production possibility curves in accordance with the pre-existing comparative cost situation, will tend to push up and out the production possibility curve.

I have stated my conclusions rather boldly and uncompromisingly. Some qualifications and reservations are obviously called for, because trade may have also unfavorable indirect (or direct) effects. But I shall discuss these exceptions and qualifications after I have discussed and considered opposing views.

......

I now discuss three important theories which assert that foreign trade often has a negative effect on the economies of the LDCs. The most important one probably is the Prebisch–Singer theory of secular deterioration of the LDCs' terms of trade; it asserts that the prices of the LDCs' main exports, raw materials and foodstuffs – primary products for short – have a pronounced secular tendency to decline in relation to the prices of manufactured goods. This theory is largely the consequence of the misinterpretation of the Great Depression of the 1930s. It is true that during the depression commodity prices declined much more sharply than prices of manufactures. But later research has definitely shown that this was a cyclical decline, and that there has been no secular deterioration.

Prices of primary products exhibit, as a rule, sharper cyclical fluctuations than prices of manufactured products. That implies that the terms of trade of LDCs deteriorate in recessions. But it does not imply that the LDCs, the 'periphery' in Prebisch's terminology, suffer more in recessions than the industrial centers; the LDCs suffer from a deterioration of their terms of trade – the industrial countries from unemployment. I leave open the question of which is more painful.

......

To what extent world trade is subject to quantitative restrictions we can only guess, but as far as the United States is concerned two recent authoritative studies provide a depressing answer. According to the Bergsten study, in 1986 18.3 per cent of all US imports were covered by quantitative restrictions compared with 5.1 per cent in 1980. This retreat from liberalism occurred under an administration dedicated to reducing the role of government in the economy. What will happen when the Congress, swayed by special interests, passes the omnibus trade bill?

Eight major American industries are now protected by quantitative restrictions, automobiles, carbon steel, dairy products, machine tools, meat, specialty steel, sugar and textiles and apparel. Most American quantitative restrictions, not merely the restrictions on Japanese automobile imports, are administered by the exporting countries. The authors estimate that in 1984–85 this policy resulted in an annual 'transfer of $9 billion from the United States to other countries', at the expense of the US taxpayer. This policy goes under different names: 'voluntary export restraint' (for Japanese automobiles), 'voluntary restraint agreements', and 'orderly marketing arrangements' (OMAs).

All this is very sad, but the United States is by no means the worst offender of liberal principles. For one thing, the United States has no exchange control, which still can be found in quite a few industrial countries, France among them, not to mention scores of LDCs. Now consider US farm policy and agricultural protectionism, which are nothing to brag about. On the contrary, over the past thirty years or so while agricultural employment has shrunk from almost six per cent of the adult population to less than two per cent, spending by the Department of Agriculture per person employed in agriculture has ballooned from less than $2,000 to almost $18,000. Real income per person employed in agriculture has remained practically the same since 1954. This means that the bulk of the spending of the Department of Agriculture represents the cost of the huge bureaucracy needed to administer the policy and the cost of storing the huge surpluses of agricultural products the government acquires to support the prices above market clearing levels. Governments – American, Japanese, European – on the one hand stimulate production with high support prices and on the other hand try to keep production down by compensating farmers in various ways for keeping some of their land idle. This is about as rational as driving a car with one foot on the accelerator and the other foot on the brake. The cost of this policy to the consumers and taxpayers of the industrial countries is now estimated at about $150 billion a year.

I now discuss an extreme but very important case of American agricultural protectionism – that of sugar. Sugar has a long history of protection both in the United States and in Europe, going back to the early nineteenth century. In its present vicious form it is a legacy of the New Deal. I quote D. Gale Johnson: in 1994.

> President Franklin D. Roosevelt sent a message to Congress outlining the structure of a sugar program. He said that one of the objectives was 'to provide against further expansion of this necessarily expensive industry'. Another objective was to keep down the price of sugar to consumers. A third objective was to retain sugar beet and sugar cane farming within our continental limits.

Only the third objective has been achieved. This 'evil system', as Johnson calls it, has been in force ever since.

To make a long story short, the sugar policy was reconfirmed and revised in 1982, the import restrictions were tightened, and the volume of raw sugar imports declined from 4.6 million tons in 1979 to 2.9 million tons in 1985. As a consequence, the US price of a pound of sugar is now (July 9, 1987) five times that of the world market price. This means that the US produces sugar at a great disadvantage compared with the countries of the tropics, implying a staggering waste of productive resources. If the quotas were decreased and production of sugar reduced, labor and capital would shift from producing and refining sugar to other industries, and the price of sugar would fall because sugar would be imported in exchange for additional exports at much lower real cost than the cost of producing it at home.

A drastic liberalization of the US sugar policy would be highly desirable, not only on economic grounds but also on grounds of national security. The present sugar policy has serious political and strategic implications. It has locked Cuba more firmly in the Russian orbit because the Soviets buy a large part of the Cuban sugar crop at prices substantially above the world market price, and there is danger that they may get a foothold in some other Central American or Caribbean countries. This danger was dramatized by a desperate attempt of ten Caribbean Basin countries to persuade the United States to save their economies and social structures from crumbling. In a letter to Secretary of State George P. Schultz they pointed out that the steady closing of the US markets to imports and the decline of the price of sugar in the world market have had a devastating effect on their economies.

The conclusion is that US farm policy and agricultural protectionism are misguided and indefensible. But again it must be said that the United States is by no means the worst sinner. The Common Agricultural Policy (CAP) of the European Community (EC) is even worse. This follows from the fact that in Europe natural conditions for most crops are much less favorable than in the United States. Especially in sugar, European disadvantage compared with the tropics is surely much greater than that of the United States. Sugar production in Europe is heavily subsidized and surplus sugar is dumped on world markets. The huge cost of CAP puts a terrific strain on the EC budget. Under the title 'Europe's Farmyard Follies', *The Economist*, (London, June 6, 1987) reported about the latest protectionist moves.

> The tax on vegetable oils and fish oils that the Brussels Commission wants levied on millers and refiners ... will hurt European consumers by putting up the price of cooking oil and margarine. It will make those consumers less healthy by tempting them back to their old high-cholesterol habits of buying butter instead of less-dangerous oils. The tax will damage the economies of those mainly poor, largely Asian countries that export oils and oilseeds to Europe, just as the EEC's sugar policies have damaged Asian, African and Caribbean sugar-cane growers.

The United States, too, will be hurt because it 'sells nearly half of its oilseeds and more than half of its fish to the EEC'. *The Economist* speaks for a good many Europeans when it implores the United States: 'Please, America, lose your temper .... It is worth America risking a trans-Atlantic trade skirmish to block a European tax on imported oilseeds', in other words, to save Europe from its own follies.

READING 26

John Richard Hicks

Biography

John Richard Hicks (1904–1984) was born in 1904 in Leamington

Spa, Warwickshire, England. He was educated at Oxford University (1922–1926) and served as lecturer at the London School of Economics from 1926 to 1935. Between 1935 and 1946 he was a professor at Manchester University and from there he moved to Oxford. He retired from teaching at Oxford (but not from writing) in 1972.

In 1935 he married Ursula Wells, also an economist, who acquired her reputation in the area of public finance. Together they prepared numerous studies in this field. John Hicks was knighted in 1964 and shared the Nobel Prize for Economics with Kenneth J. Arrow in 1972. Sir John Hicks died at the age of 85.

The Work

Hicks was an economist who could turn his mind to almost any economic subject and add some innovative refinements as is evidenced in the reading below. Hicks' work mostly represents a highly perfected development of current doctrine especially in the field of utility and equilibrium analysis.

His first major contribution was in the area of wage theory. His *Theory of Wages* (1932) was a closely reasoned attempt to validate the marginal productivity theory. In addition he elaborated a unique theory of bargaining. In a famous article 'Mr Keynes and the Classics' (*Econometrica*, 1937) Hicks gave a lucid account of the essentials of Keynes' arguments as presented in the 'General Theory'. By working with a two-sector model, Hicks produced a framework which resulted in the well-known IS/LM diagram found in all current macroeconomic textbooks.

His major work is his *Value and Capital* (1939). Here he resuscitated and refined indifference curve analysis and made many other contributions to economic theory.

In one of his latest books, *Theory of Economic History* (1969), Hicks departed from his usual theoretical work and entered the field of economic history. In this remarkable little book he made the case that the market is the motive force of economic history.

The following reading has all the Hicksian qualities. It adds several theoretical refinements to the free trade versus protectionism argument.[90] It is clear, however, that this paper was written in the immediate post—war period when the European economies were still very fragile and preoccupied with the idea of full employment.

Extract

Free Trade and Modern Economics

The subject which I have chosen for this paper is one on which I have long wanted to address the Society. During the years when I was an active member, I often felt an urge towards it, and nearly offered it to you as a subject on more than one occasion. Now that you have done me the kindness of asking me back among you, I feel that the occasion I was looking for has at last arrived. I want to state as carefully as I can what I believe on this matter of Free Trade, and there could be no more suitable place for doing this than the Manchester Statistical Society.

The Free Trade movement of the nineteenth century, in which Manchester played so great a part, is distinctive among the great movements of history in having been founded on economic analysis. It would, of course, be absurd to claim that the rational foundation of its central argument was the main thing which led it to victory. So far as the most spectacular part of the Free Trade movement was concerned, we have been shown by a not unsympathetic modern historian to what extent the Anti-Corn-Law League was based upon the same social foundations as Chartism; and Chartism, whatever its merits, was hardly a product of scientific social diagnosis. Much more impressive than the sudden flurry over the Corn Laws, to one who looks for intellectual influences in politics, was the gradual erosion of the old British tariff under the thirty-year efforts of Huskisson, Graham, Peel and Gladstone. Even this, in its turn, can be ascribed, by those who insist in interpreting all history in terms of material forces, to the increased power of manufacturing industry as a 'pressure group'. But the form which the demands of industry took, the insistence, not on special favor but on no favor, is surely to be attributed to the climate of opinion. The fact that the abolition of protective duties came to be regarded as a general symbol of political

90   J.R. Hicks, 'Free Trade and Modern Economics', *Manchester Statistical Society* (March 14, 1951).

progress and economic reform is surely to be attributed to its association with the accepted economic teachings of Adam Smith and David Ricardo.

Thereafter, during the seventy or eighty years during which the British economic policy remained faithful to the principle of Free Trade, the presence of this 'sound' economic principle among the cardinal tenets of British liberalism was a guarantee, both to statesmen and to political thinkers, of the intellectual status of the liberal creed. It drew much of its life from the other liberal principles of freedom and internationalism, but it gave life to them in its turn. It was part of the intellectual assurance that a liberal world, the goal of liberal endeavor, was a possible and viable thing.

To-day we are very far from all that. Instead of advancing confidently towards a desired objective, we are 'shoring fragments against our ruins'. Our immediate objects are closely limited by practicability, much more limited than they would have seemed to be fifty years ago. But though changes in circumstances change what is practicable, they do not necessarily change ideals. Even in these days, it is right to have principles, though the gap between principle and practice has to be wider than we should desire.

It is therefore not unreasonable for us to reconsider, at this time of day, the principle of Free Trade. And certainly there is a need for reconsidering it, for we have to recognize that it has been called into question, not only by changes in circumstances, but also by changes in economic thinking. The doctrine which used to derive much of its strength from its association with accepted economic theory, has lost much of that strength too. Free Trade is no longer accepted by economists, even as an ideal, in the way that it used to be. Economics has not lost authority, but the preponderance of economic opinion is not longer so certainly as it was on the Free Trade side.

I had better make it clear from the start that my own mind still tends in what for economists is the traditional direction. Twenty years ago, just before the final abandonment of Free Trade by the British Government, I took part in the writing of a co-operative work on the economics of the matter, much of which reads now as if it belonged to another world. Looking back now on what was said in that book, there is much which seems to me to be clearly wrong. I admit that the opposing view has made many points since the time when we wrote, and that it had made some points at that time which we ought to have comprehended, but did not altogether comprehend. One cannot honestly be so uncompromising as we thought it possible to be in

1930. Yet in spite of all that my view still is that the main thesis stands.

In a certain sense it is admitted, even by the most protectionist of economists, that the thesis stands. For however much economists may differ, economics is one; the unity of economics does indeed become better established with every decade that passes. The positive argument for Free Trade is as valid as ever; what has happened is that the exceptions have grown up and, in the minds of many, have overshadowed the positive argument. We can, I think, grant that these exceptions (many of which have long been familiar) were given too little weight in the past; but we should be wary of giving them too much weight now.

The positive argument rests, as it has always rested, upon the advantage of specialization. Any two groups of people will produce the greatest possible output, from their combined resources, if each group specializes on the production of those things which it can produce with the greatest comparative (or relative) advantage. Imports are paid for by exports; thus the quantity of goods which a nation can obtain by the use of its productive resources will be larger if it seizes every opportunity of acquiring goods by trade – by producing those things for the production of which it is itself especially favored and exchanging them for things which it wants but is less favored for producing – whenever it can get more goods by the indirect method than it could by producing those goods directly at home. I really do not need to enlarge upon this basic principle; for, as I have said, it is not the thing which is nowadays in question.

There is, indeed, one school of thought which would admit the principle, but deny its applicability. Granted that specialization according to comparative advantage maximizes output, is maximization of output the thing we really need? Is not security as important as progress, and the distribution of income as important as its absolute size? We can, I think, admit these qualifications and still claim that they do not make much difference. The high value which people set upon security and equality has been shown by experience; but experience has also shown that any large movement towards fulfilling these aims at once encounters the obstacle of deficient productivity. The fact surely is that the wealthier communities of the world have indeed, at various dates in the twentieth century, reached a point where additional wealth of old types is of diminishing interest to them; but new types are continually appearing which put off – perhaps indefinitely – the point of satiation. The great present demand for wealth is in the form of social services; the demand expressed in that way is so great that, even in a world at peace, the resources available are bound to be strained to their utmost in order to satisfy it.

I shall therefore take it for granted that we do need productive efficiency; and I shall take it as agreed that specialization according to comparative advantage is one way, and an important way, of ensuring that the resources available are used as productively as possible. Having got so far, the nineteenth century economist would have jumped, without hesitation, to the conclusion that the case for Free Trade was established. The modern economist, on the other hand, is much more nervous about this next step. The main reason for his diffidence is his uncertainty about a thing which his predecessor took for granted – the extent to which costs, as ordinarily reckoned by business men, do properly reflect the comparative costs implied in the above argument.

If business costs do properly reflect true social costs, then it does seem to follow that the mere fact of it being profitable to import an article, instead of producing it at home, shows that it can be acquired in that way at a smaller sacrifice of other things than would be entailed by the use of resources to produce it at home. And this leads straight to the Free Trade conclusion. But if there is a failure in the correspondence between the two sorts of costs, the conclusion does not follow. It does then become possible that it appears to be profitable to import an article, because it appears to be cheaper to acquire it from abroad than to produce it at home, though there is not any real net advantage in so doing. This may happen either because a failure in the correspondence has caused the cost of the home product, which might replace the import, to be set too high, or because it has caused the cost of the exports, which must pay for the import, to be set too low. In either case the argument from Comparative Cost might fail to lead to the Free Trade conclusion.

It is not difficult to think of simple examples where a failure of this sort may occur. When agricultural production is carried on in such a way as to damage the fertility of the soil, it may be said that the neglect of such damage causes business cost to be put at a figure which is lower than true cost. Thus the development of an export industry, which suffers from a disharmony of this sort, may cause trade to take place which does not really offer the advantage it appears to offer. Then there is the often-quoted possibility that the growth of a home industry, which is prevented by free imports, might entail advantages to the community which would not be directly reflected in the profits of producers (external economies, as economists call them). An example of this might be the growth of internal transport, which would be stimulated by the growth of this particular industry, but which, having grown, would benefit other industries as well. In this case the true social costs of home production would be less than the apparent costs, so that a correct interpretation of the Comparative Cost principle would not lead to Free Trade.

These arguments are, in my view, perfectly respectable and perfectly valid, though they certainly are capable of misuse. For one thing, these remoter advantages and disadvantages are nearly always difficult to assess, and are therefore easy to exaggerate. It is perhaps even more important to remark that they have no systematic tendency to support the *restriction* of trade. The advantage of trade is always a matter of comparison, of comparative cost or comparative advantage. The considerations we have just been examining give no reason why the apparent costs of export industries should always be put at a lower figure than they should be, and the apparent costs of industries competing with imports at a higher figure than they should be. It is *equally* possible for the thing to be the other way about. The growth of export industries is indeed just as likely to induce external economies as the growth of industries which will serve the home market. Historically, it may well be that such economies have been induced more frequently by export industries than by the other sort, at least in the early stages of development; for it is the growth of export industries which most readily leads to import of capital, out of which general development can be financed. However this may be, we can agree that the 'infant industry argument' does draw our attention to considerations of importance, while questioning the protectionist conclusion which is generally drawn from it. Properly interpreted, the argument is quite as likely to call for measures of encouragement of a non-protectionist as of a protectionist type.

Nowadays, however, all such arguments as these are rather *vieux-jeu*; our present-day protectionists have taken to stronger meat. The three arguments which have really counted in recent discussion are (1) what we may call the Monopoly–Competition argument; (2) the Employment–Balance of Payments argument; (3) the Terms of Trade argument. there is ample material under these three heads to last me for the rest of this paper.

Number One, the Monopoly–Competition argument, is of much less practical importance than the others, but it deserves at least a passing mention, because of the great influence which it undoubtedly exercises – in a negative sort of way – upon the minds of economic students. Even apart from the external economies (and diseconomies) which we have just been discussing, it is theoretically true that we can only be certain of finding an exact correspondence, between the apparent costs of business and the true costs which are relevant to the Comparative Cost principle, in certain very special circumstances – circumstances which it is easy to define in so exacting a way that they can practically never occur. If apparent costs only equal true costs under conditions of perfect competition, and competition hardly ever is perfect, the bottom seems to drop out of the Free Trade argument. This is in fact a fair description of the state of mind which quite a number of economic students seem to have reached.

Actually, it is hardly necessary to say, the matter needs to be taken much further than that. It is in fact admitted by everyone who looks at the matter at all carefully, that the Comparative Cost argument is only affected by discrepancies between true and apparent cost due to imperfection of competition if the degree of monopoly (or, as it might be preferable to say, the degree of competition) is different in the two industries which are being compared – the export industry and the industry competing with imports. Further, even if there is a difference, it only tends to improve the case for Protection if the discrepancy is less in the export industry than in the other industry – that is to say, if the export industry is more competitive than the other industry. Now it is true that the mere fact of producing for a world market is a thing which often tends to make an export industry more competitive than other industries (though in these days that is not a thing about which one feels included to generalize with much confidence). But it is also true that the fact of active competition with foreign imports is also a thing which tends to make an industry competitive; thus it is not by any means a clear rule that the one type of industry is likely to be more competitive than the other – which is the thing which is needed to make the Free Trade argument break down on this score. It is, on the other hand, a much safer generalization that the restriction of imports does itself have some tendency to encourage combination and cartellization in the protected industry, and so to make it less competitive. (This is a point which used to be much emphasized by American Free Traders such as Taussig; it must be said that more recent experience tends to support it very strongly.) If now we take that lessened degree of competition for granted, the Monopoly–Competition argument seems to provide a case for further restriction, even in instances where it would not, if correctly used, have provided any case for the original introduction of protective measures. An argument of that sort must surely be regarded as fallacious. Surely the fact is that we must allow for the probable effects of restrictive measures on the degree of competition; when we do so, the Monopoly–Competition argument is not made entirely ineffective, but it does become apparent that there is a good deal less in it than is commonly supposed.

I turn to more serious matters. The main thing which caused so much liberal opinion in England to lose its faith in Free Trade was the helplessness of the older liberalism in the face of massive unemployment, and the possibility of using import restriction as an element in an active program of fighting unemployment. One is, of course, obliged to associate this line of thought with the name of Keynes. It was this, almost alone, which led Keynes to abandon his early belief in Free Trade. As we follow the development of Keynes' thoughts in the pages of Mr. Harrod's 'Life' we are tracing the intellectual counterpart of the retreat from Free Trade, just as we follow the intellectual approach to Free Trade in the work of Smith and Ricardo.

In a certain sense, the Employment argument is another aspect of the distinction between true and apparent costs. If there is a serious amount of unemployment among the workers attached to a certain industry, the true cost of increasing the output of that industry ceases, for that reason alone, to have any close relation with the apparent cost. For the apparent cost includes the cost of additional labor, valued at the ruling rate of wages, but the ruling rate of wages has ceased to have any relation to the sacrifice imposed upon anyone as a result of the increase in output, for labor is not being taken away from any other use (or even from desired leisure); it is only being taken away from undesired unemployment. In order to get the true cost, we ought to value the additional labor at some much lower figure than its nominal wage – perhaps at zero or even at a minus quantity! No wonder that the case for Free Trade gets into serious trouble in a state of widespread unemployment.

Even so, however, we must go carefully. If it should so happen that a country was to find itself in a position where there was serious unemployment in industries competing with imports, but no serious unemployment in its export trades, then it would be possible to argue directly that the cost of acquiring imported goods by producing exports to pay for them was greater than the true cost of producing them at home, and that a case for restricting imports could therefore be made out on a straightforward Comparative Cost basis. But it would still not follow necessarily that this was the best way of dealing with the emergency; and the same argument would not hold without qualification in the more interesting, and practically more important, case where there is unemployment in the export trades as well. What are we to say about that case?

We now reach the point where Keynesian economics begins to break away from the classical moorings. But it does so, let us be clear, in two stages. First of all there is the case in which there is widespread unemployment in one country (extending to export industries, import–competing industries, and – perhaps – to purely home market industries as well), but in which there is no serious unemployment in the outside world. Traditional theory would have explained this case by saying that wages and prices in the affected country were too high in relation to the world level; it is not that comparative costs are wrongly assessed, but that absolute costs, measured in money, are too high all over the country. The trouble could therefore be put right by a general cut in money wages, which would be followed by a general cut in internal prices. Keynesian theory does not question the traditional diagnosis in this case (this was indeed the diagnosis which Keynes himself made of the British situation between 1925 and 1929), but because of the stress which it lays upon rigidity of wage-rates, it looks for other ways out. One of these would be by devaluation of the currency, which has much the same effect as a general cut in wages, though it has other effects too; if this also is ruled out, less simple solutions can be looked for. The scheme, which was put forward in 1930, of imposing a uniform tariff on all imports, the proceeds of which would be used to give a uniform subsidy to all exports, is especially interesting, whatever its practicability may have been. For it is strictly in accordance with Comparative Cost doctrine; it is designed to remedy the disequilibrium of money costs, without upsetting Comparative cost relations. Although it infringes the letter of Free Trade, it is in precise accordance with the spirit. Since it is nowadays the spirit rather than the letter which there is some hope of preserving, devices of this kind are very worthy of attention.

The second stage of the Keynesian argument comes when we allow for the possibility of acute unemployment abroad as well as at home. In these circumstances, the trouble cannot be ascribed to a disequilibrium between wage-levels at home and abroad; it goes deeper. The remedies appropriate to the preceding case now cease to be appropriate. Any reduction in costs by country A (whether directly by a cut in wages, or indirectly by devaluation, or still more indirectly by a device such as the tariff-subsidy plan) may indeed tend somewhat to increase employment in country A, but it will only do so at the expense of a more or less corresponding reduction in employment in other countries. If other countries are in more or less the same position, then it must be expected that they will reciprocate, and then we are back more or less where we were before. There is no way out along that road.

Nor, it should be noticed, is there any way out by straight protection. The restriction of imports can, it is true, increase employment in the import-competing industries, but it will do so, as before, by pushing unemployment abroad, with, in all probability, similar results. Simple protection is not a solution; but protection may come in as part of a more recommendable solution in another way.

The direct way of dealing with a situation of widespread unemployment, as everyone now knows, is by increasing purchasing power, either directly through government spending, indirectly through remission of taxation, or more indirectly still by improving credit facilities, through monetary or other means. In principle it is an easy remedy and an attractive remedy; but in practice there are snags. The particular snag which most concerns us here arises out of the fact that these expansionary measures can most readily be undertaken by National Governments; and any National Government is liable to be restrained from adopting such measures by fear of the consequence of the expansion upon its Balance of Payments. This is the way in which the question of Employment slides into the question of the Balance of Payments.

I have managed to get so far in this paper without saying anything about the Balance of Payments; but since the Balance of Payments figures so largely in current discussions of these problems, some of you will probably have been asking how I have been able to get so far without referring to it earlier on. I think that my procedure can be justified – as follows. The arguments which we were discussing in my first few pages were essentially long-term arguments; they were not arguments for and against the introduction of import restrictions to meet particular emergencies; they were arguments for and against the use of such restrictions as a long-term policy. When discussing such arguments as these it seems reasonable to assume that in that long term the Balance of Payments will on the whole be in equilibrium. Certainly a country cannot go on losing international reserves for a long period, so that some rough sort of equilibrium must hold, at least on the average. The Balance of Payments is a short-term problem, in the same sense (and it is no way a minimizing sense) in which unemployment is a short-term problem. Both are questions of what shall we do now, rather than questions of what, we shall do *as a rule* in the future. It is natural, therefore, that they come up for consideration together.

In my first unemployment case, where there is unemployment in country A, but no serious unemployment elsewhere, there was implicitly a Balance of Payments problem, though I did not stress it. Country A could in principle have absorbed its unemployed, or at least reduced its unemployment, by adopting expansionary measures at home - and by public spending or by monetary expansion. If it were to find itself in a position where it had widespread unemployment while at the same time its Balance of Payments was favorable (a thing which can happen) then there would be everything to be said for the expansionary solution, since there would be no difficulty on the Balance of Payments side. By neglecting attention to the Balance of Payments question, I implicitly assumed that the unemployment co-existed with an even Balance of Payments; in that case, or in the still worse case where the Balance of Payments is already unfavorable, expansionary measures are not, by themselves, a way out. For it is a general rule, which applies in all cases, that an expansion of spending, occurring in one country alone, tends to weaken the Balance of Payments of that country; the reasons why it does so are obvious enough. An expansion of home demand increases imports - whether of raw materials to be used in industry, or of consumer goods to be bought out of the increased consumer incomes; it also tends, in many cases, to diminish exports, since goods which might have been exported are diverted to satisfy the home demand.

This difficulty arises in the case of general many-country unemployment, just as it does in the case of one-country unemployment; in the general case it is perhaps even more upsetting than it is in the one-country case. For if, amid a situation of world-wide unemployment or under-employment, a single country adopts expansionary policies, or if it adopts policies which are more effectively expansionary than those adopted by others, it will find its Balance of Payments turning against it, and if it cannot afford that unfavorable balance, it must take counteracting measures of one sort or another. The position in which it then finds itself is in some ways analogous to that which we discussed previously, of the country which has a wage-level which is out of line with that of other countries; in principle the same set of alternatives is open. But the practical alternatives are distinctly more limited. In conditions when home demand is being deliberately stimulated, wage-cuts are not likely to be a plausible remedy; while devaluation is hardly an appropriate way-out for what may well be (and in principle ought to be) a very temporary trouble. If we are to make it a rule to use exchange variation to deal with troubles of this sort, then it is going to be very hard to maintain the desirable degree of stability in the exchanges; we have got to go right over to a system of flexible exchange rates. If we are unwilling to do that, we have got to admit that there is a strong case for Import Restriction, as a means of facilitating expansion without weakening the Balance of Payments. This is a much stronger case than any we have found previously. It is this, more than anything else, which has undermined the intellectual foundations of Free Trade.

Is there any way by which this conclusion can be avoided? It should be noticed that the argument we are now discussing is not an answer to the traditional Free Trade case, which I tried to restate in a modern form at the beginning of this paper, and which, as I said, still stands. It is not denied by those who stress the Employment argument that Free Trade with Full Employment may be expected, on the whole, to lead to greater productivity than Protection with Full Employment; but that, they say, is not the choice. Protection with Full Employment may still be preferable to Free Trade with Unemployment; if that is the choice, then they are surely right. But the question remains whether Full Employment with Free Trade (or with the advantages of Free Trade) really is out of reach. It is not right to abandon the pursuit of the higher goal until we are assured that it really is unattainable.

There seems to be a good deal of evidence for the view that this is indeed more or less the way in which Keynes himself came to conceive of the problem in his later years. Certainly it is remarkable that the project on which he spent so much of the last three years of his life is an embodiment of one of the ways out which naturally suggests itself. An adverse Balance of Payments is an immediately serious threat only to a country which is short of international reserves – of gold, that is, or of something else which is internationally acceptable in place of gold. If international reserves could be readily created when they were needed, they could be put at the disposal of a country which could make use of them, whenever such use was to the advantage of that country itself and to the general advantage. It was the possibility of this way-out which led to the Bretton Woods conference and to the creation of the International Monetary Fund.

What really are the prospects of substantial help from the creation of the Fund and of related institutions I am incompetent to assess; but the general opinion seems to be that they are not very rosy. That opinion may be too pessimistic; it may be too early to say that the Fund itself cannot be made a success, and even if the Fund does not work in its present form, new institutions with the same general end can be created. It would be wrong to give up hope too soon. But it is hardly reasonable, in the light of what has happened, to entertain more than moderate hopes. It cannot be expected that the creation of international reserves will be sufficiently automatic to come to the rescue in all cases where it is desirable that it should come to the rescue. Other methods will have to be used as well. Thus it is hardly possible to avoid the conclusion that there really is something in the Employment argument for Protection, something from which we can hardly escape. We must expect that occasions will arise when the use of protectionist measures as an anti-unemployment device is the least bad of the alternatives which are open, but before we allow this concession to break down all our defenses, there are several further things which need to be said.

In the first place, it may be asked – how relevant is this stuff about unemployment to the situation in which the world finds itself now, has found itself for the last five years, and is perhaps likely to find itself for some time to come? For some time now unemployment has ceased to be a major worry; does that mean that the Employment argument has ceased (at least for the time being) to be relevant to our problems? Unfortunately that is not the case.

All that has happened, during these years of Full Employment, is that the lesson of how to increase employment by expansionary measures has been learned, though the accompanying problem of how to maintain order and efficiency in international trade has remained unsolved. International Full Employment has led in practice (just where, in accordance with the preceding argument, we might expect it to lead) to a succession of Balance of Payments crises; that is true, not for this country only, but for many others. As long as a contraction of internal purchasing power is ruled out as a method of dealing with such crises, they can only be dealt with by expedients. We have witnessed a great variety of such expedients, and it is not surprising that many of them should have been highly protectionist in character. That is what, in accordance with our previous analysis, we should expect to happen.

It is true that not all of the expedients adopted can be described as protectionist. Marshall Aid was such an expedient, and there is no call to criticize that; devaluation was another, and that does not fall to be criticized from our present point of view, whatever may be the case when it is looked at from other viewpoints. It is indeed very possible to argue that the acute Balance of Payments difficulties of the years 1946–49 were made much worse than they need have been by an over-valuation of sterling; that this over-valuation was too great to have any chance of being corrected by such changes as might naturally have occurred in the conditions of international demand and supply; and that in consequence an adjustment of the exchange rate was the correct remedy. But if this were so, it might well have been expected that the need for other measures to maintain equilibrium would have been much less after devaluation than it was before, so that a relaxation of restrictions ought to have been possible. Some traces of relaxation there have been, but they certainly have not amounted to very much. Why, when the employment argument for Protection has become weaker, as it has done during the past eighteen months, have we not been able to move further in the direction of Freer Trade?

In order to throw light on this question, it will be well to turn our attention to the last of the three main modern arguments for protection – the one which I called the Terms of Trade argument. This it is which at the present time is the very center of the whole dispute. It has an even closer relevance than the Employment argument to the situation in which we now find ourselves, and it throws up in a sharp form the same divergence between Liberal and Nationalist, which was the root of the opposition between Free Trader and Protectionist in time gone by.

I have, in the course of this paper, expressed my sympathy with the Free Trade viewpoint, but I have nevertheless at several points, especially in connection with the Employment argument, shown a willingness to make concessions. I have however made these concessions with a clear conscience, because, when it came to the Terms of Trade argument, I proposed to stand rather firm.

The Terms of Trade argument is, for the most part, a modern addition to the Protectionist armory; but it has an ancestor which used to figure in older controversies. This was the idea that by imposing import duties, it was possible to 'tax the foreigner'. It was, I think, never denied by reputable economists that some shifting of the burden of taxation on to foreign suppliers was theoretically possible. If for some reason the Danes (say) must sell us just so much butter, or if the British consumer will not pay more than so much a pound for his butter, then the imposition of an import duty on butter will lower the price which the Danes have to take, without raising the price the British consumer pays. The revenue which flows into the British exchequer will come out of the pockets of the Danes and not out of those of the British consumer.

The old answer to this was (1) to say that the supposed circumstances were very improbable; consumers don't often behave like that, and Danes usually have somewhere else to sell their butter – at the worst they can eat it themselves. I think, however, that there was usually implied a second answer also: (2) even if you could push your taxes off on to other people in this way, it was a pretty nasty thing to do, not exactly a piece of international good-neighborliness. But the first answer was generally found to be sufficiently convincing, without much stress having to be laid on the second. It might, however, have been wiser to put the emphasis rather differently.

For in fact the possibility of making gains of this sort at the expense of one's neighbors is not so easily disposed of. Take another case, which was until very lately of little practical importance, but has now become very important indeed – the case of export taxes. The imposition of an export tax will usually raise the price of the export to the foreign buyer, who will accordingly reduce his purchases; reduced sales may cause the home exporter to reduce his selling price. Cases are however possible, and do in fact occur, in which the foreigner's demand is very urgent, so that he is willing to pay the higher price, with only a small reduction in the volume of trade. The export tax has then been thrown on to the foreigner, who has been made to contribute to the national exchequer, in just the same way as he would have been made to contribute by a suitable import tax, if one could be found.

It is easy to see why, in the past, exploitation of the foreigner through export taxes was a less attractive idea than exploitation through import taxes. For, excepting in an extreme case, exploitation through export taxes will involve a fall in the volume of exports,and that has usually meant the creation of unemployment in the export trades. But this check is removed once we pass from a condition of unemployment or underemployment to one of Full Employment – especially when Full Employment is carried so far as to produce actual shortages. For in the latter case we reach the position that a reduction in the volume of exports, if it can be achieve without implying a large reduction in imports, becomes a thing which is positively desired. The reduction in exports will then no longer lead to unemployment – it will simply enable more goods to be diverted to the home market. And that is precisely the thing which is so badly wanted.

I am, of course, not suggesting that trade restriction through export taxes is a charge which can be brought against our own British Government. But it is a very common practice in other countries, even in some of the countries of the British Commonwealth. There are many countries which happen to be in a fairly good position at the moment with respect to their Balance of Payments, but are nevertheless troubled by inflationary pressure at home; such countries naturally turn to export taxes as a promising anti-inflationary device, which has the particular attraction that it pushes a part of their troubles off on to other people. We in England are to-day suffering a good deal from this sort of restrictionism on the part of some of our suppliers.

This case of export taxes is relatively easy to understand; its effects are substantially the same as those which would follow if the country's export industries were formed into a cartel, which just pushed up prices to foreign buyers as far as it could. It is a little harder to see that import restrictions can be used in what is at bottom almost exactly the same way. But it is so – as may perhaps be explained in the following manner.

If a country's demand for imports increases, it is likely that (in some cases at least) it will have to pay more per unit for the goods it imports; while if it is trying (or is obliged) to pay currently for its imports by exports, it will have to find some way of forcing its exports in order to bring in the larger export proceeds which it requires. In some cases, at least, it will only be able to do this by cutting the prices at which it sells. Thus in general (though there are in practice many ways by which the tendency in this direction may be masked) we may say that it will only be able to acquire the increased volume of imports by turning the 'terms of trade' against it – by giving a larger amount of exports in return for a unit of imports. This is really nothing else but the old 'law of demand and supply', which in these large matters seems to work pretty surely and infallibly.

Contrariwise, a country which restricts its imports, and consequently its exports, will usually turn the terms of trade in its favor, so that it has to give less exports for a unit of imports. When one is dealing with an under-employed economy, this is an obvious bad mark against a policy of import restriction; it is one of the reasons why import restriction has so little to be said for it as an anti-unemployment measure, *when it is taken by itself.* (The good case for import restriction in these circumstances depends upon its use to buttress other measures.) But when one is dealing with a fully employed economy, the case is altered. We can still not conclude that any restriction of imports will be advantageous to the restricting country, merely because it tends to turn the terms of trade in favor of that country. Obviously the point will be reached (and may soon be reached) when a further restriction of imports imposes sacrifices on home consumers which cannot be compensated by a diversion to the home market of things which might be exported, or of things which can be made by the labor which might have produced exports. Thus the case for import restriction, which can be made on these lines, is limited. But there is some case; there is here a possibility of gain which was left out of account in the old Free Trade argument. In principle, a country can gain somewhat (quite apart from Employment considerations) by departing to some degree from Free Trade; though we should be quite clear how this gain arises – it is a gain which only arises at the expense of other countries.

Exploitation of this sort is, however, a game that two can play. Take the simplest case (it is all I have time for here, thought it would be interesting and instructive to go further) of trade between two countries, A and B. We start off, let us suppose from a Free Trade position. A then restricts imports in order to turn the terms of trade in its favor; we will suppose that the tariff, or other restriction, which A imposes is cleverly chosen, so that A is actually better off as a result of the restriction than it was before. The net result then is that A gains and B loses, but in a significant sense (assuming that there was no case for restriction along any of the other lines which we have considered, so that what has happened is a pure piece of terms of trade exploitation), A will have gained less than B has lost, because the restriction of trade has caused them both to lose some of the advantages of international specialization. Call this Stage I. In the next stage, surely, B will try the same game on its side. B now restricts, with the result that, as compared with Stage I, B gains and A loses – but B's gain is less than A's loss, for the same reason as before. This is Stage II. Now if we compare Stage II with the initial Free Trade position, both A and B have gained at one step and lost at the other; but we cannot conclude that the gains and losses will cancel out. We cannot say for certain that A will not retain some gain as a result of the whole proceeding; it may do so if its general bargaining position is stronger than B's. But it surely is very likely that A's loss to B on the second round will be more or less similar to its gain from B on the first; in that case each party must have a net loss on the whole proceeding. The gains at the expense of the other party cancel out, and each is left with nothing but its share of the general loss due to restriction of trade.

Even that is not the end of the trouble. For the imports which B has lost, as a result of the first two rounds, will in all probability be those with which B could dispense most easily; the urgency of B's demand for its remaining imports will therefore be greater than the urgency of its demand for imports was previously – and that makes B more exploitable than it was before. Thus if the two go on, just looking one stage ahead as they have done, there is no reason why the process we have described should not be repeated. This may seem unbelievably silly; but in a world of many countries it is not at all unbelievably silly. For countries playing this game have then got to allow for much more complicated reactions than appear in our two-country case; to see right through to the consequences of their actions may then involve much more foresight than we can expect to be forthcoming at all easily.

The mess which I have just been describing does look extraordinarily like the mess we are in now – especially since the beginning of the Reign of Full Employment. I am not suggesting that deliberate exploitation of this sort has been a common practice – at least since the days of Dr. Schacht – but countries have blundered into a situation where they are in fact behaving in this way, and the terms of trade motive then operates strongly as a deterrent against resolute measures for getting out of it. What then is to be done? It is tempting to say – have done with the silly business, go back to Free Trade, and trust in your virtue being an example to others. That was the Cobdenite prescription, and one has a yearning for it. But I am afraid that as things are, it will hardly do. So long as people believed in the old principles of sound money and balanced budgets, it was possible to rely upon governments being at least as anxious to encourage their export trades as to protect their home industries from foreign competition; this state of mind, whatever its defects (which I do not of course deny) did at least ensure that the use of foreign trade policy to exploit other countries would not be carried too far. That safeguard is at present largely removed. The danger of being exploited by other countries is therefore far larger than it used to be. I do not think that any sensible person who appreciates the situation could recommend a Cobdenite policy now. We have to look in another direction.

The only visible alternative is international agreement, agreement to abstain from, or to limit the use of such forms of exploitation. The pessimist will no doubt say that has been tried, and that the prospects of I.T.O. (or G.A.T.T.) look hardly brighter than those of I.M.F. That is as it may be; but even if we accept the view that there has been one failure, it would still be too soon to give up hope. In fact it would not be at all surprising if a failure should occur. We are dealing, as I have tried to emphasize, with a very different situation from that which was experienced in the past – different from that experienced in the (relatively) Free Trade nineteenth century, and different also from the experience of the great unemployment in the nineteen-thirties. It could not be expected that people would adjust themselves to the new situation all at once, and until they have done so they cannot know the dangers against which they ought to be guarding. Fumbling in the dark, they are bound to be too ambitious in some ways, and in others not ambitious enough; the principles on which a real move in the Free Trade direction could be based have hardly yet been discovered.[91]

The most I hope to have done in this paper is to have made a little progress in clearing the ground for such discovery. I have, to a large extent, been clearing my own mind; and I am very conscious that what I have said can be no more than the beginning of what ought to be said. I do not claim to have covered the whole subject, even by implication. But I think that I have got so far that I could finish by laying down some tentative principles, which one could honestly put forward as a basis for future endeavor.

(1)   The greatest danger, as things are at present, lies in the Terms of Trade argument – or, as I should say by now, the Terms of Trade motive. The relaxation of restrictions on trade, which have been imposed (directly or indirectly) with this motive, ought to be the first objective.

(2)   The Employment motive, on the other hand, must be dealt with tenderly. It has to be expected that countries will require, from

91   What chance is there of progress while the ablest economic thinking devoted to these matters is pulling as hard as it can be in the other direction? I allude in particular to the writings of Mr. Balogh and Mr. Kahn. See, in particular, Mr. Kahn's intellectually admirable article, 'The Dollar Shortage and Devaluation', in *Economica Internazionale* [sic] (1950).

time to time, to restrict imports in order to safeguard employment; they cannot be expected to abandon this right, nor is it necessarily to the interest of other countries that they should do so. The problem is to find a means of distinguishing between restrictions imposed with this motive and those imposed with the other.

(3)   It is a necessary condition, in order that import restrictions imposed with the Employment motive should be harmless to others, that the country imposing them should not rely upon them as the main element of its Employment policy. Such restrictions should only be regarded as justifiable when they are a means of safeguarding an Employment policy which depends upon other measures, or of safeguarding a state of Full Employment which has been reached by other measures. This condition is becoming widely accepted as necessary; it is necessary, but for the purpose in hand it is not enough.

(4)   The reason why it is not enough becomes most evident when we consider the second type of justification which we have just admitted. Import restrictions, imposed on the overt ground of maintaining Full Employment by preventing disequilibrium in the Balance of Payments, do in fact turn the Terms of Trade in favor of the country imposing them; it is therefore inevitable that a free license to impose restrictions on Balance of Payments grounds will give unlimited opportunity to Terms of Trade abuse. Something less than a full license must therefore be given, but it must be given in a form which does not prevent governments from taking such measures for the maintenance of employment as seem to be desirable.

(5)   Is this possible? In principle it is possible, though I can well believe that a long process of education will be needed before the solution becomes acceptable. The solution depends upon the fact that imports and exports enter into the Balance of Payments (or Employment) relation, and into the Terms of Trade relation, in different ways. Improving employment can be brought about by restricting imports or by *encouraging* exports; turning the Terms of Trade in your favor can be done by restricting imports or by *restricting* exports. If therefore it could be laid down that a restriction of imports, if it was to be regarded as justified on employment grounds must be accompanied by an equivalent encouragement of exports, no harm would be done to Employment policy, but Terms of Trade exploitation would be largely prevented. It is most important to emphasize that the condition stated above under (3) must continue to hold.

(6)   We have therefore to start thinking again about export subsidies. Export subsidies have a bad name, because, when they are applied to a particular export, they offer a fine weapon of economic warfare by aggressive competition. Particular export subsidies of this sort should be frowned on as much as ever. But general export subsidies, according to which *any* exporter is entitled to an allowance equal to a uniform percentage of export value, are not open to this objection. It does seem as if some international approval of such subsidies, in appropriate conditions, may be the only way which is now open to retain for the world some of the benefits of what used to be called Free Trade.

(7)   If this principle were once accepted, it would follow that an exactly parallel provision ought to be made for the case of export taxes. Export taxes are used for the opposite 'employment' reason – as a weapon against inflation, not against deflation. They can retain this virtue, without giving rise to Terms of Trade exploitation, if it is laid down that export taxes are not to be imposed without countervailing concessions in the way of reducing import taxes.

(8)   These are the main things I have to say. I do however agree that the pursuit of Full Employment complicates the issue in other ways than those which I have mentioned. Any contraction of an uneconomic industry (and the necessity for such contraction, when the industry becomes uneconomic, is a necessary part of the Free Trade position) must be expected to create unemployment; if even frictional unemployment, such as this, is always to be prevented, then there is no hope at all for any rational organization of trade. Full Employment as I have used the term in this paper, is not intended to mean that there should never be any frictional unemployment; the true ideal is not one of 'Full Employment in every industry', but one in which there are always jobs for those seeking work, even though they may be jobs which take a little finding. It has, however, to be recognized that the distinction is a difficult one; thus one of the most unfortunate consequences of the modern emphasis on Full Employment is that it increases the force of those claims by special interests on which old-fashioned protectionism was always based, and with which Free Traders have always had to reckon. On this issue we have no call to do anything else but to stand firm.

(9)   The old Listian motives for protection (encouragement of infant industries and long-range economic development) can, I think, be looked upon a little more kindly. They have nowadays become mainly a problem of the so-called under-developed countries, which

might reasonably be given special privileges to experiment in ways not allowed to those countries which have passed that stage. We can be fairly critical of these arguments, without denying that there may be something in them in particular cases. The whole thing can now be looked at as a part of the general problem of spreading, so far as possible, a tolerable level of development to the more backward parts of the world.

I am well aware that these points do not add up to a possible basis for a Charter or Treaty. That is not their object. What they seek to show is that there does still remain an ideal, not in principle unattainable, in which those who prize the inheritance of Adam Smith can still believe, with open eyes and honest minds.

READING 27

Milton Friedman

Biography

Milton Friedman was born in Brooklyn, New York in 1912, the son of an immigrant family from Carpatho–Rumania. When he was one year old, the family moved to Rahway, New Jersey. The family income was always small and precarious. When Milton was fifteen years old, his father died leaving his mother and three sisters to provide for the family.

Under a scholarship, he attended Rutgers University where he was introduced to economics in a course taught by Arthur Burns who in 1970, became chairman of the Federal Reserve Board (appointed by President Nixon). Homar Jones was another economics instructor at Rutgers who impressed Friedman. On Jones' recommendation, Friedman was offered a tuition scholarship at the University of Chicago to study economics. Here he met such stimulating teachers as Frank Knight, Jacob Viner, Henry Simons and Henry Schultz. He also met Rose Director whom he was to marry six years later (1938). They wrote several books together and had two children.

Friedman's poor financial circumstances did not allow him to complete his education at Chicago. However, he was fortunate enough to receive a generous scholarship at Columbia University where Harold Hotelling, Wesley C. Mitchell and John M. Clark exposed him to the mathematical, empirical and institutional approaches.

Before 1935 and 1945, Friedman took up various appointments.

During the war years, he was for some time with the Division of Tax Research of the US Treasury. From 1945 to 1946, he spent a year teaching at the University of Minnesota, whereafter he moved to the University of Chicago where he stayed until his retirement in 1977.

In 1967, Friedman was elected president of the American Economic Association. In 1976, he was awarded the Nobel Prize in economic science. Since his official retirement in 1977, Friedman has been senior research fellow at the Hoover Institution. There is no doubt that he has been one of the most influential economists of the twentieth century. His creativity has been exceptional and he invariably brings fresh insight to any problem that has seized him.

The Work

Friedman's accomplishments are many:

(a)   he painstakingly reconstructed and tested the quantity theory of money,
(b)   he brought to the fore the importance of monetary policy,
(c)   he vigorously defended the case for fluctuating exchange rates,
(d)   he questioned the commonly accepted trade-off between inflation and unemployment and replaced it with a new theory,
(e)   he developed a new hypothesis of consumer behavior,
(f)   he restated the classical liberal philosophy in terms pertinent to the second half of the twentieth century and beyond.

In the field of social philosophy, Friedman has expressed fully the case for freedom as seen by a classical liberal. Many contemporary doctrines and policies stress welfare and equality over freedom, the latter being, in his view, slowly but surely crushed by an ever expanding government. Freedom implies the right to the individual to make and act on one's own decisions. Economic and political freedom are inseparable. By ensuring that economic activity remains in the hands of the private sector, a market economy eliminates some of the threat to the concentration of coercive powers in the hands of government officials. This applies also to international trade.

According to Friedman, the market is by far the best socioeconomic device ever conceived for ordering human affairs. History shows that the market system raises living standards faster than any alternative order. The market can also be envisaged as a procedure of voluntary cooperation of thousands or millions of individuals freely producing the goods and services they want to consume. It satisfies people with different and even competing preferences without causing social disorganization. At the same time, the market by its very decentralization prevents heavy concentration of power and, therefore, protects individual freedom much more effectively than statist alternatives. The welfare state, which always transfers power from the private sector to the public sphere, is therefore a serious threat to individual liberty. Moreover, each time the government takes over an economic function, that activity tends to be operated according to the self-interest of those who are in charge. And when the government becomes increasingly the main source of economic power, special interest groups emerge attempting to extract special rulings for their own benefit from the ruling politicians and civil servants. Thus, government activity has the tendency to become increasingly dominated by special interest groups. Influence and advantages go to the few with the best connections and the most effective lobbying skills while the wants of the electorate are often neglected or inadequately met. This leads Friedman to the conclusion that government should be limited and benign. Government should maintain law and order, take care of defense, protect property rights, provide and enforce the rules of the free market economy, provide a stable monetary framework, overcome externalities and protect the very weak, including children and the insane. The typical welfare state of the second half of the twentieth century has moved away from the above ideal and is now implicated in many activities it should never have become involved in. The result is that government fails at almost everything, especially at those things it ought to be doing.

Milton Friedman is the author of such classics as *A Monetary History of the United States, 1867–1960* written with the cooperation of economic historian, Anna J. Schwartz. His popular writings such as *Capitalism and Freedom* (1962), *Free to Choose* (1979), and *Tyranny of the Status Quo* (1984), are marked by a forceful and combative style as well as unity of vision. Milton's wife, Rose, co-authored the latter three books. In 1966, Friedman began to write a column for *Newsweek* that appeared once every three weeks until 1984. A number of these essays have been republished in such books as *An Economist's Protest: Columns in Political Economy* (1972), and *Bright Promises, Dismal Performance* (1983). Most of Friedman's discussions of international trade and finance are to be found in his more popular writings.[92]

In his analysis of trade barriers. Friedman argues that we are caught in a jungle of constraints because people always vigorously promote their own interests while opposing those of others. Only *their* special interests are in line with those of the country, they say. But in the end people lose more from measures that serve other people's special interests than they gain from measures that fit their own. This, says Friedman, is especially clear in the field of international trade.

Producers of such products as electronics, textiles, and sugar as well as the associated trade unions keep complaining about unfair competition and ask the government for protection. In order to hide their naked self-interest, they speak of the national interests, the need to protect employment, and the requirement to promote national security. However, what protection really means is exploitation of the consumer. But, because the individual consumer's voice is usually overwhelmed by the clatter of special interest groups, the whole trade issue is seriously distorted.

Even governments which should know better, says Friedman, have acted upon the pressures of those groups. Between 1980 and 1988, President Reagan often defended free trade in his speeches. Yet, he has approved one protectionist measure after another such as voluntary quotas on imports of Japanese cars or on imports of textiles.

Talk of 'voluntary' restrictions, says Friedman, is hypocrisy pure and simple.[93] Japanese exporters, for example, will not hurt themselves voluntarily. They will restrict their exports only under government pressure. And the Japanese government will only put pressure on its exporters if the American government puts pressure on its Japanese counterpart. Thus the possibility of international friction and conflict arises. Then remains the question who benefits and who is harmed by 'voluntary' quotas on, say, automobiles. In the US the automobile factories, their owners, their employees and their suppliers

92   M. and R. Friedman, *Free to Choose, A Personal Statement* (New York: Harcourt Brace Jovanovich, 1979) pp. 31–54.
     M. and R. Friedman, *Tyranny of the Status Quo* (London: Secker Warburg, 1984) pp. 124–129.
     M. Friedman, *An Economist's Protest: Columns in Political Economy* (New Jersey: Thomas Horton, 1972) pp. 107–109.
     M. Friedman, *Bright Promises, Dismal Performance: An Economist's Protest* (San Diego: Harcourt Brace Jovanovich, 1983) pp. 359–369.
93   M. Friedman, *Bright Promises ...*, p. 367.

obviously benefit from the reduction of car imports. The Japanese car factories, their owners, their employees and their suppliers suffer. The American consumers are also hurt because they have a smaller range of choice of cars while at the same time they must pay a higher price. What is less obvious is that American farmers and lumbermen are equally afflicted. Large amounts of farm and timber products are exported to Japan. If the Japanese earn fewer dollars by selling fewer cars they have less money to purchase American farm and timber products. Exports decline and those who provide the farm and timber products are hurt. The jobs 'saved' in the US are visible while the 'lost' jobs are invisible. But, says Friedman, the self-nullifying character of trade barriers goes even further. If, for instance, the US steel industry gets protection which reduces or eliminates foreign competition, steel prices in the US will rise. This increases the costs of production of the steel users such as the domestic car manufacturers, who now become less competitive relative to the Japanese auto makers. At the same time the higher prices of American cars and trucks tend to increase the operational costs of the steel and other industries, which implies that everybody lives at the expense of everybody else.

According to Friedman, there is not only an economic case for free trade but also a political case. Both in a free trade world and in a free unhampered economy, transactions take place because buyers and sellers each gain from exchange transactions. If they did not, those dealings would not take place to begin with. Thus the interests of the parties involved are harmonized. Cooperation is the outcome. When governments interfere the case is different. Suppose business firms in a given country seek protection in order to evade competitive pressures from abroad. The victimized firms in other countries will seek help from their government and so private quarrels between firms become disputes between governments. Trade negotiations become political issues and conflict not cooperation is the likely outcome.

READING 28

Mancur Lloyd Olson

Biography

Mancur Lloyd Olson (1932–) an Economics Professor at the University of Maryland was born in Grand Fork, North Dakota, the son of a farmer of Scandinavian descent. Olson obtained his BS at North Dakota State University in 1954. Between 1954 and 1956 he was a Rhodes Scholar at Oxford University (UK) where he obtained his MA In 1959 Mancur Olson married Alison Gilbert. They have three children. Olson completed his PhD at Harvard University in 1963.

Between 1960 and 1967 he was associated with Princeton University, first as a lecturer and later as an Assistant Professor. After a two year stay at the US Department of Health, Education and Welfare, he joined the faculty of the University of Maryland, first as a Professor of Economics (1970) and later as a Distinguished Professor (1979). Olson is past president of the Public Choice Society (1972–74) and of the Southern Economic Association (1981–82).

The Work

The unifying idea of Olson's work is that individuals or firms rather than simply functioning as independent units can associate. But formidable obstacles must be overcome for this to take place. Moreover, whatever the actual or perceived benefits from association may be, once collective action occurs, it usually has negative implications for innovation, economic performance and social peace.

Collective Action Organizations (CAOs) which Olson also calls Distributional Coalitions (DCs) are combinations of individuals or enterprises which as a result of their joint action secure additional market power or political influence or both. Examples are professional organizations, labor unions, cartels, trade associations and the like. They are so-called special interest groups and are supposed to serve the common interest of some assemblage of individuals or firms.

Traditional theories of group behavior, says Olson, assume that if a group of rational and self-interested individuals recognizes that gains are to be made by collective action of some kind, they will engage in such action especially if they have similar goals and objectives. Moreover, conventional theorists have assumed that small or large groups tend to attract members for the same reasons. Olson however calls these ideas to question. In his view there exists a relationship between the size of a group and the incentives for the individual unit to contribute resources to the achievement of group goals.

The paradox of collective action, says Olson, is that if a group has some reason to promote its interests, individual members of the group, if they are rational, do not necessarily have the incentive to make the voluntary sacrifices necessary to help their group to attain its collective objectives. One important reason is that even if the group has a common purpose, the benefits of collective action are a public or collective good to that group. Contrary to private goods such as cars or watches, public goods such as defense or firework displays are indivisible and their nature is such that once the good is provided it is impossible or very costly to restrict its use to selected persons. The 'exclusion principle' does not prevail. Consequently, there is no practical way of barring noncontributing third parties from enjoying the benefit of the public good. If, for example, a domestic farm organization obtains a tariff on foreign cheese, it thereby raises the price of cheese for all domestic cheese producers and not merely the members of the organization.

If individuals or firms obtain the benefit from a public good whether or not they helped to generate it, they do not have an incentive to devote any resources to such activities. Thus they become freeloaders or 'free-riders'. If everybody has an incentive to be a free-rider, the collective or public good will not be provided. The state can supply such public goods as law and order or defense, only because it has the coercive powers to tax the benefiting citizens. The state could not support itself by relying on voluntary contributions. Collective organizations face the same dilemma. This condition makes collective action difficult to achieve because in the absence of special arrangements or circumstances, groups, composed of rationally acting individuals or firms will not act in their group interest, even if those individuals value the collective good that the organization could provide through their efforts. This is more of a problem for large organizations than for small ones.

When it comes to voluntarily organizing themselves, small groups have a significant advantage over the large 'latent' ones.[94] The reason is that in groups with few members a handful of insiders, or perhaps only one, may actually receive enough benefit from the public good that he or they may be willing to bear the entire cost of providing it. The larger the group, assuming that the members are of approximately equal size or importance, the less likely this is to be the case. Another strategic advantage of groups with only a few members

---

94   By 'latent' groups Olson means that they exist but they are not developed or active (ed.).

is that the possibility of bargaining and agreeing on sharing efforts or costs in common endeavors increases.

With intermediate size groups the outcome depends on the structure of the group. Usually no member gets such a large part of the benefits that it pays him or her to undertake the action even if all the other members remain passive. If, however, the group has a sufficiently limited number of associates so that each member will notice whether any other member is contributing, then the outcome is indeterminate.[95]

The larger groups have the greatest difficulty in establishing themselves. There may be substantial benefits to persons or firms acting in the group interest but there are costs as well. In large groups, assuming the initiative is successful, each potential provider will tend to get a disproportionately small amount of the total benefit. With public goods, non-providers cannot be excluded from benefiting from the good, but the potential provider will not take the benefits to others into account, only his own. Thus in large groups potential providers may not receive enough additional benefit from the public good to justify the extra cost of supplying it. As Olson states, if there are ten identical members of a group with a common interest, each gets a tenth of the benefit of unilateral action in the common interest of the group. However, if there are a million each gets one millionth. Therefore, assuming that the potentially acting units are of equal size, any single individual, or small subset of the group will not gain enough from getting the collective goods to be willing to bear the burden to create and maintain a collective action association. A large share of the advantages would go to non-contributing individuals or firms while participating in the costs puts the contributors, if they are firms, at a competitive disadvantage. Also, striking bargains becomes more difficult as the group increases in size. This explains why large dispersed groups like consumers, taxpayers, or the unemployed have great difficulty in getting organized and often never make it.

Yet many groups, even some large ones, have organized. As a general rule one might submit, according to Olson, that the rational individual unit will only act to achieve a common interest if there is coercion or if it has to support this group in order to obtain some

95   This may explain why religious congregations can often finance successfully public goods for their members through voluntary contributions. As long as the congregation is not too large it may be relatively easy to detect whether or not someone is contributing his or her share (ed.).

noncollective benefit. Such special devices are called 'selective incentives'. These incentives or special devices are functionally equivalent to taxes imposed by governments. They either punish (negative selective incentives) or reward (positive selective incentives) individuals selectively depending on their contribution or non-contribution to the cost of obtaining a collective good. Labor unions, for example, often obtain their dues through union shop or closed shop types of arrangements which make paying dues more or less compulsory and automatic. In a union shop or closed shop, union membership is a condition of employment. Professional organizations of, say, physicians or lawyers, typically have either discreet forms of coercion or provide subtle rewards such as access to professional publications, insurance policies, group air fares, club facilities and other private goods or services only available to members. The American Medical Association, for example, assists its members with helpful defense against malpractice suits, medical journals needed by practitioners and the like. This bundling or combining of a public with a private good is quite a common practice. Most CAOs that have lasted had access to selective incentives. If dispersed groups like consumers don't get organized it is because no selective incentives are available to them.

The implications of the model previously outlined are obvious. Groups with few members, if successful in organizing themselves, may end up with disproportionate power in society. Large groups usually have little or no tendency to promote their collective interest. The disproportional power of small groups over large ones is shown, for example, when an oligopolistic industry with relatively few firms seeks and obtains a quota or tariff on certain imports, even if the vast majority of the population loses as a result. Just like a small, disciplined, coordinated army may triumph over an undisciplined leaderless mob, so do small organized groups often prevail over numerically superior forces. The large group may remain unwilling or unable to organize and their members suffer in silence. At the same time there will be no country that will attain equity or efficiency through comprehensive bargaining between collective action groups because some very large groups such as the consumers, the unemployed and the taxpayers are left out.

Olson also emphasizes that once CAOs have secured selective incentives they tend to last even if the collective good they once provided is no longer needed. For example, an organization that represented lamplighters may take on the task of representing public utility workers. Therefore, over time, stable and peaceful societies tend to accumulate CAOs while less stable societies may have relatively few of them. Collective action is not easy, especially for large groups so it takes time for them to succeed. The longer a society has enjoyed stability and peace, the greater the chances that any given group with a common interest will find the right conditions of leadership and the selective incentives to get established.

During the 1930–45 period, countries like Japan, Italy and Germany experienced totalitarian governments. Many of the existing CAOs such as labor unions were abolished or emasculated. Once the totalitarian period was over only a few distributional coalitions still existed and they could start with a clean slate.[96] Revolutionary upheavals or unconditional defeat may produce results identical to totalitarian repression.

An unfortunate characteristic of CAOs is that they have powerful anti-social incentives. As they are producing a public good for their members they are more often engaged in redistributional struggles rather than in productive pursuits. It is obvious that successful organizations can increase the income or wealth of their members by trying to increase the economic efficiency of the society in which they live. Yet working for such policies involves a cost or burden to be borne entirely by the members of the group who cannot hope to capture the full value of the benefit they create. Non-contributing free-riders (and that could be the rest of the population) will also benefit. When a group pays the full cost of an activity and receives only part of the benefits, the incentive exists not to produce the activity or to produce less than the group-optimal amount. The removal of an inefficient tariff can be quite costly to the CAO which has lobbied for its elimination. Yet such an action conveys a benefit to all consumers in the country. Thus CAOs typically have little or no inducement to work for measures which enhance prosperity.

In contrast, the incentive to achieve redistributional benefits principally by promoting special interest legislation or combining to obtain monopoly power is strong. The costs or efforts to redistribute

96   It is true that in Nazi Germany all traditional independent labor organizations were destroyed. Cartels however did flourish and were given a special legal status of their own. Actually the Nazi government used cartels to strengthen German industrial resources for war. After Germany's defeat in 1945, however, a strong decartelization movement was fostered by the occupying British and Americans in the West German economy (ed.).

income to the advantage of the members of the CAO are borne by those members. If the redistribution of income by changing the incentives to produce in a negative manner results in lower output for society, the members of the group will share in the loss of production. However, those members are usually only a very small portion of society, so that most of the loss is borne by outsiders or third parties. However, if the CAO succeeds in appropriating a larger portion of society's production for their members, the latter get the whole benefit. Thus CAOs have an incentive to fight for the redistribution of income and wealth. They are essentially rent-seeking distributional associations.[97] At the same time resources are often diverted to a relatively inefficient industry which does not have a comparative advantage, so the economic performance of the whole society is lowered.

A trade union – which is a CAO – has the incentive to block the introduction of labor saving innovations which would reduce the demand for the labor services of its members. The protected union members benefit, but the society's productivity is damaged. Successful cartels restrict the output of their members to obtain higher prices and profits.[98] They also have the incentive to limit entry into the market. Those practices reduce society's efficiency. There are other ways too in which CAOs can result in poorer economic performance of any given economy. Rent-seeking activities tend to be cumulative. As such doings increase in a society, more resources will be devoted to them. This can only be at the expense of a more productive allocation of such resources.

Lobbying and other activities aimed at using the political process to promote private economic ends, if successful, lead to the creation of special legal provisions and exceptions. A lobby that obtains a tariff increase or a voluntary export restraint for the suppliers of a particular good makes trade regulation more complex. Someone or some organization has to administer the increasingly intricate regulations

---

97   Rent-seeking behaviour, it will be remembered, refers to unproductive behaviour. It can be defined as actions by individuals and/or special interest groups designed to restructure public policy in a manner that will either directly or indirectly redistribute more income to themselves at someone else's or society's expense (ed.).

98   A cartel is a loose organization of sellers of a product who have joined together to control price, output and entry, hoping to obtain the advantages of monopoly (ed.).

with the result that the scale of bureaucracy and the scope of government are continuously expanding, absorbing more resources again.

Finally, as a society focusses more and more on distributional activities, resentment is generated. The divisiveness of an increasingly organizational and/or political struggle over the distribution of income and property may make stable, harmonious political choices less likely and may even end up making societies ungovernable as the whole pattern of incentives has changed in the direction of unproductive regulating, lobbying, politicking, and bargaining. CAOs typically busy themselves with their parochial objectives and the furthering of their own self-interest with no concern for its costs to society as a whole.

As we noticed earlier, stable and peaceful societies tend to accumulate CAOs. This leads Olson to conclude that stable societies suffer from a kind of inner contradiction. While most people desire stability and peace, they also have an interest in a society which realizes its full economic potential. Unfortunately, these two objectives tend to clash as peaceful and stable societies tend to accumulate dense networks of CAOs over time. Thus in the long run, stable and peaceful societies may suffer from institutional sclerosis which tends to lead to economic stagnation.

Given the fact that CAOs have an incentive to promote their own interest and to disregard the public interest, Olson believes that industrial policies should not be adopted.[99] The reason is that these policies would probably give special interest groups of laborers and businesses even more privileges and income than they are getting now. This could well place the foxes in charge of the henhouse. A similar situation applies to income policies.[100] With income policies the truly powerful groups often get exemptions from wage and price controls. It is also possible that the government in return for temporary wage and/or price concessions will give more monopoly power to the CAOs that are the cause of the problem.

Olson's analytical work leads to a number of policy

99　Industrial policies are policies in which the government takes a direct and active role in shaping the structure and composition of industry. Under such policies the government would work directly with business and labor associations. The provision of funds would be part of the policy (ed.).

100　Income policy refers to a government policy for restraining both prices and incomes in the interest of price stability. Typically the idea is to curb inflation without reducing aggregate demand (ed.).

recommendations which he thinks can only be implemented when public opinion is sufficiently convinced of the destructiveness of CAOs.

(a) If CAOs are harmful to economic growth, full employment, equal opportunity, social mobility and coherent government, all special interest legislation or regulation should be repealed. Anti-trust laws should be applied to all cartels or forms of collusive behavior.

(b) The best macroeconomic policy, says Olson, is good microeconomic policy. There is simply no substitute for an open and competitive environment.

(c) Organized business interests often lobby in order to exclude or restrict the entry of multinationals or foreign firms. Therefore a more liberal policy towards foreign firms and multinationals will automatically challenge the power of CAOs.

(d) Migration has demographic, economic and social effects. One consequence of relatively free immigration is that it undercuts the power of labor unions and professional organizations. These associations cannot exercise much monopoly power when a large store of outside labor is readily available. Therefore, relatively free immigration helps to combat their economic power.

(e) Olson also favors deregulation. Regulatory agencies usually enforce market sharing and fix prices at a level which allows inefficient firms to survive. Deregulation tends to reduce monopoly power, introduce competition, decrease costs and prices and increase output. This is exactly what happened after the deregulation of the American airline industry in 1984.

(f) Barriers to international trade encourage institutional sclerosis while free trade weakens it. Freer trade can come about through regional economic integration like the German customs union (1833), the European Common Market (1957) and the North American Free Trade Association (1993). Freer trade can also be prompted by cutting tariffs and reducing non-tariff barriers such as quotas or voluntary export restraints. The GATT rounds have been a powerful force in furthering tariff reductions and encouraging trade. Free or freer trade undercuts the power of CAOs because it is very hard to organize collective action on a worldwide basis, just as it is more difficult to organize large groups than small ones for reasons mentioned earlier. Moreover, differences in language and culture all must be overcome.

Furthermore, special interest legislation can only be passed in each of the countries involved. More unhampered international trade means more competition. When a country decides to participate more fully in international commerce, its domestic firms that enjoyed some amount of monopoly power will see this power decline. Free trade therefore should, according to Olson, be encouraged by all nations that want to neutralize some of the negative effects of redistributive coalitions and thereby enhance their economic performance.[101]

Extracts

The unifying idea is that any group of firms or individuals in the economy will be able to collude or organize for collective action only slowly and with great difficulty, but that this collective action, once it occurs, is normally bad for efficiency, growth, and macroeconomic performance. Suppose firms in some industry or workers in some trade lobby for legislation that is especially favorable to them. If the collective action succeeds in getting the favorable legislation, every firm or worker in the relevant category will benefit, whether or not that firm or that worker made any contribution the collective action. Similarly, when there is collective action to raise some price or wage above competitive levels by restricting the supply, the higher price or wage will be available to every seller in the relevant market, whether or not that seller helped to restrict the supply. Thus the rational actor in large groups, at least, will not normally act voluntarily in the collective interest of the groups of which he is a part: groups composed of rational individuals will not spontaneously act in their common interest.

Large groups, at least, will be able to act collectively only if they

<hr/>

101   See: M. Olson, *The Logic of Collective Action* (Cambridge: Harvard University Press, 1965).
M. Olson, *The Rise and Decline of Nations* (New Haven: Yale University Press, 1982).
M. Olson, 'The Political Economy of Comparative Growth Rates', *The Political Economy of Growth* (D.C. Mueller, ed.) (New Haven: Yale University Press, 1983).
M. Olson, 'Why Nations Rise and Fall' (Interview), *Challenge* (March/April, 1984), pp. 15–16, 20–21, 22–23. The reading below is taken from this interview
M. Olson, 'The Productivity Slowdown, The Oil Shocks, and the Real Cycle', *Journal of Economic Perspectives*, Vol. 2, No. 4 (Fall, 1988).

can work out 'selective incentives', or individual punishments or rewards that can provide the individuals who would automatically benefit from any collective action with an incentive to contribute toward the costs of collective action.

The most obvious examples of selective incentives are the union shop and the picket line, but all large organizations for collective action that last any length of time have selective incentives, often of very subtle kinds, that account for their membership. Dispersed groups like consumers, taxpayers, the unemployed, and the poor can never organize because no selective incentives are available to them, and they are not organized in any society. Those groups that can work out selective incentives, or that are small enough to be able to act collectively without them, can eventually organize. But they will ususally succeed only when they have both good leadership and favorable circumstances. It will take quite some time before most groups that can organize will have had the necessary good fortune. So it is only in long-stable societies where such groups are not violently destroyed or repressed that many organizations for collective action will exist.

Those groups that get organized for collective action do not usually have an incentive to produce anything or to try to make the economy work better, but instead have an incentive to struggle to get a larger share of what society produces. Consider an organization that represents clients who together earn one percent of the national income. If it strives to make the country more efficient, its clients will get on average only one percent of the benefits, but will have borne all of the costs of their effort. So it has an incentive to engage in distributional struggle instead, mainly by seeking special-interest legislation or colluding to get monopoly power. Worse still, it has an incentive to continue lobbying and cartelizing even when this brings exceptionally large losses in the efficiency of the economy; an organization representing one percent of the country will have an incentive to continue until the social losses from its activities become one hundred times as large as the amount it wins in the distributional struggle, since its clients will absorb on average only one percent of the social loss. So a society with a lot of distributional coalitions is like a china shop filled with wrestlers battling over its contents and breaking much more than they carry away.

......

One thing that will help is to increase the proportion of our economy exposed to free trade. Free trade not only allows us to gain from exploiting our comparative advantage in the ways that have been understood since David Ricardo, but it also undercuts distributional coalitions. It does so partly because it is very hard for coalitions to organize on a worldwide basis, since there are so many different languages and the potential members are spread across the world. Moreover, there is no world government to pass special-interest legislation at the behest of lobbies, so when there is free trade the world market really is a free market. Increasing the size of an area within which there is a free trade also helps a lot – many of the examples of impressive growth occurred after a customs union or national unification created a wider market.

When the six nations created the initial European Common Market, for example, rapid growth occurred. Several of these countries, most notably France and Italy, had to dismantle the protective tariff cover over manufacturing industries that had often formed cartels and fixed prices. The restrictive powers of national distributional coalitions were checked when customers could buy duty-free goods from anywhere in the Common Market.

A similar widening of the market occurred in Japan in the 19th century, after the Meiji Restoration of 1867–68. Japan had been desperately poor and economically isolated from the rest of the world. What little foreign trade Japan had, went mainly through one port under very restrictive conditions. Internally, Japan was divided up into more than 200 feudal domains with separate trade restrictions, so there wasn't much trade from one feudal principality to another. The Meiji Restoration put all of Japan under one government and thus allowed free trade within the entire country. Meanwhile, because of European pressure, the Japanese had to agree to have no tariff, except a revenue tariff at rates of 5 percent or less. So until the end of the 19th century, Japan enjoyed free trade and also exceptional growth.

I believe this rapid growth occurred in large part because the Japanese guilds, called 'Za', were undercut by the competition from foreign countries and from other parts of Japan. As the guilds collapsed, the firms that they had protected were forced to adapt to the new environment or to die out. But new firms emerged, and some of them are the great Japanese corporations we see today.

......

The protectionist steps we are now taking are protecting the very areas of the American economy in which our corporations and institutions are least efficient. A classic case is protection of the American steel industry – an industry with a history of cartelization of firms going back to the Pittsburgh cartel pricing system. There has also been cartelization of the labor force in steel, which has resulted in wages that are about two-thirds above the average wage in American manufacturing. No wonder the industry has trouble with foreign competition. We prevent reform by protecting this industry from competition, with triggerprice mechanisms and the like.

Automobiles are another example: this is a highly concentrated industry in which the firms never really fought it out in terms of price. Without full price competition among producers, it was easier for the organized labor force to negotiate wages about 50 to 60 percent above the norm in American manufacturing. Once again we naturally have problems with imports, and reforms in the industry are postponed so long as the so-called voluntary quota on imports of Japanes cars restrains foreign competition.

In new industries like high technology there hasn't been as much time for cartelization and collusion to develop, and we are doing better and these are products we export. So when we protect our industries from competition, we invariably prevent the shrinking and reform of the inefficient sectors of the American economy. Foreigners also earn fewer dollars from us because of the protection, and this slows down the expansion of our efficient export sectors.

......

Well, industrial policy is a phrase that can mean lots of different things to different people. Some people say industrial policy is a good idea and some say it's a bad idea. I say it's no idea at all. It's usually just a vague expression. Some of the more specific formulations propose that the existing business and labor organizations join the government in designing and administering an industrial policy. This would just give a better opening for special-interest groups of businessmen or workers to get an even larger share of income than they are getting now. So some of the proposals for an industrial policy just put the foxes in charge of the chicken coop. It is no accident that many of the advocates of these policies are from precisely the industries where distributional coalitions have done the most damage.

......

No historical process that is generally understood is inevitable. Greater understanding of the problem I am talking about would generate political support for a wide range of measures that would greatly improve the productivity of our economy. If there was a broader understanding of the problem, there would be more support for the elimination of tax loopholes and the uniform treatment of all kinds of income. A better public understanding of economics would also bring more resistance to restraints on free international trade and to barriers to free exchange in the domestic economy. It would also help undo the damage done by the distributional coalitions in the learned professions, for example.

......

I would argue that we can get reasonable economic stability without any intervention that strengthens distributional coalitions. If we have monetary and fiscal policies that expand aggregate demand at a slow and steady rate approximating the rate of growth in the productive capacity of the country, and if we have at the same time a more open and competitive economy with sensible microeconomic policies, then I believe we will also have a relatively stable economy without any deep recessions. We certainly have evidence that recently opened or recently established economies – such as the United States in the early and mid–19th century – had no problems to speak of with depressions and widespread unemployment.

READING 29

Jagdish Bhagwati

Biography

Jagdish Bhagwati (1934–   ) currently (1996) Professor of Economics and Political Science at Columbia University, New York, was born in Bombay, India on the 26th of July. He received his education in India, England and the United States. He acquired his PhD from the Massachusetts Institute of Technology. Earlier in his career he taught at that same institution.

Bhagwati has written sixteen books and edited fourteen others. In some of his earlier works on the economy of India he provided a number of intellectual arguments for the dismantling of India's counterproductive statist economic policies. His *Economics of Underdeveloped Countries* (1966) was very successful and was translated into six foreign languages. Books such as *Protectionism* (1988) and *The World Trading System at Risk* (1991) also received worldwide attention. In addition, Bhagwati is the author of numerous articles in scientific journals.

Between 1991 and 1993, Bhagwati was Economic Policy Advisor to the Director of the GATT. His wife, Padma Desai, is an economist as well. She also teaches at Columbia University.

The Work

Bhagwati begins by noting that during World War II, the US government took the initiative, in consultation with her allies, to propose various forms of international economic cooperation for the post-war period. One institution that emerged from those steps was the General Agreement on Tariffs and Trade, popularly known as the GATT. The General Agreement included general principles of trade conduct based on multilateralism and non-discrimination. The GATT rules would enable the contracting parties to enjoy the advantages of international trade in a multi-country world according to the principles of comparative advantage. The United States threw its weight behind this liberal trading system. From the mid-1940s to the mid-1970s world GNP grew fast and world trade grew even faster. No one can be too sure about what caused the post-war prosperity, says Bhagwati, but declining trade barriers and expanding world trade were surely contributing factors.

The causes of the post-war trade liberalization were most probably due to an interplay of ideas, interests and institutions. The architects of the post-war trade system had the Smoot–Hawley Act of 1930 as the historical example of how not to organize trade policy. This highly restrictive act set off reprisals by other countries and was instrumental in demolishing the system of international trade and payments that existed at the time. It also probably helped to deepen and prolong the Great Depression. Once the implications of the Smoot–Hawley Act were understood, it served to create a pro-free trade bias, according to Bhagwati. The designers of the post-war system were also aware of what economic theory had to say on the advantages of trade. The framers of the GATT chose the cosmopolitan version of the free trade theory, that is, they established a set of agreed-upon rules. Universal free trade would guarantee the best use of the world's resources. In order to maintain fair competitive trade, some provisions were made (Article VI) to allow for the use of countervailing duties, subsidized products and anti-dumping actions.

Interests, especially US interests, also helped to shape post-war liberalization. It is also probably true that American policy makers and industrial leaders had confidence in American competitive power and thus wanted open markets. However, the belief by the Executive Branch of government that liberal trade policies were in the nation's security interest was probably more decisive. A combination of trade and aid would help to contain Soviet imperialism, it was thought.

The American sponsorship of internationalism was also buttressed by institutional changes. Within the United States, the 1934 Reciprocal Trade Agreement Act transferred much of the tariff making power from Congress to the President, i.e. the Executive Branch, which is less subject to the pressures of special interest groups. Internationally, in order to promote world peace after 1945, the US and its allies planned to set up a number of international institutions of which eventually the GATT became part. GATT became the principal agent to supervise rules with regard to international trade policies. Although GATT members were required to accept balanced market-access obligations, the US was willing to accept justifiable exceptions to this rule. This was especially true in the early post-war period when Europe was recovering and when less developed countries made their first steps towards economic progress.

Until the mid-1970s, the principle of free international exchange of goods and services without discrimination was generally accepted. Since the 1970s, however, the world has witnessed the rise of the so-called new protectionism, characterized by the extensive use of non-tariff trade barriers (NTBs). The result was that the declining tariffs resulting from the GATT sponsored rounds of multi-lateral trade negotiations (in 1994, eight series or rounds of trade negotiations had taken place) began to be offset by the increase of NTBs such as voluntary export restraints, countervailing duties and anti-dumping provisions.[102]

The proliferation of protectionist policies after the 1970s was caused by a number of factors. Bhagwati notes that there is an obvious association between recessionary conditions and the growth of protectionist pressures. The weak economic performance of the American economy in the 1970s and the sharp recession of 1981–82 unleashed protectionist forces.

A second reason was the emergence of Japan as a successful industrial nation and the appearance of other newly industrialized countries (NICs) which all became important competitors. Import

---

102　A voluntary export restraint (VER), it will be remembered, is a special kind of quota that is set on the amount of goods that are exported to a given country. For all intents and purposes it is an import quota that is technically administered by its exporter. By 1991 about 34 per cent of the American market for manufactured goods was affected by VERs (ed.).

competition inside the United States from foreign imports increased and American firms also encountered stiffer competition on world markets. Some European countries also became thriving exporters. The old labor-intensive US domestic industries, such as textiles, faced strong competition from low-wage nations while the more advanced industries had to compete with those of Japan and the other modern nations. Nationalist fears were thus awakened, including those of 'deindustrialization' (removal of industries). This double squeeze had the same effect on the industrialized countries of Western Europe.

A third factor in the resurgence of the protectionist sentiment was the strong US dollar of 1980–1985 which caused exports to fall and imports to rise thus creating large trade deficits. Concurrently, the United States witnessed the erosion of its prevailing post-war rank in the global economy.[103] Bhagwati calls this the 'diminished giant syndrome'. It relates to the relative decline in the national economy when compared with the gross world product. Britain faced an identical problem towards the end of the nineteenth century when Germany and the US emerged as powerful industrial exporters at the time. It led to a rise of protectionist sentiment and claims for a self-sufficient empire. Now the US has to face Japan, which is well equipped with high-technology and knowledge-intensive industries as well as service-intensive industries. When new economic rivals emerge, it is sometimes accompanied by the perception that their success is due to unprincipled, unbalanced trade barriers or other unscrupulous devices. This is how Japan is often seen today whereas in reality Japan's tariff barriers are now among the lowest in the world. At the same time, except in agriculture, Japan's use of NTBs is more restrained than that of either the US or the European Community.

A final factor is related to the increasing global integration of financial markets. The immense flows of financial capital create the potential of large fluctuations in exchange rates. If a country's currency ends up being overvalued, its competitive advantage can be wiped out. This condition may feed protectionist interests.

In spite of the resurgence of protectionist forces, Bhagwati notices that there are still strong pro-free trade influences at work.

---

103   In 1992, the European Community's exports amounted to $568.7 billion or 20 per cent of world exports. The figures for the US were $448.2 billion or 15.8 per cent. Japan had $339.9 billion or 12 per cent (ed.).

The example of the early post-war period (1950–1975) with freer trade and rapidly rising incomes in all the important trading nations is eloquent to all observers. Available empirical studies also confirm that free trade has paid handsome dividends. The economic achievements of such countries as South Korea, Taiwan, Hong Kong and Singapore has demonstrated to the less developed countries that freer trade can contribute to their rapid economic development.

In the early post-war period, many developing countries had been sold on the combination of import substitution and protectionism. However, the example of the Pacific Tigers has shown that there are alternatives. Export-led development combined with more liberal trade policies has prompted not only fast economic growth but also successful industrialization.

A third factor here is that increased globalization and interdependence in the world economy tend to create pro-trade interests. As more firms import and export, their outlook will tend to become more cosmopolitan. Multinationals, which by definition operate in several countries, also have a direct interest in freer trade. Any kind of protectionism could reduce the returns on their global investments.

Another pro-trade force is that increased trade and investment reshuffles various interests. If, for example, country B threatens to curtail country A's car exports, policy makers in A may warn that they will lower farm imports from B. This could well induce the farm lobby in B to put pressure on B's legislators not to restrain car imports from A.

Finally, Bhagwati recognizes that now that direct foreign investment and relocation have become easier and faster, large corporations have less incentive to lobby for protection. The foreign investment option can be seen as an alternative to attempts to conduct activities aimed at influencing policy makers.

In spite of the fact that pro-trade forces are still very much alive, Bhagwati feels that the current trade system is seriously challenged by at least four factors: the advocacy of fair trade; the endorsement of the idea of managed trade; the approval of aggressive unilateralism; and the movement towards preferential trade blocs.

An objective of a free trade system like the one created under GATT auspices, should be fairness. To accomplish that end, the trade liberalization that has taken place during the eight rounds of GATT negotiations has usually been accompanied by countervailing duties and anti-dumping provisions.[104] Nowadays, however, claims of unfair trade, accompanied by demands for protection have become a habit. It is obviously easier for special interest groups to obtain protection if the foreign competitors are 'suspected; of unfair trading practices rather than if they simply mention their own difficulty in competing. Thus allegations of unfair trade can easily become the instrument used to promote protectionism, especially when they take the form of NTBs such as voluntary export restraints and voluntary import expansions. Of course, neither of them are truly voluntary. So-called fair trade policies are little else than bilateral fixed-quantity, result-oriented policies. They tend to replace the fixed-rules, multilateral, non-discriminating GATT trade system created after World War II. The idea that seems to materialize increasingly with publicists, congressmen, labor and business leaders is that the US can only engage in free trade with countries that are willing to change their anti-monopoly policies, environmental policies, infrastructural policies and labor policies to fit American preferences.

The GATT regime is also threatened by the furtherance of the idea of managed trade. Those who endorse it base their case on three simplistic notions. First it is said that most trade is managed anyway. Bhagwati's answer to this statement is that although GATT rules and self-restraint sometimes work imperfectly, that does not mean that the system should be abandoned. A second idea is that Japan does not play it by the rules and that Japanese firms use predatory strategies. Bhagwati answers that much of this talk is a myth. Although Japan did so in the 1950s, it no longer has an explicit industrial strategy. Its tariffs are low and Japanese firms are not more or less benign than US corporations. It is true, however, that many Japanese firms are successful and that success breeds discontent and envy. Third, it is also said that high-tech industries are so important that their

---

104   Webster's dictionary states that 'fair' implies an elimination of one's own feelings, prejudices and desires so as to achieve proper balance of conflicting interests'. Yet, in the US most of the foreign trade practices that are deemed to be unfair are not considered unfair if they are used by US corporations or the US government. For example, the US has levied an import surtax on rice from Thailand because of a minuscule Thai government rice subsidy. At the same time the American government was providing a subsidy to American rice growers that was over a hundred times larger (ed.).

emergence and survival cannot be left to the market place.[105]
Bhagwati points out that this argument is often based on the alleged
existence of very substantial externalities, meaning that the actions of
these industries result in extensive but uncompensated benefits to third
parties. Even Alexander Hamilton used this kind of argument. The
problem is that phenomenal externalities are usually more obvious to
politicians and to the companies that would like the protection than to
economists. It is also an undeniable fact that some policy makers take
pride in those industries which they equate with economic progress,
power and national prestige.[106] Actually, high-tech industries
probably don't need government support. The US, Japan and the
European Community all have access to advanced skills, research and
development capacities and capital. Therefore, in an open competitive
world, high-tech industries can perfectly well survive and grow in
these regions. If anything needs to be done in this field, says
Bhagwati, it should be in the form of a GATT sponsored code,
stipulating what kind of support is permitted and what is proscribed.
Managed or result-oriented trade will always be inferior as compared
to a system based on rules.

The obsession over unfair trade practices has engendered yet
another threat to agreed upon trade rules. Large countries, especially
the US, have turned to the use of political muscle to extract
concessions from other countries, especially the weaker ones. The US
now unilaterally defines what is and what is not fair trade as implied
by section 301 of the 1974 Trade Act and the Super 301 provision of
the 1988 Trade Act. Once it has decided that a trade practice is unfair
it then uses threats or acts of retaliation to get the foreign country to
modify its trade practices.[107]

---

105   High-tech industries can be defined as those industries that spend an above
      average percentage of their net sales receipts on research and development.
      Examples include the industries that produce aircraft, scientific instruments,
      drugs and medicines and industrial inorganic chemicals (ed.).
106   As early as the nineteenth century, German writers voiced this idea when they
      discussed Germany's 'unacceptable backwardness' as compared with England
      (ed.).
107   In 1974 Congress adopted the 1974 Trade Act. Section 301 gave the President
      of the US the power to retaliate against foreign countries that limit US exports
      by non-tariff barriers and other restrictive practices. Section 301 thus
      encouraged the President to act unilaterally rather than use GATT procedures
      to settle disputes because he was allowed to retaliate by withdrawing tariff
      concessions or by imposing import restrictions. The 1988 Trade Act contained

The benevolent side of this use of aggressive unilateralism may simply be an attempt to preserve the reciprocity of trade concessions. The malevolent aspect is that, especially with countries differing in economic size, the larger nations can use their power to prey on the weaker ones by wringing out concessions. Such procedures deviate a great deal from approved GATT procedures for settling disputes. They also disregard the most favored notion principle by introducing discrimination. Finally, they ignore the tariffs agreed to under GATT since the retaliatory tariffs are commonly at 100 per cent, if not more. With actions of this kind, the global trading system may degenerate and become dominated by the politically powerful, says Bhagwati.

A last menace to the global trading system according to Bhagwati is the formation of regional trading blocs. Regional economic integration is sanctioned by article XXIV of the GATT, in spite of the fact that it is an exception to the GATT rule that all trading partners should have equal access to markets. The inclusion of article XXIV was simply an acknowledgement that possible advantages might result from customs unions and free trade areas. In 1958 the U.S. endorsed the formation of the European Community, basically because it saw political benefits in a strong united Europe able to contain communist imperialism. The architects of the GATT included article XXIV with the idea that regional economic blocs would eventually fully integrate with low common tariffs. The article was not supposed to endorse limited preferential trade agreements. Yet the fact remains that regional trading blocs discriminate in the sense that there are different levels of trade barriers, one for the trade partners and another for the outsiders. Another potential problem of these associations is that they could fragment the world economy instead of unifying it. Finally, frequently regional economic blocks involve some form of trade diversion that harms world efficiency as well as other GATT

new Super 301 provisions under which a country's entire set of trade practices could be attacked. It required the President of the US to compile a hit list of trade offenders (unilaterally defined by the US Trade Representative) and take retaliatory measures if the foreign government refused to respond. Success was to be judged by an increase in US exports over a 3-year period. In other words Super 301 introduced a results-oriented standard. The Super 301 provisions expired at the end of 1990 (ed.).

members.[108] It seems to Bhagwati that the NAFTA agreement between Canada and Mexico could indicate a major shift towards regionalism on the part of the US[109] Bhagwati hoped that this is not the case because a multiplication of trading blocs could undermine the fixed-rules multilateral GATT system.

In his various books and articles, Bhagwati makes a number of policy proposals which in his view would enhance the multilateral trade system. First, it is important that the major trading nations, such as the US give up aggressive bilateral market-opening measures. If the US uses crowbar type policies, the stronger trade partners will retaliate. Moreover, the weaker nations may make concessions by taking away trade from other nations and giving it to the US. Such policies do not promote trade, they merely divert it. Confrontation and bitterness will prevail. Besides, such policies violate the spirit of the GATT.

Special interest groups seeking protection often petition merely to harass or tie up successful foreign producers in expensive legal defense actions. In order to limit the 'unfair trade practice' petitions, an impartial bilateral or multilateral panel should be used to examine these cases. If these charges are judged to have been trivial or were intended as a nuisance, penalties should be imposed.

As institutional procedures stand in countries like the US, only domestic industries are allowed to state their case. Consumer interests are always neglected. According to Bhagwati, what is needed is an institutional procedure that outlines the costs of protection to consumers so that the two interests are more properly balanced.

Another recommendation Bhagwati makes is that if a firm or industry is in difficulty and obtains temporary protection, allowing it to survive, then it should eventually be forced to reimburse to society at least some of the social costs incurred because of the protectionist relief.

Furthermore, countries, like the United States, should not link

108   Trade diversion refers to an efficiency loss associated with economic integration because less efficient, high-cost firms from a partner country may displace more efficient producers from a non-member nation which faces a tariff. As a result the international allocation of resources worsens and shifts production away from comparative advantage (ed.).

109   NAFTA or the North American Free Trade Agreement, concluded in 1993, creates a free trade zone by eliminating trade and investment barriers between the US, Canada and Mexico over a period of 15 years (ed.).

trade policy with political objectives. Trade access on a most favored national basis is sometimes linked to lofty goals, such as free outmigration of Jews or some other minority group; respect for human rights; or the like. However, these policies are often unmindful of the costs and the available alternatives. There are, after all, less costly measures for achieving these eminent goals, such as respect for human dignity, rights and freedom, says Bhagwati.

Bhagwati admits that domestic workers can be hurt by foreign imports. He, therefore, favors mechanisms including temporary protection to ease the decline and exit of firms unable to compete. But if temporary protection is given, it should be through non-discriminating tariffs. The revenues collected from the tariffs could be used for some kind of adaptation assistance in the form of worker retraining programs and the like.

Finally, Bhagwati has some thoughts on how to make regional blocs more compatible with GATT. One way would be to interpret article XXIV strictly and only to permit customs unions with a common tariff. Free trade areas should not be allowed. This policy measure would minimize the danger of trade diversion and increase the chances that the common external tariff will be close to the level of the relatively low tariff partner of the economic bloc.[110]

Extracts

The problem is that 'unfair trade' is a two-face creature: one face is friendly to free trade; the other frowns on it. Measures against unfair trade can be misused to allege unfair trade unfairly and thus to undermine free trade. And new definitions of widening scope, of what constitutes unfair, 'unreasonable' and unacceptable trade can be invented in unending improvisations. It is this other ugly face that we currently see and must fear. Why? There are several reasons.

Perhaps the most compelling reason for the increase in allegations of unfair trade is simply the outbreak of protectionist

110   See: J. Bhagwati, *Protectionism* (Cambridge: MIT Press, 1988).
       J. Bhagwati, *The World Trading System at Risk* (Princeton: Princeton University Press, 1991).
       J. Bhagwati, 'The Threats to the World Trading System', *The World Economy*, Vol. 15, No. 4 (July 1992) pp. 444–452. Readings are taken from this article.

pressures in the early 1980s, combined with the fact that protection is easier to procure if the successful foreign rival is alleged to be unfairly trading than if one pleads for it merely by citing the difficulty to one's situation.

......

But an important role in making unfair trade concerns potent in politics has been played also by developments in the realm of ideas. In the theoretical modes that have recently been analyzed with oligopolistic competition among competing firms from different nations formally modelled, one can demonstrate that the most improbable and negligible-looking form of unfair advantage provided by foreign governments can lead to predatory and large effects on one's industry's competitiveness and survival. The loss of a few high-tech industries to Japan, the visibility of some Japanese governmental support and the assumed presence of invisible support in a myriad of other ways, and the added certitude that those industries have substantial if immeasurable external economies, have combined to make the American scene a potentially fertile ground for such analytical demonstrations to flourish in a symbiotically interacting relationship between the theorists and the interest groups, correspondingly intensifying the obsession with unfair trade.

......

The notion of unfair trade in one's export markets has led not merely to conventional concerns about subsidies to one's rivals there but to two new twists. First, the question of *intra-sectoral reciprocity* of trade barriers has become fairly widespread by now, whereas earlier only some 'average' equality (across all imports) of mutual openness of the two countries would have sufficed to meet the criterion. Second, the question of fairness is now considered important enough to justify actions which can only be described as reopening the terms of earlier trade negotiations in view of *ex post* realities. This is certainly one of the many arguments for seeking unrequited trade concessions from Japan: that the difficulty of penetrating her markets was underestimated and hence the trade concessions given to her were more than those received, and that the situation must be corrected by new concessions by Japan.

These notions are dangerous enough and have driven some of the recent GATT-illegal aggressive unilateralism that will be discussed shortly. But they are benign compared with the extension of unfair-trade notions to wholly new areas, as in the 1988 Omnibus Trade and Competitiveness Act in the United States and in the Structural

Impediments Initiative (SII) with Japan. In both instances, the notion of unreasonable unfair-trade practices has been extended to areas that range over matters as diverse as domestic anti-monopoly policies, retail distribution systems, infrastructure spending, savings rates, workers' rights and so on. The American shopping list in the initial SII talks was reported to have included 240 items.

In going down this unwise trade route, we put the world trading system at risk. If everything becomes a question of fair trade, the likely outcome will be to remove the possibility of agreeing to a rule-oriented trading system. 'Managed trade' will then be the outcome, the bureaucrats allocating the trade according to what domestic lobbying pressures and foreign political muscle dictate.

......

Indeed, the question of managed trade has arisen as a threat to the GATT regime, not just because of the outbreak of unfair-trade-mindedness. It has also derived from three other notions: (i) Most trade is managed trade anyway. (ii) Japan, a major player today, is exotic and different; she will not, and cannot, play by rules. And (iii) high-tech industries are so important that they cannot be, or will not be, left to the market place. Each contention is erroneous.

Managed Trade Anyway? That trade occurs frequently by either bypassing or flouting GATT discipline, as with VERs on goods, or outside of its framework, as in agriculture and services, is indeed true. But it is a non-sequitur to conclude that rules do not work and more managed trade must therefore be the way to go. Yet, the glass is half empty and half full. But there is little doubt that it would have been emptier still if the GATT had not provided the overall framework and ethos that kept the glass upright instead of falling on its side. Moreover, the issue surely is whether we want to empty the glass further or to fill it up. The Uruguay Round negotiations are properly about filling it further.

Japan-is-different Argument. The 'Japan question' raises different issues, but, for recent critics, leads to a similar conclusion: that managed trade with Japan is either inevitable or desirable. In particular, culturalists have had a field day with their assertion that Japan's cultural uniqueness makes fix-rule trade with her impossible to contemplate and that Japan would in fact prefer managed trade. What is perceived as the 'Japan (trade) problem' has been with us a long time. It has reflected Japan's rapid growth, her import dependence for raw materials and her consequent rapid growth of exports that has been hard to accommodate in the often more sluggish world economy. The giant among Lilliputians has in consequence been repeatedly tied down by quantity restraints on her trade. If the Japanese appear responsive to negotiating on quantities, can it not be that they have learned from their trade history that this is the only way left open to them by their trading partners?

Again, the argument is often made that the Japanese behave differently in competition. They are 'predatory' and hence need to be restrained; our rules are meaningless for such predators. This contention is amusing, and the notion that American and other companies, by contrast, are 'benign' competitors is quite silly. Surely the 'animal spirits' of capitalist entrepreneurs are manifest in the United States and Western Europe as much as in Japan; the jugular is certainly the preferred target of all, although the Japanese may be better at times in getting there. The successful always appear predatory.

High-tech Support? The Japan question, however, feeds an altogether different, more universal, argument for managed trade in the United States. This relates to fear that unless trade restrictions and targets are imposed in high-tech industries, these industries will be lost to countries such as Japan which somehow managed to spawn and support them against the firms in countries that abstain from such support.

Now, while economists have great difficulty in finding externalities in specific industries and are generally inclined to discount claims of their existence in a sufficiently disproportionate degree so as to justify selected support, the opposite is true of politicians. Today, thanks to the scientific revolution that started in informatics and biogenetics, there is virtually no politician in any major developed country who does not feel that high-tech industries must be attracted and supported for their manifest externalities and, in non-economic terms, for their identification with modernisation in view of their state-of-the-arts and at-the-frontier status.

Given these perceptions, which then become realities that economists must work with, it is evident that a rules-oriented free trade system in high-tech industries will not be workable unless

• either there is a multilateral mechanism for bringing up front the various differing ways in which different governments are alleged to be biasing the outcomes in their favour, so that the 'net balance' of such artificial advantages among the different rivals is sorted out and then eliminated;

- or one goes yet further and manages essentially to get an acceptable degree of harmonisation (that then irons out the differences) by adherence to a code of dos and don'ts.

The latter may not be possible if governments have definite and differing preferences for certain policies. The former surely is possible and would enable the Japanese to point to such artificial US advantages that may stem from higher defence expenditures and support for science through the National Science Foundation when the Americans complain about the Japanese Government's guidance and support to pooled research, etc. The multilateral format would ensure that the finger-pointing would be fair and balanced, where appropriate, without the advantage of the thicker finger in bilateral one-on-one confrontations.

......

The concerns over unfair trade have created yet another hazard for the fix-rule GATT system in the recent use of aggressive unilateralism by the United States to impose on others its unilaterally-defined views of unfair trade practices.

I refer here, of course, to the use of the Section 301 and super 301 provisions of American trade legislation, as updated in the 1988 Act, to demand negotiations from specific countries on 'priority' practices that the United States find unacceptable, regardless of whether they are proscribed by the GATT or another treaty, and to seek their abolition on a tight time schedule set by the United States, using tariff retaliation by the United States if necessary.

......

There is also the problem that means may affect ends. It is not likely that a declared willingness to break GATT commitments, and actual breach thereof, may spread cynicism towards such commitments by others rather than adherence to them in the future? I would even suggest that it undermines the credibility of the commitments accepted by nations that take the law thus into their own hands.

......

The obsession with unfair trade, the flirtation with managed trade and aggressive unilateralism: these threats to the fix—rule, multilateral GATT system are real and, in my view, few knowledgeable scholars will disagree on the issues they raise. But an altogether different, and debatable, type of threat to the GATT system is posed by the recent growth of regionalism *à la* Article XXIV of the GATT. The nature of the threat must be clearly understood therefore, and ways of containing it must be found.

READING 30

Melvin Krauss

Biography

Melvin Krauss was born on December 5, 1938 in New York City. He did his undergraduate work at Brooklyn College, New York, and continued his studies at New York University (NYU), where he obtained his MA (1965) and PhD (1968).

In 1968 he taught for one year at the London School of Economics, whereafter he went to Canada to be part of the economics faculty at McMaster University in Hamilton, Ontario. This period lasted from 1969 to 1971. In 1969 Krauss married a lady of Dutch nationality. From 1971 to 1972 he stayed with the 'Europa Instituut' of the University of Amsterdam in the Netherlands, whereafter he joined the faculty of the John S. Hopkins University in Bologna, Italy. After a two-year stay (1973–1975) at Stanford University and a one-year sojourn (1976) at the Institute for International Economic Studies in Stockholm, Sweden, he became a Professor of Economics at New York University. Between 1980 and 1982 he obtained the position of visiting fellow at the Hoover Institution at Stanford. In 1982 he became a Senior Fellow of that same Institution.

He lives with his wife in Portola Valley, California, but continues to teach at NYU.

His publications are mostly in the area of international economics. His book *The New Protectionism* was published in 1978. A second work *The Economics of Integration* came out in 1981. In 1983 a monograph entitled *Development Without Aid* was issued and his book *How NATO Weakens the West* was brought out in 1988. Most of his articles deal with the global economy and trade policy.

The Work

Melvin Krauss stresses the well-known fact that the 1960s and 1970s have witnessed the emergence of the welfare state which he defines as a non-communist egalitarian state in which substantial government intervention in economic and social affairs is accepted as normal. The Scandinavian countries, Great Britain and the Netherlands are rather pure examples of the welfare state. In other countries, such as the United States, the welfare state has made significant inroads.

The first aim of the welfare state is to redistribute income and economic power from the non-favored to the favored groups. Typically this means from capital to labor. Needless to say, the favored groups usually have more votes than the non-favored ones. The second purpose is to provide economic security to individuals by shielding them from change that could somehow affect them adversely. To satisfy these objectives, the government intervenes in the private economy thereby markedly expanding the role of government. This situation plays into the hands of politicians in democracies. As they compete for office, they make promises to the electorate which comes to think of these pledges as the legitimate functions of government. Each time a promise is fulfilled a new government function is created and with each new function the politicians acquire more power.[111]

As stated before, the welfare state makes numerous commitments. Each additional undertaking means a greater invasion into the private economy. The range of intervention typical of the welfare state is remarkable and no corner of society is left untouched. There are minimum wages, labor subsidies, capital controls, investment grants, price fixing arrangements, subsidies of all kinds, a whole array of taxes, government sponsored coercive monopolistic practices by trade unions, export subsidies, tariffs, quotas, and much more.

In a market economy, economic change is the consequence of changes in consumer preferences, in technology and in international cost structures. These alterations lead to a reallocation of resources and a redistribution of incomes. Change involves adjustment and adjustment involves change. If in the process certain resource owners are made worse off they will typically try to use the political process to avoid the adjustment. The contemporary welfare state characteristically disfavors adjustments such as resource mobility especially labor mobility. Thus, the government intervenes to bring about the 'desired result'. For instance, the government may protect weak industries with subsidies or protectionist devices. Labor may be

---

111   In fact, the welfare state like other varieties of socialism gives rise to a new class of political and economic administrators with considerable power. The additional expansion of government also erodes the freedom of the average citizen (ed.).

made immobile, occupationally and/or geographically, through a system of extended unemployment benefits. The worker receiving assistance is thus permitted to resist the necessary adjustments called for by the economy. The fulfillment of the welfare state commitments thus often means keeping resources in lower productivity uses and out of higher productivity ones. The consequence is misallocation of resources, lower economic growth and eventually economic stagnation, all attributable to the inflexibility and the rigidity intrinsic of the interventionist welfare state. The inherent contradiction of the welfare state is that this system requires a high level of productivity and economic growth to support it. At the same time, the welfare economy consists of arrangements which tend to undermine the very factors on which it depends. Thus in the long run the welfare state is self-destructive. It both depends on productivity and economic growth and at the same time lowers them. The attempt to create economic security for everybody only insures the opposite. A successful welfare state depends on policies which will ultimately undermine it. This is the great inner contradiction of the welfare state as Krauss sees it.

The new protectionism which reared its head in the late 1960s is, according to Krauss, an unavoidable by-product of the welfare state. To be in favor of the welfare state ipso facto is to be in favor of protectionism. Government interventions into the private economy are the 'lifeblood' of the welfare state. Since the welfare state wants to assist specific (usually weak) industries and specific segments of the labor force, protectionism becomes inevitable. At the same time, the welfare state weakens productivity by breaking the link between effort and income or between production and consumption. Moreover, the resulting additional decline in the growth rate of GDP leads to new protectionist demands and measures to maintain stagnating or falling incomes and employment.

The new protectionism, says Kraus, like the protectionism of the 1930s is an expression of a 'profound skepticism' as to the ability of the market to allocate resources and distribute incomes to the satisfaction of society. The new protectionism consists mostly of non-tariff barriers (NTBs) which obstruct the flow of international trade. They include such devices as export subsidies, industrial subsidies, discriminatory government procurement practices, differentially applied safety standards, voluntary export restraints and 'orderly' market arrangements. The new protectionism is more perfidious than the old. Tariffs are easily identifiable, whereas NTBs are more hidden and more difficult to prove. At the same time, their effects are more difficult to assess. Moreover, NTBs do not work through the price mechanism the way tariffs do.

One of the prime policies of the welfare state is the subsidy of domestic producers. The export subsidy is an example. Export subsidies can be direct payments, grants of tax relief or subsidized loans to the nation's exporters or potential exporters. They can also be low interest loans to foreign buyers of the nation's exports.

Industrial and export subsidies have a number of interesting implications. Because governments consider subsidies as a purely domestic matter they are less willing to subject them to international negotiations. Furthermore, these techniques, especially industrial subsidies, lead to a substantial concentration of discretionary power in the hands of policy makers and legislators. For example, it is common in some European countries that when the government gives a loan or a grant, in return it usually asks for acceptance of certain government conditions on some key issues.

Substantial subsidization of domestic firms and industries in the welfare state economies puts the exporters of the remaining predominantly free market economies at a disadvantage in the international market place. This, according to Krauss, creates an incentive for them to put pressure on their countries to similarly intervene. An international solution to this problem would be to establish a specific body of experts within the GATT system. This body should have the judicial powers and the enforcement facilities to decide the rights and wrongs of subsidization disputes. Penalties could be levied on an international basis and not merely by the injured party. The important question here is whether the participating countries will have the political resolve to agree upon such a procedure. The nationalistic solution for the remaining free enterprise nations would be to maintain the integrity of their domestically preferred economic systems by not reacting to what others do. Although some domestic industries or firms may suffer when foreign nations adopt a system of subsidies, the increased pressure may induce the free enterprise firms to become more efficient. Another consequence of subsidies is that they enhance the prosperity of consumers elsewhere who buy their products. Subsidies lower prices to foreigners at the expense of the domestic tax payers who finance the cost of the subsidy.

Krauss has clearly made an important contribution to the free trade versus protectionism debate by stressing the link between the contemporary welfare state and protectionism. A few figures show the extent to which the United States has become a welfare state. Transfer payments to individuals as a percentage of federal spending rose from 24 per cent in 1960 to 43 per cent in 1994. In order to finance its welfare expenditures, the federal government chose to borrow. Thus, the public debt as a percentage of GNP rose from 55 per cent in 1960 to 67 per cent in 1994.

It is becoming increasingly obvious that the redistribution of income as practiced by the welfare state leads to a weakening of the incentives of the price system. Suppose for example that because of a change in preferences consumers want fewer cigars and more bikes. In a market economy the 'invisible hand' compels adjustment. Profits and incomes in the cigar industry would decline while profits and revenues in the bike industry would rise. Resources would move out of cigar production into the bike industry. However, if the welfare state severely taxes the growing profits and incomes of the bike makers while subsidizing the declining profits and incomes of the cigar producers, the appropriate movement of resources is inhibited and factors of production become misallocated. The destruction of the rewards–penalty system leads to inefficiency, keeping resources in low productivity employments. In more general terms, a program of government taxation and subsidies tends to equalize incomes and makes those incomes less dependent on people's contributions to the nation's output. Such a policy neutralizes the orders of the price system. The results are predictable. People will work and save less. They will contribute fewer resources to the production process. The growth rate of GDP will suffer and may eventually become negative. In the end, the egalitarian crusaders may have destroyed the very thing they wanted to distribute. This, as Krauss pointed out in other terms, is the main inner contradiction of the welfare state.

Krauss also explains that the interventionist mentality of the welfare state will affect its commercial policies. For one thing, the combination of slower economic growth, rising unemployment, and intense international competition create an environment favorable to protectionism. The low efficiency industries of the welfare state have a greater problem surviving without it. But again the outcome is predictable. As some nations become more protectionist, others tend to follow and in the end, everyone will be worse off, as was the case in the 1930s.[112]

Extracts

The Welfare State and Protectionism

In a well-functioning market economy, government interventions should be minimized other than for the provision of essential public services. There are, however, always special interests that want to alter the outcomes that result from the free interaction of buyers and sellers in the market place in their favor, and restrictions on international trade have been a favorite interventionist mechanism. Their popularity no doubt is due to the fact that their true purpose and effects are easily hidden behind the almost universal fear of foreigners, and the fact that foreigners do not vote in domestic elections. The slogan that it is foreigners who must pay, however false, has given trade restrictions considerable political appeal.

Tariffs and quotas have been imposed for all types of reasons: simply to raise tax revenue; to redistribute income to particular groups; to reduce unemployment; to improve the balance of payments; to accumulate gold; to promote an 'infant industry'; and to prevent an older industry from dying.

Economists have consistently pointed out that trade restrictions are an inefficient means of achieving each of the above objectives. Trade restrictions are a poor way to raise tax revenue, a poor way to redistribute incomes, a poor way to promote domestic employment, and so on. The argument is that the overall economy suffers when the special interest is satisfied by the tariff or the quota. The group that gains income, gains employment, or gains gold does so at the expense of the overall community when the gain is achieved by a restriction on international trade. This argumentation is essentially one for efficient intervention. But behind this argument is the view often found that there should be no intervention at all, except when there is a true consensus for it in the community. 'A deaf ear to special interest' is the true motto of the free trade.

The issue of free trade versus protectionism is that of the conflict

---

112 M. B. Krauss, *The New Protectionism; The Welfare State and International Trade* (New York: New York University Press, 1978) pp. 24–26, 36–37, 105–114.

between special interest and the public interest. It also concerns the preservation of the market economy and the price mechanism.

Free traders are against protection not only because it subordinates the general interest to special interest but because it is feared that protection will undermine the market economy and the price mechanism. Accordingly, free traders prefer certain types of trade restrictions to others. The tariff is felt to be a 'conformable interference'. This exacerbates the conflict between free traders and protectionists, since the latter prefer the quota to the tariff; they believe the quota renders greater and more secure protection.

The New Versus the Old Protectionism

In one sense, the new protectionism is not protectionism at all, at least not in the traditional sense of the term. The old protectionism referred exclusively to trade restricting and trade expanding devices, such as the tariff or export subsidy. The new protectionism is much broader than this; it includes interventions into foreign trade but is not limited to them. The new protectionism, in fact, refers to how the totality of government intervention into the private economy affects international trade. The emphasis on trade is still there – hence the term 'protection'. But what is new is the realization that virtually all government activity can affect international economic relations.

The emergence of the new protectionism in the Western world reflects the victory of the interventionist, or welfare, economy over the market economy. Jan Tumlir writes, 'The old protectionism ... co-existed, without any apparent intellectual difficulty, with the acceptance of the market as a national as well as international economic allocation and distribution mechanism – indeed, protectionists as well as (if not more than) free traders stood for *laissez faire*. Now, as in the 1930s protectionism is an expression of a profound skepticism as to the ability of the market to allocate resources and distribute incomes to societies' satisfaction.'

It is precisely this profound skepticism of the market economy that is responsible for the new protectionism. In a market economy, economic change of various colors implies reallocation of resources and redistribution of incomes. The consensus of opinion in many communities apparently is that such reallocations and redistributions often are not proper. Hence, the government intervenes to bring about a more desired result.

The victory of the welfare state is almost complete in northern

Europe. In Sweden, Norway, Finland, Denmark, and the Netherlands, government intervention in almost all aspects of economic and social life is considered normal. In Great Britain this is only somewhat less true. Government traditionally has played a very active role in economic life in France and continues to do so. Only West Germany dares to go against the tide toward excessive interventionism in Western Europe. It also happens to be the most successful Western European economy.

The welfare state has made significant inroads in the United States as well as in Western Europe. Social security, unemployment insurance, minimum-wage laws, and rent control are by now traditional welfare state elements on the American scene. And, in its first year, the Carter administration proved particularly vulnerable to protectionists. Hardly an industry that asked the Carter administration for protectionist assistance had to walk away empty handed.

The color television industry obtained 'voluntary' export quotas. The steel industry has received subsidized loans and a reference price scheme. Sugar growers got higher prices for sugar and dairy farmers got higher prices for milk. The shoe industry got protection from foreign shoes and the trade unions got protection from illegal aliens. Under President Carter, the level of interventionism has accelerated at an alarming pace.

......

The great attraction of the welfare state to many persons is that it appears to combine high rates of economic growth with high rates of social consumption – that is, economic affluence with social justice to boot. This is because the basic relationship between economic growth and social consumption is viewed to be complementary. The higher the rate of economic growth, the greater the potential social consumption.

Economic growth is conceived to *allow* social consumption without creating strains on all society. Daniel Bell writes, 'economic growth has been a 'political solvent'. While growth invariably raises expectations, the means for the financing of social welfare expenditures ... without reallocating income ... or burdening the poor ... has come essentially from economic growth ... As the Kennedy and Johnson administrations found out ... the Congress was more willing to vote for the social welfare costs of the New Frontier or the Great Society so long as economic growth provided additional fiscal revenues, than to reform the tax structure or increase the weight of taxes in society.'

The argument of this chapter is that Bell's analysis is seriously incomplete. While economic growth may permit social consumption in the short run, in the longer run social consumption will reduce economic growth. The thesis is that the true relationship between economic growth and social consumption is competitive – that is, that there exists a trade-off between economic growth and social consumption. High rates of economic growth are thus conceived to be incompatible with high levels of social consumption.

One reason for this incompatibility is that high levels of social consumption necessarily imply protectionist measures that stagnate the economy. The new protectionism did not develop in a vacuum. It is an outgrowth of social policies that promise economic security – that labor and capital be kept in low-productivity uses where they are comfortable rather than being forced to adjust to alternative high-productivity uses. High rates of social consumption must stagnate the economy by making the economy rigid and inflexible. The new protectionism represents the means by which *rigor mortis oikonomikus* sets in.

The Inherent Contradictions of the Welfare State

It is novel to write about the inherent contradictions of the welfare state. Usually it is capitalism that is alleged to be the victim of an inherent contradiction. The Marxist view, if one sentence can do it justice, is that because of 'inherent contradictions' large imbalances between production and consumption will make the demise of capitalism inevitable. This position has been modified, as I understand it. We now have a neo-Marxist and even a neo-neo-Marxist interpretation, as well as, one might add, reasonably flourishing capitalism in some parts of the globe. I am sure I will be forgiven if I 'usurp' the inherent-contradictions theme and give it something of a new twist.

Simply stated, the inherent contradiction of the welfare state is that the welfare state requires a high level of productivity to support it, but that welfare state interventionist policies necessarily reduce productivity levels. Hence, it is argued, the welfare state is not a sustainable phenomenon in the long run. It consists of policies that undermine the factors upon which it critically depends.

Consider, for example, the case of Sweden. Since the industrialization process started in Sweden in 1870, the Scandinavian country had a good overall growth record. In the pre-World War II period, it grew somewhat faster than in the other OECD countries, while in the postwar period it grew somewhat more slowly. Since the modern welfare state in Sweden did not begin until after the war (although the Social Democratic party first came to power in 1932), Sweden's growth record by comparison with that of other OECD countries should serve as a warning to those who would argue that Sweden is wealthy because it is a welfare state. Rather, the reverse is true. Sweden has a welfare state because it is wealthy.

The ascension of Social Democratic parties in the politics of northern Europe and of the Democratic party in the United States can be interpreted as a reflection of an increased demand for *economic security* on the part of populations with steadily rising incomes. This increased demand – the 'revolution of rising entitlements' – can be taken to mean the *right* of workers to a job, at the location of their choice and at the income of their choice. Assar Lindbeck notes that during the postwar period one characteristic feature of economic policy in the Western world has been the increase in the *number* of policy targets. This is true not only in the northern European countries but in the United States as well. No longer do governments just aim for full employment; they also aim for satisfactory distributions of employment among regions, sexes and races.

To meet its expanded commitments, the government makes extensive intervention, through the kinds of protectionist devices discussed, into the private economy. Since the industries and jobs that are threatened by a changing economic environment can be expected to be weak industries, fulfillment of the welfare state commitments usually means keeping resources in low productivity and out of high-productivity uses. Protection of the shipbuilding, shoe, steel, and textile industries are examples of what economic security implies. The essential point is that the welfare economy becomes increasingly unable to adjust to a constantly changing environment because its social commitments prevent it from doing so. The result must be stagnation.

Disincentives to produce are inherent in the welfare economy. The commitment of the welfare government to provide economic security 'from the cradle to the grave' cuts the link between production and consumption for welfare state citizens. The enjoyment of economic resources becomes unrelated to economic performance. Naturally, production suffers when both employers and employees know the state will bail them out no matter how poorly they perform.

Some of the disincentives to produce are planned; others are unintended by-products of welfare policies. Planned disincentives to produce are exemplified by programs that encourage workers to take an increasing proportion of their incomes in the form of leisure. The four-day week and work rules that make sick leave too much of a temptation for many to resist are examples. On the other hand, the fact that leisure represents tax-free income in countries where marginal tax rates on work income are high – sometimes astronomically so – means that the increased demand for leisure also is an unintended by-product of other social policies. The increased demand for leisure in welfare states is reinforced by the fact that while taxes are positively related to work income, subsidies either are negatively related to work income or are not related to work income at all. It thus cannot be argued that by taking increased leisure the citizen of the welfare economy reduces the subsidies he receives as well as the taxes he must pay. In fact, the opposite is the case. Taxes are reduced and subsidies are probably increased as more leisure is consumed.

The increased demand for leisure is one of the major consequences of high taxes in welfare states. But there are other consequences that also tend to stagnate the economy of the welfare state. The increased demand for leisure is a form of tax avoidance. Another such form is the use of barter as a substitute for monetary transactions. The local dentist in a welfare state may not accept cash for his services. But he will accept the services of the person who needs dental work, because the exchange of services cannot be taxed. The point is that it is easier to hide services received in kind than cash from the tax collector. The consequences of the increased use of barter is reduced efficiency in the economy, since the efficiencies created by the use of money as a medium of exchange are lost.

There is, of course, a great deal of tax avoidance in the welfare economy. That is how many citizens come to live with high tax rates. But the danger of tax avoidance is that it can divert resources from more important to less important economic uses. Since resources respond to net of tax rather than to gross of tax returns, they flow where the net of tax return is highest. But this can very well be to a use that has less economic value than its alternatives. The result is a tax-induced misallocation of resources. The alternative that appears most profitable to the private person is not the most profitable for the community as a whole, because the tax differentials have given the private person the wrong signals.

The emphasis on economic security in welfare states undoubtedly has led to the demand that income (and economic power in general) be redistributed from capital to labor. The consequences of such redistribution on economic growth can be summarized as follows: They

1. Reduce savings if the savings propensity of capitalists is greater than that of labor;
2. Increase the demand for leisure;
3. Encourage resources to stay in low-productivity and out of high-productivity uses;
4. Encourage capital flight, which can be prevented only by efficiency-distorting controls;
5. Increase the demand for foreign labor to work in the welfare state, which can create efficiency distortions;
6. Encourage the flight of 'human capital' – that is, the exit of talented high-productivity citizens;
7. Encourage tax avoidance.

Regardless of whether one feels the redistribution of income from capital to labor to be equitable; the consequence of such redistribution surely is to undermine the national product which finances social consumption in the welfare state.

This has become a subject of some concern in Europe and America. Will there be sufficient output ten years hence to finance the pension I am paying for today? This concern reflects a certain skepticism about the younger generation by their elders. By establishing the government as an intermediary between different generations, the welfare state did not take the fate of the older generation out of the hands of the young, as some mistakenly thought. Indeed, the opposite may be the case, since a good deal of social expenditure in the welfare state consists in trading present for future consumption. If future product is insufficient to support the claims on it – including those of the older generation to pensions and the like – there is going to be one large group of disappointed Danes, Dutchmen, Swedes – and Americans – some ten to fifteen years from now. The current crisis of the US social security system bears witness to this problem.

Interestingly enough, in the northern European welfare states, the decrease in productivity levels induced by the welfare state policies has not occurred as rapidly as some might have expected. This is because the older generation of norther Europeans, raised in a competitive atmosphere, had the work ethic sufficiently instilled in them to resist the welfare state incentives to slow down and do less. However, the consistent attacks on individualism and the competitive spirit, which starts in school at an early age, along with the promise of guaranteed economic security, have made their mark on the new generation of northern Europeans. The old values have been undermined, including the Protestant religious values that were compatible with hard work and saving; productivity is down; and the welfare state is threatened for the first time in northern Europe. To put this point in the technical jargon of the economist, the 'elasticity of response' to the welfare economy's 'disincentives to produce' appears to be greater with the younger generation than with the older one. This should serve as a stern warning to those who would make 'competition and individualism' dirty words in the United States.

One important implication of the enhanced response to the welfare economy's disincentives to produce is the present inflation that affects most of the developed world. The welfare economy does little to constrain the desire to consume – indeed, it enhances it by redistributing income from savers to consumers – at the same time that it dampens both the desire to produce and produce efficiently. The inevitable result is inflation. The inflation that appears to be built in to the developed economies would be reduced if the restriction on production imposed by production taxes, social changes, minimum wages, and income taxes were removed. It also could be expected to be reduced if resources which are kept in comfortable low-productivity uses were transferred to high-productivity ones.

The thesis that high levels of social consumption restrict economic growth is supported by Charles Kindelberger's argument as to the cause of Europe's outstanding growth record during the 1950s. Kindleberger attributed Europe's outstanding growth record to the fact that northern Europe had available to it during the 1950s virtually limitless supplies of labor at reasonable rates – in economist's technical jargon, a perfectly elastic supply curve of labor. Once started, growth could gather momentum because the increased demand for labor implied by growth would not bid wages up.

Eventually, of course, rapid economic growth in northern Europe would exhaust the supply of labor available to it at a fixed wage. At this point, wages could be expected to rise and the North and the South competed for the increasingly scarce labor. Economic growth in the North would then slow down. But this would be a result of a natural economic process and not the outcome of an artificially imposed increase in the price of labor imposed by government. The word 'artificial' is used because the increase in the cost of labor to firms would not be the result of labor's scarcity but of its political power to extract income transfers from the rest of the community.

Minimum wages, social security taxes, the encouragement by government of monopolistic practices by trade unions are all part of the welfare economy, and all contribute to making the cost of labor to firms higher than the free market for labor services would dictate in their absence. It is no accident that the increased incidence of social changes to make labor artificially expensive on the one hand, and a dramatic slowdown in the growth rates of the Western economies by comparison with their growth performance in the 1950s and early 1960s on the other, have occurred almost simultaneously from the late 1960s to the present. And while correlation does not prove cause and effect, it certainly doesn't disprove it either.

The analysis of the preceding paragraphs argues that the cause of the 'stagflation' – inflation with sluggish growth – that presently affects the Western economies can be laid at the doorstep of the welfare state interventions in America and northern Europe that have made labor an artificially costly factor of production at the expense of capital. Stagflation has been the undesired though omnipresent by-product of alleged socially just income redistribution policies. The long-run implications of this are that the welfare state is self-destructive. It both depends upon economic growth and destroys it. In the long run, the demand for a secure economic income at a given level or rate of increase, regardless of the changes that are being wrought elsewhere, proves illusory because the attempt to obtain the secure income reduces the ability of the economy to produce it. It is perhaps the essential irony of the welfare state that the attempt to insure one's economic position serves only to insure the opposite!

READING 31

Paul Robin Krugman

Biography

Paul Robin Krugman, Professor of Economics in the Department of Economics at Massachusetts Institute of Technology (MIT), Cambridge, Massachusetts, was born in Albany, New York on February 8, 1953. He obtained his BA from Yale University in 1974 and his PhD from MIT in 1977. Between 1977 and 1980 he was

Assistant Professor at Yale University. He then returned to MIT, first as Associate Professor and then since 1984 as Professor. In 1983 he also became a Research Associate at the National Bureau of Economic Research. From 1982–83 he served as Senior Economist at the Council of Economic Advisors.

Many of his investigations and writings relate to international economics and his work on strategic trade policy has attracted wide attention. Apart from his more technical writings, Krugman also published (with Maurice Obstfeld) a textbook entitled: *International Economics: Theory and Policy* (3rd edn. 1994). In 1990 Krugman came out with a well written, popular book *The Age of Diminished Expectations* designed to give the practical reader an understanding of current issues. In 1996 he came out with a book entitled *Pop Internationalism* in which he criticized unauthentic international economics.

In 1991 Paul Krugman won the John Bates Clark Medal awarded by the American Economic Association every two years to an American economist under forty who has made significant contributions to economic thought and knowledge.

The Work

Krugman agrees that since the late 1970s there has been some fundamental rethinking in the theory of international trade. These new developments have challenged the traditional models based on constant returns to scale and perfect competition.[113] The more recent theories have stressed the fact that the majority of international markets are characterized by imperfect competition, economies of scale and externalities. While comparative advantage due to differences in factor prices, technology and resource availability is clearly important, so is international trade driven by increasing returns to scale, and innovation, generated through research and development.

Much, if not most, international trade is in items produced by oligopolistic firms which experience declining cost per unit over a broad range of output. The widespread prevalence of non-purely

---

113 It there are constant returns to scale, then nothing prevents a firm from expanding output without incurring any increase in long-run average cost. Consequently a firm could conceivably take over the whole market for a product. Thus there is at least a potential contradiction between constant returns to scale and perfect competition (ed.).

competitive conditions in international markets has led a number of observers to conclude that free trade is non-optimal. Some trade activists have actually used these models to build a case for government intervention in order to support advance high-tech and other glamour sectors in the United States.[114]

The first important idea is that new thinking has led to the conclusion that protection or subsidy of an industry can be beneficial when that industry generates net external economies. Externalities, or spillover effects, are the harmful or beneficial impacts of the consumption or production of certain goods or services on third parties or the community at large for which compensation is not requested and which are not reflected in decreases or increases in market prices. Consequently, when externalities are present, the market fails to do its job correctly and will not allocate resources efficiently. Examples of beneficial or positive production externalities are, for instance, the case of a firm which trains workers who eventually go to work for other firms that do not have to pay for the training costs. Or take the case of a lumber company that plants trees that in turn cause the local weather to improve. In either case, since the company providing the service is not reimbursed for the cost of it under free market conditions, less and too little of the beneficial activity will occur. Another case of externalities in production exists when certain firms in an industry grow, and that growth benefits other firms inside and outside the industry *indirectly*. For instance, if in an area certain firms expand and it pays other firms to enter and provide other services like legal, repair, consultation, transportation and financial functions at a lower cost, then not only does the firm that expanded originally benefit, but other firms in the area do also.

High-tech firms or sectors producing innovative products such as semi-conductors, are often said to yield direct positive externalities.[115] Their innovation often leads to improved or new products or processes, they can generate well-paid jobs. They frequently improve the technology in their sectors, and they may ameliorate the global competitive position of the country in which they are located. Firms investing heavily in research and development (R&D) are likely to harvest generous amounts of technical knowledge.

---

114 Needless to say that non-optimality does not necessarily make a case for government intervention (ed.).

115 It is obvious that the fact that there is social benefit from innovation does not prove the existence of externalities (ed.).

However, those firms may not be able to appropriate fully all the benefits of the know-how they create. There is not always an effective way of excluding other firms from taking advantage of the knowledge once it comes into existence. In other words, the exclusion principle may not prevail and the knowledge becomes a kind of public good.[116] If others can use the fruits of a firm's research and it is not fully reimbursed for it, such enterprises may be induced to under-invest in R&D.[117] Protection by tariffs or quotas or government subsidies could be applied to correct this situation by motivating a firm or an entire industry to raise the level of investment in R&D. However, there is only a case for government assistance when domestic firms benefit from each other's activities. If foreign firms also benefit from the new knowledge generated by domestic companies there is less of a justification for assisting them.

Rethinking of international trade theory emphasizes the fact that we live in a world in which oligopoly prevails. In such a world the number of participants in some particular industry is small. Moreover, oligopolistic rivalry exists because the actions of one firm affect the profits of others. Profit opportunities above and beyond the normal return for scarce factors of production are not ruled out. These 'excess profits' are often not easily competed away because barriers to entry into the industry exist. These barriers make it too expensive, risky or impossible for new firms to enter into production. Exclusive patent rights, trade barriers or economies of scale are examples of such obstacles. Exclusive patent rights and trade barriers which are superimposed by governments add to the impediments created by the conditions of the market like economies of scale or regional differences in factor prices. If these excess profits are not competed away, they become a form of economic rent which benefits the shareholders, the entrepreneurs and the workers in those industries. Strategic trade policy then emerges as a national attempt to capture as large a share of these profits as possible. As an example, protectionism or subsidies by a national government may make entry by foreign companies into a domestic market more difficult. With

---

116 A public good provides a nonexcludable benefit that is available to everyone even if they do not pay for it. Fireworks and weather forecasts are standard examples. But it is also true for scientific knowledge, mathematical formulas and similar creations of the mind that are part of the public domain (ed.).

117 What should not be forgotten is that America's competitors, such as Japan and Germany, face the same problem (ed.).

more home companies enjoying these rents, domestic incomes and tax revenues are raised at the expense of foreign countries. Such predatory policies could in principle be rewarding.[118] An example will clarify this. Suppose we take the extreme oligopoly case, that of a duopoly of about equal size producing a comparable product. In two hypothetical countries Somewhere and Elsewhere, we have two firms: Flyfast and Flycheap, both able to produce a comparable specific new type of aircraft. Suppose further that Flyfast, located in Somewhere has some kind of margin of advantage. However, Flyfast would like to recapture some of its R&D costs and needs the entire world market to become large enough to achieve substantial economies of scale and to enjoy some surplus profits. Somewhere's government may then step in by subsidizing Flyfast or closing its market to foreign aircraft. Over time, when Flyfast is able to produce at relatively low costs, the protective measures may be lifted. Somewhere's exports increase because only Flyfast has survived. This argument presupposes that the other governments remain passive and the market is only large enough to support one firm operating at economies of scale. In another example, protection or subsidies by the Japanese government of a particular firm or industry may lower the costs for the Japanese firm and thereby discourage foreign firms from trying a product comparable to the Japanese one. Support or the promise of support, in Japan is a signal for the foreign firms that their sales would be less profitable. In that case the Japanese firm or industry may acquire a temporary or lasting edge over its foreign rivals. One conclusion of this new theorizing is that protection or predatory practices may eventually increase exports and domestic incomes. This is more likely to work if other countries don't engage in retaliatory policies.

Another case is that of 'learning by doing.' The idea is that as firms operate in a protected home market, they may expand. As they produce more they may well move down their learning or experience curve (or do so more rapidly than their foreign rivals) which implies lower unit costs.[119] As the firm gains practical knowledge and experience with a product, unit costs may drop as practice leads to a smoother coordination of tasks and their performance. Inventory costs,

---

118   It is also true that such policies impose costs on taxpayers and consumers (ed.).
119   Economists often use the learning curve to represent the extent to which the average cost of producing an item falls in response to an increase in its cumulative total output, that is, the total number of items of this sort that it has produced in the past (ed.).

for example, may be reduced as production and marketing become better organized. Again, government support may help a firm or industry to become more competitive in the domestic and foreign market.

Although certain writers have taken advantage of the new approaches to trade analysis to advocate strategic trade policies, it should be mentioned here that many of those who have contributed to the new theorizing have themselves been critical of the possible policy implications.[120]

Krugman admits that the new trade theory provides some intellectual justification for neo-mercantilist policies. However, it does not in his view, provide simple guidelines for policy. According to Krugman there are at least seven economic problems involved here.

1. How oligopolies behave is not really too well known. The world of oligopoly can resemble a chess game with moves and countermoves and unpredictable outcomes. The effect of government support on domestic and foreign oligopolistic firms cannot always be analyzed by using simple models.
2. Although technical spillovers may be important, the net effect of these externalities is very hard to measure.
3. It is difficult to determine firms or sectors where high economic rents prevail because it is not easy to separate a high rent industry from one that simply employs higher skilled or better qualified employees. Examining profit rates and wages over the past few years will not do the job.
4. If an oligopolistic industry makes surplus profits and it is protected by government intervention, these excess profits will encourage new firms to enter the market. If that occurs, such profits may be competed away and passed on to consumers many of whom may be foreigners.
5. Even if it were possible to identify industries that are likely candidates for special concern, we cannot forget that after all, industries in any country, the US included, compete against each other for scarce resources. Government assistance to one industry draws resources away from other domestic industries.

---

120 See J.A. Brander, 'Rationales for Strategic Trade and Industrial Policy', *Strategic Trade Policy and the New International Economics* (P.R. Krugman, ed.) (Cambridge: MIT Press, 1986).

The government cannot favor one industry except at the expense of others.

6. Moreover, strategic trade policies can create domestic political problems as well. Governments do not always act in the national interest. The kind of interventions suggested by the new trade theory almost always raises the welfare of small fortunate groups, while imposing costs on larger more diffuse ones. As soon as the government is in the business of strategic trade policy it will be rational for special interest groups to spend real resources trying to influence regulators, legislators and politicians. First, there are the obvious opportunity costs of these resources. Second, the pressure of special interest groups may induce policy makers to propose and enact policies which are not likely to benefit the nation as a whole.

7. Finally, there is the international relations problem. The arguments for strategic trade policies assume that there is no retaliatory response from foreign governments. However, if a country like the US adopted a more activist trade and/or industrial policy, foreign nations would be tempted to reciprocate. This could undermine whatever international cooperation now exists and lead us to a world of beggar-my-neighbor trade policies, like the ones of the 1930s.

Krugman concluded that free trade is a fairly good if not perfect policy. The formidable obstacles of translating the new theories into real-world policies still makes unhampered international trade the policy with the most likely net social benefit.[121]

Is Free Trade Passé?

If there were an Economist's Creed, it would surely contain the affirmations 'I understand the Principle of Comparative Advantage' and 'I advocate Free Trade'. For one hundred seventy years, the appreciation that international trade benefits a country whether it is 'fair' or not has been one of the touchstones of professionalism in economics. Comparative advantage is not just an idea both simple and profound; it is an idea that conflicts directly with both stubborn

121 P.R. Krugman, 'Is Free Trade Passé?', *Economic Perspectives*, Vol. 1, No. 2 (Fall 1987) pp. 131–144.

popular prejudices and powerful interests. This combination makes the defense of free trade as close to a sacred tenet as any idea in economics.

Yet the case for free trade is currently more in doubt than at any time since the 1817 publication of Ricardo's *Principles of Political Economy*. This is not because of the political pressures for protection, which have triumphed in the past without shaking the intellectual foundations of comparative advantage theory. Rather, it is because of the changes that have recently taken place in the theory of international trade itself. While new developments in international trade theory may not yet be familiar to the profession at large, they have been substantial and radical. In the last ten years the traditional constant returns, perfect competition models of international trade have been supplemented and to some extent supplanted by a new breed of model that emphasizes increasing returns and imperfect competition. These new models call into doubt the extent to which actual trade can be explained by comparative advantage; they also open the possibility that government intervention in trade via import restrictions, export subsidies and so on may under some circumstances be in the national interest after all.

To preview this paper's conclusion: free trade is not passé, but it is an idea that has irretrievably lost its innocence. Its status has shifted from optimum to reasonable rule of thumb. There is still a case for free trade as a good policy, and as a useful target in the practical world of politics, but it can never again be asserted as the policy that economic theory tells us is always right.

Rethinking International Trade Theory

From the early nineteenth century until the late 1970s, international trade theory was dominated almost entirely by the concept of comparative advantage, which we can define loosely as the view that countries trade to take advantage of their differences. In formal models, economies were assumed to be characterized by constant returns to scale and perfect competition. Given these assumptions, trade can arise only to the extent that countries differ in tastes, technology, or factor endowments. The traditional Ricardian model emphasizes technological differences as the cause of trade; the Heckscher–Ohlin–Samuelson model emphasizes differences in factor endowments. Additional models can be generated by varying assumptions about the number of goods and factors, by placing restrictions on the technology, and so on. These alternative models have different implications in important respects; for example, income distribution effects are absent in the Ricardian model, extremely strong in the Heckscher–Ohlin–Samuelson model. Nonetheless, the underlying commonality among conventional trade models is such that until a few years ago international trade theory was one of the most unified fields in economics.

Thoughtful international economists have long known that comparative advantage need not be the whole story, that increasing returns can be an independent cause of international specialization and trade. Ohlin himself repeatedly emphasized this point. Furthermore, at least since the late 1950s empirical workers and informal observers have been dissatisfied with formal trade theory, so there has been a sort of 'counter-culture' in international trade research, a set of informal arguments stressing sources of trade other than those represented in the formal models. Authors such as Steffan Burenstam-Linder (1961) and Raymond Vernon (1966) emphasized endogenous technological change, while many authors have discussed the possible role of economies of scale as a cause of trade separate from comparative advantage. A few papers attempted formal models of trade under increasing returns. However, all such efforts were plagued by the problem of modeling market structure. Except under the implausible hypothesis that economies of scale are completely external to firms, increasing returns must lead to imperfect competition. Yet until the late 1970s, there was no generally accepted way to model imperfect competition in general equilibrium. Since mainstream trade theory derived its power and unity from being stated in formal general equilibrium terms, alternative views were relegated to the footnotes. As recently as 1980, many textbooks – and even survey articles on the theory of international trade – failed even to mention the possibility that trade might arise for reasons other than exogenous differences in tastes, technology, and factor endowments.

During the 1970s researchers in industrial organization began to develop models of imperfect competition that, while admittedly lacking generality, were easy to use and apply. In particular, Chamberlinian large-group competition was given a grounding in utility maximization and placed in a general equilibrium framework by such authors as A. Michael Spence (1976) and Avinash Dixit and Joseph Stiglitz (1977). It quickly became clear to trade theorists that these new models supplied the necessary framework for formal modeling of the role of increasing returns as a cause of international trade. Simultaneously and independently, Avinash Dixit and Victor Norman (1980), Kelvin Lancaster (1980) and this author (1979) published papers in which economies of scale led to arbitrary specialization by nations on products within monopolistically competitive industries. These models immediately established the idea that countries specialize and trade, not only because of underlying differences, but also because increasing returns are an independent force leading to geographical concentration of production of each good. Indeed, at a logical level, increasing returns are as fundamental a cause of international trade as comparative advantage.

The role of increasing returns in trade was not, as already noted, a new idea, although the new models gave it more clarity and precision than in the past. The main new insight from these models was that to the extent that trade driven by economies of scale is important in the world economy, imperfect competition is important as well. International trade theory thus becomes inextricably intertwined with industrial organization. In retrospect this conclusion is obvious. After all, most trade is in the products of industries that economists classify without hesitation as oligopolies when viewing them in their domestic aspect. For international economics, however, this was a radical reorientation.

Although the new models of trade challenged the traditional view that all trade represents exploitation of comparative advantage, the new trade theory did not at first challenge the proposition that trade is of mutual benefit to the trading nations. Indeed, if anything, the introduction of increasing returns and imperfect competition into trade theory strengthens the case that there are gains from trade. In addition to benefiting from complementary differences in resources and technology, trading countries can specialize in the production of different goods, achieving increased scale of production while maintaining or increasing the diversity of goods available. Admittedly, a second best world of imperfect competition offers no guarantee that potential benefits from trade will necessarily be realized. In most formal models, however, it turns out that the presence of increasing returns increases rather than reduces the gains from international trade. Furthermore, by creating larger, more competitive markets, trade may reduce the distortions that would have been associated with imperfect competition in a closed economy. Thus the initial implication of new trade theory seemed, if anything, to reinforce the traditional view that trade is a good thing, and thus to strengthen the case for free trade.

However, showing that free trade is better than no trade is not the same thing as showing that free trade is better than sophisticated government intervention. The view that free trade is the best of all possible policies is part of the general case for laissez–faire in a market economy, and rests on the proposition that markets are efficient. If increasing returns and imperfect competition are necessary parts of the explanation of international trade, however, we are living in a second-best world where government intervention can in principle improve on market outcomes. Thus as soon as the respectability of non-comparative-advantage models in international trade was established, international trade theorists began to ask whether the new view of the *causes* of trade implied new views about appropriate trade *policy*. Does acknowledging economics of scale and imperfect competition create new arguments against free trade?

New Arguments Against Free Trade

The new view of international trade holds that trade is to an important degree driven by economies of scale rather than comparative advantage, and that international markets are typically imperfectly competitive. This new view has suggested two arguments against free trade, one of which is a wholly new idea, the other of which is an old idea given new force. The new idea is the *strategic trade policy* argument, which holds that government policy can tilt the terms of oligopolistic competition to shift excess returns from foreign to domestic firms. The old idea is that government policy should favor industries that yield *externalities*, especially generation of knowledge that firms cannot fully appreciate.

Strategic Trade Policy

The strategic trade policy argument begins with the observation that in a world of increasing returns and imperfect competition, lucky firms in some industries may be able to earn returns higher than the opportunity costs of the resources they employ. For example, suppose that economies of scale are sufficiently large in some industry that there is only room for one profitable entrant in the world market as a whole; that is, if two firms were to enter they would both incur losses. Then whichever firm manages to establish itself in the industry will earn super-normal returns that will not be competed away.

A country can raise its national income at other countries'

expense if it can somehow ensure that the lucky firm that gets to earn excess returns is domestic rather than foreign. In two influential papers, James Brander and Barbara Spencer (1983, 1985) showed that government policies such as export subsidies and import restrictions can, under the right circumstances, deter foreign firms from competing for lucrative markets. Government policy here serves much the same role that 'strategic' moves such as investment in excess capacity or research and development (R&D) serve in many models of oligopolistic competition – hence the term 'strategic trade policy'.

The original Brander–Spencer analysis and the literature that followed it uses the machinery of duopoly analysis: firms choose levels of R&D and/or output conditional on other firms' choices, and an equilibrium occurs where the reaction functions of firms intersect. The essence of the strategic trade policy concept, however, is so simple that it can be conveyed with a numerical example. Indeed, focussing on such an example may convey the essentials more clearly than a more formal treatment.

Suppose then, that two countries are capable of producing a good. For concreteness, let the good be a 150-seat passenger aircraft, and call the 'countries' America and Europe. Also, let there be one firm in each country that could produce the good: Boeing and Airbus, respectively.

To focus attention on the competition for excess returns, assume that neither America nor Europe has any domestic demand for the good, so that the good is intended solely for export; this allows us to identify producer surplus with the national interest. Also, assume that each firm faces only a binary choice, to produce or not to produce. Finally, assume that the market is profitable for either firm if it enters alone, unprofitable for both if both enter.

Given these assumptions, the game between Boeing and Airbus may be represented by a matrix like that shown in Table 1. Boeing's choices to produce (P) or not to produce (N) are represented by upper case letters, Airbus's corresponding choices by lower case letters. In each cell of the matrix, the lower left number represents Boeing's profit (over and above the normal return on capital), the upper right number represents Airbus's profit.

As the game is set up here, it does not have a unique outcome. To give it one, let us assume that Boeing has some kind of head start that allows it to commit itself to produce before Airbus's decision. Then in the absence of government intervention, the outcome will be Pn, in the upper right cell: Boeing will earn large profits, while deterring entry by Airbus.

Clearly Europe's government would like to change this outcome. The strategic trade policy point is that it can change the outcome if it is able to commit itself to subsidize Airbus, at a point before Boeing is committed to produce. Suppose that Europe's government can commit itself in advance to pay a subsidy of 10 to Airbus if it produces the plane, regardless of what Boeing does. Then the payoff matrix is shifted to that represented by Table 2. The result is to reverse the game's outcome.

Table 1
Hypothetical payoff matrix

		Airbus	
		p	n
Boeing	P	-5 \ -5	100 \ 0
	N	0 \ 100	0 \ 0

Table 2
Hypothetical payoff matrix after European Subsidy

		Airbus	
		p	n
Boeing	P	-5 \ 5	100 \ 0
	N	0 \ 110	0 \ 0

Boeing now knows that even if it commits itself to produce, Airbus will still produce as well, and it will make losses. Thus Boeing will be induced not to produce, and the outcome will be Np instead of Pn. The surprising result will be that a subsidy of only 10 raises Airbus's profits from 0 to 110! of this, 100 represents a transfer of excess returns from America to Europe, a gain in Europe's national income at America's expense.

The strategic trade policy argument thus shows that at least under some circumstances a government, by supporting its firms in international competition, can raise national welfare at another country's expense. The example just presented showed this goal being achieved via a subsidy, but other policies might also serve this purpose. In particular, when there is a significant domestic market for a good, protection of this market raises the profits of the domestic firm and lowers the profits of the foreign firm in the case where both enter; like an export subsidy, this can deter foreign entry and allow the domestic firm to capture the excess returns. As businessmen have always said, and as economists have usually denied, a protected domestic market can – under some circumstances! – promote rather than discourage exports, and possibly raise national income.

The strategic trade policy argument is immensely attractive to non-economists, since it seems to say that views always condemned by international trade theorists as fallacious make sense after all. In defense of free trade, a number of analysts have quickly acted to point out the weakness of strategic trade as a basis for actual intervention. Before considering these arguments, however, I turn to the other justification for government intervention in trade suggested by the new theory.

External Economies

There is nothing new about the idea that it may be desirable to deviate from free trade to encourage activities that yield positive external economies. The proposition that protection can be beneficial when an industry generates external economies is part of the conventional theory of trade policy. However, the rethinking of international trade theory has given at least the appearance of greater concreteness to the theoretical case for government intervention to promote external benefits.

It is possible to imagine bees-and-flowers examples in which externalities arise from some physical spillover between firms, but empirically the most plausible source of positive externalities is the inability of innovative firms to appropriate fully the knowledge they create. The presence of problems of appropriability is unmistakable in industries experiencing rapid technological progress, where firms routinely take each others' products apart to see how they work and how they were made. In traditional international trade models with their reliance on perfect competition, however, externalities resulting from incomplete apropriability could not be explicitly recognized, because the knowledge investment by firms that is the source of the spillover could not be fitted in. Investment in knowledge inevitably has a fixed-cost aspect; once a firm has improved its product or technique, the unit cost of that improvement falls as more is produced. The result of these dynamic economies of scale must be a breakdown of perfect competition. As a result, perfectly competitive models could not explicitly recognize the most plausible reason for the existence of external economies. This did not prevent trade theorists from analyzing the trade policy implications of externalities, and in fact this is a well-understood topic. Since investment in knowledge was not explicitly in their models, however, external economies seemed abstract, without an obvious real-world counterpart. In traditional trade models, one industry seems as likely as another to generate important external economies – so that the theory seems remote from operational usefulness.

Once increasing returns and imperfect competition are seen as the norm, the problem of abstractness is reduced. The dynamic scale economies associated with investment in knowledge are just another reason for the imperfection of competition that has already been accepted as the norm. External economies can now be identified with the incomplete appropriability of the results of R&D, which immediately suggests that they are most likely to be found in industries where R&D is an especially large part of the firms' costs. So by making tractable the modeling of a specific mechanism generating externalities, the new trade theory also seems to offer guidance on where these externalities are likely to be important.

The emphasis on external economies suggested by new trade theory is similar to the strategic trade policy argument in offering a reason for government targeting of particular sectors. However, the external economies argument differs in one important respect; policies to promote sectors yielding external economies need not affect other countries adversely. Whether the effect of one country's targeting of high-externality sectors on other countries is positive or negative depends on whether the scope of the externalities is national or international. There is a conflict of interest if knowledge spills over within a country but not between countries. Suppose that the research of each computer firm generates knowledge that benefits other computer firms. This is only a case for sponsoring production of computers in the United States as opposed to Japan if US firms cannot benefit from Japanese research. In many cases it seems unlikely that spillovers respect national boundaries; a firm can 'reverse engineer' a product made abroad as well as one made at home. The best candidates for nationally limited externalities are where knowledge spreads largely by personal contact and word of mouth. This is a much more restricted set of activities than R&D in general, although it is presumably the force behind such spectacular agglomerations of high-technology industry as Silicon Valley and Route 128.

Despite the restriction that only externalities at the national level make industrial policy a source of international conflict of interest, it is clear that the changes in trade theory have strengthened the view that nations are competing over who gets to realize these externalities. This reinforces the new strategic trade policy argument in offering a more respectable rationale for deviating from free trade than has been available until now.

Critique of the New Interventionism

The positive economics of the new trade theory, with its conclusion that much trade reflects increasing returns and that many international markets are imperfectly competitive, has met with remarkably quick acceptance in the profession. The normative conclusion that this justifies a greater degree of government intervention in trade, however, has met with sharp criticism and opposition – not least from some of the creators of the new theory themselves. The critique of the new interventionism partly reflects judgements about the politics of trade policy, to which we turn below. There are also, however, three economic criticisms. First, critics suggest that it is impossible to formulate useful interventionist policies given the empirical difficulties involved in modeling imperfect markets. Second, they argue that any gains from intervention will be dissipated by entry of rent-seeking firms. Third, it is argued that general equilibrium considerations radically increase the empirical difficulty of formulating interventionist trade policies and make it even more unlikely that these policies will do more good than harm.

Empirical Difficulties

The previous numerical example assumed that the European government knew the payoff matrix and knew how Boeing would respond to its policy. In reality, of course, even the best informed of governments will not know this much. Uncertainty is a feature of all economic policy, of course, but it is even greater when the key issue is how a policy will affect oligopolistic competition. The simple fact is that economists do not have reliable models of how oligopolists behave. Yet the effects of trade policy in imperfectly competitive industries can depend crucially on whether firms behave cooperatively or non-cooperatively, or whether they compete by setting prices or outputs. Furthermore, in many oligopolistic industries firms play a multistage game whose rules and objectives are complex and obscure even to the players themselves.

The externality argument for intervention runs up against the empirical problem of measuring external economies. By their nature, spillovers of knowledge are elusive and difficult to calculate; because they represent non-market linkages between firms, they do not leave a 'paper trail' by which their spread can be traced. A combination of careful case study work and econometrics on the history of an industry may be able to identify significant external economies, but what we need for trade policy is an estimate of the future rather than the past. Will a dollar of R&D in the semiconductor industry convey ten cents worth of external benefits, or ten dollars? Nobody really knows.

By itself, the argument that making policy based on the new trade theory is an uncertain enterprise would only dictate caution and hard study, not inaction. When it is linked with the political economy concerns described below, however, it raises the question of whether the political risks associated with action outweigh any likely gains.

Entry

Suppose that government is somehow able to overcome the empirical difficulties in formulating an interventionist trade policy. It may still not be able to raise national income if the benefits of its intervention are dissipated by entry of additional firms.

Consider first the case of a strategic trade policy aimed at securing excess returns. Our example was one in which there was room for only one profitable firm. Suppose, however, that the market can actually support four or five firms, a sufficient number so that the integer constraint does not matter too much and free entry will virtually eliminate monopoly profits. In this case, as Ignatius Horstmann and James Markusen (1986) have emphasized, a subsidy, even if it succeeds in deterring foreign competition, will be passed on to foreign consumers rather than securing excess returns for domestic producers. Or as Avinash Dixit has put it, when there is possibility of new entry we need to ask, 'Where's the rent?'.

A similar issue arises with policies aimed at promoting external economies. Suppose that external economies are associated with the manufacture of semiconductor chips, seemingly justifying a subsidy to chips production. If additional resources of labor and capital are supplied elastically to the industry, the external benefits of larger production will not be confined to the promoting country. Instead, they will be passed on to consumers around the world in the form of cheaper chips. The *national* advantage can come only to the extent that some factors are supplied inelastically to the industry – Santa Clara valley real estate? – or external benefits conveyed by the semiconductor industry to other industries. The point is that entry of new factors and new firms further reduces, though it does not eliminate, the extent to which competition for external economies represents a valid source of international conflict.

General Equilibrium

Even in a world characterized by increasing returns and imperfect competition, budget constraints still hold. A country cannot protect everything and subsidize everything. Thus interventionist policies to promote particular sectors, whether for strategic or externality reasons, must draw resources away from other sectors. This substantially raises the knowledge that a government must have to formulate interventions that do more harm than good.

Consider first the case of strategic trade policy. When a particular sector receives a subsidy, this gives firms in that sector a strategic advantage against foreign competitors. However, the resulting expansion of that sector will bid up the price of domestic resources to other sectors, putting home firms in these other sectors at a strategic disadvantage. Excess returns gained in the favored sector will thus be offset to at least some extent by returns lost elsewhere. If the government supports the wrong sector, the gain there will conceal a loss in overall national income.

The implication of this general equilibrium point is that to pursue a strategic trade policy successfully, a government must not only understand the effects of its policy on the targeted industry, which is difficult enough, but must also understand all the industries in the economy well enough that it can judge that an advantage gained here is worth advantage lost elsewhere. Therefore, the information burden is increased even further.

A similar point applies to externalities. Promoting one sector believed to yield valuable spillovers means drawing resources out of other sectors. Suppose that glamorous high-technology sectors yield less external benefit than the government thinks, and boring sectors more. Then a policy aimed at encouraging external economies may actually prove counterproductive. Again, the government needs to understand not only the targeted sector but the rest of the economy to know if a policy is justified.

The general equilibrium point should perhaps not be emphasized too much. Sectors of the economy differ radically and visibly in both the extent to which they are imperfectly competitive and in the resources they devote to the generation of knowledge. There may not be a one-to-one correspondence between small numbers of competitors and excess returns, or between high R&D expenditure and technological spillovers, but there is surely a correlation. Governments may not know for sure where intervention is justified, but they are not completely without information. However, the general equilibrium critique reinforces the caution suggested by the other critiques.

To say that it is difficult to formulate the correct interventionist policy is not a defense of free trade, however. Thus the economic critique of the new interventionism is only part of the post-new-trade-theory case for free trade. The other indispensable part rests on considerations of political economy.

The Political Economy Case for Free Trade

Like most microeconomic interventions, the interventionist policies suggested by new trade theory would affect the distribution of income as well as its level. The well-justified concern of economists is that when policies affect income distribution, the politics of policy formation come to be dominated by distribution rather than efficiency. In the case of trade interventions, this concern is at two levels. First, to the extent that the policies work, they will have a beggar-thy-neighbor component that can lead to retaliation and mutually harmful trade war. Second, at the domestic level an effort to pursue efficiency through intervention could be captured by special interests and turned into an inefficient redistribution program.

Retaliation and Trade War

Strategic trade policy aimed at securing excess returns for domestic firms and support for industries that are believed to yield national benefits are both beggar-thy-neighbor policies that raise income at the expense of other countries. A country that attempts to use such policies will probably provoke retaliation. In many (though not all) cases, a trade war between two interventionist governments will leave both countries worse off than if a hands-off approach were adopted by both. For example, consider the case of the European telecommunications equipment industry. This industry is a likely candidate for targeting on both oligopoly and external economy grounds. It is also a sector where nationalistic procurement by government-owned firms allows countries to pursue protectionist policies without violating agreements on international trade. The result of such protectionist policies, however, is by most accounts harmful to all concerned. Each country tries to be largely self-sufficient in equipment, and no country is able to realize the scale economies that would come from supplying the European market as a whole. Arguably, the structure of the game between countries in telecommunications equipment, and probably in other sectors as well, is that of a prisoners' dilemma where each country is better off intervening than being the only country not to intervene, but everyone would be better off if nobody intervened.

The way to avoid the trap of such a prisoners' dilemma is to establish rules of the game for policy that keep mutually harmful actions to a minimum. If such rules are to work, however, they must be simple enough to be clearly defined. Free trade is such a simple rule; it is easy enough to determine whether a country imposes tariffs or import quotas. New trade theory suggests that this is unlikely to be the best of all conceivable rules. It is very difficult to come up with any simple set of rules of the game that would be better, however. If the gains from sophisticated interventionism are small, which is the import of the economic critique of the last section, then there is a reasonable case for continuing to use free trade as a focal point for international agreement to prevent trade war.

Domestic Politics

Governments do not necessarily act in the national interest, especially when making detailed microeconomic interventions. Instead, they are influenced by interest group pressures. The kinds of interventions that new trade theory suggests can raise national income will typically raise the welfare of small, fortunate groups by large amounts, while imposing costs on larger, more diffuse groups. The result, as with any microeconomic policy, can easily be that excessive or misguided intervention takes place because the beneficiaries have more knowledge and influence than the losers. Nobody who has followed U.S. trade policy in sugar or lumber can be very sanguine about the ability of the government to be objective in applying a policy based on the Brander–Spencer model.

How do we resolve the problem of interest group influence on decision-making in the real world? As in the case of the problem of international conflict, one answer is to establish rules of the game that are not too inefficient and are simple enough to be enforceable. To ask the Commerce Department to ignore special-interest politics while formulating detailed policy for many industries is not realistic; to establish a blanket policy of free trade, with exceptions granted only under extreme pressure, may not be the optimal policy according to the theory but may be the best policy that the country is likely to get.

The Status of Free Trade

The economic cautions about the difficulty of formulating useful interventions and the political economy concerns that interventionism may go astray combine into a new case for free trade. This is not the old argument that free trade is optimal because markets are efficient. Instead, it is a sadder but wiser argument for free trade as a rule of thumb in a world whose politics are as imperfect as its markets.

The economic cautions are crucial to this argument. If the potential gains from interventionist trade policies were large, it would be hard to argue against making some effort to realize these gains. The thrust of the critique offered above, however, is that the gains from intervention are limited by uncertainty about appropriate policies, by entry that dissipates the gains, and by the general equilibrium effects that insure that promoting one sector diverts resources from others. The combination of these factors limits the potential benefits of sophisticated interventionism.

Once the expected gains from intervention have been whittled down sufficiently, political economy can be invoked as a reason to forego intervention altogether. Free trade can serve as a focal point on which countries can agree to avoid trade wars. It can also serve as a simple principle with which to resist pressures of special-interest politics. To abandon the free trade principle in pursuit of the gains from sophisticated intervention could therefore open the door to adverse political consequences that would outweigh the potential gains.

It is possible, then, both to believe that comparative advantage is an incomplete model of trade and to believe that free trade is nevertheless the right policy. In fact, this is the position taken by most of the new trade theorists themselves. So free trade is not passé – but it is not what it once was.

7. Protectionist Opinions and the Idea of Managed Trade after 1945

PREAMBLE

1

This last chapter deals with protectionists and advocates of managed trade. Because of the structure of this work they happen to find themselves in the last chapter. This does not necessarily mean that they have 'the last word'. However, an effort has been made to give them, like the other authors, a fair and evenhanded treatment.

In the interwar period, there was a strict connection between the increasing role of governments in the economy and the spreading of economic nationalism. This was true for both predominately market and collectivist economies. As was stated earlier, the post World War II economic policies of most Western nations contained an inner contradiction. Many politicians and legislators wanted to combine the regulatory, interventionist, controlling welfare state with a free international trade order. The welfare state, with its ideals of full employment and cradle-to-grave security, implies the gradual abandonment of automatic adjustment mechanisms and personal market forces and therefore has a tendancy towards autarky – a free trade order does precisely the opposite. The free trade order, as has been explained, embodied to a large extent the preferences of the American executive branch.

The collectivist priorities of many Western policy makers after World War II reflected an erroneous reading of the history of the interwar period. They often thought that the nightmare economy of the 1930s was mainly due to the failure of free enterprise and market forces. In fact market forces were not given much of a chance. World War I, the breaking up of old empires, the peace settlement, the war loans, the reparation payments, and later the toxic policies of the Federal Reserve, all injected into the world intractable elements for which market forces were not responsible, which they were unable to digest and which they could not be expected to remove. Governments often reacted to the prevailing economic confusion and anxiety by weakening market forces even more. This was done by all kinds of interventions, controls, regimentation and the promotion of government cartels. In any case, after the Second World War, the mixed economy with systematic government intervention appeared on stage. It was the response to a demand for a political, social and economic renewal which historically speaking was retrograde.

2

At the same time, in the post war period, left of center parties in various countries gained many votes. The left-wing programs of that period, usually based on the idea of a conflict between labor and capital, were nearly all oriented towards reforms which embodied far-reaching deviations from the profit-based market economy. These reforms typically included the nationalization of basic industries, the creation of planning organizations, the guarantee of full employment, the free or subsidized provisions of public services such as health care and education, and a far reaching redistribution of the national income through steeply progressive taxes, generous transfer payments and the like.

Britain and its post war labor government, for example, opted for selective nationalization of industrial sectors such as coal, steel, energy and transportation, and most of the measures mentioned above. The French adopted a more neo-collectivist type of interventionism with a wave of nationalizations which included the biggest four banks, the Renault car factories, and Air France. Indicative planning was also adopted. It consisted of setting goals and priorities which indicated the directions in which the economy should go. Smaller European countries such as Denmark, Sweden and the Netherlands chose a type of mixed economy which promoted a form of central consultation between various economic partners such as labor and management. Cooperation between factory workers and employers' organizations under state supervision was considered essential in the new system. Such ideas were obviously based upon the corporate concept which had been tried in fascist Italy in the 1930s. In the Netherlands, a Central Planning Office was also established, but it had an advisory position only.

Between the wars the United States had already gone far down the road to a mixed economy once the Roosevelt administration had embraced the New Deal Policy. During the Second World War the government was heavily involved in the economy. After the war, many of these emergency powers were dismantled, however a fundamental change had taken place in the sense that the country had the experience of successful large scale government intervention affecting the play of market forces. This experience opened up opportunities for extensive government involvement in the economic system. The Employment Act of 1946 committed the government to work for a very high rate of employment presumably by means of a counter-cyclical policy. This act was a fundamental step towards the mixed economy. In 1961, President Kennedy brought in Keynesian economics to combat the underuse of productive resources. President Johnson's 'Great Society' introduced new social aid programs and the expansion of existing programs. As in other countries, these programs became ever more expensive. Between 1969 and 1993, transfer payments in the US, as a percentage of Federal spending, rose from 26 per cent to 42 per cent. In the same year (1993), the American public debt had risen to $4.4 trillion.

3

During the postwar period from about 1950 to 1971, there was always the possibility of a conflict between the neomercantilist domestic policies of the Western nations and the relatively free organisation of world trade. However, the combination of reconstruction and trade liberalization brought high rates of growth and rapidly increasing national incomes to the Western world and Japan. As tax receipts rose consistently, the expansion of the welfare state could be financed out of tax revenues. In the 1970s however, this 'happy' period came to an end.

When the prosperous high growth decades of the 1950s and 1960s drew to a close, it was no longer possible to finance the ever increasing social welfare expenditures from economic growth. During the 1960s, many politicians and legislators had come to believe that economic growth of the mixed economy could be taken for granted. Thus they turned their attention to the extension of the welfare state and the redistribution of income. This meant free or low-cost provision of insurance against disease, accident, disability, unemployment, and old age. Services such as education, health, and to a lesser extent housing, were also provided below market cost. The price mechanism was increasingly eliminated, while taxes and premiums were used to pay for these benefits.

What many of the policy makers of the period did not understand was that in the long run high levels of social consumption imply policies that can lead to economic stagnation. Welfare state-type of governments typically weaken the link between economic performance and consumption which means that the incentives to undertake, work, and perform are undermined. Concurrently, the old values associated with hard work and saving are weakened. The welfare state, however, is expensive and depends on economic prosperity, productivity, and growth. At the same time, all the disincentives inherent in the welfare state and the way in which social programs are usually organized decrease productivity and growth while stimulating inflation if the central bank 'accommodates' the high levels of government spending. Thus as Melvin Krauss explains (Reading 30) the welfare state undermines the factors on which it critically depends. At some point, a lower rate of economic growth occurs and with it come protectionist calls.

As has been stated on earlier occasions, if 'politics' becomes an important source of income for all sorts of groups, then those groups have a strong incentive to organize or to organize more effectively in order to extract more from the government. This can easily become a circular and cumulative phenomenon (see Reading 32). Behind every government intervention, say in the form of farm subsidies, a vested interest builds up and pressure groups arise. As these groups get better organized, their influence on the size and composition of government spending increases. Attention should also be given to the 'ratchet effect'. Along with more intervention, old pressure groups remain and new ones emerges especially if the old ones are successful.

Moreover, when Labor parties came to power, in such countries as England, France, Sweden, and the Netherlands, they easily gave in to the demands of pressure groups, such as trade unions (their comrades), for higher wages not justified by productivity increases. This often contributed to the cost-push inflation after 1969.

In the 1970s, central bank accommodation and cost-push factors were among the causes leading to relatively high levels of inflation and a depreciated dollar. Reacting to these phenomena, the Petroleum Exporting Countries (OPEC) organized themselves as a cartel and quadrupled oil prices in 1973–74. This led to higher energy costs, more inflation, and a recession starting in 1974. The phenomenon of stagflation was born. During the 1970s the conflict between an open trade system and greater government control of the domestic economic system became increasingly clear. Many examples could be given. We will limit ourselves to just two. In order to squeeze inflation out of the economic system, tight fiscal and monetary policies are necessary. This, however, leads to an economic slowdown. Then a conflict with the ideal of full employment occurs. Tight fiscal and monetary policies may also be justified on the ground that inflation leads to a decline of exports, an increase in imports and thus a trade deficit. If, to give another example, economic stagnation becomes a worldwide phenomenon, any country's exports could fall and the national income will be negatively affected via the multiplier effect. Unemployment will rise, but under a liberal trade system, higher tariffs to protect the troubled industries cannot be used.

4

During the first two decades following World War II, protectionism sat silently on the side-lines, but the 1970s, as is well known, witnessed the birth of the so-called 'new protectionism'. This neo-protectionism or the rebirth of economic nationalism of the typical welfare state can be seen as its government's prime weapon against the threat posed by a relatively free world trade order. It did not develop in a vacuum. It was a symptom of the inherent contradiction between the interfering welfare state and an open trading system.

Many other factors contributed to the rise of the new protectionism, such as the fact that countries like the United States and the members of the European Community faced increasing competition both domestically as well as abroad. Japan, among others, proved to be a formidable rival. Increased competitive pressure tends to evoke a protectionist response.

The result of this neo-protectionism was a proliferation of voluntary export restraints, so-called orderly market agreements, anti-dumping levies, subsidies to domestic industries and other non-tariff trade barriers. All these devices had one thing in common. They by-passed the treaty obligations the major Western industrial nations had accepted under GATT sponsorship.

Between 1971 and 1973, the international monetary arrangement, as established in Bretton Woods in 1944, collapsed and was replaced by a system of flexible exchange rates with a depreciated dollar. The old Bretton Woods system tried to combine the incompatible objectives of fixed exchange rates, independent national fiscal, monetary and structural policies and relatively free trade, all this with the dollar at the center and a dollar pegged at $35 an ounce of gold. When inflation overtook the US economic system, the American gold reserves vanished and the system broke down. Furthermore, the protectionist furor continued throughout the 1980s in the US and the European Economic Community. The rather pro-trade minded

American Executive Branch of government further prevented an outbreak of protectionist measures which would have undermined the GATT system even more with additional discriminatory and bilateral arrangements. A good example of the renewed protectionist mood of the US Congress was the Omnibus Trade and Competitiveness Act of 1988. After three years in the making, the 1000 page trade bill was passed by both the House and the Senate. The initial version met with President Reagan's veto. Subsequently, a somewhat modified version became law. In spite of its escape clauses the bill toughened US trade policy.

The Democrats, influenced as they are by the AFL-CIO, wanted a more protectionist bill than the Republicans. Section 201 of the bill makes it easier for domestic industries to get relief from 'unfair' trade practices. Moreover, domestic industries are allowed to petition for five years of temporary relief (through protective tariffs) if they suffer from cheap (but fair) imports. To receive such help, industries must show that they intend to use the aid to update and become more competitive. Section 301, the heart of the bill, speeds up the process for imposing sanctions on trading partners who practice 'unfair' trade with the US. This section also transfers the authority to find unfair trade practices from the President to the US trade representative, obviously giving Congress more power over trade policy.

Between 1947 and 1973, the real income of the median American family doubled. However, between 1973 and 1992, that income remained basically constant. Productivity, the main determinant of income, behaved similarly. After 1992 it rose again but at the expense of corporate downsizing and layoffs. Productivity depends heavily upon capital formation and capital formation depends on saving. Especially during the 1980s, but also in the 1990s, Western governments borrowed huge sums of money as they incurred budget deficits, at least partly the result of heavy social consumption and the failure to increase taxes. This large scale borrowing tended to deprive the non-government related private sector of the funds needed for renewing its equipment, for modernization, expansion, and for research and development. This 'crowding out' of the private sector by the public sector helped to keep unemployment at relatively high levels resulting in more pressures for protection. Although the United States climbed out of its three years of quasi-recession in 1992, with Western Europe following in 1994, protectionist appeals remained forceful.

Looking forward (these words were written in 1996), it would seem that over the next 25 years the world will witness the emergence of new economic giants. Most of these large economies will be in Asia, Latin America, and possibly also in Eastern Europe. Under the agreements implicit in the completed Uruguay Round of the former GATT, trade barriers will be low and trade will be relatively free. Competition from low-wage emerging economies will be stiff. This will probably move the protectionists of the more affluent countries to raise their voice again and attack freer trade policies if they can.

At present, protectionists in wealthier countries, who are always on the look-out for new reasons for trade barriers, are using labor and environment related arguments to back up demands for additional trade impediments. They argue that with low trade barriers and with the latest technology available almost everywhere, the cheap labor emerging economies will overwhelm the rich countries, with their low-cost products wiping out jobs in countries with historically high wages. The usual conclusion is that high tariffs, quotas (and sometimes capital controls) are needed. As previous readings show, this type of agreement is extreme protectionism in its crudest possible disguise. Other protectionists will say that there must be closer equality between developing and developed countries in terms of workers wages, working hours, standards of health and safety and so forth in order to make trade 'fair'. The point here is of course that those protectionists insist on a standard of living which relatively poor countries simply cannot afford. These countries must first produce more, and one of the best ways to encourage their economic growth is through international trade.

Trade policy activists also claim that free trade with third-world countries that have lax environmental controls make competition for the more developed nations with more rigid environmental controls very difficult. It may even lead to a relaxation of pollution controls in the high income countries themselves in order to remain competitive. Therefore, in return for access to the markets of developed countries, the emerging nations should raise their environmental standards, so goes the argument. The problem here is that such demands, if they could be imposed upon the emerging economies, would slow their economic growth and thus could delay the point at which those nations themselves start to be really concerned about their own environment. Even in the more developed countries these environmental concerns were a later consideration.

In conclusion, it may be said that to bring these labor and environmental issues into multilateral trade talks only serves to enfeeble the GATT or the WTO which are most probably unable to accommodate such controversial issues.

Another recent challenge to the proponents of free trade is policy proposals for managed trade. Managed trade consists of policies to establish and strengthen comparative advantage through temporary trade protection in certain areas at the expense of foreigners. The tools usually involve a combination of domestic market protection and subsidies. Managed trade, therefore, is a newer form of economic nationalism. The problems with managed trade, like its kin the infant industry argument are:

1. Picking the potential winners who will qualify for temporary protection will be difficult to say the least.
2. If the leading trading nations undertake such managed trade policies simultaneously their efforts will be largely neutralized.
3. Retaliation is likely if one country's managed trade policy is successful.

With all this in mind free trade still seems the best policy after all. Free trade or freer trade will always be beneficial. Economic nationalism or protectionism will always harm the long-run national interest if only because those policies reduce the national income by blocking efficiency increasing changes in the pattern of production. At the same time, they commonly merely redistribute income among various domestic groups, with the lowest income groups often bearing a disproportionately large share of the burden.

READING 32

Gunnar Myrdal

Biography

Gunnar Myrdal (1898–1987) the economist, public official and author, who was awarded the Nobel Prize in economic science in 1974 was born in Gustafs, Sweden. He studied with such famous economists as Knut Wicksell, Eli Heckscher and Gustav Cassell and received his doctorate from the University of Stockholm in 1927. Between 1933 and 1939, he taught political economy at that institution. In 1924 he married Alva Reimer a sociologist and public official. In the 1930s both Myrdal and his wife became active in domestic politics. Between

1935 and 1938, he served in the Swedish senate.

In 1938 the Carnegie Corporation selected him for a major study on the black population of the United States. That research resulted in the influential *An American Dilemma: The Negro Problem and Modern Democracy* (1944). Back in Sweden Myrdal headed the committee that drafted the postwar program of the Social Democratic Party (SDP). That agenda involved substantial planning, interference with market mechanisms, and redistribution of income. Between 1945 and 1947 he was Minister of Trade and Commerce in the SDP government.

For the next ten years he served as Executive Secretary of the United Nation's Economic Commission for Europe. In that position he had to live in Geneva, Switzerland from 1947 to 1957. After that he embarked upon a study of underdevelopment and development in Asia. It resulted in his well-known *Asian Drama: An Inquiry into the Poverty of Nations* (1968).

In his later years, Myrdal was associated with the Stockholm University Institute for International Economic Studies and the Stockholm International Peace Research Institute. He died in 1987 at the age of 89.

The Work

Myrdal considered himself an institutionalist. Institutionalism usually embraces a critical attitude towards conventional economic theory. For Myrdal, because conventional economic analysis abstracts from non-economic factors, such as attitudes and institutions, the corresponding economic models and theories lack realism. In the period just following World War II investigations of economic development, for example, used the familiar analytical tools that had been forged to study developed nations. Attitudes and institutions in less developed nations were often neglected. Because these attitudes and institutions however, were more rigid and less permissive of economic development than they had been in the earlier phases of economic progress in the more developed countries, awkward problems were avoided. Yet, these studies presented a distorted view of reality.

Myrdal has two central concepts which distinguishes him from most contemporary economists. He does not think that economic analysis is value free nor does he believe that economic systems tend towards equilibrium. Key to Myrdal's analytical system is the methodological observation that positive economics cannot be divorced from normative economics (*Objectivity in Social Research*, 1969). As a result, every economic statement involves explicit and implicit value judgments. Those value premises determine the approach, the definition of concepts used, the facts observed, the way of drawing inferences, and even the manner of presenting the conclusions reached. According to the Swedish economist, value judgments are conditioned by (a) the personality traits of the individual researcher, (b) the impact of tradition and ingrained thoughtways in the various social sciences and (c) the play of dominant interests and prejudices of the society in which the researcher lives and works. However, central as they may be to the researcher, valuations are often hidden and vague. The researcher, him or herself, may even be unaware of them. As a consequence the results of the research tend to be biased. By bias Myrdal means a systematic, though unintentional, falsification of our conception of reality. A characteristic of biases is that because the researcher is not always conscious of them they are not necessarily under control in the research. Myrdal contends that to free ourselves from the biases, the researcher must state his or her value premises explicitly at the start of the research project. Objectivity is achieved by exposing the value premises to full light and making them conscious, explicit and specific. Since value judgments cannot be avoided they should be permitted to influence research as long as they are tested for relevance, significance and feasibility. Myrdal argues that a disinterested social science never existed and can never exist.[122]

According to Myrdal, in spite of the protests of its advocates to the contrary, classical and neoclassical economic theory is not value free or free from bias. Classical and neoclassical economists often had a tendency to hide their value judgments, at least partly because they did not consider them relevant. Economic theory which developed along classical and neoclassical lines, largely retains the hedonistic psychology and the moral philosophies based on natural law and utilitarianism according to Myrdal.

Circular and cumulative causation is the second important concept in Myrdal's arsenal of ideas (*Rich Lands and Poor*, 1957). Economic analysis is largely based on the notion of equilibrium in which relevant forces return the system to a state of rest. In contrast, the principle of

---

122   In criticism of this position one might observe that what really counts is whether or not a theory is sound or unsound. This is to be established by the use of the well-known scientific methods. The motives that guided the thinker are simply immaterial (ed.).

circular and cumulative causation places emphasis on a social process which once begun feeds on its own efforts, so that departures from equilibrium tend to lead the economy away from instead of towards equilibrium.[123] In his study *The American Dilemma* Myrdal uses the idea of a circular and cumulative relationships to illustrate what happened between whites and blacks in the earlier decades of the twentieth century. White prejudice and the resulting discrimination against blacks prevented blacks from raising their living standards. The resulting poverty, ignorance and disorderly conduct then contributed to the prejudice of the whites leading to more discrimination and so on and so forth.[124] In his publication on Asian economic development, Myrdal used the concept to demonstrate that market forces tend to increase economic inequalities between regions and countries. He argued that if one country (or region) initially experiences a higher rate of economic growth than other countries (or regions), the resulting flow of resources from the slow growing area to the fast growing area will reinforce the initial advantage. The result is a widening gap in growth rates and/or per capita incomes.[125]

In this reasoning Myrdal adopts the concepts of backwash effects and spread effects. Spread effects are the beneficial results that come from the growth of a regional or national economy on the economies of other areas. Such effects mainly consist of the emergence of expanding markets within and the diffusion of technical progress from the leading regions. Backwash effects are the adverse repercussions that the leading area has on others. For one thing, it encourages an outflow of resources from the slow growing nations. Economic inequality increases when the backwash effects are stronger than spread effects, which in Myrdal's view is the usual case. Adverse cumulation thus occurs when the backwash effects dominate.

A net negative social process can be stopped or reversed by

---

123   This statement could lead to the conclusion that there are no automatic adjustment processes and that all social outcomes are explosive (ed.).

124   Yet there must be some self-limiting factors to this process. For instance, life expectancy at birth for whites in the US exceeded life expectancy at birth for blacks by 9.6 years in 1920. In 1990 the difference had narrowed to 5.7 years. In 1959, 55.1% of blacks lived below the poverty level. In 1990 this figure had fallen to 31.9% (ed.).

125   Again in the real world there seem to be adjustment processses as a number of developing countries have experienced and are experiencing rapid economic growth (ed.).

planned and applied policy interferences. Because Myrdal believed in the overwhelming importance of the principle of cumulative causation and its adverse effects, he became an interventionist and planner.[126] Myrdal contended that international trade and capital movements, for instance, if left alone, would widen the gap between the per capita incomes in the more and less developed countries. He took the position therefore that foreign trade must be controlled. The imports of the less essential commodities into low income countries must be restricted and young infant industries must be protected. Furthermore, Myrdal took the view that the wealthier nations should give special import advantages (low tariffs, etc.) to the relatively poor countries.

Myrdal recognized, however, that even though it is less effective for more developed countries to give aid it is easier to accomplish because it does not adversely affect any special interest group.[127]

Extracts

The Effects of Trade

The theory of international trade was not worked out to explain the reality of underdevelopment and the need for development. One might say, rather, that this imposing structure of abstract reasoning implicitly had almost the opposite purpose, that of *explaining away the international equality problem.*

When applying an immanent criticism to the theory of international trade, the biased approach it implies stands out in the unrealistic assumptions of stable equilibrium – and a number of other assumptions related to that assumption. Even in later writings, it has been retained more tenaciously than in other parts of economic theory.

---

126   Myrdal does have an obvious interventionist bias and can be suspected to use the reasoning of circular social processes to support it. However, it is not clear to the editor of this work that at the outset of his research Myrdal clearly stated this bias as, according to himself, researchers are supposed to (ed.).

127   G. Myrdal, *The Challenge of World Poverty* (Harmondsworth: Penguin Books, 1970) pp. 272–274.
G. Myrdal, 'Development and Underdevelopment', *Reshaping the World Economy* (John A. Pincus, ed.) (Englewood Cliffs: Prentice Hall, 1968) pp. 85–90. These pages are taken from the so-called Cairo Lectures.
G. Myrdal, *Rich Lands and Poor* (New York: Harper & Row, 1957) pp. 96–97.

Another unrealistic assumption is the notion that there are certain elements of social reality which can be characterized as the 'economic factors', and that it is defensible to analyse international trade while abstracting from all other factors.

These assumptions opened the way for the ideological predilections that since classical times have been deeply embedded in all economic theory but particularly in the theory of international trade. These predilections – harmony of interests, laissez-faire and free trade – determine, more than economists usually realize, their approach in present writings.

Biased in this way, the international trade theory developed the thought that trade worked for the equalization of factor prices and incomes, in the first instance wages of labour. Trade would permit industrial activity to adapt itself to the location of natural and population resources in different countries and different regions, and this would have a generally equalizing effect on incomes everywhere.

Two prominent compatriots of mine, the Professor Eli F. Heckscher and Professor Bertil Ohlin, perfected this classical theory long before the Second World War by carrying out the reasoning in terms of more factors of production than labour. They also drew the major conclusion about trade having equalizing effects more explicitly. After them the econometricians, particularly in the United States, have in recent decades shown a lively interest in elaborating how under very specific, abstract and usually static conditions this tendency to equalization of factor prices in different countries would be realized.

What we can here observe is indeed a very strange thing. International inequalities of income have been increasing for a long time and are still increasing. After the avalanche of the liquidation of the colonial power structure since the end of the Second World War this development toward increasing inequality has become an ever more pressing concern in international politics. At this very juncture of world history the theory of international trade has increasingly stressed the concept that international trade initiates a tendency towards a gradual equalization of incomes as among different countries – under assumptions that should stand out as obviously unrealistic and against all experience.

The reader of this book will by now not be surprised if I characterize this strange *direction of theoretical interest* – and, in particular, the almost total lack of interest among the economic theoreticians working in the field of international trade to explain the existing and growing inequalities in the world – *as a bias, opportune to people in the developed countries.* In its origin this bias had its moorings much further back in the history of economic thought than most of the other biases operating through what in the first chapter I called the post-war approach.

......

Contrary to what the equilibrium theory of international trade would seem to suggest, the play of the market forces does not work towards equality in the remunerations to factors of production and, consequently, in incomes. If left to take its own course, economic development is a process of circular and cumulative causation which tends to award its favours to those who are already well endowed and even to thwart the efforts of those who happen to live in regions that are lagging behind. The Backsetting Effects of economic expansion in other regions dominate the more powerfully, the poorer a country is.

Within the national boundaries of the richer countries an integration process has taken place: on a higher level of economic development expansionary momentum tends to spread more effectively to other localities and regions than those where starts happen to have been made and successfully sustained; and inequality has there also been mitigated through interferences in the play of the market forces by organized society. In a few highly advanced countries – comprising only about one—sixth of the population in the non-Soviet world – this national integration process is now being carried forward towards a very high level of equality of opportunity to all, wherever, and in whatever circumstances they happen to be born. These countries are approaching a national harmony of interest which, because of the role played by state policies, has to be characterized as a 'created harmony'; and this has increasingly sustained also their further economic development.

Outside this small group of highly developed and progressive countries, all other countries are in various degrees poorer and mostly also less progressive economically. In a rather close correlation to their poverty they are ridden by internal economic inequalities, which also tend to weaken the effectiveness of their democratic systems of government in the cases where they are not under one form or another of oligarchic or forthright dictatorial rule.

The relations between relative lack of national economic integration and relative economic backwardness run, according to my hypothesis of circular cumulative causation, both ways. With a low level of economic development follow low levels of social mobility, communications, popular education and national sharing in beliefs and valuations, which imply greater impediments to the Spread Effects of expansionary momentum; at the same time the poorer states have for much the same reasons and because of the very fact of existing internal inequalitites often been less democratic and, in any case, they have, because they are poorer, been up against narrower financial and, at bottom, psychological limitations on policies seeking to equalize opportunities. Inequality of opportunities has, on the other hand, contributed to preserving a low 'quality' of their factors of production and a low 'effectiveness' in their production efforts, to use the classical terms, and this has hampered their economic development.

On the international as on the national level trade does not by itself necessarily work for equality. A widening of markets strengthens often on the first hand the progressive countries whose manufacturing industries have the lead and are already fortified in surroundings of external economies, while the underveloped countries are in continuous danger of seeing even what they have of industry and, in particular, their small scale industry and handicrafts outcompeted by cheap imports from the industrial countries, if they do not protect them.

It is easy to observe how in most underdeveloped countries the trading contacts with the outside world have actually impoverished them culturally. Skills in many crafts inherited from centuries back have been lost. A city like Baghdad, with whose name such glorious associations are connected, today does not harbour any of the old crafts, except some silver smithies, and they have adapted patterns from abroad requiring less craftsmanship; similarly it is only with the greatest difficulties that one can buy a book of Arabic literature, while cheap magazines in English or Arabic are in abundance.

If international trade did not stimulate manufacturing industry in the underdeveloped countries but instead robbed them of what they had of old-established crafts, it did promote the production of primary products, and such production, employing mostly unskilled labour, came to constitute the basis for the bulk of their exports. In these lines, however, they often meet inelastic demands in the export market, often also a demand trend which is not rising very rapidly, and excessive price fluctuations. When, furthermore, population is rapidly rising while the larger part of it lives at, or near, the subsistence level – which means that there is no scarcity of common labour – any technological improvement in their export production tends to confer the advantages from the cheapening of production to the importing countries. Because of inelastic demands the result will often not even be a very great enlargement of the markets and of production and employment. In any case the wages and the export returns per unit of product will tend to remain low as the supply of unskilled labour is almost unlimited.

The advice – and assistance – which the poor countries receive from the rich is even nowadays often directed towards increasing their production of primary goods for export. The advice is certainly given in good faith, and it may even be rational from the short term point of view of each underdeveloped country seen in isolation. Under a broader perspective and from a long term point of view, what would be rational is above all to increase productivity, incomes and living standards in the larger agricultural subsistence sectors, so as to raise the supply price of labour, and in manufacturing industry. This would engender economic development and raise incomes *per capita*. But trade by itself does not lead to such a development; it rather tends to have Backsetting Effects and to strengthen the forces maintaining stagnation or regression. Economic development has to be brought about by policy interferences which, however, are not under our purview at this stage of the argument when we are analysing only the effects to the play of the market forces.

Neither can the capital movements be relied upon to counteract international inequalities between the countries which are here in question. Under the circumstances described, capital will, on the whole, shun the underdeveloped countries, particularly as the advanced countries themselves are rapidly developing further and can offer their owners of capital both good profits and security.

There has, in fact, never been much of a capital movement to the countries which today we call underdeveloped, even in earlier times – except tiny streams to the economic enclaves, mainly devoted to export production of primary products which, however, usually were so profitable to their owners that they rapidly became self-supporting so far as investment capital was concerned and, in addition, the considerably larger but still relatively small investments in railways and other public utilities which had their security in the political controls held by colonial governments. The bulk of European overseas capital exports went to the settlements in the free spaces in the temperate zones which were becoming populated by emigration from Europe. After the collapse of the international capital market in the early 'thirties, which has not been remedied, and later the breakdown of the colonial system, which had given security to the foreign investor, it would be almost against nature if capital in large quantities were voluntarily to seek its way to under-developed countries in order to play a role in their economic development.

True, capital in these countries is scarce. But the need for it does not represent an effective demand in the capital market. Rather, if there were no exchange controls and if, at the same time, there were no elements in their national development policies securing high profits for capital – i.e., if the forces in the capital market were given unhampered play – capitalists in underdeveloped countries would be exporting their capital. Even with such controls and policies in existence, there is actually a steady capital flight going on from underdeveloped countries, which in a realistic analysis should be counted against what there is of capital inflow to these countries.

Labour migration, finally, can safely be counted out as factor of importance for international economic adjustment as between underdeveloped and developed countries. The population pressure in most underdeveloped countries implies, of course, that they do not need immigration and the consequent low wages involve that immigrants are not tempted to come. Emigration from these countries would instead be the natural thing. For various reasons emigration could, however, not be much of a real aid to economic development, even if it were possible.

And the whole world is since the First World War gradually settling down to a situation where immigrants are not welcomed almost anywhere from wherever they come; people have pretty well to stay in the country where they are born, except for touristing by those who can afford it. And so far as the larger part of the underdeveloped world is concerned, where people are 'coloured' according to the definition in the advanced countries, emigration is usually stopped altogether by the colour bar as defined by the legislation, or in the administration, of the countries which are white-dominated and at the same time better off economically.

If left unregulated, international trade and capital investments would thus often be the media through which the economic progress in the advanced countries would have Backsetting Effects in the underdeveloped world, and their mode of operation would be very much the same as it is in the circular cumulation of causes in the development process within a single country. Internationally, these effects will, however, dominate the outcome much more, as the countervailing Spread Effects of expansionary momentum are so very much weaker. Differences in legislation, administration and *mores* generally, in language, in basic valuations and beliefs, in levels of living, production capacities and facilities, etc., make the national boundaries effective barriers to the Spread Effects to a degree which no demarcation lines within one country approach.

Even more important as impediments to the Spread Effects of expansionary momentum from abroad than the boundaries and everything they stand for is, however, the very fact of great poverty and weak Spread Effects within the underdeveloped countries themselves. Where, for instance, international trade and shipping actually does transform the immediate surroundings of a port to a centre of economic expansion, which happens almost everywhere in the world, the expansionary momentum usually does not spread out to other regions of the country, which tend to remain backward if the forces in the markets are left free to take their course. Basically, the weak Spread Effects as between countries are thus for the larger part only a reflection of the weak Spread Effects within the underdeveloped countries themselves.

Under these circumstances the forces in the markets will in a cumulative way tend to cause ever greater international inequalities between countries as to their level of economic development and average national income *per capita*.

The underdeveloped countries are thus thrown back upon their own resources. They have one asset, the national state, and the possibility it implies of regulating their own economy. To speak in Hegelian terms: 'the road to international integration must go over national integration; nationalistic policies by the poor countries and an increase of their bargaining power, won through these policies and through increased cooperation between them as a group, is a necessary stage towards a more effective world-wide international cooperation'.

......

Returning to the trade regulations and their employment for protective purposes, I would insist that quite obviously they cannot be rationally framed by reference to the 'objective' economic criteria of the price system, i.e. by means of a simple application of the static theory of comparative costs. Many manufacturing industries are thwarted in their growth or prevented from ever coming into existence because of the small size of the domestic market. This market is frequently flooded by foreign imports from sources to which this demand is often only marginal. By providing protection against outside competition the local industries can be given their chance.

Another general reason for protection is the fact that, as I have already pointed out, almost every new industrial enterprise yields benefits for the economy as a whole, which are not reflected in the profit calulations, in the form of external economies of all sorts, an increase in the number of trained workers, and so on. These effects are for various reasons relatively much more important in an underdeveloped country than in a developed one.

An underdeveloped country is also characterized by the fact that a large portion of its working force is unemployed or eking out a bare subsistence through various forms of 'disguised unemployment.' This fact that labour is not productively employed is from one point of view a way of stating that the country is underdeveloped; from another point of view it represents its opportunity to become developed. If part of this 'free' labour can become gainfully employed, it is a net advantage for the country even if, for this purpose, a shelter against competition needs to be erected.

In an underdeveloped country, the span between wages in manufacturing industry and in agriculture tends, furthermore, for many reasons, to be particularly broad. This will hamper industry if it is not given protection to a corresponding degree.

Interferences in international trade, motivated by considerations of these types, are only part of the general efforts, defined in the national plan, to recondition the price system in such a way that a sustained cumulative process toward economic development is engendered. The action part of a national plan consists of nothing else than a system of interferences with the price system, which must be judged in terms of the practical contribution which they make toward the cumulative upward process which is the goal of the plan.

READING 33

Raul Prebisch

Biography

Raul Prebisch (1901–1986) was born on April 17, 1901 in Tucuman, Argentina. He studied economics at the University of Buenos Aires. When he graduated in 1923 he had already written nine articles on economic subjects.

Prebisch taught economics at the School of Economics of the University of Buenos Aires from 1925 to 1948. In addition, from 1930 to 1932 he was undersecretary of Finance and from 1935 to 1943 he was the first Director General of the Argentine Central Bank.

In 1950 he was appointed executive secretary of the Economic Commission for Latin America (ECLA). In January 1963 he became the Secretary General of the United Nations Conference on Trade and Development (UNCTAD). He was also its leading ideologist.

When the first UNCTAD Conference was held in Geneva in 1964, it endorsed Prebisch's platform. When his term in office with the UNCTAD was over in 1969, Prebisch went to Santiago de Chile as Director of the United Nations Latin America Institute for Economic and Social Planning. Prebisch died at the age of 84 in Santiago de Chile.

The Work

Prebisch makes a major distinction between the 'periphery', that is the less developed countries producing primary products, and the industrial 'center', the industrialized nations of North America and Europe producing manufactured goods. Both Gunnar Myrdal and Prebisch argue that in an unregulated international market system the gains from trade are biased in favor of the advanced industrial countries, the center, and that foreign trade inhibits industrial development in the periphery.

One major problem, according to Prebisch, is that the peripheral countries have experienced and presumably will continue to experience, a long-term deterioration in their terms of trade with the center. As a consequence the periphery has to export ever larger quantities of primary products in order to be able to buy the same amount of industrial products from the center. Agricultural protectionism in the more developed nations is a major cause of this phenomenon. Prebisch argues however, that the most important contributor to this occurrence is that income elasticity of demand, that is, responsiveness of quantity demanded to changes in income, for manufactured imports is high in the periphery. Therefore economic growth and higher incomes in the periphery translate into a very large increase in demand for the industrial products of the center. On the other hand, the income elasticity of the center countries for the traditional export goods of the periphery is low so that increases in their national incomes do not have much effect on the exports of the periphery.

Another problem further contributing to this deterioration in the terms of trade of the periphery is related to price elasticity of demand, that is the measure of responsiveness of quantity of a commodity demanded to a change in market price. Prebisch's hypothesis is that the price elasticity of demand is relatively low for primary products and relatively high for manufactures. The fact that the periphery sells primary goods in inelastic markets means that the gains from productivity increase in the periphery are channeled to foreign consumers. Technological improvements in the periphery increase output and in order to sell it those countries must lower their prices so much that their total receipts fall. Thus the center becomes the primary beneficiary of the technological progress in the periphery. On the other hand, the increases in productivity in the manufacturing sector of the center have a tendency not to be translated into lower prices because wages and prices in both product and labor markets are inflexible downwards. Therefore, the gains in productivity are kept in the center in the form of rising factor incomes. The result of the mechanisms described above is that the export earnings of the less developed countries are inevitably reduced below the levels they would reach if the structure of world trade were different. Thus, according to Prebisch, a new trade policy is needed.[128]

Prebisch proposes five major remedies:

1. Protectionism. Selective protectionism in the periphery including high tariffs on consumer items, would allow these countries to economize scarce foreign exchange and use it for imports which their policy makers believe will contribute to economic development.
2. Duty-free entry for the industrial products of the less developed countries in the markets of the center.
3. Commodity agreements designed to stabilize and increase the prices of primary products.
4. Compensatory financing to low income countries to remedy previous and future deterioration in their terms of trade.
5. Economic cooperation and integration among the peripheral countries to expand their markets and connect their economies with one another.

Prebisch's proposals, sometimes called the Myrdal–Prebisch view

128   Because Prebisch wrote during the 1945–1972 period of fixed exchange rates, he opposed devaluation by the periphery which would ease exports but at a price (ed.).

became accepted doctrine by many officials and politicians in less developed countries. This was especially true for the 1960s and 1970s although much less since then.

The Prebisch thesis has been challenged by the following four counterarguments:

1. The empirical basis of the terms of trade hypothesis is weak. It relies too much on older British statistics. The choice of the base year has a marked effect on the conclusions. The indexes use mixed primary products exported by non-industrial and industrial countries which creates a false impression. Moreover, no proof is provided that the terms of trade must deteriorate in the future.
2. Prebisch's work does not adequately take into account the fact that the center countries are also major producers of primary products and that the periphery increasingly produces and exports manufactures as part of the overall development process.
3. If wages are inflexible downwards in the center but flexible in the periphery, it should be possible for the peripheral countries to compete more and more effectively on a price basis in the fields where both more and less developed countries produce the same products, and they should be able to enter fields where the center was formerly the only producer, especially if they have the inputs available locally.
4. Although it is true that in the center countries there are monopolistic elements in their product and factor markets, that does not mean that the center as a whole is a monopolist in the markets for its exports. In the real world, there is substantial price competition in world export markets among different industrialized nations.

Both supporters and critics of the Prebisch thesis tend to agree that the more developed countries should give wider access to the products of the periphery. They should also reduce their levels of agriculture protection.

The first reading deals mostly with Prebisch's contention that there is a secular tendency of the terms of trade to deteriorate for primary producers. It is taken from the Economic Bulletin for Latin

America.[129] The second reading discusses the slow growth of exports from the periphery and agricultural protectionism by the center. It is taken from the report written by Prebisch for UNCTAD.[130] The third reading, taken from an article in the *American Economic Review*, discusses the implications of different elasticities of exports and imports as well as some issues surrounding economic protectionism.[131]

Extracts

Center and Periphery

In Latin America, reality is undermining the out—dated schema of the international division of labor, which achieved great importance in the nineteenth century and, as a theoretical concept, continued to exert considerable influence until very recently.

Under that schema, the specific task that fell to Latin America, as part of the periphery of the world economic system, was that of producing food and raw materials for the great industrial centers.

There was no place within it for the industrialization of the new countries. It is nevertheless being forced upon them by events. Two world wars in a single generation and a great economic crisis between them have shown the Latin-American countries their opportunities, clearly pointing the way to industrial activity.

The academic discussion, however, is far from ended. In economics, ideologies usually tend either to lag behind events or to outlive them. It is true that the reasoning on the economic advantages of the international division of labor is theoretically sound, but it is usually forgotten that it is based upon an assumption which has been conclusively proved false by facts. According to this assumption, the benefits of technical progress tend to be distributed alike over the whole community, either by the lowering of prices or the

129 R. Prebisch 'The Economic Development of Latin America and its Principal Problems', *Leading Issues in Development Economics* (G.M. Meier, ed.) (New York: Oxford University Press, 1964) pp. 339–343.

130 R. Prebisch, 'Towards a New Trade Policy for Development', *Leading Issues in Economic Development*, 2nd edn. (G.M. Meier, ed.) (New York: Oxford University Press, 1970) pp. 484–491.

131 R. Prebisch, 'Commercial Policy in Underdeveloped Countries', *American Economic Review*, Vol. 49, No. 2 (May 1959), pp. 254–257, 264–265.

corresponding raising of incomes. The countries producing raw materials obtain their share of these benefits through international exchange, and therefore have no need to industrialize. If they were to do so, their lesser efficiency would result in their losing the conventional advantages of such exchange.

The flaw in this assumption is that of generalizing from the particular. If by 'the community' only the great industrial countries are meant, it is indeed true that the benefits of technical progress are gradually distributed among all social groups and classes. If, however, the concept of the community is extended to include the periphery of the world economy, a serious error is implicit in the generalization. The enormous benefits that derive from increased productivity have not reached the periphery in a measure comparable to that obtained by the peoples of the great industrial countries. Hence, the outstanding differences between the standards of living of the masses of the former and the latter and the manifest discrepancies between their respective abilities to accumulate capital, since the margin of saving depends primarily on increased productivity.

Thus there exists an obvious disequilibrium, a fact which, whatever its explanation or justification, destroys the basic premise underlying the schema of the international division of labor.

Hence, the fundamental significance of the industrialization of the new countries. Industrialization is not an end in itself, but the principal means at the disposal of those countries of obtaining a share of the benefits of technical progress and of progressively raising the standard of living of the masses.

......

It was stated in the preceding section that the advantages of technical progress have been mainly concentrated in the industrial centers and have not directly extended to the countries making up the periphery of the world's economic system. The increased productivity of the industrial countries certainly stimulated the demand for primary products and thus constituted a dynamic factor of the utmost importance in the development of Latin America. That, however, is distinct from the question discussed below.

Speaking generally, technical progress seems to have been greater in industry than in the primary production of peripheral countries, as was pointed out in a recent study on price relations. Consequently, if prices had been reduced in proportion to increasing productivity, the reduction should have been less in the case of primary products than in that of manufactures, so that as the disparity between productivities increased, the price relationship between the two should have shown a steady improvement in favor of the countries of the periphery.

Had this happened, the phenomenon would have been of profound significance. The countries of the periphery would have benefited from the fall in price of finished industrial products to the same extent as the countries of the center. The benefits of technical progress would thus have been distributed alike throughout the world, in accordance with the implicit premise of the schema of the international division of labor, and Latin America would have had no economic advantage in industrializing. On the contrary, the region would have suffered a definite loss, until it had achieved the same productive efficiency as the industrial countries.

The above supposition is not borne out by the facts. As can be seen in the indexes of Table I, the price relation turned steadily against primary production from the 1870s until the Second World War. It is regrettable that the price indexes do not reflect the differences in quality of finished products. For this reason, it was not possible to take them into account in these considerations. With the same amount of primary products, only 63 per cent of the finished manufactures which could be brought in the 1860s were to be had in the 1930s; in other words, an average of 58.6 per cent more primary products was needed to buy the same amount of finished manufactures.[132] The price relation, therefore, moved against the periphery, contrary to what should have happened had prices fallen as costs decreased as a result of higher productivity.

During the expansion of the last war, as in the case of all cyclical expansions, the relation moved in favor of primary products. Now, however, although there has not been a recession, a typical readjustment is taking place, with the result that prices of primary products are losing their former advantage.

The pointing out of this disparity between prices does not imply passing judgement regarding its significance from other points of view. It could be argued, on grounds of equity, that the countries which strove to achieve a high degree of technical efficiency were in no way obliged to share its fruits with the rest of the world. Had they done so, they would not have reached their enormous capacity to save,

132   According to the report already quoted. The figures for the thirties go only as far as 1938 inclusive. The data given are the Board of Trade's average price indexes for British imports and exports representative of world prices for raw materials and manufactured goods respectively.

without which it might well be asked whether technical progress would have achieved the intense rhythm which characterizes capitalist development. In any case the productive technique exists and is at the disposal of those with the capacity and perseverance to assimilate it and increase their own productivity. All that, however, is outside the scope of this report. The purpose is to emphasize a fact which, despite its many implications, is not usually given the importance it deserves when the significance of the industrialization of the peripheral countries is discussed.

TABLE I. RATIO OF PRICES OF PRIMARY COMMODITIES TO THOSE OF MANUFACTURED GOODS (AVERAGE IMPORT AND EXPORT PRICES, ACCORDING TO DATA OF THE BOARD OF TRADE)
(1876–80 = 100)

Periods	Amount of finished products obtainable for a given quantity of primary commodities
1876–80	100
1881–85	102.4
1886–90	96.3
1891–95	90.1
1896–1900	87.1
1901–05	84.6
1906–10	85.8
1911–15	85.8
—	—
1921–25	67.3
1926–30	73.3
1931–35	62.0
1936–38	64.1
—	—
1946–47	68.7

Source: 'Post War Price Relations in Trade Between Under-developed and Industrialized Countries,' document E/CN.1/Sub.3/W.5,23 February 1949.

Simple reasoning on the phenomenon in question brings us to the following considerations:

First   Prices have not fallen concomitantly with technical progress, since, while on the one hand, costs tended to decrease as a result of higher productivity, on the other, the income of entrepreneurs and productive factors increased. When income increased more than productivity, prices rose instead of falling.

Second   Had the rise in income, in the industrial centers and the periphery, been proportionate to the increase in their respective productivity, the price relation between primary and manufactured products would have been the same as if prices had fallen in strict proportion to productivity. Given the higher productivity of industry, the price relation would have moved in favor of the primary products.

Third   Since, as we have seen, the ratio actually moved against primary products in the period between the 1870s and the 1930s, it is evident that in the center the income of entrepreneurs and of productive factors increased relatively more than productivity, whereas in the periphery the increase in income was less than that in productivity.

In other words, while the centers kept the whole benefit of the technical development of their industries, the peripheral countries transferred to them a share of the fruits of their own technical progress.

In short, if, in spite of greater technical progress in industry than in primary production, the price relation has moved against the latter instead of in its favor, it would seem that the average income, *per capita*, has risen more in industrial centers than in the producer countries of the periphery.

The existence of this phenomenon cannot be understood, except in relation to trade cycles and the way in which they occur in the centers and at the periphery, since the cycle is the characteristic form of growth of capitalist economy, and increased productivity is one of the main factors of that growth.

In the cyclical process of the centers, there is a continuous inequality between the aggregate demand and supply of finished consumer goods. The former is greater than the latter in the upswing and lower in the downswing.

The magnitude of profits and their variations are closely bound up with this disparity. Profits rise during the upswing, thus tending to curtail excess demand by raising prices; they fall during the downswing, in that case, to counteract the effect of excess supply by lowering prices.

As prices rise, profits are transferred from the entrepreneurs at the center to the primary producers of the periphery. The greater the competition and the longer the time required to increase primary production in relation to the time needed for the other stages of production, and the smaller the stocks, the greater the proportion of profits transferred to the periphery. Hence follows a typical characteristic of the cyclical upswing; prices of primary products tend to rise more sharply than those of finished goods, by reason of the high proportion of profits transferred to the periphery.

If this be so, what is the explanation of the fact that, with the passage of time and throughout the cycles, income has increased more at the center than at the periphery?

There is no contradiction whatsoever between the two phenomena. The prices of primary products rise more rapidly than industrial prices in the upswing, but also they fall more in the downswing, so that in the course of the cycles the gap between prices of the two is progressively widened.

Let us now look at the explanations of this inequality in the cyclical movement of prices. It was seen that profits rise in the upswing and decrease in the downswing, thus tending to offset the disparity between demand and supply. If profits could fall in the same way in which they rose, there would be no reason whatsoever for this unequal movement. It occurs precisely because they cannot fall in that way.

The reason is very simple. During the upswing, part of the profits are absorbed by an increase in wages, occasioned by competition between entrepreneurs and by the pressure of trade unions. When profits have to be reduced during the downswing, the part that had been absorbed by wage increased loses its fluidity, at the center, by reason of the well-known resistance to a lowering of wages. The pressure then moves toward the periphery, with greater force than would be the case, if by reason of the limitations of competition, wages and profits in the center were not rigid. The less that income can contract at the center, the more it must do so at the periphery.

The characteristic lack of organization among the workers employed in primary production prevents them from obtaining wage increases comparable to those of the industrial countries and from maintaining the increases to the same extent. The reduction of income – whether profits or wages – is therefore less difficult at the periphery.

Even if there existed as great a rigidity at the periphery as at the center, it would merely increase the pressure of the latter on the former, since, when profits in the periphery did not decrease sufficiently to offset the inequality between supply and demand in the cyclical centers, stocks would accumulate in the latter, industrial production contract, and with it the demand for primary products. Demand would then fall to the extent required to achieve the necessary reduction in income in the primary producing sector. The forced readjustment of costs of primary production during the world crisis illustrates the intensity that this movement can attain.

The greater ability of the masses in the cyclical centers to obtain rises in wages during the upswing and to maintain the higher level during the downswing and the ability of these centers, by virtue of the role they play in production, to divert cyclical pressure to the periphery (causing a greater reduction of income of the latter that in that of the centers) explain why income at the centers persistently tends to rise more than in the countries of the periphery, as happened in the case of Latin America.

That is the clue to the phenomenon whereby they great industrial centers not only keep for themselves the benefit of the use of new techniques in their own economy, but are in a favorable position to obtain a share of that deriving from the technical progress of the periphery.

The Slow Growth of Exports

As has been pointed out, the trend towards external imbalance in the developing countries is mainly a manifestation of the disparity between the rate of growth of their primary exports and that of their imports of industrial goods. While primary exports, with certain exceptions, develop fairly slowly, demand for industrial imports tends to accelerate. This is a spontaneous feature of economic development.

The slow growth of primary exports is an inevitable result of technological progress in the industrial centers. On the one hand, there are direct consequences, since technological progress leads to the increasing substitution of synthetics for natural products; and it is also reflected in one way or another in the smaller raw material content of finished goods. On the other hand, there are indirect consequences, since only a small part of the increased per capita income generated by technological progress goes into the demand for foodstuffs and other staple consumer goods, as compared to the demand for industrial goods and services which tends to rise rapidly.

In western Europe, cereals and meats, milk products, vegetable fats and oils, sugar and other foodstuffs are thus well-protected by the fixed or flexible tariffs and import quotas. Thanks to this protection, it is possible to pay domestic producers, as stated above, prices much higher than those prevailing on the international market, or to grant them substantial subsidies. While the effects on consumption vary, depending on the nature of the measures adopted, all these measures serve to stimulate increased domestic production at the expense of imports, which have thus dropped to a level where they are merely residual.

In the United States, too, the impact of protectionism is significant and is intensified, in the case of some agricultural products, by the sale of surpluses abroad, which, despite efforts to prevent them from invading traditional markets, have a harmful effect on other producing countries.

It is often asserted that the weight of the restrictive measures applied to agricultural products from the temperate zones falls mainly on the primary exports of industrial countries and that they consequently have little effect on developing countries. But there are two reasons why this is not so. The first is that certain Latin American and Mediterranean developing countries which export such temperate-zone products are seriously affected by these restrictions. The other is that the sale of surpluses in world markets often displaces tropical or semi-tropical products. One example is rice in the consumption of countries in the Far East and Canada. Furthermore, oils and fats from the industrial countries are tending to oust imports from developing countries; temperate-zone fruits are tending to take the place of tropical varieties; and the competition between beet sugar and cane sugar is seriously harming the developing countries, as are highly subsidized exports of cotton, maize and tobacco from industrial countries.

In addition to the foregoing, the following consideration must also be borne in mind. International trade cannot be arbitrarily fragmented, and the unfavorable effect that sales of surpluses have on exports from other developed countries also impairs their capacity to import from the developing countries.

Thus, for example, the difficulties experienced by such countries as Australia, Canada, the United States and New Zealand are bound to affect the ability and willingness of these countries to open up their internal markets to larger shipments from developing countries.

Tropical products are not subject to import restrictions in the markets of the industrial countries, but their consumption is discouraged in some of them by internal taxes which are usually more than the value of the items imported. Furthermore, the preferences granted to certain countries which export these tropical products are detrimental to the interests of other developing countries.

Imports of many mineral products tend to rise as industrial development progresses. This is happening in the countries of western Europe, which continue to depend on imports for most of their requirements in minerals and non-ferrous metals, which the United States has become a net importer rather than a net exporter of this group of products. Nevertheless, the United States continues to restrict imports in the interest of domestic production of lead, zinc and petroleum. Similarly, certain coal-producing western European countries levy duties and taxes on petroleum products that compete most directly with coal.

The foregoing remarks relate to the advanced private-enterprise countries. The socialist countries too have obviously made great efforts to stimulate their primary production, and the technological revolution in agriculture is proceeding there also. In recent years, as will be seen elsewhere, their imports of primary commodities from the developing countries have increased rapidly, although not yet commensurately with their economic potential. Consequently, the aforesaid objectives as regard a reasonable share in consumption hold good in the case of the socialist countries as well.

Why the Prices of Primary Commodities Tend to Deteriorate in Relative Terms

The easing or elimination of protectionism in the industrial centers could have a far-reaching effect on the prices of the goods benefiting thereby. But it would be idle to believe that this can have any decisive effect on the downward trend of the terms of trade for primary commodities in relation to industrial products, which has again prevailed in the past decade. The factors operating in this direction have deeper roots in the peripheral countries than in the industrial centers. The former suffer from a congenital weakness that makes it extremely difficult, if not impossible, for the deterioration to be checked by a decision on their part and on their part alone.

Owing to the slowness of the growth of demand for primary commodities, only a dwindling proportion of the increment in the economically active population in the developing countries can be absorbed in their production, and the more productivity in primary activities rises as a result of the assimilation of advanced techniques, the smaller will that proportion be. The economically active population therefore has to be shifted to industry and other activities.

This shift is a lengthy process, even in the industrial countries where the proportion of the economically active population employed in primary production is already relatively small. Hence the phenomena discussed above. If the switch-over were effected rapidly and primary production were quick to adjust itself to the slow growth of demand, one of the requisites for obviating the deterioration of the terms of trade would be fulfilled.

For this to happen, industry and other sectors would have to develop very rapidly in the peripheral countries and achieve a rate of growth much higher than that heretofore attained in those countries, particularly if efforts to introduce advanced techniques into primary production and other low-productivity activities were intensified.

The magnitude of this process is indeed enormous. It should be remembered that, although there are differences from country to country, about 60 per cent, on the average, of the economically active population of the developing countries is still engaged in agriculture and other branches of primary production, working generally at a low rate of productivity, and that to this figure must be added that part of the economically active population engaged in artisan activities and personal services at very low scales of remuneration. All these sectors of the population exert constant pressure on the real level of wages in the developing countries and make it extremely difficult for this level to rise in direct proportion to productivity as the latter improves with technological progress. The increase in income generated by higher productivity in the agricultural sector thus tends to shift to other parts of the domestic market or abroad, as the case may be, provided that the shortage of available land does not absorb the increase in income by raising the rent for the benefit of landowners and provided that the play of market forces is left undisturbed.

In the industrial countries, on the other hand, the relative shortage of labor and strong trade-union organization allow wages not only to rise as productivity increases but even, as often happens to outstrip the increase.

Thus there is a fundamental disparity in these trends. It is a consequence of the structural differences between industrial centers and peripheral countries and it explains the tendency of the terms of trade to worsen. The protection enjoyed by the primary commodities of the industrial centers obviously encourages this tendency because it accentuates the disparity between demand for primary commodities in the centers and demand for imports of manufactures in the periphery.

This should not be regarded as an immutable law. It is a trend which can be slowed down or halted when the demand for primary commodities in the major centers expands very rapidly either because of the speed with which income rises or because of extraordinary requirements, and it cannot be immediately followed by a corresponding expansion in primary production. The terms of trade will then become favorable; and if, as is usually the case, both land and manpower are available, production will expand to the point where it exceeds demand and the tendency of the terms of trade to deteriorate will reappear, particularly if techniques which increase productivity are applied and the demand of the industrial countries is restricted at the same time.

With an effort of the imagination it is possible to visualize a situation of dynamic equilibrium in the distant future in which the trend in question disappears as a result of the world-wide process of industrialization. If the advanced centers themselves have not yet succeeded in reaching that stage, the countries on the periphery of the world economy can hardly be expected to do so within a short space of time. The readjustment will come about in the end when the structural change is completed, but the period of transition will be very long. In the meantime, it is precisely through this period of transition that the present and successive generations are destined to live, and it is those generations which will have to bring about the change. The change will also require capital formation on a vast scale, to say nothing of time. In the developed economies, capital formation, intrinsically very strong, is facilitated by the very increase in productivity which accompanies technological progress whereas in the developing countries, owing to the transfer abroad of income caused by the deterioration in the terms of trade, the capacity for capital formation, intrinsically very feeble, will be further diminished.

It is obvious that, if technological progress in primary production is intensified and if technology in the developing countries also undergoes a revolution, without which they cannot grow faster, the tendency of the terms of trade to deteriorate may be even stronger than in the recent past. This is not a prediction. But, what factors can we descry on the economic horizon that they are capable of countering this tendency?

There are those who are inclined to set great store by the recent firmness of primary commodity prices and indeed, the United Nations index of world commodity export prices, having declined by the beginning of 1961 to a level of 8 per cent below that of 1953, remained stable during 1961 and 1962 and has since recovered more than half of the loss since 1953. But can it be argued that the general trend has finally reversed itself and that there is no longer any need to worry about the possibility of further deterioration? Or ought we, on the contrary, to face up to this phenomenon with a great sense of foresight?

There are various ways in which this can be done: by means of commodity agreements, which not only improve prices but also facilitate access to the markets of the industrial countries, or by compensatory financing. These are in fact convergent measures, the nature of which will be analyzed in the appropriate part of this report. Suffice it to say here that there are difficulties but that they can be solved. However, for the technical discussion to be profitable, it must be preceded by a political decision of the first importance, namely, a decision to transfer, in one way or another, to the countries exporting primary commodities the extra income accruing to the industrial countries as a result of the deterioration in the terms of trade.

From a pragmatic point of view this means recognizing that countries experiencing a deterioration in the terms of trade have a *prima facie* claim upon additional international resources – resources over and above those which they would have received in the normal course of events.

Some aspects of this matter are rather delicate and might lead the discussion on to barren ground unless we keep these pragmatic considerations uppermost in our minds. Practically speaking, the position is this. The foreign earnings of the developing countries have suffered severely from the deterioration in the terms of trade. Unless these countries succeed in obtaining additional resources, they will be unable to achieve the reasonable rate of growth set as a target in their plans. The situation will be worse still if the terms of trade deteriorate further in the future.

External Bottlenecks Obstructing Development

There is one dominant note in this report. On the international economic scene we are faced with new problems, new in kind, in some cases, and new because of the magnitude they have acquired, in others. We therefore need different attitudes from those prevailing in the past, and these attitudes should converge towards a new trade policy for economic development.

The problems that beset the developing countries are very grave indeed. They have to assimilate modern techniques swiftly in order to raise their levels of living. But new techniques, while they bring enormous advantages with them, are fraught with dangerous consequences, because we have not yet learnt fully to control the forces of development in a rational way.

The direct and indirect effects of technological progress are responsible for the fact that world demand for primary commodities is growing so slowly, to the detriment of the developing countries. The effects of the protectionism prevailing in the industrial countries are an added factor. Even through access to the markets of the latter countries is facilitated, the primary production of the developing countries should adjust to this slow tempo of demand, but structural difficulties prevent it from doing so to the extent necessary to prevent primary commodity prices from deteriorating in relation to those of manufactures. The further modern techniques permeate primary production, the stronger may be the tendency towards such a deterioration. Action by Governments is therefore imperative to deal with this paradox of development.

Such action is also essential for rapid industrialization to become the dynamic factor in the development of the world periphery, just as primary exports were the dynamic factor in the development of the world periphery in former times. But in those days development had no social depth. Today it must. This makes the problem of development more complex and pressing.

The circumstances in which industrialization must proceed are, moreover, very adverse. The developing countries are still suffering the consequences of the disintegration of the world economy that followed upon the great calamity of the 1930s. They do not export industrial goods, except in very small quantities. Since their primary commodity exports are growing so slowly and their terms of trade tend to deteriorate, they lack the resources necessary to import, on an adequate scale, the goods required for a satisfactory rate of development.

These imports are mostly industrial goods, and only part of them have been or could be produced domestically on an economic basis owing to the smallness of national markets. They must export in order to enlarge these markets. But it is usually difficult to increase exports because costs are high because of the difficulty of realizing economies of scale in the absence of exports. Here too a policy is needed, action by Governments to break this vicious circle by providing reasonable access to the markets of the industrial countries for manufactures from the developing countries, and a decided effort to promote the exports of such manufactures.

The developing countries should also form their own groupings in order to plan and develop their industries in wider markets. In some cases they have only just embarked on this policy and they should be given firm international support in the technical and financial fields, within a more favorable institutional framework than now exists. Such co-operation is needed to help import substitution within the groupings with respect not only to goods but also to services, since maritime transport and insurance, for example, represent very substantial external payments.

......

Protection

In the changing pattern of employment associated with the process of development, a declining proportion of the continuously increasing active population is needed for the growth of existing activities for the internal market, due to improvements in productivity. Therefore a part of the growing manpower is not required in these existing activities. Moreover, there is manpower that for the same reason is not needed to produce the present level of exports. All this redundant manpower has to be employed in the expansion of these exports and in new branches of industries for substitution purposes, as well as in other new activities. These new forms of employment are geared to internal and external demand elasticities and to different rates of increase in productivity.

In other words, in a dynamic economy redundant manpower is continually emerging as a result of technical progress, and it tends to be absorbed to meet the increasing demand generated by that very same technical progress.

In addition, there is a second form of manpower that has to be so absorbed. There are indeed vast numbers of marginal workers of low productivity rendering poorly paid personal services, as well as people engaged in other forms of precarious employment or disguised unemployment of a precapitalist character who should be moved to new jobs.

In the process of growth, at every level of per capita income, a certain proportion of this manpower is made available for transfer to other forms of employment, through shifts in demand as well as through technical changes in production.

For the sake of brevity, we will use the term 'surplus manpower' to describe both these sources of labor and we will confine ourselves to that part of the surplus to be transferred to exports or new branches of industry for import substitution.

Redundant manpower as such does not produce any income and the real measure of the fruits of technical progress is the increment that accrues to the community when such manpower is transferred to new forms of employment. In addition to this increment, there is the net increase in income obtained by transferring available manpower from these precapitalist forms of employment of very low productivity to exports or industrial activities of much higher productivity.

Let us first clarify one important point. Industrial costs higher than import prices do not necessarily mean that an industry is not economic for a country as is sometimes assumed. Of course the smaller the difference the better.

The problem has to be considered from another angle. It is not really a question of comparing industrial costs with import prices but of comparing the increment of income obtained in the expansion of industry with that which could have been obtained in export activities had the same productive resources been employed there.

I am afraid that it is not possible to arrive at the optimum solution of this problem if market forces are left unrestricted. The classical mechanism of the free play of market forces, either in its original form of wage adjustments or in its contemporary version of price adjustments through exchange rate movements, does not bring about that optimum solution. On the contrary, the periphery transfers to the outer world a greater part of the fruits of increased productivity than if the market forces had been contained at a certain point, either through customs protection or some other form of interference in the process.

I have strong doubts about the advisability of exchange rate adjustments as an instrument to correct foreign trade disparities in demand elasticities. The main appeal of depreciation as compared with protection is that it leaves private initiative rather than government agencies to decide which branches of industry will be profitable substitutes for imports. But this could also be achieved through a uniform protective duty.

Protection (or subsidies) seems a more direct and simple solution, as it limits the adjustment to those new branches of industries that should be developed within a given period of time. To obtain the same result, depreciation forces the adjustment of the whole price system. In my view, a policy of depreciation or devaluation should be used only to correct an externally overvalued currency and not as an instrument for effecting structural changes in the economy. A selective protection policy is a preferable instrument, notwithstanding the obstacles that have to be overcome in practice; and if it is applied gradually, higher import prices, affecting a relatively small proportion of imports each time, could be absorbed by general increments of productivity without affecting the price level of the entire economy, provided that protection has not been exaggerated to shelter inefficiency.

In any event, this is not relevant to our main line of argument. What is highly relevant is that the cost of spontaneous industrialization – by the unrestricted play of market forces through exchange depreciation – is a transfer abroad of part of the increment in real income derived from the employment of the surplus manpower, and that this transfer could be reduced or avoided by protection, subsidies, an export tax, or other forms of interference.

......

Reciprocity

Protection has different meanings in the peripheral countries and in the industrial centers. In the former it is, up to a certain point, the instrument for correcting the effects of the disparity in income elasticity of demand for exports of primary commodities and for imports of industrial goods and does not hamper the rate of growth of world trade. In the industrial centers, by contrast, protection of primary production accentuates this disparity and tends to depress peripheral development and to decrease the rate of growth of world trade.

The reduction or elimination of such protection at the centers has an implicit element of reciprocity, since the resultant increase in exports of primary commodities from the periphery will be followed by a corresponding increase in its imports of industrial goods, in response to their high income elasticity of demand, and there is no need for any reduction or elimination of duties to obtain this result.

The traditional form of reciprocity, under which peripheral

countries are asked to grant duty concessions, similar to those introduced by the centers, does not take into account this implicit element of reciprocity.

Moreover, these reciprocal duty concessions may have an unfavorable influence on the periphery's rate of growth. The development process requires a continual change in the composition of imports. These changes usually start with the decline in the proportion of imports of light consumer goods in favor of imports of basic material, capital goods, and durables. At more advanced stages of industrialization, when import substitution of these light consumer goods has been nearly completed, new changes relating to the other categories of goods are necessary, so that by reducing or eliminating imports of some of them it is possible to increase imports responding to the needs of the development process. Now, if these duty concessions interfere with these changes, then the increased peripheral capacity to import resulting from duty concessions at the centers in stead of helping to attain a higher rate of growth might be accompanied by a real decline in the rate of industrial development. This might be a very harmful use of the increase in the periphery's capacity to import deriving from such duty concessions at the centers.

READING 34

John Mathew Culbertson

Biography

John Mathew Culbertson was born in Detroit in 1921. Now (1996) at 75 he is emeritus Professor of Economics at the University of Wisconsin, Madison. He earned his PhD in economics from the University of Michigan in 1950. Early in his career he taught as a visiting professor at the University of Michigan and at the University of California at Berkeley. From 1950 to 1957 he was an economist with the Board of Governors of the Federal Reserve System. In 1957 he joined the faculty of the University of Wisconsin. He has toured Southeast Asia for the US Information Agency and lectured on monetary economics at the University of Paris.

The Work

Professor Culbertson's writings have been mainly on macroeconomics, monetary economics, economic development and international economics. In his writings on international trade and finance he expounds the institutionalist view. Like Myrdal he strongly criticizes neoclassical economics which in his view is based on 18th century beliefs of natural harmony. According to Culbertson mainstream economics is too individualistic and governed by an outdated framework. Moreover, it does not pay sufficient attention to the nation state which, in his view, is the most important organization in the existing system of human life. This explains why Culbertson takes the national view and not the world view.

We noted in previous readings that economists like Prebish and Myrdal believed that international trade operates with a fundamental bias in favor of the richer nations. They thought free, unregulated trade would tend to create or perpetuate stagnation in the less developed countries. Culbertson argues just the opposite. Unregulated international trade, like free international migration, works in favor of (often densely populated) low wage countries (LWCs) and against the relatively prosperous high wage countries (HWCs).

Culbertson's argument can be thought of as a new and more sophisticated version of the so-called 'pauper labor argument' a discussion of which is found in most texts on international economics. According to the pauper labor argument (a) wages in HWCs, by definition are much higher than in most less developed nations. Therefore (b) the costs of production are lower in LWCs. Under free trade (c) foreign goods will flood the market of HWCs such as the United States, forcing producers in HWCs to lower wages to a level approximating foreign wages in order that companies in HWCs can remain competitive.

The usual reply to this type of argument is that it fails to recognize the link between efficiency and wage costs. Wages in HWCs are higher because their labor is more productive when compared with foreign labor. The higher productivity can be explained by the greater skills and by the fact that those HWC workers are usually assisted by a large supply of capital, a sophisticated infrastructure, up-to-date technology and sometimes the advantages of large scale production.

Another problem with the pauper labor argument is that it treats wage costs as if they are the only costs of production. Wages represent a single item in production costs and the return to the factors of production other than labor may dominate the cost structure.

As stated previously, Culbertson believes that free international trade can lead to an impoverishment process which would first affect the HWCs and then spread to the LWCs. His explanation reminds one of Myrdal's concept of circular and cumulative causation.

Assuming that labor cannot move freely across boundaries and that we live in a world of HWCs and LWCs the succession of events according to Culbertson runs as follows. The LWCs often experience overpopulation, one of the major causes of low wages. Consequently they have low production costs. As a result, they can undersell the HWCs in their domestic markets as well as in their traditional export markets. As long as LWCs can increase output and sell it in HWCs, industries and work will shift to the cheap labor nations.[133] Therefore, free trade deindustrializes HWCs like the USA. Firms in those countries increasingly establish production facilities in the LWCs in order to take advantage of the lower wage costs.

In all this the multinational corporations or transnational enterprises intensify the process. Revolutionary changes in transportation and communications have made it possible for corporations to organize, manage and finance production in the LWCs. Thus the transnational enterprises are capable of shifting operations to other nations thereby providing technology, capital and skilled managers to LWCs and using their efficient ties to the markets of the HWCs. As industries move from HWCs to LWCs, exports from the more prosperous countries fall while imports rise resulting in a deficit on the balance of trade. Moreover, the drop in exports and rise in imports causes the exchange rates of the HWCs to decline. The terms of trade shift against them and the standard of living falls.

In the end, in order to remain competitive the high wage country must lower its wage levels and its standard of living drops further. Culbertson calls this 'degenerative competition'.[134] This also implies that the HWC must eventually lower its environmental standards and relax rules pertaining to the health and safety of workers to avoid losing even more industries and jobs. The drop in incomes and the

133 It may be observed here that in the real world increased output is frequently associated with higher costs which would also be true for the less developed countries Culbertson has in mind. In that sense the process he describes is self-limiting.

134 In the 1930s and even later, a number of American companies located in the Northern part of the country moved to the South, taking advantage of lower wage costs and taxes. Their products were sold in all parts of the United States. One may wonder whether according to Culbertson this is another instance of 'degenerative competition' (ed.).

rise in unemployment cause a decline in tax receipts in the HWCs while at the same time expenditures on unemployment compensation and other income supplements go up. The inability of the national and local governments to adjust quickly, results in large budget deficits. This in turn leads to more public borrowing at the expense of privately financed productive investment.

In the long run, however, Culbertson contends, the course of events is self-defeating. As the economies of HWCs suffer a progressive decline in living standards, the profitable high income markets in which LWCs can sell the 'advanced manufactured products' die away leaving the whole world worse off. In the countries which were once prosperous, the demand for mass produced items such as appliances, cars and aircraft shrinks. Similarly, the demand for advanced medical and dental treatment, high levels of education, scientific and technological research and so on also declines. All this involves a return to backwardness. The way in which HWCs will react to declining standards of living is hard to predict, according to Culbertson. However, a rise in political disorder and extremism cannot be excluded.

Culbertson extends the argument by stating that free migration can also destroy the more prosperous nations. High income nations have achieved prosperity mainly because they have avoided a high density of population and high demographic growth rates. The low income countries usually suffer from demographic congestion, high levels of fertility and high rates of population growth. In a world with free migration, migrants would travel in very large numbers from the crowded LWCs to the less densely populated HWCs, pulling down wage rates and standard of living in the areas of destination. People in the HWCs would find their salaries and wages undercut, having to accept levels of income well below the accustomed ones. HWCs would also experience accelerated environmental degradation, crowding, and resource depletion. Thus through free migration, overpopulation and poverty would spread throughout the entire world.

Conscious limitation of births as is practiced in the HWCs only makes sense if large scale migration is not allowed to occur. Otherwise the low fertility populations will simply be outbred by high fertility populations or sink to a position of relative insignificance.

It is of course true, says Culbertson, that outmigration from the LWCs may promote some relief to them, but a cumulative improvement process will only occur if successful population policies reduce fertility levels in those areas.

Suppose, however, that because of outmigration from the LWCs incomes begin to rise and mortality is reduced. If people react by marrying earlier while maintaining high fertility levels, population growth will accelerate and a return to extreme misery will become inevitable.

In summary, Culbertson argues that free migration and free trade might integrate the world but the equalization of wage rates and living standards will bring HWCs to the poverty levels and overpopulation LWCs are currently experiencing. Culbertson obviously embraces the mercantilist idea that trade usually benefits one country and damages another.[135] Therefore international integration through trade is not desirable. On the contrary, he states that often enough, a relatively high degree of national insulation best serves that nation's interests.[136]

Trade between what Culbertson calls 'harmonious trade areas' could be relatively free. Such harmonious areas are areas with common or approximately common goals, wages, rates of population growth, social economic and environmental standards and policies.[137] Such trade would not result in degenerative, standards-lowering competition among sub areas. Trade between 'disharmonious' areas should be managed by negotiated trade agreements among governments. These largely bilateral agreements should keep trade and payments between nations in balance. Trade between countries in this category would consist of deals, concluded between trade officials (government agencies, etc.) of the relevant nations. Only mutually advantageous bargains will be consummated. Central planning of the entire economy is not needed, says Culbertson. Yet, because trade will be regulated, guided and restricted by national governments, a national trade plan will be required. Most deals will be bilateral but multilateral trade packages are not impossible.

Having presented Culbertson's ideas, it may be useful at this point to take a more critical look at them. There is admittedly some force

---

135   Culbertson states that pre-Adam Smith economists had a better understanding of international commerce than Adam Smith and his followers. See Culbertson, *International Trade and the Future of the West*, p. 48.

136   *Ibid*, p. 209.

137   Needless to say that his idea denies the logic of comparative advantage (ed.).

in Culbertson's argument that free migration: or even systematic immigration in such countries like the US, Canada, or Western Europe can generate negative socioeconomic effects in the countries of destination. In 1991 the world population of about 5.4 billion was growing at an annual rate of 1.6 per cent. In total numbers that amounted to some 93 million people per year. Of the 5.4 billion inhabitants of the earth some 4 billion or 77 per cent lived in the less developed areas of Asia, Africa, and Latin America. A fair estimate of the annual excess of births over deaths in all less developed nations is at least 75 million. Should the US, Canada, Western Europe and Japan take in these numbers in order to provide some relief? In a world where the high income/low fertility countries constitute a small minority surrounded by a high fertility majority, free migration becomes a somewhat unrealistic proposal.

Looking judiciously at Culbertson's ideas on free and managed trade reveals many problems, as is to be expected when someone makes a large number of personal statements unsupported by empirical evidence.

1. The type of argument advanced by Culbertson calls for cost comparisons. Trade in harmonious areas can be relatively free, he says, because the costs of production are about equal. The problem is: whose costs are to serve as a frame of reference? Producers in any country have different and constantly changing costs for the same products.

2. There is no doubt that wages differ and are sometimes very low in LDCs. However, differences in factor prices reflect to a large extent differences in the relative availability of those factors in various countries. Opportunities for gainful trade emerge precisely from those differences in comparative costs.

3. Free trade can be compared to technical progress. Free trade generates adjustment problems that are sometimes just as difficult and painful as those created by technical progress. People who lose their jobs suffer. Yet nobody is arguing that the government of an HWC such as the US should pass a law banning all innovation.

4. In a market-oriented economy firms will always attempt to lower their costs and in doing so they will search for cheaper sources for their inputs. Sometimes, this search for lower cost resources such as labor can cross national frontiers. This makes the world economy more efficient and the consumer benefits. At

this moment a restructuring of the world economy is taking place which should result in an improved resource allocation.

5. It is true that some intermediate and finished products are now made abroad by American companies and then imported into the US. This process is called 'export platforming' or 'outsourcing'. However, it would be an exaggeration to believe that multinationals merely shift jobs and industries from HWCs to LWCs. American companies build plants in other countries but foreign corporations such as Honda and BMW build factories in the US providing employment. Moreover, multinationals continue to manufacture in MDCs because they do not want to subject all their manufacturing to 'country risk' problems which are particularly dominant in LDCs.

6. Corporations do not always go abroad in search of lower labor costs. American companies such as Ford and General Motors built plants in Europe, not because labor is cheaper (because it is not), but because they want to be closer to the market they serve. Insofar as their operations increase business profits in the US and consumers' income abroad they can, in the long run, increase the demand for American products and contribute to an increase in domestic American jobs.

7. Sometimes writers such as Culbertson seem to regret the shift from manufacturing to the service sector in HWCs because they tend to identify manufacturing with high productivity and services with low productivity. However, the argument can be misleading when it comes to modern highly progressive service sectors such as air transportation services and banking. In 1995 receipts from American services sold to foreigners exceeded payments by almost $65 billion.

8. The basis of Culbertson's thinking is the decline in the US international competitive position resulting in such problems as a negative trade balance. He expresses the belief that it is the moving of industries and jobs from America to low wage nations that lies at the heart of the problem. There are, however, other explanations. Competitiveness depends on productivity which in turn is determined by saving and investment. In the US the rate of personal saving as a percentage of GNP dropped from 5.7 per cent in 1980 to 3.9 per cent in 1991. Net private investment fell from 5.7 per cent of GNP in 1980 to 1.8 per cent in 1991. Also, the education system was allowed to deteriorate while the absence of Federal

fiscal discipline resulted in large budget deficits. Therefore the Federal government had to borrow annually huge sums of money, thus depriving the private sector of the funds needed for renewing its equipment, for modernization, expansion, and for research and development. Japan's economic success was not due to its wage levels but to the fact that it had relatively high rates of saving and investment. The government practiced restraint and did not 'crowd out' the private sector while corporations were willing to take the long run view. Japan's educational system moreover, was exacting and put great emphasis on science and mathematics.

9.   It may be observed here that the idea that Third World competition is a threat to First World countries is often used by politicians and the media to put the blame on Third World countries instead of placing the responsibility on the wrongheaded policies of those First World nations. This is even more true for the European welfare states where excessive redistribution of incomes discourages effort, enterprise and initiative and makes for economic stagnation.[138]

10.   In search of a policy solution Culbertson distinguishes between harmonious and disharmonious trade areas. However, it may well be difficult to establish objective criteria as to what exactly these concepts involve.

11.   Trade between disharmonious regions should, according to Culbertson, be negotiated by trade agreements among governments. In fact, in the interwar period (1920-1940) numerous countries and policy-makers advocated state control trade over foreign trade. Soviet Russia, Fascist Italy and Nazi Germany actually practiced it. It cannot be denied that state controlled trade represents an important step in the direction of state socialism. A probable first result of state controlled trade will be that bureaucracy will grow by leaps and bounds. Second, if international trade is taken out of the orbit of private enterprise and becomes state directed it becomes part of international relations in general and will be subject to political influences and pressures. International friction may thus be generated. The price of sardines and the quantities that may be

138   See on this: P. Krugman, *Pop Internationalism* (Cambridge: The MIT Press, 1996).

delivered may become an important source of political discord between two nations. Finally, bilateral trade agreements play into the hands of the more powerful countries because they may acquire the ability to enforce some of their decisions on the smaller nations. Nazi Germany which in the 1930s developed to the full its system of bilateral trading, was often able to impose agreements upon the weaker nations and force them into a state of quasi-dependency.[139]

Extracts

Free Trade and the West

For most of this century, United States trade policy has been based on the belief that unregulated international trade, or 'free trade', fits a theoretical pattern that automatically makes it beneficial to the nations involved. Thus, 'barriers to trade' and 'protectionism' are harmful. The difficulty with this elegantly simple theory is that it bears little relation to reality.

The evidence shows that not all trade is the same – different patterns of foreign trade exist, and they have different effects. Some are very damaging. The pattern of foreign trade that has caused the extraordinary shift of industries from the United States in recent years is of the destructive kind.

The stereotype within which economists have viewed international trade was developed by Adam Smith, in the 18th century. It depicts each nation as specializing in products to which it is peculiarly suited, in which it has low relative costs or a *comparative advantage*. Thus, a nation rich in iron ore might trade with a nation that produces steel efficiently. Both would gain by the trade.

In this 'comparative-advantage rule', the gain in efficiency from international specialization benefits both nations. Further, the trade is

139   J.M. Culbertson, 'Free Trade is Impoverishing the West', *New York Times* (July 28, 1985).
J.M. Culbertson, *The Dangers of Free Trade* (Madison: 21st Century Press, 1985) pp. 19–20, 22–24, 33–34.
J.M. Culbertson, *International Trade and the Future of the West* (Madison: 21st Century Press, 1984) pp. 219–223.

assumed to be in balance, so there is no general shift of industries from one nation to another – with the chain of serious consequences it can bring.

The error in the theory gained new importance in the modern era, when changes in technology, transportation and communications began to break down the conventional economic barriers between countries. Today, most United States trade is not based on comparative advantage and is not efficient. There is no gain in efficiency from shifting factories that are producing goods for the domestic market from the United States to Asia or Latin America. There is little comparative advantage in today's manufacturing industries, since they produce the same goods the same ways in all parts of the world. Why, then, is industry after industry moving out of the United States?

These industry shifts are based on the transfer of industries and jobs to countries with low standards of living and low wage rates. American factories are closed because foreignmade goods are cheaper. These goods are cheaper because the workers who make them earn wages one-half, one-fifth and even one-tenth as high as those of American workers. This trade is not comparative-advantage trade, but 'wage-cutting trade'.

Wage-cutting trade does not offer the benefits arising from comparative-advantage trade. It does not increase economic efficiency; often it reduces efficiency by adding transportation costs. Thus, it cannot possibly make both nations, and the world, better off. If wage-cutting trade benefits one nation, it does so by damaging the other one. In an immediate sense, such trade commonly benefits the low-wage nation that is gaining industries and jobs and damages the high-wage nation that is losing them. In the long run, it may be damaging all around, dragging all nations down to a low standard of living; there are signs that even Japan is becoming concerned with this trend.

The debilitating, long-run effects of wage-cutting trade derive from its out-of-balance character. The high-wage nation cannot go on forever losing industries and jobs, importing more than it exports and running up its foreign debt. It is forced by rising unemployment and burgeoning foreign debt to 'become competitive', which it must do by accepting declining wage rates – as the United States has begun to do.

How much does the high-income nation's standard of living have to decline to make it 'competitive' under 'free trade'? That depends entirely on the circumstances of the case. With cheap transportation, instant communications, multinational corporations to shift technology and management around the world, low-wage and unemployed people now numbering in the billions and population rising very rapidly in some already populous nations, the economic decline suffered by the United States and Europe under 'free trade' could be a shattering one.

More broadly, 'free trade' in an increasingly overpopulated world would cause wage-cutting trade to pull all nations down to the lowest-common-denominator level. It would put all nations into a shared 'population trap' in which no accomplishments would permit a nation to improve its lot. Thus, a nation that perfected a particular industrial process would not be enriched. It would simply lose its industry to a lower-wage nation. In this respect, 'free trade' has the same effects as 'free migration'.

The implications for the United States of comparative-advantage trade and of wage-cutting trade are as different as night and day. When the facts are considered, it is impossible to deny that recent economic developments in the United States have been dominated by wage-cutting trade. To argue for a policy of 'free trade' – and to terminate the import quota on Japanese automobiles, and seek further reductions in tariffs and quotas – on the basis of comparative advantage is not just erroneous but dangerously misleading.

Past economic progress has occurred through an evolutionary process in which one nation finds a way to put together a more effective economy. Other nations advance by copying the success. This pattern requires that nations have the economic independence to experiment, to create constructive patterns – rather than being helpless within a worldwide commune forced by 'free trade'.

A reasonable trade policy in today's world, then, must encourage mutually beneficial, comparative-advantage trade by curbing destructive wage-cutting trade and other destructive patterns of foreign trade. The starting point for a realistic interpretation of trade is the recognition that different patterns have different effects, and some are destructive.

To curb wage-cutting trade requires balancing arrangements. Balance in trade prevents excessive imports from low-wage nations from undercutting the standard of living of high-wage nations. Balanced trade thus provides the framework within which mutually beneficial trade between nations can develop. Actions to limit a nation's imports, and mutual agreements between nations to prevent damaging trade developments, have been common. We need to use such policies more coherently and cooperatively, with a new understanding of the patterns of trade that are to be encouraged or curbed.

The recent trade policy of the United States has encouraged the wage-cutting foreign trade that has been draining away the nation's industries and jobs and created an enormous trade deficit. Given this starting point, the economic state of the nation can be radically improved simply by adopting realistic policies that limit imports so as to bring the nation's foreign trade into balance.

......

The undercutting and disappearance of high-income nations would affect the future course of all nations. For one thing, the loss of high-income societies would drastically reduce the demand for the output of what have been the attractive industries – and the migrating industries – of recent years. The production of autos, say, shifts to South Korea and China, which undercuts American production and incomes, and then it turns out that there no longer is much of a market for autos. Many goods, and the technology that is used to produce these goods, would become obsolete in a world in which no large group of people had incomes high enough to buy them. With the shift back down to simpler and more basic consumer goods, recent 'technological progress' would be reversed. Many of its innovations were geared to a high-income world, and would be useless in a low-income world.

Another kind of effect of the loss of high-income nations would be the cutbacks in research and development, and in scientific capabilities. Some kinds of technological know-how would remain relevant – indeed, essential – to the new low-income world. The population situation requires the knowledge and the technical and organizational capabilities lying behind the flow of chemical fertilizers, insecticides, genetic improvement of food plants and animals, and the capability to keep ahead of the evolving diseases and pests that threaten the food supply. These have been achievements of the well organized, high-income nations, which could and did carry their overhead costs and meet their demanding organizational requirements. The loss of these capabilities because of poverty and disorder would have dire consequences.

......

What determines whether wage–competition across national boundaries prevails, say, between the United States and China – and thus whether the rule of one price, i.e., of one wage rate, does or does not apply? One obvious way in which wage-competition could prevail across two nations is for them to have 'free migration', or the free movement of people. In the absence of 'barriers to population movement', people would act in such a way as to bring about equalization of wage rates and living standards. People would move from the low-wage nation to take better-paid jobs in the high-wage nation. This movement of people would raise the wage in the low-wage nation and lower the wage in the high-wage nation. Such migration would tend to occur until the wage rates in the two countries were made equal.

As a matter of fact, this kind of movement of people, both legally and illegally, from lower-wage nations to take jobs in higher-wage nations is an important feature of the present-day world, and a problem for a number of nations. Not only the United States and Europe are suffering such an influx of people. India, for example, is subject to illegal immigration from nations with a still lower standard of living and worse unemployment than it suffers.

Nations do not accept any principle of 'free migration'. It is widely understood that for a nation to permit unlimited immigration – in a world with billions of low-wage workers and hundreds of millions of unemployed or only partially employed workers – would invite an influx of people that could radically reduce its wage rate and standard of living.

But it is not so well understood that wage-competition across two nations will occur if industries and jobs are free to move to the low-wage nation, with the goods shipped back for sale in the markets of the high-wage nation. Workers in the lower-wage nation can take away the jobs of workers in the higher-wage nation as effectively by the jobs moving to them as by them moving to the jobs. Either way, the workers of what had been the higher-wage nation are thrown into wage-competition with those of the lower-wage nation. If the workers in both countries are available to do the same kinds of work and do it equally well, there will tend to be one, equalized wage rate.
......

The population explosion of recent decades – which has added 2 billion people and doubled world population since the Second World War – has enormously increased the pool of low-wage labor available for wage-competition with Western workers. This is true not only in absolute numbers of available low-wage workers but also in relative terms. Population has grown most rapidly, and continues to grow most rapidly, in low-wage nations – their rapid population growth being a major reason, in some cases *the* reason, why they *are* low-wage nations.

When international wage-competition and the shift of industries and jobs from high-wage to low-wage areas works to equalize world wage rates, the level of the equalized wage rates depends on the relative size of the groups of high-wage and low-wage workers. Given the numbers of people now in the two groups, such equalization of wage rates would bring a great fall in the wage level and the standard of living of the United States and other high-income nations. The fact that some large, low-wage nations have very high rates of population-growth tellingly affects the future prospects of nations that are economically merged with these nations by international trade and wage-competition.

In theorizing, or thinking about the world in terms of words or conventionalized 'models', one may assume that, say, 'free trade is free trade', and it will have the same effects in one case as another. Thinking in terms of 'principles' tempts us to neglect the influence on events of changing circumstances. In truth, a revolutionary change in conditions implies that 'free trade' now has effects very different than in the past. The world now faces the challenge of dealing with a problem that has not existed in the past, and that can be understood only by escaping from traditional slogans, theories, and viewpoints.

......

Among the potential problems that must be dealt with by reasonable arrangements for trade across national boundaries is the tendency toward degenerative competition in production standards. A nation that requires standards in the work-place that protect the health and safety of employees thereby imposes on its producers costs that do not have to be incurred by firms producing in nations that do not enforce such standards. Under these conditions, competition among them will tend to force firms to shift production from high-standards nations to low-standards nations. This may be accomplished in part by the firms of high-standards nations failing and being replaced by those of low-standards nations. The same kind of problem applies to all kinds of cost-affecting standards: standards in environmental protection, in resource conservation, in the preservation of historical treasures and aesthetic values.

The competition imposed upon firms under unregulated international trade will tend to lower such standards without limit. The movement of industries and jobs from high-standards to low-standards nations will cause a competition among nations to retain industries and jobs by lowering their standards. The effect will be not only to prevent nations imposing standards that are unreasonably high, but to prevent them from maintaining any standards at all. The force of competition is to require firms to avoid all costs that can be avoided. Such competition includes no in-built mechanism that distinguishes reasonable from unreasonable regulations and standards. If this ingredient is to be supplied, it must come from national governments.

In seeking arrangements for international trade that would avoid standards-lowering competition without damaging the interests of any particular nation, what kind of approach is to be considered?

......

Once it is recognized that trade that is mutually beneficial to the nations involved cannot possibly result from unregulated dealings across national boundaries by firms and individuals, it is natural to turn to the one arrangement that actually is capable of bringing about such mutually beneficial trade. That is the management of international trade by negotiated trade agreements among governments. It is for the governments to bring about the condition that trade, say, between 'England' and 'Portugal' actually be beneficial to both England and Portugal.

Though explicit and comprehensive trade deals between governments have been largely limited to the centrally planned economies, many governments have guided their international trade in one way or another. Governments have placed barriers in the way of imports thought to be detrimental to the nation's interests, because of the character of the imports and the industry they represented, the rapid growth of the imports, or the general excess of the nation's imports. Direct negotiations between governments over trade have occurred in cases like the agreement between the United States government and the government of Japan through which a quota was imposed on sales of Japanese automobiles in the United States.

Arrangements for trade that are negotiated directly between the two governments involved thus would be more balanced, would, as it were, put the cards on the table, and would open up the potential for kinds of mutually advantageous trade deals that could not be worked out at lower levels but require the larger perspective and powers of the national governments. The positive side of such arrangements is that they would open the way to mutually profitable arrangements for international trade and international economic specialization that are not feasible now because the only agency with the breadth of viewpoint and authority to make them is the national government. The decisions that have to be made are decisions involving the interests of nations. Despite the rhetoric about 'competition' and 'the free market', firms cannot act effectively or responsibly on behalf of a nation.

For national governments to oversee and guide international trade through such arrangements with other governments would not require an extension of central planning of production, or the nationalization of industries. The production of goods could be left as much as desired in the hands of private firms. The needed limitation or guidance of trade could be achieved through requiring licenses for certain kinds of transactions – as is done now in special cases. The licenses would be issued by the government in the required volume and under the required side-conditions to private firms. Even in cases in which governments made direct contracts with one another for the delivery of specified goods, the actual operations could be carried out by private firms acting under contracts with the governments. Perhaps in many cases trade could be permitted to proceed without such arrangements, and only kept under surveillance by governments to assure that it does not expand or change in form in a way that is inconsistent with the over-all program of mutually advantageous trade between the nations involved.

Surely such management of international trade by national governments could involve many kinds of problems. Differences among governments in competence could seriously affect the outcome. Some governments would find it difficult to create an agency that could act knowledgeably and intelligently on behalf of the nation in trade matters.

There is a hazard that nations that are in a strong position because of their size, their lack of dependence on international trade, or their possession of something that other nations badly need would take advantage of nations that are in a weak bargaining position. Some nations might make trade agreements and not live up to them. For some nations, the government's assumption of a role in guiding international trade could seriously increase the burdens imposed by a poorly organized, red-tape-bound, or corrupt government bureaucracy. The new regulations could become the basis for new kinds of graft and bribery of government officials.

All such potential difficulties need to be taken seriously. But the fact that managing international trade involves difficulties and inconveniences does not imply that managing international trade is not necessary. Dealing with a heart ailment involves difficulties and inconveniences, but the fact that it is difficult does not imply that it is superfluous. Management by governments of trade between nations can prevent patterns of trade that are seriously disadvantageous to nations, even ruinous to them. This is a requirement that must be met.

There seems to be no other way of meeting it.

It is often cited as a positive feature of unregulated international trade that it can construct multilateral patterns of trade: United States sells machinery to Venezuela, which sells oil to Japan, which sells automobiles to the United States. In economic theory, all of this balances out nicely and has no indirect effects, but we are aware that the reality is very different from the theory.

Can trade regulated and guided by national governments generate patterns of three-way trade, or more complex patterns of trade? Or does the existence of such national guidance of trade force it into a strictly bilateral framework?

Clearly, it is feasible for trade packages to be arranged by more than two nations. Where there exists a potential for a set of nations to gain from a trade package of this type, their governments will have an incentive to work out the necessary arrangements. The ability to keep the trade under control, in accordance with a plan, and to make larger and longer commitments than would be feasible for firms, may permit the working out of some constructive patterns of trade that could not have been developed under individualistic trade.

The systems of contractual arrangements among firms on which the ordinary operations of economics are based are extremely complex. The development of such intricate patterns of dealings depends on the use of explicit contracts among firms. Such contractual arrangements bring to the system of activities the order, predictability, and controllability that make possible the planning of elaborate sets of dealings that are mutually advantageous to the firms involved. If firms could not operate through such contracts and had to flounder along on the basis of week-to-week dealings, they could not arrange such complex patterns of mutually advantageous specialization.

Trade contracts or formal trade agreements among nations would involve the extension to a higher organizational level of the planning and guidance instrument through which firms achieve the wonders of modern production. In an economic world that is based on mutually advantageous contractual arrangements among firms, it is anomalous that mutually advantageous contractual arrangements among nations are not made – and that contracts between firms are assumed to be a substitute for contracts between nations. Correcting this anomaly should make possible new kinds of benefits from international trade – as well as protecting nations against the greater hazards of unregulated trade.

READING 35

Robert L. Kuttner

Biography

Robert L. Kuttner (1943–) was born in New York City. He was educated at Oberlin College, the University of California at Berkeley and the London School of Economics. Kuttner now lives in Brooklyn, Massachusetts with his wife and two children.

Kuttner is the author of several books, including *The Economic Illusion* (1984) that discusses social justice and economic growth, *The Life of the Party* (1987) that deals with the Democratic Party, and *The End of Laissez Faire* (1991) in which Kuttner goes into his views on international economics. Besides this, he is the co-editor of *The American Prospect*, a journal of politics, policy and culture, which he founded with Robert Reich and Paul Starr in 1989. Kuttner is also one of the four contributing columnists to *Business Week*'s *Economic Viewpoints*. In addition, he writes for other publications such as the *New Republic*, *The Atlantic* and the *Boston Globe*.

Kuttner has lectured at Harvard's Institute of Politics, at Brandeis University, at Boston University and the University of Massachusetts. He won several awards including the Jack London Award for Labor Journalism. Robert Kuttner describes himself as a social democrat. As a tract writer he is a devout Keynesian and a follower of Roosevelt-style New Deal politics. Consistent with those philosophies, Kuttner believes that the solution to economic ills rests with the extension of government as a provider of welfare services and substantial government interference in industry and trade.

The Work

In his books and articles Kuttner heralds the end of 'laissez–faire' both in theory and policy. Especially in his book *The End of Laissez–Faire*, he starts from a number of premises which to him seem self-evident. He believes for instance, that unless the domestic and the global economies are regulated, they tend to be systematically unstable. An unstable market economy, says Kuttner, is vulnerable to cycles of overproduction and underconsumption as well as to competition based on low wages. The result is a short-fall of aggregate demand. New technologies are fine in that they can improve manufacturing efficiency. However, they can also displace jobs and destroy communities.

In discussing international finance, Kuttner holds that financial markets are chaotic. He views their history as a record of speculative bubbles followed by panics. Exchange rates, if left alone, have a tendency to overshoot and to fluctuate wildly with the result that they play havoc with enterprises trying to invest in the long run. In the end, markets are not self-correcting mechanisms in a way that is politically tolerable. These 'brute' market forces have to be 'channeled', 'stabilized', 'tamed', and 'civilized' if social harmony is to prevail.

As Kuttner sees it, the United States has ardently promoted unrestrained laissez–faire. This commitment to unbridled laissez–faire in global commerce is due to the fact that since 1945 the US has emerged as the strongest military and economic power. Consequently, it had a strong interest in open world markets. At the same time the US committed as it was to containing Soviet imperialism, offered its Cold War Allies the advantage of free access to its huge domestic market. Open American markets were the glue of the Anti-Soviet Alliance. But now that the Cold War is past says Kuttner, the US commitment to laissez–faire is outdated and it must share economic power with the European Community and Japan. Redefinition of the American interest is in order and a 'new' (ed.: read 'more nationalistic') trade policy is required.

According to Kuttner there are other reasons as well why the US must chart a different course. One is that while the US promoted a laissez–faire commercial policy, its trade partners played the global trade game by different, more mercantilist-nationalistic rules. The Japanese for example, had a coherent industrial policy based on supporting promising industries. They used cheap loans and subsidies, they waived anti-monopoly laws, they promoted temporary research and recession cartels while Japan's distribution and retailing systems were organized in such a way that made it difficult for foreign companies to break in. Thus the US was put at a competitive disadvantage and lost numerous high-technology, high-wage industries, according to Kuttner.

A major problem with globalization is that, combined with deregulated financial markets and free trade policies, domestic political autonomy is reduced. International competition damages the high-cost social welfare programs and trade union practices by making those nations that abide by them less competitive. So, unless foreign goods can be locked out to some extent and domestic financial capital locked in, trade unions are left out in the cold and social welfare programs have to be reduced in size. These consequences are highly regrettable in Kuttner's view.

Kuttner equally believes that the global economy is systematically unstable. That conviction leads him to advocate international institutions in the spirit of Keynes and Roosevelt. The International Monetary Fund, for instance, is now, according to Kuttner, very far removed from where Keynes would have liked it to be. At present, it has become an agent of austerity, economic orthodoxy and private capital. Less developed countries that want access to the financial capital of the Fund, usually have to accept stabilization packages including currency devaluation, tight monetary policies, public spending cuts, reduced government intervention and the liberalization of capital flows. Instead, Kuttner advocates an IMF with an operating philosophy based on more plentiful and cheaper credit. Countries which are in economic difficulty could be asked to try income policies, higher taxes on the wealthy and capital controls.[140] In Kuttner's view, countries which run chronic trade surpluses, export unemployment and should be penalized. Finally, the IMF should have enlarged powers to create reserves that would increasingly replace the dollar as an official reserve currency. The IMF, as Kuttner sees it, should be much more sympathetic to the mixed social-democratic economy.

Discussing the General Agreement on Tariffs and Trade (GATT), Kuttner regrets that during the Uruguay Round negotiations, US negotiators did not focus more on the 'neo-mercantilist' policies of such countries as Japan, South Korea and Brazil. Over the years of the GATT's existence, too many non-tariff trade barriers were allowed to persist. Moreover, no judicial enforcement mechanisms were developed to settle disputes. As Kuttner sees it, the new trading order of the 1990s should contain rules to allow for national industrial and technology strategies. This would include departures from laissez-faire policies such as domestic development subsidies, domestic content requirements and flexible quotas and cartels.[141] Thus Kuttner believes that the GATT should move away from the principle of

---

140   Income policies involve government manipulation of incomes (ed.).
141   It seems that Kuttner criticizes new-mercantilist policies and proposes them at
      the same time (ed.).

unconditional free trade and toward the concept of conditional free trade. Countries that have identical rules and standards should have free access to each other's markets. The conditions of access to those countries which adopt different rules and/or protectionist–mercantilist policies should be negotiated bilaterally.

When it comes to domestic policy recommendations, Kuttner basically advocates a return to the welfare state heritage of the New Deal. Public sector spending has to increase to pay for a continuously growing list of social programs. Governments of industrial countries with relatively high per capita incomes such as the US have to be active and involved and deal with such domestic issues as: (a) education and training, (b) labor relations, (c) the structure of capital markets, (d) public infrastructure, (e) the accountability of corporate managers, (f) corporate raiding, (g) environmental regulation and (h) health care.

Recalling that Kuttner believes that contemporary economies are systematically unstable, his recipe for getting out of a recession consists of such fiscal policies as: (1) steeply progressive surtaxes on earners of high incomes, (2) wage and price controls, (3) forced savings, and (4) massive public work programs.

Since Kuttner prefers a managed, planned, regulated, mixed domestic economy, it is not surprising that he also advocates the international economic arrangements and institutions needed to match the controlled welfare state. Thus he advocates the kind of supranational institutions as envisaged by Keynes in the early 1940s. Moreover, the international trading system should allow for the growth and development strategies mentioned earlier, including domestic subsidies, domestic content provisions, flexible quotas and cartels, limited use of other market closing devices and bilateral deals.[142] According to Kuttner, the Multi-Fiber Agreement (MFA) which regulates the international textile trade is a good illustration of a successful managed trade policy. The MFA permits the US to place stringent limits on imports of textiles and garments without violating GATT obligations.[143] Assured of some protection, investments in the

---

142   Domestic content requirements limit the purchase of foreign components by domestic companies. Such requirements usually stipulate the percentage of a product's total value that must be produced domestically (ed.).

143   The Multi-Fiber arrangement is a mammoth global voluntary export restraint including over forty countries and covering about half of all world trade in textiles and clothing. It allows nations to negotiate bilateral quantitative

textile industry have increased, says Kuttner, and in the 1980s American textile exports began to exceed textile imports.

For nations that want to preserve such industries as the steel industry, Kuttner would recommend the use of quotas. A portion of the domestic market, say 75 per cent, could be reserved for domestic suppliers while the remaining 25 per cent could be made available for imports.[144]

A last question to address is how to choose industrial candidates to be included in a managed trade regime. The solution, says Kuttner, is to look for those industries that already enjoy some form of needed protection. Moreover, if governments wish to retain or develop new industries or technologies, there is also room for government involvement, protection and state intervention.

While it is not possible here to examine critically all of Kuttner's propositions, some deserve comment.

As we have seen, Kuttner relies heavily on selecting a straw man: undiluted laissez-faire. This permits him to rail against the ruthlessness and the disorder of markets and to advocate government involvement and intervention to 'channel', 'civilize', and 'tame' those brutal market forces. Authors like Kuttner believe in the fundamental disharmony of the market. Consequently, they insist upon the negative. Whatever does not work gets attention, whatever works is often neglected. This view proceeds on the premise that whenever markets are in disarray it is because of market failure. They perceive as a logical consequence the desirability of government interference or management. The possibility that such intervention may not improve the situation is left out of the picture. Yet in the minds of many students of the era, the history of the twentieth century seems to show that free markets usually do a better job in allocating resources than policy makers and planners.

It is true that the governments of some of the economically more successful Pacific countries initially practiced some measure of sectoral intervention. Whether or not that explains their fast economic growth will never be known. It is noteworthy however that at the same time these countries had very high rates of physical and human capital accumulation. The governments of Japan, South Korea, Hong

restrictions on textile trade. In the early 1990s it encompassed about 3000 bilateral quotas on different countries' products within the arrangement (ed.).
144   Apparently Kuttner's choice of percentages is purely arbitrary and not based on any kind of research (ed.),

Kong and the Republic of China also did a remarkable job in maintaining macroeconomic and political stability, while their economic approach was always market friendly. Hong Kong probably had the freest economy in the world while government interference was reduced to the bare minimum. Taxes were low, it had no quotas or tariffs and virtually no restraints on entry into business. Since the mid-1960s the per capita income of Hong Kong has doubled every 12 years.

Kuttner also wants the government to select and support those business firms or industries which deserve special care. This approach has the same problem as the infant industry case. When it comes to industrial targeting there are no clear usable economic criteria to target 'desirable' industries as opposed to those which are not deserving support. Moreover, governments have shown no particular genius for picking industrial and technological winners better than the free market does. Political clout is frequently the main determinant. Kuttner suggests that the criteria for relief be those industries that utilize emerging technologies as well as those that already enjoy some form of 'needed' protection, because they are vulnerable. However, if one takes the losers which must be protected and adds all the potential winners to them, close to the entire economy will be locked up.

Kuttner states that the Multi-Fiber arrangement was a good model for managed trade. After all, it allowed the American textile industry to become productive to the point where textile exports surpassed imports. Yet this achievement becomes less impressive if it is remembered that the MFA limits imports. Besides, the MFA relies on bilateral quantitative restrictions. Bilateralism in general usually means that two nations make concessions to each other or conclude some specific deal. Bilateralism does affect third parties which are by definition excluded. Therefore, there is always an element of discrimination in bilateralism which tends to breed hostility, retaliation and possibly very substantial diplomatic friction.

Multilateralism as promoted by the GATT tries to avoid the problem of discrimination inherent in bilateral deals. In spite of all its shortcomings the GATT is probably still the most practical approach to bring order into that anarchy of independent nations which often lies at the bottom of the world's problems.

Domestic content legislation cannot be thought of as a 'normal' element of commercial policy as Kuttner seems to suggest. Domestic or local content rules reduce imports and are examples of pure and unadorned protectionism which displace employment without creating it.

In commenting upon the practices of America's trade partners such as Japan, Kuttner discusses the fact that they often play the global trade game by rules which are to the detriment of US owned companies. Nobody would deny that when that happens the US has to take notice. For example, specific government procurement practices of America's trade partners may result in significant losses for some American businesses. Kuttner apparently wants the US to resort to managed trade to deal with these situations and thereby put commercial policy on a different, more collectivist basis. As an alternative one could argue that when emergency situations arise there is a case for special negotiation or the adoption of special expedients preferably within the GATT framework. Why replace a set of arrangements which have so far proven to be generally beneficial?

In his book *Pop Internationalism*, Paul Krugman complains that writers such as Kuttner (*The End of Laissez Faire*, 1992), Lester Thurow (*Head to Head*, 1992), and Robert Reich (*The Work of Nations*, 1993), view the world as a place of difficult struggle among market economies for markets and capital. The problem, according to Krugman, with this type of discourse is that it is totally unrelated to the kind of well-known international trade theory that academic economists teach.

Finally, one may observe that in a sense Kuttner takes us back to Fichte. Just as Fichte needed protectionism to preserve his redistributional objectives in a closed commercial state, Kuttner needs protectionism to retain his welfare state and its trade unions.[145]

---

145   R.L. Kuttner, 'Managing U.S. Economic Destiny', *Challenge*, Vol. 34, No. 1 (Jan.–Feb. 1991) pp. 18, 22.
R.L. Kuttner, 'The Free Trade Fallacy', *The New Republic*, Vol. 188, No. 12 (March 28, 1983) pp. 16, 17, 20.
R.L. Kuttner, 'Another Great Victory of Ideology over Prosperity', *The Atlantic*, Vol. 268, No. 4 (October 1991) p. 39.
See also: R.L. Kuttner, *The End of Laissez Faire*, Chs. 4, 7, 8 (New York: A.D. Knopf, 1991).

Extracts

The essential argument is that the pursuit of laissez-faire as an ideal for the global economy has a lot to do with the role that the United States has played geopolitically since World War II. That role no longer fits the self-interests of either the United States or the world economy, for reasons that ought to be pretty well established by now.

Laissez-faire is systematically unstable within one country and it is systematically unstable globally. The critique of laissez-faire is interesting not just because of the political debate between the right and the left over economic justice and fairness. There is also a perfectly good critique of laissez-faire based on the economic instability it generates, and another critique for economic development reasons. So you do not have to be a social democrat, a trade unionist, or a liberal proponent of the welfare state to be skeptical about whether laissez-faire can produce optimal economic results. Nor do you have to be an economic nationalist. You can simply be someone who understands economic history and, based on that knowledge, appreciates that laissez-faire is a utopian idea, not a workable economic system.

......

Just fifty years ago, Keynes, having dissented from the nineteenth-century theory of free markets, began wondering about free trade as well. In a 1993 essay in the *Yale Review* called 'National Self-Sufficiency', he noted that 'most modern processes of mass production can be performed in most countries and climates with almost equal efficiency'. He wondered whether the putative efficiencies of trade necessarily justified the loss of national autonomy. Today nearly half of world trade is conducted between units of multinational corporations. As Keynes predicted, most basic products (such as steel, plastics, microprocessors, textiles, and machine tools) can be manufactured almost anywhere, but by labor forces with vastly differing prevailing wages.

With dozens of countries trying to emulate Japan, the trend is toward worldwide excess capacity, shortened useful life of capital equipment, and downward pressure on wages. For in a world where technology is highly mobile and interchangeable, there is a real risk that comparative advantage comes to be defined as whose work force will work for the lowest wage.

In such a world, it is possible for industries to grow nominally more productive while the national economy grows poorer. How can that be? The factor left out of the simple Ricardo equation is idle capacity. If America's autos (or steel tubes, or machine tools) are manufactured more productively than a decade ago but less productively than in Japan (or Korea, or Brazil), and if we practice what we preach about open trade, then an immense share of US purchasing power will go to provide jobs overseas. A growing segment of our productive resources will lie idle. American manufacturers, detecting soft markets and falling profits, will decline to invest. Steelmakers will buy oil companies. Consumer access to superior foreign products will not necessarily compensate for the decline in real income and the idle resources. Nor is there any guarantee that the new industrial countries will use their burgeoning income from American sales to buy American capital equipment (or computers, or even coal), for they are all striving to develop their own advanced, diversified economies.

......

Against this background of tidal change in the global economy, the conventional reverence for 'free trade' is just not helpful. As an economic paradigm, it denies us a realistic appraisal of second bests. As a political principle, it leads liberals into a disastrous logic in which the main obstacle to a strong American economy is decent living standards for the American work force. Worst of all, a simple-minded devotion to textbook free trade in a world of mercantilism assures that the form of protection we inevitably get will be purely defensive, and will not lead to constructive change in the protected industry.

The seductive fallacy that pervades the hand-wringing about protectionism is the premise that free trade is the norm and that successful foreign exporters must be playing by the rules.

......

The argument that we should let 'the market' tease us out of old-fashioned heavy industry in which newly industrialized countries have a comparative advantage quickly melts away once you realize that precisely the same nonmarket pressures are squeezing us out of the highest-tech industries as well. And the argument that blames the problem on overpaid American labor collapses when one understands that semi-skilled labor overseas in several Asian nations is producing advanced products for the US market at less than a dollar an hour. Who really thinks that we should lower American wages to that level in order to compete?

In theory, other nations' willingness to exploit their work forces in order to provide Americans with good, cheap products offers a deal we should not refuse. But the fallacy in that logic is to measure the costs and benefits of a trade transaction only in terms of that transaction itself. Classical free-trade theory assumes full employment. When foreign, state-led competition drives us out of industry after industry, the costs to the economy as a whole can easily outweigh the benefits. As Wolfgang Hager, a consultant to the Common Market, has written, 'The cheap (imported) shirt is paid for several times: once at the counter, then again in unemployment benefits. Secondary losses involve input industries ... machinery, fibers, chemicals for dyeing and finishing products.'

As it happens, Hager's metaphor, the textile industry, is a fairly successful example of managed trade, which combines a dose of protection with a dose of modernization. Essentially, textiles have been removed from the free-trade regime by an international market-sharing agreement.

......

What, then, is to be done? First, we should acknowledge the realities of international trade. Our competitors, increasingly, are not free marketeers in our own mold. It is absurd to let foreign mercantilist enterprise overrun US industry in the name of free trade. The alternative is not jingoist protectionism. It is managed trade, on the model of the Multi-Fiber Arrangement. If domestic industries are assured some limits to import growth, then it becomes rational for them to keep retooling and modernizing.

It is not necessary to protect every industry, nor do we want an American MITI. But surely it is reasonable to fashion plans for particular key sectors like steel, autos, machine tools, and semiconductors. The idea is not to close US markets, but to limit the rate of import growth in key industries. In exchange, the domestic industry must invest heavily in modernization. And as a part of the bargain, workers deserve a degree of job security and job retaining opportunities.

Second, we should understand the interrelationship of managed trade, industrial policies, and economic recovery. Without a degree of industrial planning, limiting imports leads indeed to stagnation. Without restored world economic growth, managed trade becomes a nasty battle over shares of a shrinking pie, instead of allocation of a growing one. And without some limitation on import, the Keynesian pump leaks. One reason big deficits fail to ignite recoveries is that so much of the growth in demand goes to purchase imported goods.

......

The challenge is to replicate the institutions of a mixed economy on a global scale. That is much more difficult because of the problem of national sovereignty. A nation state can have a variety of mechanisms to prevent complete economic permeability. These are used to wield the power to regulate commerce. It can pursue monetary and fiscal policies, it can set labor standards, it can have various regulatory policies. But carrying out such policies becomes very difficult in a system with complete globalization of commerce.

You can attempt to run a big deficit and stimulate your economy, but a lot of that incremental purchasing power leaks out and buys imports, which in turn causes balance-of-payments crises. You can attempt to have a monetary policy, but it is partly captive to the monetary policies of other countries if you have free international flows of capital. You can attempt to regulate labor standards, but there is a risk of a competitive race to the bottom of the wage structure, if other countries are willing to pay workers less and allow their labor standards and working conditions to deteriorate. So the dual challenge of stabilizing and civilizing a market economy becomes more difficult when the economy is globalized.

......

I see a system with a central bank along the lines Keynes envisioned, but that seems politically improbable. You could imagine a stronger IMF built around three key currencies, which I think is rather more probable, and that would increase the pressure for macro-economic convergence. If you want to have a yen, a European Currency Unit (ECU), and a dollar that do not fluctuate wildly against each other, you need two things: an interventionist monetary policy that is the collective work of the US Federal Reserve, a Euro-Fed, and the Bank of Japan; and a convergence of macroeconomic fundamentals. Otherwise, you are constantly having to adjust exchange rates and domestic policies. A successful system needs to countervail the tendency of central bankers to run a monetary policy that has a continual deflationary bias, when the world really requires a bias toward real growth. We need cheap money for development purposes with credit allocated to poor countries – complete violations of laissez-faire, in which markets are supposed to allocate credits.

......

A more modest but attainable trade-policy goal would be to acknowledge the radical disparity in the rules by which diverse economic systems play, and to seek a trading system that accommodates diversity rather than demanding nominal comformity. Concretely, this would mean a shift in the operating principle of the GATT, from unconditional to conditional free trade. Nations that agreed to a common set of practices on subsidies, pricing, intellectual-property protection, social standards, and, generally, the right to do business would enjoy free access to one another's markets. Nations that did not agree would retain the right to operate more mercantilist or exploitive economies internally – but their access to other nations' markets would be conditional and would have to be negotiated, country by country and sector by sector. Ironically, a step backward from the utopian ideal of perfect free trade would enhance both the health of the multilateral trading system and the competitiveness of the United States.

The stakes are anything but academic. It matters whether the products made in the United States – and the jobs, the investment capital, and the knowledge embedded in those products – get roughly equal access to world markets. By viewing the trading system in utopian terms, denying that the policies of other nations affect our access, and insisting that the only kind of national security is military, the United States is slowly squandering both its standard of living and its economic influence in the world. To revise our trade strategy will require an acknowledgement that we have economic interests to defend and advance, in addition to ideological goals for the world.

READING 36

Robert Reich

Biography

Robert Reich was born on June 24, 1946 in Scranton Pennsylvania. He grew up in South Salem, New York, where his father owned and operated two women's clothing stores. After graduating from high school he went to Dartmouth College in Hanover, New Hampshire, where he graduated Summa Cum Laude in 1968. The summer between his junior and senior years he worked in the office of Senator Robert F. Kennedy in New York.

That year, Reich was awarded a Rhodes scholarship to Oxford University in England. There he met Bill Clinton who became President of the US in 1993. In 1970 he received a Master's degree in Political Science and Economics from Oxford University. He then enrolled at Yale Law School where he received his Doctor of Jurisprudence degree. However, he decided not to practice law.

For one year Reich served as a law clerk to Frank M. Coffin, the chief judge on the United States Court of Appeals in Boston. Reich then entered government service as an assistant solicitor general with the Justice Department. Two years later in 1976 he was appointed director of policy planning at the Federal Trade Commission where he witnessed the growing foreign challenge to American industry.

In 1981 Reich joined the faculty of the John F. Kennedy School of Government at Harvard University. He, his wife and two children lived in Cambridge. As a lecturer on Political Economy he was responsible for courses on public policy, business strategy and public management. In spite of his full teaching schedule, Reich still managed to advise and influence the Democratic presidential nominees Walter F. Mondale, Michael S. Dukakis and Bill Clinton in 1984, 1988 and 1992.

Following his election as President of the United States in November 1992, Bill Clinton chose Robert Reich to lead his economic policy transition team. Later, in December 1992, Clinton chose Reich to be Secretary of Labor. Reich remained in that position until 1996.

The Work

In all his writings, Reich has been a proponent of an active role of government in economic affairs.[146]

In an earlier book written with Ira Magaziner, entitled *Minding America's Business* the two authors contend that since the early 1970s, the United States has become increasingly dependent on international trade. This increased dependency raises new issues.[147]

Along with other advanced countries, the United States must deal with business firms which face long-term competitive declines in an increasingly integrated world economy. The decline in competitive advantage may be due to increasing costs of raw materials or the easy migration of capital and technology across nations. Advanced nations, the US included, must also concern themselves with industries and enterprises that are developing rapidly and are capable of gaining

---

146   The criteria for intervention are never explicitly stated in Reich's work (ed.).
147   I.C. Magaziner, R.B. Reich, *Minding America's Business* (New York: Random House, 1983).

long-term competitive leadership in world markets. According to Reich and Magaziner, the US needs a 'comprehensive industrial policy' to facilitate the adjustment of its economy to the rapid changes in the world economy.[148]

As a matter of fact, says Reich, the US already has an industrial policy. However, he contends that it is irrational and uncoordinated. It consists mostly of trade barriers, voluntary export restrictions, loan guarantees, targeted subsidies, and occasional bail-outs for major companies near bankruptcy. Such policies often delay structural adjustment instead of facilitating it. Although the two authors advocate an active industrial policy, they caution against too heavy-handed an approach. As far as they are concerned a rational industrial policy must:

1. Develop programs to assist workers facing industrial displacement, including assistance in retraining and relocation.
2. Adopt corrective measures in situations where the social benefits of investment exceed the private benefits. Programs in this category would include subsidies for investments in research and development, education and the like.
3. Support high–risk, large scale investment or investments that yield a return only after a long period of time.

Moreover, according to the authors, for an industrial policy to be effective, it should emanate from only one or two agencies of government. When too many agencies share the responsibility, overlap and confusion prevail. They argue that many current US policies have this fault. They also think that such tools as tax credits, accelerated depreciation and subsidies are preferable to government contracts, quotas, tariffs and licenses.

In most of his later writings however, Reich de-emphasizes the importance of industrial policy. In its place he promotes the ideas of 'market design' and 'managed trade'.[149]

In an article entitled 'Of Markets and Myths', Reich argues that the debate on the role of government often takes place in terms of total laissez-faire versus interference in the market.[150] This type of

---

148   Here the two authors obviously take the normative view (ed.).
149   Again these concepts are not clearly and explicitly defined (ed.).
150   R.B. Reich, 'Of Markets and Myths', *Commentary* (February 1987).

debate, says Reich, obscures the more subtle question of market design. Good government should concern itself with making up the right market rules rather than trying to dictate the right market outcomes.[151]

The same reasoning applies, according to Reich, to international trade. In an article published in *Challenge* he states that the choice is not between free and managed trade.[152] The relevant question is 'how are we to manage our trade and for what ends?' According to Reich free trade is usually meant to denote the absence of tariffs and quotas.[153] However, says Reich, the concept of free trade becomes increasingly obscured in a world in which tariffs and quotas are superseded by a broad range of nontariff barriers. If trade is to be managed anyway the first question is 'What do we seek to accomplish?' We must ask ourselves such questions as 'do we want trade to be balanced or are we striving for a higher standard of living'? Once we agree upon the ends we have to decide upon the strategies of getting there. For example a nation will have to choose between rule oriented or outcome oriented trade agreements. The General Agreement on Tariffs and Trade is a system of rules. A voluntary export restraint is an example of an outcome oriented accord.

Reich's latest book, *The Work of Nations*, shows some change in his vision of the world. In it he argues that after the late 1960s profound changes have taken place in the world economy.[154] For example, Japan and Western Europe have emerged as powerful exporters of advanced industrial products. Technological developments in communication and international transportation have made it possible for manufacturing processes to be fragmented and parceled out across the globe. At present a large number of low-income countries are exporting the simpler consumer goods.

Many factors of production such as various types of equipment, financial capital and technology now move 'effortlessly' across borders. These changes have helped to bring about a fundamental alteration in the structure and policies of traditional American

---

151 The criteria for the 'right' market rules are not plainly spelled out (ed.).
152 R.B. Reich, 'We need a Strategic Trade Policy', *Challenge* (July/August 1990).
153 It seems more logical to define free trade as government noninterference in exports, imports and capital movements (ed.).
154 R.B. Reich, *The Work of Nations* (New York: Random House, 1993).

corporations. The typical corporation of the 1950s used to plan and implement the production of a large volume of goods and services. More recently many of these corporations have shifted from high volume to high value-added production. They have also become more global. The 'new corporation has become a kind of decentralized network or 'web' of contractors, subcontractors, licenses, franchises, partnerships and other temporary alliances. The final product is often an international composite. Each part of the web provides something such as product design, marketing services, financing or fabrication. Much of the trade between people and departments within the same interactive network crosses national borders. Fabrication or assemblage of standardized products often takes place in low-wage countries. Frequently, the more sophisticated operations are done in advanced countries where the appropriate skills are found.

Many governments in the more developed countries have reacted to these changes by raising trade barriers. Those barriers include anti-dumping levies and voluntary export restraints. Some governments have also altered the cost structure of selected industries with subsidies, subsidized loans, tax credits, research grants and the like. Yet, the US government has failed to put together a coherent national strategy to respond to these changes. The outcome is a confused and contradictory trade policy which *de facto* tends to inhibit the adjustments in the US and elsewhere.

According to Reich what the US should have done or should do is to work out an explicit strategy for encouraging higher skilled, knowledge intensive, higher value-added forms of production. Instead of doing what it has been doing in the past, i.e. embracing preservationist policies, the US government should design policies to ease and accelerate the transition to higher value-added and more competitive production. However, such policies require an involved and active government, according to Reich.

The 'new' global enterprise which has emerged in recent times is based on 'insights', says Reich. Problem solving and brokering occurs wherever the right skills are found and they are usually available in the more advanced nations. High volume standardized production increasingly takes place in low-wage countries. The highest incomes go to the most skilled people within the corporate network. These incomes may be in the form of salaries, bonuses, licensing fees or partnership shares.

For a nation such as the United States a major problem is not that American corporations are not profitable enough. It is a more important issue that too many Americans do not have the skills and insights to add enough value to the global output to guarantee them a high standard of living. These considerations lead Reich to propose his own version of the so-called immiseration doctrine which we will define here as the case in which the evolution of the economy leads to a situation in which large groups of the population experience a decline in their standard of living.

In the 1950s and 1960s, says Reich, the distribution of income in the US was such that most Americans enjoyed medium middle class incomes. In the mid-1970s however, this began to change as wage differentials began to widen. With the shifts of routine production jobs from advanced countries to low income-low wage nations, the revenues of the 'routine producers' (workers with low skilled jobs) in the US fell.

The fortunes of low-skill service providers, the 'in-person servers', are also declining. Although they are sheltered from the direct effect of global competition, they are confronting former routine producers who lost their jobs and who seek employment in the service sector.[155] Besides, many new entrants in the labor market will seek jobs in the service sector because of the absence of the traditional blue collar jobs. Also, the in-person servers face ever growing competition from legal and illegal immigrants who have weak skills. Finally, low skilled services providers face rivalry from labor-saving equipment. Automatic tellers and self-service gas stations are the examples. At the same time, the incomes of well-educated, skilled Americans able to do complex, knowledge-intensive tasks, the so-called 'symbolic analysts', are rising because there is an expanding world-wide demand for their services and expertness. The end result of all these trends is that the income gap in the United States is rising. According to Reich, other nations are experiencing the same trend. Only an increased and rather stiff tax burden on the incomes of the symbolic analysts will slow down the process.

In view of this general direction of the global economy, says Reich, the obvious aim of the US government policy should be to help Americans to become technologically more sophisticated. American economic policies should be designed to increase the value of what US

155　The fact that the service sector is continuously expanding and that there must be an explanation for this phenomenon is not discussed in *The Work of Nations*.

citizens can add to the world economy.

In earlier writings Reich sometimes advocates subsidies to firms in declining sectors to scrap excess capacity, and subsidies and other benefits to retain and attract high value-added firms in the United States.[156]

In his most recent book *The Work of Nations* Reich no longer sees in subsidies the ultimate solution, because so many corporations are losing their national identities. Government benefits, he argues, should go to the heart and soul of the economy, i.e. the relatively immobile labor force and the country's infrastructure. It is the skills of a nation's labor force and the quality of its infrastructure that make a country attractive for investment. Business of all national origins thrives on a well-trained workforce and an up-to-date infrastructure. That is what attracts global investors and keeps national firms from moving abroad.

Reich then presents a long list of activities which in his view deserve government support and financing.[157] Most of it goes under the name of 'positive economic nationalism'. The agenda includes:

(a) Measures to ensure the health and nutrition of small children.
(b) Stimulating preschool programs.
(c) High quality public schools.
(d) Financial assistance to all high school graduates who want to go to college.
(e) Investments in colleges, universities and research parks.
(f) Subsidies to any corporation regardless of nation origin that agrees to undertake research and development and manufacturing in the US using American personnel.
(g) Subsidies to facilitate the movement of the work force out of their older industries and technologies. Such subsidies might include severance payments, relocation assistance, retraining assistance and prolonged unemployment insurance.

The money needed for all these programs would have to come from higher taxes on the fortunate, highly skilled, 20 per cent of Americans whose incomes are steadily rising, according to Reich.

---

156   R.B. Reich, 'Beyond Free Trade', *Foreign Affairs* (Spring 1983) pp. 784, 803.
157   There is no cost-benefit analysis of these policy proposals in Reich's work (ed.).

In comment on Reich's propositions one has the impression that he somewhat exaggerates the extent to which American and foreign companies have globalized their businesses and shed national markets and identities. Most US firms still fit the traditional mold of national companies. He also seems to overestimate the impact of the global economy. US exports of goods and services amount to some 10 per cent of GDP, while imports account for 11 percent. These are still comparatively modest figures. The major problem of the US economy in the 1970s, in the 1980s, and in the early 1990s is not some massive global shift but low productivity growth. The annual average rate of increase of productivity was 0.5 per cent for the 1973–1980 period; 1.1 per cent for the 1980–86 period and 0.5 per cent for the 1986–1990 period. In other areas of the American economy such as fiscal policy, monetary policy and structural policy the major determinants are also still mainly, although not exclusively, domestic. Against these facts it is also difficult to accept Reich's argument that the expansion of the global economy explains the widening gap between America's higher and lower income groups. Earlier versions of the immiseration doctrine have ultimately proven to be invalid and that raises some doubts about this one as well.

In his work Reich advocates American economic policies designed to promote industries with high value-added per worker which he believes to be identical with high-tech industries. Krugman points out that according to his research these two types of industries are not synonymous. Industries with a really high value-added per worker tend to be those with very high ratios of capital per worker. Here we find traditional industries such as tobacco manufacturers, oil refineries and car makers. High-tech sectors like electronics and aerospace are only average. Sure enough, says Krugman, Reich would not want capital and labor to flow increasingly towards industries like steel and tobacco.[158]

Reich, like Kuttner (discussed earlier in this text) would like to increase the role of government with the associated increase in public sector spending and taxes on persons with the higher incomes to pay for their list of social programs. Unfortunately recent history suggests that all these programs often fail to achieve their intended results. Governments are not very good at allocating resources and the public

---

158 P. Krugman, *Pop Internationalism* (Cambridge: The MIT Press, 1996) pp. 13–14.

seems to resist tax increases. Besides, in these days of easier mobility, increased taxes on highly skilled persons and/or corporations may induce a brain drain or the movement of the domestic company's resources and operations to more hospitable locations. In a basic sense, the mobility of businesses, of their employees, capital and technology now imposes relatively tight controls on political decisions. Moreover, there remains the age-old issue of the impact of taxes on the incentives to work, save and invest. Consequently, Reich's list of taxes, grants, subsidies and other forms of government involvement in the economic system may not be entirely realistic and certainly requires a close examination of likely costs and benefits of the specific proposals before they are adopted.[159]

Extracts

Although most politicians, pundits, academics, and editorial writers continue to disavow protectionism, the concept of managed trade has gained a certain cachet recently. Largely because of America's continuing $50 billion a year trade deficit with Japan, it now is respectable to argue that the United States should abandon free trade and 'manage' its trade relations with Japan.

......

The debate is hopelessly confused. In trade policy, as in most other areas of public policy-making, the way choices are posed and goals tacitly accepted can make all the difference. The real choice is not between free trade and managed trade. The question should be: How are we to manage our trade, and for what ends? Herewith, an attempt to sort out the issues.

One problem is that no one any longer knows what free trade is. The world over, formal tariffs and quotas are superseded by a broad range of what are euphemistically called 'nontariff barriers'. Formal tariffs and quotas clearly block trade; their purposes and effects are indisputable. But nontariff barriers are often in the eyes of the beholder. Thus, while free trade obviously means the absence of tariffs and quotas, its meaning quickly becomes relative in the face of

159 R.B. Reich, 'We Need a Strategic Trade Policy', *Challenge*, (July–August 1990) pp. 38–39.
R.B. Reich, 'Beyond Free Trade', *Foreign Affairs* (Spring 1983) pp. 788, 789, 803, 804.

nontariff barriers.

......

The term 'managed trade' conjures up visions of government restrictions and intrusions upon what is an otherwise free trading system. But once we accept the proposition that, in the absence of formal quotas and tariffs, free trade is coming to have no meaning apart from international agreement about how it is to be defined, then the distinction between free trade and managed trade collapses. International agreement itself is a form of management.

The policy choices concern how trade is to be managed – what is to be the area of potential agreement, who is to be party to it, and how is it to be enforced.

......

The practical policy choices facing the United States and every other industrialized nation are whether (and to what extent) to preserve existing jobs and industries, and whether (and how) to help move capital and labor to higher value-added and more competitive production. Both choices imply an active role for government. But the first is politically and administratively easier to accomplish than the second, at least in the short run. Most people are afraid of change, particularly when they suspect that its burdens and benefits will fall randomly and disproportionately. By the same token, many policies to preserve the status quo – like barriers against foreign competition and special tax benefits propping up deteriorating balance sheets – do not entail active and visible government intervention. No bureaucrats intrude on corporate discretion. Congress votes no budgets. The costs do not appear on any national accounts, and those who bear them are seldom aware of the source or extent of the burdens.

On the other hand, policies designed to ease and accelerate an economy's transition to higher value-added and more competitive production often require that governments work closely with business and labor to ensure that the sharp changes required do not impose disproportionate costs on some or windfalls for others; that workers have adequate income security and opportunities for retraining; that emerging industries have sufficient capital to cope with the high costs and risks of starting up when these costs and risks are beyond what private investors are willing to endure; and that industries in difficulty have sufficient resources to reduce capacity in their least competitive parts and restructure their most competitive. All of these activities entail an active and explicit government role.

......

The United States must understand that government expenditures in the form of subsidies, loan guarantees, and tax benefits designed to keep or lure high value-added emerging businesses within the United States, are no less legitimate investments in the education of America's labor force than are investments in the public schools. Properly conceived, these are not zero-sum efforts to increase employment at home at the expense of employment elsewhere; they are positive-sum policies to enhance the skills and know-how of American workers while increasing the wealth-creating potential of the world. In the long run they may constitute our most important strategy for emerging businesses.

Conclusion

The controversy this book examines – free trade versus protectionism – has existed from mercantilist times to the present. This book reviews schools of thought and individual writers in their settings and their contributions to economic analysis. Some of the ideas have developed and become part of accepted thought, while others have long since been discarded as untenable.

The study of economic thought in general, and of the free trade versus protectionism issue in particular, gives us a better perspective and understanding. It shows how the past and the present are linked and it provides a continuity of ideas. We get a sense of direction from it, and it improves understanding which neither a contemporary treatise nor a textbook in international economics alone could provide.

The period surveyed has been divided into four segments. The first interval runs from the end of the Middle Ages to the late eighteenth century. The second era deals with the nineteenth century and the very early part of the twentieth century. The third time span covers the years between the two World Wars. Period four starts after 1945 and ends with the last decade of the twentieth century.

For the issue of free trade versus protectionism to come into play, we must be dealing with (1) an open economy, (2) a state of affairs in which production, trade and consumption decisions are in the hands of the private sector, (3) the existence of a State and finally (4) a situation in which a significant portion of GDP finds its way across borders. Once the conditions are met, a debate will start as governments under pressure from local constituencies attempt to influence or control the nature and extent of international trade. In fact what is involved is the superimposition of the political process on the economic process. During medieval times, people lived in a world of local self-sufficiency. Money and credit were not widely used. Consequently, systematic economic thinking about trade issues did not evolve.

Up to 1800

With the emergence of nation states with integrated economies, the situation changed. Domestic and foreign trade expanded rapidly and the importance of money and credit increased substantially. New technologies which led to reduced transportation costs, the opening up of new sea routes, the discovery of America, the revolution of prices, periodic inflation and recessions and the infiltration of capital into industry, all led to the waning of feudalism, the passing of the village economy, the consolidation of populations into new national units and the concept of national wealth.

The bulk of mercantilist literature discussing these phenomena was pre-analytic, the work of unprofessional minds. Most mercantilist authors simply stated their views and then moved on quickly to specific policy proposals. Growing out of the development of nation states, the spirit of the age was non-individualistic, nationalistic and authoritarian. As mercantilists saw it, the power of the newly created states had to be strengthened. None of the new nations had all they wanted and each of them had something the others coveted. Precious metals, which served as the bases for money, were seen as the main form of wealth. Consequently, a positive balance of trade was sought to insure an inflow of gold and silver. Mercantilist authors believed that to achieve this, a positive balance of trade required the protection of domestic agriculture and industry from foreign imports. Mercantilist writers and policy makers also advocated and considered essential, the regulation of economic behavior and state intervention in economic dealings. State interference in economic affairs became the rule during that period. It was mitigated around 1750, in such countries as England, the Netherlands and France.

1800–1914

Towards the end of the eighteenth century, economic conditions in Europe and the United States began to change slowly, a trend that reinforced itself as the nineteenth century wore on. In Britain, for example, the economic structure began to shift from agriculture to industry. As the population kept growing it became cheaper to import food and pay for it with industrial exports. This prepared the ground for free trade ideas. Other European countries such as Germany eventually followed this trend. In Britain the economic transition sparked a debate in which David Ricardo took part. He welcomed the change and argued in favor of lower duties on corn,

Early in the nineteenth century, the United States was still a predominantly agricultural country. Most of its exports consisted of primary commodities and food, such as cotton, tobacco, sugar and cereals. Most imports consisted of manufactured goods. The westward expansion after the 1830s brought huge supplies of rich natural resources under American control which served the developing factory system well. Thus the United States was basically self-sufficient with exports and imports well below ten per cent of GDP. Economic growth accelerated after the 1830s and as young industries began to develop, infant industry arguments were proposed by such American authors as Daniel Raymond and Henry Charles Carey.

During the eighteenth century, mercantilism and the mercantilist doctrine slowly disintegrated. The new ideas advocated by the Physiocrats; philosophers such as John Locke; and writers on economic, historical and philosophical subjects, like David Hume and Adam Smith, contributed to its decline. The Classical School of Economics, which began with Adam Smith and included other well-known thinkers like David Ricardo and John Stuart Mill, dominated economic reasoning in all advanced countries during the first five decades of the nineteenth century. The social philosophy underlying what became political and economic classical liberalism contained several important components. Following Adam Smith, classical liberals, who are now often called libertarians, believed that the most important principle supporting the economic life of a nation was economic freedom. They held that governments should not interfere in the economic choices and decisions of individuals. That policy was expected to yield greater returns – both to the individual and society – than any other alternative. This approach applied to international trade as well as to all other economic activities. All should be free. Towards the middle of the nineteenth century and later, economic and political liberalism was the basis for the policies of many governments. They included England and the Netherlands, countries that relied heavily on foreign trade. It also obtained a significant degree of qualified acceptance elsewhere. There is no question that this philosophy and approach led to a substantial liberalization of international trade. It was backed up by sophisticated economic analysis.

During the second half of the nineteenth century, the economic trends under way continued, and in some countries accelerated. Factors involved in the quickening economic pace included large economic establishments based on growing markets and a greater specialization and division of labor. The development of the steam engine for transportation once again lowered the costs of ocean shipping and land transportation. Both in Western Europe and in the United States, greater quantities of goods per unit of human endeavor were steadily produced while per capita incomes rose. The United States became an industrial power and by 1894 it had become the leading manufacturing nation in the world. Both Europe and the United States relied increasingly on the exploitation of the natural resources of other continents. International trade expanded rapidly. Between 1850 and 1900 both US and UK imports increased by a factor of five.

However, the hostile reactions to free trade and to the underlying classical liberal outlook also grew stronger. Fast capitalist evolution combined with free trade and the relatively cheap imports it created evoked hostile resistance from groups that were threatened and who could not easily adapt to a new form of existence. Cheap imports are likely to affect domestic producers of manufactured products which are substitutes for the imported goods. Broad sectors of the economy, such as the farmers or urban workers, can be disturbed when, because of international trade, changes in the domestic resource allocation adversely affect them. It is obvious that during the transitional periods some sectors will feel more pressure than others. As these categories experience the squeeze of the market mechanisms they are likely to turn to the political system for help. Typically, the kind of solutions they look for inhibit the signals of the market mechanism required for improved resource allocation. Moreover, the policy solutions which the groups under pressure propose, typically benefit them while making the other members of society worse off.

During the second half of the nineteenth century, many European farmers, landlords, artisans, and industrial workers in domestic industries found themselves in a difficult situation. They could not easily compete with foreign imports. Germany and France were cases in point. Not surprisingly these two countries produced economic theorists defending government intervention and providing a theoretical justification for protectionist measures. Names like Friedrich List, Adolph Wagner and Paul Emile Cauwès come to mind.

During the 1850–1900 period tariff policy in the US differed sharply from that of England. For 1861 the US adopted the protective principle on a large scale with the Morill Act. In 1860 there was apparently no widespread demand by manufacturers for a high tariff but it was promoted by the Republicans who believed that protectionism would bind together the discordant elements of the North where about 90 per cent of the nation's manufacturing was located. As usual, the South favored low tariffs. Once the Civil War had started, Congress raised the import duties again and again until the 47 per cent level was reached. Money to finance the war had to be obtained. War industries in the North now demanded protection and with the Southern congressional opponents of the tariff no longer in the Congress there was practically no opposition. Once the tariffs were in place they created vested interests, and after 1864 special interest groups defeated almost every effort at a reduction of the duties.

Although the second half of the nineteenth century produced a certain number of adversaries of conventional economic doctrines, orthodox economics, as exemplified by John Stuart Mill's principles, did not stand still. During the latter decades of the nineteenth century classical economics underwent a profound transformation often designated as the 'Marginal Revolution'. With economists such as Karl Menger, Leon Walras and Alfred Marshall well in evidence, neo-classical economics made its appearance. It contained many advances, innovations and refinements, yet it basically maintained the economic liberalism's outlook in its attempts to explain the functioning of the free enterprise economy. Most neo-classicals also believed that individuals should be left free as much as possible to live and trade as they chose.

Nevertheless, between 1850 and 1900 there were some important changes in the intellectual climate of the western world. The ideas of classical liberalism and the teachings of classical political economy came under widespread attack. For instance, the German Historical School strongly opposed the ideas and analytical apparatus of the Classical School. In Germany, as in other countries, rival creeds and gospels including socialism, syndicalism, nationalism and racism arose or re-emerged. They all opposed the political and economic classical liberalism of the earlier thinkers.

Furthermore, the industrial revolution with its rising real wages produced a quasi-literate proletarian urban class which had no sympathy for the classical liberal outlook. With the progressive introduction of universal suffrage, much of the urban proletariat voted for political parties that advocated social reform. Those parties increasingly tried to use state power to deliver specific privileges to the urban industrial workers and other low income groups they represented. With the ascendancy of these political forces the state once again provided a host of special interest groups with a preferred position.

The increase in interventionist, protectionist and imperialist policies persisted until 1914, especially in Germany and France and, to a lesser degree, the United States. The policies of economic and political nationalism led to increasing friction between the great powers, with World War I as the final outcome.

1914–1945

The First World War is generally recognized as, and in effect was, the very end of the nineteenth century. The war caused a radical change in the economic conditions and policies of nearly all nations. During the war, those nations directly involved, turned to a policy of government intervention; one that included an almost complete control of foreign trade and financial flows during wartime. After the hostilities had come to an end many of those wartime regulations were abandoned, yet the readiness to intervene became greater.

While the Western European powers were concentrating on their war efforts, they inevitably neglected their overseas markets. The post-war need to rebuild their economies and the additional competition of new traders, such as the US, Japan and Canada, made a return to pre-war markets difficult. Exports to the US were made more difficult by the Fordney–McCumber tariff of 1922, which raised import duties. Russia turned towards a regime of socialist totalitarianism, characterized by state control of all imports and exports. The Austrio-Hungarian Empire was subdivided into a number of small countries with nearly all of them adopting protectionist policies.

As indicated earlier, during the 1869–1914 period the United States had become an industrial giant, with merchandise exports exceeding merchandise imports after 1880. During World War I the US was insulated from the devastation that racked Europe. The interruption of imports during the war gave American industry more protection than any tariff could provide. In addition, the war created a prodigious domestic and foreign demand for American war materials and food. Thus both the industrial and agricultural sectors expanded. However, that rate of growth was not sustainable after the war. Between 1919 and 1921, American exports dropped by one half as war demands vanished and international competition gained strength. Many voices arguing for increased protection were heard and the government listened. During the 1923–29 period the average US duty on all dutiable imports was about 38 per cent.

During the same period, and even up to 1939, many important contributions were made to the theory of economics. It was a time too when the belief in political and economic classical liberalism was broken. The prevailing climate of opinion moved increasingly towards a greater role for government, which meant more neo-mercantilism, statism and interventionism.

Just as World War I was a watershed, so was the Great Depression of the 1929–1933 period a turning point, along with the economic hardship it created. In the US it undermined faith in free market institutions and gave rise to the interventionist New Deal. In England and other democratic countries, government involvement in the economic system became ever more common and free trade policies were increasingly abandoned. In 1932 England ended its free trade policy altogether, a policy introduced in 1846 by Sir Robert Peel. The interwar version of the gold standard was also abandoned, along with most of the remaining vestiges of political and economic liberalism.

Russia, Germany, Italy and Japan all adopted totalitarian institutions, subordinating the individual to the state. Foreign trade and payments came under integral government control. The return to extreme economic nationalism practically brought international trade to a halt and contributed to a worsening of the depression. With unemployment at high levels, governments raised tariffs and introduced quotas to protect domestic employment. That in turn gave rise to a vicious cycle of additional intervention and protectionism. Because the international monetary system had collapsed as well, governments often reacted with unilateral devaluations to foster exports. Others placed restrictions on the purchase and sale of foreign exchange.

Writers in the neo-classical economic tradition continued to explain and advocate the advantages of free trade. However, policy makers did not listen. In the 1930s, the western world was suffering from mass unemployment and it was the voice of the English economist, John Maynard Keynes, which caught the attention of many legislators.

Keynes argued that classical self-adjusting mechanisms of the private economic system would not necessarily guarantee full employment of existing resources. Thus he recommended a greater role for government. During the 1930s he also stood firmly in favor of increased economic self-sufficiency and protectionism. His work seemed to provide answers to the burning questions of the time and his thoughts gradually conquered economic and political opinion. Because Keynes focussed on a greater role for government in economic affairs, he contributed to the creation of a climate of opinion characterized by a greater degree of economic and political nationalism and interventionism.

Like World War I, the Second World War unleashed widespread destruction on the world's populations. After the war the United States emerged as the world's leading economic power with enormous bargaining strength. In 1945, GNP in current dollars reached a level of about $212 billions more than twice that of 1940. Inflation accounted for much of this gain. Nevertheless real GNP rose by 56 per cent. Merchandise exports increased from $3.2 billion in 1939 to some $9.8 billion in 1945. During the same period merchandise imports rose from $2.2 billion to $4.2 billion. This left the US with a very favorable merchandise trade balance and a vested interest in free international trade. When normal trade relations returned after the war, both merchandise exports and imports maintained their upward trend.

After 1945

During World War II, it was generally understood that once the war was over, a new system of international cooperation was needed to avoid a recurrence of the events that characterized the 1930s. After the war the US assumed the major responsibility for postwar relief and rehabilitation which most of the war-torn nations badly needed. The US also provided leadership in establishing a system of nondiscriminatory economic multilateralism and international cooperation. New institutions such as the General Agreement on Tariffs and Trade (GATT), the International Monetary Fund (IMF) and the International Bank of Reconstruction and Development (IBRD) became part of the redesigned international economic system.

The two decades running from the early 1950s to the early 1970s were a period of relatively high economic growth in the western world and Japan. International trade grew rapidly and prosperity increased. Simultaneously, the new international trade order was also a success. As a trading partner the US grew in importance. Between 1946 and 1970 its exports almost quadrupled while imports multiplied by a factor of eight. As the size of the foreign trade sector grew in importance, the US became actively involved in negotiations to reduce tariffs world-wide. Non-tariff issues also received increasing attention.

After the early 1970s however, the rapid rate of growth of the economies of the western world began to slow down. The negative incentives implicit in the ever-expanding welfare reforms with their required higher taxes and encroaching regulations began to lower the productivity of the private sector of the North American and European economies. In order to combat the prevailing inflation, monetary policies became tighter. At the same time, as a result of international oil cartel practices, oil prices rose, increasing both production and transportation costs. With the economic slowdown came increased unemployment and the so-called 'new protectionism' emerged. This movement was characterized by the ascent of non-tariff barriers, such as voluntary export restraints. Those non-tariff barriers were an attempt to bypass GATT obligations. In the United States, the administrations of Presidents Reagan and Bush were able to exert pressure which slowed down this movement toward increased trade restraints, even if their support for free trade was not always wholehearted. The new treaty obligations of the eighth GATT round concluded in 1994 also inhibited the introduction of non-tariff barriers.

As the 1980s wore on, some economic writers and talkers proposed the idea of 'managed trade'. As they saw it, the government should work out policies which would yield a competitive trade advantage for a country, usually their own. These arrangements involved subsidies to research centers, allowances to corporations developing new products, and support for high-tech industries. Many well-known economists severely criticized this aggressive unilateralism. With the increasing prosperity of the 1990s and the improved competitiveness of American industries, these voices calling for trade management weakened again in the United States, Japan and Europe, even though the French and German unemployment levels exceeded 10 per cent.

Finally, the last decades of the twentieth century have witnessed a dramatic increase in the flows of trade and investment between countries. Globalization is the word that is mostly used to indicate the fact that economies around the world are becoming more and more interrelated. A number of factors are responsible: the tangible declines in tariff barriers; the reductions in capital controls; the falling transportation costs; and the greater speed of information flows. With globalization, economic isolationism seems an anachronism. Yet, protectionist voices can still be heard from those who believe in it. Consequently, we can expect to continue to hear about free trade versus protectionism.

During the 1930s, Keynes brought aggregate theory into the foreground of attention. After World War II, Keynesian analysis dominated academic circles. By the 1960s, it formed the foundation for the macroeconomic policies of many western nations. In the 1970s, the new phenomenon of stagflation tempered the confidence of economists in the Keynesian system and led to many amendments in it. Concurrently, microeconomic issues once again began to receive more attention.

The collapse of the communist variety of statism in Eastern Europe and the difficulties experienced by the welfare state led to a re-emergence of the philosophy of classical liberalism. Private initiative, the importance of free markets and free trade, and the desirability of a more limited role of government were recognized once again. This was quite a departure from the interventionist position many thinkers had adopted during the 1945–1975 period.

It is obvious that during the period under investigation the science of economics has become much richer, which makes it possible for us to better understand the nature and consequences of economic policies. The increased use of the scientific method and the patient investigations of the many highly capable scholars have produced a copious and solid body of economic theory and analysis. This has led to a greater sophistication in the kinds of arguments we have surveyed here. Along with this important understanding, a very large part of the economics profession now supports the free trade doctrine. Many, if not most contemporary economists feel that the myopic view of protectionism does not work in a global economy because it inhibits economic adjustment and leads to a serious misallocation of the world's scarce resources.

Name Index

Subject Index